KT-424-518

# HARRIS'S GUIDE

TO

## CHURCHES AND CATHEDRALS

EBURY
PRESS

# HARRIS'S GUIDE

## ── TO ──

## CHURCHES AND CATHEDRALS

*Discovering the unique and unusual in over 500
Churches and Cathedrals*

Brian L. Harris

First published in Great Britain by Ebury Publishing in 2006

1 3 5 7 9 10 8 6 4 2

Text © Brian Harris 2006

Brian Harris has asserted his right to be identified as the author of this work under the Copyright, Designs and Patents Act 1988.

Ebury Publishing
Random House, 20 Vauxhall Bridge Road, London SW1V 2SA

Random House Australia (Pty) Limited
20 Alfred Street, Milsons Point, Sydney, New South Wales 2061, Australia

Random House New Zealand Limited
18 Poland Road, Glenfield, Auckland 10, New Zealand

Random House South Africa (Pty) Limited
Isle of Houghton, Corner Boundary Road & Carse O'Gowrie, Houghton, 2198, South Africa

Random House Publishers India Private Limited
301 World Trade Tower, Hotel Intercontinental Grand Complex, Barakhamba Lane, New Delhi 110 001, India

The Random House Group Limited Reg. No. 954009
www.randomhouse.co.uk

A CIP catalogue record for this book is available from the British Library.

Editor: Anne Newman
Designer: Peter Ward
Map on p.xvi by Rodney Paull
Picture Researcher: Isobel Sinden
For picture credits and permissions please see page 482.

ISBN: 0091912512
ISBN-13 [from January 2007] : 9780091912512

Papers used by Ebury Press are natural, recyclable products made from wood grown in sustainable forests.

Printed and bound in Italy by Graphicom

This book is dedicated to my wife, Ann, my son, David, and Chris North, my brother-in-law. For 40 years they have patiently accompanied me on many of my travels to numerous churches and cathedrals throughout England and Wales and have given of their time unselfishly to allow me the opportunity to visit these wonderful buildings.

*Exton, Rutland. A fine country church with an outstanding tower and spire.*

# Contents

Foreword by Chris Smith  ix

Introduction  xi

Map  xvi

County-by-County Gazetteer  xvii

Introduction to Selected Churches  1

A-Z of Churches and Cathedrals in England and Wales  3

ARTICLES

*Hodnet, Shropshire – the only octagonal tower in the county.*

# Foreword

It was as a young schoolboy that I first began to discover the glories of our churches and cathedrals: their beauty, and architecture and history, and the sense of awe when you cross the threshold. And it was Brian Harris then, my teacher nearly half a century ago, who led me to that discovery. He is leading us still, and this book is testimony to that.

Brian Harris is much more than a teacher, though. In this book he is a guide, a mentor, a leader, an opener of doors and eyes. He takes us through some of the most moving places in our land, and does so with grace and wisdom. These are the very qualities I remember from all those years ago, and it's a real pleasure to encounter them again, now, in the pages of this book. He has done us all an inestimable service.

CHRIS SMITH
*Rt Hon. Lord Smith of Finsbury*
*27 October 2005*

*G. F. Bodley's fine tower which dates from 1903 at Long Melford, Suffolk.*

# Introduction

I have been researching and visiting churches for over 50 years. My curiosity was first aroused by my mother and grandmother, both of whom I used to accompany to church on Sundays. Their enthusiasm in pointing out each intriguing detail and feature, and taking me to other neighbouring churches, fostered my love of the subject, and as a schoolboy in the 1940s I would cycle to various churches and sketch them. I also joined my local village church choir and helped to ring the bells! When the *King's England* books by Arthur Mee (who visited most of the towns and villages of England before the Second World War) were reissued immediately after the war I started to collect them and his many lovely descriptions of churches and cathedrals compelled me to explore further.

It is difficult to single out one church or cathedral over another but certain memories do linger. I shall never forget the first time I saw Long Melford's magnificent church dominating the Suffolk village – I was awestruck by its immense size, glorious flintwork and superb tower. Equally outstanding was my first glimpse of the beautiful spire rising majestically above the church at Patrington, in the East Riding of Yorkshire, as I motored down Holderness to the remote outpost of Spurn Head. Walking above the plaster vaulting of Lichfield Cathedral and looking up inside the glorious central spire and, on another occasion, admiring the wonderful octagon at Ely Cathedral from the great west tower, are experiences that have made me feel truly privileged. And indeed, such experiences will remain with me for ever.

For centuries our parish churches have been an integral part of our national heritage and with 16,000 ancient churches to choose from, there are infinite treasures to see and appreciate. A visit to any one of them

Shottesbrooke Church, Berkshire.

*My sketch of Shottesbrooke Church, drawn when I was 15 years old.*

reveals just how these buildings encapsulate our history. The fact that some of them, for example, contained dovecotes, that nine men's morris was played inside them and fairs were held nearby on the great church festivals, indicates the key part played by the church in the lives of each parishioner.

These old churches, which so dominate our towns and villages, contain much evidence of the love and care lavished on them by generations of worshippers over hundreds of years. Ancient customs and traditions still

'Adderbury for strength,
Bloxham for length,
King's Sutton for beauty.'

'If Hanslope spire
Were a little bit higher
I would take off my shoe
And jump over it!'

survive, such as 'yew clipping' at Painswick, Gloucestershire, rush-bearing at Grasmere, Cumbria, as well as the many distributions of bread and money under the wills of former wealthy parishioners. There is also keen competition between villages and towns even today in the form of church flower festivals.

On 21 September 1967 Canon William Ernest Purcell (1909–99), a canon of Worcester Cathedral, gave a talk on BBC Radio about 'holy places' and in particular detailed the church at Little Gidding, Cambridgeshire. I have reproduced a transcript of this talk in the Appendix (see page 457) because I feel it sums up what every church and cathedral is – not a museum containing beautiful objects, but a holy place, a place where God is worshipped and has been, in many cases, for hundreds of years.

I have personally visited nearly all of the churches I describe in these pages. You must be prepared, however, to find, as I did, that some are locked and that you might have to travel some distance to collect a key and to return it afterwards. (I had to travel to a neighbouring village to obtain the key to Gaddesby Church, Leicestershire, for example, but the effort was most definitely well rewarded.)

It can be both frustrating and disappointing to travel great distances to visit a particular church or cathedral only to discover, on returning home, that you missed out on seeing the most intriguing feature because you did not know it was there! This book, I hope, will prevent this from happening, highlighting as it does the unique, the unusual and the fascinating – things that can so easily be missed by the casual observer with only limited time to spend.

*'Bosham for antiquity*
*Boxgrove for beauty,*
*Clymping for perfection.'*

*'Shalfleet's poor and simple people*
*Sold their bells to build a steeple!'*

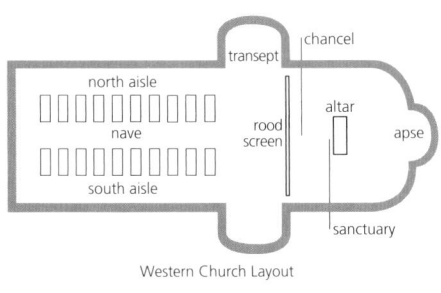

Western Church Layout

| | | | |
|---|---|---|---|
| 1 East Window | 6 Altar | 11 Chancel | 16 Memorial brass |
| 2 Cross | 7 Choir pews | 12 Lady chapel | 17 Font |
| 3 Hymn board | 8 Pulpit | 13 Chancel step | |
| 4 Crucifix | 9 Organ | 14 Pews | |
| 5 Lectern | 10 Altar rails | 15 Nave | |

Armed with this book, you might like to be reminded of the basic layout of a church. Most churches (Wilton, Wiltshire, being a notable exception) face East; that is the Holy Table or altar is at the East end. South, therefore, is on the right as you face East, North on the left and West behind you. (Incidentally, the word 'altar' is more correctly called the 'Holy Table' since Holy Communion replaced the Mass in the Church of England following Henry VIII's break with the church of Rome in 1533.)

It is somewhat surprising to learn that some churches and cathedrals make claims that are disputed by others. On a visit to Chichester I recall hearing a lady telling her friends, 'This is the only cathedral with a separate bell tower with bells!' Someone else was heard to say, 'Chichester is the only cathedral that can be seen from the sea!' Nikolaus Pevsner (who compiled most of the splendid *Buildings of England* series) and Arthur Mee had differences of opinion also, as is well seen in my entry on Thursford Church, Norfolk (see page 359).

Complete lists and locations of notable features such as round towers, wooden effigies and medieval brass lecterns, as well as the burial places of famous people, are just some of the things you will find in these pages. You may choose to pursue a particular feature and plan a holiday or car journey around it – some years ago a friend of mine took me on a 'church crawl' around East Anglia during which we saw several superb medieval brass lecterns in one day! Or, you may prefer to use the book as a guide to churches in general. Either way, I hope that it will add to your pleasure in visiting churches and help you to see how and why these buildings enshrine such a wealth of our heritage.

*Little Gidding, Cambridgeshire.*

SCOTLAND

Northumb

Tyne and Wear

Durham

Cumbria

Redcar & Cleveland

North Yorkshire

York

East Riding

Lancashire

West Yorkshire

Merseyside

Greater Manchester

South Yorkshire

Cheshire

Derbys

Notts

Lincolnshire

Conwy

Denbigh

Wrexham

Gwynedd

Staffs

Shropshire

Leics

Rutland

Norfolk

Powys

West Midlands

Cambs

Suffolk

Ceredigion

WALES

Worcs

Warks

Northants

Beds

Pembroke

Herefs

Monmouth

Herts

Essex

Carmarthen

Glos

Oxon

Bucks

Cardiff

Berks

Greater London

Kent

Wiltshire

Surrey

Somerset

Hampshire

West Sussex

East Sussex

Devon

Dorset

Cornwall

Isle of Wight

| 0 | 50 miles |
| 0 | 80 kilometres |

# County-by-County Gazetteer

*Kilpeck, Herefordshire. The magnificent Norman south doorway.*

*Ledbury, Herefordshire. A picturesque street leading to the church.*

*Clifton Reynes, Buckinghamshire – a north Buckinghamshire treasure house.*

*Lavenham, Suffolk. The superb west tower of a great 'wool' church.*

# Introduction to selected churches

In the following section you will find my choice of churches and cathedrals in England and Wales – buildings containing (with just a few exceptions) either unusual or one or more unique features. It is true to say that every church is unique in itself, but these particular features are well worth seeing and make visits to these churches especially rewarding.

In a few cases one may not always be able to see the features mentioned, except by special permission and /or arrangement. In the case of rings of bells, for example, it is easier to listen to them than it is to see them because viewing is normally forbidden to the general public for obvious safety reasons.

If your favourite church is omitted from the list, I apologise, but hope that others previously unknown to you will enrich your church-visiting experience. Whether you wish to view the church as a whole or see a particular feature I trust this book will help you to enjoy our rich heritage of religious buildings in which so many of our ancestors worshipped God and on which they lavished their care and love.

Whilst consulting this book you will frequently come across references to the famous Victorian architects named Scott. Their family is as follows: Sir George Gilbert Scott (1811–78) had five sons, two of whom became architects. They were John Oldrid Scott (1842–1913) and George Gilbert Scott, Junior (1839–97). The latter had a son named Giles Gilbert Scott (1880–1960).

The reader should be aware that there is a slight discrepancy between the date of Mary Queen of Scots's execution at Fotheringhay Castle, Northamptonshire. At Peterborough Cathedral, Cambridgeshire, it is recorded as 8 February 1587, but in Westminster Abbey, London, it is shown as 6 February 1587 on the side of her tomb.

*Page xxx: Fotheringhay, Northamptonshire*

## Abbotsham
DEVON

ST HELEN is situated between Bideford and the north Devon coast. It has a squat tower on its N side, a little higher than the nave and with buttresses only at the base.

▨ A superbly carved bench-end depicts the Crucifixion, but the faces of Mary and John have been mutilated. This is one of only three medieval examples of the Crucifixion scene on a bench-end (the others being at Osbournby, Lincs., and Woolfardisworthy or Woolsery, Devon).

▨ Following the Bishop of Exeter's Commission in 1723, the backs of some of the pews carry brass plates, each differently engraved, indicating where people from every house and farm in the parish should sit.

## Abbots Langley
HERTFORDSHIRE

ST LAWRENCE THE MARTYR The only Englishman ever to become Pope was born in this parish. The church's low W tower with a plain brick parapet was probably commenced when he was a boy!

▨ In the N aisle is the font, dating from 1400 and one of the finest in England. The eight sides are decorated alternately with the symbols of the four Evangelists and symbols connected with Baptism.

▨ Near by on the wall is a Table of the Ten Commandments. Notice how 'maid-servant' has been omitted from the last commandment.

▨ In the floor of the nave is a fine brass showing Thomas Cogdell (d. 12 February 1607) with his two wives, Jane and Alice.

▨ On each side of the E window in the S aisle chapel are wall paintings showing St Thomas à Becket and St Lawrence carrying a grid-iron. They date from c.1400.

▨ In this chapel is an imposing monument to Anne Combe (whose husband left his library to Sidney Sussex College, Cambridge), dated 1640. She is shown kneeling and on the left is a skeleton in bridal robes (she died at 24) and on the right Father Time with his hour-glass.

▨ In the S aisle is a stained-glass window commemorating Robert and Eliza Henty who lived at Breakspear College. Robert was born in Chichester and the Cathedral appears at the base, together with Abbots Langley Church.

▨ Near by on the wall a tablet records, 'At Bedmond in this parish about the date of the building of this present church was born Nicholas Breakspear, Pope Adrian IV (1154–59) the only English Pope. This tablet is erected by the Hertfordshire Historical Association. 1924.'

▨ At the W end of the S aisle is an impressive monument to Sir Robert Raymond, Lord Chief Justice of England, 1724–32. He is shown holding 'Magna Carta' in his right hand while his left hand reaches out to receive a coronet! This monument was sculptured by H. Cheere.

▨ At the W end of the N aisle is a similar monument to Lord Raymond's son, erected in 1756 by Scheemakers. The allegorical figures depict 'Hope' and 'Plenty'.

Over the s door is a well-preserved Charles II coat of arms dating from 1678.

## Abbotts Ann     HAMPSHIRE

ST MARY This red-brick church dates from 1716.

There are box pews and a gallery at the w end but the interior has been spoilt by seven stained-glass windows dating from *c.*1860 to 1880. These have been inserted in Gothic frames, thus ruining the eighteenth-century window design, of which there are four original ones at the w end.

The octagonal wooden font dating from 1716 is decorated with three acorns on top and a very large one in the middle. (See Wooden Fonts, page 34.)

Attached to some of the bench-ends are 17 servants' seats, which were used by the servants of the families occupying those pews.

High on the N and s sides of the nave walls is a collection of maidens' garlands, or virgins' crowns as they are otherwise known. These are and were placed here following the death of an unmarried woman or man of unblemished character.

The crowns are made of hazel wood, ornamented with paper rosettes. Attached to them are five parchment gauntlets which represent a challenge to anyone wishing to dispute the good character of the dead man or woman who must have been born, baptized, confirmed and died in the parish.

At the funeral the crown is carried in procession by two young girls dressed in white, after which it is hung from the gallery inside the church. After three weeks, if there is no challenge, it is hung on the wall and remains there until it decays. The earliest remaining name is that of someone called John Morrant, 1740, but his crown has disappeared.

In April 1984 there were 41 crowns hanging in the church, but only a few had gloves still attached. Among those which can be seen easily from the floor on the N side are:

† Florence Jane Wisewell, aged 72 (1953)
† William George Annetts, aged 15 (1918)
† Mary Jane Baker, aged 45 (1921)
† Lily Myra Annetts, aged 73 (1973)

On the s side these are clearly seen:

† Marianne Geraldine Fenwick, aged 43 (1919)
† Elizabeth Annie Edmonds, aged 45 (1915)

Apart from the crown of John Morrant, several others have also disappeared completely. Other examples of maidens' garlands can be seen across England but this is the only place in where the medieval custom still continues. (See Maidens' Garlands, page 24.)

## Abingdon     OXFORDSHIRE

ST HELEN is impressively situated near the River Thames.

The 45.72 m (150 feet) spire makes this church a notable landmark. Rebuilt *c.*1850, it is slightly out of the perpendicular.

The plan of the church is unusual in that it has a nave and four aisles of approximately equal width and the total width – 32.91 m (108 feet) – exceeds the total length, 29.56 m (97 feet). After St Nicholas, Great Yarmouth (Norfolk), it is the second widest parish church in England.

Between the tower and the N porch is a two-storey building that still has the remains of a fireplace in the upper storey. It was erected *c.*1450 and may have been a priest's lodging – a rare feature.

At the E end of the inner northern aisle is the lady chapel. The famous painted ceiling (the second oldest in England, the oldest being at Peterborough Cathedral, Cambs.) dates from *c.*1390 and contains representations of Kings and Prophets. Its theme is the Tree of Jesse and this Jesse ceiling is unique in England. The painted figures are very similar to those found on medieval rood screens. Originally there were 52 panels but now only 38 remain. On one panel is the extremely rare depiction of a lily crucifix – the only one painted on a ceiling. (See Lily Crucifix, page 338.)

In the nave is a fine chandelier dating from 1710.

Between the baptistery and the lady chapel is the table tomb of John Roysse, a London merchant who refounded the old Grammar School in 1563. The slab of stone on his tomb came from his London garden.

## Acton SUFFOLK

ALL SAINTS Not far from Lavenham, situated in a quiet village, the church is famous for arguably the finest military brass in England.

In a recess under the tower is a bomb that was dropped by a zeppelin on 7 August 1916.

On the N side of the N chapel, nearest the wall, is the magnificent brass of Sir Robert de Bures, 1302. He is depicted in mail armour with a shield that is separate. His crossed feet rest on a lion. This brass is 1.99 m (6 feet 6½ inches) long.

In the s chapel, which doubles as a vestry, is a monument to Robert Jennens (d. 25 February 1725 aged 54). He reclines while his wife looks on sadly. Everything is beautifully carved including his wig, coat buttons and embroidery.

## Aldborough NORTH YORKSHIRE

ST ANDREW This long church with a low w tower is reputed to have in its walls materials from the Roman town of Isurium Brigantum situated near by. Several fine Roman mosaic pavements can still be seen in numerous places.

A brass to William de Aldeburgh *c.*1360 at the NE corner of the N aisle is the last one to show a shield carried on the arm.

The tower clock was made by M. Climeshaw in 1783. The pendulum is 9.32 m (30 feet 7 inches) and is the longest in the British Isles. To accommodate its unusual length, a 1.82 m (6 feet) pit had to be dug in the ground under the tower. The time of the pendulum swing is 3.04 seconds.

A beautiful window at the w end of the s aisle commemorates Colonel John Kelby Holdsworth (d. 24 November, 1905, aged 72). All kinds of animals and birds are depicted and across the middle are the words, 'In singleness of heart fearing God'. Colonel Holdsworth's arms are in the left light and the Royal Arms in the right. The window was made by Hemingway.

## Aldeburgh SUFFOLK

ST PETER & ST PAUL is a large Perpendicular town church on a hill, overlooking the sea.

An unusually long s porch has entrances on the w, s and E. The w and E openings would have been used for processions around the church since the s entrance projects on to the road.

The nave roof was replaced in 1934 with Suffolk oak and copies the original sixteenth-century roof.

In the nave are ten very attractive brass candle holders and two in the chancel now converted to electricity.

🔲 At the E end of the s aisle is the 1914–18, 1939–45 war memorial showing a dying soldier and these words: 'These laid the world away, poured out the red sweet wine of youth, gave up the years to be of work and joy and that unhoped serene that men call age.' The memorial is in the style of Eric Gill but was designed by someone called Gilbert Bayes.

🔲 Opposite the war memorial is a large standing monument to Lady Henrietta Vernon (d. 11 April 1786). Lady Henrietta leans on an urn while an angel overhead beckons her heavenwards. A huge curtain is draped in front.

🔲 In the N aisle there is a bust to George Crabbe (24 December 1754–3 February 1832), poet of nature and truth.

🔲 At the NE end of the N aisle is the Benjamin Britten memorial window designed by John Piper and depicting three operas by Britten. It was dedicated on 6 June 1980.

🔲 Bullet holes made by German aircraft during the Second World War can still be seen in the main E window.

🔲 The fine pulpit dates from 1632.

🔲 Immediately in front of the steps to the communion table are two coffin-shaped pieces of wood inlaid in the floor. One commemorates 'Thomas Eliot, 1654' and the other the 'daughter of Captain Elyot, 1662'. They are very crudely inscribed.

🔲 To the N of the church in the new churchyard extension Benjamin Britten (1913–76) and Peter Pears (1910–86) are buried, their graves marked by two large slate headstones. Also buried near them is Imogen Holst (1907–84), whose stone is inscribed with the words, 'The Heavenly Spheres make music for us. All things join in the dance'.

🔲 To the E of the church a large memorial commemorates the lifeboat disaster of 1899. The inscription reads:

'On December 7th, 1899, in response to signals of distress, a crew of 18 brave men manned the lifeboat "Aldeburgh", which was speedily launched in the teeth of an Easterly gale and a heavy rolling sea. At duty's call to rescue others, with their own lives in their hands, these brave men went afloat, when alas! the boat capsizing seven of them met their end and lie buried here.

By a large fund promptly raised to provide for those thus suddenly bereft as well as by this monument fellow townsmen and fellow countrymen near and far pay tribute to an example of noble self-forgetfulness.'

## Aldworth      BERKSHIRE

ST MARY On a slope of the Berkshire Downs, just s of the ancient Ridgeway leading to Goring-on-Thames, this church is famous for it fine collection of stone effigies.

🔲 The interior of the church is dominated by nine stone effigies of members of the De la Beche family. These date from 1300 to 1350 and are known locally as the 'Aldworth Giants'. Some have been broken over the centuries. The largest monument commemorates Sir Philip de la Beche, who was a valet to Edward II. A dwarf is shown at his feet as if to emphasize his size.

🔲 Near the outside of the church is a railed tomb in which are buried the parents and grandparents of Emily Sellwood, who married the poet Alfred Lord Tennyson at Shiplake Church near Henley-on-Thames (Oxon.) in 1850.

🔲 The poet Laurence Binyon (10 August 1869–10 March 1943) is also buried in the churchyard. He is famous for the words used annually on Remembrance Sunday each November: 'They shall not grow old as we that are left grow old . . .'

*Alnwick, Northumberland. This church vies with the castle in splendour and position.*

## Alfriston EAST SUSSEX

ST ANDREW is also known as the 'Cathedral of the Downs' and boasts very fine external flint work.

 In the tracery of the N window of the N transept is a small piece of ancient stained glass depicting St Alphege, Archbishop of Canterbury. The figure of St Andrew nearby is modern.

 In the Easter sepulchre on the N side of the chancel is a sculpture showing Jesus calling Peter to abandon his nets, Andrew with his cross and a bishop with an axe.

 On the easternmost beam in the chancel are hooks which were used in pre-Reformation times to attach the Lenten veil – a rare survival.

 At the w end of the nave is a bell inscribed 'Anno Dni 1587'.

 To the s of the church the old Clergy House (dating from *c.*1350) was the first building to be acquired by the National Trust after it was founded in 1895.

## Alnwick NORTHUMBERLAND

ST MICHAEL & ALL ANGELS is one of the finest examples in northern England of Perpendicular architecture.

 The four hexagonal pillars on the N side of the nave have two incised panels down the entire length of each face – a very unusual feature.

 At the w end of the N aisle is an ancient chest, *c.*1320, one of the finest Flemish chests in England. Note the hunting scene in the upper panel.

 A window in the N aisle has fifteenth-century glass showing the Pelican in her Piety.

 In the chancel are 22 choir stalls carved in the nineteenth century by local craftsmen

*Altarnum, Cornwall.*

taught by Italian carvers engaged on restoring the castle.

▦ On the N side of the communion rail is the Hotspur Pillar bearing the Percy badges. Henry Percy 'Hotspur', son of the first Earl of Northumberland, was killed at Shrewsbury on 21 July 1403.

▦ Near the s door stand two medieval statues of Henry VI, benefactor of the church, and St Maurice, a local saint.

## Alstonefield        STAFFORDSHIRE

ST PETER is situated in the Peak District, of which the churchyard commands magnificent views.

▦ The two-decker pulpit is dated 1637 with a curious abbreviated text from Revelation 2, v.10.

▦ At the E end of the N aisle is the elaborate Cotton family pew painted green and dating from c.1640. (Charles Cotton (1630–87) was a poet and jester who entertained Isaac Walton, author of *The Compleat Angler*). Among the pew's carvings are flowers and grapes.

▦ In the churchyard in line with the s porch are two interesting gravestones. The first, dating from 1518, commemorates a woman named Anne Green and is reputed to be the oldest gravestone in Britain. The other commemorates a Margaret Barclay, who died at the age of 107 in 1731! This was a most unusual age at that time.

## Altarnun        CORNWALL

ST NONNA is a unique dedication and may mean that the saint herself built the first church here, known as the 'Cathedral of the Moors'.

▦ A carved bench-end near the font depicts an angel holding a shield bearing the words, 'Robart Daye maker of this worke . . .' This is a unique example of a woodcarver actually stating that he has carved the bench-end in question. There are 79 carved bench-ends by Robert Daye dating from between 1510 and 1530.

▦ On the s side of the church is a gravestone to George Burnard (d. 23 May 1805, aged 52) and his wife Elizabeth (d. 1 August 1819, aged 71).This was carved by N. N. Burnard, aged 14, who later became a famous sculptor; he used a nail to carve this slate memorial stone to his grandparents.

▦ Near the church gate is a fine Celtic cross dating from c.550.

## Alwalton        CAMBRIDGESHIRE

ST ANDREW In the former county of Huntingdonshire, this church and village

*Amberley, West Sussex. There are two particularly interesting people buried in the churchyard.*

are situated very close to the A1 and the city of Peterborough.

 A plaque in the church reads: 'Sir Frederick Henry Royce, Bart. Born at Alwalton 27 March, 1863. Died 22 April, 1933.' After his death at West Wittering (W Sussex) he was cremated at the Golders Green Crematorium and his ashes taken to the Rolls-Royce works at Derby. They were later interred underneath a stone in this church directly below the plaque. The stone bears his initials and a cross. Tradition says that Henry Royce was so unhappy in his childhood at Alwalton that he never returned here.

## Amberley    West Sussex

ST MICHAEL The church lies at the end of a delightful village street, overlooked by the South Downs and right up close to the walls of Amberley Castle.

 In the lower part of the churchyard on the E side is the grave of Edward Stott, ARA (25 April 1855–19 March 1918) surmounted by a memorial showing the artist's sculptured head by Francis Derwent Wood. Underneath are the words, 'By his works ye shall know him'.

 Near Stott's grave is the grave of Francis Derwent Wood, RA, sculptor (1871–1926), and Florence Derwent Wood (1873–1969). A bronze relief depicts the Entombment of Christ executed by Francis Derwent Wood in 1909.

 Opposite the S door and occupying the top of the Norman N doorway is a semi-circular stained-glass window depicting the Deposition of Christ with sheep, chickens and singing angels. It is by the sculptor Anning Bell and was placed there in 1919 in memory of his artist friend, Edward Stott.

 The magnificent Norman chancel arch dates from c.1100.

9

To the right of the chancel arch are wall paintings dating from c.1150 to 1250. Among them is the Crucifixion, the Resurrection and Christ in Majesty.

In the s aisle is a unique brass showing a man wearing a surcoat over his armour. It commemorates John Wantele (d. 29 January 1424).

On the N wall near the pulpit is an hour-glass stand dating from c.1570. The hour glass was stolen in September 1970.

The five bells dating from 1742 are rung anticlockwise and is the lightest ring of five in Sussex. The tenor bell weighs 298.01 kg (5 cwt 3 qr 13 lb).

## Appledram or Apuldram    West Sussex

St Mary the Virgin. This little church is in an idyllic setting quite close to Chichester Harbour.

The chancel is an outstanding example of Early English architecture dating from c.1290. The e wall comprises three lancet windows with richly moulded heads and Purbeck marble shafts. Smaller groups of lancets can be seen in the N and s walls.

On the N side of the chancel is a slab of Purbeck marble carved with an elaborate cross which may have covered the grave of the builder of this chancel.

Note the graffiti scratched on the inside jambs of the windows in the fifteenth-century s porch. A scratch dial, merchant's mark, letters and a cockerel can be seen.

## Arreton      Isle of Wight

St George is situated in the centre of the island, on the road from Newport to Sandown. The church is long with a bold w tower.

Immediately opposite the priest's door on the N side of the churchyard is the grave of Elizabeth Wallbridge (1770–1801) who was 'The Dairyman's Daughter' in the famous gospel tract by the Reverend Legh Richmond (1772–1827). She is buried next to her sister.

Near the gateway on the s side of the church is the grave of James Urry, who was gored to death by a bull on 17 June 1815, aged 53. The inscription reads,

'Death is most certain you may see
For suddenly it came to me.
In perfect Health to me'twas sent
By Accident most violent.'

Near the w corner of the porch is the red-brick tomb of Oliver Cromwell's grandson William (1720) and his wife, Martha.

On the sanctuary floor is the headless brass of Harry Hawles, who fought at Agincourt (1415).

The Burma Star Memorial Window can be seen in the s aisle – this was unveiled on 12 May 1992 by Countess Mountbatten of Burma.

## Arundel      West Sussex

St Nicholas is a cruciform church with central tower and spire.

This was originally a parish church whose chancel was used by a college of secular priests. The chancel was separated from the remainder of the church by an iron screen erected c.1380 and this has never been removed! At the Dissolution of the Monasteries, 1538–40, the College was closed and the chancel became ruinous. It was purchased from the Crown in 1544 by the Duke of Norfolk and became the mortuary chapel of this great Roman Catholic family, who lived in the nearby castle. It was renamed the Fitzalan chapel and it can only be entered from *inside* the castle grounds, although one can look into it through the iron and glass screen. Interestingly, the Fitzalan chapel and parish church nave are both the same length at 24.99 m (82 feet).

⬣ Behind the choir stalls under the tower is a medieval stone pulpit complete with stone canopy. (The only other examples in England of medieval stone canopies are at Brockley, Somerset, and Cold Ashton, Gloucestershire. See Medieval Stone Pulpits, page 348.)

⬣ On the N wall is a painting dating from c.1450 showing the Coronation of Our Lady.

⬣ Around the inside walls is rare stone seating – the origin of the saying, 'the weakest should go to the wall'.

THE FITZALAN CHAPEL

On the N side of the chapel, separated by arches, is the lady chapel. The following tombs are noteworthy:

† In the centre of the choir is the tomb of Thomas Fitzalan (1381–1415) and Beatrix, his wife. Except for the Purbeck marble base it is made entirely of alabaster. Note the unusual niches at the back of the canopies over their heads.

† To the w of the Thomas tomb is that of Henry, fifteenth Duke of Norfolk (1860–1917), who restored this chapel in 1886. His effigy is of bronze.

† On the N side of the choir is the tomb of John Fitzalan (1408–35). He wears plate armour and underneath is a gruesome cadaver.

† To the E of John's tomb is the chantry chapel of Thomas Fitzalan (d. 1524). A large canopy is supported on four columns and is Renaissance in design.

† Also opposite Thomas's chantry on the s side of the choir is that of William Fitzalan (d. 1488) and Joan, his wife. Made of Petworth marble the huge canopy is supported on four pillars. Separated from

these, about 30cm (1 foot) away, are unusual twisted columns resembling barley sugar. Note the pendants hanging from the roof inside and the fine effigies of the earl and countess.

## Ashbourne      DERBYSHIRE

ST OSWALD vies with Tideswell in being called the 'Cathedral of the Peak'.

⬣ The 64.61 m (212 feet) high octagonal spire is known as the 'Pride of the Peak'. It is pierced with 20 canopied windows, which greatly reduce the wind force.

⬣ In the w wall, near the figure of St Oswald, are the marks of the cannon balls fired by Parliamentarian troops in 1644.

⬣ The stained-glass window above the priest's door on the s side showing David and Goliath is Victorian. When John Ruskin visited the church in 1875 he was appalled by it and afterwards wrote to the vicar describing it as the worst glass he had ever seen!

⬣ In the N transept are five medallions of stained glass in the lancet window next to the N door. Dating from c.1250 they depict scenes from the birth of Christ. Some of the details are interesting – Herod's men wear chain mail and toadstools grow on the ground where the angel appears to the shepherds!

⬣ On the E side of the N transept is the Boothby chapel. At the SE corner of the chapel is a beautiful marble monument to Penelope Boothby by Thomas Banks, RA. She died in 1791, aged five, and is said to have spoken, if only a few words in each, the four languages around the base of the tomb – English, French, Italian and Latin. The English inscription is on the N side, part of which reads, 'To Penelope, only child of Sir Brooke Boothby and Dame Susannah Boothby, born April 11, 1785: died March 13, 1791. She was in form and intellect most exquisite. The unfortunate parents ventured their all on this frail bark, and the wreck was total.' The monument is carved out of a single slab of Carrara marble of which it is difficult to obtain large pieces without any flaws; it was shown at the Royal Academy, London, in 1793 and moved Queen Charlotte, wife of George III, to tears.

Penelope also sat for a portrait by Sir Joshua Reynolds (1723–92) in 1788, entitled 'Penelope Boothby'. This portrait is now owned privately but was last exhibited at the Royal Academy in 1986.

In the NE corner of this chapel is the table-tomb of Sir Thomas Cockayne (d. 1537) and his wife, Barbara FitzHerbert. Part of the inscription of what is the earliest rhyming epitaph in existence reads:

'And did his house and name restore
　Whiche others had decayed before
　And was a Knight so worshipfull
　So virtuous wyse and pitifull'

In the chapel adjoining the s transept behind the organ on the s wall is the church's original dedication plate, which translated from the Latin, reads, 'In the year one thousand two hundred and forty-one [1241] from the Incarnation of Our Lord on the eighth [day] before the Kalends of May this church was dedicated and this Altar consecrated in honour of Saint Oswald, King and Martyr, by the Venerable Father, the Lord Hugo de Patishul, Bishop of Coventry.' The date of the dedication was 24 April 1241 and is the oldest contemporary dedication plate in the British Isles as well as the oldest example of Arabic lettering in Britain.

The stained glass in the SE window of the s aisle was designed by Christopher Whall in 1905. It depicts St Barbara, St Cecilia and St Dorothea and is in memory of Monica and Dorothea Peveril Turnbull

(2 June 1880–27 April 1901), who both died from burns received in rescuing their father when a lighted lamp he was holding exploded at their home, Sandybrook Hall.

At the NE corner of the s transept is the door which formerly led to the ringing chamber. It has Norman serpent hinges on it. The staircase behind the door was blocked by the Victorians when it was found necessary to strengthen the tower piers. At the same time the unsightly buttress *inside* the church was added at the E end of the nave – diagonally opposite the blocked staircase.

At the entrance to the churchyard at the NE corner the gate posts are crowned with skulls and flames dating from c.1700. John Ruskin deplored these too and said the stones should be used for making roads!

## Ashbrittle　　　　　　　SOMERSET

ST JOHN THE BAPTIST can be found in a lovely village, high up on the border between Devon and Somerset. With the exception of the nave, the church was rebuilt in Victorian times.

In the churchyard is a 3000-year-old yew tree. It is the largest yew and one of the oldest recorded trees in England.

## Ashby-De-La-Zouch LEICESTERSHIRE

ST HELEN is delightfully situated on the N side of the ruined castle, surrounded by a beautiful churchyard and the small town.

The ancient heraldic glass in the E window of the chancel came from the ruined castle chapel near by.

The Hastings chapel on the s side of the chancel also contains ancient heraldic glass.

In the Hastings chapel is the splendid tomb of the Second Earl of Huntingdon (d. 1561) and his wife, Katherine (d. 1576).

His feet rest on a lion with a grinning human face.

🔹 Near by is a monument to the famous Countess of Huntingdon (d. 17 June 1791, aged 84) who admired John Wesley, George Whitfield and other great eighteenth-century preachers. A memorial brass on the chancel floor also commemorates her.

🔹 The oak reredos in the chancel is in the style of Grinling Gibbons.

🔹 The piers supporting the nave arcades have battlemented tops – a very rare feature.

🔹 To the left of the door leading up to the tower is a unique finger pillory, 1.09 m (3 feet 8 inches) long, 12 cm (4½ inches) wide and 14 cm (5 inches) deep. It consists of 13 grooves of varying sizes hinged to another piece of wood with corresponding grooves into which different-sized fingers could be locked – a principle similar to that of the stocks.

## Ashover DERBYSHIRE

ALL SAINTS The church, with its imposing spire, sits in an impressive churchyard encircled by numerous trees.

🔹 The spire is 39.01 m (128 feet) high.

🔹 The Norman font, dating from c.1150, is the only lead font in Derbyshire. It is circular and is 0.6 m (2 feet) across the top and 0.35 m (1 foot 2 inches) deep. Around the outside are 20 figures of men holding books, 0.20 m (8 inches) high, each standing under an arch.

This font is unique as it has stone inside – all other lead fonts are made of solid lead, inside and outside. It was probably saved from destruction during the Civil War by being buried by the rector, Immanuel Bourne, in his kitchen garden at Eastwood Hall. (See Lead Fonts, page 74.)

🔹 The third bell in the ring of eight is the only bell in England to bear the name of Napoleon Bonaparte. It cracked while ringing the news of his retreat from Moscow in 1814 and his subsequent abdication and had to be recast. The inscription states that it 'rung the downfall of Bonaparte and broke April 1814'.

🔹 A very fine alabaster table-tomb at the E end of the S aisle depicts Thomas Babington (d. 1518) and Edith (d. 1511), his wife. Erected in 1511, it shows Edith wearing a kennel headdress. Thomas has a large purse attached to his belt. On the end of the tomb is St Catherine holding a wheel. Both effigies are attractively coloured. Around the sides of the tomb are carved figures of the Babington family's 15 children. This is arguably the finest sixteenth-century tomb in Derbyshire.

🔹 The rood screen was given by Thomas Babington in 1511.

## Ashurst WEST SUSSEX

ST JAMES is a little church in remote countryside on the N side of the South Downs, not far from Steyning.

🔹 On the NE side of the churchyard a wooden cross marks the grave of Margaret Fairless Dowson (d. 24 August 1901, aged 33). Under the pseudonym Michael Fairless she wrote a book called *The Roadmender* (1902) which relates to this area, as well as other novels.

🔹 Inside the church over the N doorway in a transparent plastic case given in memory of Archibald Robert Piper (1903–68) is a vamping horn 0.91 m (3 feet) long with a bell 0.17 m (7 inches) in diameter. Inside, about 0.20 m (8 inches) from the end, is a framework of wires that may be to prevent obstructions from being put inside or to increase the tone.

This vamping horn is made of iron, is painted a dark green and in yellow lettering says: 'Praise Him upon ye strings &

pipe', a quotation from Psalm 150. It also has the words 'Palmer Fecit' and the date 1770.

Of the nine vamping horns in England this one is unique because unlike the others – which are trumpet-shaped – it is conical with the bell set at an angle to the mouthpiece. It is also the smallest, the most recent and the only one with wires inside. (See Vamping Horns, page 245.)

▨ At the w end of the nave is a font dating from c.1250.Three of its four faces are plain but the E face (visible to the congregation) is decorated with five incised arches.

▨ E of the s doorway is a wall tablet surmounted by a fluted urn to Sarah Wilson, the eldest and last surviving daughter of Thomas Wilson of Tenterden, Kent. The memorial by John Flaxman was erected by Edward Wilson, DD, rector of Ashurst, 'as a testimony of his affection and regard for his justly lamented niece. She departed this life whilst on a visit at his parsonage house, the 7th day of July, 1798 in the 33rd year of her age.' She was buried in the family vault at Tenterden. 'She died in a well grounded hope through the merits of her Saviour of a joyful resurrection to life eternal, the happy effect of a pious remembrance of her Creator in the days of her youth.'

## Ashwell      RUTLAND

ST MARY THE VIRGIN nestles in a delightful village in the countryside, N of Oakham.

▨ In the churchyard to the s of the tower is the grave of the Reverend J. W. Adams (24 November 1839–20 October 1903), who, on 11 December 1879, was the first clergyman to win the Victoria Cross. He received the award for rescuing from drowning some men of the North Lancers, in the immediate presence of the enemy, under heavy fire from the Afghans and up to his waist in water at a muddy watercourse at Villa Kazi, Afghanistan.

▨ On the floor of the s chapel is a wooden effigy of a knight which probably represents Sir Thomas Touchet, c.1350. The effigy, at 1.88 m (6 feet 2 inches) long, has a mail head-covering, surcoat and hauberk. On his left side are the remains of a sword. His damaged hands are in prayer, his right leg is crossed over his left and a mutilated lion lies at his feet to which spurs are attached.

The effigy is in fair condition. (See Wooden Effigies, page 246.)

▨ Near by is the top stone of a table-tomb commemorating John and Rose Vernam, 1400. Their figures are incised on the stone like brass but have been defaced – graffiti was a problem as early as 1651!

▨ In the N chapel, now a vestry, is the alabaster figure of a priest, sadly now defaced. Some of the graffiti is dated 1783 and 1795.

## Astley      WORCESTERSHIRE

ST PETER can be found on a hill, surrounded by trees.

▨ Built c.1160, the doorway has typical Norman zigzag carvings.

▨ In the churchyard is buried the great hymn writer Frances Ridley Havergal (14 December 1836–3 June 1879). On her tombstone are inscribed the words, 'By her writings in prose and verse she being dead, yet speaketh.' Among her hymns are, 'Take my life and let it be' and 'Who is on the Lord's side?'.

## Aston Ingham      HEREFORDSHIRE

ST JOHN THE BAPTIST was almost entirely rebuilt in 1891.

▨ The lead font is 0.32 m (1 foot 1 inch)

deep externally and has a top diameter of approximately 0.6 m (2 feet).

🔲 On the E and W sides appears the date 1689 and some beautiful decoration. The initials W. R. appear on the N side and W. M. on the S. They are not the names of the church-wardens at that time as these names are *not* in the registers. They may refer to William of Orange, who was invited to become king in 1689 with Mary, the initials denoting William Rex and William/Mary our only joint sovereigns. (See Lead Fonts, page 74.)

🔲 The two stone coffin lids fixed to the E wall date from *c.*1300 but the figures have not been identified.

🔲 The beautiful E window showing the Adoration by the Wise Men dates from 1923. It commemorates three generations of the Whatley family who were rectors here successively from 1785–1914 without a break: Charles Whatley, MA 1785–1835, his son Henry Lawson Whatley, MA 1835–73 and his son, Henry Lawson Whatley, BA 1873–1914. The last rector's wife, Isabella Margaret, is also commemorated, as well as their elder daughter, Florence Isabella, who was organist from 1891 to 1922.

## Awliscombe      Devon

ST MICHAEL & ALL ANGELS is built on a hill; this explains why the nave and N aisle slope *up* towards the chancel.

🔲 The magnificent stone chancel screen dates from *c.*1510 and has six angels at the front of the tracery acting as corbels. They all hold scrolls but one has a wing missing. Along the top of the screen runs a cornice of vine leaves; the battlements were added in 1838.

🔲 Note the panelled chancel arch and also the arches leading to the N aisle and S transept.

🔲 A particularly beautiful stained-glass window at the W end of the N aisle commemorates a well-known parishioner, Margaret Ruth Wilmington (1934–69). It shows Ruth with a bundle of corn and the words, 'The Lord recompense thy work and a full reward be given thee of the Lord.' On either side of the S window in the S transept is unusual tabernacle work dating from *c.*1500.

🔲 The S porch dates from *c.*1510 and is unusual in having two openings. At the base of the SW buttress the words 'Bride's hand, 1708' are inscribed.

## Aylesbury      BUCKINGHAMSHIRE

ST MARY is a large church set in the centre of a busy county town.

🔲 This fine church has an unusual spirelet (*c.*1650) sheathed in lead on top of its central tower.

🔲 The superbly carved chalice font dates from *c.*1180 and is one of a local group of similarly carved fonts known as 'Aylesbury fonts'.

🔲 In the vestry is a fine canopied tomb commemorating Lady Lee (d.1584) and her children. She is shown kneeling at a little stool on which is a vase containing a red flower, regardless of season. The reason for this is explained in the inscription on the tomb, part of which reads:

'Good friend stick not to strew with
  crimson flowers
This marble stone wherein her cinders
  rest.
For sure her ghost lives with the
  heavenly powers
And guerdon hath of virtuous life
  possessed.'

This tomb is said to have come from the ruined church of St Peter, Quarrendon, about 2.4 km (1½ miles) NW of Aylesbury.

*St Andrew in Banwell – the superb Somerset tower dominates this busy village.*

## Bacton SUFFOLK

ST MARY THE VIRGIN can be found in an idyllic setting near a little stream. To enter the churchyard from the village one has to cross a bridge.

 On the outside of the clerestory are excellent examples of knapped flintwork including triangles, the triple crown, St Catherine's wheel and monograms of Christ and His mother.

 Above the nave is a magnificent double hammer-beam roof dating from c.1450. It is decorated with numerous detailed carvings, especially over the clerestory windows.

 Over the chancel arch are the remains of a 'Doom' painting. On the lower right can be seen a dishonest ale-wife who is being tipped from a wheelbarrow into the pit of everlasting fire! This ale-wife and wheelbarrow combination is unique in an English wall painting.

 The E window was designed by Sir Edward Burne-Jones and dates from c.1920.

 The font dates from c.1550 and is decorated with angels and Tudor roses. One side is plain, showing that it used to stand against a pillar or wall.

## Bamburgh NORTHUMBEFRLAND

ST AIDAN is situated at the opposite end of the village to the magnificent castle. It has a long and very impressive chancel.

 To the W of the tower is the grave of Grace Darling (1815–42) the heroine. It consists of a recumbent effigy under an elaborate Victorian canopy.

 In the N aisle is the original effigy from Grace Darling's grave which was brought inside for greater preservation at the end of the nineteenth century. The sculptor of this effigy carved the replica outside.

 On the N side of the chancel is a beautiful modern electric lamp enclosing a cross. Inscribed on a plaque underneath are the words, 'This is the site where St Aidan died in the year 651 A.D. Remember him and this his church.'

 At the E end over the altar is a fine historical reredos in Caen stone depicting 16 men and women who contributed to the spread of Christianity in northern England.

 Underneath the chancel is a beautifully groined thirteenth-century crypt.

## Banwell SOMERSET

ST ANDREW The church tower dominates the busy village and is well seen from across the bowling green.

 The magnificent tower, similar to Winscombe and Cheddar, dates from c.1450 and contains a ring of ten bells.

 Inside the church on the E side of the tower is a statue of St Andrew which was originally *outside* before the roof level was raised.

The medieval stone pulpit is a superb example of fifteenth-century work. Note the delicate stone carving. (See Medieval Stone Pulpits, page 348.)

*South doorway, Barfreston, Kent.*

🔲 In the E window of the s aisle is a piece of medieval glass showing the miraculous preservation of the life of a child who had been left in a bath over a fire while his mother attended the consecration of St Nicholas, Bishop of Myra.

🔲 In the vestry on the N side of the chancel are some panels of sixteenth-century Flemish glass depicting scenes from the Apocrypha and the Bible.

🔲 The magnificent chancel screen was erected in 1521, the two doors being cut from a single block of oak!

🔲 Among the hundred wooden roof bosses is one that is unique. It shows Christ rising vertically from a tomb wearing the Crown of Thorns. The Cross, spear and sponge are depicted at the sides. This is the only complete roof boss devoted to this subject

and is near the N door. Eleven other roof bosses depict St George killing the Dragon.

## Barfreston                           KENT

ST NICHOLAS dates from *c*.1170 and is a superb example of a late Norman or Romanesque church.

🔲 Part of the church is composed of stone from Caen in Normandy.

🔲 The wheel window at the E end is particularly outstanding.

🔲 The s doorway has a magnificent carved tympanum and elaborate mouldings.

🔲 The one bell hangs in the nearby yew tree – a unique position for a bell. It was placed there in 1900 and is rung from inside the church, the bell rope passing through a metal tube.

## Barkham                           BERKSHIRE

ST JAMES is situated in beautiful rolling countryside; it is a Victorian church and replaces an earlier building.

🔲 On the s side of the church is a beautiful cedar tree planted *c*.1770.

🔲 In a recess of the E wall of the s porch which forms the base of the tower is a wooden effigy believed to commemorate Anne or Agnes (d. 1336), daughter of Thomas Neville. The effigy, at 1.53m (5 feet 1 inch) long, wears a wimple and loose gown; her arms are in prayer position but the hands are missing. Her head rests on two cushions but the features of her face have been destroyed. No feet are visible as, presumably, these would have been hidden under her gown. The effigy is quite well preserved. (See Wooden Effigies, page 246.)

🔲 In the same porch is an ancient door now used as a notice board.

🔲 The font, which may be early nineteenth century, is adorned with two

**B**

cherubs' heads and two winged horses. Underneath the latter appears the motto '*Audacter et sincere*'.

🔳 This same Latin motto appears on a wall plaque on the NE side of the nave to Henry Clive (18 October 1777–16 March 1848) and Charlotte Jane Clive (15 August 1784–12 May 1874). Perhaps this family gave the font?

## Barnby                              SUFFOLK

ST JOHN THE BAPTIST lies close to the busy A146 between Beccles and Lowestoft.

🔳 On the S side of the nave is a banner locker complete with its original door – a unique survival. It is now used for storing service books. It is 1.85 m (6 feet 8 inches) high, 28 cm (11 inches) wide and 30 cm (12 inches) deep. There is a quatrefoil at the top of the door and window tracery at the bottom.

🔳 On the N wall of the chancel is a charming relief showing Jesus and the woman at Jacob's well.

🔳 The E window depicts Jesus, John the Baptist and two disciples in memory of one Grace Hilda Dudgeon. It was made by M. E. A. Rope in 1963.

## Basildon                            BERKSHIRE

ST BARTHOLOMEW This church is found between the main London to Bristol railway line and the River Thames, both being very near.

🔳 Jethro Tull (1674–1741), inventor of the seed drill c.1701, is buried in the churchyard. His invention was first used on his farm at Howberry near Wallingford (Oxon.).

## Bath                                SOMERSET

THE ABBEY CHURCH OF ST PETER & ST PAUL was commenced in 1499 on the foundations of the Norman cathedral following a dream by Bishop Oliver King (1495–1503).

🔳 This is the last great church to be built in the Perpendicular style of architecture.

🔳 The W front has two turrets on the faces of which are ladders carved with angels ascending and descending from heaven. The descending angels are shown with their heads downwards. These ladders were in the dream of Bishop King, who also heard a voice say, 'Let an Olive establish the crown and a King restore the church.' On each side of the turrets are carvings of the 12 apostles and on the W faces of the buttresses flanking the N and S aisles is the rebus of Bishop Oliver King – an olive tree and a crown.

🔳 The great W door, carved in oak, was given by Sir Henry Montague, Lord Chief Justice, in 1617. On each side of the doorway are figures of St Peter and St Paul dating from c.1580.

🔳 The entire abbey is roofed with fan vaulting – the only church in the world completely roofed in stone with this unique English invention. The vaulting in the aisles and chancel was designed by Robert and William Vertue, master masons to Henry VII, but that in the nave, following the chancel design, was carried out by Sir Gilbert Scott between 1864 and 1874 and is an excellent copy. (See Fan Vaulting, page 152.)

🔳 Against the SE pier of the central tower is the beautiful processional cross of silver made by Omar Ramsden in 1925 and given in memory of Frederick W. S. Shelton. One side shows the Adoration of the Shepherds and the other the Adoration of the Kings.

▨ On the same pier, near by, is a beautiful mace rest given *c*.1920 in memory of Second Lieutenant Roy Leslie Box, killed at Gueudecourt, France, in the First World War, aged 23.

▨ At the E end of the S choir aisle is a rare portable oak font dating from *c*.1750. The finial of the cover is an acorn. (See Wooden Fonts, page 34.)

▨ Bath Abbey has more tablets and memorials than any other English church (apart from Westminster Abbey). There are 614 wall tablets, many dating from the eighteenth century when Beau Nash helped to attract visitors to this fashionable spa. These memorials inspired Henry Harington, MD (d.1816) to write:

'These walls so full of monument and bust,
Show how Bath waters serve to lay the dust.'

The most interesting monuments are:

† At the W end of the N aisle, a memorial to Robert Walsh (d. 12 September 1788), aged 66. It shows a broken pillar and is the second oldest depicting this motif. (The oldest is in Canterbury Cathedral dating from 1752.)

† At the NE end of the N aisle, a memorial commemorating Sir Isaac Pitman, KT (1813–97), the inventor of Pitman's shorthand.

† Just opposite the Pitman memorial, the imposing monument of James Montagu, Bishop of Bath and Wells, 1608–15, and Bishop of Winchester, 1615–18. He lies on a table-tomb surrounded by iron railings with iron banners at the corners. This monument was designed by William Cuer (the younger) and Nicholas Johnson and is one of only two effigies in England depicting a bishop wearing the badge of the Order of the Garter. (The other is of Bishop Lancelot Andrewes (d. 1626) in Southwark Cathedral, London. He was a Bishop of Winchester.)

† At the E end of the N choir aisle is a wall tablet commemorating the Reverend Thomas Haweis (d. 11 February 1820), aged 87, the founder of the London Missionary Society.

† On the S side of the sanctuary is the magnificent chantry chapel of Prior William Birde (d. 1515), who helped Bishop King build the Abbey. His rebus, a 'W' with the figure of a bird, frequently appears in the carving and at the E end in the vaulting is his mitre, staff and coat of arms. The cost of this chantry is said to have made Prior Birde very poor.

† On the E side of Birde's chantry is a lovely memorial by Chantrey to William Hoare, RA (d.1792) the painter and a contemporary of Gainsborough. The monument is dated 1828.

† In the S choir aisle is a memorial to Sir Richard Bickerton (1759–1832) also by Chantrey and dated 1834.

† To the W of this memorial is a tablet by Flaxman to the botanist John Sibthorp (d.1796).

† On the E wall of the S transept is the oldest relief monument in the abbey. It commemorates Jacob Bosanquet (d. 9 June 1767), aged 54, and was executed by W. Carter. Underneath the superb relief depicting the Good Samaritan are the words, 'Go and do thou likewise. So shalt thou die the death of the righteous and thy last end be like his.'

† At the S end of the S transept under the Jesse window is the fine monument by Epiphanius Evesham to Jane, the wife of Sir William Waller, who commanded the Parliamentary forces against the Royalists under Sir Ralph Hopton and was defeated at the Battle of Lansdown in 1643. The monument was erected *c*.1634. At the back are two arches, the left one recording

*Angels ascending and descending on the west front of Bath Abbey, Somerset.*

Jane's virtues and the right one blank because her husband was buried in the Tothill Street chapel, Westminster, London.

† At the E end of the S aisle is a plain tablet to Richard (Beau) Nash (d. 1761), who as Master of Ceremonies made Bath into a fashionable resort in the first half of the eighteenth century.

† Across the N transept is a magnificent wrought-iron screen, probably by William Edney, which was given in 1725. It was originally an altar rail but was discarded in 1833 and used on the balcony of a house in Bath (1 Lansdown Place West) before being returned to the abbey in 1960 through the generosity of the Dowager Lady Noble. It was then made into a two-tiered screen.

⬚ In the floor near the lectern is a stone slab commemorating 1000 years of English monarchy. It reads, 'On the ninth day of August AD1973 the Queen and the Duke of Edinburgh gave thanks here for one thousand years of the English Monarchy since the Coronation of King Edgar on Whit Sunday AD973 in the Saxon abbey on this site.'

⬚ At the E end of the N aisle is the 1949 Edgar window also commemorating the Coronation of King Edgar on 11 May 973.

⬚ The large E window of the chancel is unique in being *square-headed*. It contains 75.9 sq m (817 sq. feet) of stained glass which portrays 56 scenes from the Life of Our Lord. This window was badly damaged by a landmine on 26 April 1942 and restored by M. C. Farrar Bell, great grandson of the original designer. It was unveiled on 13 March 1955.

⬚ The central tower, containing ten bells, is unusual in being rectangular in plan instead of the usual square. It is 49.4 m (162 feet) high.

# Bathampton        SOMERSET

ST NICHOLAS is today mostly Victorian in construction except for the eastward extension, which was dedicated on 30 April 1993. Note how well it blends with the new building, the balustrade copying that of the S aisle.

⬚ In the S aisle is located the Australia chapel, which contains the grave of Arthur Philip (1738–1814), founder of Australia and First Governor of New South Wales. On the Friday nearest to his birthday (11 October) a service is held in the church attended by representatives of the Australian High Commission and the Australian flag is flown from the tower.

⬚ The graves of three particularly interesting people can be found in the graveyard:

† On the S side of the church near the path is the grave of William Harbutt, ARCA (13 February 1844–1 June 1921), inventor of plasticine. Among relatives buried with him and his wife is his youngest son, Owen C. Harbutt, who died December 1993, aged 104.

† Also on the S side of the church is the grave of the artist Walter Sickert (1860–1942) and his third wife, Therese Lessore (1884–1945), also a painter. If you stand on the S side of the large conifer tree, look towards two o'clock, then take about 15 paces you will see the grave.

† Just N of the W face of the tower and near the wall is a flat grave slab commemorating John Baptiste Viscount Du Barry, died 18 November 1778. He was the last person to be killed in a legal duel in England.

# Beaulieu        HAMPSHIRE

THE BLESSED VIRGIN AND HOLY CHILD is the former refectory of the abbey and is orientated N to S with the altar at the southern end.

*Beaulieu, Hampshire.*

In the w wall is a rare example of a monastic pulpit from which a monk would read during meal times. This pulpit, built into the thickness of the wall, is approached by 18 steps. The pointed arches and Purbeck marble pillars are beautiful examples of thirteenth-century work. (See Medieval Stone Pulpits, page 348.)

The wagon-shaped plaster roof contains several interesting wooden roof bosses, including the following:

† Near the altar, the head of a pope, possibly Pope Boniface IX. (Other roof bosses depicting popes are only found at Burwell, Cambridgeshire, and there are two at Exeter Cathedral, see page 131.)

† Two modern bosses on the first and fourth ribs depict the arms of the abbey (a crosier over a crown) and have the date 1204 on them.

† Another boss near by has a blue strap with 1856 inside it. This probably records the year in which the roof was repaired.

† On the seventh rib from the N is a boss depicting a bearded man with a red hat holding a heart between the star of David. Was he a Jew?

Above the altar are triple lancets, the middle one of which is blocked because of a huge buttress outside which was built in 1743. In the recess of this former window is a beautiful plaque of the Virgin and Child by Martin Travers, installed in 1942. Underneath are the words, 'The nations shall walk in His light.' (See page 288 for a similar bas-relief in Romsey Abbey.)

The outstanding memorial in the church is on the E wall of the chancel and commemorates a woman called Mary Do (1611–51).

Near this monument is a bronze tablet, the work of Lady Scott, widow of the famous Antarctic explorer, to the memory of Eleanor Thornton, drowned in the sinking of the SS *Persia* on 30 December 1915. She was secretary to the second Lord Montagu and the original model for the 'Spirit of Ecstasy' on the bonnet of Rolls-Royce cars.

Near the pulpit is the 'Tubby' Clayton Memorial dedicated in June 1984 to the memory of the founder of Toc H who lived in Beaulieu as a boy.

In the churchyard on the NW side is a tombstone to the memory of Michael Silver (1732–78) master carpenter of HMS *Agamemnon* built at nearby Bucklers Hard.

Near this tombstone there is a narrow horizontal opening low in the church wall. This was a serving hatch through which dishes were passed into the refectory from the monastic kitchen, which stood on this site.

# MAIDENS' GARLANDS

From the seventeenth to the nineteenth centuries it was the custom in many English counties to carry a garland (also called a 'crown' or 'crant') in the front of the funeral procession of either a maiden who had died while still a virgin or a girl who was engaged but who had died before marriage. Afterwards the garland would be hung in the church above the dead girl's parents' pew until it decomposed. In some churches garlands of white ribbons were hung from the crown on the anniversary of the person's death.

The garland comprised a circular wooden frame like a lantern on which were fixed coloured paper rosettes and inside, suspended from the centre, were hung paper gloves or handkerchiefs. The name, age and date of death of the young girl commem-

*Maiden's Garland, Ilam, Staffordshire.*

orated were also fixed to the framework and sometimes a verse of poetry.

The following verse could once be seen on the garland of Ann Swindel, who died on 9 December 1798, aged 22 at Ashford-in-the-Water, Derbyshire, but has now disappeared:

'Be always ready, no time delay,
I in my youth was called away:
Great grief to those that's left behind,
But I hope I'm great joy to find.'

The origins of the garland custom are obscure but it may have come from Scandinavia. It is interesting that Shakespeare's only reference to it is in the play *Hamlet* in connection with the death of Ophelia, when the priest protested against Ophelia wearing them:

'Yet here she is allowed her virgin rites
[or 'garland' or 'crown']
Her maiden strewments, and the
bringing home of bell and burial'
(Act 5, Scene 1).

He thus incurred the anger of Ophelia's brother Laertes at the graveside.

The maiden's garland at Springthorpe, Lincolnshire, commemorates Mary Hill, who was killed on Shrove Tuesday in 1814 while ringing one of the four church bells. The rope coiled around her arm and carried her up to the ceiling from where she fell on to the edge of the font below, dying instantly. The garland, made of white parchment stretched over an arched wooden crown, is the only surviving example in Lincolnshire.

At Theydon Mount, Essex, a maiden's garland made of iron and decorated with evergreen leaves hangs from the nave roof, while in Flamborough, East Yorkshire, a pair of white paper gloves is now preserved in a frame. They were used at the funeral of a virgin called Miss Major in 1761.

The maidens' garlands formerly in Robin Hood's Bay at St Stephen in Flyingdales, North Yorkshire, are now in the care of the Yorkshire Museum Services.

Only a few churches in England still contain examples of maidens' garlands because of their fragility. The largest collection can be seen at Abbotts Ann, Hampshire.

As far as I know, maidens' garlands can be seen in the following churches:

1. Abbotts Ann (St Mary), Hampshire
2. Ashford-in-the-Water (Holy Trinity), Derbyshire
3. Astley Abbots (St Calixtus), Shropshire
4. Beverley (St Mary), East Riding of Yorkshire
5. Great Musgrave (St Theobald), Cumbria
6. Ilam (Holy Cross), Staffordshire
7. Matlock (St Giles), Derbyshire
8. Minsterley (Holy Trinity), Shropshire
9. Oxhill (St Laurence), Warwickshire
10. Springthorpe (St Laurence & St George), Lincolnshire
11. Theydon Mount (St Michael), Essex
12. Trusley (All Saints), Derbyshire
13. Walsham le Willows (St Mary), Suffolk
14. Warcop (St Columba), Cumbria

## Beccles

SUFFOLK

ST MICHAEL Approaching the church from the town on its s side, one is drawn to it by its massive tower.

 At 28.04 m (92 feet) high, the detached bell-tower erected *c.*1515 commands a good position overlooking the River Waveney. It boasts a unique feature – four staircases, one in each corner. One leads to the belfry, another to the clock, a third to the ringing chamber and the fourth to the top of the tower.

In the ringing chamber there is another unique feature – the top of the cupboard standing on the w wall in the window acts as a 'shove ha'penny' board, complete with straight lines especially cut for the purpose.

The superb chancel screen was erected *c.*1913 by members of the Crowfoot family who practised medicine in Beccles from 1751 to *c.*1920; Joseph Arnold (see below) was apprenticed to one of them. The two side screens were added as a memorial to those who died in the First World War.

On the s wall of the s chancel aisle is a monument by Chantrey to Joseph Arnold MD (1784–1818), surgeon to the Royal Navy, who died in Sumatra of a pestilence. The inscription reads:

'In memory of Joseph Arnold, MD, Surgeon of the Royal Navy, and fellow of the Linnean Society of London and of the Royal Medical Society of Edinburgh who, after having, in the pursuit of science and his profession, circumnavigated the globe and suffered numerous privations and been exposed to many dangers by sea and land, fell a victim to the pestilential climate of Sumatra, at the moment of entering upon the career most congenial to his wishes having been appointed naturalist in that island to the honourable East India Company.

He was born at Beccles AD1784 and died in Sumatra July 19, 1818.

Reader! If entire devotion to the cause of science, unbiased by interest, unchecked by perils, unappalled by disease, if genuine simplicity of character, and if the kindest disposition, joined to the most steady attachment can excite thy respect, thy admiration, and thy regret, those feelings are due to Him for whose Name this marble strives to ensure a short existence: his virtues are happily recorded in the everlasting tablets of God.'

## Bellingham      NORTHUMBERLAND

ST CUTHBERT This interesting church is situated quite near the Pennine Way and the North Tyne river and is almost completely hidden by houses.

An unusual stone roof in the nave comprising 15 ribs dates from 1609 and is unique in England. There are also seven ribs in the s transept. Many buttresses outside support the great weight of these roofs.

The stone font and wooden cover are encased in a metal circle on which are inscribed the names of those men from the parish who died in the Second World War.

## Bere Regis      DORSET

ST JOHN THE BAPTIST

Over the s door are two large iron hooks which were used to pull off the thatch from the roofs of burning cottages.

The magnificent nave roof is unique and dates from 1475. It was given by Cardinal Morton, who was born here in 1425. At the extreme E end is a boss which reputedly depicts him. On each side of the roof are carvings of the 12 apostles dressed in Tudor costume.

On the s side of the church is the Turberville chapel containing several tombs and the entrance to the vault. Thomas Hardy (1840–1928) wrote a story around this family.

## Berkeley      GLOUCESTERSHIRE

ST MARY THE VIRGIN is close to the famous castle and stands on part of its original outer defences.

The detached bell-tower dates from 1753 and contains a ring of ten bells.

The N door contains several bullet holes and the marks of an axe sustained during the siege of 1645 when the castle was surrounded by Roundheads.

The rood screen dates from c.1450 and is unusual in being of stone.

On the N side of the high altar is the Jenner family vault in which is buried Dr Edward Jenner (1749–1823), who was among the first to prove the efficacy of vaccination against smallpox. He inoculated an eight-year-old boy, James Phipps, on 14 May 1796 although Benjamin Jesty, a Dorset farmer, had inoculated his wife and two sons in 1774 (see Worth Matravers, Dorset, page 435). The stained-glass E window is Jenner's memorial.

The priests' stalls are fine modern work by Robert Thompson of Kilburn (N. Yorkshire). Notice his signature – a carved mouse.

On the s side of the chancel is the Berkeley burial chapel built by Lord James, 11th Lord of Berkeley (1417–63). Apart from his tomb other tombs include Lord Henry, Seventeenth Lord of Berkeley (1534–1613).

In the churchyard, on the left of the path leading to the vestry, is the table-tomb of Dicky Pearce, the Earl of Suffolk's jester, who was killed in revels at the castle in 1728.

## Beverley      EAST RIDING OF YORKSHIRE

THE MINSTER CHURCH OF ST JOHN THE EVANGELIST has, since 1548, been the largest church in England used as a parish church. It is *not* a cathedral.

It has a floor area of 2772.13 sq m (29,840 sq feet) as compared to its nearest rival, Hull Parish Church, which covers an area of 2530.13 sq m (27,235 sq feet).

The magnificent w towers are the finest pair of towers in England and were built c.1450. They are rectangular, being broader E to w than N to s and are both 49.68 m (163 feet) high. They are thought to have inspired Nicholas Hawksmoor, who was architect to Beverley Minster, when he designed the two w towers for Westminster Abbey in 1745.

◈ On the sw tower is a sundial inscribed 'Now or When', and on the nw tower on the nw pinnacle a wind vane dated 1802.

◈ On the n side of the nave is the Highgate porch (over which is a room), which was built c.1410 and is a superb example of Perpendicular architecture.

◈ Above the nave vaulting, invisible from the floor, is brick infilling. Dating from 1308 this is the earliest brickwork still in its original position.

◈ An interesting engineering feat was carried out in c.1710 when the whole of the n transept gable was forced back to the vertical using an enormous wooden framework and many men and horses. Before it was done, the gable was leaning dangerously over the street. A picture in the n transept shows how the work was done. Inside, one can see near the floor how distorted the pillars were.

◈ In the n choir aisle is a beautiful thirteenth-century double staircase with Purbeck columns which led to the chapter house, demolished in 1550.

◈ On the n side of the choir is the famous Percy tomb, a magnificent example of stone carving. Dating from c.1350 it may commemorate Lady Eleanor (d.1328). Among the carvings are figures holding coats of arms, fruits, leaves and numerous angels. Fortunately the details are only slightly damaged.

◈ Opposite the Percy tomb is a rare *wooden* sedilia also dating from c.1350.

◈ In the choir is the famous Frith-Stool or Sanctuary Chair dating from c.980. (The only other Frith-Stool is in Hexham Abbey, Northumberland, but what may have been others are in Chewton Mendip,

Somerset, Sprotbrough, S. Yorks., and Welsh Newton, Herefordshire.)

◈ Also in the choir are 68 misericords, more than in any other church or cathedral in the British Isles. They date from c.1400.

◈ Under the vaulting at the back of the reredos below the great e window is more exquisite carving dating from c.1350. Note particularly the boss showing the Coronation of the Blessed Virgin Mary on the s side.

◈ The great e window contains a variety of medieval stained glass. Some of it comprises jumbled fragments. Observe how the tracery on the s side leans into the centre of the window.

◈ Inside the tower over the crossing is a tread-wheel dating from 1716 but built to a medieval design. It is still used to lift a movable boss in the centre and to carry materials up to the roofs. Other tread-wheels are preserved at Canterbury, Durham and Peterborough cathedrals, Salisbury Cathedral and Louth (see pages 61, 110, 270, 303 and 226 respectively).

◈ Also in the crossing is a movable circular communion table which was presented by the Friends of the Minster in 1970.

◈ At the e end of the nave is the tomb of St John of Beverley, founder of this church, Bishop of Hexham AD687–705, Bishop of York AD705–18. He was born at Harpham in c.640 and died at Beverley AD721.

◈ On the w wall of the s transept an interesting plaque reads:

'Your late Pastor T.M. being dead, yet speaketh.

Be daily and devout in private and (if opportunity serve) in publick [sic] Prayer

Frequently receive the holy Communion with humble, penitent, faithful, charitable, and thankful Hearts. Live soberly, righteously and Godly. Fear God and keep his Commandments. The peace of God be with you all in Christ Jesus. Amen. Died Feb. 1, 1750 aged 84.'

On the E wall of the S transept another plaque records:

'This tablet is dedicated by subscription to the memory of Caroline Elizabeth Hanks, mistress of the Beverley Minster Beckside Infant School, in consequence of whose timely warning a fire which had broken out on 15 Nov. 1889 in the roof of the choir of this minster and threatened irreparable damage was extinguished. She died at Prees in Shropshire 21 April, 1890 Aged 23.'

At the entrance to the choir is a magnificent wooden screen designed by Sir George Gilbert Scott and carved by James Elwell from 1876 to 78. It supports the organ.

The fine W door has carvings of the Four Evangelists and dates from c.1750.

This church contains the largest collection of carvings of medieval musical instruments in the world. They are found on the misericords and elsewhere, including a large number at the head of the nave piers and on the superb arcading in the N nave aisle.

The Minster clock is the only one to strike on bells in two towers. The quarters are chimed on the ten bells in the N tower and the hours are struck on 'Great John', weighing in at 7112.44 kg (7 tons) in the S tower. The chimes are also unique.

# Beverley   EAST RIDING OF YORKSHIRE

ST MARY is one of the most beautiful parish churches in England and dates from c.1220–1530.

In 1520 the central tower collapsed and damaged the nave. It was rebuilt 1520–24 and also the nave. The cost was met by the town guilds and individual parishioners. Over each of the piers are figures bearing shields and the donors' names.

The most outstanding one is at the NE end. Known as the Minstrels' Pier it was paid for by the Minstrels' Guild. Five quaint figures wearing brown or blue coats and pink shoes formerly held different musical instruments, but unfortunately three have lost theirs and only the lute and oboe are left. The dress is typically Tudor.

Adjoining the N transept is the choir vestry dating from c.1310. Below it is a crypt built 1280–90 with fine stone vaulting.

To the E of the choir vestry is the vicar's vestry. On the right of the doorway is a stone figure of a rabbit carved c.1330. It is reputed to have inspired Sir John Tenniel when he produced his drawing of a white rabbit for Lewis Carroll's book *Alice in Wonderland*.

In the NE corner is St Michael's chapel, dated 1325–40. It is a superb example of Decorated architecture with a lovely ribbed vault.

Adjoining St Michael's chapel in the E wall of the church is a doorway, surmounted by the Beverley Imp (a mythical creature, similar to the famous Lincoln Imp, see page 200) which leads to two rooms over St Michael's chapel. In these rooms is a collection of interesting objects, including a maiden's garland (see Maidens' Garlands, page 24).

The chancel ceiling is unique and was painted in 1445. Forty kings are depicted. It was repaired and repainted in c.1860 and cleaned in 1939 when George VI was added at the extreme SW corner.

In the chancel are 28 stalls dated 1445 with an interesting and amusing set of misericords. Several depict foxes and there is also an excellent carving of an elephant with a seat on its back.

🔲 Throughout the church are nearly 600 carved wooden roof bosses. The following are specially interesting:

† At the E end of the nave is a soldier on horseback (probably St George) trampling a dragon.

† In the nave and chancel are two bosses depicting St John of Beverley and King Athelstan side by side. They are unique.

† In the N chancel aisle is a boss showing an axe, an L-square and a pair of compasses.

🔲 The octagonal marble font in the NW corner is unusual in that it carries an inscription recording the name of the donor, William Leryffaxe, and the date, 1530.

Near by is a wooden font (1963) from the workshop of Robert Thompson – notice the mouse! It is inscribed, 'To the dear memory of Catharine Murrey, died Jan. 3rd. 1963. Aged 31. A chorister of this church.' (See Wooden Fonts, page 34.)

🔲 Outside, the W front dates from c.1411 and may have inspired King's College Chapel, Cambridge, which was started in 1446.

🔲 Also outside on a buttress in the SE corner of the church is a plaque which states:

'Here two young Danish Souldiers lye
The one in quarrel chanc'd to die;
The others Head, by their own Law
With Sword was sever'd at one blow.
December the 23d. 1689.'

Above the verse are two crossed swords.

## Binton                              WARWICKSHIRE

ST PETER is reached via a flight of stone steps and commands fine views across the Avon valley from its porch.

🔲 The W window is a memorial to Captain Robert Falcon Scott (1868–1912), who came here just before his last Antarctic expedition in 1911.

## Birling                                    KENT

ALL SAINTS stands high above the village and is approached through a lych gate up a flight of 20 deep steps.

🔲 Just to the S of the church are the graves of two highly talented painters, Rowland and Edith Hilder. The beautifully engraved headstone reads:

'ROWLAND HILDER 1905–1993
Landscape Painter
EDITH HILDER 1904–1992
Flower Painter'

The carving in the roundel depicts two oast houses, trees, convolvulus and ivy.

🔲 Near the plain fourteenth-century stone font is an elaborate three-tiered oak font cover carved by the three daughters of the Reverend William Nevill in 1853. The Nevill family originally came to England from France with William the Conqueror. One of them became Warwick the King-maker and the Reverend W. Nevill was descended from the family. The font cover, rising to 3.04 m (10 feet), is no longer used.

🔲 In the chancel are 12 shields relating to the Nevill family dating from 1536 to 1720.

🔲 In the centre of the chancel is a huge cast-iron cover to the Nevill vault bearing heraldic devices.

## Bisham (pronounced 'Bizzum') BERKSHIRE

ALL SAINTS is situated right on the edge of the River Thames and its churchyard borders the river.

🔲 The fine W tower dates from c.1160.

🔲 On the SE side is the Hoby chapel, which was built c.1550. It contains some superb monuments and heraldic glass dating from 1609 in the E window.

🔲 A magnificent monument against the s wall commemorates Lady Elizabeth Russell (d. 1609). She died a widow and is depicted kneeling at a prayer desk with her sons and daughters. Notice her detailed headdress, so characteristic of this period.

🔲 Near by is a monument which Lady Elizabeth erected to her first husband, Sir Thomas Hoby (d. 1566), and his half-brother, Sir Philip (d. 1558). These are the earliest examples of reclining effigies in England. Up until this time people were normally depicted as recumbent or lying on their backs, with hands usually at prayer.

🔲 An unusual monument comprises an obelisk with four swans at its base and a heart at the top. It commemorates Lady Margaret Hoby (d. 1605), wife of Sir Edward Hoby. They lived at nearby Bisham Abbey.

🔲 An elaborate marble monument commemorates George Kenneth Vansittart (1890–1904), an Eton schoolboy who died of peritonitis. He is depicted kneeling at a prayer desk with his pet dog, a spaniel, asleep in front of it!

🔲 Near the N aisle chapel is a reredos comprising four painted saints. It dates from c.1500.

## Bishop Burton     EAST RIDING OF YORKSHIRE

ALL SAINTS is situated in a pretty village just off the main road. The church was much restored in Victorian times but still retains some interesting features.

🔲 At the w end of the N aisle is a fine alabaster monument to a Rachel Gee (d. 1684) in her shroud. It was found in a vault under the chancel in 1865.

🔲 In the s aisle is a fine bust of John Wesley carved from an elm tree blown

down in 1836 and under which he preached.

🔲 In the N and s aisles are ten Kempe stained-glass windows, some of them bearing his wheat-sheaf signature.

🔲 On the N side of the chancel is a chalice brass to Sir Peter Johnson, vicar (d. 1460). This is reputed to be the oldest chalice brass in England.

🔲 Down the centre of the nave the bench ends are carved with beautiful figures of saints, that of St Martin of Tours being especially fine.

🔲 At the NW corner of the nave a black floor slab commemorates a Tobias Hodson (d. 1664). His Latin inscription ends, 'As you see, reader, this inscription is rude and uncouth. Do you wish to know the reason? Tobias Hodson is dead.'

## Blakeney     NORFOLK

ST NICHOLAS, THE BLESSED VIRGIN MARY AND ST THOMAS OF CANTERBURY This unusual church with its two towers stands on rising ground 30.48 m (100 feet) above the sea, to the s of the town.

🔲 At the NE corner of the chancel is a small, square, tapering tower crowned with pinnacles. It may have served as a lighthouse to Blakeney Harbour below, but its original purpose was to provide a stair turret to the chamber above the vaulted chancel.

🔲 The nave and w tower were built in 1435 but the chancel was built in the thirteenth century. The tower is 31.69 m (104 feet) high.

🔲 The chancel is unusual in possessing a vaulted roof with a room above it. The E window consists of seven graded Early English lancets – a very rare feature. (The only other ancient example is at Ockham, Surrey, although there is a Victorian copy in Southampton.)

◉ On the s side of the churchyard are some fine eighteenth-century headstones.

## Blaxhall     SUFFOLK

St Peter is in a remote village in beautiful countryside near Wickham Market, with several roads converging on it.

◉ Situated a long way from the village in a large churchyard, the flint tower has been repaired in brick at the top.

◉ On the splay of a n window is a beautiful plaster relief depicting an angel directing a little child.

◉ On the n wall of the nave is the war memorial in bronze showing Jesus bending over a dying soldier, above which are the words, 'Even there also shall Thy rich hand lead me.' It was made by Ellen Mary Rope.

◉ The magnificent e window was made by Margaret A. Rope. It depicts the Nativity and underneath are the figures of St Peter and St George. St George was modelled on the brother of the artist, Michael Rope, who died tragically when the R101 airship crashed near Beauvais on 5 October 1930.

◉ A granite cross near the hedge inside the gate on the left marks the grave of Marjorie Wilson, a contributor of poems to the former *Children's Newspaper* founded by Arthur Mee in the 1920s. The inscription reads, 'In loving memory of Marjorie Wilson much beloved daughter of the Rector of Blaxhall entered into life June 4, 1934. "I will fear no evil for Thou art with me."'

## Bletchingley (or Blechingley)    SURREY

St Mary the Virgin An impressive Perpendicular church with a large Norman w tower.

◉ The magnificent monument to Sir Robert Clayton, 1710, Lord Mayor of London, and Lady Clayton, is considered to be the finest Baroque monument in England. It was carved by Richard Crutcher.

## Blewbury     OXFORDSHIRE

St Michael is set in a beautiful village that still retains some original Saxon thatched walls of wattle and daub!

◉ The four arches at the e end of the nave originally supported a Norman central tower. Until 1968 the four bell-rope holes in the vaulting were still visible, but the chafe marks made by the bell ropes can still be seen on the inner edges of the arches.

◉ On the n wall of the sanctuary is an iron ring which, together with a now-vanished one on the s wall, was used to hang the Lenten veil before the Reformation.

◉ In the s chapel is a brass to Sir John Daunce (1545) and Alice, his wife (1523). He was Surveyor-General to Henry VIII.

◉ In the s transept is a pastel drawing of a special service held on the downs s of Blewbury at Churn Knob or St Birinus Mound on 4 August 1942 to mark the 400 years of the foundation of the Oxford diocese. It was attended by the Bishop of Dorchester-on-Thames, Oxon.

◉ In the churchyard n of the tower is an effigy with an unusual brass plate to the vicar's son, John Macdonald (1841), aged 13. Faith is depicted as Britannia.

## Blythburgh     SUFFOLK

Holy Trinity is known as 'the Cathedral of the Marshes'. Dating from 1442, it is a large spacious building which dominates the countryside.

◉ With 36 clerestory windows and small amounts of stained glass, including some fifteenth-century fragments, the interior is very light.

The wonderful nave roof was damaged in 1644 by Cromwell's soldiers, who used the angels' wings for target practice! New ones were added in 1954. The roof retains much of its original colouring.

In the Hopton chapel at the E end of the N aisle is a Peter's Pence alms-box dated 1473, the finest pre-Reformation alms-box in England. It has traceried panels on three sides and is secured with a padlock and a pair of handcuffs.

The bench-ends in the nave with modern backs and book rests date from c.1475. Among the carvings is a man in the stocks, the Four Seasons and the Seven Deadly Sins.

In the chancel is the famous Clock Jack holding an axe which strikes a bell just before the service begins. Dating from 1682, it is one of only a few 'Jacks' remaining in England. (See also nearby Southwold, page 329 and Minehead, Somerset, page 241.)

The old choir stalls have holes which originally held inkwells when a school was held in the Hopton chapel in the seventeenth century for the children of Dutch immigrants who came to Blythburgh to work on the river dykes. One pupil has carved his name on the s side: 'DIRCK LOWERSEN VAN-STOCKHOLM. ANNO 1665.'

On the pillar behind the pulpit are three masons' marks. Several more can be found on other pillars.

Outside, the s side of the parapet is richly ornamented but the N side away from the village is plain.

Below the E window outside the church is some curious lettering which may stand for the first letters of Latin words which, translated, mean: 'In the Name of the Blessed Jesus, the Holy Trinity (and) in honour of Holy Mary, Anne and Katherine, this church was rebuilt.'

Outside, s of the tower, is a grave with an unusual headstone inscribed on both sides.

The weathercock on the tower dates from 1768.

## Bodelwyddan DENBIGHSHIRE

ST MARGARET, known as 'the Marble Church' (actually magnesium limestone), was built 1856–60 to the design of John Gibson by Lady Willoughby de Broke in memory of her husband.

The spire is 61.56 m (202 feet) tall.

The quality of carving inside is superb and over 14 varieties of marble have been used.

The wooden hammer-beam roof has been constructed without the use of nails or screws – each of the timbers is secured by wooden pegs.

In the graveyard are the graves of 83 Canadian soldiers, most of whom died from flu and pneumonia during the First World War.

## Bosham
(pronounced 'Bozzum') WEST SUSSEX

HOLY TRINITY is situated quite near an inlet of the sea, part of Chichester Harbour. The church occupies the oldest Christian site in Sussex dating back to c.650.

The tower and nave are Saxon dating from c.1030. The Saxon chancel arch is shown in the Bayeux Tapestry. King Harold entered this church in 1065 before sailing to Normandy. (Apart from Westminster Abbey, London, Bosham is the only English church depicted in the Bayeux Tapestry.)

The magnificent chancel arch is horseshoe-shaped with unique capitals comprising a large square stone placed on top of a round one, reversed at the base. The arch is 2.11 m (6 feet 11 inches) wide and 2.63 m (8 feet 8 inches) high to the lower side of the capitals.

*Angels adorn the roof of Blythburgh's impressive church in Suffolk.*

# WOODEN FONTS

Of all the materials used to make fonts, wood is one of the most vulnerable and therefore very few wooden fonts survive. Furthermore, the Church also disapproved of these fonts, believing wood to be a material unworthy for use in the service of baptism.

In order to prevent the water used in baptism from seeping through the wood, nearly all wooden fonts were lined with lead. Sometimes the water was poured into a metal or china basin placed inside the font.

Some of the surviving wooden fonts are very elaborately carved, such as the one at Croome d'Abitot, Worcestershire, and the one in Parham House, West Sussex – this formerly stood in the chapel there and came originally from the church of St Peter-in-the-East, Oxford.

The font at Plympton St Maurice, Devon, was used for the baptism of the famous artist Sir Joshua Reynolds (1723–93).

The octagonal wooden font at Grove, near Wantage, Oxfordshire, was made *c.*1750; it came originally from Pusey Church, Oxfordshire, where it was used for the baptism of Dr Edward Bouverie Pusey (1800–82), a leader of the Oxford Movement. The inscription on the font states: 'Dr Pusey was baptised from this font September 14, 1800.' Apparently there was either no font at Pusey Church, or Edward was privately baptized and the font was provided for this. At a later date a Pusey church-warden of the time gave the font to the vicar of Wantage, who later presented it to Grove Church, where Dr Pusey had preached his first published sermon at the consecration of an earlier Grove Church in 1832. The present building dates from 1965.

It is interesting that many of the existing wooden fonts date from the eighteenth century and generally take the form of an elegant baluster.

 To the s side of the chancel arch is the reputed grave of King Canute's daughter, buried there in 1020. The tomb was discovered in 1865 and carries the Black Raven of Denmark.

The superb E window in the Early English style dates from *c.*1180 and comprises five lancets with Purbeck marble shafts.

In the s aisle is an unusual crypt, partly above and partly below the level of the nave. Dating from *c.*1250 it has a vaulted roof and may be built over the cell of Dicul, an Irish monk, mentioned by the Venerable Bede.

 The window in the s aisle above the crypt displays four roundels of medieval glass depicting angels which came from Norwich Cathedral.

The Saxon tower has an original arch opening into the nave with a gable-headed doorway above. (This has now been converted to a window but originally opened on to a now-vanished gallery.) Outside, on its w face, is an original window complete with central baluster shaft.

As far as I know, the following is a complete list of all the old wooden fonts still surviving in churches in England and Wales (excluding some stone fonts completely encased in wood like those at St Botolph, Cambridge, Stanford-in-the-Vale, Oxfordshire and Swimbridge, Devon):

1. Abbotts Ann (St Mary), Hampshire
2. Arborfield (St Barthlomew), Berkshire
3. Ash (St Peter), Surrey
4. Bath Abbey (St Peter & St Paul), Somerset
5. Chobham (St Laurence), Surrey
6. Cottesbrooke (All Saints), Northamptonshire
7. Cricket St Thomas (St Thomas), Somerset
8. Croome d'Abitot (St Mary Magdalene), Worcestershire
9. Dinas-Mawddwy (St Brynach), Gwynedd
10. Dymock (St Mary the Virgin), Gloucestershire
11. Efenechtyd (St Michael), Denbighshire
12. Fulmer (St James), Buckinghamshire
13. Gayhurst (St Peter), Buckinghamshire
14. Grove (St James), Oxfordshire
15. Ickenham (St Giles), Greater London
16. King's Pyon (St Mary), Herefordshire
17. Marks Tey (St Andrew), Essex
18. Marton (St James & St Paul), Cheshire
19. Oxhey Place Chapel (dedication unknown), Hertfordshire
20. Passenham (St Guthlac), Northamptonshire
21. Plympton St Maurice (St Maurice or St Thomas), Devon
22. Poole (St James), Dorset
23. Prestbury (St Peter), Cheshire
24. Rushbrooke (St Nicholas), Suffolk
25. Sandy Lane (St Nicholas), Wiltshire
26. Teigh (Holy Trinity), Rutland
27. Tushingham (Old St Chad), Cheshire
28. Tynemouth (Christ Church), Tyne & Wear
29. Udimore (St Mary), East Sussex
30. Well (St Margaret), Lincolnshire
31. West Wycombe (St Laurence), Buckinghamshire
32. Windsor Castle (St George's Chapel), Berkshire

# Boston LINCOLNSHIRE

ST BOTOLPH is one of the largest and grandest parish churches in England, almost cathedral-like in its proportions.

The magnificent w tower, known as the 'stump', is the loftiest in England. Rising to a height of 82.91 m (272 feet) to the top of the wind vanes, it was begun c.1450 and completed c.1520. Under the tower can be seen the superb stone-vaulted roof, erected in 1853 on the springing which medieval masons had provided. It is 41.76 m (137 feet) above the floor. The central roof boss represents the Agnus Dei; it is surrounded by many angel bosses.

The tower is crowned by a beautiful octagon enriched with pinnacles and once carried a beacon to guide ships into Boston Harbour. From the top can be seen Tattershall Castle and, on a very clear day, Lincoln Cathedral.

The s door is enriched with elaborate flowing tracery dating from c.1350.

In the room over the s porch is one of the finest parish libraries in England. It contains nearly 1200 books mostly printed from c.1500 to 1690. There is a copy of the first *English Prayer Book* (1549) and a first

*Boston's glorious 'stump' in Lincolnshire is seen from across the River Witham.*

edition of *The Book of Martyrs* by John Foxe (1516–87), who was born in Boston.

🔲 At the w end of the s aisle is a huge Royal Arms erected in 1634.

🔲 The floor at the w end of the nave is largely made up of grave slabs. Eleven have incised figures, formerly inlaid with brass or marble. The most interesting incised slabs are in the third bay of the nave from the E, between the pillars on each side. Many of the slabs are of Tournai marble from Belgium.

This is the most remarkable collection of grave slabs in England, but see also Wadhurst, E. Sussex, page 379.

🔲 At the sw corner of the nave is a superb bronze knocker dating from *c*.1250 and older than the church itself.

🔲 There are many interesting misericords on the 64 seats of the fourteenth-century choir stalls. One of the most famous is on the N side, second from the E in the front row; it shows a choirmaster birching a boy who is trying to protect himself with a book! Three other boys wait their turn!

Other misericords show a wolf dressed as a bishop with a fox as his chaplain and bears playing an organ – one of the oldest representations of an organ.

A unique misericord shows a mermaid trying to lure a ship to its doom and another shows Sir Yvaine's horse sliced in two by a portcullis.

🔲 Note the little carved heads on the canopies of the choir stalls and on the heads of the pillars – at least 576.

🔲 Outside the tower on the sw buttress are high-water marks dated: 19 October 1781, 10 November 1807, 10 November 1810, 31 January 1953 and 11 January 1978 (the highest mark).

# Bottesford                LEICESTERSHIRE

ST MARY THE VIRGIN is known as 'the Lady of the Vale', the vale being the Vale of Belvoir.

🔲 The tower is 26.52 m (87 feet) high and is crowned by a superb spire which rises a further 37.49 m (123 feet), making it – at 64.01 m (210 feet) – the tallest spire in Leicestershire on the county's biggest village church. The whole dates from *c*.1450.

🔲 The church has the unique distinction of having in its chancel a series of monuments to eight earls of Rutland (including six Knights of the Garter), the first six in alabaster and the last two in marble, consecutive from the first earl (1543) to the eighth (1679). The marble effigies (1641 and 1679) were carved by Grinling Gibbons.

🔲 On the s side of the chancel is the very large elaborate tomb to Francis, Sixth Earl, 1632 and his wives. Known as the 'witchcraft' tomb, it is the only tomb in England which records the death by witchcraft of two heirs to an earldom. In 1608 Francis married his second wife, Lady Cecilia Hungerford '. . . by whom he had two sonnes both who dyed in their infancy by wicked practice and sorcerye,' as the inscription states. This monument is so tall that it touches the roof.

🔲 In the centre of the chancel is the tomb of Henry Manners, Second Earl of Rutland, 1563. The effigies lie beneath an ornate example of an Elizabethan dining table supported on heavy bulbous legs – a unique representation.

Earl Henry's armour is also unique in that he wears a breastplate made, not in one piece, but of laminated plates. In his right hand he holds a closed book – an unusual feature – while his left hand grasps his sword.

🔲 The font is unique in being a pseudo-Gothic octagonal bowl resting on a

Renaissance base with bulbous legs, again like an Elizabethan dining table.

▨ Over the chancel arch is a fine Victorian coat of arms carved in elm and plaster.

▨ The five-light E window of the chancel has an unusual and disproportionately high transom without any cusping. It was inserted c.1650.

▨ On the chancel floor is the famous Codyngton Brass, which commemorates Henry de Codyngton (d. 1404.) It is noted for the rich embroidery on the cope.

▨ On the N wall of the chancel a small effigy, only 45 cm (18 inches) high, shows Robert de Ros (d. 1285). The lower part of the effigy is missing. It came from Croxton Abbey.

▨ A Victorian stained-glass window on the N side of the chancel commemorates one Richard Norman (19 March 1853–29 November 1874). His picture appears in the tracery of the window – a very unusual feature in England.

▨ This church was the very last place to be attacked in the Second World War by German aircraft, on 20 March 1945. Fortunately no damage was caused.

# Boulge                     SUFFOLK

ST MICHAEL & ALL ANGELS is near Bredfield in a peaceful situation in the middle of fields and quite difficult to find.

▨ The brick W tower dates from c.1450–1530.

▨ To the W of the tower is the grave of Edward Fitz-Gerald (31 March 1809–14 June 1883), marked with the simple verse, 'It is He that hath made us and not we ourselves' (Psalm 100, v.3).

A rose bush at the W end has this inscription: 'Translator of "Rubaiyet of Omar Khayyam". This rose tree raised in Kew Gardens from seed brought by William Simpson, Artist Traveller from

the grave of Omar Khayyam at Naishapur was planted by a few admirers of Edward Fitz-Gerald in the name of the Omar Khayyam Club. 7th October, 1893.'

A pink rose bush with a beautiful scent was blooming on the grave when I called!

▨ Near by is the huge Fitz-Gerald Mausoleum with the words, 'Lord Jesus receive my spirit' over the door. It has a pyramid roof, cross-like windows on three sides and a door at the bottom of steps. It is constructed of stone and flint over a brick core but is in a poor state of repair.

▨ The churchyard is designated as a wildlife sanctuary by the Suffolk Wildlife Trust.

▨ Under the tower is a Tournai marble font dating from c.1210. Its square bowl rests on an enormous circular shaft which measures 1.4 m (55 inches) in circumference. The bowl is plain and uncarved except for foliage carvings underneath at the four corners and at the base. (See Tournai Fonts, page 439.)

▨ The S aisle and transept contain several memorials to the Fitz-Gerald family, who moved into Boulge Hall in 1835.

▨ A fine window in the S aisle commemorates Sir Robert Eaton White (1864–1940) and depicts local agriculture and this church.

# Boxgrove                 WEST SUSSEX

THE PRIORY CHURCH OF ST MARY AND ST BLAISE At the Dissolution, Lord Thomas de la Warr of Halnaker bought the Priory from the Crown and later exchanged it for the dissolved nunnery of Wherwell in Hampshire. Having reverted to the Crown again, the Priory became a parish church with the monastic buildings and nave unused, but was again sold, to Sir John Morley, in 1587 when the original chancel continued in use as a parish church, the remainder falling into ruins.

◈ Opposite the entrance to the s porch inside the church are two Norman arches. The w one is interesting because it shows how the builders began to decorate the arch with chevron work and then stopped. Why was it never completed?

◈ Each of the two transepts are covered with beautiful fifteenth-century oak ceilings and have screens which form galleries on the sides facing the choir. The reason for these galleries is unknown. The s gallery is reached via the newel stair that leads to the clerestory, but the n one can only be reached using a ladder! However, this n gallery has the remains of a stone fireplace and a door which led from the monks' dormitory. As this was the only means of access, it may have been used by sick monks who kept warm by the fire and followed the offices being chanted in the church below.

◈ The vaulting of the church is known as 'double bay vaulting' and is the earliest example of this type in England. The round Norman arches on each side enclose two pointed arches inside each of them. The pillars between these pointed arches support the vaulting of the choir aisles. This rebuilding of the Norman chancel dates from c.1210.

◈ The delicate paintings on the vault showing flowers and fruit are by Lambert Bernard c.1530, who was employed by Thomas de la Warr. Bernard painted another ceiling in Chichester Cathedral.

◈ On the s side of the choir is the De la Warr chantry, built of Caen stone in 1532. The date is carved on the NE pendant. It is a magnificent example of Gothic and Renaissance architecture.

Above the site of the altar at the E end is the unfinished reredos on which appears the following inscription: 'Of your charity pray ye for the soule of Thomas La Warr and Elizabeth his wife.'

Inside the chantry notice the angels upside down on the central hanging pendant (see Fan Vaulting, page 152). Outside the chantry at the top of the s side is a grotesque carving depicting three naked men fleeing from a two-headed dragon. On the NE column two boys raid a pear tree while a girl accomplice collects the fruit in her skirt! These and several other subjects appear as marginal illustrations in a French *Book of Hours* printed in Paris c.1500 by Thielmann Kerver. This book was probably bought by Thomas de la Warr and used by the craftsmen he employed to build his chantry chapel.

The entrance to the chantry is at the w end through the original gate of Sussex iron. The chantry was never completed as the Priory was suppressed in 1536 and Lord de la Warr was buried at Broadwater near Worthing in 1554.

◈ Towards the E end of the choir are three separate pillars comprising a central column surrounded by four shafts of Purbeck marble. (A fourth pillar was removed to make way for the de la Warr chantry.) This design of clustered columns is only found here and in the retro-choir of Chichester Cathedral.

At the E end of the s chancel aisle on the floor are a number of beautiful medieval tiles showing lions, stags, cockerels, etc.

◈ At the E end of the N chancel on the right of the altar is a rare example of a pillar piscine. There is another one in the s transept in the chapel of St Blaise.

◈ The second central roof boss from the E end of the building is pierced with a hole The boss is carved with eight heads but there are only eight eyes between them, each head sharing an eye with its neighbour. Every alternate head has a small stem proceeding from the mouth and disappearing under the chin. (Similar bosses in which heads share eyes can be found in Chichester and Canterbury cathedrals). This particular boss at Boxgrove is the earliest in the British Isles with this motif.

◈ On the N wall of the N transept is a marble monument in memory of Mary, Countess Dowager of Derby (d. 28 March 1752). A beautifully detailed relief depicts the countess putting money into a poor man's hat while his wife and child follow behind. It was probably carved by Thomas Carter.

◈ In the S aisle is the bronze effigy of Admiral Philip Nelson-Ward (d. 27 June 1937) resting on a tomb-chest in a recess. The bronze was executed by Cecil Thomas in 1947.

◈ In the extreme SE corner of the church-yard is a grave bearing this inscription: 'Pilot Officer W. M. L. Fiske III. Born 4 June 1911 in Chicago. Killed in action 17 August 1940. He died for England.' P. O. Fiske was the first American airman to die in the Second World War.

A tablet in the crypt of St Paul's Cathedral, London, unveiled on 4 July 1941 to his memory, reads: 'William Meade Lindsley Fiske III, an American who died so that England might live.'

## Brabourne                          KENT

ST MARY THE VIRGIN In beautiful country-side below the North Downs, the church boasts a short W tower with enormous buttresses.

◈ The tower staircase, made of oak, dates from c.1150.

◈ The large chancel arch is an excellent example of Norman carving.

◈ The small Norman window on the NE side of the chancel is unique. Dating from c. 1090 this is the oldest complete stained-glass window in the British Isles that is

still in its original position. The glass is patterned in delicate, pale colours.

◈ On the S side of the chancel is a rare heart-shrine dating from c.1300. It probably contained the heart of John Balliol, founder of Balliol College, Oxford. The blank shield would once have been painted.

## Bradford-on-Avon            WILTSHIRE

HOLY TRINITY The parish church of Bradford-on-Avon stands on the N side of the river, quite close to the famous bridge and the lock-up in the centre.

◈ From the Horton chapel in the N aisle a hagioscope or squint stretches nearly 6.1 m (20 feet) to the chancel which was extended c.1300. This is exceptionally long and makes it the longest squint in England.

◈ On the S side of the chancel is a fine memorial to someone called Anthony Methuen (d. 1737) by J. M. Rysbrack.

◈ At the E end of the N aisle is a fine brass commemorating Thomas Horton (d. 1530), a clothier in Bradford. Note his 'merchant's mark' and the representation of the Holy Trinity.

◈ On the S side of the chancel a brass plate commemorates Henry Shrapnel (1761–1842). It reads, 'To the Memory of Lieut. General Henry Shrapnel, Colonel Commandant 6th Battalion of Artillery. Obiit 13 March 1842. Aetat 80 years.'

Shrapnel was the inventor of a shell containing bullets that increased the number of casualties when exploded. It was first used in the Peninsular War in 1804 and his name has given us the word 'shrapnel' to describe fragments of any shell, bomb, etc.

*An original Norman window at Brabourne, Kent.*

# BRIDGE CHAPELS

In the Middle Ages, long before the invention of the train or car, there was obviously far less travel than there is today. Journeys were often hazardous with travellers encountering many dangers such as highwaymen, poor roads, floods and so on.

Crossing large rivers, in particular, always posed a problem and often the Church would build a bridge at a strategic place and chapels would be erected either on or near the bridge. Travellers could then call in to pray and ask God's blessing on their journey out or offer thanks for a safe return. Most travellers had to pay tolls towards the upkeep of the bridge or payment of the priests who conducted services in the bridge chapels.

The remains of one bridge chapel can be seen at Cromford (Derbyshire). High up in the wall overlooking the river is a small, round window in which the priest would have placed a light to guide people to the bridge.

Many of the bridge chapels were also chantry chapels with an appointed priest to pray for the soul of the founder. When Henry VIII suppressed the monasteries (1538–9) this was followed by the closure of the chantries under Edward VI from 1547 onwards. Many bridge chapels which had been chantry chapels fell into ruin which is why so few exist today.

Not all the surviving bridge chapels are actually on a bridge but some are quite near.

The following chapels are on a bridge:
1. Rotherham, (Our Lady), South Yorkshire
2. St Ives (St Leger), Cambridgeshire
3. Wakefield (St Mary and the Virgin), West Yorkshire

These chapels are near a bridge:
1. Cromford, Derbyshire
2. Derby (St Mary on the Bridge)
3. Rochester (All Souls or the Holy Trinity), Kent

Although Bradford-on-Avon (Wiltshire) once had a bridge chapel, the present building is an old lock-up

## BRADFORD-ON-AVON

The structure on the famous bridge over the River Avon replaces a chapel that was built in the thirteenth century and dedicated to St Nicholas. It belonged to the Hospital of St Margaret, which stood at the southern end of the bridge. The historian John Aubrey (1626–97) said that there used to be a 'chapel for masse in the middest of the bridge' at Bradford-on-Avon.

In 1621 the medieval bridge was widened and rebuilt but two of its thirteenth-century arches were retained. The bridge chapel was reconstructed as a watch house, which later became a lock-up with an attractive domed roof and two small windows overlooking the river. On the top of the roof is a wind vane in the shape of a fish and known as the Bradford Gudgeon. This fish caused locals to refer to those held in the lock-up as being 'Over the river and under the fish'!

The famous preacher John Wesley actually spent a night in one of the two cells of the lock-up in 1757, presumably for his own safety to escape the mob of people who did not approve of his preaching!

## DERBY

The Chapel of St Mary on the bridge has been described as 'Derby's unsung treasure'. It is not actually situated over the River Derwent but a short distance from the beautiful bridge built by Thomas Harrison from 1788 to 1793. When this was completed, the medieval bridge dating from c.1350 was demolished, thus isolating the bridge chapel.

Records of a bridge chapel go back to c.1250 but the present building dates from c.1350. In 1547 it ceased to exist as a chapel and in 1554 became the property of the inhabitants of Derby. Over the years that followed it lapsed into decay until, in the eighteenth century, it was converted into a pair of cottages. In 1826 Thomas Eaton, a well-known Derby surgeon, moved into Bridge Chapel House, which stands on the site of the priest's house and dates from c.1650–1750. The chapel subsequently became a carpenter's shop until 1873, when it was returned to use as a religious building. However, by c.1928 it was once again in a state of disrepair and was rescued by the Archaeological Society. The adult children of Sir Alfred Haslar bought it outright in memory of their father and following an appeal, it was restored in 1930. Since 1932 the chapel has been in regular use as a place of worship.

Inside, there is a fine modern stained-glass window designed by Mary Dobson in memory of Sean Ferguson (1951–72). He was the son of Commander and Mrs H. R. M. Ferguson of Derby; he died of cancer and his ashes rest in a vault on the N side of the communion table. The glass reflects the dedication of the chapel to the Blessed Virgin Mary with numerous symbols associated with her.

## ROCHESTER

The bridge chapel here traces its origins to the fourteenth century when Sir Robert Knollyes and Sir John de Cobham both provided money to build a new bridge across the River Medway, a short distance from the Norman castle. Soon after the building of this bridge in 1392, a chapel was founded at the E end of the bridge dedicated to All Souls or the Holy Trinity. Although used as a chapel by travellers crossing the bridge, this was also a chantry chapel with a chantry priest appointed to pray for the soul of Sir John de Cobham and other members of his family.

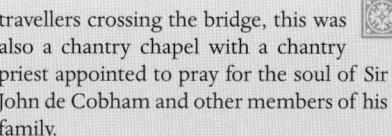

In 1549 this chantry, like all the others, was suppressed and the plate and vestments sold in 1552. In the years that followed the chapel served many purposes, including its use as a greengrocer's shop up until 1879. After this, the building fell into a ruinous condition until it was restored in 1937 at the expense of the Rochester Bridge Trust and to the plans of Sir Herbert Baker.

The Court of Wardens and Assistants of the Rochester Bridge Trust is charged, among other things, with the maintenance of the road bridge. This was rebuilt in 1856 and another road bridge, reconstructed from a former railway bridge in 1965, came into use a little way downstream from the former medieval bridge – hence the isolation of the old bridge chapel.

## ROTHERHAM

The second-most elaborate bridge chapel, Rotherham's stands in the middle of a bridge over the River Don which ceased to be used for traffic in 1930 following the opening of a new road bridge for the A630.

Dedicated to Our Lady, this chapel was endowed by the will of John Bokyng in 1483 and became a chantry chapel, closing in 1547. In 1569 it was converted into an almshouse and only survived because it was an integral part of the bridge!

Between 1778 and 1779 the almshouse was converted into a prison and the crypt served as a jail with the deputy constable occupying the chapel above. In 1826 the jail became redundant, following the construction of a new courthouse and cells and so the chapel was rented out as a dwelling house until 1888 when it became a tobacconist's and news-agent's shop. It continued in this way until 1913 when it was bought out by Sir Charles Stoddart.

44

After the First World War it was completely restored and reconsecrated as a chapel on 22 July 1924. It has been used for occasional services since. In 1975 a new E window was installed, designed by Alan Younger. It charts the history of the building with the initials of numerous persons associated with Rotherham.

## St Ives

The chapel over the River Ouse at St Ives is possibly the most famous example of a bridge chapel. Dedicated to St Leger it was probably constructed at the same time as the stone bridge in c.1426. It forms part of the actual bridge and is situated in the middle of the river. In 1716 the southern two arches of the bridge were rebuilt and over the years numerous repairs have had to be carried out on the bridge.

The bridge chapel has also witnessed great changes, not least the addition of two upper storeys in brick in 1736, making it into a private house. However, with the coming of motorized vehicles and an increase in traffic on the bridge, the original chapel began to feel the effects of the two-storey building on top of it. It was therefore decided to demolish these in 1930. (A photograph of the bridge showing the chapel with its upper storeys can be seen on page 272 of Arthur Mee's *Bedford and Huntingdon* in the King's England series (first edition, published 1939).

The chapel was subsequently restored to its original condition – or as near as possible – with a new parapet in stone. The balcony and doorway on the downstream side, which were not original, however, were retained.

From time to time services are still held in the chapel, thus fulfilling its original function.

## Wakefield

The chapel in the middle of the bridge over the River Calder is the largest and finest of our surviving bridge chapels, although most of it has been restored. It was founded in 1356 as the Chantry Chapel of St Mary the Virgin. Before it ceased functioning in 1548, chantry priests officiated there, not only saying masses for the dead but also collecting tolls for the upkeep of the bridge.

Following the departure of the chantry priests, the chapel was kept in good repair, the most extensive work being done by the West Riding Magistrates when the bridge was given its present width (1797–8). The bridge chapel was then sublet for numerous uses including offices for a corn merchant and, later on, a tailor's workshop.

From 1847 to 1848 Sir George Gilbert Scott devised and effected a scheme for the almost complete demolition of the chapel down to bridge level, followed by rebuilding using much of the original stonework, except for a new w front. The medieval w front was taken to Kettlethorpe Hall, south of Wakefield, where it can still be seen gracing the front of a boathouse!

The newly rebuilt chapel was opened on 22 April 1848 and has functioned as a place of worship ever since. Unfortunately the new stonework of the w front weathered badly and had to be renewed from 1939 to 1940. Much of the other external stonework (including window tracery) has also had to be replaced due to air pollution. However, the portion of the chapel below street level is still essentially medieval work, as are the pointed arches of the bridge on the E side which can be viewed from downstream.

Inside the chapel is some fine Victorian stained glass and at the NE corner is a turret with a stairway to the roof and stone stairs leading down to a small crypt; this used to be a home for the chantry priest.

*Opposite: England's finest surviving Bridge Chapel at Wakefield, West Yorkshire.*

# Bradford-on-Avon      WILTSHIRE

ST LAWRENCE is the most notable Saxon church in England. Dating from c.920, it was hidden between numerous buildings until being 'discovered' in 1858. The w front had ordinary house windows inserted in it and the chancel was used as a separate house. In 1871, through the efforts of Canon Jones, the church was bought back from private owners.

The chancel arch, measuring 2.95 m (9 feet 8 inches) high and 1.06 m (3 feet 6 inches) wide, is not only the narrowest and smallest in England but also leads to the narrowest chancel in England.

The wall arcading on the outside walls is similar to that found on churches in northern Italy.

# Brading      ISLE OF WIGHT

ST MARY THE VIRGIN

On the s side of the chancel is the Oglander chapel containing three wooden effigies as follows:

† On a table-tomb on the s side of the chapel is the wooden effigy of Sir William Oglander (d. 27 March 1608). His effigy, at 1.85 m (6 feet 1 inch) long, is shown in plate armour with a herringbone pattern. His hands are in prayer, he wears a ruff and his feet rest on a lion. His sword has a pommel carved with a woman's face. This figure was carved from oak between 1625 and 1640. It is painted and is well preserved.

† On a table-tomb exactly opposite on the N side of the chapel is Sir William's son, Sir John Oglander (d. 28 November 1655), who was MP for Yarmouth (Isle of Wight) and entertained Charles I at Nunwell in 1647. His effigy, at 1.9 m (6 feet 2 inches) long, is depicted in plate armour with a scroll pattern. He lies on his right side with his right hand supporting his head. His right leg is crossed over his left and his feet rest on a lion. He wears a helmet with raised visor showing his face and moustache.

† In a niche above Sir John's tomb is a small wooden effigy, 0.53 m (1 foot 9 inches) long, commemorating George Oglander, only son of Sir John, who died of smallpox at Caen, Normandy, in 1632. It is similar in detail to Sir John's effigy except that George does not have a moustache or wear spurs and his sword is curved near the point. (This is the smallest wooden effigy in the British Isles.)

These three effigies were repainted c.1870. (See Wooden Effigies, page 246.)

On the s wall inside the church is a brass plate which commemorates the curacy of the Reverend Legh Richmond at Brading from 1797 to 1805. He wrote numerous religious tracts called 'Annals of the Poor' in which he describes particular Island people. One of them was 'the Young Cottager' or Jane Squibb ('Little Jane'), who died of consumption at the age of 15 and is buried immediately E of the Oglander chapel. Legh Richmond composed the epitaph on her tombstone, 1779.

Also in the s aisle is a plain octagonal font dated 1631.

In the N aisle is the beautiful marble effigy of Elizabeth Theresa Agnes Rollo (23 June 1874–1 September 1875), daughter of Lord and Lady Rollo.

# Bramfield      SUFFOLK

ST ANDREW is a lovely thatched church.

It is one of only two churches possessing a circular tower standing detached from the building – the other is at Little Snoring, Norfolk. (See Round Towers, page 398.)

The fine fifteenth-century screen retains much of its original colouring and is considered to be one of the loveliest in Suffolk.

On the N side of the chancel is the beautiful tomb of Arthur Coke (d. 6 December 1629) and Elizabeth, his wife (d. 14 November 1627). He is shown kneeling at prayer while below, his wife lies recumbent on two cushions holding a little baby. The sculptor was Nicholas Stone.

# Brampton                    CUMBRIA

ST MARTIN, designed by Philip Webb and built in 1877–8, is unique in being his only church.

The stained-glass windows are a complete set designed by Burne-Jones and executed by William Morris. Their themes are Worship, the Good Shepherd, Heroes of the Bible, Virtues, Childhood and Paradise. The E window is particularly impressive and is a blaze of intense colour, red being the dominant one.

Over the altar in the chapel on the N side of the chancel is a very unusual painting called 'The Neglected Invitation'. It shows Christ seated alone at a table laid for a feast with eight empty cups, while through the windows the busy world goes about its business. The painting uses gesso and jewels and is by Byam Shaw.

On the window sill behind the altar of this chapel is a beautiful framed relief panel of St Martin dividing his cloak. He is shown again in a similar panel to the left of the main entrance porch on the N side.

# Bray                        BERKSHIRE

ST MICHAEL is famous for its turncoat vicar, Simon Aleyn, who was vicar from 1540 to 1565.

Thomas Fuller, author of *Worthies of England* (1662), wrote of him, 'The vivacious Vicar living under King Henry VIII,

King Edward VI, Queen Mary and Queen Elizabeth, was first a Papist, then a Protestant, then a Papist, then a Protestant again. He had seen the martyrs Filener, Peerson and Testwood burnt 2 miles off at Windsor in 1543 and found the fire too hot for his tender temper. The Vicar being taxed by one for being a Turn-coat and an unconstant Changeling, "Not so," said he; "for I always kept my principle, which is this, to live and die the Vicar of Bray."'

He died a natural death and is buried in an unknown grave in the churchyard.

The well-known song, which declares:

'And this is law I will maintain,
Until my dying day, Sir,
That whatsoever King shall reign,
I'll still be the Vicar of Bray, Sir'

was written c.1720 and describes Dr Francis Carswell, who became vicar in 1667 and held the living during the reigns of Charles II, James II, William III, Anne and George I. He is buried in the centre of the nave of the church.

The author of this celebrated ballad is said to have been an officer in Colonel Fuller's regiment during the reign of George I. (See complete song in Appendix, page 459).

The beautiful lych gate on the s side of the churchyard dates from 1448. The date is carved in Arabic numerals on a beam at eye level on the right-hand side as one enters underneath the oriel window from the road into the churchyard. Note how the '4' is actually carved as half an eight!

On the N side of the chancel is a fine wall monument to William Goddard and his wife, Joyce Mauncell. His hands are resting on a skull showing he died before his wife in 1609. He left money to build the Jesus Almshouses in the village in 1627.

Against the N wall is a fine brass to someone called Sir John de Foxley (d. 1378)

*The Lych Gate in Bray, Berkshire, leads to a beautiful churchyard.*

with his two wives, Maud and Joan. Note the differences between their two dresses.

On each side of the pillars in the nave are carved heads of past villagers. All date from *c.*1310 except the two nearest the chancel arch depicting the Bishop of Oxford and the Vicar of Bray in 1860, when the two easternmost arches were enlarged and rebuilt.

On the N side of the churchyard is the former chantry chapel of St Mary. It was used as a school *c.*1610 until the nineteenth century. Note the carved Norman stone on the S wall.

# Breamore                    HAMPSHIRE

ST MARY is a basically Saxon church (built *c.*980) situated about 0.8 km (½ mile) from the village and picturesquely surrounded by beautiful trees in Breamore Park.

A rare feature is the Saxon central tower resting on piers and arches. Few Saxon builders had acquired the necessary constructional techniques.

Over the arch leading to the S transept, in letters 15 cm (6 inches) high, is the largest only remaining stone-carved text in Anglo-Saxon in the British Isles. It reads, 'HER SWUTELATH SEO GECWYDRAEDNES THE,' which means 'Here the covenant is made plain to you'. Over the arch between the nave and the chancel are the letters 'DES', fragments of another text. These words were cut *c.*1000.

Seven Saxon windows remain and are characteristic of the late Saxon period, being 'double-splayed' – outwards and inwards. Other windows have been blocked up or destroyed at varying periods.

Above the new upper storey of the S porch is a Saxon rood (similar to others

*Bray Church and Jesus Almshouses, seen from the south across the fields.*

at Romsey and Headbourne Worthy, Hampshire) but it has been badly damaged. The rood is surrounded by fifteenth-century wall paintings.

On each side of the E window, which dates from c.1340, are remains of other wall paintings.

Under the tower are 12 well-preserved hatchments providing rich examples of heraldry.

## Bredwardine HEREFORDSHIRE

ST ANDREW is not far from the lovely River Wye, crossed here by a fine six-arched bridge.

The Georgian tower, built in 1790, contains a ring of six bells, the oldest dating from 1729.

Near the N side of the tower in the churchyard is the grave of the Reverend Francis Kilvert, the famous Victorian diarist who spent the last two years of his life here as vicar. He married on 20 August 1879 and returned with his bride, Elizabeth Rowland, to Bredwardine on 13 September, dying ten days later from peritonitis. His tombstone is inscribed, 'In Loving Remembrance of the Reverend Robert Francis Kilvert, MA, Vicar of this Parish. Died Sepr.23rd, 1879 aged 38. "Until the day break, and the shadows flee away," *Song of Songs* 2, v.17. "He being dead yet speaketh." *Hebrews* 11, v. 4.'

In the SE corner of the new churchyard across the lane is the grave of Francis Kilvert's widow. A white cross is inscribed, 'In loving memory of Elizabeth Anne, widow of the Rev Robert Francis Kilvert. Born April 10th 1846. Died January 16th, 1911. "At Rest".'

The chancel is deflected to the N.

49

On the N wall of the chancel is a memorial to Harriott Thomas (d. 13 April 1778, aged 16). The inscription reads:

'GOD takes the Good, too Good on Earth to stay
And leave's [sic] the bad, too bad to take away.'

The S doorway is Norman and the lintel is carved with geometric designs, even underneath.

The lintel of the blocked N doorway has carvings representing a bird and a grotesque animal, possibly a monkey.

The enormous font (c.1190) has a bowl 1.17 m (3 feet 10 inches) in diameter. It is carved out of a single block of breccia stone resting on five pillars

## Breedon on the Hill LEICESTERSHIRE

ST MARY & ST HARDULPH is situated on top of a hill, inside ancient earthworks and near the edge of a quarry.

The existing building is the chancel of the former priory church, which was dissolved in 1539 and then claimed by the parishioners.

The N aisle is almost entirely occupied by monuments to the Shirley family, who purchased the church from Henry VIII. Their family pew, dated 1627, is constructed of wood, ornately carved.

The earliest monument commemorates Francis Shirley (d. 1571) and his wife and the last, George Shirley (d. 1588). This latter memorial is very large and an excellent example of the period. Note the cadaver underneath.

All around the inside of the church are about 30 fragments of a Saxon frieze dating from c.800. This is the largest collection in the British Isles and depicts numerous animals and birds and interlaced designs.

Under the tower in the ringing chamber is the famous Breedon Angel, perhaps the earliest known carved angel in England and a superb example of Saxon figure sculpture.

At the W end of the N aisle are three sections of free-standing Saxon crosses. Before being rescued, the largest piece had been re-used as a staircase step!

## Brent Knoll SOMERSET

ST MICHAEL is conspicuously placed on the side of a 137.16 m (450 feet) high hill or knoll and commands fine views from its churchyard.

The fine tower, about 22.9 m (75 feet) high, has a series of interesting gargoyles.

Three very famous bench-ends on the left of the S aisle depict Reynard the Fox as an Abbot preaching to various birds, being stripped of his robes, put in the stocks and finally being hanged by some geese. Dating from the fifteenth century, the bench-ends represent the contempt of the parish priest for the Abbot of Glastonbury.

On another bench-end, dating from c.1450, is a carving of the winged ox, emblem of St Luke, and underneath is a unique carving of a donkey which appears to have the stumps of two wings on its back!

On the S wall of the nave is a large memorial to a John Somerset (d. 1663) and his two wives. The one on the left wears a large hat that is red underneath, rather like a Welsh hat. This is the largest hat on any memorial anywhere.

John Somerset's inscription ends, '. . . and when th'Almighty found him fit for bliss He called him to his proper happiness.'

The N aisle has a beautiful roof dating from c.1450 and divided into 96 different panels with angels on each side.

The baptistery window dates from 1973 and is gloriously coloured modern glass. Given by a Mrs Gladys Lee Kimble in memory of her parents and brother, it was made by James Crombie.

## Bridlington EAST RIDING OF YORKSHIRE

PRIORY CHURCH OF ST MARY THE VIRGIN is situated in the old town a long way from the sea.

The two towers of the w front are completely different. Between them is a large Perpendicular window which has a unique feature – the window above the horizontal transom is set back about 23 cm (9 inches). This is also noticeable inside.

The three westernmost piers on the s side of the nave have been encased in fifteenth-century panelled work – a very unusual feature.

The chancel stalls were carved in the workshops of Robert Thompson of Kilburn and contain numerous mouse carvings. There are 16 carvings of mice in the church and one of the most difficult to see is under the canopy of the pulpit.

Attached to a chain under the sw tower is an iron collar. This was used as a punishment for troublesome people and was fixed outside the church.

At the w end of the s aisle is a superb block of Tournai marble, richly decorated, which may have covered the grave of the founder of the priory. If so, it dates from 1113.

At the w end of the N aisle, where the tower arch meets the nave arch, is a carving of a smiling woman looking down with leaves above her.

## Brightwell Baldwin OXFORDSHIRE

ST BARTHOLOMEW is in a little village about 4.82 km (3 miles) from Chalgrove

Field, the site of a Civil War battle in 1643. It has a fine old yew for a neighbour.

A brass to John the Smyth (d.1371) is the earliest inscription in English on a brass and also the earliest example of an epitaph warning the living. It is difficult to read easily.

In the chapel is much ancient stained glass including depictions of Michael the Archangel, Gabriel appearing to Mary and the Weighing of Souls.

## Bristol GLOUCESTERSHIRE

THE CATHEDRAL CHURCH OF THE HOLY AND UNDIVIDED TRINITY This former Augustinian abbey church, which became a cathedral in 1542, forms a superb backdrop to College Green, particularly when it is floodlit at night.

The nave and two w towers date from 1868 to 1888 and were built by G. E. Street, following the architecture of the choir. Notice that all the roofs go up to the *same* height, aisles as well as the nave. This makes Bristol Cathedral a 'hall church' and as such unique among the cathedrals of England. (St Michael, Bath, is also a 'hall church'.)

In the choir, the ribs of the vaulting form a pattern in the centre instead of the more usual continuous ridge. Dating from c.1311 to 1340 this is the earliest lierne vault in England.

The arches from which the vaulting springs are unbroken in their rise from floor to apex and at 15.24 m (50 feet) are the highest in England.

In the N transept are some richly gilded bosses, the most interesting being as follows:

† One carved with two saddles. This is the only boss showing saddles alone, although saddles on horses are depicted.

† A boss showing a naked king except for his crown. This is probably Edward II.

† Another boss shows Edward II pointing to the spot where the red-hot iron pierced his body and killed him in 1327 at Berkeley Castle.

All these bosses are unique.

▨ To the E of the N transept is the elder lady chapel, dating from c.1220. Notice the exquisite carving including a bird, fox, lizard and numerous monkeys.

▨ At the E end of the N choir aisle is a memorial to the poet Robert Southey (1774–1843).

▨ At the extreme E point of the cathedral is the Eastern Lady Chapel dating from c.1298 and superseding the earlier chapel now known as the Elder Lady Chapel. Much of the glass in the E window dates from c.1350 and shows the arms of Lord Berkeley and his relatives who fought at the Battle of Crécy in 1346.

▨ Round the walls of this lady chapel are star-shaped niches containing the effigies of former abbots who contributed towards the building of this abbey church before it became a cathedral in 1542.

▨ Above the altar is an elaborate parapet which was built by Abbot Burton, 1526–30. His initials W. B. and a rebus on his name, a thistle or burr on a barrel or tun – burr-tun – can be clearly seen.

▨ In the s choir aisle is a unique double star-shaped niche and other star-shaped niches along the walls. Notice the vaulting of this and the N aisle which is unique. The little bridges supporting the vaults above are very beautiful and worthy of inspection.

▨ At the E end of the s choir aisle is the sacristy or ante-room to the Berkeley chapel. Notice the 'flying ribs' supporting the roof and the beautiful bosses. Among the carvings on the w side is a snail crawling over an oak leaf. This is known as the 'Bristol snail'. Other examples of 'flying ribs' may be seen at Lincoln Cathedral, St David's Cathedral, Southwell Cathedral and Warwick (see pages oo, oo, oo and oo respectively).

▨ In the Berkeley chapel is the only medieval candelabrum in England. It shows the Virgin and Child above with St George and the Dragon below. It was given to the Temple Church, Bristol, in 1450 but after that church was destroyed in 1940 during the Second World War it came to this cathedral.

▨ In the choir are several interesting ancient misericords including a mermaid, a husband and wife tilting with brooms and a man trying to whip a slug with a pack on its back, to make it go faster!

▨ In the s transept is an interesting Saxon coffin lid depicting the Harrowing of Hell.

▨ In the s wall of the s transept is the entrance to the former monks' dormitory with the night stairs.

▨ s of the s transept is the Norman chapter house dating from c.1154 to 1164. It is the finest Norman chapter house in England.

▨ On the NE side of the N aisle a plaque records, 'In this Cathedral on 12 March, 1994 Barry Rogerson, Bishop of Bristol ordained the first women as priests in the Church of England.'

## Bristol    Gloucestershire

St Mary Redcliffe In 1574 Queen Elizabeth I described this magnificent church as 'the fairest, goodliest and most famous parish church in England' and no parish church can compare with it in its cathedral-like splendour.

▨ Behind the high altar is an ambulatory and lady chapel. This is the only medieval parish church in England to be entirely vaulted in stone.

▨ The spire, dating from 1872, is 89 m (292 feet) high.

▨ There are over 1200 roof bosses in the vaulting, some of which are very unusual:

† Window tracery is found on four bosses, two of which depict fine rose windows in the N aisle of the nave. Only two other bosses show window tracery and these are at Sherborne (see page 313).

† A boss in the E aisle of the N transept shows vaulting that is an actual model of the roof vaulting in the transept.

† On another roof boss is an excellent example of a maze. This is in the N aisle of the nave. (There is one other example of a maze, at South Tawton, Devon, but it is not so fine as this one.)

† Other roof bosses in the N aisle of the nave depict elaborate geometrical designs.

† At the W end of the nave is a boss showing Christ crucified, His arms resting on His Father's knees.

† In the nave also is a boss depicting a sheila, a grotesque female fertility figure possibly pre-dating Christianity. This is one of only four roof bosses depicting sheilas – the others are at South Tawton, Devon, and at Wells Cathedral (see page 388).

† The most unusual bosses can be found in the nave and at the W end of the N aisle under the tower in what is known as the chapel of St John the Baptist or the American chapel. They depict men at stool – a curious subject for the carving of a roof boss! The one in the American chapel is on the NE side nearest to the wall near the bell rope and is the finest example of this subject in England. (Only one other church has a boss depicting men at stool and that is in the W cloister of Wells Cathedral.)

Other crude bosses can be seen in the N aisle of the nave.

All the bosses in the church, except those in the American chapel, are beautifully gilded with pure gold.

◈ In the American chapel is a wooden statue of Queen Elizabeth I, originally a ship's figurehead, and the rib of a cow-whale which was given to the church by John and Sebastian Cabot after they had discovered Newfoundland in 1497.

◈ The outer N porch is hexagonal in shape and is a superb example of Decorated architecture dating from c.1280. Note the curious windows with inverted points and the delicate carving. Over the porch is the church treasury, reached by a door in the E wall of the inner porch. The inner porch dates from c.1180. (See Porches, page 265.)

◈ In the SW corner is the octagonal medieval font built into a pillar of the baptistery – an unusual feature.

◈ Over the S door are the fine arms of Charles II dating from c.1660.

◈ In the S aisle of the nave are three star-shaped tomb recesses. The only other examples are in Bristol Cathedral (see page 51).

◈ In the S transept is a four-poster monument to William Canynges (d.1474) and his wife. He was mayor five times and is depicted in rich merchant's robes. He has the unusual distinction of being depicted again on the left as a priest because after the death of his wife he entered holy orders.

◈ The superb brass eagle lectern was given in 1638 by James Wathen, churchwarden and 'pinn maker'.

◈ Outside, near the S transept is the grave of the church cat, 1912–27.

◈ Also on the S side of the churchyard is a tramline embedded in the grass. This was flung here on 11 April 1941 when a high-explosive bomb fell on Redcliffe Hill. How narrowly the church escaped!

## Brithdir                          GWYNEDD

ST MARK, surrounded by a glorious blaze of rhododendrons in June, was consecrated on 26 April 1898.

◈ In the churchyard is buried the Reverend

Ivor Farrar, son of Dean Farrar, and his wife, Constance, who was aunt of Lord Montgomery of Alamein.

Several features inside the church reflect the art nouveau style – the chancel walls are of red ochre while the roof is a pale blue.

The pulpit is encased with beaten copper and carries motifs of grapes.

The altar and reredos are also of beaten copper – unique in the British Isles.

The choir stalls are carved from Spanish chestnut and depict numerous animals including a tortoise, hare, squirrels with nuts, rabbits, an owl and several others.

At the w end under the w windows stands a circular lead font on an octagonal stone pillar. Made in 1898 this is the only lead font in Wales. It is 34 cm (1 foot 1½ inches) deep with an internal diameter of 51 cm (1 foot 8 inches) and an external diameter of 65 cm (2 feet 1½ inches). Around the sides is a large wavy-leaf pattern and numerous motifs including cockle shells, roses and the Dove-symbol of the Holy Spirit. There are three seams.

This lead font was cast at the Central School of Arts and Crafts, London, designed by Henry Wilson and modelled by Arthur Grove. (See Lead Fonts, page 74.)

# Brockhampton -by-Ross          HEREFORDSHIRE

ALL SAINTS is situated in a beautiful churchyard with fine views. It has a w tower, low central tower and thatched roof. Built by Alice Madeline Foster in memory of her parents, Ebenezer D. and Julia M. Jordan, the church was consecrated on 6 October 1902. The architect was W. R. Lethaby.

In the tower there is a dovecote (see Church Dovecotes, page 182).

Over the s door in the porch are plaques of six doves and a cross. The s door has unusual ironwork.

The building is an excellent example of the Arts and Crafts movement with notable triangular arches inside and windows with cylindrical shafts in the nave and chancel.

The stone font depicts vine leaves and fruit and is very similar to the lead font at Brithdir, Gwynedd (see previous entry), which dates from 1898 but carries different motifs.

The E window depicts angels and Saints John, Peter, Agatha, Edward and Elizabeth. It is by C. Whall.

In the chancel is an ancient bell (c.1210), which came from the old church and was badly damaged by fire during the Second World War.

The chancel stalls have 48 carved panels of different wild flowers and the pulpit shows Christ preaching to the crowds. Note the boys playing at the left and another boy in the tree on the right.

At the w end a plaque commemorates the younger son of Arthur and Madeline Foster, Arthur Cedric Foster, Grenadier Guards, who was killed in France on 12 March 1915, aged 23.

At the w end is a framed altar cloth embroidered with 60 different wild flowers. Many of the hymn books have embroidered wild-flower covers.

To the w of the church, under a crucifix, are the graves of Arthur W. Foster (18 June 1855–13 September 1929), Alice M. Foster (12 April 1863–29 September 1932) and their son, Arthur Foster.

# Buckland          OXFORDSHIRE

ST MARY THE VIRGIN is a beautiful church situated quite near the impressive Buckland House and little Roman Catholic church.

54

With the exception of a four-light Perpendicular window on the s side of the nave to the E of the porch, and a small Victorian window on the w side of the s porch, all the windows in the church have straight mullions to the top with *no tracery* (a very unusual feature). No church possesses so many such windows. (See Cheddleton, Staffordshire, page 70 and Uffington, Oxfordshire, page 377.)

It is not certain why so many windows are without tracery. Perhaps they were constructed like this in *c.*1290 as an experiment, although another theory is that the tracery was cut out in 1787 (the date on the outside of the s transept).

The stained glass is very fine, especially the following:

† The large E window of five lights is called the *Te Deum* window, with verses from this ancient hymn of the Church. At the top is Christ in Glory with His left hand on a blue orb, and numerous figures below representing Poetry, Philosophy, Agriculture, Spinning and so on.

At the base is a scroll with the words, 'To the Glory of God and in ever devoted memory of Francis Mourilyan Butler, Captain R. A. who fell in action October 8th 1917 near Ypres and was laid to rest near Elverdinghe.' The glass was made by Henry Holiday.

† At the w end of the chancel in the N wall another memorial window commemorates the Newhouse family – Hugh and George, who died in the Second World War and their parents, the Reverend R. L. C. Newhouse (vicar 1910–33) and Marion E. Newhouse. The three saints depicted are St Edward crowned as King, St Hugh as Bishop of Lincoln and St Francis of Assisi. This window was originally intended by the vicar, the Reverend Newhouse, to be a memorial to his son Hugh, who died early in the war serving in the RAF. By the time the war ended another son, George, had also been killed. The vicar and his wife died before the window could be installed, so this was done by the surviving son, the Reverend John Newhouse, and his sister Kate as a memorial to their two brothers and their parents.

† Below the s windows of the chancel are five shields framed in wood. Dating from *c.*1330 they were originally in the side windows above and then *c.*1900 incorporated in the E window until 1919. They are the largest shields in the diocese of Oxford.

† The large w window depicts the Crucifixion in the top five lights and the Nativity in the lower five lights. It commemorates Warren Green, a churchwarden of 1923, and was designed by Burlisson and Grylls.

The s transept is richly decorated with panels of mosaic and pictures painted on engraved marble, much of it again depicting the *Te Deum Laudamus*. This was executed 1890–2 at the expense of William West in memory of his wife, Clara Jane. The work was probably designed by Henry Holiday.

In the N wall of the chancel is buried the heart of preacher William Holcott (d. 1575) in a casket behind a triangular door – a rare survival.

On the N wall of the N transept is a fine brass to John Yate (d. 1578), his wife Mary Justice and their five sons and seven daughters – an important family who lived N of the church. Note that the date of Mary's death has been left blank and the most unusual feature of stubble on John's face!

## Bucklebury      BERKSHIRE

ST MARY THE VIRGIN The church and pretty village with its large common are situated in a peaceful valley near the River Pang.

*Bucklebury, Berkshire. This church is noted for its stained-glass sundial.*

The magnificent s Norman doorway dates from c.1150–70. At the apex is a strange face surmounted by a carved orb and Maltese cross.

The interior is like that of an eighteenth-century church, complete with high box pews, w gallery, six hatchments and a three-decker pulpit.

On the N side of the chancel is the famous 'Sundial' window, dated 1649, and lighting the squire's box pew. The shield shows the coats of arms of the families of Stephens and Stone. This glass panel came from one of the houses of the Stephens family. The dial has lost its gnomon, which would have been useless in its present position.

The realistic-looking fly to the left of the shield has wings painted on one side of the glass and the body and legs on the other! It reminds us that 'time flies'. (See Stained-glass Sundials, page 312.)

In the N aisle is an ancient oak chest which is said to have come from Reading Abbey.

In the vestry is an eighteenth-century hudd used by former vicars at burial services to protect them from rain. (See Graveside Shelters, page 111.)

The splendid E window was made by Sir Frank Brangwyn. It is very rich in colouring and depicts Christ crucified looking up to Heaven – a rare feature since He is usually shown with head bowed. Three other Brangwyn windows can be seen – two smaller ones on either side of the chancel and one in the N aisle, all distinguished by their vivid colouring. (See also Kingsland, Herefordshire, page 189.)

Near the pulpit is a window designed by

56

Allen W. Seaby and made by Charles Earthy in memory of the Reverend E. M. Thorp (possibly a former vicar of the parish). It shows a trout swimming through reeds with a kingfisher above and was dedicated on 24 September 1944.

## Bucknell　　　　　　　　OXFORDSHIRE

ST PETER boasts a fine Norman central tower.

In the chancel, two low-side windows (those placed lower than the normal windows in the church), face each other with two more at the E end of the nave. This is the only church in England possessing so many low-side windows which have always puzzled ecclesiologists.

It has been suggested that low-side windows may have been used for the purposes of administering the host during mass to 'lepers', or for the priest to ring the bell at the elevation of the host or even as a means of ventilating the E end of the church when the smell of incense and candles became stifling.

## Burghfield　　　　　　　　BERKSHIRE

ST MARY THE VIRGIN was rebuilt in stone and brick in 1843.

An unusual W tower starts with four sides and rises through eight to finish with 16, the whole being surmounted by a small spire very similar to Quarr Abbey on the Isle of Wight.

On the N side of the chancel in a glass case is the carved wooden effigy of Sir Roger de Burghfield (d. 1327). The effigy, which is 1.98 m (6 feet 6 inches) long, dates from c.1330 and was probably carved in London. Sir Roger's head rests on a cushion supported by one angel. He wears a mail head covering and his left leg is crossed over the right. The left side of the effigy has been cut away but the existing work is of excellent design and craftsmanship.

When the church was rebuilt, the effigy was hidden away in the porch under the belfry steps! It was rediscovered in 1931 and placed in its present position in the chancel, where it is safely padlocked after being stolen in 1978. (See Wooden Effigies, page 246.)

In the S transept on the W wall are the brass portraits of Nicholas Williams and his wife dating from c.1580. His wife wears a Mary Queen of Scots bonnet and has a scent bottle hanging from her waist.

The ten-sided font has cable moulding at its base and is probably Norman.

Under the tower in the W porch are the battered effigies of Richard Neville, Earl of Salisbury (b. c.1400), and Alice or Eleanor his wife. He was the father of Warwick the Kingmaker and was executed at Pontefract (West Yorkshire) in 1460.

## Burrington　　　　　　　HEREFORDSHIRE

ST GEORGE lies in a lonely village in the hills near Ludlow and was virtually rebuilt in 1864.

*Outside* the E end are six cast-iron grave slabs, commemorating the following: Robert Seward (d. 1619), Joyce Walker (d. 1658), Maria Hare (d. 1674)', William Walker (d. 1676), Jane and Barbara Knight (d. 1701 and 1705), Richard Knight (d. 1745) and Ralph Knight (d. 1754).

Originally inside the chancel, the slabs were left outside when the church was rebuilt smaller. They were cast at Bringewood Forge near Downton Castle on the River Teme.

As a rare feature of our churches, they should be returned to the inside of the church. (See Wadhurst, E. Sussex, page 379.)

## Bury          WEST SUSSEX

ST JOHN THE EVANGELIST From the A29, at the foot of Bury Hill, a little road leads down towards the River Arun and terminates at the church; from there are fine views towards Amberley.

On the outside wall of the s porch to the left of the doorway is a holy-water stoup dating from *c.*1500 – an unusual position as it is usually found inside the porch to the right of the doorway.

The s aisle is separated from the nave by massive circular pillars dating from *c.*1220. At the E and W ends the arches rest unusually on three small corbel capitals, beautifully carved.

The octagonal font is decorated with quatrefoils and roses dating from *c.*1450.

On the w wall of the nave is a brass plaque inscribed, 'The Fellowship of the Services. To perpetuate the founder of this brotherhood of ex-servicemen Cresswell Fitzherbert Tayler White of the parish of Bury. Born 13 December, 1888. Died 26 July, 1962. We will remember him.'

His grave is in the churchyard right near the NW corner and is marked by a plain cross.

Under the tower, hanging on the s wall, is an ancient bier dated 1697 and on the floor is a large bell inscribed, 'Roger Tapsil 1611'.

The chancel screen dates from *c.*1450. The holes in groups of four at the base were made to allow kneeling worshippers to see the altar.

Under the middle window of the nave hangs a polished wrought-iron bas-relief from Gloucestershire of the Last Supper by Leonardo da Vinci.

## Bury St Edmunds        SUFFOLK

ST EDMUNDSBURY CATHEDRAL OR THE CATHEDRAL CHURCH OF ST JAMES

became in 1914 the Cathedral Church of the Diocese of St Edmundsbury and Ipswich.

From 1943 to 1988 Stephen Dykes Bower (1903–94) was appointed as architect. The Victorian chancel was demolished *c.*1959 and Dykes Bower designed a new quire and crossing which were built from 1963 to 1970.

The impressive nave and N and s aisles date from 1503. The hammer-beam roof was erected by Sir George Gilbert Scott *c.*1870.

Thanks to grants from the Millennium Commission, the Stephen Dykes Bower Trust and other generous donations, the magnificent central lantern tower was built. Costing approximately £12.5m it was designed by Hugh Mathew, a former partner of Dykes Bower, and its completion was celebrated on 22 July 2005 after five years' work.

The 45.72 m- (150 feet-) high tower, comprises a core of 600,000 bricks faced externally and internally with stone. It is unique in that the external stone is mainly Barnack, the best English limestone in the Middle Ages. Clipsham stone has also been used on the tower and Doulting stone elsewhere.

Note the letter 'E' for St Edmund surmounted by a crown in flint and stone flush-work below the battlements on each face of the tower. (See also, Southwold, Suffolk, page 329.)

There is no public access to the top of the tower but touch-screen computers allow visitors to see the view from the top and even to zoom in on more distant buildings.

The E side cloister, St Edmund's chapel, a crypt chapel, the N transept and Cathedral Centre are some of the other new buildings erected through the inspiration of Stephen Dykes Bower to enlarge the original medieval church.

The superb Norman tower on the s side

of the cathedral contains a ring of ten bells dating from 1785.

▣ At the w end of the s aisle is the Susanna Window with Flemish glass in the lower lights dating from c.1480 and English medieval glass at the top.

▣ The w window dates from c.1900 and depicts the Last Judgement.

▣ The gold and silver cross on the high altar was made in 1921 in memory of the only daughter of the Greene family who died at four years old. An inscription states that 'life is eternal, love immortal and death only the horizon, the limit of our sight'.

▣ On the bishop's throne is a carving of the head of St Edmund the Martyr (d. 870) being held by a wolf.

▣ At the head of the treasury stairs is a piece of sculpture entitled 'Crucifixion' by Elizabeth Frink – probably the most important modern work in the cathedral.

## Bury St Edmunds          SUFFOLK

ST MARY is a magnificent Perpendicular church, built 1424–33.

▣ There is a superb hammer-beam roof.

▣ Among the many wooden bosses in the chancel are a number depicting animals and birds. An unusual one shows a snail among leaves. Snails are only found in three other churches – Bristol Cathedral, Great St Mary, Cambridge, and Lacock, Wilts.

▣ On the N side of the chancel is the grave of Mary Tudor (1495–1533), Queen of France, third daughter of Henry VII and sister of Henry VIII. She was first married in 1514 to Louis XII, King of France, and then in 1517 to Charles Brandon, Duke of Suffolk. She died at Westhorp Hall, Suffolk, was buried in the Abbey church and re-interred here in 1784.

▣ At the SE end of the s aisle a window given by Queen Victoria shows Queen Mary Tudor (called Princess Mary Tudor) – her two marriages and death.

▣ On the E wall of the s aisle is a painting by John Williams called 'The Incarnation'. Mary is shown in the centre with the Nativity in the top left corner, Jesus instructing His disciples in the top right, the Crucifixion in the bottom left and the Resurrection and Ascension in the bottom right.

▣ Over the chancel arch is a window with Star of David tracery. The stained glass (1840) depicts the Martyrdom of St Edmund.

▣ On the N side of the church is the Notyngham porch with an unusual pierced pendent boss showing angels worshipping God.

## Bywell          NORTHUMBERLAND

ST PETER is situated high up and very close to the River Tyne, creating a dramatic impression.

▣ On the N side of the nave is a beautiful fourteenth-century chapel which was formerly a chantry chapel. It was used as a school until 1849 when the present arcade was built which opened it to the church. The windows are excellent examples of fourteenth-century work.

▣ On the s side of the chancel are two lancets filled with Victorian glass. The one nearer the altar bears the inscription, 'To the cherished memory in this House of God of the Reverend Henry Parr Dwarris, MA, Curate of this parish accidentally drowned opposite this church, May 8th, 1855, aged 33 years.'

The other window carries the inscription, 'To the cherished memory in this House of God of Georgiana G. Dwarris, wife of the vicar who was taken from us March 4th 1853, aged 28 years. ROM VIII V. 34.'

Such tragedy lies behind these two windows!

*The magnificent central tower of Canterbury Cathedral in Kent, known as 'Bell Harry'.*

# Cambridge

KING'S COLLEGE CHAPEL is a magnificent building and a supreme achievement of the Perpendicular period.

◈ It was begun by Henry VI in 1446 but not finally completed until 1515 by Henry VIII. After Henry VI's murder in the Tower of London in 1471 the work was resumed using a different stone. The difference is noticeable on the N side.

◈ The superb fan-vaulted roof was designed by John Wastell. It took three years to build. At 24.38 m (80 feet) high, it measures 12.19 m (40 feet) between the piers supporting the fan tracery. It is 88.09 m (289 feet) long and with 13 fans on each side is the largest fan vault in existence.

The poet Wordsworth (who was a student at St John's College) described it as '. . . scooped into ten thousand cells, where light and shade repose, where music dwells lingering – and wandering on as loth to die.' He also described this chapel as 'this immense and glorious Work of fine intelligence'. (See Fan Vaulting, page 152.)

◈ The wooden organ screen (1533–36) is decorated with the initials of Henry VIII and Anne Boleyn, who was executed in 1536. The choir doors carry Charles I's arms and date from 1636.

◈ The windows are the largest most complete series of Tudor stained glass in England. Most of it dates from 1515–31 and was made by glaziers from Belgium, assisted by Englishmen, the most famous being Bernard Flower.

The last window inserted was the w window in 1879. Made by Clayton and Bell it depicts the Last Judgement.

◈ At the E end is Rubens's oil painting on wood of 'The Adoration of the Magi'. Dating from 1634 it was given to the chapel in 1961 by Major A. E. Allnatt, who bought it for £275,000.

◈ The brass desk lectern dates from c.1520 and supports a statuette of Henry VI holding an orb and sceptre. It is inscribed 'Robertus Hacomblen' who was Provost, 1509–28. (See Medieval Brass Lecterns, page 362.)

# Canterbury Cathedral     KENT

THE CATHEDRAL CHURCH OF CHRIST is the mother church of the Anglican communion. On 29 May 1982 an historic meeting occurred here when Pope John Paul II, on the first visit of a Pope to the United Kingdom, met the Archbishop of Canterbury (Reverend Robert Runcie) at a special service of friendship between the Anglican and Roman Catholic churches.

◈ The magnificent nave was constructed by Henry Yevele c.1400 and encases the pillars of the ancient Norman nave.

◈ In the N aisle of the nave is the fine font dating from 1639. This was given by John Warner, Bishop of Rochester.

◈ Also in the N aisle of the nave is a bust depicting the musician Orlando Gibbons (d. 1625) which was carved by Nicholas Stone. This is the earliest example of a pedestal bust in England.

Separating the nave from the quire is the Screen of the Six Kings. Its delicate Gothic stone carving dates from c.1450 and is some of the finest in existence. Above the kings – Edward the Confessor, Ethelbert, Henry IV, Henry V, Henry VI and Richard II – are tiny faces carved on the canopies. These are all original.

In the N wall of the NW transept (known as the Martyrdom) is the tomb of Archbishop William Warham (1503–32) surmounted by a tall Perpendicular canopy of three ogee arches. His chantry chapel, to the N of his tomb, is squeezed in between the wall of the transept and the wall of the chapter house – the most curiously situated of all chantry chapels. (But compare Bishop Grandisson's chapel in Exeter Cathedral, see page 134.)

When I saw this chantry chapel of Archbishop Warham in May 1982 it was being used as a store for brushes and buckets!

Also in the N wall of the NW transept is the tomb of Archbishop John Peckham (1278–92). His wooden effigy is 2.23 m (7 feet 4 inches) long and lies on an original table-tomb underneath an elaborate arch. The archbishop is depicted in full ecclesiastical vestments including mitre, his hands are in blessing, his head rests on two cushions and his feet are on an animal now mutilated. The left side of the figure is damaged and also the mitre. (See Wooden Effigies, page 246.)

On the E side of the NW transept is the lady chapel with a fine fan-vaulted roof. On the s wall is a monument to Dean John Boys (d. 1625) which shows him seated in his study, his left elbow resting on a table draped with a cloth on which is an open book. (See Fan Vaulting, page 152.)

Also in the lady chapel on the s side is the gruesome tomb-chest of Dean Fotherby (d. 1619) which is adorned with carvings of skulls.

In the NW transept, near the entrance to the lady chapel, is the site of the martyrdom of St Thomas à Becket on 29 December 1170.

Behind the quire stalls on the N and s sides are stone screens erected by Prior Eastry c.1300. The many cinquefoil heads consist of plain cusping except at the E end near the transept gates, where there are two clusters of delicate foliage facing each other. Why were only these carved?

In the N quire aisle, opposite the NE transept, is the fine tomb of Archbishop Henry Chichele (1414–43) which was erected during his lifetime. His figure in splendid vestments on the top contrasts well with his cadaver on a shroud below! Chichele founded All Souls College, Oxford, in 1438 and provided £7 a year for the upkeep of his tomb.

Behind the high altar is St Augustine's chair of Petworth marble which dates from c.1205 and was only moved to its present and original position in 1977. It is used at the enthronement of every Archbishop of Canterbury.

To the E of the high altar is the Opus Alexandrinum or marble pavement, which was a gift from the Pope in c.1220. It consists of a geometrical pattern of squares and circles.

On the N side of the Opus Alexandrinum (this is situated in the Trinity chapel) is the tomb of Henry IV (1367–1413) and his queen, Joan of Navarre – the only monarchs buried in the cathedral. The tomb was completed in 1437. Henry IV was the nephew of the Black Prince.

On the s side of the Trinity chapel, opposite the tomb of Henry IV, is the tomb of Edward, the Black Prince (1330–76), the son of Edward III who fought at the Battle of Crécy in 1346. In 1363 he founded a chantry chapel in the crypt which was first used by French Protestants (the Huguenots' Church) in 1575 and where services are still held in French every Sunday.

Replicas of his 'achievements' were hung over his tomb in 1954 – the originals are now placed for safer preservation in a glass case near by.

The Black Prince's magnificent effigy is made of bronze and rests inside on an iron grille dated 1400. The sword is now missing, reputed to have been stolen by Cromwell c.1650.

◈ In the SE corner of the Trinity chapel is the curious tomb of Odet de Coligny, a cardinal who fled from France in 1568 and died mysteriously in 1571, probably from poisoning. His tomb comprises brickwork plastered over with cement – a temporary measure while he awaits removal to France for burial, which now seems unlikely after more than 400 years!

◈ To the s of the Trinity chapel is St Anselm's chapel. In the NE corner of the apse is a well-preserved medieval wall painting dating from c.1150 showing St Paul and the snake on Malta (Acts 28, vv1–6).

◈ In the SE transept are two brilliant modern windows by Erwin Bossanyi (1956–62).

◈ On the E side of the sw transept is St Michael's chapel or Warriors' chapel under the altar of which is the stone tomb of Archbishop Stephen Langton (d. 1228) which extends outside the wall! (See Slindon, W. Sussex, page 321.)

◈ Under the E part of the cathedral is the largest Norman crypt in the world, the w part of which dates from c.1110. It covers an area of approximately 1587 sq m (17,080 sq feet) and contains some very fine and interesting capitals including apemen, peculiar beasts and animals playing musical instruments.

◈ Around the crypt are numerous chapels. On the s side is St Gabriel's, containing finely carved capitals; in the corresponding Holy Innocents' chapel on the N side is a pillar carved with a unique design similar to fish scales.

◈ In the crypt, protected by glass, are two of the most famous graffiti in the cathedral. On the N wall of the passage leading to the E crypt is a knight on horseback and on the E crypt's w wall is Christ in Majesty.

◈ In the crypt, on the s side of the Chapel of Our Lady Undercroft, is the tomb of Archbishop John Morton (1486–1500). On the E side of the tomb is a beautiful Annunciation scene with four lilies in a pot.

◈ A monument in the s nave aisle to John Sympson (d. 1752) by Rysbrack shows a broken column with two cherubs – the earliest example in the British Isles of a broken column.

◈ The chapter house was built between 1304 and 1320 and heightened c.1400–12. It is covered with a vast barrel-vaulted roof of Irish oak and is the second greatest wooden roof in England (the greatest being Westminster Hall, London).

◈ The cloisters were vaulted c.1400 and contain more than 820 roof bosses showing coats of arms (largely of subscribers to the work). This is the greatest collection of medieval heraldry in Europe.

One of the bosses on the s side of the E walk is thought to depict Henry Yevele, the architect.

◈ In addition to the cloister bosses, the cathedral contains the following interesting roof bosses:

✝ In the centre of the E crossing of the quire is one of the most outstanding roof bosses in the country showing the *Agnus Dei*. The lamb is carrying a cross and banner and the boss is surrounded by four angels. These angels are the earliest representation on a roof boss and are the most important example in England. The boss dates from 1178 and was carved by a craftsman working under William of Sens.

† Directly above the spot where the shrine of St Thomas à Becket stood is a large foliate boss near to which is a curious crescent moon which may have been brought from the Holy Land by Crusaders c.1200.

† In the N aisle of the nave there is a boss with one head on one side and two heads on the other. The two heads share three eyes between them, the central eye being common to both heads!

† In the Black Prince's chantry chapel in the crypt are some fine bosses dating from c.1360 including the Black Prince's wife, Joan, in typical fourteenth-century head-dress, a pelican feeding her young, a lion and the Green Man.

▦ On the N side of the cathedral is the unique Norman water tower built c.1160.

▦ The central tower, known as Bell Harry Tower at 76.2 m (250 feet) high, is a superb example of Perpendicular architecture and was finished c.1500. Although faced with stone, the inside core comprises about 500,000 bricks. Above the vaulting is an old tread-wheel. Other tread-wheels exist at Beverley Minster, Durham, Peterborough and Salisbury Cathedrals and Louth (see pages 26, 110, 270, 303 and 226 respectively).

▦ The most famous treasure of the cathedral is the magnificent stained glass, some of it in the quire dating from as early as 1180. In the first window on the left of the steps leading up to the Trinity chapel is a portrait of Becket himself. Others, dating from c.1250, are the finest remaining examples of thirteenth-century glass in England.

▦ Among other treasures is a Saxon pocket-sundial or 'watch' dating from c.900. This unique object, beautifully made from gold

and silver, measures 6 cm (2.5 inches) long and was found in 1937 when soil was being removed from the cloister garth.

▦ In the cloister garth is the grave of the Reverend Hugh Richard Lawrie Sheppard ('Dick', 1880–1937), who was a famous vicar of St Martin-in-the-Fields (London) from 1917 to 1927. He kept the church open 24 hours a day and attracted many home-less people. The church also featured in early religious radio broadcasts.

Dick Sheppard became Dean of Canterbury in 1929 and, as a staunch pacifist, founded the Peace Pledge Union in 1936. A special pilgrimage is made annually from London to his grave.

## Canterbury       KENT

ST MARTIN Parts of this church dating from AD560 cover an earlier Roman build-ing of c.AD90, making it the oldest church in the British Isles.

▦ When St Augustine came in AD597 Queen Bertha, wife of King Ethelbert, was already worshipping on this spot!

▦ The fine Norman font made of Caen stone stands on a plain base. It has inter-esting arches around the top and rows of unevenly spaced interlocking circles at the bottom.

## Cardington       BEDFORDSHIRE

ST MARY Most of the church dates from 1898–1902, when it was rebuilt in the Perpendicular style of architecture.

▦ On the outside S wall of the tower is a sundial erected by Samuel Whitbread I in 1782. Below this is a rare and well-preserved example of an Anglo-Saxon sundial.

▦ In the Whitbread chapel on the N side of the N aisle is a rare Wedgwood font in black basalt which was the gift of Harriet

*The truncated nave of Carlisle Cathedral, Cumbria.*

Whitbread in 1783. The foot, which was damaged, has been replaced in wood painted black. It stands on a wooden plinth. (See Wedgwood Fonts, page 302.)

▨ On the N wall of the Whitbread chapel is an imposing memorial to Samuel Whitbread I (1720–96), the founder of the famous brewery, who was born in Cardington. The monument was carved by J. Bacon, RA in 1799.

▨ Also on the N wall of this chapel is a memorial to Charles Whitbread (29 January 1839–31 July 1845): '. . . to the deep distress of his Family accidentally killed at Cardington by the fall of a Tree.'

▨ On the E wall is a memorial by H. Weekes, 1849, to Samuel Whitbread II (1764–1815).

▨ On the W wall is a monument to Ive Whitbread by Peter Scheemakers, c.1766. The two busts are very impressive.

▨ On the E wall of the S chapel are some ancient coffin lids and a wall tablet comprising a beautiful marble wreath to William Charles Whitbread (3 April 1789–5 May 1791).

▨ On each side of the chancel are beautiful tomb-chests with elaborate canopies, the S one boasting Renaissance details.

▨ In the S aisle is the R101 memorial commemorating the 48 victims of the airship which crashed at Beauvais, France, on 5 October 1930 while on the first airship flight to India. Overhead in a glass case is a portion of the RAF blue ensign flag which flew on the airship. It was installed in the church on 28 September 1931.

Forty-eight victims are buried just inside the gate of the churchyard extension NW of the church on the opposite side of the road. The simple monument over their grave was designed by Sir Albert Richardson.

It is a curious fact that 49 deaths are recorded as victims of the disaster but only 48 are commemorated inside the church. Who is the missing one?

# Carlisle                    CUMBRIA

THE CATHEDRAL CHURCH OF THE HOLY AND UNDIVIDED TRINITY is unique in possessing a chancel and two transepts but only a truncated nave which is now a chapel, the remainder of the site being laid to lawn. Following the siege of 1644–5 during the Civil War, six bays of the nave were demolished and the stones used to repair other buildings!

▨ The piers supporting the central tower have Norman capitals halfway down. This is a very unusual feature.

▨ In the head of the N tower arch is a Perpendicular strainer arch put in to strengthen the tower. It used to act as a window when the roof of the N transept was lower.

▨ Notice how the Norman arch that leads from the S transept into the truncated nave has been depressed – further evidence of weak foundations.

▨ The beautiful choir is a superb example of Decorated architecture. The E window 15.54 m (51 feet) high displays excellent curvilinear tracery, the finest in England. It is also unique in being the only fourteenth-century window in England with nine lights. Most of the glass dates from 1861.

▨ The arches on each side of the choir are thirteenth century while the piers supporting them are fourteenth. On the capitals of the piers, beginning with January on the S side, nearest the large E window, are detailed carvings showing the Occupations of the Months. This is the most perfect stone calendar in England and will reward careful study. Notice how Janus has three heads – to look back, view the present and look forward to the future.

On the piers themselves, especially on the NW side, are numerous interesting examples of medieval graffiti.

◈ The attractive roof, repainted in 1970, has the remains of a hammer-beam roof still left in position at the sides, the ends of which are decorated with angels. (Not all authorities agree with this; some think these are the sawn-off ends of tie-beams.)

◈ The beautiful pulpit dates from 1559 and came from St Andrew's, Antwerp. From 1826 to 1963 it was in the little church at Cockayne Hatley, Bedfordshire, when it was sold to this cathedral.

◈ On the N side of the choir is the Salkeld Screen erected by Lancelot Salkeld, the last prior and first dean. Dating from c.1540 it is contemporary with the pulpit and exhibits beautiful early Renaissance work.

In the s choir aisle is a small brass to Bishop Henry Robinson (d. 1616) showing the old buildings of Queen's College, Oxford, three dogs, weapons of war and this cathedral.

◈ The 46 stalls in the choir date from c.1400 and have a variety of interesting misericord seats including a mermaid with her glass, a fox killing a goose and the coronation of the Virgin.

◈ Above the E window on the outside is a small statue of the Virgin and Child and above this an elaborate triangular window, which lights the roof space over the choir but is invisible inside the cathedral.


# Carno      POWYS

ST JOHN THE BAPTIST was designed by J. W. Poundley and built in 1863; it lies at the foot of a Welsh hillside called Clorin.

◈ Laura Ashley (1925–85) the famous Welsh-born designer, is buried in the churchyard. She died tragically after falling downstairs.


# Cartmel      CUMBRIA

PRIORY CHURCH OF ST MARY THE VIRGIN AND ST MICHAEL It is the tower on this church that leaves a lasting impression on visitors.

◈ The square central tower dates from c.1400 and is unique in possessing another and smaller square tower set diagonally on top of it.

◈ The stalls and misericords in the choir date from c.1450. Among them may be seen the Pelican in her Piety, a mermaid with two tails, the elephant and castle, the Holy Trinity and the oak tree and the unicorn. These misericords and choir stalls survived 83 years of exposure to the weather after the dissolution of the monastery in 1537 when the choir became roofless until 1620. The result of the exposure can be seen in the poppy heads of the benches.

◈ The magnificent choir screen and canopies of the choir stalls were carved in 1620 and given by George Preston. They are an excellent example of Renaissance work.

◈ In the E window of the choir are fragments of glass dating from 1350 to 1450.

◈ On the s side of the choir is the very interesting tomb of the first Lord Harrington (d. 1347). The small figures of mourners at the top bow over the effigies and are not separate from them – a unique feature.

◈ The Priory Church treasures include one of the first umbrellas (dating from c.1760) and an interesting library dating from c.1630 which has, among its 300 books, a Vinegar Bible of 1716 and a first edition of Spenser's *Faerie Queene*, printed in London in 1596.

# Castle Combe                    WILTSHIRE

ST ANDREW is situated in what many people consider to be England's prettiest village.

High on the outside E face of the tower, near the N side, is a carving of sheep shears, comb and shuttle put there by the builders of the tower. Above this is inscribed: 'Vivat regine ani 1575'. This was placed here during the reign of Queen Elizabeth I.

The font dates from c.1450 and is unique in possessing a bookrest on the s side.

The chancel arch is richly decorated with carvings of six saints – an unusual feature. Above the arch is another rare feature – a rose window in this position (but Burwell, Cambridgeshire, also has one).

The clock is one of the oldest in England and dates from c.1450 but has no face. The mechanism can be seen under the fan-vaulted tower. (See Fan Vaulting, page 152.)

# Castle Hedingham                    ESSEX

ST NICHOLAS has a beautifully attractive churchyard with roses among other flowers.

The fine brick tower dates from 1616.

The superb Norman nave has plain moulded arches. Notice two pillars at the extreme E end which have capitals half square and half round. This would indicate they were changed when the easternmost arches were inserted.

The nave is crowned by a magnificent double hammer-beam roof dating from c.1540. It is decorated with crowned angels and the emblems of the earls of Oxford – a star and a boar. The craftsman who built this roof was Thomas Loveday.

The Norman chancel has pointed windows inserted in the round arches and a Norman wheel window at the E end – a very rare feature.

On the N side of the chancel is the large tomb of the De Vere, Earl of Oxford and his wife. They are shown in relief on top of the tomb while their daughters Elizabeth, Anne, Frances and Ursula kneel below. The monument dates from 1539.

There are three Norman doorways complete with three Norman doors – no other church in England has so many. One of the doors is fixed and cannot be opened.

A large wooden viewer contains photographs of the church and lights up when a coin is inserted. It was made by Brian Maurice Westrop in 1958. He drowned on the Norfolk Broads on 21 July 1960 aged 22.

# Chantry                    SOMERSET

HOLY TRINITY was built 1844–6 and designed by Sir Gilbert Scott and W. B. Moffatt.

At the w end are two lancet windows. The s one contains a rare depiction of Christ crucified on a lily. The glass was made by William Wailes in c.1846. (See Lily Crucifix, page 338.)

In the chancel are eight misericords. Among the carvings is a green man and a phoenix rising from the flames. A particularly lovely one shows a squirrel with acorns.

On the N side of the chancel is the tomb of Jacob Fussell, 1846. He was a priest and founder of this church.

The roof is very interesting outside, being covered with immensely large stone slabs which give the appearance of lead sheeting.

# Chasetown                    STAFFORDSHIRE

ST ANNE was built c.1863–5 by the Cannock Chase Colliery Company as a place of worship for the miners and their families

*The rare circular Norman window in Castle Hedingham, Essex.*

who were working and living in the new coalfields. It was consecrated on 14 September 1865.

⊞ In 1883 this church became the first in England to be lit by electricity, the supply coming from the nearby no. 2 colliery. A piece of the original cable is preserved inside the church.

⊞ In 1938 an electrical device was arranged to ring the church bell, thus making it the first church bell in the country to be rung in this way.

## Cheddar        Somerset

St Andrew Down the hill to the s from the famous caves is the little village of Cheddar, the lofty tower of its beautiful church rising behind the houses.

⊞ There are unusual fine, modern gates to the churchyard on the n side.

⊞ The tower, rising to 33.53 m (110 feet), dates from c.1400 and has a ring of eight bells.

⊞ To the s of the church, about 45.72 m (150 feet) from the door, under a huge sycamore tree, is the grave of William Chatterton Dix. It bears the inscription, 'Here lies William Chatterton Dix, hymn writer, 1837–1898'. He wrote such hymns as, 'Alleluia sing to Jesus', 'As with gladness men of old' and 'Come unto Me, ye weary'.

⊞ On the s side of the nave attached to the easternmost pier is a fine, richly coloured medieval stone pulpit dating from c.1450.

⊞ In the s transept or Chantry Chapel of Fitzwalter or St Nectan's chapel are fragments of ancient glass, including shields, dating from c.1485. Over the altar is a beautiful painting by Jan Erasmus Quellinus of Antwerp (1629–1715) entitled 'The Supper at Emmaus'.

⊞ Among the good pre-Reformation bench-ends, the best are in the n aisle,

several of which depict the 'Sins of the Tongue'.

## Cheddleton        Staffordshire

St Edward the Confessor lies in a little village near the River Churnet, picturesquely situated on a hillside on the A520 between Stone and Leek.

⊞ The window in the e wall of the s aisle is unusual in possessing mullions but no tracery in the arched head. (See also Buckland and Uffington, Oxon, page 54 and 377 respectively).

⊞ Several of the windows contain stained glass by William Morris, Madox Brown, Rossetti and Burne-Jones.

⊞ The magnificent brass eagle lectern is medieval Flemish and was brought from Belgium in 1864 by Reverend C. S. Hassalls. (See Medieval Brass Lecterns, page 362.)

⊞ The central portion of the triptych over the altar is medieval Flemish, but the side paintings of the Annunciation were added by William Morris c.1860.

## Chester        Cheshire

The Cathedral Church of Christ and the Blessed Virgin Mary Chester Cathedral was originally the Abbey of St Werburgh and at the dissolution of the monasteries it became the cathedral of the newly formed Diocese of Chester on 26 July 1541.

⊞ In 1645 Charles I watched the Battle of Rowton Heath from the cathedral tower.

⊞ Near the e end is the new detached bell-tower, which was commenced in October 1974 and opened in 1975. It is 26.21 m (86 feet) high and houses a ring of 12 bells which are named after famous saints. The tower, designed by George Pace, was the first detached bell-tower for a cathedral to be built since the fifteenth century.

*New bell-tower, Chester Cathedral, Cheshire.*

On the ground floor of the unfinished sw tower is one of only two examples in England of an ancient consistory court. It dates from 1636 and the bishop and diocesan chancellor preside here over ecclesiastical affairs. (Another similar court dating from 1617 can be seen in St Nicholas' chapel, King's Lynn, Norfolk.)

In the sw porch is some beautiful fan vaulting dating from *c*.1870. (See Fan Vaulting, page 152.)

The magnificent choir stalls (the finest in England) date from *c*.1380 and contain some superb misericords, including one depicting the first Easter Day and another showing wrestlers. On the end of the dean's stall on the s side is a beautiful tree of Jesse above which is the coronation of the Virgin. On the elbow rest is a quaint carving of a pilgrim who has visited St Werburgh's shrine. The elbow rest on the N side shows the Pelican in her Piety.

There are a few interesting roof bosses, the two most notable being the following:

† In the lady chapel the w boss depicts the murder of St Thomas of Canterbury. This is the earliest representation of St Thomas on a roof boss and dates from *c*.1275. (St Thomas is only found on roof bosses in two other places – Exeter and Norwich cathedrals.)

† On the abbey gateway is a unique roof boss depicting St Werburgh.

The N transept is the oldest part of the cathedral and dates from 1092. The large monument dating from 1864 depicts Bishop Pearson (1672–86).

On the N side of the cathedral are the cloisters and adjoining buildings, which were the domestic buildings of the abbey. The refectory was the abbey dining hall and contains a beautiful wall pulpit. The magnificent hammer-beam roof dates from 1939.

# Chesterfield      DERBYSHIRE

OUR LADY & ALL SAINTS The town is dominated by this church's world-famous twisted spire which attracts many visitors.

The twisted spire was built in 1362, the exact date being given by Nottingham University's tree-ring dating laboratory after they took a pencil-sized core sample from a beam in the spire. No definite reason is given for its unique shape but the most likely one is that it was caused by the heat of the sun on green timber which resulted in the splitting of one of the main supports.

The lean is 2.29 m (7 feet 6 inches) to the S, 2.39 m (7 feet 10 inches) to the SW and 0.96 m (3 feet 2 inches) to the W. The entire spire is covered with lead plates laid herringbone fashion. This gives the illusion that the spire is channelled and has 16 faces although it is octagonal in plan and all its faces are perfectly flat.

It has been estimated that the total weight of the lead plates is 50,803.2 kg (50 tons). Rising 69.5 m (228 feet) high, this is the highest lead spire in England. Its original position in relation to the building is marked by brass studs in the floor under the crossing. (See Lead Spires and Spirelets, page 229.)

▨ Opening off the E end of the s transept is the lesser lady chapel, dating from c.1350 and formerly known as the Calton chapel. It has a polygonal E end, which is rare in an English parish church.

▨ In the lady chapel on the SE side of the church is an astonishing collection of tombs of the Foljambe family, the earliest dating from 1510. A kneeling figure represents Sir Thomas Foljambe, who died in 1604 aged 13, but the head does not belong to the body!

On a wall monument in the corner (c.1580–90) an allegorical representation of Death is shown with spear and spade and underneath is a corpse completely wrapped in a shroud. (See also Fenny Bentley, Derbyshire, page 142.)

▨ In a case on the N wall is a processional cross dating from c.1500. At the four points of the cross are the emblems of the gospel writers and on either side of the cross are Mary and John.

▨ The fine Jacobean pulpit dates from c.1620 and may have been carved by the same team who did the work on the Long Gallery at nearby Haddon Hall.

▨ The fine w window depicting the Supper at Emmaus dates from 1874 and is a copy of a window dating from c.1550 in Lichfield Cathedral.

# Chichester WEST SUSSEX

THE CATHEDRAL CHURCH OF THE HOLY TRINITY The spire of this cathedral can be seen for many kilometres and, apart from Portsmouth (which is much smaller), it is the only cathedral that can be seen from the sea.

▨ The central tower and spire, at 84.43 m (277 feet) high, were rebuilt by Sir Gilbert Scott following their dramatic telescopic collapse on 21 February 1861. The rebuilding of the tower and spire commenced on 2 May 1865 and was completed in just over a year. On 28 June 1866 the original weathercock was refixed to the top of the new spire by Gilbert Scott, Junior.

▨ The detached bell-tower (campanile) on the N side was built c.1450 and contains a ring of eight bells. It is the oldest detached bell-tower of any English cathedral which was built specifically as a bell-tower. (Bury St Edmunds Cathedral has a Norman bell-tower which was originally the gatehouse tower of the abbey.)

▨ In the baptistery under the sw tower is a painting of the baptism of Christ by Hans Feibusch (1952).

▨ Also in the baptistery is a font of dark green Cornish marble, 1.09 m (3 feet 7 inches) square engraved with the words 'One Lord, One Faith, One Baptism' (Ephesians 6, v. 5) which was dedicated on 4 February 1983 to commemorate the centenary of the birth of Bishop George Bell. Carved by John Skelton, assisted by nine other people, the font took two years to complete.

▨ In the s nave aisle is a brass to William Broadbridge (d. 1546, but corrected from 1552), Alice, his wife, and their six sons and eight daughters. He was three times Mayor of Chichester.

This and the heart brass (see below) are the only brasses in the cathedral.

*Chichester Cathedral and superb Market Cross (1501) in 1970 before the cathedral became partly obscured by a new building.*

I first became interested in lead fonts when I was a boy of ten, primarily because I used to stay with my grandmother at a village in Oxfordshire and the church there possessed a lead font. The village is Childrey and the church's lead font is unique in that it is the only one decorated around the top with large figures of bishops or abbots holding croziers (although Long Wittenham and Warborough – both in Oxfordshire – do have smaller figures around the base).

Despite the fact that there are thousands of churches in England and Wales, it is a curious fact that only 33 lead fonts survive. Over the centuries numerous fonts have suffered at the hands of iconoclasts (see Seven Sacrament Fonts, page 318) but none more so than the lead ones. Many have disappeared completely, having been melted down during the Civil War for bullets and other ammunition. Perhaps others have been used to repair roofs. Being soft and easily worked, a lead font was an ideal target for the destroyer before the days when such a treasure was appreciated.

Several lead fonts unfortunately disappeared during the Victorian period. Clifton Hampden, Oxfordshire, had its font melted in 1840 by the vicar and church-wardens 'because it was unshapely' and it was used to repair the church roof! Chilham, Kent, lost its font in 1860 and St Nicholas-at-Wade, Kent, in 1878. Hassingham, Norfolk, also lost its font but the exact date is unknown. The font at Great Plumstead, Norfolk, melted as the church burnt down (probably in Victorian times)!

Many of those lead fonts that have survived have done so because people hid them in some form or other during the turbulent days of the Civil War. The font at Ashover, Derbyshire, was hidden by the rector in his kitchen garden at Eastwood Hall. The church-wardens at Long Wittenham, Oxfordshire, surrounded their font with a wooden case packed with rubbish and it remained hidden thus for nearly 200 years until the case was removed in 1839.

The parishioners at Lower Halstow, Kent, had no idea that their church possessed a lead font until the early summer of 1921 when their vicar, the Reverend E. R. Olive, sent for a local mason to repair the cracks around the basin of the font. (These had been caused by powerful anti-aircraft guns operating on the banks of the River Medway during the First World War.) When the workman opened out the plaster he revealed a square lead font which, following restoration, was altered back to its original circular shape. This is yet another example of ingenuity in hiding a lead font.

The lead font at Pycombe, West Sussex, was painted white during the Civil War and white flecks still remain on it. Penn, Buckinghamshire, was also whitewashed.

The font at Edburton, West Sussex, has a white mark around the base confirming a theory that it was buried a few centimetres deep in a field by Roundhead soldiers in the Civil War and used as a horses' drinking trough.

Barnetby-le-Wold, Lincolnshire, consigned its lead font to the church coal shed for many years, while that at Wichling, Kent, was discovered during the incumbency of the rector the Reverend T. Norton between 1880 and 1916. He instituted major repairs including raising the chancel and sanctuary. Under the altar were graves of former rectors and in one of these the font was discovered. It had obviously been hidden there, probably during the Civil War.

On the grass in front of Greatham House, West Sussex, is a lead bowl which may be a lead font, but which is more likely to be the lining from a stone font or even a non-ecclesiastical object.

Lead fonts were normally cast as one, two, three or four flat slabs bent into circles, half-circles or even quarter-circles and then soldered together, often defacing the design. A circular piece of lead was then soldered on to one end of the cylinder to form the base and complete the font.

A few lead fonts have only one seam, such as those at Tangley, Hampshire, and Long Wittenham, Oxfordshire. Some have two and only one has three – Walton-on-the-Hill, Surrey. The majority, however, have four seams. Wareham, Dorset, is believed to be the only one cast in one complete piece and it is also the only one that is hexagonal.

With nine lead fonts, Gloucestershire has more than any other county. Those at Frampton-on-Severn, Gloucester Cathedral (from Lancaut and Tidenham), Oxenhall, Sandhurst and Siston were all cast from the same mould, although there are variations because when the sheets were curved to form the font, some of the arcades were omitted. Hence Frampton-on-Severn, Oxenhall, Siston and Tidenham each have 12 arcades, Sandhurst has 11 and the font from Lancaut has 10 arcades.

Edburton and Pyecombe, West Sussex, have similar fonts which may have come from the same mould or been designed by the same person.

As for age, there are 16 Romanesque (1066–1200) lead fonts in England, but it is impossible to say which is the oldest. Some authorities hold that the font at Walton-on-the-Hill, Surrey, dating from c.1150–60, is the oldest but the font at Lower Halstow, Kent, also dates from c.1150 and the six in Gloucestershire cast from the same mould may well date from c.1130.

The newest lead font is at St Alban, Leicester, and dates from 1905. It was

designed by G. P. Bankart and features bunches of grapes in its decoration. It is similar to the font at Moddershall, Staffordshire, dating from 1903. The font at Brithdir, Gwynedd, dates from 1898 and was designed and cast at the Central School of Arts and Crafts in London (founded 1896).

The finest font is that at Brookland, Kent. It has the signs of the zodiac around the top and the Labours of the Months below. This should be compared with the Norman stone font at Burnham Deepdale, Norfolk. Dorchester Abbey, Oxfordshire, also possesses a fine lead font. This is unique in being the only one inside a former monastic church and which was not destroyed at the Dissolution of the Monasteries.

The lead font at Ashover, Derbyshire, is unique in that it is the outside casing around a stone font. The usual form is a stone font with a thin lead lining to prevent the water seeping through the stone, or a font made solely of lead.

The font at Parham, West Sussex, dates from c.1351; it is the only one cast in the fourteenth century and also the only one to be covered in heraldry.

The largest lead font is at Barnetby-le-Wold, North Lincolnshire. It has a depth of 49 cm (1 foot 7¼ inches) and a top diameter of 81.3 cm (2 feet 8 inches). The smallest is at Parham, West Sussex, with a depth of only 21.6 cm (8½ inches) and a top diameter of 51 cm (1 foot 8 inches).

For the first time in their history the fonts from Barnetby-le-Wold, Gloucester Cathedral and Lower Halstow were displayed in London at a special Arts Council Exhibition entitled 'English Romanesque Art, 1066–1200' at the Hayward Gallery in London from 5 April–8 July 1984.

How many lead fonts are still hidden, awaiting discovery by future generations? Time alone will tell.

*A complete list of all the lead fonts in England and Wales:*

✠ BUCKINGHAMSHIRE
1. Penn (Holy Trinity)

✠ DERBYSHIRE
2. Ashover (All Saints)

✠ DORSET
3. Wareham (Lady St Mary)

✠ GLOUCESTERSHIRE
4. Down Hatherley (St Mary)
5. Frampton-on-Severn (St Mary)
6. Gloucester Cathedral (font from Lancaut, St James)
7. Gloucester Cathedral (font from Tidenham, St Mary)
8. Haresfield (St Peter)
9. Oxenhall (St Anne)
10. Sandhurst (St Lawrence)
11. Siston (St Anne)
12. Slimbridge (St John)

✠ GWYNEDD *(Wales)*
13. Brithdir (St Mark)

✠ HAMPSHIRE
14. Tangley (St Thomas)

✠ HEREFORDSHIRE
15. Aston Ingham (St John the Baptist)
16. Burghill (St Mary)

✠ KENT
17. Brookland (St Augustine)
18. Eythorne (St Peter & St Paul)
19. Lower Halstow (St Margaret of Antioch)
20. Wichling or Wychling (St Margaret)

✠ LEICESTERSHIRE
21. Leicester (St Alban), Harrison Road

✠ LINCOLNSHIRE
22. Barnetby-le-Wold (St Barnabas)

✠ NORFOLK
23. Brundall (St Lawrence)

✠ OXFORDSHIRE
24. Childrey (St Mary the Virgin)
25. Dorchester Abbey (St Peter, St Paul & St Birinus)
26. Long Wittenham (St Mary)
27. Warborough (St Lawrence)
28. Woolstone (All Saints)

✠ STAFFORDSHIRE
29. Moddershall (All Saints)

✠ SURREY
30. Walton-on the-Hill (St Peter)

✠ SUSSEX *(West)*
31. Edburton (St Andrew)
32. Parham (St Peter)
33. Pyecombe (The Transfiguration)

*Lead Font, Brookland, Kent.*

❦ + ❧

*Chichester Cathedral, West Sussex.*

 The nave pulpit was designed by Robert Potter and Geoffrey Clarke (1966). It is made of reinforced concrete, stone, cast aluminium and wood.

 The Bell-Arundel Screen across the nave dates from c.1475. It was removed in 1859 and stored in the base of the bell-tower. In 1961 it was restored to its original place as a memorial to Bishop George Bell (1929–58).

 In the s transept on the w wall is a series of unique paintings by Lambert Bernard. One of the large paintings shows Bishop Sherburne (d. 1536) asking Henry VIII to renew the charter of the cathedral; the other shows St Wilfrid receiving a grant of land at Selsey for the first cathedral in 680.

The medallions show kings of England but some were so badly damaged by Puritan soldiers in the seventeenth century that they could not be restored. They also suffered from the fall of the spire in 1861.

 Under a canopy on the NW side of the s transept is a memorial to Charles Eamer Kempe (d. 29 April 1907), the famous stained-glass artist, who is buried at Ovingdean near Brighton, E. Sussex.

 In the s choir aisle is a roof boss showing a group of six heads with only six eyes between them. From the mouth of each face protrude two large leaves. In the same aisle another boss shows a group of six heads but here the eyes are 12 in number, none being shared between neighbours!

 At the E end of the s choir aisle is a fragment of a second-century Roman mosaic pavement discovered in 1966. Note its depth below the present floor level of the cathedral.

 Near the Roman mosaic floor are two of the finest medieval carvings in England. Dating from c.1130 (although some authorities say they may be as early as 1000) the easternmost panel is the earlier and depicts Christ arriving at Bethany and being greeted by Mary and Martha. In the other panel the Raising of Lazarus is shown. The figures are arranged in size, not according to perspective but according to importance. The figure of Christ is the largest and the apostles, workmen and others are much smaller. Originally the panels were coloured with semi-precious stones in the eyes.

Both Eric Gill and Henry Moore, the famous sculptors, were influenced by these unique carvings, which may have formed part of a twelfth-century stone screen. They were found behind the choir stalls and moved to their present position in 1829.

 Above the altar at the E end of the s choir aisle is a painting by Graham

Sutherland of Christ appearing to Mary Magdalene on the first Easter morning.

◈ In the lady chapel, at the E end of the cathedral, is a fine pelican lectern dated 1879. The pelican is feeding three hungry young ones.

◈ The paintings on the roof vault of the lady chapel are similar to other foliage designs at Boxgrove Priory, W. Sussex. They were the work of Lambert Bernard, c.1520.

◈ In the NE corner of the retrochoir, near the lady chapel, is a stained-glass window by Marc Chagall which was unveiled on 6 October 1978. Illustrating Psalm 150, the predominant colour is red. (This is one of only two churches in the British Isles possessing a Chagall window; the other is at Tudeley, Kent.)

The window at the E end of the N choir aisle (near the Chagall window) depicts St John the Baptist surrounded by a wreath of flowers, all of which can be found in bloom in Sussex on 24 June – St John the Baptist's day.

◈ In the retrochoir behind the high altar the pillars consist of a central column surrounded by four shafts of Purbeck marble. (This particular arrangement is only found here and at nearby Boxgrove Priory.)

The retrochoir was built 1187–99 and the architect was probably Walter of Coventry. Here, immediately behind the high altar screen, stood St Richard's Shrine until its destruction at the Reformation in 1538.

◈ Near the site of St Richard's Shrine, attached to the wooden screen, is the Anglo-German tapestry, which was designed by Ursula Benker-Schirmer and dedicated on 15 June 1985. The tapestry relates the life of and legends about St Richard of Chichester. The central portion was woven at Marktredwitz in Bavaria and the two outer sections at West Dean College near Chichester. The tapestry commemorates the great work of Bishop George Bell, whose ashes rest near by.

◈ On the other side of the Anglo-German tapestry, immediately behind the high altar, is the John Piper tapestry. This represents the Holy Trinity, the four elements and the four evangelists. It was woven by Pinton Frères at Felletin, Aubusson, France, and installed in 1966.

◈ In the N transept are sixteenth-century paintings by Lambert Bernard showing bishops of Chichester. (Note that they all have the same face!)

◈ Also in the N transept rest the ashes of the famous composer Gustav Holst (1874–1934).

◈ Near by is the back of the main organ, which was originally built in 1678 by Renatus Harris and represents the work of nine English organ builders in succeeding years. Its original pipework by Harris is the oldest in any English cathedral. The present front case, dating from 1888, was designed by Dr Arthur Hill. It incorporates fragments of the old case, which was destroyed when the spire collapsed.

The organ was completely rebuilt, renovated and first used in 1986.

◈ On the floor of the N transept is a stone marked 'Site of the sub deanery font'. This was the site occupied by the fifteenth-century font used by the congregation of St Peter who worshipped in this part of the cathedral, occupying the N transept and the chapel of the four virgins, now the treasury, which served as the chancel.

The font was moved to the new St Peter's Church opposite the cathedral in 1850 and to St Paul's in 1982 when St Peter's closed.

This font was used for the baptism of William Juxon (1582–1663) on 24 October 1582. He became Bishop of London in 1633 and was with Charles I on the scaffold on 30 January 1649. His last words to the King were, 'You are exchanging a temporal for an eternal crown, a good exchange!'

Juxon died on 4 June 1663 and is buried in St John's College chapel, Oxford.

At the E end of the N nave aisle is the tomb chest of Maud, Countess of Arundel (d. 1270). It is the oldest tomb in England to have 'weepers', or mourning relatives, on its sides. There are three on each of the longer sides but they are defaced.

At the w end of the N nave aisle is a life-size statue of William Huskisson, who was MP for Chichester for ten years before becoming MP for Liverpool. He died on 15 September 1830 at the opening of the Liverpool and Manchester Railway and so became the first person in the world to be killed in a railway accident. (In fact the 'Rocket' ran over and crushed his left foot and he died a few hours later at Eccles vicarage.)

In the cathedral library is an unusual heart brass dating from c.1500 showing two hands issuing from clouds holding a heart which is inscribed 'I H C'. The heart is coloured red, which is probably original, and is mounted on a block of wood with three rivets. On the side is a brass plate inscribed, 'Found in the triforium under the clock, July 18, 1829 by Thos. King.'

Between the bell-tower and the w front of the cathedral is a beautiful statue of St Richard of Chichester (c.1197–1253). Sculpted by Philip Jackson, it was dedicated by the bishop on 15 June 2000.

On the s side of the plinth is inscribed St Richard's famous prayer:

'Thanks be to Thee my Lord Jesus Christ for all the benefits which Thou hast given me. For all the pains & insults which Thou hast borne for me. O most merciful redeemer. Friend & brother. May I know Thee more clearly. Love Thee more dearly & follow Thee more nearly.'

On the sw side of the cathedral is the bishop's chapel. Inside, on the N wall is the exquisite and famous Chichester roundel depicting the Virgin and Child. Dating from c.1250 it features gold, silver and the blue of lapis lazuli. According to Pevsner, this is 'the first known example of their use on a wall painting'.

## Chiddingly      East Sussex

DEDICATION UNKNOWN The beautiful countryside of the Weald is dominated by the stone spire of this church, standing as it does at 39 m (128 feet) high.

On the tomb of Sir John and Lady Jefferay (an influential couple in Tudor times) are two standing effigies representing Sir Edward and Lady Montagu, their son-in-law and daughter. Dating from 1578 these are the oldest standing effigies in England.

## Childrey      Oxfordshire

ST MARY THE VIRGIN is situated at the end of a leafy cul-de-sac to the N of the village with beautiful views from the N side of the churchyard.

The clock on the tower of c.1450 dates from 1763 and is one-handed. (See Church Clocks, page 121.)

Inside the s porch is a round-headed doorway with dog-tooth decoration dating from c.1200, pilgrims' crosses and old graffiti.

At the w end of the nave is a unique lead font dating from c.1175. Around the outside of the bowl are 12 raised figures of bishops or abbots holding croziers and books. The bowl has only one seam. (See Lead Fonts, page 72.)

On the s wall of the nave are the remains of a wall pulpit – a very rare feature.

On the N side of the chancel is a fine

*North transept window, Childrey, Oxfordshire. The picture of heraldry in the second light has now been moved to another window.*

Easter sepulchre dating from *c.*1400. The carvings of dogs chasing a hedgehog in the E spandrel of the arch are exquisite in their detail.

In the chancel are seven different brasses, three of which commemorate priests. The brass immediately to the s of the communion table is very large at 2.9 m x 1.12 m (9 feet 6 inches x 3 feet 8 inches), and dates from 1444. It commemorates William Fynderne and Elizabeth, his wife. The cross-crosslet device on William's sleeves and surcoat and on Elizabeth's dress also appears on the Marney brass at Little Horkesley, Essex, where Lady Marney's first husband, Thomas Fynderne (d. 1523) appears on her right. The families may well have been related.

Much of the Childrey brass has been stolen and some of the indents filled with lead. On the N side of the communion table is the brass to John Kyngeston (d. 1514) and his wife, Susan. Her date of death (1540) is left blank. She is commemorated again in brass at Shalstone, Bucks., where she died as a nun.

The N window of the N transept dates from *c.*1350. The yellow glass fragments are of the same date and show scenes from the life of the Virgin Mary including the Annunciation, her Assumption and the Ascension of Christ.

Underneath this window is a fourteenth-century effigy of a knight drawing his sword and near by some fine medieval floor tiles. Other medieval tiles can be seen in the s transept.

The s transept was the Fettiplace chantry from 1526 until its dissolution in 1547. It contains some ancient glass in its E window.

In the s transept are five more brasses, the most interesting being in the NE corner

*East window, Childrey, Oxfordshire. This window was given in memory of all those from the Berkshire Hunt who died in the First World War.*

on a marble altar-tomb. It depicts Elizabeth and William Fettiplace in shrouds rising from their coffins with the lids falling off. Latin inscriptions proceed from their mouths; the woman's reads, 'Set us free, save us, justify us, O Blessed Trinity' and the man's, 'Holy Trinity, one God, have mercy upon us'. Elizabeth died in 1516 and William in 1528.

The Fettiplace family moved to Swinbrook (Oxon.) *c.*1610 where several monuments still exist to them.

Outside the church on the sw side of the tower near the path is a small gravestone inscribed:

'JP 1821
AP 1816
This world is wide
And full of crooked streets:
Death is the market place

Where all men meet:
If life was merchandise,
As men could buy,
The rich would live
And the poor must die.'

The last line is now impossible to read.

## Chilham KENT

ST MARY is set in a very pretty village dominated by the castle at one end of the street and the church at the other.

Remains of fifteenth-century glass adorn the tracery and surrounds of the N aisle windows.

In the N chancel aisle is an imposing memorial by Sir Francis Chantrey to James Wildman (20 March 1747–25 March 1816) and James Beckford Wildman (19 October 1788–25 May 1867). On the left a woman holds her head while a girl buries her head in her lap; a young man sits on the right. Chantrey's signature and the date 1822 are on the back left. The Wildmans owned the castle from 1792 to 1861.

Near by, a beautiful monument commemorates Arthur and Edmund Hardy who died October 1858. The Hardy family owned the castle from 1861 to 1918. This monument by Alexander Munro shows the two boys reading the book *Babes in the Wood* while at their feet are a battledore and shuttlecock – the only representation of children's toys on a church monument in England (but see also Elford, Staffs, page 125.)

In the s chancel aisle is an unusual monument to Mary Kemp, Lady Digges, wife of Sir Dudley Digges. A black central column, 3.35 m (11 feet) high, has an urn on top surrounded by the four cardinal virtues depicted as women – Justice, Prudence, Temperance and Fortitude. The sculptor was Nicholas Stone.

At the w end of the N aisle is another unusual memorial, to Lady Margaret Palmer, 1619. Made of Bethersden marble, the beautiful decoration includes honeysuckle, roses and vines.

At the w end of the s aisle is a memorial to Frederick Lacy Dick, who was assassinated on 29 August 1847, aged 32. The inscription reads, 'Accompanied by a few of the police he went to a lone house in the country (Ceylon) to recapture a notorious criminal, whom the native police feared to encounter, and was shot through a window by an unseen hand.'

# Christchurch                    DORSET

THE PRIORY CHURCH OF THE HOLY TRINITY This former Augustinian priory makes an attractive picture across Christchurch harbour.

The N porch was built c.1290 and is the largest in England. Its large size, 12.19 m (40 feet) long, is traditionally due to the great amount of business the prior had to conduct with the townspeople.

The reredos over the high altar dates from c.1320 and is a fine piece of sculpture. In the centre is Jesse, the father of David. The mural above is by Hans Feibusch and represents Isaiah's vision (*Isaiah 6*).

Near the reredos is a beautiful sculpture by the artist Flaxman to the memory of Viscountess Fitzharris. It was exhibited at the Royal Academy in 1817.

The misericords in the choir are extremely interesting. The fourth from the w end on the N side in the front row dates from c.1210 and is one of the oldest in England. It shows bold foliage with two central dragons. Other carvings on the misericords show a mermaid with two tails, the Christchurch salmon, a beautiful bat, a rare contemporary carving of Richard III (d. 1485) and several jesters.

On the NE side of the choir, adjoining the high altar, is the Salisbury chantry chapel, which was built c.1530 by Margaret, Countess of Salisbury for herself and her son, Cardinal Pole. Made of Caen stone it shows Italian and English work side by side and is noted for its extremely delicate carving. There is a fan vault inside with a carving depicting the coronation of the Virgin in the centre. Countess Margaret was executed by Henry VIII in 1541 at the age of 69 because her son had denounced the king and fled to Italy. The Countess was buried in the Tower of London instead of Christchurch Priory.

At the E end of the s choir aisle is the chantry chapel of John Draper, the last prior of Christchurch before the priory was dissolved in 1539. The chantry bears the date 1529 and over the door are the

*Norman blind arcading at Christchurch Priory, Dorset.*

initials 'J.D.' (John Draper) and a representation of the earlier central tower and spire of the priory which collapsed c.1450.

▨ To the w of the Salisbury chantry is the Berkeley chapel of the stone-cage type with a flat wooden roof and dating from c.1500.

▨ Opposite the Berkeley chapel is the chantry of Robert Harys (d. 1525) which he constructed c.1520. Look for his rebus in the panels – a hare with the letter R.

▨ The circular turret adjoining the N transept is one of the finest examples of Norman blind arcading in England.

▨ Over the arch on the s side of the lady chapel is the 'miraculous beam', which was originally found to be too short by 30 cm (1 foot) when it was about to be used in the construction of the church. Legend says that after being left overnight it was found to be long enough the next morning and so was fixed in place! A mysterious workman who had been helping to build the church also disappeared and the builders recognized this man as Jesus, the Carpenter of Nazareth, and so the name was changed from Twynham to Christchurch in honour of Him.

▨ At the w end is a fine font of Purbeck marble dating from c.1900.

## Cirencester     GLOUCESTERSHIRE

ST JOHN THE BAPTIST is a magnificent Perpendicular church that takes pride of place in this beautiful Cotswold town.

▨ The magnificent three-storey s porch was built c.1490 and was used by the abbey until its dissolution in 1538. After the dissolution it became the town hall, the name it still retains. It is the second largest porch of any parish church in the British Isles, Christchurch, Dorset, being the largest.

▨ The medieval stone pulpit on the N side

of the nave dates from c.1450. It is of the wine-glass type and its open tracery work is unique. The colour was retouched in 1865. Near by is a Puritan hour-glass.

In a safe at the E end of the s aisle is the Boleyn Cup, which was made for Queen Anne Boleyn (the second wife of Henry VIII ) in 1535. After her execution in 1536 it passed to her daughter, Queen Elizabeth I, then her physician, Dr Richard Master, who finally gave it to this church.

▨ In the SE angle of the s aisle is the Garstang chapel, founded by Henry Garstang (d. 1464). It is enclosed on the N and w sides by wooden screens and is a rare example of a timber chapel.

▨ Between the lady chapel and the chancel is St Catherine's chapel, which has a beautiful fan-vaulted roof given in 1508 by the penultimate abbot of the Augustinian abbey, John Hakebourne. The third boss from the E end carries Abbot Hakebourne's initials and the date 1508. G. H. Cook says that this fan vault is said to have been removed from the abbey cloisters at the Dissolution.

In the apex of the window over the chancel arch are carved the Arms of Henry VIII.

▨ At the E end of the N and s aisles are the arms of George II and Charles II, those of Charles II being rare.

▨ Many of the windows contain fifteenth-century glass. The figure of St Catherine in the great w window is exactly the same as one in the E window of Oddingley, Worcestershire, and must have come from the same workshop.

▨ The tower contains the first ring of 12 bells in the world. First cast by Rudhall in 1722 some have since had to be recast. (See Bells, page 293.)

▨ In the Trinity chapel on the N side are several brasses, including people connected with the wool trade.

*Cirencester's magnificent tower and porch dominate the market place.*

## Clayton                    WEST SUSSEX

ST JOHN THE BAPTIST is a little church nestling under the Sussex Downs.

🔲 The well-preserved wall paintings date from c.1150. They may have been done by Cluniac monks. The subject of the paintings is the Last Judgement and they are on the N and S walls and over the chancel arch. Pevsner says of them that they 'are unique in England for their extent, preservation, and date'.

🔲 The chancel arch dates from c.1040 and is a good specimen of Saxon architecture.

🔲 On the S wall of the chancel is a brass to Richard Idon,1523, who is shown holding a chalice and wafer.

🔲 The wind vane dates from 1781 and is unusual because the vane is *below* the cardinal points.

🔲 In the churchyard is the grave of Sir Norman Hartnell (12 June 1901–8 June 1979), former dressmaker by appointment to HM Queen Elizabeth II and to HM Queen Elizabeth the Queen Mother.

## Clifford                  HEREFORDSHIRE

ST MARY THE VIRGIN Almost on the border with Wales, this church stands high on a wooded hill, with extensive views to the River Wye.

🔲 In a recess on the N side of the chancel is an oaken effigy of a priest, dating from c.1280. It is 1.93 m (6 feet 4 inches) long. His hands are in prayer, his head rests on a damaged cushion and his feet, in pointed shoes, rest on a bracket. The effigy is well preserved and there is still a trace of orange paint in the folds of his chasuble. This is the oldest wooden effigy of a priest in England and Wales. (See Wooden Effigies, page 246.)

🔲 The three panels on the reredos were painted in 1921 by James Clark, RI

(1858–1943) and originally commemorated Oscar S. C. Blakstad, who was killed in action on 28 March 1917. The left-hand painting shows him kneeling before Jesus with the words, 'Let my cry come unto Thee'. Others who died in the two world wars are also commemorated.

🔲 The N arcade is Victorian and is remarkable for its four supporting oak pillars. The woodwork, including the nave roof, is excellent.

## Clifton Campville          STAFFORDSHIRE

ST ANDREW is one of the least well-known of the great parish churches of England.

🔲 There is a beautiful W tower and spire with three large windows at the base and a high arch opening into the church.

🔲 Above the stone-vaulted N transept is a priest's chamber complete with fireplace and garderobe – one of only two medieval toilets in an English church! (The other is at Warmington, Warwickshire, where a similar room is situated over a vestry on the NE side of the chancel.)

🔲 At the E end of the S aisle is the table tomb of Sir John Vernon (1543) and his wife, Maud Camille. She wears a kennel headdress. Carved in alabaster the details are exquisite, though defaced.

🔲 Another monument commemorates Charles Watkins (1813) by Chantrey.

🔲 In the S aisle is an ancient chest hewn out of solid wood.

🔲 Also in the S aisle is a semicircular recess containing remains of a wall painting dating from c.1310 showing the Coronation of the Virgin.

## Clifton Reynes            BUCKINGHAMSHIRE

ST MARY THE VIRGIN is found in a beautiful little village on the E bank of the River Great Ouse in N Buckinghamshire. In the distance one can see the church spire at Olney.

⬧ Here is a unique group of four oak figures – the largest number in any English church (apart from Westminster Abbey). They are all in the N or Reynes chapel.

⬧ In a recess of the N wall is a wooden effigy depicting Thomas Reynes, c.1300. It is 1.52 m (5 feet) long and wears a mail head-covering. His right hand is sheathing a sword while the left is holding the scabbard. Two cushions are under his head, his right leg is crossed over his left and a dog lies at his feet.

⬧ Near by is the effigy of a lady, probably Joan Borard, c.1310. It is 1.47 m (4 feet 10 inches) long and has a wimple and long, flowing gown as well as a long veil falling to the shoulders. At her feet is a mutilated dog. Her hands are at prayer.

⬧ On a table-tomb under the western of the two arches separating the chancel from the Reynes chapel are two more wooden figures. One probably represents Ralph Reynes (d. 1350). He is 1.65 m (5 feet 5 inches) long and wears a mail head-covering. His right leg is crossed over his left, which rests on a lion. His broken right hand is sheathing a sword (which is missing) and he holds a shield in his left hand. He wears a short surcoat.

⬧ Nearby is Ralph Reynes's wife, also dating from c.1350. She is also 1.65 m (5 feet 5 inches) long and wears a wimple and long, flowing gown. Her hands are at prayer and a mutilated dog lies at her feet.

All of these four figures are well preserved but notice the hole in one of them that shows that they are hollow and were originally filled with charcoal to absorb the moisture.

For some years these wooden effigies were encased in plaster until c.1830, when the vicar scraped the covering away. (See Wooden Effigies, page 246.)

⬧ On the E table-tomb are the stone effigies of Sir Thomas Reynes III (d. 1390) and his wife. Around the base are 16 mourners, men and women alternately, who give us interesting glimpses of medieval costume. Sadly, much of Sir Thomas's effigy has been mutilated with graffiti.

On the collar of the dog at the feet of the knight is the name 'Bo', set between the lilies of France. This feature is unique on a medieval stone monument. Over his tomb hangs a visored helmet and breastplate.

⬧ On the floor is a brass to John Reynes (d. 25 March 1428) and two shroud brasses dating from c.1500.

## Clyffe Pypard     WILTSHIRE

ST PETER This peaceful church is situated at the foot of a hill, in a large churchyard surrounded by many trees.

⬧ The entry gates and railings to the churchyard were given in 1963 in memory of Nikolaus Pevsner's wife Lola. They bear the initials LP and NP, with one on each gate.

⬧ Just beyond the E end of the church near the path a simple slate headstone reads:

'LOLA
PEVSNER
Born Kurlbaum
1902–1963
and NIKOLAUS
her husband
1902–1983'

The church guide states, 'Nikolaus Pevsner, an architectural historian, undertook a lifetime's work of surveying the notable buildings of England, county by county. From this we have inherited a unique record of the architectural features of buildings of all ages from the most imposing stately home to the humblest parish church.'

▦ Some of the foreign glass in the N windows of the nave is Flemish and one piece may have been designed by Holbein the Younger (1497–1543) and originates from Switzerland.

▦ The fine Jacobean pulpit dates from 1629 and is richly carved with many Renaissance features. Note the unusual *iron* bookstand.

▦ At the w end is the parish bier for holding a coffin. It is probably nineteenth-century.

▦ In the sw corner of the s aisle is an imposing monument by John Devall to Thomas Spackman, who was a carpenter and is depicted with his tools in a basket, including an axe and hammer. Hanging on the sides are a plane, T-square, mallet and saw. Two children stand at his feet holding books and quill pens. Everything is beautifully carved.

The monument states that Spackman died 13 October 1786 aged 76, and after providing for his wife and six nephews and nieces, he bequeathed £1000 to be invested, among other things, 'to pay a schoolmaster to teach the poor children in the parish, Reading, Writing and Arithmetick and to provide Loaves of Bread to the Poor of this Parish every Sunday Morning in this Church.'

▦ High up on each side of the chancel arch standing in the recesses which formerly led to the rood loft, are two Tudor figures, traditionally known as John and Elizabeth Goddard.

# Cobham                    KENT

ST MARY MAGDALENE With its unique collection of brasses, this beautiful church attracts visitors from all over the world.

▦ Its wide thirteenth-century chancel contains the largest collection of medieval memorial brasses in the world (19 in all). The largest are arranged in two rows in front of the communion rails and are a spectacular sight when the sun shines on them through the stained-glass windows.

They are described in great detail in *The Buildings of England, West Kent and the Weald*, and a leaflet obtainable in the church.

▦ Several of the brasses commemorate the Cobham family, one of whom, Lord John Cobham, founded a chantry college in 1370 on the s side of the church. In 1598, after the Reformation, the chantry college buildings were converted into 20 almshouses for old people.

▦ Among the most interesting brasses is one to Dame Joan de Cobham (c.1320) which has the earliest surviving inscription in England. This grants an indulgence of 40 days pardon to whoever will pray for her soul. This brass is also the oldest brass of a lady shown under a canopy and the second oldest brass to a lady in England. (The oldest female brass is at Trotton, see page 371.)

▦ The brass of Ralph de Cobham (d. 1402) is unique. His half figure holds the inscription plate.

▦ The brass of Sir Nicholas Hawberk (1407) is crowned by a magnificent canopy surmounted by the Holy Trinity.

▦ Inside the communion rails is the fine alabaster tomb of Sir George Brooke, ninth Lord Cobham (d. 1558) and Anne, his wife. Their ten sons and four daughters kneel inside shell-headed recesses and wear heraldry. At the heads of the effigies is a tilting helmet with a Saracen's head on top.

This is the finest alabaster tomb in Kent.

▦ In the chancel hang four tilting helmets dating from c.1450.

*Cockayne Hatley in Bedfordshire is famous for its unique woodwork, mostly brought from Belgium.*

# Cobham     SURREY

ST ANDREW, with its Norman w tower, lies in a large, scattered village, quite close to the busy A3.

On the s wall of the chancel is a unique brass dating from c.1500 depicting the Adoration of the Shepherds. Mary is in the foreground with Jesus lying by her side in a manger. The shepherds stand at the end of her bed while Joseph (drawn out of proportion) stands at the head of the bed. Note the ox and ass peering into the manger.

# Cockayne Hatley     BEDFORDSHIRE

ST JOHN THE BAPTIST is famous for its woodwork, which is unique in England. It was installed by the Hon. Henry Cockayne Cust, Squire and Rector 1806–61, mostly in 1826 when he shortened the chancel to fit the woodwork!

The panelling in the chancel consists of 16 carved heads of saints and writers of the Roman Catholic Church. Below are stalls and 24 misericords. These all came from the Abbey d'Alne near Charleroi and are dated 1689.

The communion rail came from Malines and has magnificent carvings of cherubs drinking water, gathering corn, pressing grapes and gathering manna.

The lectern, with St Andrew in relief, came from St Andrew's Church, Antwerp, and other woodwork at the w end under the tower came from Louvain and other places in Belgium. The main pulpit was sold to Carlisle Cathedral in 1963.

The E window of 1829 shows scenes from Christ's life in rich colours. It was made by Thomas Willement, a London glazier. Other glass in the chancel is heraldic and dates from 1839.

In the E window of the N aisle is superb glass dating from c.1250 and showing four saints, St Dunstan, St Oswald, St Edward and St Sebald. It was saved from destruction and came from a small church in Yorkshire.

In the nave is the brass of Lady Ida Cockayne, c.1410, showing a 'butterfly' head-dress, a short-lived fashion at this time.

To the s of the church is the large gravestone of the poet William Ernest Henley, 23 August 1849–11 July 1903. He was a one-legged playwright and friend of Robert Louis Stevenson and also the inspiration for Long John Silver. The stone bears the inscription:

'So be my passing
My task accomplished and the long
   day done
My wages taken and in my heart
Some late lark singing
Let me be gathered to the quiet west
The sundown splendid and serene
Death.'

Also commemorated is his wife, Anna, who died 5 February 1925, and his only child, Margaret Emma Henley (4 September 1888–11 February 1894). This daughter was the inspiration for Wendy in J. M. Barrie's *Peter Pan*. She referred to Barrie as a 'Fwendie' of her father and Barrie subsequently devised the name 'Wendy'!

# Coggeshall     ESSEX

ST PETER-AD-VINCULA This beautifully restored church is well seen behind the attractive sixteenth-century Woolpack Inn.

On 16 September 1940 a bomb dropped on the NW side of the church destroying a large part of the tower, N aisle and nave. The tower seen today is a complete rebuilding, together with some of the

*Coggeshall, Essex – the church as it appeared immediately after its restoration.*

nave and N aisle. The work was completed in 1956 at a cost of £86,000. The belfry windows are similar to those at Maids Moreton, Bucks.

Apart from the rebuilding, the remainder of the church dates from c.1400–25 when it was built by wealthy wool merchants, including the famous Paycockes, whose house in West Street now belongs to the National Trust.

◈ At the SE corner of the tower is a vestry door with interesting hinges. The top hinge portrays a cock crowing for dawn, the lower hinge a star and crescent moon for night and the door handle a blazing sun for midday.

◈ In the S porch is a large central boss depicting a pelican feeding her young.

◈ The seven-light Perpendicular E window is an excellent example of its period.

◈ In St Katherine's chapel on the N side of the chancel are three Paycocke brasses, John Paycocke (d. 1533) and his wife, Joan, and Thomas Paycocke (d. 1580).

◈ In the sacristy off the chancel is a monument to Mary Honywood (d. 1620). When she died at 93 she had 367 descendants!

## Colmworth           BEDFORDSHIRE

ST DENYS is supposed to be unique in that it was started in 1426 and finished in 1430 – very quick by fifteenth-century standards. (One authority, however, states that it was built from c.1390 to 1396.)

◈ The S porch has springers for a vaulted roof which was never completed.

◈ In the window on the NW side of the chancel are fragments of fifteenth-century glass including a complete angel standing on a wheel, mostly of yellow stain.

On the N side of the chancel is a large monument to Sir William and Lady Katherine Dyer, erected in 1641. Lady Dyer's head rests on a skull. At her feet is her grandson, Henry, who died on 22 September 1637, aged 1 year, 11 weeks and 3 days. On the right side of this monument is the following epitaph:

'My dearest dust could not thy hasty day
Afford thy drowsy patience leave to stay
One hour longer; so that we might either
Sat up, or gone to bed together?
But since thy finished labour hath
  possessed
Thy weary limbs with early rest,
Enjoy it sweetly; and thy widow bride
Shall soon repose her by thy slumbering
  side
Whose business, now is only to prepare
My nightly dress, and call to prayer.
Mine eyes wax heavy and ye day grows
  old,
The dew falls thick, my blood grows cold
Draw, draw ye closed curtains and make
  room
My dear, my dearest dust; I come, I come.'

At the base of the monument are the figures of Faith, Hope and Charity and between them stand four sons and three daughters.

The E window is very unusual in having complicated tracery in its head.

## Compton       SURREY

ST NICHOLAS is one of the most interesting churches in England, situated just off the busy A3.

Above the chancel arch is an ancient mural showing a lozenge-type pattern uncovered in 1966.

The E part of the Norman chancel is divided into two storeys with a small chapel above – unique in England.

In front of the upper sanctuary is a Norman wooden screen which, dating from c.1180, is the oldest woodwork in England.

On the S side of the chancel is a former anchorite's cell dating from c.1170. A staircase inside the cell leads to the chapel above.

In the Norman E window is a beautiful panel of stained glass showing the Virgin and Child dating from c.1210 – one of the earliest pieces of stained glass in England.

On the piers of the chancel arch are crude graffiti, one depicting a Norman knight, which may have been made by pilgrims on their way to Canterbury. This church is near the Pilgrims' Way.

At the E end of the N aisle is a modern stained-glass window by Sir Ninian Comper. It depicts St Michael and St Francis.

## Conington       CAMBRIDGESHIRE

ST MARY is near the town of St Ives to the S of the A14 between Cambridge and Huntingdon (not to be confused with another Conington to the S of Peterborough).

The spire rises to 28.96 m (95 feet) and forms a conspicuous landmark.

In the nave are what has been described as 'the finest collection of funerary monuments in East Anglia'. These include a stone portrait medallion of Robert Cotton (1697) by Grinling Gibbons and the only marble monument carrying his signature, 'G. Gibbons fecit'. Robert Cotton was a descendant of the Cotton family who saved many books when the monasteries were dissolved; these can now be found in the British Library. (It is curious that another branch of the Cotton family owned the other village of Conington from c.1680 to 1720.)

*Coventry's new cathedral viewed from the tower of the old one.*

The nave was rebuilt in 1737 and the monuments are placed in recesses between the windows.

## Cookham                    BERKSHIRE

HOLY TRINITY is situated near to the River Thames and the famous iron bridge immortalized by Sir Stanley Spencer.

In the churchyard is the grave of the famous painter Sir Stanley Spencer (1891–1959), who featured Cookham and its church-yard in many of his paintings. An art gallery in the village displays some of his work.

Also buried in the churchyard is the Victorian artist Frederick Walker (1840–75). One of his paintings depicting the Jesus Alms-houses at Bray and called 'The Harbour of Refuge' is now in the National Gallery, London.

A tablet on the w wall of the church commemorates him.

The medieval stone altar slab has five inlaid brass crosses on it – a rare survival.

## Cotehele                    CORNWALL

ST CATHERINE & ST ANNE (CHAPEL OF COTEHELE HOUSE) Cotehele House, a property of the National Trust, stands on high ground among woods above the River Tamar, NW of Plymouth.

A clock in the sw corner dating from c.1488 is the oldest unaltered clock in England still in working order and in its original position. It has no face or pendulum and is regulated by a horizontal balance known as a foliot. It is driven by two weights, each of about 40.82 kg (90 lbs). (See Church Clocks, page 121.)

Among the interesting wooden roof bosses in the roof is one dating from c.1530 depicting three hares with three ears between them.

## Coventry                WEST MIDLANDS

CATHEDRAL CHURCH OF ST MICHAEL was designed by Sir Basil Spence and completed in 1962 to replace the medieval cathedral which was destroyed on the night of Thursday 14 November, 1940, and which, with the exception of the magnificent tower and spire – 89.9 m (295 feet) high – now lies ruined to the s of the new cathedral.

At the liturgical E end (the cathedral is actually built N to S) is a tapestry designed by Graham Sutherland and woven at Felletin, France. At 24.08 m (79 feet) high and 11.6 m (38 feet) wide it weighs nearly 1016 kg (1 ton) and is the largest tapestry in a church anywhere in the world. Christ is shown in glory with 'Man' between His feet and four panels showing the symbols of the four evangelists.

Below the tapestry are six unique pottery candlesticks designed by Hans Coper. They are the largest 'thrown' pots in the world.

The baptistery window designed by John Piper comprises 195 lights made by Patrick Reyntiens. At 24.7 m (81 feet) high and 15.54 m (51 feet) wide it is the largest stained-glass window in the British Isles.

Below the window is a boulder brought from near Bethlehem and used as the font, the top having been cut as a scallop to hold the water.

Outside on the wall near the baptistery window is a huge bronze sculpture of St Michael defeating the Devil. Executed by Sir Jacob Epstein, this was his last religious work.

Off the 'N side' of the nave is the Chapel of Unity. Used by all denominations it was the first to be built for an English cathedral. The marble mosaic floor was designed by Einar Forseth, a Swedish artist, and the windows by Margaret Traherne.

The unique choir stalls and bishop's throne are surmounted by representations of thorns.

To the 's' of the lady chapel below the tapestry is the Gethsemane chapel. The beautiful mosaic designed by Steven Sykes shows an angel holding a chalice. The iron screen at the entrance depicting the crown of thorns was made by the Royal Engineers at Chatham.

At the 'w' end of the cathedral is a magnificent screen of clear glass containing incised figures by John Hutton. Among the figures is that of St Alban, the first British martyr. Through the screen can be seen the ruins of the old cathedral.

## Cowfold     West Sussex

St Peter The village is located on the busy A272 at the intersection with the A281, but the beautiful church dominates the scene with its large, yellow sandstone w tower.

In the windows on the N side of the chancel is stained glass dating from c.1250 and c.1350. This is some of the oldest glass in England.

Also in the chancel is a memorial to Richard Pierce, who at the age of 22 was seriously wounded at the Battle of Edgehill in 1642 but lived until he was 94!

In the nave is the impressive brass to Prior Thomas Nelond, 1433. It is the largest brass in Sussex and one of the largest in England, measuring 3.1 m (10 feet 2 inches) long by 1.3 m (4 feet 3 inches) wide. The standing effigy of the prior measures 1.7 m (5 feet 10 inches) and is life-size. From his praying hands issue three scrolls to the saints above the canopy, St Pancras on the left, the Virgin Mary and the Child in the centre and St Thomas à Becket on the right. The triple canopy is one of the finest in existence. The prayer to St Pancras, the patron saint of Lewes Priory, reads, 'Holy Martyr of God, lead me to the abodes of rest'. The one to Mary reads, 'Holy Mother of Jesus preserve us from the sting of death', and the one to St Thomas à Becket, Prior Nelond's patron saint, reads, 'May the supplication of St Thomas on my behalf be duly heard'. Thomas Nelond was prior of St Pancras at Lewes from 1421 to 1429 and when he died, was buried in the priory church, but how did this brass, the only full-length representation of a prior in England, come to Cowfold Church? This fact undoubtedly saved it from destruction when the monasteries were dissolved by Henry VIII in 1538–40.

In the s aisle on a pillar is the brass of churchwarden John-a-Gate, c.1500, depicting him in civilian dress and wearing a pouch and rosary at his waist.

## Coxwold     North Yorkshire

St Michael With its distinctive w tower, this church stands at the top of the village street commanding lovely views over the moors.

The imposing w tower is octagonal with crocketed pinnacles rising from buttresses between the windows.

The chancel, which was rebuilt in 1774, is filled by a unique communion rail resembling an elongated 'U'. It compensates for the narrowness of the chancel, caused by the enormous Fauconberg tombs on either side.

Queen Mary and the Princess Royal visited the church on 15 September 1938 and their names appear on the chancel wall.

On the NW side of the chancel is an imposing monument to Henry Belasyse (d. 1647) in Roman costume and his son Thomas. Some of Henry's ancestors became Earls of Fauconberg and Anthony Belasse was one of the commissioners appointed to survey the closure of the monasteries; he was given Newburgh Priory by Henry VIII. This marble group was carved by Grinling Gibbons, more famous for his wood carving.

On the floor of the nave is a brass to a Sir John Manston (d. 1464) and his wife, Elizabeth. The date of her death has never been filled in.

In the tracery lights of the nave windows is stained glass dating from c.1450. Among the saints depicted is Mary Magdalene – a figure rarely found in medieval glass.

E of the porch is the grave of the Reverend Laurence Sterne, vicar from 1760 until his death in 1768. Among the books he wrote here are, *The Life and Opinions of Tristram Shandy*, *A Sentimental Journey* and *The Journal to Eliza*. Originally buried in Bayswater, London, Sterne was reburied here in 1969.

# Crockham Hill                    KENT

HOLY TRINITY is beautifully situated on the s slope of the North Downs and has commanding views from its churchyard. The church was built in 1842 by a father and son, using local stone. It was paid for by Charles Warde, who lived at Squerryes Court, a seventeenth-century house near Westerham (Kent).

The window on the NW side of the nave shows St Francis preaching to the animals and birds. It was given in 1970 in memory of Mr S. D. Gladstone. The robin sitting on the branch on the right is very lifelike.

Another window on the N side of the nave near the pulpit commemorates Lilian Polkys Campbell Colquhoun, wife of Captain H. T. A. Bosanquet, CVO, RN. She was born at Chartwell on 3 November 1872, married in this church and died on 20 February 1947. The picture underneath

shows her family home, which was later that of Sir Winston and Lady Churchill.

Another window, installed in 1995, commemorates Octavia Hill and 100 years of the National Trust, 1895–1995.

On the N side of the sanctuary is the marble effigy of Octavia Hill (3 December 1838–15 August 1912). The inscription on the side of the chest reads, 'Noble in aim, wise in method, unwavering in faith and courage and renewing the spiritual strength of her fellow citizens she was a pioneer in the matter of housing reform and a founder of the National Trust for securing places of national beauty and historic interest for the public.'

On the right-hand side of the inscription is a carving of St Christopher carrying the Christ child and on the left is a beautiful depiction of the Blessed Virgin Mary holding a crucifix surrounded by lilies – a rare example of a modern lily crucifix. (See Lily Crucifix, page 338.)

Octavia Hill's feet rest on some books, she holds a scroll in her left hand and her right hand rests on her breast. The effigy was carved by Dora Abbott. Octavia is buried with her sister under a yew to the s of the church on the left of the path as one leaves the church.

# Croft                    LINCOLNSHIRE

ALL SAINTS is one of the great marshland churches of Lincolnshire, set in a beautiful village.

The fine Jacobean pulpit and tester bear the name 'William Worship, Doctor in Divinitie' on the reading desk. He gave the pulpit in 1615 in memory of his wife, Agnes.

Near the chancel step in the s aisle is a memorial brass to Agnes inscribed, 'Here lyeth the bodie of Agnes Worship, a woman matchless, both for wisdom and Godlyness. Shee was the wife of William

*Croft, Lincolnshire – a most interesting church standing in a lovely village.*

Worship, Doctor of Divinitie, and Minister of Croft, and departed this life the 6th Daie of Maye Ano 1615.'

The fifteenth-century chancel screen has birds for crockets above the central doorway and in the spandrels below are carvings of numerous animals including, on the s side, a fox with a bird in its mouth.

On the floor of the s chantry chapel is the demi-effigy of a knight in armour, c.1370, and portions of a border in Norman-French. This is the second oldest brass in Lincolnshire, the oldest being at Buslingthorpe.

The magnificent medieval brass eagle lectern has three lions at its base and an iron bar supporting the tail whose slot has been sealed. The eight silver claws are missing but the eyes are perfect and never had jewels in them.

The lectern stands about 1.5 m (5 feet) high (see Medieval Brass Lecterns, page 362.)

In the chancel are two fine monuments to the Brownes who lived at Old Hall. One shows Sir Valentine Browne of 1606 and his wife and 15 children below. The other depicts their second son, John (d. 1614), with one of his two wives. The monuments show excellent examples of seventeenth-century costume.

On the s side of the chancel arch is a monument to William Bonde (d. 1559), father of Nicholas Bonde DD, President of Magdalen College, Oxford, from 1590 to 1608.

The s door bears the inscription, 'God save the King 1633'.

## Croft                                NORTH YORKSHIRE

ST PETER Located on the River Tees, which forms the boundary with County Durham, this lovely red sandstone church makes a splendid picture with the fifteenth-century bridge near by.

In the nave is the huge Milbanke family pew dating from c.1670. Raised on oak pillars it is like a house on stilts and is approached by an imposing staircase. At about 4.6 m (15 feet) long it dominates the nave.

On the E wall inside the chancel is a crudely carved stone relief panel depicting a smiling cat. Charles Lutwidge Dodgson (alias Lewis Carroll) was 11 years old when his father moved from Cheshire to become vicar of this parish from 1843 to 1868. This cat may well have been the inspiration for the vanishing Cheshire Cat in Carroll's *Alice in Wonderland*.

Another church that has a claim to the inspiration for the Cheshire Cat is Pott Shrigley, Cheshire. Carroll was born about 40.23 km (25 miles) away at Daresbury, Cheshire in 1832. (See also Lichfield Cathedral, Staffs, page 199.)

## Cropredy

(pronounced 'Cropriddy')        OXFORDSHIRE

ST MARY THE VIRGIN The village lies in quiet countryside near the River Cherwell, which flows into the Thames at Oxford; it is dominated by its lovely church.

An unusual feature of the interior is the fact that the tower and chancel arches and nave piers are all without capitals.

The Civil War armour that was formerly on display behind a grille in the s aisle was stolen in May 1986.

In the s aisle is a fine chest dating from c.1250. Note the excellent ironwork.

In the s aisle chapel of St Fremund a tablet records:

'Nearby lie the ashes of Richard Howard Stafford Crossman of Prescote. Teacher. Writer. Politician. 1906–1974.
And of his only son Patrick Danvers Crossman 1957–1975.'

 In the second window from the w in the

N aisle there is a beautiful piece of medieval glass depicting the head of the Virgin Mary. It was found in the churchyard.

▨ In the N aisle, above the organ, is a little window cut from a single stone which enabled the priest to look down into the church from the priest's room above the vestry.

▨ The beautiful medieval brass eagle lectern dates from c.1490. The eagle has eight talons, its beak is open but closed at the tip and its wings are complete. The slot in the base of the tail is sealed up. The overall height of this lectern is 1.78 m (5 feet 10 inches). (See Stories About Medieval Brass Lecterns, page 136.)

▨ The fifteenth-century screen separating the choir from the Chapel of St Fremund on the S is interesting because some of the wooden blocks halfway down remain uncarved. Other parts of the screen show good carvings of grapes and vine leaves.

## Cuckfield                          WEST SUSSEX

HOLY TRINITY From the churchyard to the S there are magnificent views over the beautiful Sussex countryside.

▨ This is the only church in England to have two brasses commemorating the same man – Henry Bowyer (d. 1589). In the first (1589) he is shown in armour, alone, but in the second (1601) he is depicted with his wife, Elizabeth, three sons and two daughters, engraved on a rectangular plate.

## Culbone                            SOMERSET

ST CULBONE is situated in a remarkable setting in the woods, 121.9 m (400 feet) above sea level. It is inaccessible by car.

▨ This is the smallest complete medieval parish church in England in regular use. It is 10.67 m (35 feet) long, its nave is 3.76 m (12 feet 4 inches) wide and its chancel is 3.05 m (10 feet) wide.

▨ One of the windows is cut from a single block of stone.

▨ The seat at the front left-hand side of the nave has been patched with a piece of linen fold panelling which probably came from the former rood loft.

## Cullompton                         DEVON

ST ANDREW is usually approached from the W, down Church Street, some distance from the town centre; the superb sandstone tower, at 30.48 m (100 feet) high, is a notable landmark.

▨ The fine rood screen, one of the longest in Devon at 16.46 (54 feet), extends right across the church. The original colouring on the E side is well preserved. Above the screen is the rood beam to which is fixed the Royal Arms. This is the only division between nave and chancel as, unusually, there is no chancel arch.

▨ The nave and chancel are covered with a richly carved wagon roof of 24 bays. Note the numerous interesting bosses.

▨ On the S side of the nave is the magnificent Lane Aisle dating from 1526. Built by John Lane, a wealthy wool stapler, it has a beautiful fan-vaulted roof springing from angel corbels holding implements used in the wool trade. (See Fan Vaulting, page 152.)

▨ At the W end of the Lane aisle is a unique piece of medieval woodwork called Golgotha. Consisting of two huge pieces of oak, it depicts rocks, skulls and bones and three holes for crosses. It was probably used for the foundations of the rood on top of the screen.

*Dunster, Somerset. This church is best seen from the spectacular castle towards the southeast.*

## Daresbury      CHESHIRE

ALL SAINTS Situated quite near the busy A56, this village will forever be associated with the writer Lewis Carroll.

🔲 A stained-glass window by Geoffrey Webb commemorates Charles Lutwidge Dodgson (27 January 1832–14 January 1898), better known as Lewis Carroll, author of *Alice in Wonderland*. The Mad Hatter and the March Hare hold the following message:

'We have heard the children say,
Gentle children whom we love,
Long ago on Christmas Day,
Came a message from above.'

Dodgson was born in Daresbury and died at Guildford. He is buried in Guildford Cemetery.

🔲 The fine Jacobean pulpit is carved with angels' heads.

## Deerhurst      GLOUCESTERSHIRE

ST MARY is located near the fast-flowing River Severn and a sharp, right-angled bend in the road. This famous church was founded by the Saxons but omitted by the Normans in the Domesday Survey of 1086.

🔲 This is the only example in England of a Puritan chancel dating from c.1650. Seats are provided on the N, S and E sides of the communion table. The communion rails dating from c.1600 enclose the altar on all four sides – an unusual arrangement. (See also Lyddington, Rutland, page 228.)

🔲 The font is the best-preserved Saxon one in existence.

🔲 A brass dating from 1400 to Sir John Cassy, Baron of the Exchequer, and Alice, his wife, shows her dog lying at her feet. The dog is named 'Terri' and this is the only surviving example of a dog being named on a brass.

🔲 The W window of the S aisle contains a beautiful panel of glass dating from c.1310 showing St Catherine with her wheel.

🔲 Looking into the nave from the E face of the tower are some unusual Saxon windows.

🔲 At the tops of the piers or pillars in the nave are carvings of leaves dating from c.1180 – an early example of this form of decoration, considered by some to be the most beautiful in the British Isles.

## Dennington      SUFFOLK

ST MARY THE VIRGIN is a beautifully light church.

🔲 The windows of the N aisle are filled with flowers and leaves executed in pale green glass made by E. Woolnough in 1858.

🔲 Magnificent wooden parclose screens enclose the N and S chapels at the E end of the two aisles. Complete with projecting lofts and original colouring they date from c.1450. Before the Reformation a rood screen would have connected the two.

🔲 In the S chapel is the tomb of Sir William Phelip or Lord Bardolph and his wife (1441). (Lord Bardolph was a friend of Henry V. He fought at Agincourt and became Governor of Calais.) His feet rest on an upright eagle and hers on a wyvern. The alabaster has been defaced over the years. Note the elaborately carved surrounds to the window on the s side of this tomb and some original floor tiles.

▨ The chancel windows are very fine with curved shafts inside and heads supporting the hood moulds. Original fourteenth-century glass remains in the heads of five of the windows.

▨ The bench-ends are superb examples of fifteenth-century woodwork. Note particularly the unique carving of the Sciapod in the centre of the nave at the end of the sixth bench from the back on the s side. This is a mythical figure which was supposed to have lived in the Libyan desert. It had *one* huge foot which it used as a sunshade when lying down, but the Dennington carver gave his beast two.

▨ Hanging over the communion table is a rare pyx canopy, partially restored, dating from 1500. Only four exist in England, the other three being at Milton Abbey, Dorset, Tewkesbury Abbey and Wells Cathedral (see pages 354 and 388).

▨ In the first two rows of the box pews are 12 hat pegs.

▨ In the N aisle is a rare sand table used from *c.*1830 to 1860 to teach Dennington children how to write and do arithmetic.

## Derby

THE CATHEDRAL CHURCH OF ALL SAINTS Most of the present building dates from 1723 when the medieval church, except for the Perpendicular tower (begun in 1511), was pulled down and rebuilt in the classical style to the design of James Gibbs.

▨ In 1972 Sebastian Comper (son of Sir Ninian Comper) erected a *baldacchino* over the high altar and the E end was extended to his design.

▨ Stretching right across the building is a magnificent wrought-iron screen incorporating the Royal Arms of George II and made by the great craftsman Robert Bakewell, *c.*1725–50.

▨ At the s end of the wrought-iron screen is a fine wooden effigy on a tomb-chest which may represent Robert Johnson, canon *c.*1527. The effigy is 1.7 m (5 feet 8½ inches) long and shows a priest in clerical dress including a cope, which is an uncommon feature. His hands are in prayer and his head, resting on two cushions, is supported by two reclining angels.

▨ In a recess under the tomb-chest is a wooden male cadaver 0.8 m (2 feet 10 inches) long. A shroud covers the head but the face is visible. These are the only wooden effigies in Derbyshire. (See Wooden Effigies, page 246.)

▨ At the E end of the s aisle is a superb monument to Elizabeth, Countess of Shrewsbury ('Bess of Hardwick', 1518–1608). In the vault below one of her descendants – Henry Cavendish (1731–1810), the famous scientist who discovered hydrogen in 1766 – is buried.

▨ In the tower hangs a ring of ten bells. Incorporating six older bells, the ring was increased to ten in 1677 and none of the bells has been recast. This not only makes them unique but also makes them the oldest ring of ten bells in the world. (See Bells, page 293.)

## Detling        KENT

ST MARTIN OF TOURS Below the North Downs and quite near Maidstone, this little church keeps company with an ancient yew tree.

▨ By the churchyard path is the grave of Stanley Stock, who died on 7 October 1923, aged 13. He is depicted in his chorister's robes.

The magnificent pale oak lectern dates from c.1340 and probably came from Boxley Abbey. It comprises four faces, richly carved. The top would have been adorned with a statuette. This lectern was exhibited at the 'Age of Chivalry' exhibition in Burlington House, London, 1987–8.

In the N aisle, fixed to the wall between the arches, is the upper half of a monumental slab representing a tonsured priest. It was found inserted face downwards in the lean-to wall of this aisle in 1887.

On the s side of the chancel is a memorial to Mary Foote (d. 17 March 1778 aged 60). It is in the style of Strawberry Hill 'Gothick' with three recessed ogee arches. Pieces of it have been broken. The memorial rests on a black marble tomb-slab.

## Dibden                                    HAMPSHIRE

ALL SAINTS was destroyed by German bombs on 20 June 1940 and restored and consecrated on 2 April 1955. It was the first village church in England to be burnt by enemy action in the Second World War.

The church formerly possessed N and s aisles but the N aisle was demolished and a sunken garden has taken the place of the s one. Stone from the original outside walls of the aisles has been used to construct the new nave walls.

The font dates from c.1210 and was badly damaged by the falling bells during the bombing as it used to stand under the tower. It has been carefully repaired.

In the window N of the font are the arms of Canterbury and Winchester.

The E window depicts the Risen Christ and the W window in the tower the Royal Arms of Queen Elizabeth II.

All the stained glass is by Derek Wilson, ARCA.

There are some interesting eighteenth-century tombstones in the churchyard.

## Digswell                               HERTFORDSHIRE

ST JOHN THE EVANGELIST The church is sited on the hillside, overlooking the River Mimram and the magnificent railway viaduct.

On the N side of the sanctuary a fine brass commemorates John Peryent (standard-bearer to Richard II) and his wife, Joan, 1415. She wears a most impressive head-dress that is unique in its design. The swan on her collar and the hedgehog at her feet are also unique features.

## Doddiscombsleigh                          DEVON

ST MICHAEL is a remote church approached by narrow, winding lanes.

The w tower is unusual in possessing two buttresses, but these are situated in the centre of the N and s faces, not on the corners.

Five windows in the N aisle are almost completely filled with fifteenth-century glass, although some restoration has been done.

The E window contains a central picture of Christ seated which is a Victorian replacement, but the scenes around it are original. They depict scenes from the Seven Sacraments and are delightful pictures of medieval life. Note particularly the bottom right-hand panel showing a man receiving Communion on his death-bed, while his wife looks on thoughtfully. In the blue pane to the right of the lady's head has been scratched:

'Pr Coles
Glazr Done
this window
March 1762
Whom God
Preserve
Amen'

The glass must have required serious attention at this time for a glazier to be employed, as the late eighteenth century is not recognized as the most enlightened time for conserving such treasures!

## Dorchester     OXFORDSHIRE

THE ABBEY CHURCH OF ST PETER, ST PAUL & ST BIRINUS At the Dissolution of the Monasteries by Henry VIII this church was bought by Richard Beauforest, who gave it to the villagers in 1539 for their parish church. Before this, they had only used the nave.

▨ The lead font dates from c.1120. It shows figures of the Apostles in relief but only Peter with his key can be clearly identified. It is the only lead font in a former monastic church to have escaped destruction at the Reformation, probably because it was hidden. (See Lead Fonts, page 74.)

▨ Cantilevered from the pier near the font is a most unusual bracket depicting sleeping monks. It dates from c.1340 and was intended for a statue.

▨ The great E window behind the high altar is most impressive with tracery filling the entire window from top to bottom. The rather ugly buttress in the centre was probably added for stability as the E end of the abbey is built on an artificial embankment above the River Thame to the E. Much of the stained glass dates from c.1350.

Carved on the tracery, halfway up the window, are scenes from the life of Our Lord.

▨ On the S side of the sanctuary is a superb sedilia with rich canopies enclosing a double piscina. Behind the seats are four unusual windows containing glass dating from c.1250 and showing scenes from the life of St Birinus.

▨ On the N side of the sanctuary is the famous Jesse window – a gallery of medieval sculpture unique in the British Isles. On the window sill is the recumbent figure of Jesse from which grows a tree. On its branches rest the figures of Old Testament prophets and kings (notice King David playing his harp), but the figures of Christ and the Virgin and Child were destroyed by Cromwell's soldiers during the Civil War. Some of the original glass remains. This window was boarded up during the Second World War.

▨ In the lady chapel is the new shrine of St Birinus which was dedicated in June 1964. It incorporates fragments of the medieval shrine, discovered c.1875 in a blocked-up doorway of the N transept.

▨ Below the altar steps are three tombs; the one in the centre depicts Sir John Holcomb, who died in the Second Crusade, c.1148. This is one of the most impressive effigies in England. He is shown cross-legged, his right hand withdrawing his sword – a magnificent piece of medieval carving.

## Down Ampney     GLOUCESTERSHIRE

ALL SAINTS Ralph Vaughan Williams (1872–1958) the famous composer was born here, the son of the vicar. His tune to the hymn 'Come down, O Love Divine' is named after his native village.

▨ The original spire dates from c.1350 and is a rare feature in the Cotswolds.

▨ A fine oak screen separates the nave from the chancel and dates from c.1900.

▨ Near the church is the site of 'St Augustine's Oak', claimed to be the place where St Augustine met the English bishops in AD 603.

# THATCHED CHURCHES

Complete or partly thatched churches are comparatively rare. The Victorians replaced many roofs with tiles because they considered thatching was not good enough for an ecclesiastical building. As far as I know, these are the only remaining fully or partially thatched churches in England:

✠ CAMBRIDGESHIRE
1. Long Stanton (St Michael)
2. Rampton (All Saints)

✠ ESSEX
3. Duddenhoe End, near Saffron Walden (The Hamlet Church)
4. Silver End, near Braintree (St Francis)

✠ HEREFORDSHIRE
5. Brockhampton-by-Ross (All Saints)

✠ ISLE OF WIGHT
6. Freshwater Bay (St Agnes)

✠ LINCOLNSHIRE
7. Markby (St Peter)

✠ NORFOLK
8. Acle (St Edmund)
9. Babingley (St Felix)
10. Bacton (St Andrew)
11. Banningham (St Botolph)
12. Barton Bendish (St Mary)
13. Beechamwell (St Mary)
14. Beighton (All Saints)
15. Billockby (All Saints)
16. Brumstead (St Peter)
17. Burgh-next-Aylsham (St Mary)
18. Burgh St Margaret (St Margaret)
19. Burgh St Peter (St Mary)

*Thatched church at Irstead, Norfolk.*

20. Burlingham St Edmund (St Edmund)
21. Claxton (St Andrew)
22. Coltishall (St John the Baptist)
23. Cranwich (St Mary)
24. Crostwight (All Saints)
25. Drayton (St Margaret)
26. Eaton, near Norwich (St Andrew)
27. Edingthorpe (All Saints)
28. Filby (All Saints)
29. Fritton (St Edmund)
30. Hales (St Margaret)
31. Hassingham (St Mary)
32. Heckingham (St Gregory)
33. Hempstead, near Stalham (St Andrew)
34. Horsey (All Saints)
35. Horsford (All Saints)
36. Hoveton (St Peter)
37. Ingworth (St Lawrence)
38. Irstead (St Michael)
39. Lessingham (All Saints)
40. Mautby (St Peter & St Paul)
41. Norton Subcourse (St Mary)
42. Old Buckenham (All Saints)
43. Ormesby St Michael (St Michael)
44. Paston (St Margaret)
45. Potter Heigham (St Nicholas)
46. Ranworth (St Helen)

47. Reedham (St John the Baptist)
48. Rockland St Peter (St Peter)
49. Rushford (St John the Evangelist)
50. Scoulton (Holy Trinity)
51. Sea Palling (St Margaret)
52. Seething (St Margaret & St Remigius)
53. Sisland (St Mary)
54. Stockton (St Michael)
55. Stokesby (St Andrew)
56. Swafield (St Nicholas)
57. Taverham (St Edmund)
58. Thorpe-next-Haddiscoe (St Matthias)
59. Thurgarton (All Saints)
60. Thurlton (All Saints)
61. Thurton (St Ethelbert)
62. Thwaite St Mary (St Mary)
63. Trowse Newton (St Andrew)
64. West Somerton (St Mary)
65. Wickhampton (St Andrew)
66. Woodbastwick (St Fabian & St Sebastian)

✠ SHROPSHIRE
67. Little Stretton (All Saints)

✠ SOMERSET
68. Tivington (St Leonard)

✠ SUFFOLK
69. Ashby (St Mary)
70. Barnby (St John the Baptist)

71. Barsham (Holy Trinity)
72. Bramfield (St Andrew)
73. Bures (St Stephen's Chapel)
74. Butley (St John the Baptist)
75. Coney Weston (St Mary)
76. Covehithe (St Andrew)
77. Great Livermere (St Peter)
78. Harleston (St Augustine)
79. Henstead (St Mary)
80. Herringfleet (St Margaret)
81. Icklingham (All Saints)
82. Iken (St Botolph)
83. Ixworth Thorpe (All Saints)
84. Kessingland (St Edmund)
85. Kingsfield (All Saints)
86. Lindsey (St James Chapel)
87. North Cove (St Botolph)
88. Pakefield (All Saints & St Margaret)
89. Ramsholt (All Saints)
90. Rushmere (St Michael)
91. South Cove (St Lawrence)
92. Theberton (St Peter)
93. Thornham Parva (St Mary)
94. Uggeshall (St Mary)
95. Westhall (St Andrew)
96. Westleton (St Peter)

✠ WILTSHIRE
97. Sandy Lane, near Chippenham (St Mary the Virgin & St Nicholas)

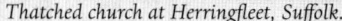

*Thatched church at Herringfleet, Suffolk.*

## Drinkstone                    SUFFOLK

ALL SAINTS is a little church in peaceful countryside off the busy A14, between Bury St Edmunds and Ipswich.

On the outside of the building, to the right of the N door of the nave is a curious construction built into the wall which may be the base of an ancient churchyard cross.

At the E end of the chancel, on the outside, are two unusual buttresses.

Built into the base of the westernmost pillar of the S aisle is a curious chevron carving on a piece of stone which may have come from an earlier church.

In front of the lectern are several rare glazed tiles dating from c.1350.

Under the chancel arch is a well-proportioned oak screen dating from c.1450. It contains much of its original colouring. The rood loft is missing.

Exquisite fragments of medieval stained glass remain in the tracery of some of the chancel windows, but some is restored.

On 11 September 1923 Sir Malcolm Sargent, the famous musician and conductor, was married in this church to Miss Eileen Horne, a niece of the Reverend Frank Horne, rector of Drinkstone.

The W brick tower dates from 1694.

## Droxford                    HAMPSHIRE

ST MARY & ALL SAINTS is located in a beautiful village in the lovely Meon Valley.

The flint W tower has a very unusual square stair turret projecting diagonally at the NW corner. Over the W door is a stone bearing the date 1599. This may refer to the insertion of this doorway and the windows above which are characteristic of this date, and also to the construction of the tower. Although the tower is battlemented, the stair turret is not.

On the S side of the chancel is the S chapel, which contains a fine (albeit mutilated) niche with an ogee arch and Tudor roses in the roof.

Also in the S chapel is a beautiful effigy of a lady dating from c.1280. She clasps a heart to her breast. This effigy was found buried in a nearby ditch (c.1850), where it had probably been hidden during the Civil War to escape destruction.

The corbels on the arch separating the S chapel from the chancel depict two fourteenth-century characters, although the one on the E side appears to have been restored.

The seventeenth-century altar rails have large finials on the end posts – a rare feature, but seen again at nearby Bishops Waltham.

In the lady chapel is a stained-glass window by Martin Travers (1886–1948) depicting the Blessed Virgin and four saints – St Francis, St George, St Stephen and St Wilfrid. Dated 1938, the window was given in memory of the Reverend S. Bridge and his wife.

As one leaves the churchyard, on the right of the path is the table-tomb of the Reverend Thomas P. White. Among other things it has a very unusual inscription:

'Born in sin 19 September MDCCLXXVIII (1778)
Born again A.D. MDCCCI (1801).'

## Duncton                    WEST SUSSEX

HOLY TRINITY From the vantage point on Duncton Hill, to the S of the village, a magnificent view of the Sussex countryside can be seen, with the church and village nestling immediately below.

The third oldest *dated* bell in Britain hangs in the tower of this Victorian church. Cast in MCCCLXIX (1369) the

*Dunsfold – a beautiful church in rural Surrey.*

inscription is very unusual in being at the top of the bell. The primitive lettering is unique in England and some authorities believe the bell came from Normandy, perhaps stolen. In this case it is the oldest dated foreign bell.

🔲 In the churchyard Florence Gertrude de Fonblanque (22 July1864–3 January 1948) is buried, the originator and leader of the women's suffrage march from Edinburgh to London in 1912.

## Dunsfold                    Surrey

St Mary & All Saints was called by William Morris 'the most beautiful country church in all England'. It lies about 0.8 km (½ mile) from the village just above the flood level of a tributary of the River Arun.

🔲 Near the stream below the church is the holy well with a reputation for miraculous cures for eye diseases. It is protected by a shrine on the side of which is a statue of the Blessed Virgin Mary holding the infant Christ. Underneath are the words, 'To the Glory of God and in honour of the Blessed Virgin Mary. This Shrine was erected in 1933 by Members of the Dunsfold Amateur Dramatic Society.'

🔲 The whole of the exterior of the church is covered with 'galleting' (ironstone chips inserted into the mortar ), which was done in 1882.

🔲 A very unusual feature on the outside of the n wall of the nave, the w wall and the w wall of the s transept are three low openings through which water was sluiced over the brick floor and swept outside. They are now blocked on the inside but

*One of the original wooden plugs at Dunsfold, Surrey.*

the original wooden plugs attached to chains can still be seen on the outside.

▨ Some of the oak pews dating from *c*.1200 are among the oldest in England although they have had backs added. The holes in the pew ends were made to hold tapers.

▨ Note two uncarved blocks of stone on each side of the chancel arch, which was raised to its present height in 1882.

▨ The w respond of the s transept arch is an almost complete octagonal column. Perhaps it was the medieval builders' intention to enlarge this into a s aisle?

▨ The piscina on the s side of the chancel is unusual in having two bowls rather than one.

▨ On 9 July 1987 members of 320 Dutch Squadron RAF who had been stationed at Dunsfold between February and October 1944 visited this church and presented a flag and plaque which are now on display.

## Dunster SOMERSET

ST GEORGE served, until 1539, two communities. The villagers worshipped in the nave and Benedictine monks used the portion E of the screen. When Henry VIII closed all the monasteries, the monks

*Dunster Church, Somerset, seen from the castle.*

were ejected and the whole church reverted to the villagers' use.

▨ Following a dispute between the monks and parishioners, the superb wooden screen was erected in 1500 to prevent the parishioners from entering the monks' church, which included chancel, tower and transepts.

The screen has 14 unequal compartments and at 17.7 m (58 feet) is the second longest in England. The longest is at Uffculme, Devon, and is 20.4 m (67 feet) long.

▨ On the N side of the church is the old sacristy, paved with thirteenth-century tiles.

▨ On the N side of the choir are the mutilated effigies of Sir Hugh Luttrell and Catherine Beaumont, his wife (*c*.1440).

▨ At the E end of the s aisle is an alabaster

slab with an incised effigy to Lady Elizabeth Luttrell (1493) – a rare depiction.

▨ Notice the unusual arch at the E end of the s aisle. Near by is a memorial plaque to Sir Henry Maxwell Lyte, grandson of Henry Francis Lyte, author of 'Abide with Me'.

▨ Near the s door is an alms-box dated 1634 with two quotations engraved on it.

▨ The tower clock plays a different tune daily on the hours of one, five and nine.

# Durham

THE CATHEDRAL CHURCH OF CHRIST, BLESSED MARY THE VIRGIN & ST CUTHBERT OF DURHAM occupies a commanding position overlooking the River Wear. A spectacular view of the church can be seen from the train window on the London to Newcastle line.

▨ This was the first great church in Europe to be planned with stone-ribbed vaulting. It was built from c.1093 to 1133.

▨ The nave vault has buttresses in the form of pointed arches hidden in the galleries of the triforium. These arches are the earliest examples of flying buttresses in England and the earliest pointed arches.

▨ The incised decoration on the circular Norman piers of the nave is unusual and the best example of its kind. Some of these patterns also vary from each other. They must have been incised *after* the piers were erected. Other churches possessing incised Norman piers are Kirkby Lonsdale, Cumbria, Norwich Cathedral and Waltham Abbey (see page 380).

▨ Underneath the windows all around the inside of the cathedral is a continuous arcade of interlocking arches – the earliest in the British Isles. Can you see how the pointed arch might have evolved?

▨ The bishop's throne was built by Bishop Hatfield (bishop from 1318 to 1333) above his altar-tomb. It is made of stone and is the highest bishop's throne in existence.

▨ The E transept is called the Chapel of the Nine Altars. Built between 1242 and 1280 it is unique, as the only other one is in ruins at Fountains Abbey, North Yorkshire.

▨ The Neville screen behind the high altar was given by John, Lord Neville c.1380 and is made of Caen stone.

▨ Behind the Neville screen is the tomb of St Cuthbert (d.687), above which was his shrine which existed until the Reformation.

▨ The font and font cover at the w end were given by Bishop Cosin c.1650 and are superb examples of Renaissance work.

▨ In the sw corner of the s transept is one of only two fireplaces to be found in a Norman cathedral. (The other example is in Hereford Cathedral, where it is in the same position.) These fireplaces were probably used for baking the Mass wafers.

▨ At the w end of the cathedral is the rare Galilee chapel. It was erected by Bishop Hugh de Puiset in c.1175 and comprises beautiful Norman arches enriched with much ornamentation.

▨ On the s side of the Galilee chapel is the tomb of the Venerable Bede (673–735). His bones were brought to Durham in 1022 and laid in this tomb c.1350. The Latin inscription translated means, 'In this tomb are the bones of the Venerable Bede'. On the wall behind Bede's tomb are these words written by him:

'Christ is the morning star
Who, when the night of this world
is past,
Brings to His saints the promise of
the light of life
And opens everlasting day.'

▨ In the original monks' dormitory on the w side of the cloisters are many treasures, including the following:

# GRAVESIDE SHELTERS OR HUDDS

Graveside shelters or hudds were used from *c.*1700 to *c.*1900 but few have survived, as they were usually made of wood and had to be quite light and flimsy for ease of transportation. They normally resembled a sentry box or even a sedan chair and were used by clergymen officiating at a churchyard burial when the weather was particularly inclement. (The mourners had to make do with umbrellas!) There are a few recorded instances of clergymen contracting pneumonia and subsequently dying as a result of excessive exposure to the elements so the advent of the shelter must have been very welcome.

To the best of my knowledge, graveside shelters can still be seen in the following churches:

1. Beaumaris, Isle of Anglesey (St Mary), Wales
2. Brookland (St Augustine), Kent
3. Bucklebury (St Mary the Virgin), Berkshire
4. Crondall (All Saints), Hampshire
5. Deeping St James (St James), Lincolnshire
6. Donington (St Mary and the Holy Rood), Lincolnshire
7. Friskney (All Saints), Lincolnshire
8. Ivychurch (St George), Kent
9. Maxey (St Peter), Cambridgeshire
10. Pinchbeck (St Mary), Lincolnshire
11. Quadring (St Margaret), Lincolnshire
12. Silverton (St Mary), Devon
13. Walpole St Peter (St Peter), Norfolk
14. Wingfield (St Andrew), Suffolk

† part of the coffin of St Cuthbert (AD698)

† a unique Anglo-Saxon embroidered stole from St Cuthbert's coffin

† the gold cloisonné pectoral cross of St Cuthbert taken from his coffin in 1827

† the beautifully illuminated Bible belonging to Bishop Hugh de Puiset

† the famous Norman bronze sanctuary knocker (*c.*1150), which was formerly fixed on the N door on the NW side of the cathedral. A replica has replaced it.

(Clinging to this knocker, criminals could seek sanctuary inside the cathedral until the monarch had pardoned them, if innocent.)

 Inside the SW tower at triforium level is a tread-wheel, similar to a capstan, used for raising stone. Only five others exist – at Beverley Minster, Canterbury Cathedral, Louth, Peterborough Cathedral and Salisbury Cathedral (see pages 26, 61, 226, 270 and 303 respectively).

*The Saxon tower of Earls Barton, Northamptonshire. Note the two 'sound holes' on the east face.*

# Earls Barton    NORTHAMPTONSHIRE

ALL SAINTS This well-known church and spectacular tower dominate the village, which slopes away to the s.

 Dating from *c.*970 this is the most famous and magnificent Saxon tower in the British Isles. Apart from the battlements, added *c.*1450, and the clock *c.*1650, it remains essentially as the Saxons built it. Note the characteristic 'long and short' work at the four corners.

 The fine w doorway has a semicircular arch which springs from two stone slabs on which are carved miniature arcading – a feature unique to this doorway.

Above the belfry windows, high up on the E face, are two circular holes, not placed centrally, and sometimes referred to as 'sound holes', although their original purpose remains unknown. The Saxon belfry openings with characteristic baluster shafts between the five lights can be seen on all four faces of the tower. This tower is unique in having them on every face.

Like most Saxon towers, Earls Barton does not have any external buttresses, but there is one *inside* the church near the SE corner. Note also the corner stones of the tower on the NE side inside the church on the opposite side to the internal buttress.

There are eight bells in the tower, the heaviest (tenor) weighing 608.3 kg (11 cwt 3 qr 25 lb).

The tower is 18.3 m (60 feet) high and featured on the 4p British postage stamps of village churches issued on 21 June 1972.

 In the chancel is beautiful Norman arcading and the s doorway also shows fine Norman work including chevrons, beak heads and miniature arcading around the outside.

 The rood screen dates from *c.*1450 and the painted panels below it were done by Henry Bird in 1935.

 Near the screen is a fine Jacobean oak pulpit dating from about *c.*1620.

 The E window of the lady chapel on the N side of the nave commemorates Canon L. A. Ewart (vicar 1930–59), who did a great deal for this church. Below a representation of Earls Barton tower are numerous saints and famous Christian women – Edith Cavell, Mary Sumner, Florence Nightingale and Elizabeth Fry. The window is signed by Christopher Webb and dated 1960.

 The adjacent window in the N aisle depicts an aerial view of Earls Barton with villagers from different centuries. Designed by Francis Skeat (a former pupil of Webb) in 1980, this is probably the only stained-glass window in existence that includes an aerial view of its church.

 The church register records the death of Daniel Sheffield, 'Sunday School Teacher and Labourer', who was buried on 29 January 1791. This is possibly the oldest reference to a Sunday school teacher in any church register.

 On the N side of the church is a huge tree-clad mound called Berry Mount. It may have been a pagan burial site or part of some defences or the result of digging

*The unique Bell Cage in East Bergholt, Suffolk.*

the ditch in front of it! At present we can only guess at its purpose.

## East Bergholt SUFFOLK

ST MARY THE VIRGIN The famous painter John Constable, RA (11 June 1776– 31 March 1837) was born here and the priest's room above the S porch is the subject of one of his paintings.

In the NE corner of the churchyard lie Golding and Ann Constable, parents of the artist.

The centre window of the S aisle is in memory of John Constable.

The tower was begun in 1525 at the expense of Cardinal Wolsey. His downfall and death in 1530 stopped the work through lack of funds.

On the N side of the churchyard is the 'bell-cage' erected as a temporary measure

in 1531! It houses five bells, the oldest of which (the second) is dated *c.*1450. The ringing of the bells is done in a unique manner because they are rung by force of hand applied directly to the bell and not by the usual rope and wheel method.

These bells are the heaviest five bells – the tenor weighs 1324.51 kg (1 ton 6cwt 0qr 8 lb) in the world. (See Bells, page 293.)

In the N aisle are fragments of the tomb of someone called Anna Parker (d. 1656) which shows a bear's head and camels.

On the N wall of the chancel is a memorial to Maria, wife of John Constable.

## East Budleigh DEVON

ALL SAINTS In a village near the River Otter in south Devon, it is a short distance from Hayes Barton farmhouse, where Sir Walter Raleigh was born in 1552.

Most of the fine bench-ends were carved *c.*1500 and show Renaissance details. Some depict instruments associated with the wool trade such as a pair of scissors and sheep shears. Others show a representation of a sailing ship, numerous Tudor faces and the head of an American Indian. A modern bench-end commemorates those who died in the First World War.

In the centre of the nave near the step leading to the screen is the grave slab of Joan Raleigh (née Drake), the first wife of Walter Raleigh. (He was the father of Sir Walter Raleigh with his third wife.)

The Latin inscription translated means, 'Pray for the soul of Joan Raleigh, wife of Walter Raleigh, Esq., who died the tenth day of the month of June, Anno Domini...' The date of death is missing but it should be *c.*1530.

Interestingly this inscription is carved in reverse like 'mirror-writing' and may have been done by an illiterate sculptor. This mirror writing is very rare on a tomb, but painted examples occur on an arch (see Trent, Dorset, page 368 and Morwenstow, Cornwall, page 244) and also on a gravestone (see Stow, Lincs., page 342). (On a frieze over the w doorway of the tower at Stawley, Somerset, is an inscription to Henry Howe and his wife dated 1523, with the words 'Pray for the soule', again engraved backwards.)

Also in the nave are a number of interesting roof bosses dating from *c.*1450. They were restored to their medieval colours in 1974.

To the s of the chancel arch are the former stairs to the rood loft which were only uncovered in 1891 having been plastered over and hidden *c.*1560.

# Eastbury     BERKSHIRE

ST JAMES THE GREATER was built in 1853 of flint and Bath stone and is one of G. E. Street's early works.

The fine E window depicts the Ascension.

On the s side of the nave is a memorial window to Edward Thomas (3 March 1878–9 April 1917) and his wife, Helen. He died fighting near Arras, France, and she spent the last 12 years of her life here. She is buried at the top of the churchyard near the fence. The window was engraved by Laurence Whistler on 9 April 1971 and across it are lines from Thomas's poems.

In the centre light is the spire of Steep Church, Hampshire, and in the right light Hodson Wood Cottage, Wiltshire, where Edward and Helen enjoyed much happiness. Hanging on a nearby tree is a soldier's helmet and Sam Browne leather belt. In the left light are the dates and initials of Edward and Helen Thomas, cut in the bark of another tree: E.T. 1878–1917 H.T. 1877–1967.

# East Chinnock     SOMERSET

ST MARY is located in one of three Chinnock villages (the other two are West and Middle) that lie along the hills between Yeovil and Crewkerne.

Nine of the stained-glass windows were designed, made and given by Herr Gunther Anton of Leonberg, Stuttgart, Germany, the first being given in 1962 and the last being installed in July 1982. Gunther was a rear-gunner in the German Luftwaffe and was shot down over Southampton in 1944 at the age of 17. He came to East Chinnock in 1945 and when he returned to Germany in 1948 he helped his father to build up a stained-glass business. Before he left England he had resolved to make a stained-glass window (later to become eight more) for this church as a thanksgiving to God for the kindness shown to him by the people of East Chinnock, for his safe return from the war and as an act of reconciliation.

The window by the lectern on the SE side of the nave was the first to be installed. It depicts scenes from Christ's life including the Crucifixion and Ascension. The colours are predominantly blue, purple and yellow.

Next to be installed was the window on the NE side of the chancel. It shows Mary holding the Infant Jesus in one light and Christ the King in the other. It was given in 1967.

In 1969 two more windows on the s side of the chancel were installed. From E to w they depict the archangels Michael and Gabriel in one window and Raphael and Uriel in the other. Also in 1969 the window on the NE side of the nave was installed and it shows the healing of the blind beggar, the woman who touched Christ's robe and the raising of Jairus's daughter.

In July 1982 four more windows were installed, completing the nine given by Gunther Anton. These are:

† the small centre window in the s wall of the nave showing scenes from the life of the Blessed Virgin Mary

† w of this window, another depiction of the Crucifixion with scenes from Christ's life

† over the NW door of the nave, a window showing the Slaughter of the Innocents and the Flight to Egypt

† the final window – on the NW side of the nave and known as the 'Anna Window' – depicts Anna holding her baby, the Blessed Virgin Mary, surrounded by scenes from the lives of Anna and Joachim.

Herr Gunther Anton died in 1988.

# East Coker                    SOMERSET

ST MICHAEL This church, found in a beautiful village near Coker Court, will forever be associated with the writer T. S. Eliot.

At the w end of the N aisle is a wall plaque to the memory of the famous poet T. S. Eliot, whose ashes rest below. The inscription on the plaque reads:

'"in my beginning is my end."
Of your charity pray for the repose of
the soul of Thomas Stearns Eliot. Poet.
26 September, 1888–4 January, 1965.
"in my end is my beginning."'

In the second of his Four Quartets (1944) Eliot commemorates East Coker.

Near by is a beautiful modern stained-glass window given by Walter Graeme Eliot of New York whose ancestors lived in East Coker. Made by Leonard Walker in 1936 it depicts Faith, Love and Hope.

A wall plaque in the s aisle commemorates William Dampier (1651–1715), a navigator described as a 'buccaneer, explorer, hydrographer'. He brought home Alexander Selkirk, whose adventures gave Daniel Defoe the basis for *Robinson Crusoe*. Dampier's book *A Voyage Round the World* was published in 1691. Dampier was the first Englishman to land in Australia in 1688.

The brass eagle lectern was given in 1897 to commemorate '60 glorious years of Queen Victoria's reign' and 600 years since the first rector of East Coker, Robert de St Nicholas, was inducted in 1297.

Descendants of Andrew Eliot, who emigrated to America in 1627, joined in the memorial.

The N door dates from c.1360 and its original lock still works.

Two piers of the N arcade lean markedly northwards.

The tower occupies an unusual position at the E end of the N aisle.

*The tower at East Lulworth, showing projecting corbels between the tops of the three belfry windows.*

# East Grinstead     West Sussex

St Swithun The High Street of the busy town in which this church is located is dominated by this beautiful church.

In the se corner of the churchyard is the grave of the Reverend John Mason Neale (1818–66), the famous hymn translator and church historian. Among his best-known hymns are, 'Good King Wenceslas' and 'O come, O come, Emmanuel'.

On the s side of the nave steps near the chancel is the oldest-dated iron tombstone in England. Dating from 1570 it was used, upside down, as a doorstep in the old vicarage.

The mosaic pavement of the sanctuary was made by Constance Kent while a prisoner at Portland. She murdered her young brother in 1844 but did not confess to it until 1865. She was sentenced to death but later reprieved.

# East Hagbourne     Oxfordshire

St Andrew is situated picturesquely at the end of a lane leading from an ancient stepped cross located between attractive timbered cottages.

The fine w tower, dating from c.1490 and containing a superb ring of eight bells, has an unusual medieval stone sanctus bellcote high on its e side.

On the n door is a rare sanctuary knocker dating from c.1350.

In the n aisle is a beautiful depiction of the Nativity in stained glass dating from c.1310.

# East Knoyle     Wiltshire

St Mary Here was born Sir Christopher Wren (1632–1723), the great English architect who designed St Paul's Cathedral and many other churches and buildings after the Great Fire of London in 1666. His father was rector of East Knoyle.

In the chancel is most unusual plaster decoration depicting scenes from the Bible including Jacob's dream of the ladder ascending to heaven with angels on it on the e wall, and elsewhere the Ascension and Elijah being fed by ravens.

This scheme was devised by Dr Christopher Wren and completed seven years after young Christopher was born.

On the Second World War memorial is an unusual quotation from 1 *Maccabees* 3, v. 59, 'Better for us to die in battle than to behold the calamities of our people and our sanctuary.'

# East Leake     Nottinghamshire

St Mary the Virgin This church is situated in a small village about 6.44 km (4 miles) n of Loughborough; it has a prominent spire.

There are some good Swithland slate gravestones in the churchyard, boasting fine eighteenth-century script.

A table-tomb on the e side of the church commemorates John Bley, a local benefactor, and has a very attractive inscription on the side.

On the w wall above the font is a shawm or vamping horn; at 2.36 m (7 feet 9 inches) long it is the largest in existence. A plaque underneath states, 'This Trumpet was formerly used in the Gallery of this Church for one of the singers to sing the Bass through. Only three similar instruments are known to exist, and this appears to have been the last used in England, having been in use as late as the year 1850. Having become much decayed, it was saved from destruction and repaired by Ch. Angrave, Esq. of Berwick, Sussex, late of this parish by whom it was sent to the "Inventions Exhib", London, 1885 and replaced in this Church, 1888.' (See Vamping Horns, page 245.)

⊞ The tower clock is one of the most accurate in England, having a radio link to the atomic time piece at Daventry which keeps it in time – accurate to 1 second in 15,000 years.

## East Lulworth     DORSET

ST ANDREW The Anglican church of St Andrew stands in a beautiful setting in Lulworth Park, near to Lulworth Castle. This small village has two churches – one Anglican and the other Roman Catholic.

⊞ The fine tower (c.1460) has certain unique and unusual features. All four corners have large projecting diagonal buttresses crowned with pinnacles. It is rare to find such buttresses on *all* four corners.

⊞ Inside the base of the tower, a doorway in the centre of the N wall leads to a narrow passage formed in the thickness of the wall. This in turn leads to the NE corner where a circular staircase rises to the top of the tower, not visible externally.

⊞ Between the heads of the three windows on each face of the tower are two large projecting stone corbels which make this tower unique. They are similar to uncarved gargoyles, minus the water spouts running through them, but their exact purpose has never been explained. They may have been used to support a temporary wooden hoarding to give increased means of defence if the tower was attacked or besieged. Similar corbels are found on the walls of medieval castles.

This tower may well have existed before the remainder of the church was built, which would account for the buttresses at all four corners and the unexplained corbels.

⊞ The arch between the tower and nave is very unusual in being flat and low. On the nave side are blank niches with pedestals and canopies.

⊞ On the N side of the chancel the fine coat of arms of George III dates from 1785 and was the gift of Thomas Weld. It was restored in 1973.

⊞ Near the Anglican church and close to the castle is the first Roman Catholic church to be built legally in England after the Reformation. King George III (who ruled from 1760 to 1820) gave special permission to Thomas Weld, owner of the castle, to build it. Noted for its fine dome it was completed in 1786.

## East Meon     HAMPSHIRE

ALL SAINTS is set picturesquely above the village, its lead spire forming a notable landmark.

⊞ Just inside the lovely Norman s doorway is the famous font, one of seven Tournai marble fonts in the British Isles. It was brought from Belgium c.1150 probably by Henry de Blois, Bishop of Winchester, William the Conqueror's grandson.

The font is richly carved with scenes from the lives of Adam and Eve. On the N face, God is shown creating Adam and Eve, the serpent offering Eve the forbidden fruit and Adam eating it.

On the E face the Gate of Paradise is shown with a sword-carrying angel barring the way. Another angel teaches Adam to dig while Eve spins flax.

The other two faces depict the flat earth on its pillars with all kinds of animals and birds. On the s face two beautiful doves are shown being chased by ferocious-looking dogs.

On the top of the font, around the rim, is carved a vine, while doves adorn opposite corners with a tongue of fire – the symbol of the Holy Spirit.

An iron bracket at the SE corner on the

top shows where the cover was padlocked to prevent the baptismal water from being stolen in the Middle Ages.

As this beautiful font is situated in a fairly dark part of the church it is a good idea to examine it with a torch, but *do not touch it* in case some damage may be done. (See Tournai Fonts, page 439.)

◻ On the w wall of the s transept is an inscription which reads: 'Heare lyeth the body of Richard Smyther who departed this life in hope of a better. March ye 16, 1633.'

◻ Also in the s transept but on the E wall is the curious inscription 'Amens Plenty', said to commemorate some soldiers who died in 1644 during the Civil War.

◻ The colourful E window by J. N. Comper commemorates men who died in the First World War.

# East Pennard                   SOMERSET

ALL SAINTS This church is situated on high ground just w of the A37 (Fosse Way) with lovely views over Somerset.

◻ On the outside N wall of the tower between the two windows is a Glastonbury rose, linking this church with the abbey in medieval times.

◻ In the NW corner of the churchyard is an ancient cross that was restored in 1920.

◻ The tower houses the second-heaviest ring of five bells in the world. The tenor weighs 1261.46 kg (1 ton 4 cwt 3 qr 9 lb), has a diameter of 1.40 m (4 feet 8 inches) and dates from 1740. The inscription records the list of donors who 'cast mee July 26 1740. God send good luck.'

From 1910 to 1970 the bells were silent as the frame and tower were considered unsafe. It is thought, however, that in 1910 the rector gave this as his reason for stopping the ringing after a dispute with the ringers!

In 1970 the then rector, the Reverend C. Vernon Francis, called for an inspection of the bells and frame after an itinerant band of ringers had rung them successfully. Following reports from two bell-founders, no exceptional movement was detected. The Reverend Francis then sent a letter to his parishioners to find out what support there would be for restoring the bells and people began donating money immediately. Enough money was raised to replace the wooden frame with a steel one, lower the bells in the tower (they were originally only 30 cm/1 foot from the roof of the tower!) and recast the second bell, which was cracked.

The five bells were rededicated on 15 April 1972. An interesting story is told that a former elderly lady parishioner who had emigrated to Australia planned to leave some money in her will for the eventual restoration of the bells. When the appeal was launched, she immediately sent £1000. Subsequently, when the bells were being rung, her friend in the village telephoned her in Australia from a kiosk near the church and she heard them over the phone. She was then nearly 90 years old. (See Bells, page 293.)

Near the N door affixed to a pillar is an old iron pulley which supported the rood light – a rare survival.

◻ The fine nave roof dates from *c*.1420 and contains numerous bosses depicting flowers and leaves.

◻ The font dates from *c*.1170 and has fine carvings of salamanders and toads.

◻ On the s side of the chancel is a modern chalice brass to the Reverend Edward Armstone Ducket (d. 1913) and his wife, Maria Hester (d. 1930).

Medieval mass or scratch dials are a series of holes, usually in a half circle, with a hole in the centre into which a gnomon was placed to cast a shadow (similar to a sundial), in order to indicate the times of services. They are often found on the s side of churches, but apart from these there are many other interesting clocks to be seen.

The oldest church turret clock is at Rye, East Sussex, and the largest dial in the world is at Coningsby, Lincolnshire, with a diameter of 5.02 m (16 feet 6 inches). The pendulum of the Rye clock hangs down inside the tower and is visible from the nave, but the largest pendulum in the British Isles is 9.32 m (30 feet 7 inches) long and hangs in Aldborough, North Yorkshire.

*Coningsby, Lincolnshire.*

Some church clocks have letters in place of numerals. For example, the one at Buckland-in-the Moor, Devon, has 'MY DEAR MOTHER'.

At Wootton Rivers, Wiltshire, the clock proclaims 'GLORY BE TO GOD' and West Acre's (Norfolk) commands 'WATCH AND PRAY'. The clock at Cheadle, Cheshire, was installed in 1988 and instead of Roman numerals it has lettering on three of its faces. This lettering is as follows: on the s side – FORGET NOT GOD; on the w side – TRUST THE LORD; and on the E side – TIME IS FLYING.

These last three churches are the only ones in England whose clocks carry a biblical message.

The clock face on the Eastern wall of the tower at Baslow, Derbyshire, bears the patriotic inscription 'VICTORIA 1897' in place of numerals, while Littledean, Gloucestershire, has a clock in which the Roman numeral 'XI' is incorrectly shown as 'IX'.

The clock outside St Dunstan-in-the-West, Fleet Street (London), dates from 1671 and was the first to show minutes and also the first with two dials. Several other interesting clocks with beautiful carved cases can be found inside many of London's churches.

The oldest working clock in Europe is at Salisbury Cathedral, Wiltshire, and dates from 1386, although it has no face or quarter-jacks. The clock at Wells Cathedral, Somerset, is the oldest complete mechanical clock with a face and quarter-jacks. It dates from c.1390 and was probably given by the same bishop (Bishop Erghum) who gave the clock at Salisbury Cathedral. The Wells clock no longer has its original mechanism, which was renewed in 1838. The old mechanism is on loan to the Science Museum in London.

The earliest working clock in England that remains unaltered and still in its original position dates from c.1488 and can be found in a recess in the chapel of Cotehele House, Cornwall.

Several ancient clocks have quarter-boys, which strike the quarters of an hour. Among the most famous are:

1. Exeter (St Mary Steps), Devon
2. Leicester (All Saints)
3. London, Fleet Street (St Dunstan-in-the-West)
4. Rye (St Mary the Virgin), East Sussex
5. Wells Cathedral (St Andrew), Somerset
6. Wimborne Minster (St Cuthburga), Dorset

There are four astronomical clocks showing the phases of the sun and moon as well as the time. These are at:

1. Exeter Cathedral (St Peter), Devon
2. Ottery St Mary (St Mary the Virgin, St Edward the Confessor and All Saints), Devon
3. Wells Cathedral (St Andrew), Somerset
4. Wimborne Minster (St Cuthburga), Dorset

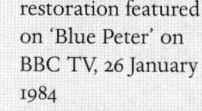

*Astronomical clock, Wimborne Minster, Dorset.*

5. Edenbridge (St Peter & St Paul), Kent
6. Edith Weston (St Mary), Rutland
7. Exeter (St Mary Steps), Devon
8. Farthinghoe (St Michael), Northamptonshire
9. Galby (St Peter), Leicestershire – its restoration featured on 'Blue Peter' on BBC TV, 26 January 1984
10. Great Glemham (All Saints), Suffolk
11. Holt (St Andrew), Norfolk
12. Kedington (St Peter and St Paul), Suffolk
13. Long Stratton (St Mary), Norfolk
14. Nether (or Lower) Winchendon (St Nicholas), Buckinghamshire
15. Northill (St Mary), Bedfordshire
16. North Stoneham (St Nicholas), Hampshire
17. Penn (Holy Trinity), Buckinghamshire
18. Rustington (St Peter & St Paul), West Sussex
19. Saxlingham Nethergate (St Mary), Norfolk
20. Selborne (St Mary), Hampshire
21. Stratford-sub-Castle (St Lawrence), Wiltshire
22. Sutton Courtenay (All Saints), Oxfordshire

With the exception of the Wells clock, these show the Earth as the centre, around which the Sun and Moon revolve – a view widely held in the Middle Ages until the Church admitted its error!

There are reputed to be 22 one-handed clocks in England at the following churches:

1. Antony (St James), Cornwall
2. Childrey (St Mary the Virgin), Oxfordshire
3. Coningsby (St Michael), Lincolnshire
4. Crosthwaite (St Kentigern), Cumbria

The hour-hand-only clock at Rustington, West Sussex, was bought in 1905 for £2. How times have changed!

# Eaton Bishop     HEREFORDSHIRE

ST MICHAEL & ALL ANGELS is a landmark for miles around being 103.6 m (340 feet) above sea level.

🔲 The fortress-like tower is crowned with a short wooden spire and has four louvered dormer windows on the cardinal faces.

🔲 Over the chancel arch is a five-light window – a feature usually found in the Cotswolds.

🔲 The five-light E window contains magnificent stained glass dating from c.1320 which was removed for safety during the Civil War and again in 1940. In the left-hand light is an exquisite panel showing the Virgin and Child. She holds Him in her left hand; He holds His mother under her chin and holds a Dove in His left hand. She holds a spray of flowers in her right hand. This is one of the most beautiful panels of medieval glass in existence.

Another panel depicts St Michael weighing souls.

The window was releaded in 1928 and again in 1970.

🔲 At the E end of the N aisle is a beautiful alabaster group of Christ blessing the children given in memory of Lady Irva Keenan Pulley, who died 28 January 1942. Note especially the lambs.

# Edenham     LINCOLNSHIRE

ST MICHAEL The village is set in beautiful countryside NW of Bourne with the fine church dominating it from its little hill.

🔲 In the N aisle are the remains of an Anglo-Saxon cross-shaft.

🔲 At the W and E ends on the inside wall, separating the S aisle from the nave, are two Anglo-Saxon roundels which were once part of the exterior decoration before the aisle was built.

🔲 On the SW wall near the tower arch is a replica of a small brass depicting Thomas à Becket. Dating from c.1500 the unique original was fixed 12.19 m (40 feet) up on the *outside* W face of the Somerset-type tower to the right of the clock. (An indentation marks the spot quite clearly.) In 1910 it was moved to the NW wall of the chancel. When Henry VIII ordered that all depictions of Thomas à Becket be destroyed, this brass escaped. Someone has said that the ladders of the iconoclasts couldn't reach high enough to prise it off the tower!

🔲 On the N side of the N aisle opposite the S doorway is a re-erected Norman arch which came from a derelict barn at Scottlethorpe. It was placed here in 1967 by the Ministry of Public Buildings and Works.

🔲 In the chancel are six memorials to the dukes and earls of Ancaster, all superbly carved by sculptors such as Scheemaeckers, Roubiliac and Nollekins. The one by Scheemaeckers depicts Robert Bertie (20 October 1660–26 July 1723). He is dressed in a Roman toga. The monument almost touches the roof.

🔲 Over the vestry door a beautiful memorial commemorates Frederick Burrell (d. 17 May 1819, aged 15 months). The baby is shown asleep in a sheet supported by an angel which, in turn, is supported by two other angels. A fourth angel waits to receive the child.

🔲 The font dates from c.1180 and has unusual two-lobed arches to the decorated columns.

# Edington     WILTSHIRE

THE PRIORY CHURCH OF ST MARY, ST KATHERINE AND ALL SAINTS This magnificent building lies just below a steep hill from which there is a superb view of the church and surrounding countryside,

*Edington, Wiltshire, built by William of Edington.*

including the beautiful church of Steeple Ashton to the N.

🔲 This church was built between 1352 and 1361 for the Augustinian order of monks by William of Edington, Bishop of Winchester. It is an important example of the transitional period in architecture from Decorated to Perpendicular.

🔲 Out of originally 24 consecration crosses, 12 remain inside and 11 outside which is very unusual. (See also Ottery St Mary, Devon, page 260 and Uffington, Oxon., page 377.)

🔲 The S porch is also unusual in possessing three storeys. Inside there is much graffiti including the date 1677.

🔲 Against the outside wall of the N transept are four shell-headed niches dating from c.1650. They were probably garden seats when the grounds of the mansion extended to the church.

🔲 On the turret of the S transept is a mass dial complete with gnomon.

🔲 The pink and white plaster ceilings of the nave, N transept and under the tower date from the seventeenth century. In the N transept or lady chapel are four vases of tulips and the date 1663. This is an early representation of this then newly imported flower. (See Tolleshunt D'Arcy, Essex, page 367.)

🔲 The chancel screen dates from c.1500 but the ceiling dates from 1789. Originally all the windows were closed (as the lower parts are now) and the grooves on each side of the central iron bars show where the wood was fitted. Before the windows were opened, the only view into the monastic choir was through the upper part of the central doors.

🔲 At the W end of the S aisle are furnishings from St Giles' Church at Imber, the evacuated village on Salisbury Plain used for military training. These include the Royal Arms of 1639, two fourteenth-century figures of knights and fragments of ancient glass. These were moved here in 1952.

◈ Against the s wall of the s transept is the tomb (c.1480) of a monk. A rebus of a bay (tree) in a tun (barrel) of wine suggests that his name may have been Bekington or Baynton.

◈ On the w wall of the s transept are numerous masons' marks including two pentagrams or five-sided stars.

◈ On the n side of the high altar is a white marble monument to Sir Simon Taylor (1783–1815) by Chantrey (c.1817). It shows a deathbed scene but the two female figures are probably allegorical because Sir Simon was a bachelor.

◈ In the chancel are eight canopied niches which once held statues. Two headless statues remain. Note the beautiful supporting figures underneath each bracket.

◈ On the s side of the chancel is the impressive tomb of Sir Edward Lewis (d. 1632) and Lady Ann Beauchamp (d. 1664). The cherub above holding the coronet is made of wood painted to look like marble.

◈ The e window has fine stained glass dating from c.1350 and shows the Crucifixion flanked by Mary and John.

◈ At the w end of the n aisle is the font with a cover dating from 1626. The fine Victorian marble mosaic floor has four roundels showing scenes from the life of Christ.

◈ It is interesting to note that the windows in the n aisle are short because the monastic buildings joined on to the church this side.

## Effingham                    SURREY

St Lawrence Just off the A246, between Guildford and Leatherhead, this church is mostly of flint and has been much restored.

◈ Aircraft designer Sir Barnes Wallis (1887–1979) is buried in the churchyard. He was the inventor of the bouncing bomb, which was used by the Dambusters in 1943 to breach the Mohne and Eder dams.

## Elford                    STAFFORDSHIRE

St Peter A fine avenue of trees leads to this church that is located about 7.24 km (4½ miles) n of Tamworth on the bank of the River Tame.

◈ Apart from the Perpendicular tower of 1598, the nave and chancel were rebuilt 1848–49 and the s aisle and chapel 1869–70.

◈ In the s chapel is a series of excellent medieval monuments. The best commemorates Sir William Smythe (d. 1525) and his two wives, one of whom was Lady Isabella Neville, niece of Warwick the Kingmaker and a cousin of Richard III.

◈ Another monument depicts the boy John Stanley, who was killed by a tennis ball c.1460. He is shown holding a ball in his left hand and pointing with the other to his head where he was fatally struck. This monument is unique. (See Tong, Shropshire, page 367 – also a Stanley!)

## Elmley Castle                    WORCESTERSHIRE

St Mary the Virgin The attractive village street runs s to the church, which is surrounded by several trees.

◈ In the n transept is a fine monument to the Savages. On the n side is Sir William Savage (d. 1616), in the centre his son, Sir Giles (d. 1631), and Lady Catherine Savage (d. 1674, aged 84). She is buried in Great

Malvern Priory. In her arms she holds her infant daughter, who was born after Sir Giles's death. The baby is dressed in long embroidered clothes with a ribbon tied around her waist and she holds a gold ball in her left hand. It is all beautifully carved in alabaster.

This is regarded as the most delightful long-clothed baby in England, although a similar baby in plainer clothes is held in its mother's arms at Bramfield, Suffolk.

Sir Giles and Lady Catherine's four sons kneel at their feet – Thomas, William, Giles and John.

Above the tomb hang an armorial unicorn's head and helmet used at Sir Giles's funeral.

Facing the Savage memorial is a huge monument of *c.*1700 in white and black marble to the first Earl of Coventry (d. 1699). Erected by his widow it was intended for Croome d'Abitot Church but the Countess's stepson would not allow it to be installed there because he said her pedigree was false and she did not come from noble stock!

The font has four unusual writhing dragons at its feet and dates from *c.*1250. The octagonal bowl dates from *c.*1500.

# Ely    CAMBRIDGESHIRE

THE CATHEDRAL CHURCH OF THE HOLY AND UNDIVIDED TRINITY This magnificent building dominates the surrounding countryside and can be seen from many miles away. It has been likened to a great ship sailing across the Fens and is sometimes called the 'Ship of the Fens'.

The separate lady chapel on the N side of the cathedral was begun in 1321 and finished in 1349; the span of the vault is 14.02 m (46 feet). This makes it the widest medieval vault and the largest lady chapel in England.

In the third bay from the W is a roof boss depicting the head of Christ wearing the Crown of Thorns. This subject is only found elsewhere on roof bosses in St Stephen's Cloister, Westminster (London), Wells Cathedral (see page 388) and Winchester (see page 415).

At the W end of the lady chapel is another boss depicting the translation of St Etheldreda and the marble coffin mentioned by the Venerable Bede.

The beautiful carvings and statues in this chapel were all defaced at the time of the Reformation. What a great tragedy caused by misguided zealots!

The unique Octagon Tower, 22.5 m (74 feet) wide, was built between 1322 and 1342 under the direction of Alan of Walsingham, following the collapse of the square Norman tower in 1322. England was scoured for the great oaks that form the eight corner-posts of the lantern. They are 19.20 m (63 feet) long. The architect of this fantastic lantern was William Hurley (d. 1354) and it has been described as 'the only true Gothic dome in existence'.

In the choir, the work of Alan of Walsingham, are several foliage bosses, at least three of them consisting of faces among the leaves. From the floor it is almost impossible to detect these faces except on the very brightest days.

In Bishop Northwold's presbytery, further E towards the high altar, is a fine roof boss depicting St Etheldreda, the foundress of Ely in 673. It is directly over the spot where her shrine stood.

There are two interesting chantry chapels:

† The earlier chapel is of Bishop Alcock (1486–1500) and occupies the E bay of the N choir aisle. The screens on the W and S sides comprise an amazing mass of canopies which is almost overpowering when one is inside. The chapel was built in

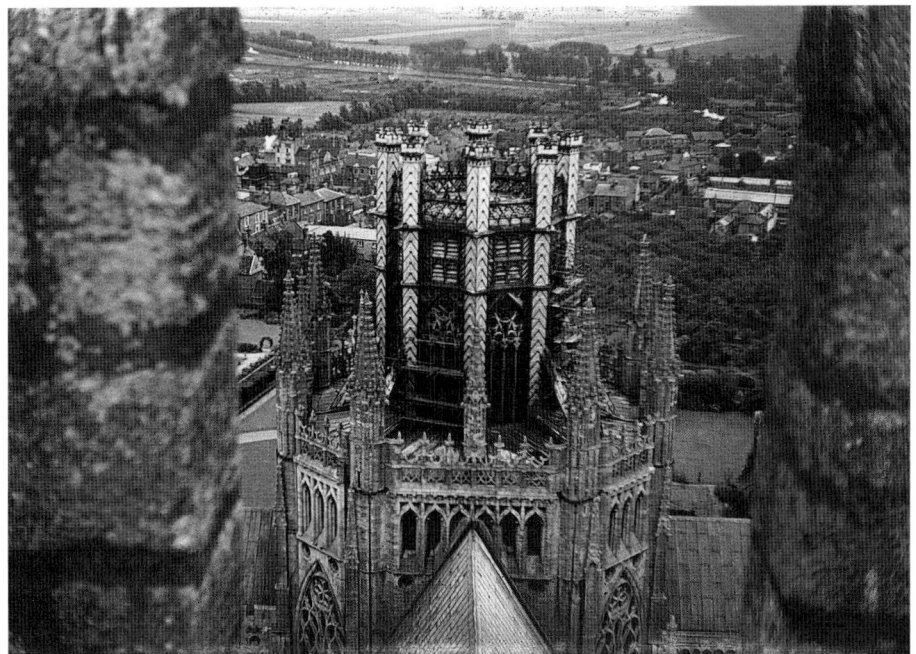

*The Octagon, Ely Cathedral, viewed from the West Tower.*

1488 and the bishop is buried under a slab in the centre of the floor although his effigy lies under the window on the N side.

The bishop's rebus, a cock on a globe, occurs quite frequently in the stonework and in the glass on each side of the doorway.

Bishop Alcock founded Jesus College, Cambridge, in 1497.

† In the corresponding bay of the s quire aisle is Bishop Nicholas West's chantry. Bishop West (1515–34) built his chantry in 1533 using an interesting blend of Gothic and Renaissance details. The chapel is famous for the large number of empty niches, which used to contain at least 200 figures! Over the entrance in the w wall is inscribed: *'Gracia Dei Sum Id Quod Sum'* (By the grace of God I am what I am).

In the N choir aisle, five bays from Bishop Alcock's chantry, the chantry tomb of Bishop Richard Redman (1501–05) is a good example of Perpendicular architecture. On the tomb is the bishop's effigy, while around the sides are shields which still contain traces of colouring.

Also in the N choir aisle is a monument in black Tournai marble to Bishop Nigel (d. 1169). Note the magnificent wings of the angel holding the napkin containing his soul.

There are 62 misericords in the choir. The second one from the w on the s side in the front depicts Tutivillus, who is mischievously eavesdropping on gossips in church.

Another misericord depicts Noah and his ark, the only example of this subject on a misericord.

In the N nave gallery is a Stained Glass Museum containing both ancient and Victorian glass.

*Ely's magnificent cathedral, known as the 'Ship of the Fens'.*

*Looking down on to one of the turrets of the southwest transept of Ely Cathedral. The matching towers on the north side collapsed in about c.1400.*

◈ Under the w tower is a maze dating from 1870 (see Church Mazes, page 278).

◈ In the porch near the s door of the cathedral is a tombstone commemorating two men, William Pickering (30) and Richard Edger (24) who died on 24 December 1845 in a railway accident. The stone is inscribed with an unusual and apt poem entitled, 'The Spiritual Railway':

'The Line to Heaven by Christ was made
With heavenly truth the Rails are laid.
From Earth to Heaven the Line extends
To Life Eternal where it ends.
Repentance is the Station then
Where Passengers are taken in
No Fee for them is there to pay
For Jesus is Himself the Way.
God's Word is the first Engineer
It points the way to Heaven so clear.
Through tunnels dark and dreary here

It does the way to Glory steer.
God's Love the Fire, His Truth the Steam,
Which drives the Engine and the Train.
All you who would to Glory ride,
Must come to Christ, in Him abide.
In First and Second, and Third Class.
Repentance, Faith and Holiness
You must the way to Glory gain
Or you with Christ will not remain.
Come then poor Sinners, now's the time
At any Station on the Line
If you'll repent and turn from sin
The Train will stop and take you in.'

## Essendon Hertfordshire

St Mary the Virgin The church is situated in the centre of the little village between Hatfield and Hertford.

◈ On the outside se wall of the church is a tablet recording the fact that the chancel,

129

organ chamber and vestry were severely damaged by bombs in a zeppelin raid on 3 September 1916 – the second church in the British Isles to be damaged in this way (the first being Snettisham, see page 322.)

▩ An ancient and magnificent Lebanon cedar stands near the tower.

▩ Against the fence of The Close is the grave of the Reverend Robert Orme, rector from 1790 to 1843. His fear was that he might be buried alive so his tomb was built above ground and in it was placed a bottle of wine and a loaf of bread, together with the key of the door to the tomb. None of these was needed!

▩ In the baptistery at the sw corner of the church is a Wedgwood font of black basalt. It was presented by Mary Whitbread in 1778. She was the daughter of Samuel Whitbread I (1720–1796), who was born at Cardington, Bedfordshire. (See Wedgwood Fonts, page 302.)

▩ In the children's corner is a charming memorial to the two children of Robert and Frances Hanbury – Robert (3 April 1866–16 May 1866) and Laura (8 November 1867–8 February 1868). Robert Hanbury, their father, died on 20 March 1867, aged 44, but his wife Frances lived on until 19 March 1916, dying at the age of 84 'after a long widowhood and much suffering'.

# Etchingham     East Sussex

THE ASSUMPTION OF ST MARY & ST NICHOLAS This magnificent fourteenth-century church is close to the busy A265 and quite near the railway line and Kent border.

On the tower is the oldest wind vane still in use in England dating from c.1370. Made of copper, it takes the form of an inverted banner and resembles the arms of Sir William de Echyngham, who rebuilt the church between 1360 and 1380.

▩ In the chancel floor is the oldest dated brass in Sussex. It commemorates Sir William de Echyngham and is dated 1388. It has been headless since 1788.

▩ The choir stalls contain 18 finely-carved misericords depicting such things as keys, foliage, fish, a woman in medieval headdress and a fox in clerical dress preaching to geese.

▩ Inside the church to the left of the s door is a memorial plaque to Sir Henry Corbould, the designer of the Penny Black, the world's first postage stamp. It is the only known pictorial representation of Corbould (d. 1844), who was a painter friend of Chantrey.

▩ The Victorian oak pulpit is noted for its fine carvings of Christ and a knight in chain mail.

▩ There is much original fourteenth-century glass in the tracery heads of many of the windows.

# Eton     BERKSHIRE

ETON COLLEGE CHAPEL This large stone chapel, standing to the s of School Yard and near the main street, can be well seen above the other college buildings.

▩ The magnificent fan-vaulted stone roof was constructed between 1957 and 1959. It replaced a wooden roof and probably fulfils the original design of its founder. It was designed by Sir William Holford. (See Fan Vaulting, page 152.)

▩ On the N side of the chapel is the small chantry chapel of Robert Lupton. Completed in 1515 it lies between a large buttress at the E and a vestry at the w. On the stone screen separating the chantry chapel from the main building is the rebus of Robert Lupton – the letters R and LUP on a tun (barrel).

▩ The fine medieval brass desk lectern dates from c.1485. It is engraved with the

college arms and the signs of the Four
Evangelists at the corners. On each side
are two scrolls above and below the coat of
arms, inscribed *'Gloria in excelsis Deo'* and
'IHC' on one side and *'In terris pax'* and
'Mercy' on the other. (See Medieval Brass
Lecterns, page 362.)

The fine E window was made by Evie
Hone between 1949 and1952 to replace one
destroyed by bombing. It shows the
Crucifixion above and the Last Supper
below.

## Eversley                    HAMPSHIRE

ST MARY is the church where Charles
Kingsley (1819–75) ministered for 31 years,
first as curate and then as rector.

Kingsley's grave in the churchyard is
marked by a Celtic cross and has on it a
Latin inscription which translated means,
'We have loved: we love: and love we
shall.' While at Eversley he wrote the
books *Yeast, Alton Locke, The Water Babies*
and *Westward Ho!*.

In the chancel is a beautiful alabaster
effigy depicting Dame Marianne Cope (d.
1862; probably an ancestor of the Cope
family who lived at nearby Bramshill
House). Her feet rest against a little dog.

## Ewelme                    OXFORDSHIRE

ST MARY THE VIRGIN is situated in a
delightful village of watercress beds above
the school and almshouses.

Near the s porch is the grave of Jerome
Klapka Jerome (d. 14 June 1927, aged 68),
author of *Three Men in a Boat*.

The church is a superb example of
Perpendicular architecture and contains a
font surmounted by a beautiful telescopic
cover reminiscent of Suffolk.

Between the chancel and the nave is a
rood screen dating from *c.*1450. It is unusual

in that it incorporates an ingenious device
allowing the doors to be opened and
closed without the use of hinges!

On the s side of the chancel is the magnificent tomb of Alice, Duchess of Suffolk
(d. 1475), granddaughter of Geoffrey
Chaucer the poet. She is shown in
alabaster, her hands in prayer and wearing
the Order of the Garter. Underneath is a
cadaver showing the Duchess in a shroud
– a grisly reminder of mortality. The tomb
is richly decorated with angels holding
shields in the lower portion, while above
they are depicted praying.

To the s of the chancel is the Chapel of
St John the Baptist, which was founded by
William de la Pole and Alice, his wife, in
1437 for the use of the people who occupy
the adjoining almshouses. The stalls are
still in use.

## Exeter                         DEVON

THE CATHEDRAL CHURCH OF ST PETER is
the only cathedral in England with a tower
on the N and s sides and transepts formed
underneath them. (Only one other church
follows this pattern – Ottery St Mary, also
in Devon, see page 260.)

At 91.44 m (300 feet) long, the magnificent roof boasts the longest unbroken
stretch of medieval vaulting in the world.
It is supported by flying buttresses outside
and on piers inside which consist of 16
shafts – more than in any other English
cathedral.

The roof bosses are very fine (there are
374 altogether) and date from *c.*1290 at the
E end to *c.*1370 at the W. The following are
particularly interesting:

† In the second bay of the nave from the
w is a magnificent boss depicting the
murder of St Thomas à Becket. The
knights are shown in the armour of 1360.
This is one of the finest roof bosses in

England. (Becket appears on roof bosses in only two other churches, namely Chester and Norwich cathedrals.)

† In the quire is a boss showing the head and shoulders of a pope, his hands raised as though supporting the vaulting ribs. (Only two other churches have roof bosses depicting heads of popes – Beaulieu, Hants., and Burwell, Cambs.)

† In the quire is a boss showing a mermaid holding her tail.

† Also in the quire is a boss showing the Crucifixion – the earliest depiction on a roof boss and one of five Crucifixions in the cathedral. (Only nine other churches contain Crucifixion bosses.)

† In the ambulatory are some magnificent bosses depicting natural foliage, one of which shows six caterpillars eating leaves! These caterpillar carvings are unique in England and the foliage bosses are among the most realistic in the British Isles.

Many of these roof bosses have had their colouring and gilding renewed so that they now look much as they would have done in medieval times.

▣ On the N side of the nave is the minstrels' gallery, dating from c.1350 and showing 14 angels playing musical instruments.

▣ In the quire is the bishop's throne, dating from c.1316. At 18.29 m (60 feet) high and made of oak, it is the finest of its kind in existence. In 1939 it was dismantled and removed to a place of safety, together with the medieval glass from the E window.

▣ In the spandrels of the quire arches are beautiful corbels supporting the vaulting. Dating from c.1310 some show foliage, the Virgin and Child with angels and the Coronation of the Virgin.

▣ The E window of the quire contains magnificent stained glass, most of it dating from 1390, but some is from the earlier window of 1303, which it replaced.

▣ The 50 misericords in the quire, most of them dating from c.1230 to 1260, are the earliest set in Britain. Among the most interesting are:

† The Exeter elephant with hooves of a cow. This dates from c.1260 and is the oldest carving of an elephant in Britain.

† A beautiful pair of gloved hands holding up the seat.

† A depiction of King Herod bathing in hot oil. Dating from c.1450 this is a rare subject in England.

▣ The medieval brass eagle lectern in the quire dates from c.1450 but the bookrest was added later. There are three lions at the base. (See Medieval Brass Lecterns, page 362.)

▣ On the S side of the quire is an elaborate canopied sedilia with three seats for the clergy. The two delicate central pillars supporting the canopy are made of *brass* instead of stone or marble – a unique survival.

▣ On the S side of the S quire aisle is the double chapel of St James. After its destruction by a bomb on 4 May 1942 it was rebuilt by George Down, whose ashes rest beneath the corbel showing his head in the SE corner.

▣ At the E end of the cathedral is the lady chapel dating from c.1280. The E window contains modern stained glass depicting the triumph of good over evil. It was made by Marion Grant in 1948 and is one of the first stained-glass windows to be made by a woman in England.

▣ Also in the lady chapel is a beautiful wood carving of the Christmas shepherds made by Devon craftsmen c.1380. Note the recorder player!

▣ On the S side of the lady chapel is the magnificent tomb of Bishop Bronescombe (d. 1280) with the canopy and base dating from 1442. This is the cathedral's finest monument.

*Exeter Cathedral, Devon. Its uniquely-placed northern tower complements the southern one.*

⊠ Opposite Bishop Bronescombe's tomb is that of Bishop Stafford (d. 1419) which is identical. Stafford's canopy and base were copied for Bronescombe's tomb.

⊠ On the NE side of the retroquire is St George's chapel occupying Sir John Speke's (d. 1517) chantry chapel. With the Oldham chantry opposite they are superb examples of the Perpendicular style.

When the cathedral was divided in two after the Civil War of the seventeenth century, a doorway was made in the E wall of Speke's chantry and was used until c.1790.

⊠ In the N quire aisle at the w end is a beautiful banner of Our Lady made in 1931 by Miss Longridge in memory of her niece Eileen O' Neill Haines and her baby, both of whom died at childbirth. Eileen's face represents the Virgin Mary.

⊠ In the N transept is an ancient clock which was probably given by Bishop Courtenay (Bishop from 1478 to 1487). The earth is in the centre with the moon revolving around it. The sun (fleur-de-lys) marks the hours. The dial above dates from 1760 and the Latin motto means, 'The days pass and are reckoned to our account'.

⊠ In the N nave aisle is a charming Elizabethan memorial to Matthew Godwin, organist, who died in 1586 aged 17 years and 5 months. He is shown kneeling in front of an organ with other musical instruments behind him. This is the earliest monument to a musician in the British Isles.

⊠ Just E of the nave pulpit is a unique corbel dating from 1310 which shows an acrobat with his feet in the air while an angel plays a musical instrument below.

⊠ On the s side of the central doorway in the w wall of the cathedral, in between the w wall and the w screen outside, is the curiously placed chantry chapel of Bishop Grandisson (Bishop from 1327 to 1369),

who completed the cathedral we see today. His body was removed in the sixteenth century. The large roof boss inside shows Christ in Majesty.

⊠ The sledge flag carried by Captain Robert Falcon Scott is displayed at the w end of the s aisle. He was leader of the national Antarctic expeditions, 1900–04, 1910–12, and died after reaching the South Pole in 1912. The flag was presented by his mother.

⊠ The w screen outside contains statues of kings, prophets and apostles. Notice the tiny windows to the s of the central doorway which admit light into the Grandisson chapel, and the fine Decorated window above with a pentagonal star in the tracery.

⊠ The chapter house on the s side of the cathedral was restored in 1969. New figures were later inserted in the niches. Sculptured by Kenneth Carter and dating from 1975 they are based on the theme of Creation.

⊠ In the cathedral library, which is housed in the bishop's palace, are 20,000 books and 6000 manuscripts including the famous *Exeter Book* dating from AD950.

⊠ In the s tower is the second-heaviest ring of 12 bells in the world. The tenor, 'Grandisson', weighs 3684.13 kg (3 tons 12 cwt 2 qr 2 lb) and 'Great Peter' weighs 4064 kg (4 tons). (See Bells, page 293.)

## Exton RUTLAND

ST PETER & ST PAUL is set in a park outside the village and is very peaceful.

⊠ The tower and spire are particularly fine, the tower having embattled turrets crowned with an eight-sided lantern and spire rising from it.

⊠ The interior contains a fine collection of sculptured monuments dating from c.1550 to c.1750.

In the N transept is an enormous monument by Grinling Gibbons commemorating Baptist Noel, Third Viscount Campden, who died on 29 October 1683, aged 71. He and his wife stand either side of an urn, and underneath a charming relief shows some of their 19 children.

Other medallions show typical Gibbons naturalistic carving which is especially beautiful. This is one of the few works carved in marble by Gibbons, who usually worked in wood.

At the W end of the N aisle a monument by Nollekens commemorates Lt G. Bennett Noel (d. 17 September 1766, aged 51).

Near by, a marble effigy on a table-tomb depicts Anne, wife of Lord Bruce of Kinlosse. She died in childbirth on 20 March 1627, aged 22. Notice she lies in a shroud with a pelican at her feet holding a snake.

In the chancel a finely carved memorial by Nollekens commemorates Baptist Noel, his wife, Elizabeth, and Thomas Noel, her second husband. Baptist (d. 21 March 1751, aged 43), Elizabeth (d. 15 December 1771, aged 64) and Thomas (d.18 January 1788, aged 83).

Notice a cherub holding medallions of the three persons commemorated. They are being 'tied' to the apex of the monument by a flying cherub.

Opposite this monument is another fine one of 1591 commemorating Sir James Harrington and his wife, Lucy. They kneel facing each other.

At the W end of the S aisle, near the door, a fine alabaster table-tomb of 1524 depicts John Harrington and Alice, his wife. Notice angels at her head and a defaced figure holding beads at his feet.

## Eyam       DERBYSHIRE

ST LAWRENCE This village will always be associated with the Great Plague of London, which reached here at the end of August 1665 in a parcel of clothes, killing 260 people out of a population of 350. Catherine Mompesson, the rector's wife, was among those who died.

High up on the walls inside the church are the remains of wall paintings dating from c.1600, discovered in 1963.

In the chancel is the chair used by William Mompesson, inscribed 'MOM 1665 EYAM'. A brass plaque states: 'This chair formerly the property of the Rev. William Mompesson, Rector, was presented for use in the church of Eyam by the Rev. Egbert Hacking, 1885–1888.' The chair was found in a Liverpool junk shop c.1880.

In the N aisle is the Plague Window, showing scenes and people associated with the Great Plague of 1665.

On the S side of the chancel, outside, is a large sundial dating from 1775, showing place names and signs of the zodiac.

Near by is the tomb of Catherine Mompesson (d. 16 August 1666). Every year on Plague Sunday (the last Sunday in August) a wreath of roses is placed on the tomb by the present rector's wife.

Also nearby is a magnificent Celtic cross dating from c.AD750. On the arms of the cross are angels. This is one of the finest Saxon crosses in England.

# STORIES ABOUT MEDIEVAL BRASS LECTERNS

Many lecterns have interesting stories attached to them or boast something unusual or worthy of note.

✠ At the Reformation (1540 onwards) several lecterns were hidden or buried to prevent their destruction. The one at Croft, Lincolnshire, was found in a ditch (having had its silver claws stolen) and Isleham, Cambridgeshire, retrieved its lectern from Isleham Fen, *c.*1850.

✠ The lectern at Cropredy, Oxfordshire (dating from *c.*1450), was retrieved from the River Cherwell, where it had been thrown during a Civil War skirmish on 28 June 1644 then subsequently lost. When it was found (which may have been quite soon after the Civil War) a lion was missing from its feet, so a new one was added in bronze on the assumption that the lectern was made of this metal (it was completely black when it was taken out of the river). It was only once the whole lectern had been cleaned that the mistake was discovered!

✠ When the Puritans wanted to sell the eagle lectern at Holy Trinity Church in Coventry, West Midlands, in 1654, the church-wardens moved it from its ancient position in the choir instead and it is said to have been used as a collection box to raise funds for

*Clare, Suffolk*

Cromwell's New Model Army. Of course, C. C. Oman would not have been convinced (see page 465)!

✠ The lectern at Wells-next-the-Sea, Norfolk, was recovered from a field near the church known as Church Marsh, where it had been buried to escape destruction. Halfway down the stem is a hole, allegedly made by the pickaxe of the workman who found it and nearby is a large dent. The exact date of its discovery is unknown but in 1879 a disastrous fire destroyed the church. The bells and lead roof melted but, miraculously, the lectern survived (if indeed it was in the church at the time). A piece of the tail feathers was cut out and stolen *c.*1970.

✠ The famous lectern at Southwell Cathedral, Nottinghamshire, was recovered from the lake at Newstead Abbey, 16.09 km (10 miles) west of Southwell *c.*1750 when the lake was drained. It was probably thrown there by the monks in 1539, together with a pair of candlesticks (also retrieved from the lake), when the abbey was dissolved by Henry VIII and sold to Sir John Byron. After the lectern's discovery it was sent to Nottingham for cleaning and was purchased in 1775 from the fifth Lord Byron (great uncle of the famous poet) by Sir Richard Kaye, who, as dean of Lincoln, gave it to Southwell Minster in 1805. Numerous accounts have been given of the abbey deeds and other documents having been hidden and subsequently found in the pedestal of the lectern but nobody can prove whether or not this is correct. It would seem unlikely that such documents could survive 200 years in a lake!

✠ A magnificent lectern that was for some time at St Stephen's Church in St Albans, Hertfordshire, was actually given originally to Holyrood Abbey, Edinburgh, in 1522 by Bishop Crichton of Dunkeld to commemorate his abbacy at Holyrood from 1515 to 1524. It was taken to St Stephen's in 1544 by Sir Richard Lee, to whom Henry VIII had granted the monastic buildings

*Oxborough, Norfolk.*

of Holyrood at the Dissolution. During the English Civil War (which began in 1642) the lectern was hidden, presumably so that it would escape destruction, and was only rediscovered in 1748 when the Montague family tomb in the chancel of St Stephen's was opened for an internment.

From 1748 until 1972 it was in continuous use in St Stephen's Church; I was often asked to read a lesson from the Holy Bible placed upon it! Then, in 1972, the lectern fell victim to thieves who, although disturbed as they tried to steal the lectern, managed to remove the three lions at the base. These were later recovered and kept in the church safe.

In November 1984 a group of Scottish Nationalists broke into the church and removed the lectern to Scotland. They then sent a photograph of it to the press, along with this message, 'This piece of our heritage is here to stay . . . patriotic Scots have asked for the eagle to be returned . . . to its rightful home. English arrogance won the day . . . all requests were refused.' In subsequent letters to the press the thieves stipulated that they would not release the lectern unless an absolute guarantee was given that it would remain in Scotland and that no action would be taken that would lead to their prosecution.

When St Stephen's agreed to support the return of the lectern to Scotland, St Margaret's Church in Barnhill, Dundee, generously offered the English church a slightly smaller but excellent Victorian replica of the Dunkeld lectern. This was delivered to St Stephen's in 1995. The eagle's feet rest on an orb; between the eagle's talons on the front of the orb and also on the back is a bishop's crozier and underneath is the following inscription: *'Joannes Jabezus Warlon In Mem Grorgii Czrichtoun Epilcopi Dunkeldenlis'*. This is the lectern that can be seen in St Stephen's Church today.

It was not until 30 April 1999 that the original Dunkeld lectern reappeared, when it was delivered anonymously to the Netherbow Arts Centre in Edinburgh. After careful examination it was found to be undamaged (except for its missing feet) and is now in the care of the National Museum of Scotland. When the legal processes are complete the lectern will remain in Scotland and will one day be joined by its feet!

✠ The eagle lectern at North Cerney, Gloucestershire, was found in pieces in a marine stores at Gloucester Docks and given to the church as a memorial c.1920. It is late fifteenth-century Flemish work, but the stand is contemporary Spanish. It is possible that when Spain ruled the Low Countries, a Spanish nobleman took the eagle back with him for a church in Spain and there supplied it with a stand. How it arrived in Gloucester Docks in numerous pieces is, so far, a complete mystery.

*Clare, Suffolk.*

✠ The lectern at Redenhall, Norfolk dates from c.1500 and is the only medieval lectern in the British Isles to have an eagle with two heads! The only other example of a two-headed eagle lectern is in Venice, Italy, but it is quite unlike the one at Redenhall.

✠ At Upwell, Norfolk, the lectern has had a cock's comb added to the eagle's head. The three lions at the base were once used as scrapers at the church door!

✠ The beautiful lectern at St Mary the Virgin in Wiggenhall, Norfolk, left the church for London in 1951 when it was exhibited at the Festival of Britain. Twenty-nine years separate my seeing it there and again at Wiggenhall in 1980.

✠ Nikolaus Pevsner, author and editor of *The Buildings of England*, names one other church as home to a medieval brass lectern – Billingford, near East

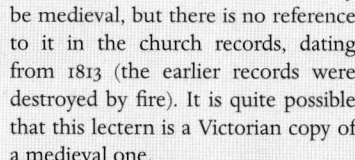

Dereham, Norfolk. However, this lectern is not brass but cast-iron, as was confirmed by the vicar, the Reverend Albert Derisley, who tested it with a magnet in 1981. It has a blackish or dark grey appearance and the surface is rather pitted. Traces of surface colour can be removed but there is not enough of it to give the impression of brass as was obviously originally intended. The eagle is broken and has been repaired with a plate, probably the work of a local blacksmith. According to tradition, the lectern was dug up from a field near the church and its date of manufacture is unknown. It may be medieval, but there is no reference to it in the church records, dating from 1813 (the earlier records were destroyed by fire). It is quite possible that this lectern is a Victorian copy of a medieval one.

✠ The lectern at Wolborough, Devon, was hidden in Lang's Copse near Bradley Manor during the Civil War and returned to the church c.1661, after Charles II had been restored to the throne.

✠ The lectern at Chipping Campden, Gloucestershire, has semiprecious stones for the eyes, eight talons altogether and a sealed tail. A lady who cleaned it told me that sometimes it rattled when she moved it, so perhaps there are some loose coins inside!

With so many medieval 'brass' lecterns having been hidden during the Civil War, how many more await discovery?

# BERTEL THORVALDSEN (1770-1844)

Bertel Thorvaldsen, the famous Danish sculptor, was the son of an Icelandic woodcarver. He was probably born in Copenhagen, where his parents had settled, and after studying there until 1797 he travelled to Rome. He spent most of his working life having been very impressed by the influence of classical sculpture and drew the attention of the noted sculptor Canova.

In 1838 he returned to Copenhagen to end his days. The following year work started on a neo-classical museum (now called the Thorvaldsen Museum), which he endowed and paid for from his fortune. The museum houses his works of art and sculpture, which he left to the people of Denmark. At his own request he was buried in the court-yard of the museum.

Among his works are several statues in Copenhagen Cathedral including 'Christ and the Twelve Apostles' and the 'Preaching of St John the Baptist'. There is also a famous monument, carved in granite (1819–21) and overlooking Lake Lucerne, Switzerland, entitled 'The Lion of Lucerne'. This commemorates some of the Swiss guards who died during the defence of the Palais des Tuileries in Paris at the commencement of the French Revolution in 1792.

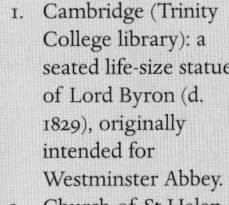

*Statue of Lord Byron,*
*Trinity College Library, Cambridge*

In England there are, as far as I know, only five examples of his work, as follows:

1. Cambridge (Trinity College library): a seated life-size statue of Lord Byron (d. 1829), originally intended for Westminster Abbey.
2. Church of St Helen, Escrick (North Yorkshire): Lady Lawley (d. 1816), shown kneeling between two angels, one of whom holds an hour-glass and the other a scroll.
3. Manchester (Heaton Park): a seated sculpture of Theseus in the entrance hall.
4. Roman Catholic church of St Richard in Slindon (West Sussex): the monument commemorates Antony, Earl of Newburgh (d. 1814) and shows a kneeling woman on one side of a column and a standing angel on the other. The details of the carving are exquisite and well worth seeing.
5. Wheathampstead (Hertfordshire): high up in the N transept a wall tablet in memory of Charles Drake Garrard (d. 1817) shows two Greek figures holding hands.

*Fairford, Gloucestershire: (Top) Window showing the 'Breaking of the Bread at Emmaus' in the Risen Christ window. (Bottom right and left) Misericords on the underside of wooden seats.*

# Fairford

GLOUCESTERSHIRE

ST MARY THE VIRGIN was almost completely rebuilt between *c.*1490 and 1500 by the wool merchant John Tame.

 The church is unique in the British Isles for its large amount of pre-Reformation stained glass dating from *c.*1497. There is a complete set of 28 windows. They were carefully restored from 1986 onwards by Keith Barley of York.

 The windows illustrate the Bible story from Adam and Eve to the Life of Jesus and the Last Judgement. In the Crucifixion scene over the high altar the heads are all missing! These were removed during the Civil War by General Morgan and in claiming that he had 'defaced' the windows the rest were miraculously spared.

 The most spectacular window in the church is the great w window comprising seven lights. It shows Christ in Majesty encircled by a rainbow and surrounded by the Heavenly Host. Below Him is the Last Judgement, and how frightening it looks!

The greatest damage to the stained glass was sustained by this window during a storm in 1703. The restorers allowed the whole of the glass in the window between the transom and tracery to be copied and used the copy as a replacement instead of the original!

 The clerestory windows on the s side of the nave show saints and martyrs of the Church while those on the N side portray the persecutors.

 Other windows in the church show apostles and prophets.

 The 14 misericords in the chancel choir stalls are very fine and also date from *c.* 1480. One shows two entwined wyverns – mythical heraldic beasts. A wyvern appears on John Tame's crest.

 Separating the choir from the lady chapel is a screen under which is the Purbeck marble tomb-chest of John Tame. On the tomb-chest are the brasses of John Tame (d. 8 May 1500) and Alice, his wife, who died 20 December 1471 after the birth of their fourth baby, Edmund. John never married again.

At their feet the following verse appears:

'For Jesus love, pray for me,
I may not pray now pray ye,
With a Paternoster and an Ave,
That my paynes relessyd may be.'

 In the lady chapel are several other brasses including one to Sir Edmund Tame (John's son) and his two wives, Agnes and Elizabeth. They are shown at the foot of the altar steps and also kneeling at a faldstool on a brass on the N wall. Over the latter brass is a fine representation of the Holy Trinity.

 The central tower has an unusual parapet comprising huge quatrefoils which are purely ornamental – a man could easily fall through its openings. The corner buttresses are also unusual with pedestals and niches for statues, many of which are now empty, although on the w face of the

middle stage is a niche complete with an original figure of the Risen Christ or Christ of Pity dating from *c*.1490.

The buttresses terminate in two pinnacles on each corner of the tower.

The inside of the tower is peculiar and similar to that in Cricklade, Wiltshire. The bells are rung by the ringers standing in the choir stalls!

Inside the church are 69 stone-carved angels supporting or finishing the roof timbers. Some carry scrolls or shields and some are better carved than others. Those in the N aisle may have been carved by an apprentice or inexperienced craftsman.

On the S wall of the sanctuary is a marble tablet erected to the memory of the father and two sisters of John Keble (1792–1866), author of *The Christian Year*, who was born at Fairford and is buried at Hursley, Hampshire.

The fine fan vault inside the S porch dates from 1892. It replaced a groined stone roof removed in 1835. (See Fan Vaulting, page 152.)

# Fenny Bentley     DERBYSHIRE

ST EDMUND This spired church is situated on the busy A515, between Ashbourne and Buxton.

The nave and chancel are covered by a fine Victorian hammer-beam roof with 26 angels, some of whom are praying, singing and playing musical instruments. At the extreme E end are two trumpet players. The roof was completed in 1895.

Across the chancel is a fine wooden screen with vaulted canopy dating from 1511. The corresponding screen across the N aisle is smaller and is called a parclose screen. It dates from 1519.

Just inside the chancel screen on the N side is the unique table-tomb of Thomas

and Agnes Beresford. They are both depicted covered completely in shrouds, tied in three places. Thomas, the larger, died in 1473 and Agnes in 1467, but the effigies were not executed until many years later. Perhaps the sculptor had no idea how the Beresfords looked so opted for shrouds as if to show that all people will end up like this!

Around the tomb their 16 sons and 5 daughters are also depicted in shrouds.

The epitaph on the tomb ends with these words:

'As you now are, soe once were wee, And as wee are soe shall you bee.'

(A single shrouded figure appears on an unknown Foljambe monument, *c*.1580–90, in Chesterfield, Derbyshire, perhaps carved by the same sculptor as the Beresford tomb.)

# Fenstanton     CAMBRIDGESHIRE

ST PETER & ST PAUL The stone spire of this church dominates the village, which lies on the busy A14, between Huntingdon and Cambridge, in the former county of Huntingdonshire.

On the N side of the chancel there is a monument to Lancelot Brown (1715–83), perhaps better known as 'Capability Brown', the famous landscape designer, who is buried here. Note the reference to his landscaping in the rhyming epitaph.

# Flamborough     EAST RIDING OF YORKSHIRE

ST OSWALD Situated in a little village not far from the famous chalk cliffs of Flamborough Head, the church has been much restored but is still well worth a visit.

Here is one of only two ancient rood

screens complete with loft remaining in Yorkshire. (The other is at Hubberholme.) It may have come from Bridlington Priory at the Dissolution.

🔲 Between the chancel and the s chapel is another old screen, on the back of which are carvings of ships done by pilgrims, including a large ship upside down!

🔲 Observe how the Norman chancel arch leans outwards – probably due to poor foundations.

🔲 At the e end of the n aisle is a modern stained-glass window designed by L. C. Evetts in 1966, inscribed, 'I am come a Light into the World'. It was given in memory of James and Catherine Woodhouse and Margaret Hephzibah and John Farrer Wilkinson.

🔲 In the vestry is a pair of white paper gloves dating from 1761, now protected by a frame. They formed part of the maidens' garlands custom. (See Maidens' Garlands, page 24.)

## Fletching                    East Sussex

St Andrew & St Mary the Virgin The church, located in a lovely village, has a fine shingled broach spire on its w tower.

🔲 In the s transept, mounted upon a stone slab, is a brass to Peter Denot. The brass shows a pair of gloves, indicating his vocation as a glover. Peter Denot (d. 1440) took part in Jack Cade's rebellion but was subsequently pardoned.

🔲 Also in the s transept is a fine brass on a table-tomb to a member of the Dalyngrugge family, probably Sir Edward or Sir Walter, and his wife, c.1386. It is unusual in possessing a central shaft between the double canopy over their heads. He built Bodiam Castle, East Sussex.

Above the tomb is a unicorn over a shield.

🔲 In the n transept below the two Early English windows is a Decorated piscina in which the apex of the hood-mould terminates as a stone bracket with a flat top for an effigy – an unusual position for a bracket. It dates from c.1340.

🔲 Adjoining the n transept is the Sheffield Mausoleum in which is buried Edward Gibbon (1737–94), who wrote *The History of the Decline and Fall of the Roman Empire.*

🔲 The chancel, dating from 1880, is wider than the nave, which is unusual, and at 15.24 m (50 feet) long it is exceptional for a village church. Its width is 6.9 m (22.5 feet).

## Fotheringhay                    Northamptonshire

St Mary & All Saints is a beautiful church standing in splendid isolation overlooking the River Nene. It is not far from the earthworks that supported the now-vanished castle where Mary Queen of Scots was beheaded on 8 February 1587.

🔲 The building we see today is all that remains of the church, choir and college built c.1370–1440. After the Dissolution, Edward VI granted the college in 1553 to Dudley, Duke of Northumberland, who demolished the choir and college, allegedly for the lead covering their roofs and for the stone, which was later used in other local buildings.

🔲 The superb lantern tower is 31.4 m (103 feet) high and inside has a fan-vaulted roof. (See Fan Vaulting, page 152.)

🔲 On the n side of the communion table is the monument to Richard Plantagenet, third Duke of York (d. 1460) and Cicely, his wife (d. 1495).

🔲 On the opposite side is a similar monument to their son, Edmund de Langley (d. 1402) and Edward, second Duke of York, his uncle.

*Fotheringhay, Northamptonshire – the beautiful church reflected in the River Nene.*

Both of these Renaissance monuments were erected in 1573 by Queen Elizabeth I, who had the Plantagenets moved from the choir after its destruction.

 On the N side of the nave is the lovely fifteenth-century wooden pulpit. At the back are the Arms of France and England quarterly, and underneath the seventeenth-century canopy is delicate fan tracery.

## Frome                          SOMERSET

ST JOHN The parish church, with its prominent spire, is built on the side of a hill, near the centre of this small town.

 Underneath the outside of the E window is the tomb of Bishop Ken (1637–1711) – a mausoleum with iron railings on the N and S sides. Inside, resting on blue and red tiles, there is an iron morte-safe on which rest a crozier and mitre, also made of iron. On a plaque on the E wall is an epitaph, ordered by Bishop Ken himself, which reads:

'May the here interred Thomas, Bp. of Bath and Wells and uncanonically deprived for not transferring his allegiance, have a perfect consummation of Bliss both of body and soul, of which God keep me always mindfull.'

Two famous hymns that he wrote are 'Awake, my soul, and with the sun' and 'Glory to Thee, my God, this night'.

 The four westernmost piers of the nave have no capitals but large bases which may have been seats. They mark the extension of the nave *c.*1410.

 Above the N porch is a parvise room approached by a flight of narrow stone steps. On the wall near by is an interesting

# MEDIEVAL BRONZE EFFIGIES

Only ten medieval bronze or latten effigies from the period *c*.1250–1530 exist in England and Wales. Being less vulnerable than wood or stone, they cost more to make and therefore only the wealthy could afford to be commemorated in this way. It is also not surprising that the biggest collection of these bronze effigies is in Westminster Abbey, England's national shrine.

The ten effigies are located as follows:

1. Canterbury Cathedral, Kent – Edward, the Black Prince, 1376.

*Westminster Abbey, London*
2. Henry III, 1291

3. Eleanor of Castile, 1291
4. Edward III, 1377
5. Richard II, 1399
6. Anne of Bohemia, 1394
7. Lady Margaret Beaufort, Duchess of Richmond, 1511
8. Henry VII, 1518
9. Elizabeth of York, 1518
   (These last three effigies were made by the famous sculptor Pietro Torrigiano, specially commissioned by Prior Bolton.)

10. St Mary in Warwick – Richard Beauchamp, Earl of Warwick, 1457.

stone corbel showing two heads with only three eyes between them!

 At the E end of the N aisle is the baptistery, the N window of which contains stained glass dating from *c*.1510.

The floor slabs represent the seven virtues and the seven deadly sins. The wall decoration is in the form of hanging curtains complete with creases – all carved in stone.

To the E of the baptistery is the lady chapel. On the N side of this chapel is an altar tomb with a gruesome cadaver underneath. This may represent Edmund Leversedge.

On the s side of the chancel is St Andrew's chapel. It is also known as the Chapel of Blessed Thomas Ken and contains portraits of him in the E window and in oils. There is a modern statue (1961) of him near the entrance.

Adjoining St Andrew's chapel is the tower which occupies an unusual position on the s side of the church. On the N side of the tower, are two carved Saxon stones, the lower depicting a galloping animal. They may have formed part of a Saxon cross.

In the nave are 18 medallions in the spandrels of the arches dating from *c*.1860. Those on the N side depict Christ's miracles; those on the s His parables.

At the w end of the s aisle is a memorial brass to Richard Antrum, 'clothyer' (d. 1597).

The spire is 42.4 m (139 feet) high.

*The ostentatious south aisle of Gaddesby, Leicestershire.*

# Gaddesby
LEICESTERSHIRE

St Luke The beautiful stone spire of this impressive church dominates the village, which lies in remote countryside.

 The N and S aisles have lovely exterior stonework, with pinnacles, a frieze and canopied niches, the S aisle being particularly elaborate.

 At the W end of the S aisle is an unusual window like a rounded triangle.

 Among the pews are 18 medieval benches and an eighteenth-century panelled box pew.

 On the N side of the chancel is a fine three-quarter-size equestrian statue depicting Colonel Edward Cheyney (d. 1848). He is shown astride one of the four horses shot from under him at the Battle of Waterloo in 1815. The inscription reads, 'Edward H. Cheyney, C.B., Colonel in the Army Late Scots Greys'. Underneath is a carved panel showing a scene from Waterloo with foot soldiers and horsemen.

Notice the wound between the horse's front legs where it has been shot.

This marble statue was carved by Joseph Gott and came from Gaddesby Hall, the home of the Cheyneys, in 1917. It is the only marble statue of a horse inside an English church, apart from one in St Paul's Cathedral, London. (See Horses in Churches, page 413.)

# Gatcombe
Isle of Wight

St Olave is situated in secluded countryside near Godshill.

 Around the top of the tower are an interesting display of corbel heads.

 Under an arch on the NE side of the chancel is the oaken effigy of a knight, 1.55 m (5 feet 11 inches) long. It may commemorate a knight of the Estur family. He holds a shield in his left hand supported on a strap and his right hand holds a short sword. His right leg is crossed over his left and both feet rest on a lion. His surcoat reaches to his knees, and on the left side of his head, which rests on a cushion, is a small angel with outstretched wings.

The whole figure rests on a low wooden bench and is in excellent condition. Several experts believe that this figure is an anachronism dating from c.1620 and not from c.1300 as the style would suggest. Some have even suggested that perhaps a village carpenter has mutilated it by later re-cutting; certainly the head would appear to be a restoration. (See Wooden Effigies, page 246.)

 In a S window of the nave the tracery contains fifteenth-century yellow glass showing four angels – the only surviving medieval glass in the Isle of Wight.

 In the chancel, which dates from 1865, the windows are all filled with Pre-Raphaelite stained glass by William Morris, Burne-Jones, Ford Maddox Brown and Dante Gabriel Rossetti.

Sir John Betjeman considered the E

window to be one of the most interesting and attractive examples of this group of artists.

■ At the w end of the nave is a marble monument carved by Sir Thomas Brock (his last work). It commemorates Charles Seely and the inscription reads:

'We pray you commend to the mercy of God the soul of Charles Grant Seely, eldest son of Sir Charles Seely, Baronet, and Dame Hilda his wife. Born on Nov. 29, 1894, and educated at Cheam, Eton and Trinity College, Cambridge, he joined the Isle of Wight Rifles at the outbreak of the Great War and, after serving with distinction in the Gallipoli and Egyptian campaigns, fell gloriously, thrice wounded, at Gaza in Palestine on April 19, 1917, while leading the advance upon the Turkish position.

Greatly beloved – for he was a very gallant gentleman – he lies in the cemetery at Gaza, surrounded by the men of his regiment who fell with him that day.
MIZPAH'

The effigy depicts the young soldier holding his sword with clasped hands. His nose and sword handle are damaged; this was done soon after completion by a patient with mental health difficulties from a local hospital.

## Gloucester

The Cathedral Church of the Holy and Indivisible Trinity The magnificent cathedral (a former Benedictine abbey) is well seen from Robinswood Hill to the s.

■ At 68.6 m (225 feet) high, the beautiful central tower dates from c.1450 and is a superb example of the Perpendicular style.

■ There are 12 ringing bells in the tower. In 1978 they were taken down, two new ones added (to make up the 12), three were recast and several retuned. The eleventh bell bears a Latin inscription dated 1626 and which, translated, says: 'I have the name of Gabriel'. The inscription has been cast back to front and inside out!

The new ring of bells was rung officially for the first time on 31 March 1979.

■ The Bourdon bell in the tower known as 'Great Peter' weighs 2946.6 kg (2 tons 18 cwt) and dates from c.1450. It is 1.74 m (5 feet 8 ½ inches) across the mouth and is the largest medieval bell remaining in England.

■ The great E window of the choir is the second largest stained-glass window in the British Isles but the largest in England containing stone tracery. (The largest is the baptistery window at Coventry Cathedral.) It measures 21.94 m (72 feet) high by 11.58 m (38 feet) wide and dates from c.1350. Known as the Crécy Window it commemorates knights and local barons who fought at the Battle of Crécy in 1346. At the base is a roundel of glass depicting a golfer! In the apex of the window is the figure of Pope Clement I, added c.1450. The predominant colours of this window are red and blue.

Notice that the window is actually wider than the choir and the walls turn outwards to meet it. Running behind the window is a whispering gallery approached from the triforium.

■ Below this huge window and in front of the high altar is the wooden effigy of Robert, Duke of Normandy, eldest son of William the Conqueror, who died in 1134 in Cardiff Castle.

The effigy is 1.78 m (5 feet 10 inches) long, dates from c.1280 and shows Robert wearing a long red surcoat open up the middle over a hauberk that fits over his

*The exquisite fan-vaulted cloisters at Gloucester Cathedral.*

head, leaving a space for his face. On his head he wears a coronet ornamented with strawberry leaves and fleurs-de-lys, fastened by a strap passing through the mail across his forehead and down the right side of his face. His head rests on a red cushion, his right leg is crossed over his left and his right hand grasps the handle of his sword. Iron spurs have been added to his feet.

The wooden tomb-chest on which the effigy rests dates from c.1400 and has ten painted shields of arms around it.

This effigy, protected by an iron hearse, is one of the oldest in the British Isles. (See also Warwick, St Mary, West Tanfield, N. Yorks., and Wooden Effigies, page 246.)

In the vaulted roof of the choir, remodelled c.1337–67, are bosses showing numerous angels, many of them holding different musical instruments including a harp, organ, bagpipes, trumpet etc. while others hold instruments of the Passion including the cross, nails, spear and Crown of Thorns.

Being so high up, at 28.04 m (92 feet) above the floor, this wonderful roof escaped the iconoclasts at the time of the Reformation.

In the choir is an interesting graffito showing a medieval archer complete with his bow and quiver.

Among the interesting subjects depicted on the misericords in the choir are the following:

† a unique carving on a misericord showing Delilah cutting off the hair of sleeping Samson

† a hawking scene showing a rider on horseback wearing a peculiar hat and suit

† two men playing with a ball, which may be an early form of football!

† Eve giving Adam the forbidden fruit while the Devil grins at both of them.

On the N side of the high altar in the N ambulatory is the tomb of King Edward II, who was murdered in Berkeley Castle in 1327. The beautiful pinnacled canopy and superb effigy of the king attracted many pilgrims in the Middle Ages and their gifts made possible the rebuilding, remodelling and enlarging of the Norman cathedral we see today.

E of King Edward's tomb is a little stone cross, which was carved by Lieutenant Colonel J. P. Carne VC, DSO, Commander of the First Battalion Gloucestershire Regiment, during his captivity in N Korea in 1951.

At the extreme E end of the cathedral is the lady chapel, built 1457–83. Most of the roof bosses comprise foliage designs, but some show strange animals and fishes.

In the lady chapel is a lead font dating from c.1130 which came from the ruined church of St James, Lancaut. Another lead font came from Tidenham, about 3.2 km (2 miles) from Lancaut. These are the only lead fonts inside a cathedral. (See Lead Fonts, page 74.)

At the w end of the choir at the entrance to the N and s transepts, notice how cleverly the fourteenth-century vaulting of the roof is carried down to the Norman piers on graceful flying arches – a wonderful medieval achievement.

The s transept is considered to be the first place where the Perpendicular style of architecture was experimented with and which is uniquely English.

In the s transept is a beautifully carved bracket in the shape of an 'L' which probably carried a sculptured figure. Known as the 'Prentice Bracket' the outstretched figure carved underneath is supposed to depict a young apprentice who fell to his death during the construction of the cathedral.

The two w bays of the nave, which had to be rebuilt after the w towers collapsed, show the difference between the Norman and Perpendicular styles of architecture.

⊞ On the pipes of the organ is unique seventeenth-century painting which was restored by an expert picture restorer, Anna Plowden, in 1971.

⊞ On the N side of the nave (an unusual position) are the beautiful fan-vaulted cloisters, which were rebuilt from *c.*1360 onwards, commencing with the E cloister walk. These are the oldest fan-vaulted roofs in existence. Notice the 20 alcoves where monks sat to read and write and the places where they washed, with miniature fan vaulting above. (See Fan Vaulting, page 152.)

⊞ The great Norman piers of the nave, 9.32 m (30 feet 7 inches) high, are comparable with those of nearby Tewkesbury Abbey.

⊞ A spectacular wall monument in the N aisle by Flaxman commemorates Sarah Morley, who died in childbirth at sea on 25 May 1784 on her way to England from Bombay. The mother of seven children, she is shown rising from the waves holding her baby while three angels hold out their hands to guide her to Heaven.

# Godshill Isle of Wight

ALL SAINTS Situated on one of the highest points in the village and approached between charming thatched cottages, the churchyard commands fine views to the south.

⊞ On the E wall of the S transept is a unique wall painting dating from *c.*1450, depicting Our Lord crucified on a triple-branched lily which resembles a tree. Two angels watch over Him. This painting was lime-washed at the Reformation and only discovered in *c.*1850. (See Lily Crucifix, page 338.)

⊞ Between the two chancels and under an exquisitely carved canopy lies Sir John Leigh (d. 1529) and his wife, Agnes, carved from Derbyshire alabaster. On the soles of his feet are carved bedesmen or monks holding rosary beads. This is a very rare feature, especially figures showing the 'telling of beads'.

⊞ In the nave is a large painting entitled 'Daniel in the Lions' Den', after Rubens.

⊞ Behind the organ is the huge monument to Sir Richard Worsley (d. 1805) known locally as 'The Bath'!

# Grantham Lincolnshire

ST WULFRAM is a magnificent building dominating the town.

⊞ The 86.2 m (282 feet 10 inch) spire was built between 1280 and 1300 and was the first great spire in England. It is now the sixth highest. Only Salisbury and Norwich cathedrals, Louth (Lincs.), Coventry (St Michael) and Bristol (St Mary Redcliffe) are higher.

John Ruskin is said to have nearly fainted when he saw the W front with tower and spire for the first time!

⊞ This is one of only two churches in England dedicated to St Wulfram.

⊞ Projecting from the N aisle is St Katharyn's chapel (now a vestry), a former chantry chapel for Thomas Hall, a wool stapler, built *c.*1490. It is unusual in being longer from N to S, than E to W.

⊞ Over the S porch is a chained library presented to the church by the Reverend Francis Trigge in 1598 – the oldest parochial library in England.

⊞ From the S side of the chancel, steps lead down to a vaulted crypt under the lady chapel. The door is the original one.

# FAN VAULTING

*The Lady Chapel, Gloucester Cathedral.*

Fan vaulting is the most sophisticated form of roof decoration inside a building and is a purely English invention, although Francis Bond (a great authority in the early twentieth century on ecclesiastical architecture) says that examples can be found in the Baltic lands.

Fan vaulting developed originally in the west of England and is believed to have started in the chapter house of Hereford Cathedral – completed *c*.1364, but sadly demolished in 1769.

It is generally accepted that the earliest existing fan vaulting is in the E walk of the cloisters at Gloucester Cathedral, dating from *c*.1360, although author Walter C. Leedy Jnr (see Bibliography, page 465), suggests a date of *c*.1400. He goes on to say that 'the identification of the first example of the fan vault is not of real importance to the understanding of the origins of the form. What is important, however, is the realization that fan vaulting was an evolutionary rather than a revolutionary building innovation.'

Fan vaulting consists of trumpet-shaped half cones of masonry (not unlike half ice-cream cones), above which equidistant ribs radiate. The half cones have concave faces that usually just touch opposite each other. The overall effect when you look up is a beautiful display resembling open fans – each one touching or overlapping the next.

In addition to the ribs that start from the base or springer, other ribs cross at right angles. Between all the ribs there is beautiful cusped panelling, characteristic of the Perpendicular period.

Some fan vaults were made of blocks of stone, carved on the ground, joined together and then lifted into position. This technique was probably employed at Chewton Mendip, Somerset, because the fan vaulting under the w tower is now twisted out of shape – this would probably not have occurred had carving been done in situ as the tower rose upwards.

Other fan vaults are made of ribbed stone infilled with separate pieces of stone. It is interesting to observe the technique employed. The earliest vaults tend to be made of stone ribs as at Sherborne Abbey, Dorset. Wooden screens, especially those in Devon and Somerset, are often enriched with simplified fan-vaulted coving supporting the cornice and cresting above and originally a rood loft as well. Many canopies of niches also contain miniature fan vaults.

Inside the chantry chapel of Edward Despenser on the s side of the choir of Tewkesbury Abbey, Gloucestershire, is a miniature fan vault dating from c.1375. The fan vaulting in the cloisters of Gloucester Cathedral was the first to be developed on a scale larger than a chantry chapel, but the fan vaulting in the choir of Sherborne Abbey, Dorset, was the first high vault to be built c.1440, followed by the fan vaulting of the nave c.1490.

An interesting insight into the construction of a fan vault is recorded in the annals of Fairford Church, Gloucestershire. In 1835 it was found necessary to enlarge the seating capacity in the church, so a gallery was built under the pitched roof of the s porch and an opening made into the church above the door. It would appear that the old groined stone roof of the porch was taken down to accommodate the gallery. In 1854, however, new pews were installed in the church and the gallery, being no longer required, was removed and the opening into the church was closed.

In 1890 the vicar (the Reverend F. R. Carbonell) expressed a wish that the groined stone roof of the porch be replaced and £230 was the amount estimated for a new fan-vaulted roof. The architect, a Mr Waller, prepared drawings of the roof and a stonemason, a Mr Frith, did most of the work in his Gloucester workshop.

The stones were carved and fitted  together on the ground, and were then taken to Fairford. The roof was fixed in position (the actual fixing took about six weeks) and the work was completed on 17 September 1892.

Although it was comparatively easy to construct a fan vault under a square tower or porch, and many excellent examples do remain, unfortunately the cost was often too great for many churches and fewer still could afford to vault other parts such as aisles or chapels. This was left to wealthy benefactors: John Lane, a wool merchant, left money to vault the s aisle at Cullompton, Devon; Cicely Bonville, Marchioness of Dorset built the outer N aisle at Ottery St Mary, Devon; and Elizabeth Wilcote built a chantry chapel for her two husbands and two sons at North Leigh, Oxfordshire.

Occasionally money ran out after a fan vault had been started, as at Leigh-on-Mendip, Somerset, where the start of the springing ribs can still be seen under the tower. The s porch at Shelton, Norfolk, and the N and s porches at Littlebury, Essex, also show evidence of projected vaulting but these may have been for lierne vaults rather than for fan vaults. Old Wardour Castle, Wiltshire, also has signs of fan vaulting, which may have been executed but is now in disrepair.

The spaces or spandrels between the fans in the upper part of the vault were sometimes filled with elaborate carving inside circles, or decorated with hanging pendent bosses as at Cullompton and Ottery St Mary, Devon. In St George's chapel, Windsor Castle, Berkshire, the spandrels are filled with octagons – these are not found anywhere else. Occasionally, figures of angels were included in the spandrels as at Torbryan, Devon, or heraldic devices as at Bath Abbey, Somerset, or St George's Chapel, Windsor Castle.

Under many fan-vaulted towers there is usually a large circular spandrel between the fans and Pevsner suggests this is used for bell ropes. The most likely reason for its construction is to provide an opening when the bells need to be lowered for maintenance purposes or when new bells are installed. The opening is usually covered by a wooden trap door as at Castle Combe, Wiltshire. In many towers containing bells, the ringers do not stand on the ground floor but on the first floor *above* the vaulting or ceiling.

The finest achievement of the pure fan vault is King's College chapel, Cambridge, which is also the one with the greatest span – 12.66 m (41.53 feet). Some people, however, consider Henry VII's chapel in Westminster Abbey, London, to be superior, although Nikolaus Pevsner is careful to point out that the roof of the choir and nave of that chapel is actually 'a groin-vault divided into bays by strong transverse arches'. This vault would appear to be a refined development of a lierne vault, echoing the earlier lierne vaults with pendants at the Divinity School, Oxford (*c.*1480–3), and the choir at Oxford Cathedral (*c.*1478–1503).

Only one church in the world is vaulted entirely with stone fan vaulting, namely Bath Abbey, Somerset. It was not finally completed, however, until 1864–74 when the Victorians, under the guidance of Sir Gilbert Scott, vaulted the nave, copying that of the medieval chancel beyond the crossing tower.

After the seventeenth century, stone fan vaulting virtually ceased. St Mary Aldermary, London was rebuilt by Wren in 1682 and has *plaster* fan vaults in the nave, choir and aisles but the central spandrels are unique to Wren.

Around 1950 it was decided to renew the roof of Eton College Chapel, Berkshire which had become seriously damaged by rot and death-watch beetle. Instead of replacing the existing wooden roof with a similar one, a fan vault was planned, designed by Sir William Holford and using the existing shafts that were constructed *c.*1450 when the chapel was built. Since Eton College and King's College, Cambridge, were both founded by King Henry VI and King's College chapel has a fan-vaulted roof, it was argued that probably a fan vault was intended for Eton. The Eton vault is not a true fan vault because the fans are made of concrete faced with stone and suspended from steel beams. The overall effect, however, is excellent although the ribs of the fans lack the cusped decoration that is common to most medieval fan vaults, with the exception of the lady chapel or dean's chapel at Canterbury Cathedral, Kent.

Soon after the new fan vault was completed at Eton in 1959 (the chapel was closed for three years for its construction) an American tourist was heard to remark after looking up, 'They can't do work like that today'!

The following is a complete list of all examples known to me of fan vaulting in religious buildings in England and Wales today, under various counties, with their approximate dates of construction.

✠ ANGLESEY *(Wales)*
1. Holyhead (St Cybi) s porch, 1877–9 by Sir Gilbert Scott.

✠ BERKSHIRE
2. Eton College Chapel, Lupton chantry chapel, 1550; nave and chancel, 1956–9.
3. Shottesbrooke (St John the Baptist), inside two tomb recesses for Sir William Trussell and his wife in N transept, *c.*1380.
4. Windsor Castle (St George's chapel), N and s choir aisles, *c.*1490; nave aisles, *c.*1505; crossing, *c.*1528; organ screen of Coade stone, 1790.

5. Hillesden (All Saints), N porch, c.1870. Designed and presented by Sir George Gilbert Scott, who was born in the neighbouring village of Gawcott in 1811.

6. Maids Moreton (St Edmund), under w tower, N and S porches, vestry and outside W door supporting a canopy, c.1475.

✠ CAMBRIDGESHIRE

7. Burwell (St Mary), N porch, c.1500

8. Cambridge (King's College Chapel), 1512–15

9. Ely Cathedral. Bishop Alcock's chantry chapel, c.1488.

10. Peterborough Cathedral. The 'New Building' or retrochoir, 1500–28.

✠ CHESHIRE

11. Chester Cathedral. SW porch, c.1870. Organ screen on N side of crossing, over three arches, 1876.

✠ CORNWALL

12. Bodmin (St Peter), S porch, c.1500.

✠ DEVON

13. Clyst Hydon (St Andrew), S porch with central boss, c.1500.

14. Cullompton (St Andrew), Lane aisle, c.1526.

15. Exeter Cathedral, N porch inside the w front, c.1420. (This is the only fan vaulting in the cathedral.)

16. Holcombe Rogus (All Saints), S porch, c.1500.

17. Ottery St Mary (St Mary), Dorset, aisle, N porch, c.1530.

18. Paignton (St John), under three openings to the Kirkham chantry chapel, c.1490.

19. Torbryan (Holy Trinity), S porch, c.1490.

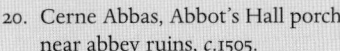

20. Cerne Abbas, Abbot's Hall porch near abbey ruins, c.1505.

21. Christchurch Priory, Salisbury, chantry chapel, c.1530; Draper chantry chapel, inside a piscina, c.1500, predating the chapel.

22. Forde Abbey near Thorncombe, porch below tower, c.1530.

23. Hilton (All Saints), S porch, c.1490. (Brought from the destroyed cloisters of nearby Milton Abbey.)

24. Milton Abbey, under crossing tower, c.1500. Miniature fan vaulting along the top of the stone reredos at the E end, restored in plaster by James Wyatt in 1789.

25. Sherborne Abbey, choir; under crossing tower; N transept; Wykeham chapel; St Catherine's chapel, c.1430; nave, c.1490; retrochoir, 1921.

26. Silton (St Nicholas), N chantry chapel, c.1500. (This is now a vestry and has a locked door, but the roof can be seen through a little four-light Perpendicular window on the S side in which are portraits of Paul, Timothy, Barnabas and Luke.)

✠ ESSEX

27. Saffron Walden (St Mary the Virgin), S porch, c.1490.

✠ GLOUCESTERSHIRE

28. Bishop's Cleeve (St Michael & All Angels), over w end of S aisle, c.1450.

29. Bristol (St Mark or the Lord Mayor's chapel), Poyntz chapel, 1536.

30. Bristol (St Stephen), S porch, c.1480.

31. Cirencester (St John the Baptist), N porch, c.1450; S porch, c.1500 (rebuilt in 1865); Chapel of St Catherine and St Nicholas, 1508.

32. Fairford (St Mary), S porch, 1892.

33. Gloucester Cathedral, E walk of cloisters, c.1360; remaining three

walks of cloisters, 1380–1412; w entrance to nave, ᴇ entrance into cloisters from ɴ side of nave, c.1430; two chantry chapels on ɴ and s sides of lady chapel, c.1470.

34. Iron Acton (St James), under w tower, c.1439.

35. Newent (St Mary), porch under sw tower, c.1500.

36. Prinknash Abbey, inside oriel window on ɴw side of library, c.1510.

37. Tewkesbury Abbey, Trinity chapel or chantry chapel of Edward Despenser, c.1375; chantry chapel of Robert Fitzhamon, c.1395; Beauchamp chantry chapel, c.1430.

38. Wickwar (Holy Trinity), under w tower, c.1500.

Kings College Chapel, Cambridge.

⊹⊢ GREATER MANCHESTER
39. Manchester Cathedral, under w tower, 1867.

⊹⊢ HAMPSHIRE
40. Winchester Cathedral, Cardinal Beaufort's chantry chapel, c.1450; Bishop Waynflete's chantry chapel, c.1470; Bishop Gardiner's chantry chapel, above ᴇ sacristy, 1555; under crossing tower, 1635 (wood).

⊹⊢ HEREFORDSHIRE
41. Bosbury (Holy Trinity), Morton chapel, c.1510.
42. Hereford Cathedral, Vicars' College porch; Bishop Stanbury's chantry chapel, c.1490; Bishop Audley's chantry chapel, c.1500.

⊹⊢ HERTFORDSHIRE
43. St Albans Abbey, tomb of Humphrey, Duke of Gloucester, 1447, s of St Alban's shrine; chantry chapel of Abbot Ramryge, 1519, ɴ of the high altar.

⊹⊢ KENT
44. Canterbury Cathedral, Henry IV's chantry chapel or St Edward the Confessor's chapel, 1438, under sw tower, c.1455; lady chapel or dean's chapel, c.1460; under Bell Harry or crossing tower, c.1510.

⊹⊢ LEICESTERSHIRE
45. Leicester (St Margaret), s porch, c.1444.

⊹⊢ LINCOLNSHIRE
46. Belton, near Grantham (St Peter & St Paul), mortuary chapel on ɴ side of chancel, 1816.
47. Morton, near Bourne (St John the Baptist), under crossing tower, c.1500.
48. Spalding (St Mary & St Nicholas), ɴ porch, c.1500.

⊹⊢ LONDON
49. Westminster Abbey, Henry VII's chapel, aisles and chapels, c. 1503–12, not choir and nave.
50. Putney Bridge, Putney (St Mary), Bishop West's chantry chapel,1533.
51. St Mary, Aldermary, nave, choir and aisles, 1682; plaster by Wren.

⊹⊢ NORFOLK
52. King's Lynn, Red Mount chapel,

the walks; crossing vault of the upper chapel, *c*.1485.

53. Norwich (St Giles), s porch, *c*.1450. (This is the only fan vaulting in Norwich.)

✦ NORTHAMPTONSHIRE
54. Fotheringhay (St Mary & All Saints), under w tower, 1529.
55. Great Brington (St Mary), Spencer chapel, over bay window, 1846.
56. Wellingborough (St Mary), nave and chancel, 1931 (plaster).

✦ NOTTINGHAMSHIRE
57. Nottingham (St Mary), under crossing tower, 1807 (oak and stucco).

✦ OXFORDSHIRE
58. Burford (St John the Baptist), s porch, *c*.1450.
59. Deddington (St Peter & St Paul), N porch, *c*.1690.
60. Minster Lovell (St Kenelm), under crossing tower, *c*.1440.
61. North Leigh (St Mary), Wilcote chapel, *c*.1438.
62. Oxford (Brasenose College), chapel, *c*.1665. (This is a plaster fan vault underneath a fifteenth-century hammer-beam roof brought from the former St Mary's College, *c*.1580.)
63. Oxford (Christchurch) Cathedral, chantry chapel, underneath watching loft, *c*.1490.
64. Oxford (Magdalen College), chantry chapel on N side of chapel, *c*.1480.
65. Oxford (St John's College), chapel, inside the Baylie chapel, 1662 (plaster).

*Wellingborough, Northamptonshire.*

66. Oxford (St Mary the Virgin) University Church, s porch, *c*.1492. (This fan vault came from a previous porch and was adapted to fit the existing porch in 1637.)

✦ PEMBROKESHIRE (*Wales*)
67. St David's Cathedral, the Holy Trinity chapel or Vaughan chantry, between the eastern side of the N and s choir aisles, *c*.1520.

✦ SHROPSHIRE
68. Tong (St Bartholomew), Vernon chapel, *c*.1520.

✦ SOMERSET
69. Axbridge (St John the Baptist), under crossing tower, *c*.1420.
70. Batcombe (St Mary), under w tower, *c*.1540.
71. Bath Abbey, choir, N and s aisles; N transept, *c*.1502; crossing tower, *c*.1580; s transept, *c*.1610; nave, 1864. Chantry chapel of Prior Birde in chancel, *c*.1515. Miniature fan vaulting at top of reredos at E end of chancel, 1875.
72. Bath (St Saviour), chancel, 1882.
73. Beckington (St George); under w tower, *c*.1510.
74. Bruton (St Mary), under w tower, *c*.1878.
75. Buckland Dinham (St Michael), s porch, *c*.1590.
76. Burrington (Holy Trinity), under w tower, *c*.1500.
77. Chewton Mendip (St Mary

Magdalene), under w tower, *c.*1540.

78. Crewkerne (St Bartholomew), s porch, *c.*1490; under crossing tower, 1904 (oak).
79. Croscombe (St Mary), under w tower, *c.*1476.
80. Crowcombe (Holy Ghost), s porch, *c.*1520.
81. Curry Rivel (St Andrew), under w tower, S porch, *c.*1590.
82. Ditcheat (St Mary Magdalene), under crossing tower, *c.*1540.
83. Doulting (St Aldhelm), s porch, *c.*1500. Rebuilt *c.*1850.
84. Glastonbury (St John), under w tower, *c.*1490.
85. Ilminster (St Mary), under crossing tower, *c.*1500.
86. Isle Abbots (St Mary), under w tower, s porch, *c.*1500.
87. Kingsbury Episcopi (St Martin), under w tower, *c.*1500.
88. Kingston St Mary (St Mary), S porch, *c.*1500.
89. Langport (All Saints), under w tower, *c.*1500.
90. Mells (St Andrew), under w tower, 1470; s porch, *c.*1500.
91. Mulcheney Abbey, s walk of cloisters, *c.*1490.
92. Mulcheney (St Peter & St Paul), under w tower, *c.*1500.
93. Nash Priory, North Coker, supporting an oriel window, *c.*1450.
94. North Curry (St Peter & St Paul), s porch, *c.*1500.
95. North Petherton, under w tower, *c.*1510.
96. Shepton Beauchamp, under w tower, *c.*1500.
97. Shepton Mallet, under w tower, *c.*1540.
98. Stavordale Priory (now a private house), N or Jesus chapel, *c.*1525.
99. Taunton (St James), under w

tower, *c.*1500. Rebuilt 1871–3.
100. Taunton (St Mary Magdalene), under w tower, *c.*1500. Rebuilt in 1862.
101. Wedmore (St Mary Magdalene), under crossing tower, *c.*1500.
102. Wells Cathedral, Bishop Beckington's chantry chapel, *c.*1450; E end of Dr Sugar's chantry chapel, *c.*1490; under crossing tower, *c.*1500.
103. West Cranmore (St Bartholomew), under w tower, *c.*1500.
104. Weston Zoyland, under w tower, *c.*1510.
105. Woodspring Priory, under former crossing tower, *c.*1828; carried out under the guidance of John Buckler. Property now owned by the Landmark Trust.
106. Wrington (All Saints), under w tower, *c.*1500.

✠ SUFFOLK
107. Denston (St Nicholas), s porch, *c.*1480.
108. Eye (St Peter & St Paul), W porch, under W tower, *c.*1500.
109. Lavenham (St Peter & St Paul), s porch, *c.*1865.
110. Long Melford (Holy Trinity), vestibule near Clopton chantry chapel, *c.*1500.
111. Mildenhall (St Mary & St Andrew), under W tower gallery, *c.*1540.

✠ SUSSEX *(West)*
112. Boxgrove Priory (St Mary and St Blaise), De la Warr chantry, 1532.

✠ WARWICKSHIRE
113. Warwick (St Mary), tiny chantry chapel between the chancel and the Beauchamp chapel, *c.*1449

✠ WEST MIDLANDS
114. Walsall (St Matthew), nave ceiling. Fans and pendents, Georgian Gothic, 1820–21.

✠ WILTSHIRE

115.   Bromham (St Nicholas), s porch, s transept, c.1500.
116.   Castle Combe (St Andrew), under w tower, c.1490.
117.   East Knoyle (St Mary), under w tower, c.1500.
118.   Highworth (St Michael), under w tower, c.1510.
119.   Malmesbury Abbey, porch leading to ruined cloisters, c.1450.
120.   Pewsey (St John the Baptist), under W tower, c.1500.
121.   Salisbury Cathedral, Bishop Audley's chantry chapel, c.1520.
122.   Trowbridge (St James), N porch, under w tower, c.1500.

✠ WORCESTERSHIRE

123.   Evesham (All Saints), Lichfield chapel, c.1500.
124.   Evesham (St Lawrence), s chantry chapel or St Clement's chapel,1530.
125.   Great Malvern Priory, sunken chantry chapel in s aisle of chancel, c.1460.

✠ YORKSHIRE *(South)*

126.   Rotherham (All Saints), under crossing tower, c.1500.
127.   York Minster, inner porch of pulpitum under crossing tower, c.1450.

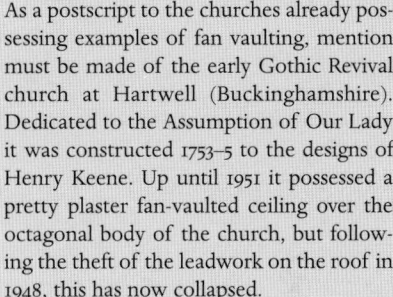

As a postscript to the churches already possessing examples of fan vaulting, mention must be made of the early Gothic Revival church at Hartwell (Buckinghamshire). Dedicated to the Assumption of Our Lady it was constructed 1753–5 to the designs of Henry Keene. Up until 1951 it possessed a pretty plaster fan-vaulted ceiling over the octagonal body of the church, but following the theft of the leadwork on the roof in 1948, this has now collapsed.

On 23 July 1975 the church was vested in the Churches Conservation Trust and among numerous repairs effected by the Trust and others, a new roof has been constructed over the octagon. The plaster fan vaulting, however, has not yet been restored owing to its prohibitive cost.

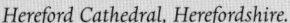

*Hereford Cathedral, Herefordshire.*

## Great Barrington   GLOUCESTERSHIRE

ST MARY THE VIRGIN A walk past the walls of Barrington Park leads to this little church.

▨ At the NW end is the finest child monument of the early eighteenth century and one of the finest in England. Dating from c.1720 it commemorates Jane Bray who died in 1711 aged eight, and her brother, Edward, who died in 1720 aged 15, both from smallpox. The boy (who looks older than his 15 years) and girl both hold the hands of an escorting angel as they walk across the clouds of Heaven.

This monument was carved by Christopher Cass. It is believed to have been designed by Francis Bird.

## Great Brington   NORTHAMPTONSHIRE

ST MARY THE VIRGIN This large, ironstone-built church stands on a hillside away from the village; there are fine views from the churchyard.

▨ On the NE side of the chancel, surrounded by a blue iron grille with locked gates, is the Spencer chapel.

▨ In the E bay between the chancel and chapel is the earliest tomb. It commemorates Sir John Spencer (d. 14 April 1522) and his wife, Isabella Graunt. A rosary hangs from her girdle and from the roof above an angel holds the Spencer arms.

▨ Underneath the E window of the chapel is the plain altar tomb of their son Sir William Spencer (d. 22 June 1532) and his wife, Susan Knightley. Notice the heraldic shields in the quatrefoils below.

▨ The central monument of the bay is that of Sir William's son, Sir John Spencer (d. 1586), and his wife, Katherine Kitson, who lies under a coverlet. He wears armour and she has a head-dress similar to that worn by Mary Queen of Scots.

Notice the Renaissance influence on this tomb and successive ones.

▨ Near this tomb, on the chancel floor of the church between the choir stalls, is the tomb of Laurence Washington (d. 13 December 1616). He was the great-great-great-grandfather of George Washington. His grave slab carries the Washington arms – the origin of the stars and stripes.

▨ In the NE corner of the chapel is the imposing tomb of Sir John Spencer (d. 1599) and his wife, Mary Catelin.

▨ In the W bay adjoining the chancel is the tomb of Sir Robert Spencer (d. 1625) and his wife, Margaret Willoughby (d. 1597). She rests under a coverlet decorated with heraldry.

▨ On the opposite side to this tomb is that of Sir Robert's son, William (d. 1636), and his wife, Lady Penelope Wriothesley (d. 1697). Carved out of black and white marble it was designed by Nicholas Stone.

▨ In the SE corner of the chapel is a remarkable bust of Sir Edward Spencer (d. 1655) rising from a funeral urn, carved by John Stone, son of Nicholas.

▨ The chancel contains a fine E window by William Morris depicting the Adoration of the Lamb and in the SW window are fragments of old glass including a monk blowing a horn, a kneeling nun and John the Baptist with a lamb.

▨ There are fine bench-ends in the chancel and the nave. Those in the nave are carved on one side only and date from c.1450. Others date from 1400, 1606, 1848 and 1903. There are 181 altogether.

▨ Outside the church on the S side is a rare recessed wall tomb containing the worn figure of a priest. It dates from c. 1200 and is contemporary with the pedestal of the font.

▨ Diana, Princess of Wales (1961–97) is buried on an island in the lake at nearby Althorpe House.

*Great Malvern Priory, viewed from the south.*

## Great Malvern <sup>WORCESTERSHIRE</sup>

THE PRIORY CHURCH OF ST MARY & ST MICHAEL is situated in the centre of this spa town on the slopes of the beautiful Malvern Hills. At the Dissolution of the Monasteries, this former Benedictine priory was bought from the Crown by the townspeople for £20!

 The central tower is very similar to the one at Gloucester Cathedral and was probably designed by the same architect.

 Outside the E end are 11 wooden crosses set in stone. These are in memory of ten men killed in the First World War but buried overseas and Major D. H. Acworth, who died of pneumonia at Port Said on 6 February 1919, aged 33.

 The nave comprises ten Norman pillars with a fifteenth-century clerestory above.

The contrast between the Norman nave and Perpendicular chancel is very striking.

 Around the E end are tiles decorating the choir screen. There are over 1,200 altogether comprising 90 different patterns. Dating from 1456 to 1520 they make up the most varied collection of tiles surviving in any English church and the only extant examples of mural tiles in England.

A large collection of fifteenth-century medieval glass – the most complete collection in England and predominantly blue and red – fills many of the windows as follows:

† The N transept window was given by Henry VIII and depicts the Joys of Mary. Notice how the Coronation of the Virgin inside the circle could not be placed in the exact centre of the window because of the stone mullion. Along the base are the

kneeling figures of Henry VIII and Arthur, Prince of Wales.

† The N and S choir clerestory windows depict various figures with the Annunciation at the extreme NE and the Crucifixion in the central window on the S side. The Annunciation shows Mary with three white flowers in an ornamental vase with a handle.

† The S choir aisle is filled with ancient glass depicting scenes from the Old Testament.

† The magnificent E window, although composed of fragments, contains panels depicting the Passion of Jesus from Palm Sunday to the Ascension and the Coming of the Holy Spirit. The Annunciation is again shown. In front of Mary on her left is a gold vase with three flowers.

† The W window depicts various saints and bishops with Mary and the infant Jesus.

† In the N nave aisle is yet another window in medieval glass depicting the Annunciation. Mary is shown kneeling at a desk with her rosary beads and a black-handled knife. In the centre is a lily with three flowers in a two-handled vase.

There are 22 misericords in the choir, ten of which depict months of the year.

On the S side of the high altar is the Knotsford monument. John Knotsford (d. 1589) and his wife, Jane (d. 1582), are shown lying on a cushion, hands at prayer. Their daughter, Anne, who erected the monument, kneels at a prie-dieu at their feet. The three alabaster figures show excellent examples of Elizabethan costume.

At the E end of St Anne's chapel (S choir aisle) are two modern statues of St Ursula and St Anne teaching the Virgin Mary to read. They were carved by Robin Pancheri of Bromsgrove in 1976.

On the W face of a Norman pier on the N side of the nave is a fifteenth-century tile with these words:

'Think, man, thy life may not ever endure; what thou dost thyself of that thou art sure, but what thou keepest for thy executor's care, and whether it avail thee is but adventure.'

On the W wall of the N porch are six clappers from the old ring of bells, inscribed:

'Our duty done in belfry high,
Now voiceless tongues at rest we lie.'

## Great Waltham    ESSEX

ST MARY & ST LAWRENCE The little village of beautiful old houses is dominated by this church.

Many of the pews on the S side of the nave date from c.1420.

At the E end of the N aisle is a magnificent alabaster and marble monument to Sir Anthony Everard and his wife, Anne (a cousin of Oliver Cromwell), dated 1611. The unique feature of this memorial are the two little coffins at its foot with the couple's three sons – two who died unbaptized and are sadly called 'Anonymous' and one called Richard. Note the two unusual windows in the back of the monument with original glass.

A pre-Reformation paten dating from 1521 is the oldest piece of church plate in Essex.

A tombstone in the churchyard to Hugh Western was carved by Eric Gill.

## Great Witley    WORCESTERSHIRE

ST MICHAEL & ALL ANGELS was completed in 1735, probably to the designs of James Gibbs working for Thomas, first Lord Foley (d. 1732) but whose widow actually completed it. This is England's finest Baroque church.

The church was built of brick with

*Great Waltham, Essex. The unusual Everard monument is lit by windows with original glass.*

stone dressings but was encased in stone *c.*1861. The cupola, balustrade and urns are original.

▨ The coved ceiling of the nave is adorned with magnificent plaster work. In the centre is a huge painting depicting the Ascension and two small circular paintings on either side. That at the w end shows the Nativity while the one on the e shows the Descent from the Cross. Both were painted by Antonio Bellucci (1654–1726).

▨ The ten round-headed windows in the church are filled with painted glass by Joshua Price of York working to the designs of Francesco Sleter (or Slater), a Venetian painter. They are all dated 1719 (bar one of 1721) and depict incidents in the New Testament (except one showing the golden calf (*Exodus*, 32).

These painted windows, the ceiling paintings and plaster work all came from the chapel of Canons near Edgware in 1747 when the second Duke of Chandos sold the house. The second Lord Foley bought these items and adapted them for this church.

▨ The organ case also came from Canons but the organ occupying it was built 1858–60 by John Nicholson of Worcester.

▨ In the s transept is the great monument to the first Lord Thomas Foley by John Michael Rysbrack (1694–1770), erected in 1735. Seven figures are depicted with Lord Foley in the centre reclining on one arm. This is the largest eighteenth-century church monument in England and cost £2,000 – a huge amount at that time.

▨ In the nw corner of the n transept is a monument to Thomas Foley (d. 1677) and a door which used to lead to the house.

▨ The door opposite in the s transept is a dummy to lend symmetry to the e end of the church.

*Greensted, Essex. Note the original Saxon wooden walls.*

## Greensted-juxta-Ongar     ESSEX

ST ANDREW is the only surviving wooden church in the British Isles dating from c.1000 (although carbon dating on some of the uprights in the nave claims a date c.850).

The nave consists of oak trees split in two with the rounded part on the outside and the flat side forming the inside walls. In places outside where the oak has split, the cracks have been filled with cement! I wonder when the acorns were planted from which these oak trees grew?

A stained-glass window on the NE side of the church commemorates the martyrdom of St Edmund, whose body rested here in 1013 on its way for burial at Bury St Edmunds, Suffolk.

This church featured on the 3p British postage stamps of village churches issued on 21 June 1972.

## Guildford     SURREY

THE CATHEDRAL OF THE HOLY SPIRIT is situated on Stag Hill and dominates the town and countryside. It is approached by a beautiful drive up to the w front. Designed by Sir Edward Maufe in 1932, the foundation stone was laid by Dr Cosmo Lang, Archbishop of Canterbury, in 1936 and consecrated by Dr George Reindorp, the fifth Bishop of Guildford, on 17 May 1961.

The cathedral is built of red brick with Somerset stone dressings. Much of the clay for the bricks came from the hill on which the cathedral is built.

The bronze doors at the w end contain

*Guildford Cathedral seen from the east, before new buildings encroached on the site.*

plate glass 2 cm (¾ inch) thick engraved with angels by John Hutton.

🔲 The beautiful Rose window over the high altar at the E end was designed by Moira Forsyth and depicts the Dove and the gifts of the Holy Spirit.

🔲 On a pier of the nave is a stone carving of the Virgin and Child by John Cobbett.

🔲 At the crossing, set into the floor under the tower, is a brass stag marking the highest point of the hill on which the cathedral is built.

🔲 In the S transept are more engraved glass doors by John Hutton showing angels and tongues of flame. On the w wall is a children's window, also by Moira Forsyth.

🔲 In the N transept is the Jarrow stone, which came from the monastic remains at Jarrow (Tyne & Wear).

🔲 On the exterior of the S transept is the figure of John the Baptist by Eric Gill.

🔲 On the outside of the E end, above the Rose window, is a sculpture designed by Eric Gill and carved by his pupil, Anthony Foster.

🔲 The 47.54 m (156 feet) tower is surmounted by a 4.6 m (15 feet) copper-gilded angel weighing nearly 1016kg (1 ton). The angel was designed by Alan Collins.

# BRASSES

## BRASSES DEPICTING MONARCHS

Monumental brasses were placed in churches and cathedrals to commemorate people who had died. Images and inscriptions were engraved on sheets of 'latten' – an alloy of copper, zinc, tin and lead. Of the many hundreds of monumental brasses in England and Wales, there is only *one* that specifically commemorates an English monarch, although there are smaller representations of other monarchs appearing as part of larger brasses to other people. They are located as follows:

*Ethelred the Unready, Wimborne Minster, Dorset.*

✠ Wimborne Minster, Dorset: a small brass here is the only separate one made to commemorate an English monarch. It depicts St Ethelred (d. 871) but was not actually made until *c.*1440. The stone in which it is set is reputed to have been part of the original grave slab over St Ethelred's grave.

✠ Elsing (St Mary), Norfolk: in the border of the brass commemorating Sir Hugh Hastyngs (1347) is a small representation of Edward III.

✠ Hereford Cathedral: a small brass preserved in the chained library depicts St Ethelbert (d. 866), king and martyr. Dating from *c.*1290 it came from the larger brass of Thomas de Cantilupe and is now the oldest surviving memorial brass to an English king. Other portraits of St Ethelbert are among figures on the side of a brass to Richard Rudhale (1476) on the W wall of the SE transept

and among similar figures on a brass to Precentor William Porter (1524) on the S wall of the same transept.

✠ St Albans Abbey, Hertfordshire: on the right, inside the large brass of Abbot Thomas de la Mare (*c.*1370) is a small representation of King Offa. He is shown standing above three pairs of saints, wearing a crown and holding a spear in his right hand.

## BRASSES TO ARCHBISHOPS

Although there are a large number of brasses to ecclesiastics, only five ancient brasses survive to archbishops because they were usually placed in cathedrals where much damage was done , especially during the Civil War. Samuel Harsnett (d. 1631), Archbishop of York, cleverly had his brass placed in Chigwell Church (Essex), where he was once vicar, and so this escaped the despoilers.

A small brass made *c.*1500 commemorating Thomas à Becket (d. 1170) at Edenham, Lincolnshire, is unique in being the only ancient brass to an Archbishop of Canterbury. Until *c.*1910 it was fixed high up on the outside W face of the tower and so escaped the hands of Henry VIII's agents who were ordered to destroy all depictions of the hated 'Thomas-cult'.

The surviving brasses to archbishops are located as follows:

1. (1315) William de Grenefeld, Archbishop of York in York Minster – mutilated
2. (1397) Robert de Waldeby,

Archbishop of Dublin and York in Westminster Abbey

3. (1417) Thomas Cranley, Archbishop of Dublin in New College, Oxford
4. (c. 1500) St Thomas à Becket, Archbishop of Canterbury in Edenham (St Michael), Lincolnshire
5. (1631) Samuel Harsnett, Archbishop of York in Chigwell (St Mary), Essex

### EXTERNAL BRASSES

Although many hundreds of monumental brasses still survive inside our churches, as far as I know only six churches have brasses *outside* the church building. These are located as follows:

1. (1609) Burford (St John Baptist), Oxfordshire – John Hunt on a small rectangular plate
2. (1601) High Halden (St Mary), Kent – Stephen Scott on a tomb-chest near the porch
3. (c.1600) Ringsfield (All Saints), Suffolk – Nicholas Garneys and his wife, Ann, on a small rectangular plate fixed to the S wall of the chancel
4. (1617) Mudford (St Mary), Somerset – William Whitbye and his wife, Annis, on a small brass fixed to a table-tomb on the SE side of the churchyard
5. Sapperton (St Kenelm), Gloucestershire – perhaps the finest collection of brass memorial plates *outside* a church in England and Wales; they range from 1687 to c.1930
6. (1592) Staverton (St Paul de Leon), Devon – John Rowe on a rectangular plate

A brass fixed outside a church is obviously more susceptible to damage or theft by vandals than one placed inside, so there may well come a time when they will all be removed from the outside. In recent years  a brass to Elizabeth Popeley (1632) at Birstall, West Yorkshire, and another depicting St Thomas à Becket (c.1500) at Edenham, Lincolnshire, have been brought indoors.

### KNIGHTS OF THE GARTER BRASSES

Monumental brasses depicting knights wearing the Order of the Garter are extremely rare and, as far as I know, only five exist, although one authority states there are six.

The five are located as follows:

1. (1409) Exeter Cathedral, Devon – Sir Peter Courtenay, KG
2. (1416) Felbrigg (St Margaret), Norfolk – Sir Symon Felbrygge, KG
3. (1538) Hever (St Peter), Kent – Sir Thomas Bullen, KG
4. (1483) Little Easton (St Mary), Essex – Henry Bourchier, KG
5. (1419) Trotton (St George), West Sussex – Thomas Lord Camoys, KG

Of these five, only Sir Thomas Bullen and Henry Bourchier are shown wearing robes and the insignia of the Order of the Garter.

### BRASSES TO ABBESSES

Only two brasses to abbesses survive in England. They are located as follows:

1. (c.1540) Denham (St Mary), Buckinghamshire – this depicts Dame Agnes Jordan, Brigitine Abbess of Syon Abbey, Middlesex
2. (c.1520) Elstow (St Mary & St Helen), Bedfordshire – here is seen Dame Elizabeth Herwy, with crosier, Benedictine Abbess of Elstow Abbey.

### BRASSES TO PRIORESSES

Only one brass portrait to a prioress is known to exist in England. It depicts Lady Maria Gore (d. 1436) and can be seen at Nether Wallop (St Andrew), Hampshire.

*The Victorian tower at Hambleden, Buckinghamshire.*

## Hadstock Essex

St Botolph The church is situated in a small village N of Saffron Walden, near the Cambridgeshire border; it commands wonderful views from its churchyard.

▦ One of the windows contains a rare Anglo-Saxon wooden window frame.

▦ The N door, which is partly restored, dates from c.1050 and is one of only two Saxon doors in England. (The other is at the entrance to the chapter house in Westminster Abbey, London, see page 222.) A piece of skin from a 'sacrilegious' Dane that used to be nailed to it is now in Saffron Walden Museum.

▦ The gravestone of Michael Ayrton (d. 1975) features a maze (see Church Mazes, page 278).

## Hale Hampshire

St Mary is found on a hill, with fine views of the River Avon.

▦ The nave and chancel were built between 1631 and 1632 but the transepts were added by Thomas Archer in 1717.

▦ The S transept contains the memorial to Thomas Archer (d. 1743), designed by himself and executed by Peter Schiemaker (1692–1786). Archer designed several churches including St Philip's Cathedral, Birmingham.

▦ Another memorial commemorates Joseph May (d. 1796) and shows an urn resting on a marble block with rams'

heads at the corners. It was carved by Richard Westmacott.

## Hambleden Buckinghamshire

St Mary the Virgin The very attractive village is dominated by the tower of this church, standing as it does in a beautiful churchyard containing several interesting trees.

▦ W. H. Smith (1825–91), founder of the famous chain of bookshops, is buried in the churchyard.

▦ The large W tower dates from 1883 and encases an earlier tower dating from c.1720.

▦ The great stone font dates from c.1120. In it was baptized the last Englishman to be made a saint before the Reformation, St Thomas de Cantelupe, who was Bishop of Hereford (1275–82) and whose shrine is in the N transept of Hereford Cathedral. (See Hereford Cathedral, page 174.)

▦ A beautiful alabaster carving showing the Adoration of the Christ Child dates from c.1450.

▦ In the N transept aisle is a charming alabaster monument to Sir Cope D'Oyley (d. 1633), his wife and ten children, all kneeling. This is considered to be the finest sculpture in England depicting a loving, united family.

▦ The nave altar comprises two beautifully carved oak panels dated c.1525 which may possibly have come from a bed belonging to Cardinal Wolsey. His coat of arms and cardinal's hat appear among the carvings as well as the arms of Richard Fox, Bishop of Winchester (1501–28). Cardinal Wolsey succeeded Bishop Fox in 1528.

On the monument to Edward Marjoribanks (d. 1868) is a small urn from which a butterfly is trying to escape!

## Hanbury                          STAFFORDSHIRE

ST WERBURGH is situated on a hill, commanding glorious views over the countryside towards the River Dove.

At the E end of the S aisle is a monument to Sir John de Hanbury (d. 1303), who is depicted cross-legged in armour with a shield and sword. It is covered with much graffiti, including the date 1580 on the sword. This is the oldest alabaster effigy in England, the alabaster coming from the Chellaston quarries.

In the SW corner of the chancel are busts of two sombre-faced Puritan ladies – Katherine Agard (d. 1628) and her daughter, Ann Woollocke (d. 1657). Both wear broad-brimmed black hats, white ruffs and black gowns. Such busts are rare because the Puritans despised statues as imagery.

In the S aisle are fragments of medieval stained glass dating from c.1350. These were placed here in memory of parishioners who died on active service in the Second World War and 62 people who were killed when an underground ammunition dump near by exploded on 27 November 1944.

On the S side of the chancel is a large effigy of Sir Charles Egerton (d. 1624). He is depicted reclining with a circular shield, his left arm around a helm and a pair of gauntlets at his feet. He was an axe bearer in the forest of Needwood.

At the E end of the N aisle is a fine monument to Sir John Egerton (1585–1662), son of Sir Charles. His sister, Mary, had his memorial erected here away from the Puritan ladies' gaze in the chancel!

On each side of the exterior E window of the chancel are small stone effigies of Queen Victoria and Prince Albert – a very unusual feature and probably unique.

## Hardham                           WEST SUSSEX

ST BOTOLPH This church is unique in possessing the earliest nearly complete series of wall paintings in England. Dating from c.1100 they are most difficult to see clearly.

Above the chancel arch is the Lamb adored by two angels (*Rev.* 5, v.8).

On the S side of the chancel arch are the Annunciation and Visitation. Above the Visitation is the inscription: '*Virgo salutatur sterilis fecunda probatur*' ('the Virgin is saluted. The barren is proved fruitful').

On the S and N walls of the nave are paintings of the childhood of Jesus.

At the bottom of the N wall at the W end is a painting of St George on horseback – the oldest painting of St George in England.

Other paintings adorn the chancel. On the NE face of the chancel arch, Eve is shown milking a curious-looking cow and on the S wall are figures of six of the Apostles uncovered in 1950.

On the W wall of the nave is the Punishment of the Lost or Torrents of Hell.

On the S side of the chancel is a squint, which probably indicates the site of an anchorite's cell.

In the little tower is the oldest tower bell in the British Isles. Dating from before 1100 it weighs 50 kg (1 cwt). (See Bells, page 293.)

## Harefield GREATER LONDON

ST MARY THE VIRGIN possesses over 40 monuments dating from 1440 to 1936 – almost like a miniature Westminster Abbey.

The most spectacular monument is in the SE corner of the chancel commemorating Alice, Countess Dowager of Derby (d. 1637). She is shown dressed in her robes lying as if in a four-poster bed, the curtains of which are tied around the posts in a very realistic manner.

To the left of the altar in the NE corner of the chancel is a large stone monument to Mary (d. 1692), wife of Sir Richard Newdigate (d. 1710), an important landowner around Harefield. The sculptor was Grinling Gibbons.

In the churchyard and on the outside church walls are several other interesting homely memorials to less important people, including over a hundred Australians who died in Harefield Park Hospital between 1915 and 1919, casualties of the Gallipoli campaign.

## Hartington DERBYSHIRE

ST GILES This church is situated in the centre of a gorgeous village in the Peak District National Park, about 1.6 km (1 mile) from the River Dove.

On the outside of the tower at the w end are two lead crosses and on the sides of the window are engravings of a chalice, a wafer and an open book.

Hanging high up in the s transept are 12 panels dating from c.1700 depicting the 12 tribes of Israel. Restored in memory of Thomas Joseph Brindley (1890–1970) they are the only complete set on wooden panels in the country.

## Hawkhurst KENT

ST LAURENCE contains much fine modern stained glass replacing that destroyed by a flying bomb on 13 August 1944. The remains of the bomb can be seen on the sill of the w window in the s aisle together with fragments of glass in the w window.

Over the N door is a coat of arms of Queen Elizabeth II dated 1957 – the year the church was reopened after bomb damage.

Against the E wall of the N chapel is a propeller cross in memory of Captain A. T. Loyd, killed 28 September 1917, aged 23, while flying near Ypres.

On the s wall is a memorial to Sir John Herschel (1792–1871) and his wife. Among other things he was a great astronomer and an early pioneer of photography.

## Haworth WEST YORKSHIRE

ST MICHAEL & ALL ANGELS The church and village are both much associated with the famous Brontë family.

In the s nave aisle is a stained-glass window in memory of Charlotte Brontë. It was given by Thomas Hockley, an American.

At the E end of the s aisle is the Brontë Memorial chapel dedicated on 4 July 1964. Underneath is the vault of the Brontë family where all the family is buried except for Anne, who died in Scarborough (N. Yorkshire) and is buried in St Mary's churchyard there.

With the exception of the tower, which would have been known to the Brontës, the remainder of their church was replaced by the present building in 1879.

*The superb Easter Sepulchre at Hawton, Nottinghamshire.*

## Hawton                        NOTTINGHAMSHIRE

ALL SAINTS In the pleasant countryside just
s of Newark, this church has a fine
fifteenth-century tower crowned with eight
pinnacles. Across the fields the twin towers
of Southwell Cathedral can be seen.

▦ Dating from c.1320 the Easter sepulchre
in the N wall of the chancel is the finest in
England and Wales. Much of the carving
has been damaged but the Risen Christ is
still clearly visible inside the recess with
four sleeping Roman soldiers below.

▦ The E window is a superb example of
Decorated architecture with curvilinear
tracery.

▦ Note the fine sedilia on the s side of the
chancel, dating from c.1350, with richly
carved canopies comparable to the Easter
sepulchre.

## Hayling Island               HAMPSHIRE

ST PETER, North Hayling, originally built
c.1150, this church was enlarged c.1250.

▦ On the E jamb of the N door some pilgrims' crosses are scratched.

▦ Several of the pillars in the nave rest on
huge, uncarved sarsen stones and there is
another one under the buttress at the sw
corner.

▦ The grating in the centre of the nave is
a fine example of Victorian wrought ironwork.

▦ An oval wall tablet commemorates a
Sarah Rogers, who died as a child in 1812.
Her epitaph reads:

'Ye virgins fair, your fading charms
    survey,
She was what'er your tender hearts
    can say.
Let opening roses, drooping lilies, tell,
Like these she bloomed, and ah! like
    these she fell.'

▦ The bells comprise the oldest set of
three in England dating from c.1350. They
are still on their wooden axles and wood-
en half wheels. The largest bell is inscribed
'Sancta Maria ora pro nobis' ('Holy Mary
pray for us'). (See Bells, page 293.)

▦ Outside, on the sloping part of the SE
buttress of the chancel, is a mass dial and
above it are carvings in the shape of the
Star of David entwined with a pentagram.

▦ In the churchyard are some interesting
gravestones commemorating others of
Sarah Rogers's family. One very unusual
one is over John Rogers's grave. He died in
1808 and his stone shows a man in a top
hat accompanied by a weeping woman
gazing at a coffin on a table!

▦ In the NW corner of the churchyard is
an ancient yew tree and not far from it,
near the car park, is the grave of Princess
Catherine Yourievsky (22 September
1880–22 December 1959). She was a member of the ill-fated Russian royal family
and lived in North Hayling for many years.

## Heathfield                    EAST SUSSEX

ALL SAINTS In a busy little town at the
intersection of the A265 and A267, the
church stands quite near Heathfield Park.

▦ The 30.5m (100 feet), thirteenth-century
shingled spire is one of the most graceful
in England.

▦ Inside the tower is scratched the date
1445 in Arabic numerals – one of the oldest
examples of such numerals in the British
Isles.

▦ In the nave is an alms-box dating from
c.1610. It is hollowed out of a tree trunk
and has wrought-iron hinges, staple and
lock of Sussex iron.

▦ A stained-glass window depicts the
Reverend Robert Hunt, vicar of
Heathfield (1602–8), who was chaplain to
the first English settlement in Jamestown,

Virginia, in 1607 and was the first known celebrant of Holy Communion in what was to become the USA.

## Hedon     EAST RIDING
(pronounced 'Heddon')     OF YORKSHIRE

ST AUGUSTINE dominates the small town and is known as 'the King of Holderness'.

🔲 An unusual stained-glass window in the N aisle commemorates Samuel and Mary Rimmington. It depicts Christ in Majesty in the centre and underneath, St Augustine of Hippo. In the left-hand light are the words, 'From this slavery can nothing deliver man but the Grace of God through our Lord Jesus Christ A.D.426.'

Above is a bull about to be sacrificed and other creatures and in the right-hand light are a couple chained to a post and others kneeling with the words, 'My son, hast thou sinned? Do so no more, but pray for thy sins past that they may be forgiven thee. A.D.1951.'

🔲 Blocked arches on the S side of the chancel once opened into a now-demolished chantry chapel of St Mary.

## Helpringham     LINCOLNSHIRE

ST ANDREW This church featured on the 7½p British postage stamp illustrating village churches issued on 21 June 1972.

🔲 The fine tower and spire date from c.1400 and form an imposing landmark.

🔲 The E window of the N aisle depicts Christ the King with St Andrew and St Hugh of Lincoln. It was made by P. E. Lemmon of Bromsgrove.

🔲 Another nearby window by the same artist depicts St Luke with St Gilbert, Abbot of Sempringham, 1131, and Edward of Lincoln, 1885–1910.

🔲 Another window in the S aisle by P. E. Lemmon shows the Virgin Mary as Queen

of Heaven with the Seven Sacraments. Note the Boston 'stump' in the head of the window and Croyland Abbey and Sleaford Church.

## Hempstead     ESSEX

ST ANDREW Situated on a hill above the village, the tower was rebuilt c.1934 as a tribute to William Harvey.

🔲 In the Harvey chapel is an impressive bust of William Harvey (1578–1657). He was chief physician to Charles I and in 1628 announced that blood circulates around the body by means of the heart.

🔲 In the crypt underneath are 13 lead coffins with the modelled faces of members of the Harvey family – a unique collection.

## Hereford

THE CATHEDRAL CHURCH OF ST MARY & ST ETHELBERT The cathedral is partly enclosed by other buildings but is well seen from the medieval bridge over the River Wye.

🔲 The 42.7 m (140 feet) tower was built c.1320 and is unique because of the hundreds of small 'ball-flowers' carved around windows and buttresses. Unfortunately many have weathered badly.

🔲 The W tower collapsed in 1786. James Wyatt subsequently decided to rebuild only the upper part of the nave above the Norman pillars and to reduce it by one bay. The vaulting is of plaster. Wyatt's W front was replaced by that we see today built by J. Oldrid Scott between 1902 and 1908.

🔲 The crypt dates from c.1217 to 1220 and is one of only two Early English crypts in England. (The other is at Rochester Cathedral, see page 286.)

🔲 The N transept dates from c.1250 to 1260

and is a unique example of Geometrical architecture. Notice how the arches are almost triangular!

Also in this transept is the shrine of St Thomas de Cantelupe (1287).

▣ In the new cathedral library (opened 3 May 1996) at the w end of the cathedral, is the largest chained library in the world containing nearly 1500 books.

Other treasures include:

† The famous *Mappa Mundi* (World Map). Drawn on vellum by Richard de Bello (*c.*1275) this unique map shows Jerusalem as the centre of the world. It measures 1.65m (5ft. 5in.) x 1.35m (4ft. 5in.). Its original oak case is also preserved but was only rediscovered in 1989.

† The *Hereford Breviary* with music. Dating from *c.*1265 to 1270 this is the only known breviary with music. It disappeared from the cathedral *c.* 1550 and was found by a musician, William Hawes, *c.*1830 in a London bookshop and sold back to the cathedral.

† A copy of the Anglo-Saxon gospels dating from *c.*750 to 850.

† A manuscript dating from *c.*1150, reputed to have the earliest drawing of an abacus, which was introduced to England by Bishop Robert Losinga (1079–95).

† The oldest brass effigy to an English king. Dating from *c.*1290 it depicts St Ethelbert (860–866) and once formed part of a larger brass to St Thomas de Cantelupe. A choirboy stole it in 1819 but returned it in 1865.

† A fine twelfth-century reliquary depicting the martyrdom of St Thomas à Becket in 1170.

▣ In the wall of the s transept is a fireplace, one of only two in a Norman cathedral. (See also Durham Cathedral, page 110.)

▣ On the s side of the lady chapel is the chantry chapel of Bishop Audley

(1492–1503). He later moved to Salisbury, where he is buried in a similar chapel.

▣ One of the three original doors is carved with linen-fold panels – the earliest linen-fold carving in England.

▣ Near the Audley chantry is the tomb of John de Swinfield (1310). Note the 16 swine carved around the arch – a rebus or pun on Swinfield's name.

▣ In a window on the s side of the lady chapel is stained glass dating from *c.*1250 showing Jesus carrying a *green* cross to Calvary. This is meant to signify the living power of the Cross.

▣ In the N choir aisle is John Stanbury's chantry chapel. Dating from *c.*1480, it contains beautiful fan vaulting.

# Hever　　　　　　　　　　KENT

St Peter is situated on high ground overlooking the valley of the River Eden.

▣ The famous brass of Sir Thomas Bullen (d. 1538) in the Bullen chapel is one of only two in England (the other is at Little Easton, Essex) showing a knight wearing the full insignia of the Order of the Garter. He was the father of Anne Boleyn, Henry VIII's second wife. This brass has been described as 'the finest post-Reformation brass in England'.

▣ A stained-glass window of 1986 in memory of the second Baron Astor incorporates ancient glass originally in the Bullen chapel.

# Hexham　　　　　　NORTHUMBERLAND

ABBEY CHURCH OF ST ANDREW The Abbey dominates the marketplace of this small town.

▣ The font is part of a Roman column on a thirteenth-century base. The cover dates from the eighteenth century.

▣ In the s transept are the unique night

stairs dating from the thirteenth century. They led from the canons' dormitory into the church.

🔲 At the foot of the stairs in the s transept is a magnificent memorial stone to a Roman standard bearer dating from c.80.

🔲 Opposite the Roman's memorial stone is Acca's cross. This stood at the head of the grave of Acca, Bishop of Hexham (709–32), who died in 740.

🔲 In the chancel is a superb set of 38 misericords dating from c.1450.

🔲 Above the altar is a reproduction painting of the Holy Family. The original, by Andre Del Sarto, is in the Pitti Palace, Florence, Italy.

🔲 In the chancel is the famous Frith stool ,which is reputed to have been brought from Italy by St Wilfrid in 674 to be his episcopal throne.

🔲 To the N of the sanctuary is a fine fifteenth-century screen with beautiful paintings including four of 'The Dance of Death'. Incorporated in the screen is a reading desk. This probably came from the canons' refectory.

🔲 Near this screen in the N choir aisle is the chantry of Prior Leschman, made between 1480 and 1491. It is decorated with sculptures, many of which are amusing, including a fox preaching to geese and the symbol of gluttony.

🔲 In the s choir aisle in a wall recess is a small Anglo-Saxon chalice, 13 cm (5 inches) high made of copper-gilt. In respect of size and material it is unique and is one of only two Anglo-Saxon chalices in existence. (The other, known as the Trewhiddle chalice, is made of silver and is in the British Museum, London.)

🔲 At the w end of the nave, under the w window, is a copper wall plate to the memory of William Chipchase Henderson (d. 1914), a great benefactor of Hexham Abbey. It concludes with these words: 'His heart was rich of such fine mould that if you sowed therein the seed of hate it blossomed charity.'

🔲 The beautiful organ was built by Lawrence Phelps in 1974. It is unusual in that when services are held in the choir, special electronically controlled doors in the back of the case will allow for projection of the sound to that area. Normally the sound projects to the nave.

🔲 In the s choir aisle is an unusual wooden chantry erected for Sir Robert Ogle (d. 1490). At the E end is a triptych contemporary with the chantry, with an interesting story attached to it. From c.1830 to 1860 it was covered with green baize and then claimed by a joiner as part of his contract to remove old material, which the abbey authorities allowed him to do! After spending two years in his attic it was sold to Mr R. F. Wilson, an architect of Alnwick, and it remained in the possession of this man's widow until 1895 as no one would buy it. Mr Bond of Newcastle then purchased it, but after only a few days it was sold on to Mr W. D. Cruddas of Haughton Castle in December 1895. In 1960 it was returned to the abbey under the will of his daughter, Miss Eleanor Cruddas, and replaced in its original position.

The paintings in the triptych depict Our Lord, Our Lady and St John.

🔲 At the E end of the nave is the entrance to the crypt, built by St Wilfrid c.674 using stones from the Roman camp of Corstopitum. One of the stones bears an Imperial inscription and others have Roman carvings on them.

## Hillesden                    BUCKINGHAMSHIRE

ALL SAINTS & ST NICHOLAS is situated at the end of a winding country road that finishes at the church on a hilltop commanding magnificent views.

*Modern RAF fighter jet aircraft fly over ancient flying buttresses at Hillesden, Buckinghamshire.*

This is a real gem of the Perpendicular period. On the NE side is a two-storey vestry and stair turret which is topped by a stone 'crown' of pinnacles and flying buttresses.

The Victorian architect Gilbert Scott was born at nearby Gawcott. At the age of 15 he made a drawing of Hillesden Church which is preserved in the vestry.

The beautiful fan-vaulted N porch still has its original door of c.1450 complete with bullet holes from the days of the Civil War. (See Fan Vaulting, page 152.)

The E window of the S transept contains beautiful stained glass dating from c.1510 in its upper eight panels. Depicting the story of St Nicholas, some of the faces are quite amusing. Note the boy and the gold cup falling from the ship in the extreme left-hand panel.

The S window adjoining the St Nicholas window is in the same style but dates from 1875. It illustrates numerous parables including the Good Samaritan and Prodigal Son.

The E window of the chancel contains fragments of fifteenth-century glass in its tracery, while other fragments in the SE window of the S aisle show heads of bishops.

Below the chancel ceiling on the N and S sides are carved angels, 18 on each side, some bearing traces of the original blue colouring. Sixteen on each side carry scrolls but the two nearest the altar carry instruments. Four more angels on each side of the altar also carry instruments including a portable organ.

On the N side of the chancel in the N aisle is the tomb of Thomas Denton, who died in 1644 at the Battle of Abingdon. The tomb was damaged by the Cromwellians.

# Hindringham      NORFOLK

ST MARTIN lies off the A148, between Cromer and King's Lynn. It stands on a little hill and, with its tall tower, it dominates the village below.

The treasure of this church is an ancient chest dating from c.1175, considered by some to be the oldest in England. The front is decorated with interlaced Norman arches.

# Hodnet      SHROPSHIRE

ST LUKE With its unusual tower, this beautiful church stands on raised ground to the NW of the village.

This is the only octagonal tower in Shropshire and dates from c.1350.

At the E end of the S aisle the paving of the chancel commemorates Bishop Heber, who was born here and was rector of Hodnet 1807–23, then Bishop of Calcutta. Notice the tiles with the initials R. H. and the bishop's mitre.

On the S side of the chancel is a suit of armour dating from c.1550 which may have belonged to the Vernon family. The sword is a genuine Andrea Ferrara.

On the N side of the N aisle is the Heber Percy chapel, built in 1870 to commemorate members of the family. On the N wall of the chapel is a medallion of Bishop Reginald Heber (21 April 1783–3 April 1826) by Chantrey. While here, Heber wrote many of his famous hymns including, 'Holy, Holy, Holy, Lord God Almighty', 'Brightest and best of the sons of the morning' and 'God that madest earth and heaven'.

In the centre of the Heber Percy chapel is a beautiful recumbent figure of a granddaughter of Bishop Heber who died in 1870. This was sculptured by Reginald Cholmondeley.

At the W end is a curious font which has

eight differently carved panels. It probably dates from *c.*1650.

# Hope under Dinmore     HEREFORDSHIRE

ST MARY THE VIRGIN can be found on the slope of Dinmore Hill, in beautiful countryside, not far from Hampton Court (the ancestral home of the Conyngsbys).

A unique monument to the Earl and Countess Conyngsby (*c.*1740) shows the countess seated with her infant son on her lap. The baby died in 1708 by choking on a cherry and he is depicted holding one!

# Horsmonden
(pronounced 'Horsm'nden')     KENT

ST MARGARET OF ANTIOCH is situated some distance s of the village.

In the s wall are *two* rood stairways dating from *c.*1455. Two stairways are very unusual and it is thought the E one was abandoned when weaknesses were noticed on a pier of the chancel arch.

A bust in the s aisle commemorates the rector's gardener, John Reid (d. 3 May 1847, aged 87). He invented the stomach pump and 'many other useful implements for the benefit or relief of suffering humanity'. He demonstrated the pump to members of the Royal Society in 1823.

In the centre of the chancel floor is a brass to Henry de Grofhurst, *c.*1340. This is one of the finest episcopal brasses in existence and shows a priest wearing full Eucharistic vestments and standing underneath a pedimented canopy. Around the brass is a border which states that it was restored in 1867 when new symbols of the Evangelists were added at the corners and columns and finials to the canopy.

At the E end of the nave, abutting the chancel step, is the iron grave-slab of Martha Browne, wife of John Browne, the gun-founder. It dates from *c.*1660.

In 1944 a German flying bomb fell just NE of the church and destroyed all the stained glass on that side. The beautiful E window dates from 1946 and depicts Christ Triumphant on the Cross. The w window dates from 1948 and shows Christ in Majesty. Both windows were designed by Rosemary Everett.

# Hove     EAST SUSSEX

ST ANDREW (Old Church), Church Road, was rebuilt in 1836 to its original design, using much original stonework inside and incorporating the old chancel. The architect was George Basevi.

Sir George Everest (4 July 1790–1 December 1866) is buried on the s side of the churchyard, close to the front wall and near the E end of the church. He was born at Gwernvale House, Crickhowell (Powys), and was a military engineer and Surveyor General of India (1823–42). Mount Everest was named after him in 1856.

He did not marry his wife Emma until he was 56. They had two sons and four daughters. Two daughters, Emma Colebrooke (died 10 February 1852, aged 2 years 10 months) and Benigna Edith (died 24 January 1860, aged 4 months), are buried with him.

His sister, Lucetta Mary Everest, is buried next to him (1787–10 January 1857).

Also on the s side of the church (1789-1871) Charlotte Elliott is buried. She wrote such hymns as 'Just as I am – without one plea' and 'Christian, seek not yet repose'.

# Howden     EAST RIDING OF YORKSHIRE

THE MINSTER AND COLLEGIATE CHURCH OF ST PETER & ST PAUL This magnificent church dominates this small town and is seen clearly from the M62 motorway. The tower rises to a height of 41.15 m (135 feet). The chancel became ruinous in 1696 and the chapter house in 1750. The latter received a new roof in 1984.

Inside, at the E end, notice the massive piers supporting the central tower. Underneath is a fine medieval pulpitum; this originally divided the nave from the choir.

Affixed to a pier on the S side of the tower in the S transept is a rare statue of 1340 depicting the Blessed Virgin Mary. Note the Dove, symbol of the Holy Spirit, speaking into her left ear!

Off the S transept is the Saltmarshe chapel, where many members of the family are commemorated. Note the old parish coffin dating from 1664 – this would have been used for carrying bodies to the graveside only.

In the nave note the unusual figures peering down above the pillars.

## Hucknall
### or Hucknall Torkard     NOTTINGHAMSHIRE

ST MARY MAGDALENE & ST JOHN THE EVANGELIST This is a large church with a pinnacled W tower dominating the centre of the town.

In the chancel floor there is a marble slab over the grave of Lord Byron, the poet (22 January 1788–19 April 1824), and on the S wall of the chancel is a memorial tablet to him.

Near the lectern is the entrance to the Byron vault in which rest 27 members of the family including the poet's daughter, Augusta Ada, who died in 1852.

## Hughenden       BUCKINGHAMSHIRE

ST MICHAEL & ALL ANGELS is beautifully situated near Hughenden Manor.

On the N side of the chancel is a

memorial to Benjamin Disraeli (1804–81) by R. C. Belt. Below the profile likeness is the inscription, 'To the dear and honoured memory of Benjamin, Earl of Beaconsfield. This memorial is placed by his grateful Sovereign and friend, Victoria R. I. 'Kings love him that speaketh right.' – *Proverbs* 16, v.13. February 27, 1882.'

A stained-glass window on the S side of the nave, the W window, an organ, the decoration of the chancel, two candelabra and two bells (to complete a ring of eight) were also given as memorials to Disraeli, a great Victorian prime minister, whose grave is in the churchyard.

## Huish Episcopi       SOMERSET

ST MARY 'Episcopi' means 'of the Bishop' because in medieval times the manor was under the authority of the Bishop of Bath and Wells.

The magnificent tower featured on the 9p postage stamp of the British village churches set issued on 21 June 1972. It is 30.5 m (100 feet) high and is richly decorated with pinnacles and elaborate niches which once held statues. The battlemented top is particularly beautiful.

The Norman S doorway dates from 1150 to 1200 and was discoloured by a fire which destroyed much of the church *c*.1300.

The blue wagon roof of the nave is a copy of the medieval blue and was restored in 1873 when the stencilled pattern was added.

In the S chapel is a Burne-Jones window showing a Nativity scene with kings and red-winged angels.

## Hull
### or Kingston upon Hull    EAST RIDING OF YORKSHIRE

HOLY TRINITY & HOLY APOSTLES was described by Sir Nikolaus Pevsner as 'the largest of all English parish churches – that is by area'. It is the largest parish church in England that is not a minster. (See Beverley Minster, page 26.) It has a total area of 2530 sq m (27,235 sq feet), an external length of 87.8 m (288 feet) and an external width of 37.8 m (124 feet).

▨ Dating from c.1420 the transepts contain some of the earliest medieval brickwork in England.

▨ The interior is very spacious and high and is filled with light flooding in through plain glass.

▨ At the w end of the nave is the richly carved font dating from c.1380. The bowl rests on eight supporting shafts which have tiny buttresses. Among the carving is a boar with a pineapple in its mouth.

▨ The impressive chancel is very high with aisles on its N and S sides. The fine curvilinear E window is filled with good stained glass.

▨ In the N aisle of the chancel is a wall monument to Thomas Ferres (d. 31 January 1630, aged 62). Among the many offices he held was that of Mayor of Hull. His bust stands on a pedestal while an angel administers a drink to a dying man.

▨ Note the enormous piers supporting the central tower, which is 45.7 m (150 feet) high and has a ring of 15 bells.

## Hursley                     HAMPSHIRE

ALL SAINTS This church is almost a shrine to John Keble who wrote many well-known hymns, including 'Blest are the pure in heart' and 'Sun of my soul, Thou Saviour dear'.

▨ A red granite stone engraved with a cross, book and chalice near the SW corner of the tower marks the grave of John Keble, author of The Christian Year. It is inscribed, 'Here rests in peace the body of John Keble, vicar of this parish, who departed this life Maundy Thursday, March 29, 1866. Et lvx perpetva lvceat eis.'

His wife lies next to him; she died 11 May 1866.

▨ Near the Keble graves is a mausoleum for the Heathcote family, who rebuilt the church in 1752 and which was replaced 1847–8 by the present building, largely using the proceeds of The Christian Year.

▨ The spire, which dated from this time, was removed in 1960 as it was found to be unsafe.

▨ The stained-glass windows are Keble's inspiration and were modelled on his home church of Fairford (Gloucestershire) providing a history from Adam to the Last Judgement. They were made by William Wailes.

▨ On the N wall inside the tower is a large monument to the Cromwell family, descendants of Oliver Cromwell. Richard Cromwell was married here on 1 May 1649.

## Hythe                            KENT

ST LEONARD The beautiful church is very prominent on its hillside among the houses of this small town.

▨ The chancel, approached by several steps from the nave, dates from c.1200. It is unusual in possessing a triforium and clerestory (normally only found in larger churches). The vaulted roof was erected by J. L. Pearson c.1850.

▨ Under the chancel is a bone hole containing a large collection of human skulls and bones which were removed from the churchyard hundreds of years ago to make way for more burials. This charnel house is one of only two still surviving in Britain. (The other is at Rothwell, Northants.)

# CHURCH DOVECOTES

In the Middle Ages many of the farmers' cattle were slaughtered in the winter because there were no root crops to feed them. The only supply of fresh meat, therefore, came from pigeons or doves, and to house them special dove-cotes were built through-out the country. This would usually be done by the Lord of the Manor, the village priest or monks of a nearby monastery. Many of these dovecotes are distinguished by their circular design and conical roofs. In a few instances the priest of the parish had his own dove-cote either inside or near the church.

*Norton-sub-Hamdon, Somerset.*

around the walls – an amazing sight above the chancel!

In the churchyard at Broughton, Hampshire, there is a circular brick dove-cote with a conical roof and lantern dating from *c*.1650. Another, dating from *c*.1450, is in the churchyard at Norton-sub-Hamdon, Somerset, and has nest-holes for about 500 birds.

In the farm to the s of the church at Garway, Herefordshire, is a large circular dovecote with an inside diameter of 5.49 m (18 feet) and walls 1.2 m (4 feet) thick. An inscription in Latin states that it was built by Richard in 1326.

At Collingbourne Ducis, Wiltshire, Sarnesfield, Herefordshire, and Upton, Nottinghamshire, there are nesting boxes for doves inside the church tower. At Collingbourne Ducis there are 300 nest-holes and at Sarnesfield over 100 birds can be housed.

At Compton Martin, Somerset, and Overbury, Worcestershire, former dove-cotes exist above the chancel. They were reached from the *outside* of the church, but the steps are gone although the doors are still in place. At Overbury the door, at 0.91 m x 0.61 m (3 feet x 2 feet) is about 4.57 m (15 feet) above the ground on the N side of the chancel. Inside the dovecote are boxes for 200 birds. A similar arrangement occurs at Elkstone, Gloucestershire, but the dove-cote there is approached by a narrow stair-case inside the chancel wall. Above, are about 50 nest-holes arranged

As far as I know, former dovecotes exist in or near the following churches:

1. Arlingham (St Mary), Gloucestershire – facing the church
2. Avebury (St James), Wiltshire – near the church
3. Bibury (St Mary), Gloucestershire – near the churchyard gate
4. Birlingham (St James), Worcestershire – church tower
5. Brockhampton-by-Ross (All Saints), Herefordshire – church tower
6. Broughton (St Mary), Hampshire – in the churchyard
7. Collingbourne Ducis (St Andrew), Wiltshire – church tower
8. Compton Martin (St Michael), Somerset – over the chancel
9. Elkstone (St John), Gloucestershire – over the chancel
10. Fladbury (St John Baptist),

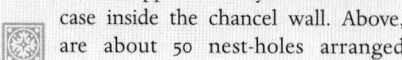

Worcestershire – former chapel

11. Garway (St Michael), Herefordshire – s of the church
12. Gumfreston (St Lawrence), Pembrokeshire – church tower
13. Lindfield (St John Baptist), West Sussex – church roof
14. Little Badminton (St Michael), Gloucestershire – near the church
15. Nassington (All Saints), Northamptonshire – near the E wall of the tower
16. Norton-sub-Hamdon (St Mary), Somerset – in the churchyard
17. Overbury (St Faith), Worcestershire – over the chancel

18. Sarnesfield (St Mary), Herefordshire – church tower
19. Sibthorpe (St Peter), Nottinghamshire – field E of the church
20. Skenfrith (St Bridget), Monmouthshire – church tower
21. Thame (St Mary), Oxfordshire – in the churchyard
22. Ugley, Essex (St Peter) – church tower
23. Upton (St Peter), Nottinghamshire – church tower
24. Witham Friary (St Mary, St John Baptist and All Saints), Somerset – near the church

# PALINDROMES

Palindromes (words that read the same forwards and backwards) appear in numerous places in churches such as epitaphs, inscriptions and so on.

One of the most interesting palindromes is a Greek one: '*NIYONANOMH-MATAMHMONANOYIN*', meaning, 'Wash my sins and not my face only'. This has been inscribed on a few fonts, font bases and font covers in England. As far as I know, this Greek palindrome is found in the following churches:

1. Caddington (All Saints), Bedfordshire
2. Dedham (St Mary the Virgin), Essex
3. Great Shefford (St Mary), Berkshire

4. Hadleigh (St James the Less), Essex
5. Hadleigh (St Mary), Suffolk
6. Harlow (St Mary the Virgin), Essex
7. Kinnerley (St Mary), Shropshire
8. Knapton (St Peter & St Paul), Norfolk
9. Leominster (St Peter & St Paul), Herefordshire
10. London (St Martin's, Ludgate Hill)
11. Melton Mowbray (St Mary), Leicestershire
12. Melverley (St Peter), Shropshire
13. Nottingham (St Mary)
14. Rufford (St Mary), Lancashire
15. Sandbach (St Mary), Cheshire
16. Woldingham (St Paul), Surrey
17. Worlingworth (St Mary), Suffolk

*Schoolchildren explore the west end of Iffley, Oxfordshire, during an educational visit in 1961.*

## Ickleton CAMBRIDGESHIRE

ST MARY MAGDALENE Much of the church was seriously damaged by fire in an arson attack during the night of 24 August 1979. Restoration was completed by June 1981.

 Four round columns in the nave are monolithic shafts of Barnack stone which probably came from an earlier Saxon church on this site. These may have been used originally by the Romans!

 The double clerestory in the nave is an unusual feature.

 On the N wall of the nave and above the chancel arch are a series of very early wall paintings. Those in the nave date from c.1170 while the one above the chancel arch dates from c.1350. These paintings were discovered during the cleaning process following the fire of 1979!

The nave paintings at the top between the windows depict, from left to right, the Last Supper, the Betrayal, the Flagellation and Christ carrying the Cross.

The lower scenes depict the martyrdoms of St Peter, St Andrew and St Lawrence.

Above the chancel arch is a doom painting illustrating the Day of Judgement. An unusual feature is the portrait of the Virgin showing her with bare breasts – unique in a wall painting in a church.

Six medieval poppy heads (some restored) have survived on the bench-ends in the nave. One bench-end shows two cocks facing each other and another shows St Michael weighing souls.

 The beautiful rood screen dates from c.1380 and also the painted font cover.

 On the S and E faces of the central tower are two crosses created from black flint – an unusual feature.

 On the outside of the lead-covered spire on the S is a small sanctus bell, which is now used as the hour bell for the clock. It dates from c.1490 to 1510.

## Idbury OXFORDSHIRE

ST NICHOLAS is found high up in the Cotswolds, N of Burford in beautiful countryside.

 The blocked N doorway dates from c.1150 and has rich carving on the outside.

 On the N side of the churchyard is an impressive tomb commemorating the Baker family. It comprises a Celtic cross supported on flying buttresses. In the grave is buried Sir Benjamin Baker, KCB, KCMG, FRS (31 March 1841–19 May 1907), his mother, Sarah Baker (5 March 1815–22 December 1891), and his sister, Fanny Maria Kemp (6 October 1838–10 February 1911).

Sir Benjamin designed the Forth Railway Bridge (completed 1890), the Aswan Dam, Egypt (completed 1902), and helped in the building of the London Underground.

## Idsworth HAMPSHIRE

ST HUBERT is situated remotely in a field not far from the main Havant to London railway line. Dedicated in 1053 this church

# PARISH ARMOURY

From the days of Edward II (1284–1327) every parish was obliged to provide fully equipped soldiers to serve at home or overseas. The necessary armour was usually kept in the church, perhaps in a room over the porch if one existed, a vestry or a specially built room, which had then to be equipped with the appropriate security.

Mendlesham, Suffolk, possesses the finest collection of armour still surviving in any church in England or Wales, although a few churches retain single items. It is housed in a room over the N porch approached by a narrow staircase. The use of this room as an armoury dates back to

1593 when it is recorded that Bartholomew Knightes was paid 16 d (7 p) 'for making of certain provision of timber work for the well hanging up of, the Town Armour, he finding the timber'. Because this work was done so well, it is still an excellent 'strong room' with barred windows and a heavy iron-plated door and three locks. The original heavy keys are still in use!

Although some of the armour has nevertheless disappeared, much has survived. In addition, the armoury also houses other valuable items such as pewter measures and pieces of stained glass.

is famous for its numerous wall paintings.  On the N wall of the chancel are two paintings separated by a border. In the upper one is St Hubert in a hunting scene, touching a wolf-like man. This is the only wall painting of St Hubert. Below is the dance of Salome in front of Herod. On a plate is the head of John the Baptist.

On the splays of the E window are paintings of St Peter and St Paul. St Peter holds keys and St Paul a book.

In the E window is a medallion of Flemish glass showing St Hubert kneeling by a tree. In the background is a magnificent stag with a crucifix between its antlers.

## Iffley                          OXFORDSHIRE

ST MARY THE VIRGIN is the finest Norman church in Oxfordshire and one of the most

famous in England. It was built soon after 1160.

The W front is very impressive with its deeply recessed doorway and three windows in the gable, all original Norman work. The doorway is particularly fine and exhibits chevron and beak-head ornament. The circular window was restored to its original form in 1858 following traces of the former Norman circular surround that had survived when a Perpendicular window was inserted in c.1450.

The arches under the tower are of three orders and contain rich chevron ornament.

The sanctuary at the E end is a fine example from the thirteenth century.

In the SE window of the nave are fragments of medieval glass showing the arms (c.1475) of John de la Pole, Duke of Suffolk, great-grandson of Geoffrey Chaucer. (See Ewelme, Oxfordshire, page 131.)

## Kemsing KENT

St Mary the Virgin The church is set to the N of this long village situated just under the North Downs and the Pilgrims' Way.

 The elaborate rood screen and loft, dating from 1894, was carved by W. F. Unsworth but it incorporates older work. The rood figures are by Sir Ninian Comper.

 In a lancet in the s wall of the nave is a roundel of glass showing the Virgin and Child dating from c.1220. The Virgin wears a green cloak.

 Underneath this window is a magnificent framed tapestry depicting Kemsing in 1991.

 Near the font is a bronze of an angel holding a child enclosed in a marble surround. It was made by Henry Wilson in 1922.

 In the centre of the chancel floor is a modern brass to Thomas Carleton Skarratt (d. 1908), who built the N aisle.

 In the N aisle hangs an unusual copper and wrought-iron lamp of c.1893.

 At the NE end of the N aisle is a wall tablet commemorating George Turner (4 March 1808–14 July 1880), probably a local farmer. It is surmounted by a beautiful model of a plough.

 Underneath are some coloured views of Kemsing painted on tiles accompanied by facts about the village in 1921 and 1934. It is interesting to note that within 13 years the population had increased from 715 to 1402.

 On one side of the churchyard is an unusual eighteenth-century brick crinkle-crankle wall, characterized by concave and convex curving of the wall. This gives it greater strength, but the original reason for such constructions is unknown.

## Kenardington KENT

St Mary is situated at the end of a winding country lane on top of a small hill with beautiful views from the churchyard over Romney Marsh. The church is approached via a narrow footpath running through the grounds of a private house.

 On the N side of the tower is an attractive stair turret crowned with a conical roof.

 The nave, which led from the w tower, has been demolished and the tower arch is blocked up.

 At the SE end of the existing aisle is an unusual blocked window. Originally a three-light window, only the middle light remains open!

## Kenn DEVON

St Andrew An impressive red sandstone church, it dominates the little village in the countryside, just off the busy A38, between Exeter and Plymouth.

 The screen stretches across the entire width of the church encompassing the N and s aisles. Dating from c.1500 it has 47 painted panels at its base.

In the centre panel of the three at the foot of the pillar supporting the arch on the s side is an unusual depiction of a lily crucifix. God is shown at the top, below

Him is the Holy Spirit with wings and below Him, Christ on the cross. The cross is shown as the trunk of a tree standing in a pot with lilies on each side. (See Lily Crucifix, page 338.)

☒ Many of the stained-glass windows were inserted c.1880 onwards during the incumbency of the Reverend R. Porter, who designed them as a series. They were made by Hardman of Birmingham and are considered very fine.

☒ Another unusual feature is to be found around the s chancel window – two angels are shown playing musical instruments although one instrument is missing, possibly a lyre or a flute.

☒ High on the w wall of the N aisle is an ancient panel showing saints and possibly the head of Richard I. It does not seem to have any connection with the screen, but may be contemporary with it.

# Kenton     DEVON

ALL SAINTS stands out in the village with its typical West Country tower of red sandstone.

☒ All the piers of the nave lean out of the perpendicular. Each of the capitals is different, but the following should be especially noted:

† The one on the NW side near the font which shows four faces with linked arms.

† Opposite this, at the extreme NW end is a king, probably Henry IV.

† On the SE side near the lectern are two grotesque faces.

☒ The magnificent rood screen extends right across the E end of the church and dates from c.1455. It was beautifully restored between 1899 and 1935. At the base are 40 panels of saints and prophets. Notice 12 figures of the Apostles, only 12.7 cm (5 inches) high, around the central doorway.

☒ The fifteenth-century pulpit was

thrown out of the church c.1870 and was discovered by the Reverend Sabine Baring Gould in 1882 dismantled in a cupboard at the village school. It was carefully restored and returned to its rightful place, thanks to scale drawings of it which he had made at the age of 17 in 1851, when it was still in the church!

☒ On the N side of the chancel is the lady chapel. On the N wall is a wooden plaque decorated with skulls, crossbones and an hour-glass commemorating a lady called Elizabeth Atwill, who died in childbirth in 1673.

# Kesgrave     SUFFOLK

ROMAN CATHOLIC CHURCH Situated on the main A12 road at Kesgrave, between Ipswich and Woodbridge, this little brick church with a western bellcote was dedicated on 8 December 1931. It was built by Mrs Doreen Rope in memory of her husband, Squadron Leader F. Michael Rope, and the 47 other people who died in the R101 when it crashed at Beauvais, France, on 5 October 1930. Squadron Leader Rope was Assistant Chief Designer at the Royal Airship Works, Cardington, and did much original work in designing and constructing the R101. (See Cardington, Bedfordshire, page 64.)

☒ Small pieces of metal from the R101 have been used as door ornaments and keyholes. Most of the metal was so hard that it was impossible to remould it.

☒ Hanging in the apex of the chancel arch is a perfect scale model of the R101.

# Kidlington     OXFORDSHIRE

ST MARY THE VIRGIN The church is quite near the River Cherwell as it makes its way to the Thames at Oxford. The spire of this beautiful church is a notable landmark.

🔲 The stately spire is 51.8 m (170 feet) high.

🔲 The choir stalls, complete with misericords, date from *c*.1250 and are the earliest stalls remaining in a parish church.

## Kilpeck  HEREFORDSHIRE

ST MARY & ST DAVID Situated in remote countryside, this is one of the most famous Norman churches in England and dates from *c*.1140.

🔲 The s doorway is magnificent and well preserved. Notice the carvings of soldiers with flared trousers and numerous mythical beasts. Until the eighteenth century this doorway was protected by a porch. (And unless protection is given again, I fear we shall lose these superb carvings.)

🔲 On each side of the chancel arch are three figures of saints, one above the other, again superbly carved.

🔲 Around the outside of the church, under the roof, is a ledge called a 'corbel table', supported by carvings of birds, mythical animals and fragments of others. There are 74 remaining as the Victorians removed some that were considered inappropriate!

🔲 The outside of the w window is beautifully carved with strap-work and on the NW and SW corners of the building are dragons with long, split tongues.

## Kingsland  HEREFORDSHIRE

ST MICHAEL & ALL ANGELS is a large spacious church with circular clerestory windows.

🔲 On the E side of the N porch is an unusually positioned chantry called the Volka chapel. It contains a miniature four-light E window, a rare type of window on the N side and an arched recess on the S containing an empty stone coffin and a four-light window looking into the church.

*Romanesque carving on the south doorway of Kilpeck, Herefordshire.*

🔲 The E window and S chancel windows contain fourteenth-century glass, the E window being almost complete. Notice Christ in Glory at the top of the E window.

🔲 In the s chapel is the original cartoon by Sir Frank Brangwyn (1867–1956) for his unusual Crucifixion window in Bucklebury Church in which Christ is shown looking *upwards*. The window was given to Bucklebury in 1912 by Mrs Nina Weobley Parry, Countess de Palatiano of the Hartley family, Lords of the Manor of Bucklebury. The glass was executed by the glass painter Sylvester Sparrow. (See Bucklebury, Berkshire, page 55.)

🔲 At the w end of the s aisle are six old bell clappers, *c*.1740.

# King's Lynn · NORFOLK

THE PRIORY CHURCH OF ST MARGARET
WITH ST MARY MAGDALENE AND ALL
THE VIRGIN SAINTS This fine, large
church, with its twin towers, stands in the
Saturday Marketplace in the centre of the
town, facing the medieval Guildhall.

▨ Outside the w door are several levels of
flood marks dating from: 11 March 1883,
1 March 1949, 31 January 1953, 20 March
1961 and 11 January 1978 – the highest level
recorded at 1.22 m (4 feet).

▨ The NW tower was built c.1150 on poor
foundations and largely rebuilt by 1453.
Notice the startling angle of the original
pillars inside the church.

▨ The ten arches of the nave were built in
1744 in 'Georgian Gothic' following the
collapse of the spire on the SW tower in the
great storm of 8 September 1741.

▨ Between the chancel and chancel aisles
are unusual quatrefoil column clusters (of
five columns!) with delightful carvings in
the spandrels between the arches, one showing a man carrying a model of a church.

▨ The unusual E window of the chancel is
circular, filled with Perpendicular tracery.

▨ In the chancel are several interesting
misericords, one showing the Black Prince
with his three feathers.

▨ The fine medieval brass eagle lectern
dates from c.1500. The wings are composed of seven graduated feathers and one
very small edge feather. Four feathers of
the right wing and two of the left have
been restored with a reddish metal – also
the colour of the bookrest. The eagle's
talons are missing. (See Medieval Brass
Lecterns, page 362.)

▨ In the s chancel aisle are the two largest
brasses in Britain. The earlier is of Adam
de Walsoken, 1349. The other commemorates Robert Braunche (1364), who gave a
peacock feast for King Edward III in 1349

and this is shown in the bottom frieze.
This brass is sometimes known as the
'Peacock Brass'. Both average 2.9 m (9 feet
6 inches) in length.

▨ The organ is by Snetzler and was built
in 1754. It had the first dulciana stop.

▨ The fine early Georgian pulpit is
decorated with marquetry panels.

▨ In the SW tower is a moon clock dating
from c.1650. It shows the phases of the
moon and, by means of a green dragon's
tongue, the time of the next high tide on
the River Great Ouse using the 24-hour
system. The letters in 'LYNN HIGH TIDE' are
each two hours apart.

# Kingston-on-Soar · NOTTINGHAMSHIRE

ST WILFRID Apart from the chancel and SE
chapel, the remainder of the church dates
from 1900. The architect was R. Creed.

▨ The font of Chellaston alabaster was
given in 1933 in memory of Margaret Lady
Belper (1852–1922).

▨ Between the chancel and SE chapel is
the Babington chantry erected in 1538. It is
a fantastic display of late Gothic, flower-
ing into Renaissance. There are 200 'babes
in tuns' – a pun on the Babington name.

The chantry commemorates Sir
Anthony and Dame Katherine Babington.
(There is a story that the great-grandson of
the builder of the original church, also
Anthony, hid on top of the monument for
some days before being captured and exe-
cuted for his unsuccessful plot to assassinate
Queen Elizabeth I and free Mary Queen of
Scots in 1586. He was then 25 years old.)

This chantry should be compared with
its contemporary at Boxgrove Priory (see
page 38).

▨ Notice the elaborate decoration around
the E window of the SE chapel inside the
church and the carved Babington arms
outside and on the chancel.

## Lacock

ST CYRIAC is situated in the middle of a beautiful village that is owned, almost entirely, by the National Trust.

On the N side of the chancel is the lady chapel or Talbot aisle. It has a stone lierne vault with pendants and numerous coloured bosses including angels holding a chalice, shields, two bears and a large snail over the E window on the left side. (A snail is only found on one other roof boss – in the chancel of St Mary's Church, Bury St Edmunds – see page 59 – although there is also a snail in the sacristy of Bristol Cathedral and one in Great St Mary's Church, Cambridge.)

Also in the lady chapel is the tomb of Sir William Sharington (d. 1553). He bought the Manor of Lacock from the Crown on 26 July 1540 after Lacock Abbey was dissolved on 21 January 1539. The carving on the tomb represents the finest example of its period in England.

The chancel was remodelled in 1902 in memory of William Henry Fox Talbot (1800–77), an early pioneer of photography.

Above the chancel arch is an unusual six-light window. The soffit of the chancel arch is ornamented with carvings of angels held in place with metal pins. Several have gone from the original 13. Notice the angel fixed upside down on the N side!

On the left side of the altar is a beautiful wall relief in memory of Horatia Gaisford, who died in childbirth in 1851.

On the exterior of the church are a number of gargoyles and grotesque carvings including, on the N clerestory, a man smoking a pipe.

## Lambourn

ST MICHAEL & ALL ANGELS Known as 'the Cathedral of the Downs' this lovely church dominates this famous 'racehorse' town.

The nave is a fine example of Norman architecture.

On the S wall of the S aisle near the entrance to the lady chapel is an unusual alabaster medallion depicting Charles I with the figures of Truth and Justice standing on Roundheads in chains. It dates from 1649.

On the S side of the tower arch facing the nave is a piscina about 3.9 m (13 feet) above the ground. This indicates that there was once an altar at this height on top of the rood screen.

On the N side of the sanctuary is a fine monument to Thomas Garrard (d. 1583) and Agnes, his wife (d. 1556).

In St. Katharine's chapel on the N side of the chancel is the alabaster tomb of Sir Thomas Essex (d. 1558) and Margaret, his wife. There is a dolphin at his feet and a winged horse (damaged) at hers. The glass in the N window of this chapel dates from 1533 and shows a figure in red and green.

In the middle of the lady chapel on the S side of the chancel is a fourteenth-century

*Lacock, Wiltshire. The south side of the church has a domestic appearance.*

arch showing a hunting scene and two men blowing horns.

On the s side of the lady chapel is Holy Trinity chapel. It contains the tomb of John Estbury (d. 1508). The inscription around the edge is interspersed with various animals including a sheep.

Near the organ is a memorial to Sir George Martin which reads:

'To the honoured memory of George Clement Martin, Knight, M.V.O., Mus. Doc., sometime organist of this church, this memorial is erected by his widow. He was born at Lambourne [*sic*] on 11 Sept., 1844 and died in London on 23 Feb., 1916. His body lies buried in peace in the crypt of St. Paul's Cathedral. His name lives in music whose secret he discovered at Lambourne [*sic*] and whose beauty he

dedicated to the worship of Almighty God during 40 years when as sub-organist and master of song and organist of St Paul's he laboured for the power and honour of the sanctuary.'

His best-known hymn tune is 'St Helen', which is sung to the hymn 'Lord, enthroned in heavenly splendour'.

On the n side of the churchyard near the railings is the tombstone of John Carter, who was executed in Reading on 16 March 1833 at the age of 30 for maliciously setting fire to Lambourn in two places on 19 November 1832. He had requested that a memorial be erected as a warning to others.

# Lancing     West Sussex

THE COLLEGE CHAPEL OF ST MARY AND ST NICHOLAS This spectacular chapel on a ridge above the River Adur is well seen from the A27 and the railway to the s.

◈ Founded by Nathaniel Woodard, the foundation stone of this imposing chapel was laid on 28 July 1868 and it was dedicated for use on the 18 July 1911.

With an external height of 45.72 m (150 feet), an internal height from nave floor to the apex of the vault of 27.43 m (90 feet) and 21.3 m (70 feet) deep foundations, it is the largest school chapel in the British Isles. The architects were R. C. and R. H. Carpenter and William Slater.

◈ The w window is not only the largest rose window in the British Isles, but also the largest rose window to be built in Europe since 1538. It is 9.75 m (32 feet) in diameter and incorporates 30,000 separate pieces of glass.

Stephen E. Dykes Bower, architect, designed the tracery and glass and Mr A. E. Buss made the glass in conjunction with Ian Eaton of the London manufacturers Clark Eaton. The heraldic glass portrays 17 schools that grew from the inspiration of Nathaniel Woodard, the founder of Lancing College Public School.

This magnificent window was unveiled in 1978.

◈ The canopied stalls (with the exception of the actual canopies, which were designed by Sir Gilbert Scott) came from Eton College chapel when they were removed following the discovery of medieval wall paintings underneath them.

◈ The large tapestries at the E end were designed by Lady Chilston in 1933 and show different saints of the Church.

◈ On the s side of the choir is the stone chantry chapel of Nathaniel Woodard (21 March 1810–25 April 1891). The recumbent bronze effigy is by P. Bryant Baker (1915) and rests on a slab of Sussex marble.

◈ On the N side of the choir is the wooden chantry chapel of William Woodard, son of Nathaniel (30 March 1842–1 June 1918).

◈ On the N aisle wall is a painting called 'The Holy Family' after Sebastiano del Piombo (Luciani) (1485–1547).

In front of the high altar are two magnificent bronze candlesticks. Note the figures at each corner supporting the weight above.

◈ Underneath the chapel is a large crypt, the s door of which leads into the War Memorial cloister. Beyond, is the vault in which Woodard and two of his sons are buried.

◈ On the N wall of the main crypt chapel is a memorial tablet to Francis Alwyne Woodard (1889–1974), priest, grandson of the founder, boy, master and housemaster at Lancing.

# Lastingham     North Yorkshire

ST MARY was built c.1078 and is situated on the edge of the moors. It occupies the site of a monastery founded by St Cedd and St Chad in 659 and mentioned by the Venerable Bede in his *History of the English Church and People*.

◈ The apsidal crypt is the earliest of the Norman period now surviving in a parish church and is the only one complete with chancel, nave and aisles.

The entrance is from a modern staircase in the centre of the nave but it was originally in the NW corner so that pilgrims could enter and worship at the shrine of St Cedd.

◈ In the crypt is a small vesicular window of which only about eight examples remain in England.

◈ Also in the crypt is a Viking hog-back

tombstone dating from c.850, part of a Saxon churchyard cross also dating from c.850 which would have stood 8 m (24 feet) high, the doorposts of the Saxon monastery and the parish bier.

▣ All the five windows in the apse of the main church depict incidents in the Life of Christ and are in memory of Anne Ringer, whose parents restored the church in 1879. The architect was R. L. Pearson, who also designed the vaulting.

▣ An old Spanish wooden Calvary came from the warship *Salvador del Mundo,* which surrendered to the *Victory* at the Battle of Cape St Vincent, 1797. It was discovered in a York antique shop!

▣ At the E end of the N aisle is a painting of Christ's Agony in the Garden painted by John Jackson, RA (1778–1831) and presented to his native church in 1831.

# Lavenham                    SUFFOLK

ST PETER & ST PAUL – a magnificent church described by Pugin as 'the finest example of late Perpendicular in the world'. Apart from the chancel it was all built between c.1444 and 1530.

▣ The w tower, the highest in Suffolk, is 43 m (141 feet) high and is a superb example of East Anglian flint work. Two hundred steps lead to the top. The plinth is unique in that it is decorated with the stars and shields of the de Veres, the merchant marks of the Spryngs and other devices. (The de Veres and Spryngs were wealthy wool merchants who financed most of the building of the church.) The tower was completed by 1525/6 and is unusual in possessing a parapet instead of battlements.

▣ In the tower hangs a ring of eight bells, the most famous being the tenor bell. Cast in 1625 by Miles Graye of Colchester it weighs 1070 kg (1 ton 1 cwt 7 lb) and has been said by some to be 'the finest toned bell in England, probably in the world'. A special peal is rung each year on 21 June to celebrate its birthday!

▣ The s porch is a beautiful example of Perpendicular architecture and was erected c.1486 at the expense of John de Vere, the thirteenth Earl of Oxford. The fan vault inside dates from c.1865.

▣ The Spryng parclose in the N aisle encloses the tomb of Thomas Spryng and Alice, his second wife. The woodwork combines Gothic and Renaissance details and is very intricate. Note the Spryng coat of arms, the unusual columns and the wooden statue of St Blaise, the patron saint of wool-combers.

▣ In the Decorated chancel (which dates c.1290–1350) is a collection of interesting misericords, among them a man having his ears pulled by a spoonbill and an ibis, a pelican feeding its young and a man holding a pig under his arm.

▣ By the chancel step is a rare brass depicting a baby in his chrisom robe which shows that he was baptized privately before his mother was 'churched'. He was Clopton D'Ewes, who died in 1631 aged just ten days.

▣ The screen dividing the Branch chapel on the N side of the chancel is interesting because the tracery in the lower panels is cut out of solid wood.

▣ On the s side of the chancel is the Spryng chapel or lady chapel, erected in 1525 – one of the last features to be added to the church. Its roof, carved wall posts and beautiful painted glass dating from c.1810 are very interesting.

▣ Between the nave and chancel on the s side is a fourteenth-century crocketed spire capping a turret containing a staircase which used to lead to the rood loft and roof. In 1960 an ancient bell bearing the date 1446 was presented to the church by Mr C. Matkin and hung in the spire to

*Lavenham, Suffolk. This magnificent church is viewed from the southeast.*

replace a missing sanctus bell which used to hang there. On the top of the spire is the crown of St Blaise.

 Outside the E end of the church is a large churchyard cross in memory of Joseph Mormon Croker (10 October 1818–25 January 1891). It is unique in being covered in verses of hymns including music!

## Ledbury                     HEREFORDSHIRE

ST MICHAEL & ALL ANGELS is situated at the end of an attractive street of old houses. It has a large detached tower and spire.

 In the w window of the N aisle is a rare glass sundial, *c.*1710. (See Stained-glass Sundials, page 312.)

 On the s side of the chancel is a beautiful memorial showing John Hamilton (23 April 1850–18 March 1851), son of John

Martin and Maria Henrietta, his wife. Two angels kneel at his head, one holding a coronet. This monument was exhibited at the Great Exhibition of 1851.

 Near by is the monument to the Skynner family of 1631. Note Mrs Skynner's hat and their infant daughter lying on the ground between the parents. Below them kneel their other ten children.

 In the chancel are four Norman arches and six circular windows.

 In the vestry on the N side of the chancel is a memorial to Edward Moulton Barrett (d. 17 April 1857, aged 71), father of the famous poet Elizabeth Barrett Browning. He lies on a couch with his weeping wife at his feet. Above, an angel opens Heaven's door at the top of a flight of stairs through which can be seen three weeping figures.

 In the N aisle is a modern window

commemorating a couple called Arthur and
Biddy Heaton, 1991. It is predominantly red
and depicts the elements with doves and
animals' heads in the central light. It is
called the Benedicite window and the
artist was John K. Clark of Glasgow.

At the E end of the N aisle are fragments
of the fourteenth-century rood screen
consigned to the church tower by the
Victorians and returned to the church in
October 1995.

The N chapel is a superb example of
Decorated architecture with hundreds of
ball-flowers carved on the mullions and
tracery of the five windows, both inside
and out. This chapel may well have been
designed as a chapter house. It is now used
as a parish room and is accessed from the
church through modern glass doors.

At the w end of the s aisle is a memorial
by Richard Westmacott to Robert
Myddelton Biddulph (d. 30 August 1814,
aged 53). His wife leans on her right arm
and her left hand holds a book into which
her fingers are placed. Her children are
carved in relief on each side and a large
chalice stands in front.

# Leominster HEREFORDSHIRE

PRIORY CHURCH OF ST PETER & ST PAUL
This, a former Benedictine priory church,
is located in a quiet churchyard, some
distance from the busy shopping centre.

The N nave and aisle are part of the
original Norman church, the transepts
and choir having been destroyed in 1540.
These are good examples of Norman
architecture.

In the N aisle is an ancient ducking
stool, last used in 1809 when a woman
called Jenny Pipes, alias Jane Curran, was
ducked. Her misdeeds are not recorded
but this poem appears nearby:

'Down in the deep the stool descends
But here at first we miss our ends;
She mounts again and rages more
Than ever vixen did before.
So throwing water on the fire
Will make it burn up but the higher.
If so, my friends, pray let her take
A second turn into the lake;
And rather than your patience lose,
Thrice, and again respect the dose,
No brawling wives no furious wenches,
No fire so hot but water quenches.'

This is one of only two ducking stools
inside a church. (See also St Mary's Church,
Warwick, Warwickshire, page 384.)

The Norman s aisle was replaced by
Early English work in c.1240 and this and
the corresponding s aisle became the
parish church. The tall piers separating the
s aisle and nave are Victorian (1860–80) but
well done.

The five windows of the s aisle and
the w window are richly decorated with
ball-flowers – inside and out – and date
from c.1310.

The great w window is unusual in
having two mullions in the centre which
act as buttresses to strengthen the roof
above. (See also Dorchester Abbey, Oxon.,
page 104.)

In a wall safe in the s aisle is a fine
pre-Reformation chalice and paten.
Christ's head appears on the paten. Note
the Maundy money also.

# Lichfield STAFFORDSHIRE

THE CATHEDRAL CHURCH OF ST MARY
AND ST CHAD Perhaps the finest view of
this beautiful cathedral can be found from
the bridge to the sw, overlooking the
Minster Pool.

The floor of this red sandstone
cathedral is 86 m (282 feet) above sea level,

*The triple spires of Lichfield Cathedral viewed from the west.*

making it the second highest of the old cathedrals. (St Albans is the highest, see page 297.)

The three spires are known as 'the Ladies of the Vale' and they make this cathedral unique among England's medieval cathedrals: the central spire is 78.63 m (258 feet) high; the NW is 59 m (193 feet 6 inches); and the SW is 60.2 m (197 feet 6 inches) high.

The W front is mostly a Victorian restoration. It had been badly damaged in the Civil War when the central spire was also destroyed.

In the third row on the extreme left is a statue of Queen Victoria carved by her daughter Princess Louise.

In the E aisle of the S transept are two busts by Westmacott of Samuel Johnson (d. 13 December 1784, aged 75) and another near by of David Garrick (d. 20 January 1779, aged 63).

At the entrance to the S choir aisle is a plaque to Erasmus Darwin (1731–1802). The inscription states that he was 'a skilful observer of Nature, vivid in imagination, indefatigable in research, original and far-sighted in his views. His speculations were afterwards more successfully solved by his Grandson Charles Darwin an inheritor of many of his characteristics.'

Also near the W end of the S choir aisle is the tomb of Bishop John Hacket (d. 1670), who assisted the dean in repairing the cathedral after the damage caused during the Civil War. The stained-glass window further along this aisle depicts this event.

Below this stained-glass window are the remains of a medieval wall painting showing two angels and remains of a Trinity. Note the angels' censers.

This painting was revealed in 1979 when Bishop Hacket's tomb was removed to its present position.

Below the painting is a Purbeck monument to Bishop Walter de Langton (1296–1321), who was responsible for building the lady chapel.

Near by is a small wall painting dating from c.1398 showing the Crucifixion.

At the E end of the S choir aisle is the beautiful memorial called 'The Sleeping Children'. They were Ellen Jane and Marianne Robinson, daughters of the Reverend Robinson, who was connected with the cathedral, and who died together in 1812. Their memorial, carved by Sir Francis Chantrey in 1817, shows them lying on a mattress and two pillows. One of the girls holds a bunch of snowdrops.

The glass in seven of the lady chapel windows came from Herckenrode Abbey in Belgium in 1802. It was bought by Sir Brooke Boothby of Ashbourne (Derbyshire) for £200 and sold for the same price to this cathedral.

Five of the windows depict biblical subjects and two (on the N side) are historical portraits. The glass in the two W windows on each side is also Flemish but not as old as the other glass. This latter glass was bought in 1895 by Albert Octavius Worthington and the dean and chapter and renovated by C. E. Kempe.

The glass from Herckenrode Abbey dates from c.1580 and is the finest continental glass in any English cathedral.

At the E end of the N choir aisle in St Andrew's chapel is a beautiful memorial by Chantrey depicting Bishop Henry Ryder (21 July 1777–31 March 1836) kneeling in prayer.

In the bay next to Bishop Ryder's monument are the head and shoulders in bronze of Bishop Edward Sydney Woods (1877–1953), sculptured by Jacob Epstein.

On the W side of the vestibule leading to the chapter house is elaborate arcading in which 13 old men used to sit on Maundy

Thursday to have their feet washed by the bishop.

🔲 The chapter house on the N side of the choir is an elongated octagon. It has a central pillar and was finished in 1249. Over the inside doorway is a medieval wall painting showing the Assumption of the Virgin with Christ above. A reconstruction by Professor Tristram in 1935 is near by.

Among the carvings on the corbel of the bishop's seat is a cat with a mouse in its mouth among the foliage. This is the original Cheshire cat!

🔲 Many of the roof bosses depict foliage. The most interesting of them (and they all date from c.1350), is the following: the Annunciation showing Gabriel holding a scroll over a pot of lilies with a Dove whispering in the Virgin Mary's ear! This is situated in the easternmost point of the nave near the crossing.

🔲 Although not obvious to the naked eye, the central portion of the nave vaulting is constructed of *plaster*, not stone, as the weight of stone was proving too much for the walls to support. It is clearly visible from above the vaulting, access being obtained from a staircase inside the central tower and below the spire.

🔲 In the cathedral library is the famous St Chad's or Lichfield Gospels dating from c.750. The book comprises the complete gospels of Matthew and Mark and part of Luke.

# Lincoln

THE CATHEDRAL CHURCH OF THE BLESSED VIRGIN MARY Situated on a hill, this magnificent cathedral dominates the city and surrounding countryside.

🔲 The W front was built 1075–92 by Bishop Remigius and has been partially covered by a later Gothic screen. At the top of the pinnacle on the S side is a statue of St

Hugh and on the N side the Swineherd of Stow. The bases of the two W towers are Norman but the upper parts were added c.1380.

🔲 Projecting from the SW tower is a small chapel. Notice the little carved pilgrim sitting inside the tracery of the eastern window!

🔲 The lower part of the central tower was built 1238–55 and the upper part 1307–11 and are in the Decorated style. At 82.6 m (271 feet) high it is the highest medieval cathedral tower in England. Notice the crockets and ball-flower ornament on each face. In the central tower hangs an hour bell known as 'Great Tom' weighing in at 5486.74 kg (5 tons 8 cwt).

🔲 The nave vaulting, dating from 1225 to 1250, is a very early example of tierceron vaulting. All 12 piers in the nave comprise stone and Purbeck marble in a variety of designs but the fourth pier from the W on the N side is different, being more stone than Purbeck marble. Why is this different, as there is no corresponding one on the S side?

🔲 Around some parts of the inside walls is double arcading, which is only found at ground level in this cathedral. (Beverley Minster and Worcester Cathedral have double arcades at triforium level.)

🔲 An unusual example of crockets being used *inside* a building can be seen on the N and S sides of the choir. Acanthus-like flowers are carved inside clustered pillars. Dating from c.1250 they are unique in the British Isles and are only found in one other place – Trondheim Cathedral, Norway.

🔲 Beyond the organ screen is St Hugh's choir. Begun in 1192 it has the oldest example of a rib running along the ridge of the roof. Notice how many of the ribs curving to meet it are irregular. The same can be seen in the NE and SE transepts. Pevsner

*Lincoln Cathedral viewed from the Castle Keep.*

describes this irregular vaulting as 'overwhelmingly lopsided', otherwise known as the 'Crazy Vault'.

▣ The organ screen includes carvings of bearded bishops with mitres but the heads only date from 1792, when they replaced those lost during the Civil War. The original statues commemorated female saints! Inside the passageway are rare 'flying ribs'; other examples of these may be seen in this cathedral (see below) as well as at Bristol Cathedral, St David's Cathedral, Southwell Cathedral and Warwick (see pages 51, 300, 326 and 384 respectively).

▣ At the extreme E end of the cathedral is the angel choir. Built between 1256 and 1280 it is a superb example of Decorated architecture. Angels and other figures fill the spandrels of the triforium above.

▣ The E window, in the Geometrical style, is the largest and oldest (c.1275) eight-light window in England, measuring 18 m (59 feet) high and 9.14 m (30 feet) wide.

▣ Above the extreme NE pier in the angel choir is the 'Lincoln Imp' under foliage. He has a broad grin with two short horns behind the ears. (Many souvenirs depicting the Lincoln imp are on sale in Lincoln – look out for one!)

▣ Below the Imp is the Shrine of St Hugh's Head with modern adornments by David Poston. This was placed here in 1986 to mark the 800th anniversary of St Hugh's arrival in Lincoln.

▣ At the extreme SE corner of the angel choir is the Russell chantry containing St Blaise's chapel. The walls, adorned with paintings associated with sheep and shepherds, were executed by Duncan Grant in 1958.

▣ In the s and n transepts are two circular windows known as the 'Bishop's Eye' and

*Chapter House, Lincoln, situated on the northeast side of the cathedral.*

the 'Dean's Eye'. The Bishop's Eye in the s transept was erected c.1350. The rare flowing Decorated tracery holds medieval glass fragments. The Dean's Eye in the n transept opposite contains stained glass dating from c.1210. The tracery here is early Geometrical and is unique in the British Isles.

In the n choir aisle near the n transept is the grave of Gordon Slater, organist, 1930–66. He wrote the hymn tune 'St Botolph'.

On the n side of the n aisle of the retro-choir is the tomb of Bishop Fleming (1431), founder of Lincoln College, Oxford, in 1427. This is the oldest tomb depicting a cadaver underneath.

The chapter house on the n side leading from the cloisters has a span of 18 m (59 feet) and is, according to Harvey, the largest chapter house ever built. Dating from c.1220 to 1235 it is a decagon (ten sides) and

was also the first polygonal chapter house in England.

On the n side of the sanctuary is the Easter sepulchre, c.1290–1300. Inside are the earliest flying ribs to support a vaulted roof. Note the three sleeping soldiers at the base.

Over the n wall of the cloister, built in 1674 by Sir Christopher Wren and the only building he did for a cathedral outside London, is an extensive library containing over 240 manuscripts dating from before 1530.

In the cathedral treasury is one of only four copies of Magna Carta (15 June 1215). (There is one other at Salisbury Cathedral and two in the British Library.)

On the s side of the nave is the famous Norman font of Tournai marble. It is decorated with lions and winged beasts. (See Tournai Fonts, page 439.)

The following roof bosses are interesting:

† In the cloisters are some of the earliest wooden roof bosses in England, dating from c.1290. The E walk contains four bosses showing the Occupations of the Months – only found on roof bosses here.

† In the sw transept is a boss depicting foliage but it is only partly finished. What story lies behind this?

† Under the sw tower is a boss showing St Martin dividing his cloak. (St Martin is only found on one other boss – Norwich Cathedral cloisters, Norfolk, see page 255.)

† Some of the other bosses in the cathedral do not fit exactly between the vaulting ribs having been carved in the workshop and not *after* the stone was put in place. An example can be seen in the Galilee porch on the s side where the boss was probably meant for somewhere else.

# Lingfield SURREY

THE COLLEGIATE CHURCH OF ST PETER & ST PAUL This beautiful church is surrounded by some lovely old houses and, because of the numerous tombs inside, it is sometimes known as the 'Westminster Abbey of Surrey'.

⬚ Against the E and w faces of the tower are two unusually large buttresses.

⬚ The wind vane and iron scrollwork on top of the spire date from 1980.

⬚ On the s side of the N chapel is the tomb of the first Lord Cobham (c.1295–1361). His head rests on a helmet and a Saracen's head. He wears a jupon or short surcoat and on his breast is the Cobham Star. His feet rest on a recumbent Saracen, whose turbaned head is a replica of the one under Lord Cobham's head. Battlements extend all round the tomb.

⬚ There are several fine brasses on the floor of the N chapel including one in the centre to John Hadresham (d. 1417). It is an excellent example of the military costume of this period.

⬚ Affixed to the N wall of the N chapel are two incised memorial slabs made of encaustic tiles. One shows a half figure but the other shows a full figure in short tunic. Both men are shown in prayer.

⬚ The E window of the N chapel contains Flemish glass dating from c.1650, given by John Hayward of Edenbridge and set in position in December 1984. The centre-piece of the glass contains the Apostles' Creed. On the left is a small figure of St Paul with his left hand on a sword while St Peter is shown on the right holding two keys.

⬚ In the centre of the chancel is the finest of the Cobham tombs – that of the third Lord Cobham (1382–1446) and his second wife, Ann (d. 1453). Their alabaster effigies are superbly carved: Sir Reginald is shown in plate armour and his head rests on a bearded Moor's head and helm while his feet rest against a lion; Ann's head rests on cushions supported by gilded angels and her feet on a griffin.

This tomb is also embattled and decorated with shields.

⬚ In the s window of the chancel are fragments of ancient glass bearing a quotation from *John* 6, v.12: '"Gather up the fragments that nothing be lost." Refixed 1899. CFH.'

⬚ In the chancel are 11 remaining collegiate stalls, eight of which still retain their misericords – six on the s side and two on the N. One of the finest is on the sw side and shows the head of a bishop with mitres as supporters. Others show shields, heads and a rose.

⬚ Notice how the columns supporting the chancel arch also have three other arches springing from them and yet are no larger than the other columns in the church!

◈ Hanging in the chancel is a fine brass chandelier dating from *c.*1750. The wrought-iron pendant above is like a sword rest and is actually larger than the chandelier!

## Lissett     EAST RIDING OF YORKSHIRE

ST JAMES OF COMPOSTELLA The church stands in a little village on the A165, about 10 km (6 miles) s of Bridlington and about 3.2 km (2 miles) from the North Sea.

◈ Hanging in the bellcote of this church, which was largely rebuilt in 1876, is the oldest dated bell in England. Bearing the date MCCLIIII (1254), it was not discovered until October 1972!

◈ The fine E window was made by C. E. Kempe.

## Little Gidding     CAMBRIDGESHIRE

ST JOHN THE EVANGELIST Nicholas Ferrar lived here from 1625 until his death in 1637. He founded a strict religious community for himself and his family (comprising Nicholas himself, his mother, his sister Susanna, his brother John and their respective families – about 30 people alt gether).

Three times daily – for matins at 06.00, for the litany at 10.00 and for evensong at 16.00, the family walked across to the church. Apart from worship, the family undertook numerous charitable works in the neighbourhood and did much beautiful needlework and ornamental bookbinding. King Charles I visited Little Gidding on three occasions and because of the family's loyalty, Cromwellian soldiers later destroyed the Manor House and badly damaged the church in 1646.

The death of Nicholas's brother John followed in 1657, and with this the eventual break-up of the community.

One of T. S. Eliot's Quartets is entitled 'Little Gidding' and describes this holy place as follows:

> 'You are not here to verify, instruct yourself, or inform curiosity or carry report. You are here to kneel where prayer has been valid.'

◈ The w façade is dated 1714 and over the doorway is the text, 'This is none other but the house of God and the gate of Heaven' (*Genesis* 28, v.17).

◈ The impressive E window of 1853 dominates the church and depicts the Crucifixion in vivid colours. St Mary and St John stand either side of the cross. Note the skull at the base of the cross and the chalice in St John's hand.

◈ The entire church is wood-panelled with seating arranged college-wise (i.e. the seats face inwards, as in a college chapel, as opposed to the conventional E towards the altar or communion table).

◈ The beautiful five-branched candle sconces on the walls were designed by W. A. Lee and presented *c.*1920.

◈ The rare brass font was presented by Nicholas Ferrar in 1625. It is fixed to a stone base on which are two brass lions.

◈ The fine medieval brass eagle lectern was also presented by Nicholas Ferrar in 1625 and probably came from nearby Sawtry Priory. The eagle's eight talons are missing and also the jewels from the eyes. The beak is open. At the base are three lions turning to the right. The lectern is in excellent condition. (See Medieval Brass Lecterns, page 362.)

The candelabrum in the nave dates from 1853 and was the gift of William Hopkinson in memory of his father, who died in 1841.

◈ Outside the w door is the table-tomb of Nicholas Ferrar and between this and the w door, the sunken grave of his brother, John (d. 1657).

# FONTS – AN INTRODUCTION

*Wareham, Dorset.*

Almost every church in England and Wales has a permanent font, although some are not in use today. Fonts are made of different materials and usually take the form of a receptacle for holding water and administering the rite of baptism or dedication into the Church, usually for an infant. Portable wooden fonts are more convenient when baptism is administered in front of the whole church (during a family service, for example); a font situated in a separate baptistery can be a disadvantage if the whole congregation is involved.

Some fonts are Saxon and many more are Norman, Early English, Decorated and Perpendicular. They may be plain or elaborately carved and the shape can vary from circular to square (with four faces), hexagonal (six faces) and so on. The majority of later fonts have eight faces but All Saints in Bigby, Lincolnshire, has one with nine and this is unique. The font in St Mary in Foy, Herefordshire, has ten faces, while St Mary in Marden (also in Herefordshire) has 12; both of these are extremely rare.

In certain areas there are regional

similarities. For example, near Aylesbury, Buckinghamshire, there is the Aylesbury type of font and in Cornwall, the Bodmin type. In East Anglia the Seven Sacrament font proved popular in the fifteenth century and around Herefordshire there is a group of fonts known as chalice fonts.

*Covers*, first published in 1908 and still the classic work on the subject. What Bond's book does not do, however, is to list all the examples of the various fonts that still survive, so the information on pages 74, 302, 318 and 439 should prove useful to anyone wishing to pursue this fascinating subject further.

*Badingham, Suffolk.*

*Cley-next-the-Sea, Norfolk.*

Apart from these variations, fonts can be made of materials other than stone. To the best of my knowledge there are in England and Wales: 33 lead fonts, 33 old wooden fonts (many churches now have a portable wooden font, as explained above), 7 Tournai fonts, 5 Wedgwood fonts, 3 brick fonts, 2 bronze fonts, 2 old brass fonts and an iron font. The brick fonts are at Chignal Smealy, Essex, Polstead, Suffolk, and Potter Heigham, Norfolk; the bronze are at Buckfast Abbey (RC), Devon, and Langworth, Lincolnshire; the brass fonts are at Birmingham Cathedral, West Midlands, and Little Gidding, Cambridgeshire; and the iron font is at Blaenavon, Torfaen.

All of the various types of font are described and illustrated in Francis Bond's excellent book *Fonts and Font*

FONT CANOPIES

Although almost every font has some form of cover over it, whether a simple, flat one or a huge, exquisitely carved one (like the one in Ufford, Suffolk, which can be telescoped above the font when not in use), only four churches in England have elaborate walk-in canopies over their fonts. They are located as follows:

1. Durham Cathedral – wood
2. Luton (St Mary), Bedfordshire – stone
3. Norwich (St Peter Mancroft), Norfolk – wood
4. Trunch (St Botolph), Norfolk – wood

The oldest is at Luton, dating from *c*.1350.

## Little Grimsby        LINCOLNSHIRE

ST EDITH nestles in a quiet, rural setting, access being obtained by walking in front of the Hall. It is a small, aisleless building dating from *c.*1500 and completely white-washed.

The E window is in memory of Dawn Mountain (1921–89) and shows numerous flowers on both sides. Dawn was a lover of flowers and among those depicted are a rose, hydrangea, anemone, daffodil and lily. Butterflies and a bee are also shown.

The window was made by D. J. B. Sear in June 1990.

On the s side of the nave another beautiful window shows trees against a blue sky behind which are numerous churches and houses and the text, 'And I saw a new heaven and a new earth' (*Revelation* 21, v.1). This window is in memory of Tom Wintringham, MP of Little Grimsby Hall, who died suddenly in the House of Commons on 8 August 1921, aged 53. The window was given by his wife.

At the E end are two finely carved oak angels playing musical instruments.

Hanging from the nave roof is an iron candelabrum with four little fawns boasting enormous tails.

On the N side of the chancel there is a fine marble bust of Lady Jemima Beauclerk, 1875, sculptured by her son, William Nelthorpe Beauclerk. Lady Beauclerk was the wife of Lord Frederick Beauclerk, who restored the church in the nineteenth century.

## Little Horkesley        ESSEX

ST PETER & ST PAUL The old church was completely destroyed by a German parachute mine on 21 September 1940 at 21.55 during the Battle of Britain. It was rebuilt from 1957 to 1958 (the foundation stone being laid on 5 January 1957) and reconsecrated on 24 May 1958 by Dr S. F. Allison, Bishop of Chelmsford. The architects were Duncan Clarke and Marshal Sissons. The builder was Everett of Colchester.

The church comprises a nave and s aisle and is beautifully light and spacious.

At the w end of the s aisle on a brick plinth are three wooden effigies representing members of the Horkesley family.

† The effigy nearest the wall depicts Sir Robert de Horkesley (d. 1296) and is 2.41 m (7 feet 11 inches) long. He is shown in a suit of mail, wears a short sword and his hands in prayer clasp what may represent a heart. The shield on his left arm is badly damaged. His right leg is crossed over his left just *above* the knee and his feet rest on a lion whose head is turned away from the effigy. Some repair work has been done to this effigy following the bomb damage. The blackening of the head was caused by its lying buried in the bombed ruins for many years, long after the other pieces had been removed to Colchester Museum for safekeeping and conservation.

† The second male effigy represents Sir Robert's eldest son, Sir William de Horkesley (d. 1332), and is 2.29 m (7 feet 6 inches) long. He also wears a suit of mail. His right leg is crossed over his left just *below* the knee and his feet rest on a lion whose head is turned upwards. His sword is missing and his hands have been destroyed. The surcoat is open to the waist like the wooden effigy of Robert, Duke of Normandy in Gloucester Cathedral. The pillow that was under his head was destroyed in 1940.

† The third oak effigy is 2.31 m (7 feet 7 inches) long and depicts Sir William's wife, Emma (d. 1333). She is dressed in a robe and wears a wimple and long veil secured around her head. Her hands have been destroyed up to the elbows. There is a

*Little Horkesley, Essex – the new church, which was completed in 1958.*

small dog at each foot, tail to tail, a square pillow under her head and fragments of what may have been supporting angels.

All the figures have had some restoration work done on them but considering their ordeal they are quite well preserved. (See Wooden Effigies, page 246.)

Set in the floor near the wooden effigies is a magnificent brass depicting Sir Robert Swynbourne (d. 1391) on the left and his son, Sir Thomas Swynbourne (d. 1412), on the right. This brass was badly bent by the 1940 bomb but is surprisingly little damaged and has been carefully reset in its Purbeck marble slab.

Also set in the floor of the s chapel or lady chapel on the N side of the communion table is an unusual brass. At 48 cm (18¾ inches) high it depicts a naked woman in a shroud tied above her head and below her feet but open to reveal her face and upper part of her body. Her hands are at prayer. This brass represents a Katherine Leventhorp (d. 1502).

The glass of the E window of the chapel depicts events of the Crucifixion and was made by Hugh Powell in 1963.

On the N side of the chancel, inside the communion rail, is the memorial brass to the twice-widowed Bridget, Lady Marney (d. 30 September 1549). She first married Thomas Fynderne (d. 1523) and then John, Lord Marney (d. 1525). Lord Marney is shown on the right because he was of higher social standing! In her will, Lady Marney requested that her own coat of arms should not appear on her brass but only those of her two husbands. The injunction was ignored and her coat of arms was added, but ironically it was completely destroyed when the brass was damaged in 1940!

The bomb revealed that the two male figures of this brass are palimpsest (engraved on the reverse side). This reverse design forms part of a larger brass to a shrouded woman about 1.52 m (5 feet) long, dating from c.1490.

It is interesting that the nine cross-crosslets that appear on Thomas Fynderne's effigy also occur on the very large brass to William Fynderne (d. 13 March, 1444) and his wife, Elizabeth, at Childrey, Oxfordshire. There must clearly be a link between these two men as the cross-crosslet device (similar to a dagger) is quite rare.

The main E window was also designed by Hugh Powell and depicts St Peter and St Paul with Mary holding the baby Jesus and Joseph holding a lamb.

At the w end of the s aisle is a fragment of the German parachute mine which destroyed the old church.

## Little Walsingham          NORFOLK

ST MARY & ALL SAINTS Largely destroyed by fire on the night of 14 July 1961, the rebuilding of this church was completed by 8 August 1964, the architect being Laurence King.

The font, dating from c.1450, shows the Seven Sacraments and the Crucifixion around the bowl and has figures on all eight sides underneath. It has suffered defacement from an earlier age. (See Seven-sacrament Fonts, page 318.)

The fine E window, dating from 1964, is by John Hayward and shows the Annunciation and scenes connected with the history of Walsingham.

In St Catherine's chapel on the s side of the chancel is a tablet commemorating George Ratcliffe Woodward (1848–1934), who is buried just outside the chapel in the churchyard. He edited the Cowley and Cambridge carol books and among his best-known carols are 'Ding-dong merrily on high' and 'This Joyful Eastertide'. He was vicar of Little Walsingham from 1882 to 1889.

In the N chapel is a sculpture, 'The Risen Christ', by Sir Jacob Epstein. This is one of his early works.

## Little Wittenham          OXORDSHIRE

ST PETER This little church is situated quite near to the River Thames and just below the famous Wittenham Clumps – an ancient hill-fort about 121.9 m (400 feet) above sea level.

The rectangular tower has a unique feature – four windows shaped like the four aces, a heart, a club, a diamond and a spade!

Under the tower are the alabaster effigies of Sir William Dunch (d. 1611) and his wife, Lady Mary. Mary was Oliver Cromwell's aunt and a sister-in-law of John Hampden.

## Liverpool          MERSEYSIDE

THE ANGLICAN CATHEDRAL CHURCH OF CHRIST The lasting memory one has of this cathedral is its immense size and the quality of its workmanship. The stonework, woodwork, metalwork and glass are excellent and exhibit some of the best that the human race can offer to Almighty God. John Betjeman declared it to be 'one of the great buildings of the world'.

Built of red sandstone and occupying a commanding position on St James's Mount, this is the largest Anglican cathedral in the British Isles. It is 193.9 m (636 feet) long and covers an area of 9687 sq m (104,275 sq feet). It was designed by Sir Giles Gilbert Scott (1880–1960).

Unlike most churches, it is not oriented E to W, but N to S – like the new Coventry Cathedral); unlike Coventry, however, the liturgical 'E end' is at the S. King Edward VII laid the foundation stone on 19 July 1904 and Queen Elizabeth II unveiled a plaque on 25 October 1978 to mark its completion and consecration. The arches inside are the highest Gothic arches ever built.

The magnificent central tower or Vestey tower is 100.88 m (331 feet) high and is surmounted by an irregular octagon enriched with much beautiful decoration and terminating in eight pinnacles. The lancet windows are 21.21 m (69 feet 7 inches) high – the tallest in England.

In the tower, 66.8 m (219 feet) from the floor, hangs the highest and heaviest ring of bells in the world. The 12 bells with a total weight of 31,498 kg (31 tons) were cast in 1938–9 and the tenor bell, 'Emmanuel', weighs 4170.9 kg (4 tons 2 cwt 11 lb). Emmanuel is the heaviest bell that can be rung in the world. (See Bells, page 293.)

On a pier at the 'SW' corner of the 'NW' transept is carved 'The Lovers' Knot' which records the visit of the Queen (as Princess Elizabeth) and Prince Philip in 1949.

In the 'S' choir aisle is an effigy of Bishop Chavasse (1933) kneeling with a representation of the cathedral as it was in his lifetime.

Among the outstanding stained glass is a window showing modern women who have benefited society such as Kitty Wilkinson and Agnes Jones, and the great W window by Carl Edwards which fills the cathedral with brilliant colours.

The organ comprises 9765 pipes and is the largest working church organ in the world.

# Liverpool    MERSEYSIDE

METROPOLITAN CATHEDRAL OF CHRIST THE KING – ROMAN CATHOLIC This was designed by Sir Frederick Gibberd and consecrated on 14 May 1967.

The circular plan is almost unique in a modern cathedral.

The lantern tower surmounted by a crown and weighing over 2,032/128 kg (2000 tons) contains stained glass by John Piper and Patrick Reyntiens symbolizing the Holy Trinity. This is the largest single area of stained glass in the world.

The impressive baptistery is entered through beautiful bronze gates designed by David Atkins – the gift of the City of Liverpool.

In the E tower, next to the Chapel of St Columba, stands the bronze holy water stoup, the gift of Pope Paul VI. Around the bowl are incidents in relief from the life of Christ connected with the theme of water.

The windows of the lady chapel were designed by Margaret Traherne and the ceramic statue of Our Lady and the Boy Jesus above the altar was designed by Robert Brumby.

On the N side of the cathedral is the only part that was completed of Sir Edwin Lutyens's cathedral – the crypt. This was opened in 1958 and is connected to the new cathedral by a piazza above. In the crypt is the Chapel of Relics where two archbishops are buried. It is entered through Lutyens's famous 'rolling gate', a circular block of stone weighing 6,096.38 kg (6 tons) that rolls back into a cavity in the wall by means of a concealed mechanism.

Lutyens's cathedral was never completed as it would have been too expensive but in design its dome would have surpassed St Peter's in Rome.

This ancient game for two players was probably brought to Britain soon after 1066.

In the most commonly played version, two players have nine 'men' (counters or marbles, each team of a different colour) which they place alternately in cups on a board containing 24 holes. Each player tries to make a line of three men and when he succeeds, removes one of his opponent's men from the board. When both players have placed all their men, they take turns to move one man one cup along any line to a vacant cup, still trying to get a line of three in order to remove one of the opponent's men. Men being removed must not be taken from a line of three, unless there are no spare ones.

The winner is the player who reduces his opponent to two men or succeeds in cornering all opposing men so that they are unable to move.

The game is played in several parts of Britain, particularly in the north. Modern versions of it can still be bought in toyshops today.

Shakespeare makes reference to nine men's morris in *A Midsummer Night's Dream*. In her description of a violent summer Titania, the fairy queen says (Act 2, Scene 1):

'The fold stands empty in the drowned field,
And crows are fatted with the murrain flock;
The Nine Men's Morris is filled up with mud;
And the quaint mazes in the wanton green,
For lack of tread are undistinguishable.'

Examples of nine men's morris have been found incised in churches all over England, but there appear to be more examples in East Anglia. Is this because much of the stone used there for building is clunch, this being easier to cut than granite and some of the sandstones?

The following churches and chapels contain examples of nine men's morris:

1. Braydeston (St Michael), Norfolk – in porch
2. Cavendish (St Mary), Suffolk
3. Dunster (St George), Somerset
4. Finchingfield (St John), Essex – on window ledge
5. Gloucester Cathedral (The Holy and Indivisible Trinity) – in N walk of cloisters, on the benches
6. Great Yeldham (St Andrew), Essex
7. Chapel of St Leonard in Hazlewood Castle, North Yorkshire – on seat in porch
8. Hickling (St Mary), Norfolk – on table-tomb
9. Ickford (St Nicholas), Buckinghamshire
10. Kirby Underdale (All Saints), East Riding of Yorkshire
11. Norwich Cathedral (The Holy and Undivided Trinity), Norfolk – in NE corner of cloisters
12. Rollesby (St George), Norfolk – in porch
13. Salisbury Cathedral (The Blessed Virgin Mary), Wiltshire – on benches in the cloisters
14. Sparsholt (Holy Rood), Oxfordshire – on jamb of doorway on N side of chancel
15. Stapleford (St Mary), Wiltshire

16. Stebbing (St Mary the Virgin), Essex
17. Wennington (St Mary and St Peter), Essex
18. Windsor Castle, Berkshire – in cloisters adjoining St George's Chapel

In the church of the Holy Rood in Sparsholt, Oxfordshire, the design is scratched in a *vertical* position on a stone jamb of the priest's doorway on the N side of the chancel. This indicates that when the doorway was constructed *c*.1325 this particular stone was re-used having been in a horizontal position!

A simplified version of the game is three men's morris. This was played on boards with straight or straight and diagonal lines, but only four counters were used. It was very similar to the noughts and crosses of today.

THREE MEN'S MORRIS

Examples of three men's morris can be seen in the following churches:
1. Ashdon (All Saints), Essex
2. Birdbrook (St Augustine of Canterbury), Essex
3. Finchingfield, Essex
4. Fyfield (St John), Essex (St Nicholas)
5. Great Henny (St Mary), Essex
6. Great Sampford (St Michael), Essex
7. Norwich Cathedral (The Holy and Undivided Trinity), Norfolk – in cloisters
8. Rickling (All Saints), Essex

# Llandaff CARDIFF

CATHEDRAL CHURCH OF ST PETER & ST PAUL, WITH ST DYFRIG, ST TEILO & ST EUDDOGWY Situated within the borders of the capital of Wales, this is the only cathedral in the British Isles that has a NW tower and SW tower with spire. The spire is 59.4 m (195 feet) high.

 On the left side of the little road leading down the hill to the E end of the cathedral, against a wall, is the original well of St Teilo. The inscription in Welsh and English reads: 'Below is reputedly the site of St Teilo's Well. Saint Teilo was consecrated as the second Bishop of Llandaff in the sixth century, and was one of the three Celtic saints in whose honour the Cathedral Church here at Llandaff was originally dedicated.'

 On Thursday 2 January 1941 a landmine fell near the S door destroying the roofs of the nave, S aisle and chapter house. Fortunately the stonework was only slightly damaged, although the top of the spire had to be rebuilt. HM Queen Elizabeth II attended the service of thanksgiving for the restored cathedral on 6 August 1960.

 Along the S and N walls of the nave, on the outside of the cathedral, are sovereigns' heads beginning with Richard III and ending with Elizabeth II.

Between the nave and choir is a unique parabolic arch of reinforced concrete, designed by George Pace, which supports part of the organ case. Facing the congregation on the W side is a huge cast aluminium figure of Christ in Majesty designed by Sir Jacob Epstein. Surrounding the case on wooden seats are 64 Pre-Raphaelite gilded figures of saints and angels; these came from the Victorian choir stalls.

# JOHN BUSHNELL (1630–1701)

John Bushnell was a highly regarded English sculptor who began his career studying under the famous Bernini in Italy. From him he learned to undercut marble to make it appear transparent. He used a drill for delicate work such as cutting eyes so that they appeared to focus.

A great eccentric, Bushnell is said to have constructed a wooden horse large enough to entertain four guests for dinner in its head, light being provided through the windows of its eyes!

Although he was commissioned to execute busts of Charles I and Charles II, examples of his work in England are rare. He seldom signed his pieces and most authorities agree that only four examples can be positively assigned to him. However, the following churches contain sculptures that were probably worked by Bushnell:

1. Ashburnham (St Peter), East Sussex – William Ashburnham (d. 1675) and his wife, Jane, the Countess of Marlborough.
2. Babraham (St Peter), Cambridgeshire – Sir Richard Bennet (d. 1658) and Sir Thomas Kennet (d. 1667).
3. Great Billing (St Andrew), Northamptonshire – Henry O'Brien, last Earl of Thomond (d. 1691) and his wife.
4. Great Gaddesden (St John the Baptist), Hertfordshire – John Halsey (d. 1670); fine bust in the chancel.
5. Groombridge (St John the Evangelist), Kent – Philip Packer (d. 1686); he is shown sitting cross-legged, his head resting on one shoulder with an open book on one knee. He is said to have died in this position in the garden of Groombridge Place!

 The chapter house on the SE side of the cathedral is unusual in being of square design. Its 'pepperpot' roof is surmounted by a gilded figure of the archangel Gabriel.

 Near the chapter house in the S aisle is a Celtic cross. This was found in 1870 in the back wall of the shed over the dairy well in the garden of the bishop's palace!

 Above the superb Norman arch (also known as the Urban Arch) at the E end where the high altar stands, is a modern window of 1959 depicting the Supper at Emmaus. It was designed by John Piper and made by Patrick Reyntiens.

 In the lady chapel at the extreme E end of the cathedral is a modern brass made by A. G. Wyon in 1942 depicting Bishop Timothy Rees (1931–9). Unusually, he is shown wearing glasses!

 The fine E window of the lady chapel shows the Tree of Jesse. It was designed by Geoffrey Webb, who planned all the lady chapel windows from 1909 to 1952. Each window contains his rebus – the spider's web.

 Below the window is a fifteenth-century reredos filled in 1965 with 12 panels of gold-leafed bronze wreaths of blackthorn twigs, each containing a wild flower

6. Little Gaddesden (St Peter & St Paul), Hertfordshire – Henry Stanley (d. 1670, aged 14).

7. London, Fulham (All Saints) – Viscount John Mordaunt (d. 1675); he played a part in restoring King Charles II to the throne in 1660.

8. London, Hart Street (St Olave's) – bust of Elizabeth Pepys (d. 1669), wife of Samuel Pepys the famous diarist who worshipped here. He and his wife are buried in the vault under the chancel.

9. London, Twickenham (St Mary) – M. Harvey; commemorated as a flaming urn, c.1680.

10. London, Westminster Abbey – Abraham Cowley (1618–67). A poet, he is commemorated by a large urn but no effigy. This can be seen on the E side of Poets' Corner in the S transept.

11. London, Westminster Abbey – Sir Palmes Fairborne (1644–80), Governor of Tangier, who was killed

defending the town against the Moors. He too is commemorated with only an urn, which can be seen halfway along the nave S aisle.

12. Mid Lavant (St Nicholas), West Sussex – Lady Mary May (1640–81), rediscovered in 1981 and brought out of a vault under the chancel.

13. Peper Harrow (St Nicholas), Surrey – Sir Thomas Broderick (d. 1641) and his wife (d. 1678). Black marble tablet with superb busts of the couple.

14. South Dalton (St Mary), East Riding of Yorkshire – Sir John Hotham (d. 1689) is shown as a knight reclining on a slab of black marble.

15. West Dean (St Mary), Wiltshire – Robert Pierrepont (d. 1669), Earl of Kingston. This is a large monument with closed doors, behind which can be seen the life-size statue of the Earl kneeling on one knee with a small angel behind him. On the doors are long inscriptions, one relating to his soul and the other to his body.

named in Welsh in honour of the Blessed Virgin Mary.

 The white Madonna and Child in the centre was carved by A. G. Walker and was an anonymous gift in 1934, the donor stipulating that it was never to be coloured.

In the N aisle is the organ case. On its E side are six porcelain panels designed by Burne-Jones depicting the 'Six Days of Creation'. They are encased in a simple bronze frame and are typical of Pre-Raphaelite work.

In the chapel on the N side of the choir behind the choir stalls is a modern wooden sedilia, on the back of which is a rare oil painting on wood showing the Assumption into Heaven of the Blessed Virgin Mary (celebrated on 15 August). It was commissioned by Bishop Marshall in 1480. On the right is the kneeling figure of Bishop Marshall, who addresses Mary in Latin, translated as follows:

'O Virgin who goes up in state
Open for Marshall Heaven's Gate.'

In the S choir aisle are parts of two of the canopies from the Victorian sedilia which stood on the S side of the high altar. These were placed here 'In memory of

George Pace, CVO 1915–1975. Appointed Cathedral architect 1949–1975 for the restoration after the ravages of War.'

◈ At the sw corner of the nave is the fine modern font dating from 1952 and carved by Alan Durst. Among the carvings are the Virgin Mary kneeling before the Infant Jesus and Eve deceived by Satan.

◈ To the e of the s doorway almost opposite the font is the 'Trinity Corbel' carved by a Victorian stonemason, Edward Clarke. The three faces of the Holy Trinity have only four eyes between them! (See also Chichester Cathedral, W. Sussex, page 77, where a similar roof boss showing six heads with six eyes can be seen.)

◈ On the nw side of the cathedral is the Welch Regiment Memorial Chapel, erected in 1953. On the e wall are details of many of their exploits and brass plates on the floor commemorate former soldiers.

A window on the w side contains eight panels of French medieval stained glass.

A fine Norman doorway (originally on the outside) leads into the cathedral nave.

In the Illtyd chapel under the nw or Jasper tower is 'The Seed of David' triptych painted by Dante Gabriel Rossetti between 1856 and 1864 – again, typical Pre-Raphaelite work.

# Lodsworth     West Sussex

St Peter Located in beautiful countryside between Midhurst and Petworth, the church has lovely views from its churchyard.

◈ Below the churchyard in the new extension Ernest Howard Shepard (1879–1976) is buried, best known as the artist who illustrated A. A. Milne's 1926 children's classic *Winnie-the-Pooh*.

# London     St Paul's

The Cathedral Church of St Paul Designed by Sir Christopher Wren (1632–1723) the foundation stone was laid on 21 June 1675 and the building was finally completed in 1708.

◈ The dome is the second largest in the world (the largest is St Peter's, Rome) and the top of the cross is 111.2 m (365 feet) from the ground.

◈ The crypt, the largest in Europe, is approached by steps from the s transept. It is unusual in that it extends under the whole building, not just under the e end.

◈ In the crypt, directly underneath the dome, is the tomb of Lord Nelson. His body rests in a marble sarcophagus made in 1524 for Cardinal Wolsey. When Wolsey fell from power the sarcophagus was seized by Henry VIII and lay forgotten at Windsor Castle until Nelson's death at Trafalgar on 21 October 1805.

◈ Also buried in the crypt, on the s side, is Sir Christopher Wren. On the wall above his tomb are the famous words, '*Lector, si monumentum requiris, circumspice*' – 'Reader, if you seek his monument, look around'.

◈ At the e end of the crypt is the Chapel of the Order of the British Empire. Instituted in 1917 the chapel was designed and furnished from 1957 to 1963 by Lord Mottistone.

◈ A famous Dean of St Paul's from 1911 to 1934 was William Ralph Inge (1860–1954), who is commemorated in the crypt. His memorial is unique because it was 'Erected by the Publishers of his Writings'.

◈ Upstairs, in a hidden gallery, is a glass case containing Wren's death-mask, his penknife and measuring stick, inscribed, 'Surveyor To The Fabrick'.

◈ In the cathedral trophy room is Wren's Great Model, which was one of his early designs for the cathedral. Made of oak it took nine months to make and cost £500. It measures 6.1 m (20 feet) long.

🔲 On the N side of the nave is the colossal monument by Alfred Stevens to the Duke of Wellington (1769–1852), the man who defeated Napoleon. At the very top is the figure of the 'Iron Duke' on his horse, Copenhagen. This horse and rider, sculpted by John Tweed (d. 1933), were not added until 1912 because many people objected to a horse in a cathedral! Wellington is buried in the crypt. (See Horses in Churches, page 413.)

🔲 At the E end of the N choir aisle is the Chapel of Modern Martyrs with their names recorded in a marble casket.

🔲 The superb iron sanctuary screens on the N and S sides of the high altar were made by Jean Tijou and erected 1691–1709. The wrought ironwork is the finest of its kind in the world.

🔲 The high altar and *baldacchino* (the canopy above) were designed by S. E. Dykes Bower and Godfrey Allen from Wren's original drawings and consecrated on 8 May 1958. The previous high altar was destroyed by a bomb on 10 October 1940.

🔲 The magnificent choir stalls and organ case were designed by Grinling Gibbons, one of the world's greatest woodcarvers.

🔲 In the S choir aisle is the effigy of John Donne (1572–1631), dean of Old St Paul's Cathedral, depicted in a shroud and standing on an urn. Carved by Nicholas Stone this is the only complete statue to have survived the Great Fire of London in 1666. Donne posed for this effigy wrapped in a shroud before his death!

🔲 High up inside the dome (separated from the outer dome by a brick core) are eight frescoes depicting the life of St Paul and painted by Sir James Thornhill from 1716 to 1719. The story goes that on completion, Thornhill was about to step back

to admire his masterpiece when his assistant realized he would fall to his death. The assistant quickly started to daub paint over part of the work and Thornhill rushed forwards to stop him. Only then did he realize how narrowly he had missed death!

🔲 Below Thornhill's paintings is the whispering gallery. Anyone speaking into the wall can be heard clearly on the opposite side, 32.6 m (107 feet) away.

🔲 In the S nave aisle is W. Holman Hunt's famous painting 'The Light of the World'. Painted by him in 1900 it is a copy of his original painting, which hangs in the chapel of Keble College, Oxford.

🔲 In the SW tower is the heaviest bell hung in the British Isles. Known as 'Great Paul' it was cast in 1881, weighs 17,002.29 kg (16 tons 14 cwt 2qr 19lb) and has a diameter of 2.9 m (9 feet 6½ inches). Every day at 1300 hours it chimes for five minutes.

🔲 In the N choir aisle is Henry Moore's controversial 'Mother and Child' carved from travertine limestone. This was his last 'Mother and Child' – the first, carved in 1943, being in St Matthew's Church, Northampton.

## London SOUTHWARK

THE CATHEDRAL & COLLEGIATE CHURCH OF ST SAVIOUR AND ST MARY OVERIE
This cathedral is hemmed in by the River Thames on its N side and the railway on the S side.

🔲 The nave was completed in 1897 to the design of Sir Arthur Blomfield. It replaced a nave of *c.*1250 that was destroyed in 1839. The W front was completed in 1905 and is unique among cathedrals in not having a western entrance.

🔲 In a recess of the N choir aisle is the oak effigy of a knight, probably of the de

Warenne family, and dating from c.1290. The effigy, 2 m (6 feet 6½ inches) long, wears mail head covering, hauberk and long surcoat. His left leg is crossed over the right and there is a lion at his feet. The lion's head is missing. His right hand holds a sword and there is a cushion under his head. The face, which is modern, wears a moustache. The shield is missing. This figure has been well restored and is one of the oldest effigies in England.

In the eighteenth century the figure was very badly treated. On one occasion it was used to prop up an unsafe stairway by resting the stairway on its head! (See Wooden Effigies, page 246.)

▨ Behind the high altar is a fine reredos dating from 1520 which was restored in 1830, 1890 and 1930. The lower part was gilded and coloured by J. N. Comper, who also painted the three-light window above.

▨ At the E end of the cathedral is the retrochoir containing the lady chapel. The retrochoir was built c.1213–35. It is a unique example of Early English architecture and was nearly demolished in 1832 to make a wider approach to London Bridge! Fortunately Dr Sumner, Bishop of Winchester, in whose diocese Southwark then was, would not approve the demolition; neither would Parliament.

The NE corner of the retrochoir is famous as having been the scene of the trial and condemnation of several Anglican martyrs in 1555 under Stephen Gardiner, Bishop of Winchester. Among those sentenced to burn at the stake were John Hooper, Bishop of Gloucester, and Robert Ferrer, Bishop of St David's.

▨ On the s side of the choir is the tomb of Bishop Lancelot Andrewes (1555–1626). He was Bishop of Winchester and a member of the panel that produced the *Authorised Version of the Bible* in 1611. He is one of only two bishops wearing the Order of the Garter. (See Bath Abbey, page 20.)

▨ At the E end of the N aisle of the nave is the tomb of John Gower (c.1330–1408). This is the only effigy of an English fifteenth-century poet in existence. His head rests on representations of the three books he wrote. His monument is also a unique example of an English medieval tomb complete with a canopy.

▨ The tower is 39.5 m (129 feet 6 inches) high. The pinnacles add a further 10.4 m (34 feet).

▨ In the tower is the seventh heaviest ring of 12 bells in the world and the third oldest. (The oldest is at Cirencester, Glos., and the second oldest is at St Michael, Cornhill, London.)

## London                              WESTMINSTER

THE ABBEY AND COLLEGIATE CHURCH OF ST PETER is the second largest church in the United Kingdom (Liverpool Cathedral is longer).

▨ The length is 161.5 m (530 feet) and across the transepts its width is 61.87 m (203 feet). It has an internal height of 30.97 m (101 feet 8 inches).

▨ The two western towers were added in 1738–9 to the design of Nicholas Hawksmoor.

▨ At the W end of the nave is the Tomb of the Unknown Warrior – an unknown soldier brought from France in 1920 who symbolizes all who died in the First World War, and subsequently the Second World War and other wars.

▨ Adjoining the Tomb of the Unknown Warrior is a green marble stone commemorating Sir Winston Churchill (1874–1965) unveiled by Queen Elizabeth II on 19 September 1965.

▨ The stained-glass window at the w end

of the nave dates from 1735 and represents figures of prophets and coats of arms.

Also at the w end of the nave are two fine candelabra inscribed, 'These candelabra were given by Arthur Viscount Lee of Fareham GCB and Ruth his wife as a thankoffering 23 December, 1899–1939. *Deo gratias.'*

All kinds of figures are depicted in the branches – Adam and Eve are on one at the top, there is a man sowing seed and Jesse at the foot. On the other are scenes from Christ's life, with the Virgin and Child in the centre.

On the sw pier of the nave is a contemporary painting on wood of Richard II, who reigned 1377–99. This is the oldest known portrait of any English monarch.

On the NE side of the nave is a fine hexagonal pulpit. According to tradition Thomas Cranmer (1489–1556), Archbishop of Canterbury, is said to have preached from it at the coronation of Edward VI on 20 February 1547.

In the N transept is a wooden model of the central tower and spire proposed for the abbey by Sir Christopher Wren (1715) but never carried out. It would have resembled that of Norwich Cathedral, Norfolk.

On the N side of the N transept under the soffits of the six lancet windows of the third stage is carved a magnificent choir of angels dating from c.1260.

On the E side of the N transept are three chapels – St John the Evangelist, St Michael and St Andrew.

Inside the Chapel of St John, among the many monuments, is one by Nicholas Stone to Sir George Holles (d. 1626), who fought in the Battle of Nieuport in 1600. He is shown standing, wearing Roman armour but looking incongruous with a beard and moustache. Roman soldiers were always clean-shaven! This monument and that of

his nephew, Francis Holles, in St Edmund's chapel are the only two in existence showing Roman armour.

In the adjoining chapel of St Michael is a monument by Roubiliac to a Joseph Gascoigne Nightingale (d. 1752) and Lady Elizabeth Nightingale (d. 1731). Underneath, the figure of Death holds an arrow by its feathers and aims it at Lady Elizabeth while her husband tries to stop him. Lady Elizabeth died at 27 when a flash of lightning brought on premature childbirth.

In the N ambulatory at the entrance to St John the Evangelist's chapel is a spectacular monument to the British general James Wolfe (1727–59). The bronze relief at the base depicts the scaling of the Heights of Abraham.

Next to Wolfe's monument is the Islip chapel, founded in 1523 by Abbot John Islip (1464–1532), the last of the abbots of Westminster. It consists of two storeys with a stone screen separating it from the ambulatory. The remains of Islip's tomb are now in the upper chantry chapel, which became a memorial chapel in 1950 for all nurses who died in the Second World War. Look out for two versions of Abbot Islip's rebus – an eye inside a slip or branch of a tree grasped by a hand and a man slipping from a branch 'I-slip', and the name 'ISLIP'.

Inside the lower chapel is a beautiful window by Hugh Easton (1948) showing Abbot Islip kneeling before St Margaret of Antioch.

Next to the Islip chapel is the Chapel of Our Lady of the Pew. Just inside the door is a fifteenth-century roof boss showing the Assumption of the Virgin Mary.

A little way E on the opposite side of the Chapel of Our Lady of the Pew can be seen the iron grille protecting the top of the tomb of Queen Eleanor of Castile (d. 1290), first wife of Edward I. This was made by Thomas of Leighton Buzzard, c.1294, and is medieval ironwork at its finest. The gilt bronze effigy of the Queen was cast by William Torel.

Opposite the tomb of Queen Eleanor is the Chapel of St Paul, containing the tomb of Baron Giles Daubeney (1452–1508) and Elizabeth, his wife. Note at his feet the little figures of bedesmen with rosaries in their hands. Compare this tomb with that of Charles Somerset (d. 1514) in the Beaufort chantry, St George's Chapel, Windsor Castle (see page 420), which has similar figures at his feet; also with a brass in St Stephen's Church, Norwich, Norfolk, with two bedesmen at its base. Other examples can be found throughout England and Wales.

Before entering Henry VII's chapel go up the steps and cross back over the bridge into St Edward the Confessor's chapel. St Edward was king from 1042 to 1066 and his body still rests in the shrine erected by Henry III in 1268. The upper part, made of wood and marble, was added in 1557 by Abbot Feckenham during the reign of Queen Mary I. Note the influence of the Renaissance.

At the entrance of St Edward's chapel is an original table-tomb on which is the oak effigy of Henry V (1387–1422) showing the crowned king. The effigy is 1.6 m (5 feet 4 inches) long and was originally covered with silver-gilt plates and the head, sceptre and other regalia of silver. Everything was stolen in 1545. (See Wooden Effigies, page 246.)

Above the effigy is the chantry chapel of Henry V, which includes one of the largest collections of carved figures from the early fifteenth century.

In St Edward's chapel on the sw side of his shrine are the fine bronze effigies of Richard II (d. 1399) and Queen Anne of Bohemia (d. 1394).

Also on the s side of the shrine is the bronze effigy of Edward III (d. 1377). On each side of the recumbent king are eight little angels with their hands raised in blessing.

On the side of the tomb-chest facing the ambulatory are the figures of six of Edward's 14 children. Those on the N side have all been stolen.

Opposite the shrine's altar is the coronation chair, which stands directly behind the high altar of the abbey. The chair was made for Edward I in 1297 to hold the famous stone of Scone, which he had brought from Scone Abbey in Scotland in 1296. This stone, on which all Scottish kings were crowned, was stolen from the abbey on Christmas Eve 1950, and taken back to Scotland but was eventually returned to the coronation chair in April 1951. It was formally returned to Scotland on 30 November 1996 and now rests in Edinburgh Castle.

Note the numerous graffiti carved on the chair and, near by, the sword and shield of Edward III.

Leaving St Edward's chapel go into Henry VII's chapel at the extreme E end of the abbey. On the N side, before entering the nave of the chapel, visit the Queen Elizabeth chapel in the N aisle. Tudor half-sisters Mary I (d. 1558) and Elizabeth I (d. 1603) are buried here. On the floor is inscribed, 'Near the tomb of Mary and Elizabeth remember before God all those who divided at the Reformation by different convictions laid down their lives for Christ and conscience' sake.'

At the E end of the Queen Elizabeth chapel is a rare monument by Maximilian Colt depicting Princess Sophia (d. 1606 aged just three days), daughter of James I. She is shown as a baby in a cradle if one looks in the mirror opposite! (See also Shipley, West Sussex, page 315.)

In the E wall of this chapel are the bones

of the princes Edward V (1470–83) and his brother Richard (1472–83), who were murdered in the Tower of London by an unknown person or persons. They were deposited here in 1674 by command of Charles II.

On the s side of the entrance to Henry VII's chapel is Lady Margaret's chapel, which corresponds with the Queen Elizabeth chapel on the N side and is really the s aisle of Henry VII's chapel.

At the E end is the tomb of Lady Margaret Beaufort, mother of Henry VII (d. 1509). Her effigy is a beautiful example of bronze gilt.

Next to Lady Beaufort is the tomb of Mary Queen of Scots. The Latin inscription states that she died on:

'VI Idvs Febrvarii
Anno Christi MDLXXXVII
Aetatis XXXXVI'.

Mary was beheaded at Fotheringhay Castle, Northants., on 6 February 1587, aged 46 and her body was first interred at Peterborough Cathedral (see page 272).

In the canopy above the tomb are carved 50 Scottish thistles and golden flowers. Mary's body was brought here from Peterborough in 1612 on the express command of her son, James I.

The entrance to the nave of Henry VII's chapel is through a pair of magnificent doors comprising bronze plates fixed to a wooden framework and adorned with Tudor roses, portcullises, crowns, fleur-de-lys and so on. These gates are a unique example of this work in England.

This chapel of Henry VII is considered to be the supreme example of Perpendicular architecture. Completed in 1519 it has been described as 'one of the most perfect buildings ever erected in England'.

The roof appears to be a fan vault but is in fact a cleverly designed groin vault with rare pendent bosses dropping from a fan. It is unique and extremely beautiful. (See also Oxford Cathedral, page 263, and Fan Vaulting, page 152.)

In the triforium around the inside of the chapel are 95 carved figures of saints and famous churchmen – the finest collection of late Gothic statues in England. There were originally 107.

Below the triforium hang the banners of the Knights of the Bath with their name plates fixed to the back of each of their stalls. Underneath each of the seats are carved misericords depicting various scenes from medieval life.

Behind the altar are the tombs of Henry VII (d. 1509), Elizabeth of York, his queen (d. 1503), and James I (d. 1625).

The bronze grille enclosing the tombs has six small bronze statues of saints on the outside, but originally there were 32. This was the work of Pietro Torregiano, an Italian from Florence who also executed the effigies of the King and Queen. Professor Lethaby describes them as 'the greatest portrait sculptures ever wrought in England'.

The tombs of the King and Queen, and Lady Margaret Beaufort in the s aisle are not only the earliest-known examples in England of Renaissance craftsmanship and sculpture but also show the very first use of Roman lettering on a tomb in England.

In front of the altar erected in 1935 and incorporating fragments of the original one which was destroyed in 1643 is the burial place of Edward VI (1537–1553). On 7 October 1966 a stone marking his grave was unveiled by the boys of Christ's Hospital, Horsham, 'in thanksgiving for their founder'.

At the extreme E end of the chapel is the RAF chapel with the Battle of Britain memorial window by Hugh Easton (1947). The candlesticks, cross and altar rails are of silver.

In front of the rails is the former vault of Oliver Cromwell (1599–1658). His body was exhumed in 1661 after the Restoration of Charles II.

On the s side of Henry VII's chapel opposite Henry VII's tomb, is the impressive monument to Ludovic Stuart – Duke of Lennox and Richmond (d. 1624). Four weeping bronze figures of Charity, Faith, Hope and Truth support the canopy on which stands an angel blowing a trumpet.

Leave Henry VII's chapel and proceed along the s ambulatory. The second chapel on the left is St Edmund's chapel, containing the following items of interest:

† On the N side, just inside the door on the right, is a stone table-tomb on which is an oak chest with five small shields remaining. On top of the chest is a wooden effigy, 1.7 m (5 feet 7 inches) long, of William de Valence (d. 1296), Lord of Pembroke and Wexford and half-brother to Henry III. The effigy is covered with copper plates decorated with Limoges enamel. William wears a mail hauberk with a sword on the left side and a richly decorated shield showing red birds on the left hip. His head rests on an enamelled cushion showing the arms of England and his feet rest on a lion. His hands are at prayer. This is the only example in England of Limoges enamelwork and also the only wooden monument still covered with metal plates.

† Nearby is an alabaster monument to Francis Holles (1604–22) by Nicholas Stone. Holles is shown as a seated figure in Roman armour. The inscribed verse ends,

'Man's life is measured by the work, not days
No aged sloth but active youth hath praise.'

† In the centre of the chapel is the brass to Robert de Waldeby (d. 1397), Archbishop of Dublin and York; he was the friend and companion of the Black Prince. This fine brass is about 3.05 m (10 feet) long.

Leaving the s ambulatory enter the s transept. On the N side, backing on to the sanctuary and high altar, is the tomb of Anne of Cleves (d. 1557), fourth wife of Henry VIII. On the marble slab, dating from 1606, is a decoration of skull and crossbones – the earliest example in England.

On the E side of the s transept (known as Poets' Corner) is a monument to Abraham Cowley (1618–67), an obscure poet. The urn, encircled by leaves, was sculpted by John Bushnell.

On the s side of the s transept and E of the cloisters is the Chapel of St Faith, built c.1250. At the E end is a well-preserved painting of St Faith and below, a Crucifixion dating from c.1290. It has been described as 'the most remarkable early Gothic wall painting in England'.

On the s side of the organ loft in the s aisle is a monument to Thomas Thynne (1648–82), who was assassinated in London. The beautiful bas-relief, exquisitely done, depicts the murder as Thomas rides in a coach.

Near the gates in the s aisle, on the s wall, is another monument by Bushnell. It commemorates Sir Palmes Fairborne (1634–80), and the inscription states that he 'was wounded by a shott from the Moores then besieging the Town in ye 46 yeare of his age; Octob. 24th. 1680'. The wound proved fatal. (Incidentally, many books give the date of Sir Palmes's birth as 1644 but no date appears on the monument.) This and the monument to Cowley (see above) are the only ones by Bushnell in the Abbey.

Among the roof bosses in the Abbey, the following are particularly interesting:

# THE THREE LIVING
# AND THE THREE DEAD KINGS

The story of the Three Living Kings and the Three Dead Kings, often known as 'Les Trois Rois Vifs et Les Trois Rois Morts', was a popular legend in fourteenth- and fifteenth-century England, France, Germany, Holland and Italy. In the story, three crowned kings go hunting through a forest and are met by three grisly skeleton kings, reminding them of their mortality and that Death will come to everybody one day. The three dead kings say to the three living ones:

> 'As you are now
> So once were we.
> As we are now
> So you will be!'

In France, the three living are usually shown on horseback, while in England they are normally shown walking. The only surviving example in England showing the three living on horseback is at Charlwood, Surrey.

The inspiration for mural paintings of the Three Living in England is probably a miniature in the famous *Arundel Psalter* in the British Library, London. The book was made on the orders of John de Lyle in 1339 as a present for his daughter and the miniature shows the three living and three dead kings standing in two groups – the crowned kings face the skeletons, which are draped in tattered shrouds.

As far as I know, 22 representations of the three kings (including six complete examples) remain in the following churches:

1. Barrington (All Saints), Cambridgeshire
2. Belton (All Saints), Norfolk
3. Charlwood (St Nicholas), Surrey⋆
4. Dalham (St Mary), Suffolk
5. Edworth (St George), Bedfordshire
6. Great Livermere (St Peter), Suffolk
7. Heydon (St Peter & St Paul), Norfolk
8. Hurstbourne Tarrant (St Peter), Hampshire⋆
9. Kentford (St Mary), Suffolk⋆
10. Little Witchingham (St Faith), Norfolk
11. Lutterworth (St Mary), Leicestershire
12. North Stoke (St Mary), Oxfordshire
13. Paston (St Margaret), Norfolk
14. Peakirk (St Pega), Cambridgeshire⋆
15. Pickworth (St Andrew), Lincolnshire
16. Raunds (St Mary), Northamptonshire⋆
17. Seething (St Margaret and St Remigius), Norfolk
18. Slapton (St Botolph), Northamptonshire
19. Tarrant Crawford (St Mary), Dorset
20. Wensley (Holy Trinity), North Yorkshire
21. Wickhampton (St Andrew), Norfolk⋆
22. Widford (St Oswald), Oxfordshire

⋆ Complete examples

✝ At the N end of the N transept is a boss showing David seated in a Gothic chair playing his harp.

✝ Another boss near by shows the Virgin Mary seated, attended by angels.

✝ Immediately above St Edward's shrine in the apex of the roof are two foliage bosses separated by a short rib pierced by several large holes opening into the space immediately under the outer roof. Here there would probably have been a windlass to lower or raise a canopy or lamps over the shrine below.

✝ In the muniment room on the W side of the S transept is a boss showing a figure – half-man, half-lion – with a broken sword, fighting a robed man. Also in this room on the W side is a carved falcon capital dating from *c.*1250. The falcon's feet rest on small trefoils.

▦ S of the abbey are the cloisters. Off the E cloister are a number of interesting buildings:

✝ The chapter house dating *c.*1250–53. The door to the outer vestibule of the chapter house is Saxon – one of only two Saxon doors in England. (The other is at Hadstock, Essex, see page 169.)

✝ The pyx chamber dating *c.*1065–90.

✝ The Norman Undercroft and Abbey Museum. This contains the following treasures:

⊹ A full-length oak effigy, 1.62 m (5 feet 4 inches) long, of Queen Catherine of Valois (1401–37), wife of Henry V. The right arm and the left hand are missing. The face was probably modelled from a death mask. A groove on the head shows it was once fitted with a crown. The body is carved as if robed and is painted red.

⊹ Another full-length wooden effigy, 1.8 m (5 feet 10½ inches) long, depicts Edward III (1312–77), the father of the Black Prince. The face is modelled on the death mask and formerly carried a beard.

⊹ The death mask of Henry VII (1457–09) is the finest pre-Reformation death mask in existence.

⊹ The 'Essex Ring' traditionally given by Elizabeth I to her favourite, Robert Devereux (second Earl of Essex), telling him at the same time to return it to her if he was ever in trouble and she would save him. Under sentence of death in 1601 he tried to return the ring but it never reached her and he was executed on Tower Hill on 25 February 1601. The ring was eventually returned to his widow and descended from mother to daughter until it was presented to the dean and chapter in 1927.

⊹ The coronation chair of Mary II. This was made in 1689 for the coronation of William and Mary because the Queen was the elder daughter of James II and had an equal claim to the throne with her husband. It was only used on this one occasion. Like the original coronation chair it is covered with graffiti.

⊹ In a glass case a scale model of the royal vault under Henry VII's chapel which was used for royal burials *c.*1700–*c.*1820. The model was presented by Leslie Unwin in March 1960.

▦ Under a bench in the S cloister is the earliest surviving monumental effigy in England. Commemorating Abbot Gilbert Crispin (d. 1117) it is badly worn and unfortunately lacks detail.

▦ In the NW tower hangs a ring of ten bells – the tenor weighs 1543.6 kg (1 ton 10 cwt 1 qr 15 lb). The original ring of eight bells were recast as six and four new bells added *c.*1971. They were first rung as ten bells on 10 December 1971. Also in the tower are two bells from the original ring of eight, dating from 1583 and 1598, and a sanctus bell dated 1738.

▦ On 9 July 1998 Elizabeth II attended the dedication of ten statues to twentieth-

*Long Melford, Suffolk. The church is seen from the east showing the enormous Lady Chapel.*

century martyrs. They occupy niches in the w front which until then had been left empty. Designed by Tim Crawley, they were carved from French limestone.

## Long Melford      <small>SUFFOLK</small>

HOLY TRINITY is considered by many to be the finest church in Suffolk.

▨ The splendid w tower was built in 1903 by G. F. Bodley and encases an earlier brick tower of 1725. It is 36m (118 feet) high. Notice the beautiful flushwork on the s face.

▨ On the outside of the church on the N and s parapets, around the lady chapel and over the porch are several carved inscriptions commencing, 'Pray for the souls of . . .' No other church in the British Isles has so many inscriptions on its outer walls. These are excellent examples of East Anglian flushwork.

▨ In the N aisle is fifteenth-century glass that has portraits of the Clopton family, who rebuilt the church *c.*1470.

▨ In the NW window is a figure of Elizabeth Talbot, Duchess of Norfolk. Her portrait is said to be that which Sir John Tenniel used in his original illustrations for *Alice in Wonderland.*

▨ Over the N door is a very small half circle of medieval glass showing three

*Superb stone and flintwork at Long Melford, Suffolk.*

hares but with only three ears painted! Each hare *appears* to have two ears. This glass may represent the Holy Trinity, to whom the church is dedicated.

 In the wall of the N aisle at the E end is an alabaster reredos dating from *c.*1350 depicting the Adoration of the Magi. It was found hidden underneath the chancel in *c.*1750. Note the ox and ass at the base of the sculpture.

 Notice the fine fan vaulting, dating from *c.*1500, in the vestibule near the Clopton chantry chapel. (See Fan Vaulting, page 152.)

 In the E window of the Clopton chapel is a piece of stained glass showing a lily crucifix dating from *c.*1450. (See Lily Crucifix, page 338.)

 Also in the Clopton chapel is an Easter tomb with original paintings on it, one showing the risen Christ and a Latin text translated, 'Everyone who lives and believes in me shall not die eternally'.

Around the walls are Latin poems ending with the words, 'I gave my blood for you in sacrifice'. John Masefield used these words in 1911 for his poem 'The Everlasting Mercy'.

 On the S side of the high altar is the imposing tomb of Sir William Cordell (d. 1581), who entertained Queen Elizabeth I at Long Melford Hall in 1578. The tomb was designed by Cornelius Cure; he also designed the tomb of Mary Queen of Scots in Westminster Abbey.

 The fine reredos dates from 1877 and is of Caen stone. It is modelled on Albrecht Dürer's 'Crucifixion'.

 At the E end of the church is the lady chapel, which is unique in England for its size and shape. A rare feature is the indoor walk around the actual chapel. On the E wall is a multiplication table dating from 1670 when the chapel was used as a school for the children of Long Melford.

*Long Sutton, Lincolnshire.*

 In the churchyard, at the extreme E end of the newer part, a flat tombstone commemorates Edmund Blunden (1 November 1896–20 January 1974), one of the famous soldier poets from the First World War who lived his last days in this beautiful village. His gravestone is inscribed:

'Beloved Poet'
'I live still, to love still
Things quiet and unconcerned.'

## Long Sutton
### (or Sutton St Mary)                    LINCOLNSHIRE

ST MARY is an impressive church and, with its imposing lead spire, it provides a wonderful spectacle for motorists on the busy A17, near the Wash.

▨ The Early English tower and spire are almost detached from the main building of the church. Dating from c.1200 the spire, at 49.4 m (162 feet) high, is the oldest and finest lead spire in Britain and leans slightly. This effect is exaggerated by inward-leaning octagonal angle turrets, which look like giant candle snuffers. The wooden spire and turrets are covered in strips of lead arranged in herringbone patterns. (See Lead Spires and Spirelets, page 229.)

▨ The magnificent brass eagle lectern dates from c.1500. The eagle's talons are missing and there are three lions at the base. (See Medieval Brass Lecterns, page 362.)

▨ On the N side of the altar, entered from the vestry, is an unusual five-sided vaulted chamber with a quatrefoil boss enclosing a shield. There is another chamber above this entered by a stone spiral staircase. This room is known locally as 'the Monk's Cell'.

▨ On the N side of the chancel on the floor is a tombstone inscribed, 'Alas! poor Bailey'. Dr Bailey was murdered in 1795.

▨ In the superb S porch, which has a room above, there are numerous bosses including a Pelican in her Piety and two faces, one of which has two tongues protruding!

▨ In the churchyard are several interesting gravestones including a thatcher's tombstone (S of the S porch) showing the tools of his trade, and one to Charles Wigglesworth (S of the E end of the church; d. 1840), who guided people over the Wash.

## Long Wittenham                    OXFORDSHIRE

ST MARY As its name implies, the village is a very long one, with the little church situated at one end of it.

▨ The lead font dates from c.1170 and is embossed with figures of bishops standing under an arcade of pointed arches. It is similar to the font at nearby Warborough and probably came from the same mould. During the Civil War the font was encased in wood to prevent it from being melted down and so remained hidden until 1839 when it was restored to view again. (See Lead Fonts, page 74.)

▨ In the SE corner of the S wall of the S transept is a combined piscina and monument to Gilbert de Clare (d.1295) – the second smallest sculptured monument in England. The effigy of the knight is only 61 cm (2 feet) long. Above the arch of the piscina are two angels with outspread wings. This memorial dates from c.1300. (The smallest effigy is 46 cm / 1 foot 6 inches long and is of an unknown knight at Mappowder, Dorset.)

▨ In the choir are Jacobean stalls from Exeter College Chapel, Oxford; the screen across the S transept also came from there.

## Louth                    LINCOLNSHIRE

ST JAMES The town of Louth is dominated by the superb church spire, forming a landmark across N Lincolnshire.

▨ The magnificent tower and spire soaring to 89.9 m (295 feet) was completed in 1515. On the corners of the tower are pinnacles linked to the spire by flying buttresses. This is the highest parish church spire in England.

▨ Above the bells, near the base of the spire, is the original tread-wheel used for raising the bells and constructing the spire. It has a diameter of 3.7 m (12 feet). Only five other wheels exist – at Beverley Minster, Canterbury Cathedral, Durham and Peterborough cathedrals and Salisbury Cathedral (see pages 26, 61, 110, 270 and 303 respectively).

▨ At the E end of the N aisle are two

wooden angels from the original medieval roof.

◈ At the w end of the n aisle is an elaborate monument to William Allison, 1845. The inscription is barely legible.

◈ Behind the organ is a stained-glass window depicting the Childhood of Christ. Notice the detail of the three rabbits.

## Lower Halstow                  KENT

St Margaret of Antioch is a delightful church situated very near a creek of the Thames Estuary, separated from it only by a grassy bank.

◈ The lead font dating from c.1150 was plastered over between 1560 and 1700 to preserve it. Its shape was changed from circular to square and until 1921 no one suspected it was a lead font. In that year the vicar called in a local mason to repair cracks that had appeared during heavy gunfire in the First World War and as the plaster was pulled off the original lead font was revealed! It was later returned to its circular shape as we see it today.

The design comprises ten arcades under which are five figures of an angel and five of a king repeated alternately. No other lead font exists with angels and kings on it. The lead bowl is 30 cm (1 foot) high with a top diameter of 54 cm (1 foot 10 inches). It is encased in a Jacobean cover. (See Lead Fonts, page 74.)

◈ The e window depicts a soldier and the Risen Lord and is in memory of Harry Greensted, BA and all who died in the First World War. This window has proved quite controversial over the years. What do you think of it?

◈ Remains of a medieval wall painting are visible in the nave.

## Ludlow                    SHROPSHIRE

St Laurence Known as the 'Cathedral of the Marches', the church has a fine central tower which, at 41.14 m (135 feet) high, dominates this lovely town.

◈ On the s side of the nave is a rare hexagonal porch dating from c.1310. Above the vaulting is a small room. (See Porches, page 265.)

◈ Much of the stained glass is original, dating from c.1450. The best windows are as follows:

† The Annunciation or Golden Window on the n side of St John the Evangelist's chapel on the n side of the chancel.

† The Palmer's Window at the e end of St John the Evangelist's chapel.

† The great e window of the chancel comprising 27 panels telling the story of St Laurence.

† The adjoining window on the s side which is the only surviving example in England of a 'Ten Commandments' window. Panels illustrate the breaking of all the commandments!

† The e window of the lady chapel shows a Tree of Jesse. It was restored in 1890 but much of the glass dates from c.1330.

◈ In the chancel are 32 stalls, 16 on each side, and underneath the seats are 28 original misericords, 20 dating from c.1447 and eight (marked with a small twig) dating from c.1390. Among the most interesting are the Prince of Wales's Feathers, a fox in bishop's robes preaching to geese, a mermaid with her mirror, a man warming himself by a fire with a kettle on another fire and two sides of bacon hanging behind him and a woman disappearing bottom-up into the Jaws of Hell!

◈ One of the bench-ends on the s side exhibits a beautiful carving of Mary holding the dead Christ.

◈ On the n side of the chancel is a fine

classical monument to a judge, Sir Robert Townshend (d. 1556), Dame Alice, his wife (d. 1574), and their 12 children. He was a Roman Catholic.

🔲 On the s side of the chancel is the most elaborate monument in the church. Made of alabaster it commemorates Edmund Walter (d. 1592), Mary, his wife (d. 1583) and their five children. The railings and iron flags are contemporary.

🔲 In the tower, which has a fine vaulted wooden roof, are eight bells on which a different tune is played daily each week.

# Lydd

ALL SAINTS Known as 'the Cathedral of the Marsh' its fine Perpendicular tower is a landmark for miles around.

🔲 The tower was raised to its present height of 40.2 m (132 feet) in c.1500 when Thomas Wolsey (later Cardinal Wolsey) was rector.

🔲 The chancel was completely destroyed in the Second World War. The modern stained glass in the three lancets was made by Leonard Walker.

🔲 The 24-branched candelabra in the nave dates from 1753 and was given by a descendant of someone called Thomas Harte (d. 20 July 1557).

🔲 At the sw end of the s aisle is a fine memorial to an Ann Russell, wife of Henry Russell, who died 25 November 1780 aged 31, and her only child, Henry, who died 15 January 1781 aged four. An angel is depicted carrying the little boy to Heaven to give to his mother. This monument, signed by John Flaxman, 1814, is the first one he sculpted.

🔲 In the N aisle is the modern font – it is in the style of an elegant marble basin of c.1750.

*Lyddington, Rutland.*

# Lyddington

ST ANDREW Just to the s of Bede House in this beautiful village stands the fine, ironstone church with a short, recessed spire on its w tower.

🔲 The communion rails enclose the communion table on all four sides. Dated 1635 they are a very rare feature. (See also Deerhurst, Glos., page 101.)

🔲 In the chancel, high up in the walls, are a number of acoustic jars, which are also rare.

🔲 An unusual brass depicts a lady called Helyn Hardy (d. 1486), who is shown in the dress of a widow who has taken the vows of chastity. She wears a butterfly headdress.

# LEAD SPIRES AND SPIRELETS

Hundreds of churches throughout England and Wales have spires – many made of stone or wood and a few with modern fibreglass replacements such as Peterchurch, Herefordshire. More unusual, however, are the lead-covered timber spires and spirelets, many of which have become warped and twisted over the centuries, often due to unseasoned timber, the movement of the lead or faults in the original construction.

*Long Sutton, Lincolnshire.*

The most famous twisted spire, and the highest lead one, can be seen at Chesterfield, Derbyshire, but the oldest, considered by many to be the finest, is at Long Sutton, Lincolnshire, and dates from c.1200. This spire is embellished with four lead-covered pinnacles at the base that look like giant candle-snuffers. The spire rises from an almost-detached bell-tower and presents a magnificent spectacle to motorists as they pass through Long Sutton.

Many of these spires have four or more faces, but the way in which the lead plates are laid on the wood in herringbone fashion gives the impression that the faces are channelled. Chesterfield's spire is octagonal but looks as though it has 16 faces!

Owing to their extreme vulnerability, all spires must be protected from lightning attack, but especially so the lead-covered spire. Throughout history there are stories of spires having been damaged or even completely destroyed by lightning. The spire at Barnstaple, Devon,

originally built from 1381 to 1389, was struck by lightning in 1810. It was only slightly damaged as it still bears the date 1636 towards the base and the initials of the church-wardens at the time; this probably refers to an earlier repair. The spire now leans 0.6 m (26 inches) to the s. (Lincoln Cathedral once had three spires, but the lead spire on the central tower was blown down in 1548 and the smaller spires on the W towers were dismantled in 1807 when they were considered to be unsafe.) It is interesting to note that the tall spire at Chesterfield sways on very windy days!

The spire at Swimbridge, Devon, was releaded in 1897 to commemorate Queen Victoria's diamond jubilee. One of the lead plates taken from the spire at the time bears the date 1674, presumably when a previous restoration was effected.

The spire at Harrow-on-the-Hill, Greater London, was originally constructed c.1450 but has been damaged by fire on two occasions. It was most recently rebuilt in 1765.

Godalming, Surrey, has a beautiful oak spire dating from c.1350 and covered in lead plates. It was completely restored in 1988 when 12,193 kg (12 tons) of lead – including the original 10,161 kg (10 tons) – were processed to re-cover the original medieval wooden framework. It is curious that none of the well-known books on churches mentions the height of Godalming's spire! Duncan Mirylees, however, working for the Surrey county archivist, has

*Hadleigh, Suffolk.*

calculated from a measured scale drawing in a book published in 1900 that the height is approximately 37 m (120 feet 6 inches) excluding the weathercock.

Similarly, the height of Harrow-on-the-Hill's spire is not recorded in any of the well-known books, but Bryan Cozens of Harrow tells me its height is 45.4 m (149 feet) and says: 'Our spire is on the main flight path in and out of RAF Northolt (home of the Royal Squadron), and the MOD have four warning lights at the top of it, so it occurred to me that they would know. Sure enough when I spoke to the Air Traffic Controller in the Control Tower they very helpfully looked at their air chart and told me straight away.'

Incidentally, because the church stands on a hill 124 m (407 feet) high, the total height above sea level is 169.47 m (556 feet). Salisbury Cathedral's spire, at 123.14 m (404 feet) from ground level, stands approximately 45 m (148 feet) above sea level, making a total height of 168.24 m (552 feet). Thus the spire of St Mary's, Harrow-on-the-Hill, is the highest in England *above sea level,* surpassing Salisbury by 1.23 m (4 feet)!

Bourn, Cambridgeshire, has a spire which Pevsner describes as 'every bit as crooked as the more famous specimen at Chesterfield'. It does not twist as much as Chesterfield's, but it is, nevertheless, quite dramatic. Following an appeal in 1911, nearly £742 was raised for the restoration of the tower and spire and the project was completed in 1912. The restored spire was reduced in height and panels inscribed John Ferrar and J. F. 1620 with three shields of arms were removed from the spire and are now preserved inside the church.

The height of the spire of St Nicholas Chapel in King's Lynn, Norfolk, has also never been officially recorded. The original, which was blown down in a storm on 8 September 1741, was 51.8 m (170 feet) high. The present spire, completed 1869–70, was designed by Sir George Gilbert Scott and is a little higher at 53.3 m (175 feet).

West Harptree, Somerset, originally had a slated spire in the 1930s but when Pevsner carried out his survey of the buildings of England in the 1950s this had been replaced by a spire covered in lead plates. By the year 2000 this had again been replaced, this time by copper sheets, which have since turned green.

In Hertfordshire and the neighbouring counties a feature which is known as a 'Hertfordshire spike' can be seen on many towers; this is really a wooden spirelet encased in lead.

The following churches possess towers with short lead spires or spirelets, which nevertheless constitute an attractive feature:

1. Ash, near Sandwich (St Nicholas), Kent
2. Aston Upthorpe (All Saints), Oxfordshire
3. East Meon (All Saints), Hampshire
4. Great Baddow (St Mary the Virgin), Essex
5. Ickleton (St Mary), Cambridgshire
6. Milford-on-Sea (All Saints), Hampshire
7. Old Stevenage (St Nicholas), Hertfordshire

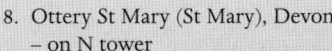
8. Ottery St Mary (St Mary), Devon – on N tower
9. Rochester Cathedral, Kent
10. Stanford Rivers (St Margaret), Essex
11. West Pennard (St Nicholas), Somerset
12. Wickham Market (All Saints), Suffolk

The following list includes, to the best of my knowledge, the highest lead spires in England and Wales, together with their approximate dates of construction or reconstruction and their heights from ground level:

1. Barnstaple (St Peter & St Paul), Devon – 1381–9, 36.3 m (119 feet)
2. Bourn (St Mary), Cambridgeshire – date of construction unknown but possibly c.1600, height approximately 41.75 m (137 feet)
3. Braunton (St Brannock), Devon – c.1250, 36 m (118 feet)
4. Chesterfield (St Mary & All Saints), Derbyshire – 1362, 69½ m (228 feet)
5. Godalming (St Peter & St Paul), Surrey – c.1350, 37 m (120½ feet)
6. Hadleigh (St Mary), Suffolk – c.1350, 41 m (135 feet)
7. Harrow-on-the-Hill (St Mary), Greater London – 1765, 45.4 m (149 feet)
8. Hemel Hempstead (St Mary), Hertfordshire – c.1350, 61 m (200 feet)
9. King's Lynn (St Nicholas Chapel), Norfolk – 1869–70, 53.3 m (175 feet)
10. Long Sutton (St Mary), Lincolnshire – c.1200, 49.3 m (162 feet)
11. Swimbridge (St James), Devon – c.1350, 36 m (118 feet)

Finally, reference should also be made to the two western towers of Southwell Cathedral, Nottinghamshire, surmounted by Victorian replicas of the original lead spires.

*England's unique triangular church tower at All Saints, Maldon, Essex.*

# Madley HEREFORDSHIRE

NATIVITY OF THE VIRGIN is a large spacious church and is unusual in possessing an apsidal E end with a crypt underneath.

 In the E window are six beautiful thirteenth-century roundels of stained glass, one showing the Adoration by the Wise Men.

 At the E end of the N aisle is the Lulham family pew incorporating fifteenth-century screen-work that was restored in 1867 by John Morris. Notice three coat hooks inside and four lions' heads on the ceiling. When the pew was originally further down the church, the little door which now opens on to the wall at the E end would have been used by the family to receive the bread and wine at Holy Communion.

 The crypt under the chancel is supported on a central pillar from which spring ten ribs to the outside walls. The crypt follows the plan of the chancel above and is approached by passageways from the E end of the N and S aisles but the S aisle door is now closed because it is behind the organ. This is the last medieval crypt to be built in England.

Just inside the entrance from the N aisle a spiral staircase leads up to what would have been the top of the rood screen, the beam of which still remains above the Lulham pew.

 Near the E end of the Chilstone chapel on the S side of the church is a gravestone commemorating a local innkeeper who died in 1793. The inscription reads:

'Famed little John a terror to many a
  boxing blade,
But now alas an insult brooks from
  sexton's dirty spade,
For coward Death waiting the time till
  Jack was weak and low
The moment seized and spite of art
  put in his favourite blow.'

# Maer STAFFORDSHIRE

ST PETER is situated high on a hill overlooking Maer Hall with 36 steps leading up to it from the road. This church was rebuilt in 1878 and reopened on 23 January 1879.

 The tower dates from 1610.

 The elevated chancel is reached by four steps from the nave.

 On the N side of the chancel is the tomb of a couple, Sir John Bowyer (d. 17 March 1604) and Lady Catherine Bowyer (d. 19 December 1631). He wears plate armour and she an Elizabethan dress and ruff.

 On the NE side of the N aisle is an impressive window depicting the Agony in Gethsemane in memory of one Jane Ellen Leslie Harrison (1882–1963).

 At the W end of the N aisle is a striking modern window comprising chunky bits of glass of every imaginable colour in memory of Dorothy Clive (d. 1942). The window was designed by Leonard Walker in 1943.

 A similar window on the SW side of the nave is in memory of Henry Clive of

Willoughbridge, husband of Dorothy. It states it was also made by Lennard [sic] Walker, assisted by E. D. Crouch.

To the w of the tower, in the church-yard, are the graves of Frances, daughter of Josiah and Elizabeth Wedgwood (d. 20 August 1832), and others including Josiah Wedgwood II (3 August 1769–12 July 1843).

Charles Darwin and Emma Wedgwood were married in this church on 29 January 1839. Emma was his cousin, the daughter of his uncle Josiah Wedgwood II.

## Maidstone                          KENT

ALL SAINTS was built in 1395 as a collegiate church by Archbishop William Courtenay. Overlooking the River Medway, this is one of the largest parish churches in England. The aisles are reputed to be the widest of any English parish church.

The magnificent wooden roofs in the Perpendicular style are Victorian.

At the w end of the n aisle is an unusual monument to Sir John Astley (d. 1639), his wife, Margaret, and their son, Sir John, and his wife, Catherine. Four life-size figures stand in their shrouds. The Astley family were royalists who supported King Charles during the Civil War.

At the w end of the nave is a wall tablet to Lieutenant Colonel William Havelock (d. 22 November 1848 aged 56 years), and several others who were killed in the Punjab campaign. An officer stands point-ing with his left hand on the shoulder of a small boy under the shadow of a palm tree. The plaque was carved by R. Westmacott Jnr.

Also near by is a plaque to Sir Jacob Astley (d. 27 February 1653) who fought at Edgehill, Naseby and Newbury. He is noted for his famous prayer before the Battle of Newbury: 'Lord, Thou knowest I

shall be very busy this day. If I forget Thee, do not Thou forget me, Amen.'

The e window of the n aisle is unusual in depicting only fruit leaves and flowers and was erected in memory of Josh Arkcoll (d. 24 July 1857). It contains notable blues and reds in the tradition of early medieval glass.

The fine stone reredos at the e end was dedicated on 6 November 1904 in memory of Herbert John Monkton, who died in the South African Campaign on 4 February 1902. It shows Christ seated in Glory wearing a crown and holding the orb adored by angels and the human race. It almost obscures the e window.

Near by, in the chancel, are four sedilia dating from c.1450. They are unusual in all being on one level.

Also in the chancel are 20 interesting misericords dating from c.1400. One on the n side shows the college cook holding a ladle in her left hand and a meat hook in her right.

At the e end of the s choir aisle is the tomb of John Wooton (d. October 1417) first master of the College of Priests founded by Archbishop Courtenay.

Also at the e end of this aisle is an unusual wall memorial in brass to a Beale family showing six generations and dating from 1593.

In the centre of the chancel is Archbishop Courtenay's tomb but the brass is missing.

At the w end of the s aisle near the s porch is the memorial to Lawrence Washington (d. 21 December 1619), great-uncle of George Washington. Note the stars and stripes in the family's coat of arms and the peculiar blue cap worn by the revolutionaries.

At the e end of the n choir aisle are a few medieval tiles showing heraldic designs.

## Maldon     ESSEX

ALL SAINTS The church stands conspicuously in the centre of the town, at the top of the hill.

▣ Here is the only triangular church tower in England, averaging 5.2 m (17 feet) on each of its three sides. It dates from *c.*1250 and is surmounted by a shingled hexagonal spire with small pyramidal roofs at the three angles. A little turret projecting from the spire contains the original sanctus bell inscribed, *'Johannes Snayn et Ricardus Lynn me fecit'* ('John Snayn and Richard Lynn made me').

Thomas Washington, the great-great-grandfather of George Washington, first President of the USA, was buried in the churchyard on 21 January 1652.

▣ The s aisle dates from *c.*1350 and has fine windows facing the street with superb arcading richly decorated inside. In the outside wall is a doorway leading to a crypt below. This sumptuous s aisle has been compared to the lady chapel at Ely Cathedral, (see page 126), constructed at about the same time.

## Malmesbury     WILTSHIRE

THE ABBEY CHURCH OF THE BLESSED VIRGIN MARY, ST ALDHELM, ST PETER & ST PAUL At the top of the hill, the remains of the abbey dominate the town.

▣ This building is the former nave of a great Benedictine abbey that was closed by Henry VIII in 1539. It was bought by a wealthy cloth manufacturer, William Stumpe, and he gave it to the townsfolk as their parish church.

▣ The s porch contains magnificent carvings of the 12 Apostles and scenes from the Old and New Testaments dating from *c.*1160. Some regard them as the finest twelfth-century sculptures in the British Isles.

▣ High up in the nave on the s side of the triforium is an unusual stone loft. The original purpose is unknown but it may have been used by monks to watch pilgrims who were visiting St Aldhelm's shrine.

▣ In the N aisle is a Perpendicular tomb-chest depicting King Athelstan (d. 939), who was buried here although the exact site is unknown.

▣ A stained-glass window in the vestry depicts the monk Elmer or Brother Oliver, who tried to fly with wings from a w tower of the abbey in *c.*1050. He crashed, breaking both legs, but survived into old age.

▣ Across the E wall of the church is the top of the original stone screen in the centre of which are the Arms of Henry VIII – a rare survival. (See Royal Arms, page 351.)

▣ In the room over the s porch is a collection of abbey treasures including four volumes of the *Vulgate* translation of the Bible written *c.*1450.

▣ In the churchyard is the tower of the former St Paul's Church which now serves as the abbey's belfry. Near by is a gravestone commemorating a woman who was killed by an escaped circus animal. The inscription reads:

' In memory of
Hannah Twynnoy
Who died October 23rd 1703
Aged 33 years.
In bloom of Life
She's snatched from hence,
She had not room
To make defence;
For Tyger fierce
Took Life away.
And here she lies
In a bed of Clay,
Until the Resurrection Day.'

## March · CAMBRIDGESHIRE

ST WENDREDA'S 42.7 m (140 feet) high spire church dominates the Fenland countryside. Ely Cathedral can be seen on a clear day from the tower parapet – a distance of 19.3 km (12 miles).

The magnificent double hammer-beam angel roof made of English oak dates from c.1500 and is among the finest in England and Wales. Comprising nine bays there are about 120 angels on the hammer-beams as well as on the wall posts. The angels at the base of the wall posts hold musical instruments, on the lower hammer-beams emblems of the Passion and on the upper beams shields or books.

In a glass case at the NE end of the N aisle is a Bible printed in 1827 and given in memory of Robert Barlow. It is the largest Church Bible in England, each page measuring 30 cm (12 inches) wide by 51 cm (20 inches) deep.

The church's dedication, 'Wendreda', is worked in flint outside the church on the N side between the clerestory windows. This is unique.

Part of the base of the tower forms a covered way outside the church – a rare survival, probably preserving an existing right-of-way before the church was built.

## Melbourne · DERBYSHIRE

ST MICHAEL WITH ST MARY is a magnificent Norman church of c.1120 with low twin towers and central tower.

The Norman W doorway is much renewed.

The nave comprises six bays with circular piers, 4.6 m (15 feet) high and 1.21 m (4 feet) in diameter. The rounded arches exhibit the characteristic zigzag mouldings.

The capitals under the tower show a grinning cat on the N side and a medieval peasant with a dog on the S side.

At the W end a gravestone states: 'Here lyeth the Body of Richard Dalman who Changed time for Eternity, June ye 1, 1747. Aged 88.'

## Mellor · GREATER MANCHESTER

ST THOMAS is situated high up above the village with spectacular views from the churchyard.

The churchyard contains a large number of gravestones, many laid flat, with superb lettering. An enormous one, on the left of the path as one enters, is a table-tomb in memory of a Thomas Ferneley (d. 14 August 1849, aged 71). The inscription reads:

'A Sinner saved by Grace.
Grace 'tis a sweet, a charming theme –
My thoughts rejoice at Jesus name –
Jesus, harmonious name, it charms the hosts above
They evermore proclaim and wonder at His love.
Jesus is worthy to receive,
Honour and power divine:
And blessings more than we can give
Be, Lord, for ever Thine.'

On the N side of the nave is England's oldest pulpit carved from solid oak c.1330. Octagonal, one of the panels is plain – probably because the pulpit was once placed close to a wall. It was removed to the tower c.1829 when a three-decker pulpit was installed. It was reinstated in 1884 when the three-decker was dismantled.

Opposite the S door is the original sounding board of the three-decker pulpit dating from 1720.

The fine Norman font, adorned with curious carving, dates from c.1190.

On the S side of the nave is a lovely

236

stained-glass window in blues, greens and yellows in memory of Lilian and Annie Reburn (members of a family called Pilkington), July, 1973.

 At the NW corner of the nave is another stained-glass window in purples, reds and yellows bearing the text, 'The righteous shall be in everlasting remembrance'. The beautiful altar frontal below showing different designs of flowers was dedicated on 19 June 1983.

## Mells                                    SOMERSET

ST ANDREW This beautiful church stands next to the manor house and is approached down a lovely street which is dominated by its magnificent tower.

 The beautiful tower is a fine example of Somerset Perpendicular, similar to nearby Leigh-on-Mendip.

 The S porch has a fan-vaulted roof with many bosses. (See Fan Vaulting, page 152.)

*Mells, Somerset.*

 Under the tower is more fan vaulting. On the S wall of the tower interior is a memorial to Raymond Asquith (6 November 1878–15 September 1916), who was killed on the Somme. Eric Gill carved the inscription while the bronze wreath above it was given by Sir Edwin Lutyens.

 On the N wall of the tower is a memorial stone to Laura Lyttelton, who was the wife of Alfred Lyttelton QC and who died 24 April 1886. Designed by Sir Edward Burne-Jones, the stone shows a peacock standing on an empty tomb and is in gesso on wood.

 On the N side of the chancel is the Horner chapel, which is dominated by a statue of a bronze horse and rider, the first horse ever sculpted by Sir Alfred Munnings. The plinth was designed by Sir Edwin Lutyens. This statue commemorates Edward Horner, who was killed at Cambrai in 1917, aged 28. The inscription

reads: 'He was greatly loved in his home of Mells but with eager valour he left his heritage to fight in France. Severely wounded at Ypres, he recovered and returned to his regiment and fell at last in Picardy...Thus in the morning of his youth he hastened to rejoin his friends and comrades by a swift and noble death.'(See Horses in Churches, page 413.)

 The E window of the Horner chapel, put up in 1930 to Sir John Horner, was designed and executed by Sir William Nicholson, the painter. It depicts St Francis preaching to the birds and fishes and was the first window designed by Sir William Nicholson.

 In the second window from the W in the N aisle are four saints in the tracery lights dating from *c.*1450. They are St Sitha

holding two keys and three loaves, St Agatha holding a sword and saw, St Mary Magdalene holding a pot of ointment and a palm and St Apollonia holding a tooth in a pair of pincers and a book.

There are eight bells in the tower and every three hours they play one of these four tunes: 'Mells Tune', 'Holsworthy', 'London New' and 'Hanover'.

On the SE side of the S aisle is an unusual two-storey hexagonal building. The bottom is used as a vestry. In the room above are four windows containing a kaleidoscope of medieval stained glass.

Near the E wall of the churchyard is the grave of Monseigneur Ronald Knox which bears the following inscription:

'Ronald Arbuthnott Knox
Priest scholar preacher and writer
He spent the last years of his life in Mells, here finished his translation of the Bible and here died on the 24 of August, 1957 aged 69 years. Pray for his soul R.I.P.
"You are dead and your life is hidden with Christ in God."'

Near by are the graves of scientist and civil servant Maurice Bonham-Carter KCB, KCVO (11 October 1880–7 June 1960) and his wife, Helen Violet, Baroness Asquith of Yarnbury DBE (15 April 1887–19 February 1969).

Also near by is the grave of the war poet Siegfried Louvain Sassoon, 1886–1967.

In the churchyard E of the E window is the grave of Canon James Owen Hannay, otherwise known as 'George Birmingham'. He was rector of Mells from 1924 to 1934.

Another gravestone commemorates Christopher Hollis, author and publisher. He is best remembered for his novel *Death of a Gentleman*.

# Mendlesham     SUFFOLK

ST MARY THE VIRGIN This is an impressive flint-built church with a fine tower.

The superb tower, dating from 1488 to 1494, is 25.8 m (84 feet 6 inches) high and contains six bells.

The sanctus bell on the church gable came from the vicarage in 1979 where it had been used to call the domestic staff to meals!

There is a magnificent set of medieval benches with poppy-heads at each end and numerous other carvings.

The fine font cover was made in 1630 by John Turner.

At the W end of the N aisle are two biers, one of which is a child's dating from c.1780 and very rare.

Near by is a clock barrel dating from c.1500.

Under the tower is a hatchment bearing the motto, *'In Coelo Quies'* ('Beside the throne of God') with the arms of the Cresacre family of Yorkshire (see Wooden Effigies, page 246) and stories associated with them (Barnburgh, South Yorkshire) and the Marshall family of Derbyshire. Dating from 1775 to 1825 it was bought by the Reverend E. R. Manwaring-White, who brought it to Mendlesham when he left Yorkshire in 1910.

In the NE window sill of the N aisle is a piscina – a very unusual position.

The E window of the N aisle comprises modern glass except for the top right-hand panel, which shows St John holding a chalice, scorpions and a palm leaf. Dating from c.1500 this glass was covered up for 400 years!

The pediment at the top of one of the legs of the seventeenth-century communion table in the N aisle has been fixed on incorrectly!

In the chancel are two 'Dan Day' (Daniel

Day) or 'Suffolk' (or 'Mendlesham') chairs made locally 1780–1820.

The N porch is an excellent example of E. Anglian flush-work. The chamber above has been used since 1593 to house the parish armoury – the most complete set in any English church! The room is approached up a narrow staircase and the little heavy door that leads up to it is secured by several locks. Despite this, thefts have taken place over the years. Among the pieces that remain are:

† part of an Elizabethan long-bow (c.1588)
† two helmets – Flemish (1590)
† a right-shoulder plate (a pauldron) c.1510 and made in Italy or the Low Countries.

Other items include a Vinegar Bible, a clock hand, seals, a mile wheel (c.1800, similar to equipment used by surveyors today) and three large chests, made in this room as they are too large to bring up! Fixed to the N wall of the armoury are pieces of glass dated between 1733 and 1849 – these came from the clerestory windows when they were destroyed in a hailstorm on 16 July 1947. (See Parish Armoury, page 186.)

## Mereworth
(pronounced 'Merryworth')                    KENT

ST LAWRENCE was built by an unknown architect from 1743 to 1746 for John Fane, the Seventh Earl of Westmorland. It is one of the few remaining in England in the Palladian style. The spire is similar to St Martin-in-the-Fields, London, which dates from 1726.

The interior follows the Basilica pattern with no separate chancel. Two lines of Doric columns, painted to imitate marble, run around the inside and carry a plaster barrel vault.

Above the colonnade along the E wall is a large lunette filled with heraldic stained glass dating from c.1560.

In the SW corner of the church are several monuments removed from the old church that stood near Mereworth Castle. The large one commemorates Sir Thomas Fane (possibly an ancestor of John Fane, Seventh Earl of Westmorland who built this church) and his widow, Lady Mary, and dates from 1639.

In the extreme SW corner is a rare 'heart shrine' dating from c.1510 and showing two cherubic hands holding a heart. It was probably built to receive the embalmed heart of a member of the Nevill family.

Near the font a wall tablet records:

'In memory of John Richard Leslie Bazley-White aged four years nine months who perished in the fire which destroyed the Hall, Wateringbury on the night of the 17 October, 1927. Born to know not Winter only Spring. Also of his father Richard Booth Leslie Bazley-White D.S.O. Captain Royal West Kent Regiment who died with him and of his mother Katharine Bechford Bazley-White who gave her life in trying to succour him and of his nurse Rosa Weeks in whose arms he was found.
The Love and Wisdom of God.'

In the churchyard on the S side of the church a large stone Celtic cross surmounts the grave of Charles Lucas and bears this inscription:

'In loving Memory of Charles Davis Lucas Rear Admiral VC. Born 19 February, 1834, Died 7 August, 1914.'

He was the *first* person to win the Victoria Cross, although owing to three officers of senior rank, he was the fourth of 62 recipients to receive it personally from Queen Victoria on 26 June 1856, shortly after it had been inaugurated. He won the distinction on 20 June 1854 for outstanding bravery in a naval battle in the Baltic off Finland during the Crimean War. While on board HMS *Hecla* he threw a live shell from the deck into the sea where it exploded harmlessly, thus saving many lives.

There is also a monument to Rear Admiral Lucas on the N side of the tower, inside the present vestry.

## Mid Lavant          WEST SUSSEX

ST NICHOLAS has been converted into a community centre but still retains facilities for worship.

On the S side of the chancel are two lancet windows containing seventeenth-century foreign glass depicting St Peter with a key, the Adoration of the Shepherds, the Descent from the Cross and a view of a city with domes.

On the N side of the church is the superb marble effigy of Lady Mary May (1640–81) sculpted by John Bushnell in 1676. She died of smallpox and in the name of artistic honesty, when Bushnell returned to add the date of death, he carved pox marks on the face of Lady May! The accompanying inscription reads:

'Here lies the Body of Dame Mary May second Wife to Sir John May of Rawmere (Roughmere) the only surviving Sister and sole Heir unto Sir John Morley of Brooms and Daughter to Sir John Morley of Chichester Son to Sir Edward Morley a second Brother of the Family of Halnaker Place. Piously contemplating ye uncertainty of this life, among other solemn Preparations for her Funerall Obsequies, Shee erected this Monument in ye time of her life, in ye

year of our LORD 1676. She departed this life in ye year or our LORD 1681 in ye 41st year of her Age.'

Because this statue was marked with the smallpox, it was buried in a vault under the chancel from 1872 to 1875 on the orders of the Reverend W.R.W. Stephens when the church was restored. In July 1981 Danny Edwardes, a workman who was laying a new floor in the chancel, put his pickaxe through the roof of the vault and revealed the statue! It was brought out in November 1981. (See John Bushnell, page 212.)

On the N side of the chancel arch is a fine modern statue in bronze of St Nicholas.

The famous theologian and Victorian writer Dean Walter Farquhar Hook (1798–1875), Dean of Chichester 1859–75, is buried in the churchyard. During his time as dean he wrote *Lives of the Archbishops of Canterbury* in 12 volumes.

Somewhere in the churchyard is buried a monument to the painter Edward Bird (1718), a half figure showing him as a young officer in a periwig holding a truncheon. Mrs Katherine Esdaile (an authority on English church monuments from 1510 to 1840, often quoted by Pevsner) says that in 1879 the vicar had the statue buried in the churchyard because he 'was ignorant of English! The inscription stated that Bird "had the misfortune to kill a waiter at a bagnio by Golden Square"; but this did not mean a house of ill fame at this time, but a reputable public bath for "sweating, bathing, washing, etc.", with days for women and men.' Mrs Esdaile adds, 'The sooner the work is dug up and restored to the church the better, while anyone remains who knows where it lies.'

Unfortunately this is what has happened and nobody knows the location of this piece of sculpture!

# Minehead     SOMERSET

ST MICHAEL is situated high up on the SE slope of North Hill and can be seen from most parts of the town. From the church-yard looking E are beautiful views over the bay and towards Dunster and the pre-served West Somerset Railway. Dr F. C. Eeles (1876–1954) stated, 'Few of our churches are more strikingly situated.'

Minehead, Somerset.

The fine tower is 26.5 m (87 feet) high and a very unusual feature is the stair turret at the SE corner which is lined up with the S wall of the church.

On the S face of the tower is a carving of God the Father holding a crucifix but no Dove is visible.

On the E face is depicted St Michael weighing souls assisted by the Virgin Mary. Note the demon trying to pull down the scales on the left!

The central window in the E face of the church outside has two figures supporting the hood mould, one of which carries the date 1529 (when the window was installed). Above this window is carved:

'We pray to Jesu and Mary
Send our neighbours safety.'

Outside, on the S side of the church to the E of the porch, is a beautiful battle-mented turret with delicate windows lighting the stairs to the rood-loft.

The magnificent rood screen dates from c.1500 and is similar to the one in Dunster (see page 109). It is about 2.4 m (8 feet) wide on top and in Victorian times was used as a gallery with the boys of the Sunday school on the N side and the girls on the S. There was no protection to prevent them from falling off!

On the S side of the screen near the stairway is the quaint figure of Jack Hammer dating from c.1640. It was origi-nally a clock-jack used to strike a bell and probably stood on a bracket near the font. A rope now attached to it hangs on the chancel side of the screen. (See also Blythburgh and Southwold, Suffolk – pages 31 and 329.)

Near the screen is a beautiful Art Nouveau lectern dating from 1903. Made of wrought iron, it is decorated with brass grapes and vine leaves and was given in memory of a Henry Astey Bosanquet. (This lectern is very similar to one at Tarrant Hinton in Dorset, dating from 1909.)

At the E end of the N aisle inside the screen is the guild chapel containing the window dated 1529 and filled with Kemp stained glass. Notice the unusual decora-tion under the inside of the arch – a unique feature.

Below the window is a beautiful Elizabethan communion table with four bulbous legs and two supporting angels in front.

On the N side of the guild chapel is the vestry with a wagon roof, visible through a massive arch made of *oak* – a most unusual feature for this part of England.

On the S wall of the chancel, inside the screen, is an unusual tureen-shaped brass plaque inscribed, 'Sacred to the memory of the Reverend William Williams. Died 27 Dec., 1812 aged 62.'

On display in a specially designed wall safe at the w end of the nave is the most precious treasure of the church – an illuminated missal or service book which once belonged to Richard Fitzjames, vicar from 1485 to 1497 and, later, Bishop of London, (1506–22). The missal is 23 cm (9 inches) high and 15 cm (6 inches) wide.

It was bought by someone called Cecil Henry Bullivant (14 October 1882–3 February 1981) on 29 November 1949 and presented to the church in memory of his mother, Nellie May Bullivant (d. 4 July 1945).

Near by is a magnificent chest which also belonged to Richard Fitzjames and bears his coat of arms.

Opposite the chest is the octagonal font dating from c.1400 with numerous figures carved underneath; unfortunately many are defaced.

The fine pulpit near the entrance to the rood-loft stairs dates from c.1650.

## Moddershall STAFFORDSHIRE

ALL SAINTS is situated in remote countryside. It was built in 1903 by the three daughters of Hensleigh Wedgwood who also built a coach house at the entrance of the drive through the churchyard.

The lead font, the second newest of all the lead fonts in England and Wales, also dates from 1903. It stands on a pink sandstone polygonal base of 16 faces and is circular, being 43 cm (1 foot 5 inches) high and with a diameter of 63 cm (2 feet ¾ inch.).

It is decorated with a band of leaves and bunches of grapes around the top and bottom and this pattern continues on the vertical shafts separating the panels. In the larger panels is the Chi-Ro monogram; in another a vine bearing three bunches of grapes and four leaves. The casting is very fine and there has not been very much defacing of the lead work.

This font is a worthy addition to our collection of lead fonts. (See Lead Fonts, page 74.)

## Monken Hadley GREATER LONDON

ST MARY THE VIRGIN Located on the A1000 and almost joined with Barnet, Monken Hadley's church looks across to the site of the Battle of Barnet (1471).

On the tower turret is a copper beacon – the only surviving one on a church. It was erected to commemorate the recovery of George III from an illness and is still lit on national occasions such as a coronation, etc.

At the junction of the nave and chancel on the capitals of the piers are carved crests of one John Goodyere (d. 1504) – a unique feature.

Near the S door is a monument to Sir Roger Wilbraham (d. 1616) by Nicholas Stone.

## Monkland HEREFORDSHIRE

ALL SAINTS This church, separated from most of the village by a busy road, is almost a shrine to a former famous incumbent, the Reverend Sir Henry Williams Baker, vicar from 1852 to 1877, and first

*Moreton, Dorset, seen from the northwest.*

Chairman of the Compilers of *Hymns Ancient and Modern* in the mid-nineteenth century.

⬚ Except for the tower, the church was carefully rebuilt by G. E. Street in 1866 using the original stones.

⬚ Just to the s of the tower is the grave of the Reverend Baker (d. 12 February 1877, aged 55 years) inscribed with a verse from his hymn 'The King of Love my Shepherd is'. On his deathbed he recited the following verse from that hymn:

'Perverse and foolish oft I stray'd,
But yet in love He sought me,
And on His Shoulder gently laid,
And home, rejoicing, brought me.'

Among his other many hymns is 'Praise, O praise our God and King', which is usually sung to the tune 'Monkland'.

⬚ The lych gate is a memorial to the Reverend Baker and also the s chancel window, which illustrates scenes from Jesus as the Good Shepherd.

⬚ The E window by Hardman depicts Our Lord in Glory and was the gift of the Compilers of *Hymns Ancient and Modern*.

⬚ In the window near the pulpit is a piece of ancient glass showing a king's head.

## Moreton DORSET

ST NICHOLAS The whole of this church (rebuilt in 1776) and especially the N wall, was badly damaged by a German bomb on 8 October 1940 and not rededicated until May 1950.

⬚ The 14 windows, including five in the apse, are filled with engraved glass, designed by Laurence Whistler (1912–2000) between 1955 and 1985. These make the church unique and allow maximum daylight inside. The service of dedication took place on 31 March 1985.

⌗ The theme of all the windows is Light with engraved candles everywhere and medallions showing the church after bombing, the four seasons, butterflies and flowers, Kentish landscapes, the sun shining on Salisbury Cathedral and the harvest of the sea.

The five apse windows were designed by Whistler but etched by the London Sand Blast Decorative Glass Works in 1958 under the direction of L. W. Legg and Dennis Richardson; the remaining nine were personally engraved by Whistler.

⌗ To the w of the church is the cemetery and at its w end is the grave of Colonel T. E. Lawrence ('Lawrence of Arabia'), who was killed in a motorcycle accident near his home at Clouds Hill. His grave is inscribed, 'To the Dear Memory of T. E. Lawrence, Fellow of All Souls College, Oxford. Born 10 Aug., 1888. Died 19 May, 1935. The hour is coming and now is when the dead shall hear the voice of the Son of God and they that hear shall live.'

## Morwenstow　　　　Cornwall

St Morwenna & St John the Baptist is situated at the head of a valley with its w tower facing the sea and no belfry window on its w face.

⌗ There is a large number of ancient bench-ends. One at the e end of the n aisle is inscribed, 'This was made in the yeare of our Lord God 1575'.

⌗ On the n side of the nave are three Norman arches. In the central arch are 26 carved faces known as beak-head ornament, extending around the inside.

⌗ On the third pier from the e at the top, on the s side of the nave, can be seen the words, 'This is the hovse of the L' (the L standing for Lord). The lettering is partly

upside down and reads from right to left, possibly the work of an illiterate craftsman. (See East Budleigh, Devon, page 114, Stow, Lincolnshire, page 342 and Trent, Dorset, page 368.)

⌗ The font probably dates from the Celtic church, c.950, that stood here before the Normans came.

⌗ Morwenstow is forever associated with its most illustrious vicar, the Reverend Robert Stephen Hawker, who was vicar from 1834 to 1875. He built the nearby vicarage with its unusual chimneys in the shape of church towers. He is most famous for introducing harvest festivals into churches, the first being on 13 September 1843. (Another church, Elton, Cambs., claims to be the first, but this was after 1845.)

⌗ In the s aisle is the Hawker Memorial Window dedicated on 8 September 1904.

⌗ On the s side of the churchyard is the former figurehead of the ship *Caledonia,* which was wrecked off the coast in September 1842 with the loss of nine lives.

## Much Dewchurch　　Herefordshire

St David The church sits in an attractive village in beautiful wooded countryside, s of Hereford.

⌗ The large tower has an unusual saddleback roof.

⌗ There are many wall monuments but the most spectacular is to the right of the chancel arch commemorating King James I's chief legal officer, Walter Pye (1625), and his wife in the rich costume of the period. Below them kneel their six sons and seven daughters, all minus their hands!

⌗ Near by, another monument depicts the recumbent effigies of John and Walter Pye (1570). The one nearer the wall holds his beard with his praying hands! The tomb-chest below shows another praying man.

# VAMPING HORNS

The vamping horn, or stentorophonica, was an instrument invented by the scientist Sir Samuel Morland (1625–95), who also called it a tuba. He had been the tutor of Samuel Pepys at Magdalene College, Cambridge. In 1671 Morland published a paper entitled 'The Tuba of excellent use as well at sea as at land, invented in the year 1670'. The instrument was a forerunner of the megaphone and King Charles II was so impressed that he ordered several for his ships. It was supposed to be effective up to a distance of 1.609 km (1 mile). Later on, the invention was adapted for ecclesiastical use and became known as a vamping horn, vamphorn or vamping trumpet.

Simon Beal, a trumpeter at the court of Charles II who also owned a shop in Suffolk Street, London, made vamping horns out of tin. They varied in length from 1.08 m (3 feet 6 inches) to 2.44 m (8 feet), and the bell measured from 18cm (7 inches) to 0.63 m (2 feet 1 inch) in diameter.

The largest existing vamping horn is at East Leake, Nottinghamshire, and is 2.36 m (7 feet 9 inches) long; the smallest is at Ashurst, West Sussex and is only 0.9 m (3 feet) long.

Nobody knows exactly what vamping horns were used for in churches but they probably assisted the choir in the leading of the singing before organs became popular, the leader blowing or humming the tune down this trumpet-like instrument, rather like a one-man band. The leader was then said to have 'vamped-up' the music.

They may also have been used on church towers in order to announce news or warnings, to summon people to church, to call workers to and from the fields and even to call grazing cattle home!

As far as I know, eight vamping horns still exist in churches in England, as follows:

1. Ashurst (St James), West Sussex
2. Braybrooke (All Saints), Northamptonshire
3. Charing (St Peter & St Paul), Kent
4. East Leake (St Mary the Virgin), Nottinghamshire
5. Harrington (St Peter & St Paul), Northamptonshire
6. Haversham (St Mary), Buckinghamshire
7. Lincoln (City & County Museum – from the church of Potter Hanworth)
8. South Scarle (St Helen), Nottinghamshire
9. Willoughton (St Andrew), Lincolnshire

The horn at South Scarle dates from c.1750 and was found in the roof space of the N aisle when it was being converted into a parish room in 1977.

On the back of the three-decker pulpit in St Mary's in Whitby, North Yorkshire, there are two horns which Pevsner and others describe as vamping horns. They are smaller than the other existing horns and more likely to have been used as ear trumpets.

It is interesting to note that the last known use of a vamping horn in a church was on Easter Sunday 1958, when the Reverend G. R. Loxton, rector of Braybrooke, sang the Magnificat and Psalm 114.

Ninety-six wooden monumental effigies remain in England and Wales today. (This does not, however, include wooden statues of Our Lord, angels and the saints, of which there are many in our churches, nor wooden figures from former roofs, rood screens or reredoses.) Most of the effigies were carved from oak that was hollowed out and then filled with pieces of charcoal to absorb the moisture in the wood. This helped to reduce cracking, a characteristic feature of oak. Holes were usually bored in the effigy to allow the air to circulate and these are conspicuous in some effigies, such as those at: Tickencote, Rutland; Pitchford, Shropshire; and Clifton Reynes, Buckinghamshire.

After the carving of the wood, the effigy was sized and pieces of linen were glued over any cracks. Gesso or gypsum was thinly coated over this with a thicker coating for any relief work that was required. It was impressed where necessary before it hardened, then painted in tempera. Finally the whole figure was varnished.

Among the various people depicted in wood, five are churchmen and can be found at: Canterbury Cathedral, Kent (Archbishop Peckham, 1292); Clifford, Herefordshire (unknown priest, c.1300); Derby Cathedral (unknown priest, c. 1500); Little Leighs, Essex (unknown priest, c.1300); and Steeple Langford, Wiltshire (Joseph Collier, 1635). The Clifford effigy is the oldest ecclesiastical one and Canterbury Cathedral possesses the only archbishop in wood.

Only three laymen are represented and they are at: Eaton-under-Heywood, Shropshire (unknown layman, c.1330); Little Baddow, Essex (unknown layman, c.1320); and Much Marcle, Herefordshire (Walter de Helyon,

c.1360). There is one lawyer depicted – at West Down, Devon.

Two kings and one queen are depicted – all in Westminster Abbey. Henry V is in the abbey itself, while Catherine of Valois, his wife, and Edward III rest in the Undercroft Museum. The effigy of Henry V was covered originally in silver plates, but in January 1545 thieves broke into the abbey and stole the silver plates and head of the king. In 1971 Louisa Bolt made a replacement head and hands from fibreglass.

The effigies of Edward III and Catherine of Valois were probably used as models by those craftsmen who made their permanent tomb effigies in Westminster Abbey. William de Valence has an oak effigy in St Edmund's chapel.

Two effigies have cadavers (emaciated figures of the deceased) underneath them. These are at Worsbrough, South Yorkshire ,and Derby Cathedral. At Keyston, Cambridgeshire, there is a cadaver without an effigy above it.

Two effigies depict knights wearing the cyclas. These are at Paulerspury, Northamptonshire, and Barnburgh, South Yorkshire. The cyclas was a peculiarly English garment that appeared c.1321–46 and replaced the surcoat, which was found to be too long when knights dismounted and fought on foot. (The last representation of a knight wearing a cyclas is the stone effigy of Sir John Lyons at Warkworth, Northamptonshire, dated 1346.)

As stated earlier, most (if not all) of the effigies would have been painted in bright colours, but few retain their original colouring and those that are coloured have been repainted several times. Some have been sanded and painted grey to resemble stone! Good examples of these can be seen at: Banham, Norfolk; Eaton-

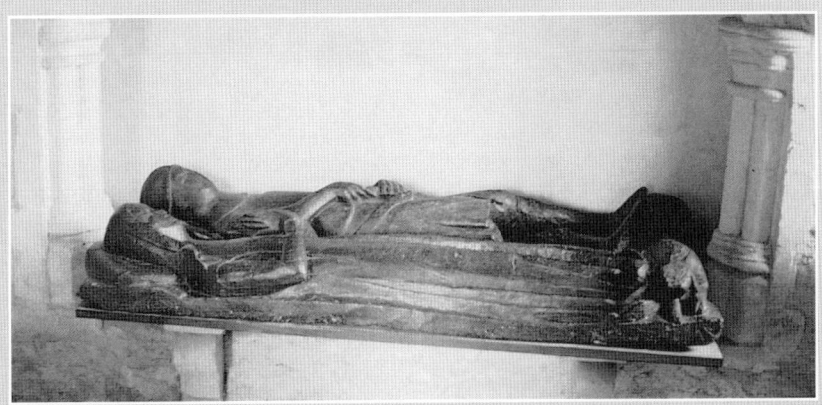
*Wooden Effigy, Clifton Reynes, Buckinghamshire.*

under-Heywood, Shropshire; and Laxton, Nottinghamshire.

Perhaps the finest coloured effigies are at: Goudhurst, Kent; Much Marcle, Herefordshire; Fersfield, Norfolk; Gloucester Cathedral; Chew Magna, Somerset; Brading, Isle of Wight; and Burford, Shropshire.

The only church in England or Wales to possess four effigies is Clifton Reynes, Buckinghamshire (excluding Westminster Abbey, which although it possesses four effigies has two in the church and two in the Undercroft Museum).

## SIZES AND AGES OF EFFIGIES

The smallest wooden effigy is that of George Oglander at Brading, Isle of Wight; he died c.1640 in Caen of smallpox. It is 53 cm (1 foot 9 inches) long and rests in a small recess above the effigy of his father, Sir John Oglander.

The largest effigies are two depicting Sir Robert de Horkesley (d. 1296) and his wife (also d. 1296) at Little Horkesley, Essex. They are both 2.39 m (7 feet 10 inches) long. They were badly damaged on 21 September 1940 when the church was completely destroyed by a German parachute mine. The effigies were

removed from the rubble to the Colchester and Essex Museum for safekeeping and conservation but Sir Robert de Horkesley's head was missing! It was found some years later among the ruins of the church, and has now been reunited with the rest of the body, although it is blackened after its long exposure to the elements.

At Great Horwood, Buckinghamshire, the smallest remaining fragment of a wooden effigy can be found. It is the lower half from the top of the thigh and is only 42 cm (1 foot 4½ inches) long.

The oldest effigies are Robert, Duke of Normandy, c.1280 in Gloucester Cathedral and a priest, also c.1280, at Clifford, Herefordshire.

The wooden effigies at Clifton Reynes, Buckinghamshire, were encased in plaster for many years until c.1850 when the vicar scraped the covering away. How many more remain to be discovered?

## THE FUTURE FOR OUR WOODEN EFFIGIES

Owing to the rarity of these wooden effigies and the theft of at least three (only one of which has been recovered) it would be prudent to ensure that all of them are padlocked. As mentioned earlier, the one at Burghfield, Berkshire, is now

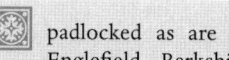 padlocked as are those at nearby Englefield, Berkshire, and Pamber Priory, Hampshire. The two effigies at Allerton Mauleverer, North Yorkshire, are padlocked to the floor and when I visited Goudhurst, Kent, in 1982, arrangements were being made to protect their magnificent effigies too.

This need for protection is a sad reflection of the age in which we live, but unless such precautions are taken, another important part of our heritage will be lost for ever.

As far as I know, the following is a complete list of the surviving wooden monumental effigies in England and Wales:

 BERKSHIRE
1. Barkham (St James)
2. Burghfield (St Mary)
3. Englefield (St Mark)

✠ BUCKINGHAMSHIRE
4.–7. Clifton Reynes (St Mary)
8. Great Horwood (St James)

✠ CAMBRIDGESHIRE
9. Keyston (St John the Baptist)

✠ CUMBRIA
10. Millom (St George)
11. Ousby (St Luke)

✠ DERBYSHIRE
12. and 13. Derby Cathedral

✠ DEVON
14. Tawstock (St Peter)
15. West Down (St Calixtus)

✠ COUNTY DURHAM
16. Bishop Auckland (St Andrew)
17. and 18. Brancepeth (St Brandon)
19. Durham (St Giles)
20.–22. Staindrop (St Mary)

✠ ESSEX
23.–25. Danbury (St John the Baptist)
26. Elmstead (St Ann & St Laurence)
27. and 28. Little Baddow (St Mary the Virgin)
29.–31. Little Horkesley (St Peter & St Paul)
32. Little Leighs (St John the Evangelist)

✠ GLOUCESTERSHIRE
33. Gloucester Cathedral
34. Old Sodbury (St John the Baptist)

✠ HAMPSHIRE
35. Pamber End (Holy Trinity, Our Lady & St John the Baptist)
36. Thruxton (St Peter & St Paul)

✠ HEREFORDSHIRE
37. Clifford (St Mary)
38. Much Marcle (St Bartholomew)

✠ ISLE OF WIGHT
39.– 41. Brading (St Mary)
42. Gatcombe (St Olave)

✠ KENT
43. Canterbury Cathedral
44. and 45. Goudhurst (St Mary)

✠ LONDON
46. Southwark Cathedral
47.–50. Westminster Abbey

✠ MONMOUTHSHIRE *(Wales)*
51. Abergavenny (St Mary)

✠ NORFOLK
52. Banham (St Mary)
53. Fersfield (St Andrew)
54. South Acre or Southacre (St George)

✠ NORTHAMPTONSHIRE
55. Alderton (St Margaret)
56. Ashton (St Michael)
57. Braybrooke (All Saints)

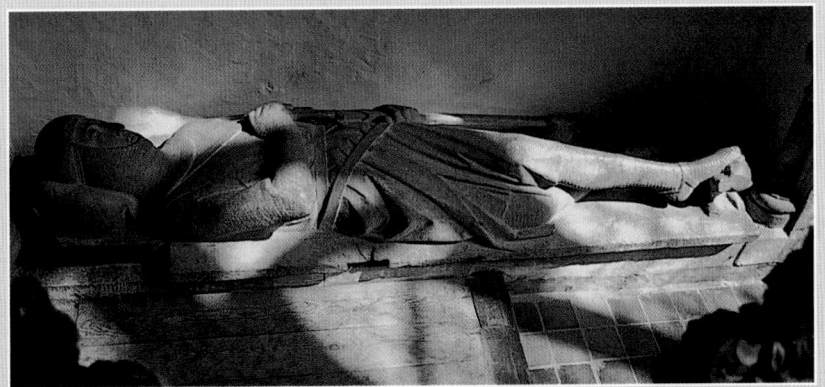

*Wooden Effigy, Danbury, Essex.*

58. Cold Higham (St Luke)
59. Dodford (St Mary)
60. Gayton (St Mary)
61. and 62. Paulerspury (St James)
63. and 64. Woodford (St Mary)

✠ NOTTINGHAMSHIRE
65. Laxton (St Michael the Archangel)

✠ OXFORDSHIRE
66.–68. Sparsholt (Holy Rood)

✠ POWYS *(Wales)*
69. Brecon Cathedral

✠ RUTLAND
70. Ashwell (St Mary)
71. Tickencote (St Peter)

✠ SHROPSHIRE
72. Berrington (All Saints)
73. Burford (St Mary)
74. Eaton-under-Heywood (St Edith)
75. Pitchford (St Michael)

✠ SOMERSET
76. Chew Magna (St Andrew)
77. Midsomer Norton (St John Baptist) –
    mutilated effigy now in Bristol
    Museum

✠ STAFFORDSHIRE
78. and 79. Weston-under-Lizard or
    Weston-under-Liziard (St Andrew)

✠ SUFFOLK
80. and 81. Boxted (Holy Trinity)
82. Bures (St Mary)
83. Heveningham (St Margaret)
84. and 85. Wingfield (St Andrew)

✠ SUSSEX *(West)*
86. Slindon (St Mary)

✠ WILTSHIRE
87. Steeple Langford (All Saints)

✠ YORKSHIRE *(North)*
88. and 89. Allerton Mauleverer (St
    Martin)
90. Whorlton (Holy Cross)

✠ YORKSHIRE *(South)*
91. Barnburgh (St Peter)
92. and 93. Worsborough or
    Worsbrough (St Mary)

✠ YORKSHIRE *(West)*
94.–96. Thornhill (St Michael)

*St Nicholas, Newbury, Berkshire, overlooks the town with its superb tower and battlemented walls.*

## Needham Market      SUFFOLK

ST JOHN THE BAPTIST is one of the most unusual ecclesiastical buildings in England and its exterior belies the treasure inside.

The magnificent hammer-beam roof dating from *c.*1470 is unique, the finest medieval roof in England. It is of uncommon design with huge posts hanging downwards supported on beams protruding outwards. The winged angels adorning the ends were added in 1892.

It is suggested that if one lies on one's back on a pew seat and looks up at the roof, the impression of gazing at a ship's hull is achieved! (Interestingly, the word 'nave', referring to the central part of a church, is derived from the Latin *'navis'* meaning ship.)

The plain screen has a rood loft supported on only four pillars.

An unusual feature is the angel on the w wall blowing a trumpet, significantly over the top of the organ!

## Nether Wallop      HAMPSHIRE

ST ANDREW The church stands in a very attractive village in the heart of the Hampshire countryside.

On the w side of the tower is a large stone pyramid surmounted by a flaming torch which covers the grave of Francis Douce (1676–1760), 'Doctor of Physick'.

The tower is unusual in being partly buried in the hillside so that one stands level with the w window outside!

At the E end of the nave is the only known portrait in brass of a prioress. The Latin inscription translated reads, 'Here lies the body of Lady Maria Gore, formerly of this house, Prioress, who died 13th day of January, 1436. On whose soul God have mercy, Amen.' She was prioress of Amesbury.

On the s wall of the nave is a fine wall painting of St George killing the Dragon dating from *c.*1450.

To the E of this is a painting called 'Christ and the Trades' or a 'Warning to Sabbath Breakers', *c.*1430.

On the w wall above the tower arch is a large painting of a bell, which is very unusual. It dates from *c.*1500.

Over the chancel arch are the remains of a painting showing flying angels dating from *c.*960 – the only Saxon wall painting still in its original position.

On the E splay of a window in the s aisle is a beautiful painting of a saint dating from *c.*1450.

## Nettlecombe      SOMERSET

ST MARY THE VIRGIN is situated in remote countryside at the end of a long lane next to Nettlecombe Court, which is a field studies centre.

The nave is entered from the N door down several steps on opening the door.

Opposite the N door, but in the s aisle, is

the famous Seven-sacrament font, one of only two outside East Anglia. It may have been given by Alice Chaucer, Duchess of Suffolk, and dates from c.1470.

In the panel depicting Holy Orders a barber is shown shaving an ordinand's tonsure – the only example of a barber shown on a Seven-sacrament font. The eighth panel shows Christ in Glory – also a unique representation of this subject on a font. (See Fonts, page 318.)

Near the font are two large recesses which project beyond the line of the s wall of the church. In the E recess, which dates from c.1300, is the effigy of a knight, and in the w recess, which is a little later, are two effigies, possibly Sir John de Ralegh and his wife, Maud (c.1360).

At the NE end of the N aisle is fifteenth-century glass showing saints and heraldry. Among the saints is St Uritha.

On the N wall of the N aisle is a delightful bronze statue of the Virgin and Child in memory of Joan Alys Wolseley (18 October 1904–10 April 1943), a member of the Trevelyan family, who founded the N chapel. Inscribed underneath are the words, 'She was greatly loved for her fearlessness, her loyalty and the loving kindness of her heart'.

In the N chapel a plaque reads, 'John Trevelyan, Knight and his wife are buried in this chapel which was erected to their memory. He died 1522. At the marriage of Prince Arthur he was created a K.C.B.'

The fine E window depicts the Virgin and Child in the central light. In the left-hand light is Nettlecombe Court and two roundels depicting spring (a sower sowing seed), and autumn (picking apples). In the right-hand light is Nettlecombe Church with roundels showing summer (cutting wheat with a scythe) and winter (trudging through snow carrying a bundle of sticks).

This window was given in memory of Sir Walter John Trevelyan, Bart. (1866–1931) and his daughter Urith, (1906–29), and was made by Martin Travers in 1935.

## Newbury        BERKSHIRE

ST NICHOLAS This famous 'wool' church, erected between 1509 and 1533, is a prominent landmark in the town with its tall, pinnacled tower.

At the ends of the roof beams are angels holding emblems of the Passion. The one on the extreme sw side holds Malchus's ear and a sword! (See John 18, v.10.)

Above the tower arch is the figure of an angel bearing a scroll with the date 1532.

Near the N door is a painting of a 'Blue Coat' boy. This replaces the original, which was stolen in 1971. A Blue Coat School was established in Newbury in 1706.

The fine pulpit dates from 1607 but the sounding board and rear panels were added in 1954. John Wesley preached from this pulpit on 3 February 1740.

The reredos behind the high altar was carved from Caen stone by Sir John Ninian Comper (d. 1960). Note the delicate carving along the top.

Under the tower is a fine brass to Jack of Newbury (John Smallwood and his wife) dated 15 February 1519. In the corners are four roundels – one depicts his children, two his initials and one John the Baptist holding the Lamb.

John, a wealthy clothier, paid for the building of the nave of the church.

## Newcastle upon Tyne    TYNE & WEAR

CATHEDRAL CHURCH OF ST NICHOLAS is England's most northerly cathedral.

The superb tower is 61.9 m (203 feet) high and supports a crown rising from flying buttresses. It is the oldest and finest 'crown spire' in the British Isles, similar to St Giles's Cathedral, Edinburgh.

The brass lectern is the only pre-Reformation eagle lectern in the N of England. Dating from c.1510 it has three lions looking right at its base. Three talons are missing on the right foot and the beak is closed. A section of the stem has been restored and a bookrest added. The whole lectern is somewhat tarnished. (See Medieval Brass Lecterns, page 362.)

At the NE end of the N choir aisle is the Danish memorial inscribed:

'In memory of Danish Seamen of all ranks who gave their lives in the service of their country in the years 1939–1945. When you read their names remember that they died for Denmark, they died for Freedom so that we, like them, might live as free Danes.'

This memorial was erected in recognition of the ties between Denmark and the Tyne.

At the E end of the S choir aisle is the Chapel of the Ascension. The beautiful stained-glass window was made by L. C. Evetts in 1962 and is inscribed, 'Thanks be to God for the Preservation of this Cathedral in time of War 1939–1945.'

In St Margaret's chapel on the S side of the nave is a roundel of fifteenth-century glass showing the Virgin and Child.

At the entrance to the S transept is an elaborate wall memorial to a Henry Maddison (d. 1634), Elizabeth, his wife, their 16 children and other relatives.

## Newland      Gloucestershire

ALL SAINTS Known as the 'Cathedral of the Forest' because it is situated in the Forest of Dean, this church has a wide, spacious interior and a fine tower dating

from c.1290 to 1320 with fine pinnacles and a pierced parapet.

A famous brass commemorates Robert Greyndour and his wife, Joan. Dating from 1443 it shows him in armour. A separate brass on this same slab shows a miner with a candle in his mouth, a pick in his hand and a hod on his back. The whole figure is placed above a helmet. Known as the 'Miner's Brass' this is the only brass to a miner and is also unique in showing the figure in relief and not incised.

There are several monuments of interest. Near the font is the unique effigy of the Forester of Fee, which shows a man in the hunting costume of 1457. Until 1950 this was in the churchyard.

Another at the E end of the S aisle depicts a bowman dating from c.1610 and is carved on a flat slab of stone. Note his horn and dagger.

## Newport      Essex

ST MARY THE VIRGIN stands on a small hill in the centre of this little village, quite close to the M11.

A superb portable altar made c.1250 and said to have been constructed for use on battlefields stands in this church. The front has 12 shields along the top and 12 indented circles along the bottom. Carrying handles are fixed to each side. On the underside of the lid, which lifts to form a reredos, are paintings of the Crucifixion and four saints. These are the oldest paintings in oil on wood in England.

## North Cadbury      Somerset

ST MICHAEL occupies a beautiful position on a little hill N of the River Cam near Cadbury Court.

It is unusual in possessing almost

identical N and S porches, both of which have two storeys.

The W window contains fifteenth-century stained glass, which was removed c.1540, stored in the Court and restored to the church in 1891 – a clever way of preserving it!

There is a fine collection of sixteenth-century bench-ends. It is interesting to note the following:

† a windmill in the centre aisle on the S side

† an unidentified church with a central tower, also on this side

† that the rear bench of this block is dated 1538 and is adorned with carving of a trailing vine

† a unique carving of a cat and Tudor mousetrap in the S aisle; the cat holds the mouse in its paws while it sits on the mousetrap!

*Northleach, Gloucestershire.*

# Northington    HAMPSHIRE

ST JOHN THE EVANGELIST This fine Victorian church, designed by the architect Sir Thomas Jackson (1835–1924), was completed in 1890 and dominates the Candover valley.

The magnificent tower of Somerset design comprises much knapped flint work and unusual gargoyles, including an eagle, frog and hare.

(It is interesting to note that the architect had planned for a low W tower with shingled spire, but when it was about 6.1 m (20 feet) high the wife of the donor, Lady Ashburton, saw the tower of St John's, Glastonbury (Somerset), and then insisted on a similar tower here!)

The stone pulpit is reached by steps inside the S wall.

All the furnishings are excellent examples of Victorian craftsmanship.

# Northleach    GLOUCESTERSHIRE

ST PETER & ST PAUL Known as 'the Cathedral of the Cotswolds', this magnificent church was rebuilt c.1410 (except for the tower of c.1350) in the Perpendicular style.

The S porch of two storeys is very fine and dates from c.1500. Over the entrance door is an original statue of the Virgin and Child. How did it escape the iconoclast?

The NW pinnacle adjoining the stair turret is an ingeniously shaped chimney!

The window over the chancel arch is an unusual feature but found elsewhere in the Cotswolds and in a few other places (e.g. Burwell, Cambs.).

Near the pulpit is the brass of John

Fortey (d. 1458), who rebuilt the church. Being a wool merchant his feet rest on a sheep and woolpack. The Latin inscription translated means, 'Behold, what is the good of anything in life, all of which is nothing unless one loves God'.

⬙ Another interesting brass commemorates Thomas Fortey (d. 1447), Agnes – his wife – and her first husband, William Scors (d. 1420). Notice the scissors at his feet indicating that he was a tailor by profession.

⬙ The octagonal stone pulpit dates from *c.*1450 and is an excellent example.

## Norwich                          NORFOLK

ST HELEN'S CHURCH IN THE GREAT HOSPITAL, BISHOPGATE This church was rebuilt *c.*1480.

⬙ In the s transept chapel are 41 bosses on the lierne vaulting, many connected with the Virgin Mary as follows:

† In the centre, a large boss depicts the Coronation of the Virgin.

† Another depicts St Katherine with her broken wheel. (She is only found on a boss in five other churches – see Roof Bosses, page 374.)

† A unique boss shows the Baby Jesus being handed by a nurse to His mother. She stands in the centre holding a large towel while Joseph kneels by looking on. This boss featured on the 4½p Christmas stamp issued on 27 November 1974.

## Norwich                          NORFOLK

ST GREGORY is located in the city centre in Pottergate, near the marketplace.

⬙ On the w wall of the N aisle is a remarkable oil painting of St George measuring 5.1 by 3 m (17 by 10 feet), the largest in an English church. It dates from *c.*1450.

## Norwich                          NORFOLK

THE CATHEDRAL OF THE HOLY AND UNDIVIDED TRINITY This magnificent cathedral, standing in the centre of Norwich and dominating the city, is well seen from the top of the City Hall in the marketplace.

⬙ The central tower, at 42.7 m (140 feet) high, is the highest Norman tower in England. The spire is 96 m (315 feet) high, exceeded only by Salisbury.

⬙ The cathedral, including the cloisters, contains about 900 roof bosses – more than any other cathedral in England.

Several of the 400 bosses in the cloisters depict stories and illustrate the life of Jesus; they date from *c.*1290 to *c.*1430. Many other bosses can be seen in the Bauchon chapel and the N and s transepts and there is a magnificent display in the nave. The following are among the most interesting:

† There is a unique boss in the N transept showing the Nativity with Mary, Joseph and the ox and ass.

† Another boss in the N transept shows the Shepherds of Bethlehem.

† In the cloisters a fourteenth-century windmill is shown and a woman carrying a sack of corn.

† Also in the cloisters is a boss showing St Martin dividing his cloak. (St Martin is found on only one other roof boss – in Lincoln Cathedral, under the sw tower, see page 202.)

(Many of the bosses are illustrated in books available from the cathedral bookshop. When viewing the bosses, especially those in the nave and transepts, a good pair of binoculars is thoroughly recommended.)

⬙ Near the entrance to St Luke's chapel in the s ambulatory a stone effigy is fixed to the wall. This may represent the founder of Norwich Cathedral, Bishop Herbert de

*England's second highest spire at Norwich Cathedral, Norfolk.*

Losinga. Dating from *c.*1100 it is England's oldest Christian effigy.

▣ In the Bauchon chapel is a unique medieval corbel of a *pietà* – Mary supporting the dead body of Christ.

▣ On the s side of the choir is the chantry chapel of Bishop Goldwell (Bishop from 1472 to 1499), who built the spire *c.*1480. The bishop's effigy is unique in England as he is shown wearing a cope instead of a chasuble over his vestments. Bishop Goldwell also built the lierne vault over the choir. Look for his rebus in the bosses – a golden bucket and well.

▣ From the e cloister into the nave one passes through the magnificent prior's doorway, over which are seven canopied figures including Christ between angels and a pope. It dates from *c.*1310. (Compare this with a similar doorway leading to the chapter room at Rochester Cathedral – see page 286.)

▣ Behind the high altar in an elevated position is the bishop's throne, which incorporates two stones from the Ancient Throne of *c.*750 – the oldest bishop's throne in use in any English cathedral and the only one in this position.

▣ The cloisters are the only two-storey monastic cloisters in England. Two of the bays have wooden tracery in the windows instead of stone. Was this a temporary measure that has yet to be replaced in stone?

▣ In the choir are some fine misericords including a schoolmaster beating a boy, a fox stealing a goose and an owl being mobbed by birds.

▣ The magnificent stone lierne vault of the nave, incorporating over 270 bosses and the w window, were erected by Bishop Lyhart (Bishop from 1446 to 1472). Notice the circular hole almost halfway down the centre. This may have been used by the monks to lower a light or relic on great occasions or for swinging a censer containing burning incense at Pentecost as a reminder of the coming of the Holy Spirit (see *Acts* 2, vvi–4).

▣ In the nave is a *medieval* brass lectern of a pelican feeding its young, unique in the British Isles. Dating from *c.*1450 it may have come from Belgium. The statuettes at the base were added *c.*1840. (A Victorian pelican lectern can be seen at Chichester Cathedral, see page 72.)

▣ In St Saviour's chapel are some fine panels from a retable (*c.*1385) that came from the church of St Michael-at-Plea, Norwich.

▣ In the nw corner of the n transept is a monument to Bishop Bathurst (1841) – the last work of Sir Francis Chantrey.

▣ In the archives of the cathedral over 3500 rolls dating from 1272 to 1539 are preserved; they records details of the monastic life at Norwich Cathedral Priory. They are the most complete collection in England.

▣ Outside the cathedral, at the se corner, is the grave of Nurse Edith Cavell, who was shot by the Germans in Brussels on 12 October 1915. Her last words were, 'Standing as I do, in view of God and Eternity, I realise that patriotism is not enough; I must have no hatred or bitterness toward anyone.'

## Ockham SURREY

ALL SAINTS is one of only two ancient churches in England with a seven-lancet E window. (The other is at Blakeney, Norfolk, see page 30.) A Victorian copy of this window exists at Holy Trinity Church, Millbrook, Southampton.

 On a pane of glass in the SW window of the chancel has been scratched 'W. Peters new leaded this in 1775 and never was paid for the same.'

 In the King chapel, opening off the N aisle, is a monument to Peter King, first Baron King of Ockham (d. 22 July 1734, aged 65) and Anne, his wife. The sculptor was Michael Rysbrach.

 The w window in the N aisle contains some stained glass commemorating William of Ockham (c.1285–1349), Franciscan friar, philosopher and theologian. It was designed by Laurence Lee.

## Old Radnor POWYS

ST STEPHEN THE MARTYR is located near the border with Herefordshire. It stands 256 m (840 feet) above sea level and commands magnificent views from its churchyard.

 The fine Perpendicular screen is richly carved with grapes and foliage.

 The organ case dates from c.1510 and is the oldest in the British Isles. A new organ was fitted inside in 1872. Note the Tudor roses and linen-fold panelling. A stained-glass window in the cloisters of Worcester Cathedral depicts this organ.

 The font, crudely carved out of a boulder, dates from c.600, and is possibly the oldest font in Britain.

## Olney BUCKINGHAMSHIRE

ST PETER & ST PAUL The spire of this famous church, which is reminiscent of Northamptonshire, dominates the little town on the River Great Ouse.

 On the S side of the churchyard under a massive granite monument are the graves of John Newton (d. 21 December 1807, aged 82) and Mary Newton (d. 15 December 1790, aged 61). These remains were removed from the church of St Mary Woolnoth in the City of London, 25 January 1893.

The tomb is inscribed: 'John Newton, Clerk, once an infidel and libertine a servant of slaves in Africa was by the rich mercy of our Lord and Saviour Jesus Christ preserved, restored, pardoned and appointed to preach the faith he had long laboured to destroy. Near 16 years as Curate of this parish and 28 years as Rector of St Mary, Woolnoth.'

 The tower and spire reach a height of 56.4 m (185 feet). The weathercock is inscribed, 'I never crow but stand to show whence winds do blow 1829'.

 At the w end of the S aisle is the pulpit from which John Newton preached at St Mary Woolnoth. Near by, on the wall, is

the brass coffin plate inscribed, 'The Reverend John Newton, Rector of this Church. Died 21 Dec., 1807 in the 83rd year of his age.'

On the N side of the chancel is a plaque to Lieutenant Charles Stanley Hipwell MC (4 September 1887– 15 October 1916). The inscription reads:

'On Sept. 23 1916 he led a successful raid into the enemy trenches which resulted in the capture of prisoners. He engaged a fire bay full of Germans and silenced them with his revolver, remaining standing on the parapet while his men crossed the hostile wire and thereafter until the last man had left for our lines – he went out again under continuous fire to search "No man's land" for a wounded man. The success of the raid was due to his determination and resourceful leading for which he was awarded the Military Cross.'

In the N aisle is a war memorial window depicting John Newton with some slaves, the church and hymn book, and William Cowper (1731–1800) with his pet hares. Newton and Cowper produced the famous *Olney Hymnal* in 1779, Newton writing 280 hymns and Cowper 68. These include 'Amazing grace, how sweet the sound' and 'How sweet the Name of Jesus sounds' by John Newton and 'God moves in a mysterious way' and 'O for a closer walk with God' by William Cowper.

Another stained-glass window depicts John Newton preaching from a pulpit and the words, 'amazing grace! How sweet the sound. John Newton' underneath.

Below this, a plaque records: 'To the Glory of God & in loving memory of Archibald Allen for many years solicitor in this town and his wife Emily Maud Allen. Their daughter Evelyn Garrard Allen caused this and the window opposite to be installed A.D. 1973.' On either side of the central panel are pictures of the boat and shipwreck which led to Newton's conversion to Christ and his relinquishing of the slave trade.

## Osmington       DORSET

ST OSMUND The village lies on the A353, just outside Weymouth and the church overlooks Weymouth Bay, with the White Horse, showing George III on horseback, as a backdrop.

The wind vane on the tower dating from 1963 depicts the famous Osmington White Horse on the hillside near by.

On the S side of the nave in the churchyard is a table-tomb with an unusual acrostic on the side.

Inside the church on the N side of the chancel is the Warham monument, *c.*1600, displaying fine Renaissance detail. It carries this inscription:

'Man's life.
Man is a glas. Life is as water that's
  weakly walld
about. Sinne brings in death. Death
  breakes the glas,
so runs the water out.
Finis.'

John Constable, RA spent his honeymoon at Osmington vicarage in 1816. He was a great friend of the vicar, Archdeacon Fisher (d. 1832), and while here he painted 'Osmington Village and Church from the Roman Road' and 'Weymouth Bay'. The latter hangs in the National Gallery, London.

## Othery       SOMERSET

ST MICHAEL is situated above the levels of Sedgemoor, dominating the village.

On a bench-end is a superb carving of

*Ottery St Mary, Devon – the east end of the magnificent church.*

two butterflies hovering around what may be a poppy. This carving is unique, as no other medieval bench-ends have insects on them!

## Ottery St Mary DEVON

THE COLLEGIATE CHURCH OF ST MARY THE VIRGIN, ST EDWARD THE CONFESSOR AND ALL SAINTS This great building, completed in 1342, was the collegiate church for a college which existed here from 1337 to 24 December 1545 when it was dissolved by Henry VIII.

The ground plan is similar to that of Exeter Cathedral (see page 131) in that it has a tower placed halfway along the N side of the N aisle together with a similar tower on the s side. Unlike Exeter, however, the northern tower is capped with a short lead spire. Transepts are placed underneath each of the towers, making this church and Exeter Cathedral the only two churches in England where the transepts are formed in the base of the tower.

On top of the spire, which is 29 m (95 feet) high, is the oldest weathercock *in situ* in Europe, dating from *c*.1340. This weathercock, measuring 69 cm (2 feet 3 inches) from beak to tip of tail and 38 cm (1 foot 3 inches) tall, is known as the 'Whistling Cock' or 'Trumpeting Cock'. This also makes it unique because it used to 'crow' or make a weird moaning sound, caused when the wind blew strongly through two trumpet-like metal tubes which run from its breast to its tail. Some authorities state that the tubes are now silenced by corrosion but another says that they were corked up after parishioners complained about the noise!

This cock may be a copy of the one

placed on the northern tower of Exeter Cathedral in 1284 but which disappeared with the spire in 1752.

In a glass case at the w end of the Dorset aisle is the tail of the original cock that braved the winds from *c*.1340 until 1908, when a new tail was put on as the old one was worn out.

▦ The bronze eagle lectern under the crossing between the transepts is a copy of the medieval one in St Nicholas chapel, King's Lynn, Norfolk.

▦ The wooden lectern is one of the oldest in England. Dating from *c*.1340 it was given by Bishop Grandisson, whose arms appear on it.

▦ The following roof bosses are worth noticing:

† In the centre of the crossing is the Founder's Boss showing Bishop Grandisson in full vestments. The hole in the centre of his body is where a light used to be suspended in front of the rood.

† In the chancel are five bosses as follows, looking from w to e:

⊹ St John the Baptist

⊹ St Anne teaching the Virgin Mary to read. This is one of two bosses depicting this subject (the other being at Nantwich, Cheshire)

⊹ the Annunciation – Gabriel and Mary

⊹ the Virgin Mary and Child (this boss featured on the 8p Christmas stamp in 1974 (from 19–27 November 1974 the Post Office staged a special preview exhibition of the new Christmas stamps inside this church – the first time such an exhibition had ever been put on inside a church!)

⊹ the Coronation of the Virgin.

▦ On the n side of the nave is the Dorset aisle built by Cicely, Marchioness of Dorset in *c*.1530. The beautiful fan-vaulted roof with five large pendent bosses of open tracery is an excellent example of Perpendicular architecture.

▦ On the piers of this aisle are some interesting carvings including two owls and a superb elephant's head on the second pier from the w end. (See Fan Vaulting, page 152.)

▦ On the w side of the s transept is an ancient clock reputed to have been given by Bishop Grandisson of Exeter (Bishop from 1327 to 1369), but the first reference to a clock does not appear until 1437–8 in the College Rolls. The Earth is shown as the centre of the solar system with the phases of the Moon. Similar clocks can be seen at Exeter, Wells and Wimborne Minster (see pages 131, 388 and 414 respectively).

▦ On the e side of the s transept is the recumbent effigy of Jane Fortescue (d. 1878), Baroness Coleridge, by Frederick Thrupp RA. At her feet is an otter, the heraldic device of the Coleridge family.

▦ Behind the high altar screen is the stone minstrels' gallery, which stands at the entrance to the lady chapel. On the s side of the lady chapel is a corbel head of Bishop Grandisson and on the n side his sister, Katharine, Countess of Salisbury (1303–49).

▦ On the outside walls of this church are 13 *stone* consecration crosses, which are rare as they were usually only painted on walls. This is the largest number of these surviving outside a church. (See also Edington, Wilts., page 123 and Uffington, Oxon., page 377.)

▦ At the nw end of the nave is an elaborate marble font designed by William Butterfield in 1850. The multicoloured marbles came from Devon and Cornwall.

## Ovingdean          East Sussex

St Wulfran is one of only two churches in England dedicated to St Wulfran or Wulfram. (The other is at Grantham, Lincolnshire.) It is approached by a road from the coast between Brighton and Rottingdean and lies in a quiet valley about 1.61 km (1 mile) inland from the sea.

Near the s porch is the grave of Charles Eamer Kemp, fifth son of Nathaniel Kemp, who died 29 April 1907, aged 69 years. Eight other members of his family are buried in the same grave. Kemp was one of the most prolific stained-glass artists of his day and most of his windows are signed with his monogram of three wheat sheaves. (Note: most writers spell Kemp's name as 'Kempe' and this appears on his memorial in Chichester Cathedral, West Sussex; however 'Kemp' is inscribed on his grave.)

To the w of Kemp's grave is the tomb of Magnus Volk (1851–1937), inventor and electrical pioneer. He invented Britain's first electric railway, which runs from the east pier to Black Rock, Brighton.

On the n side of the church is a brown obelisk marking the grave of builder William Willett (30 January 1805–8 April 1866) of West House, Brighton. Seeing his workmen idle during the hours of darkness, he would put back the clock, an early unofficial example of British Summer Time! It was left to his son, William Willett, Jnr., to suggest 'daylight saving' when he lived in Chislehurst, Kent, although it did not actually come into force until 1916, a year after his death.

The e window of the s chapel depicts the Virgin and Child with St Luke writing his Gospel. It was designed by Kemp.

Under the tower is a window showing St Wulfram. This was the last window executed by Kemp before his death.

## Ovingham          NORTHUMBERLAND

ST MARY THE VIRGIN This village church stands on the n bank of the River Tyne and has a very tall Saxon tower.

Thomas Bewick (12 August 1753–8 November 1828), well-known wood engraver and ornithologist, is buried to the w of the tower, but his gravestone is in the s porch. The famous 'Bewick Swan' was named after him in 1830.

Over the door of the s porch is a carving called 'Mother and Child' by Daniel Oates, 1986.

The magnificent Saxon tower at the w end dates from c.990.

In the s wall of the chancel is a stained-glass window by L. C. Evetts commemorating the tower's millennium, 990–1990.

## Oxborough or Oxburgh          NORFOLK

ST JOHN THE EVANGELIST is found near Oxburgh Hall; despite the absence of its tower and a ruined nave and s aisle, it is still well worth a visit.

The tower, which supported one of only three medieval stone spires in Norfolk, (the others are at Norwich Cathedral and Snettisham), collapsed at 10.10 on Wednesday 28 April, 1948, destroying the nave roof and s arcade. The nave and s aisle are now roofless and have never been rebuilt.

One of the five bells from the tower hangs in the reconstructed turret above the entrance to the former chancel.

The tall screen which formerly separated the chancel from the nave was moved to East Dereham church after the fall of the tower, and is now used in the n transept there. It has paintings of St. Withburga of Dereham and her sister St Etheldreda which were painted c.1480.

The chancel now acts as the main church for the village and contains a magnificent five-light Perpendicular e window which follows the curvature of the roof.

In the chancel is a fine medieval brass eagle lectern 1.8 m (6 feet) high, dating from *c.*1500 and inscribed '*Orate pro anima Thome Kypping quondam rectoris de Norburgh*' ('Pray for the soul of Thomas Kypping sometime rector of Norburgh'). Thomas Kypping died in 1489. (See Medieval Brass Lecterns, page 362.)

On the s side of the chancel is the Bedingfield chantry chapel, which fortunately escaped damage in 1948. This was built *c.*1500 and contains some beautiful terracotta monuments to the Bedingfield family, made of carefully screened brick clay, moulded and then fired. The craftsmen probably came from Belgium. There are only three other similar monuments – at Bracon Ash, Norfolk, Layer Marney, Essex, and Wymondham (see page 438).

# Oxford      OXFORDSHIRE

THE CATHEDRAL CHURCH OF CHRIST
This, the smallest cathedral in England, is unique in being the college chapel for Christchurch, founded by Cardinal Wolsey in 1525.

The spire, at 43.9 m (144 feet) high, dates from *c.*1210 and is one of the oldest spires in England.

The arches in the nave are unusual in enclosing the triforium below, with another arch below this. This design is only found elsewhere in England at Romsey Abbey, Hampshire (see page 287).

The choir is roofed with a unique lierne pendent-vaulted roof dating from *c.*1500.

The beautiful E end of the cathedral with two round-headed windows, arcading and rose window above, only dates from 1870–6. It is Sir Gilbert Scott's guess at what the original Norman E end might have looked like. (I think it is an excellent reconstruction.)

Among the interesting roof bosses are the following:

† S. Frideswide is shown on two bosses in the choir and on one in the chapter house. (She is not found on roof bosses anywhere else, probably because she lived near Oxford.)

† In the chapter house is a lovely boss showing the Virgin and Child with the Virgin giving some fruit to the Infant Jesus.

† Another boss in the chapter house shows four lions with one head.

In the lady chapel is the watching loft for St Frideswide's shrine. Dating from *c.*1500 it consists of a stone base with wooden structure above. (Only one other watching loft exists and is at St Alban's Abbey – see page 298.)

In the N aisle is buried Robert Burton (1577–1640), author of *The Anatomy of Melancholy.*

At the w end of the N aisle is a stained-glass window by Abraham van Linge dating from *c.*1635 showing Jonah under a large gourd tree looking at Nineveh.

In the Latin chapel are two superb stained-glass windows dating from *c.*1350 depicting St Frideswide and St Catherine.

The glass in the E window of St Lucy's chapel also dates from *c.*1350. One scene depicts the murder of St Thomas à Becket in 1170. Notice how the saint's head has been replaced by plain glass following Henry VIII's command that *all* representations of Becket should be destroyed.

At the w end of the s aisle is a fine window depicting Faith, Hope and Charity by Burne-Jones and Morris made in 1871.

Other windows by Burne-Jones can be seen at the E end of the lady chapel (Samuel, David, John and Timothy), in the adjacent N aisle (St Cecilia) and in the s aisle (St Catherine of Alexandria).

In the cloisters is an interesting graffito showing what may be a jester with a sad face.

The doorway from the cloister into the

chapter house is a fine example of Norman architecture.

⬛ The chapter house is a superb example of Early English architecture dating from c.1225 to 1250. Under the E window is the foundation stone of Wolsey's intended grammar school at Ipswich (Suffolk), laid in 1528 but never completed (like Cardinal College) owing to Wolsey's downfall in 1530.

# Oxford

MERTON COLLEGE CHAPEL is the largest and oldest college chapel in Oxford, the choir having been completed in 1294.

⬛ The fine medieval brass desk lectern is inscribed *'Orate pro anima magistri Johannis Martok'* ('Pray for the soul of school-master John Martok). John Martok, MA died in 1503. (See Medieval Brass Lecterns, page 362.)

⬛ The central tower, built c.1420, contains an unusual gallery high inside and octagonal in shape. This is used by the bell-ringers. (Only one similar gallery exists in England – at Southwell Cathedral, Notts; although Pershore Abbey, Worcester (see page 270), has an unusual 'cat's cradle' inside the tower for ringers.)

⬛ In the N transept is a monument to Thomas Bodley, 1613, by Nicholas Stone.

⬛ Note the fine E window of seven lights with a wheel at the head of the tracery – an excellent example of the Decorated style of architecture.

# Oxford

ST MICHAEL AT THE NORTH GATE, the City Church of Oxford since 1971, possesses the oldest church tower in Oxford. Dating from c.1000 it exhibits typical Saxon windows with baluster shafts in the middle. In 1953 the church was badly damaged by a fire started deliberately but was restored the next year.

⬛ In the NE window of the N aisle are fragments of stained glass dating from c.1410, including a rare picture of Christ crucified on a lily with the Annunciation. (See Lily Crucifix, page 388.)

⬛ The E window of three lancets contains four pieces of ancient glass dating from 1290 – the oldest glass in Oxford.

⬛ Set in a Victorian frame is the prison cell door through which Cranmer, Latimer and Ridley walked to their martyrdom in 1555–6.

⬛ Healing services have been held in this church since 3 February 1926 – the longest unbroken tradition for such services in Britain.

# Ozleworth      GLOUCESTERSHIRE

ST NICHOLAS OF MYRA was vested in the Churches Conservation Trust on 27 October 1972; it is situated in the seclusion of Ozleworth Park in a beautiful setting in the south Cotswolds near the Cotswolds Way.

⬛ The irregular central hexagonal tower dates from 1110 to 1120 and is unique in being the only one surviving in this position in England. It is also one of only two hexagonal towers in England. (The other is at Swindon near Cheltenham.)

⬛ The thirteenth-century crossing arch from the nave to the tower is richly carved with pierced chevrons – a rare feature.

⬛ Several interesting wall monuments dating c.1770–1880 include a fine one to a lady called Catherine Clutterbuck (d. 1805) by Thomas King of Bath. It depicts an elegant urn with a very realistic tree drooping over it.

# PORCHES

In most churches and in every cathedral there is a porch, found either on the N or S side or both, and occasionally at the W end. It is usually an addition rather than part of the original fabric and serves to protect the door and doorway from inclement weather and also provide a shelter for worshippers entering or leaving the church.

In medieval times, porches were an important meeting place for making all kinds of business transactions and the walls were later used to display public notices, times of services and so on. This practice still continues today.

Sometimes a porch had a room above it known as a parvis; this could be used as a home for a chantry priest. The porch at Northleach, Gloucestershire, has a chimney cunningly disguised inside a pinnacle on the W side of the magnificent S porch. A fireplace inside would not only have provided heating for the occupant but also could have been used to bake the Holy Communion wafers. Other uses for this room include a vestry for the priest, safe storage for the church plate or even a depository for all the village armour, as at Mendlesham, Suffolk. (See also Parish Armoury, page 186.)

The largest porch in England and Wales is at Christchurch, Dorset, and the second-largest is at Cirencester, Gloucestershire. Many fine porches can be seen throughout England and Wales, ranging from simple wooden constructions to elaborate stone ones, especially in Essex, Gloucestershire, Norfolk, Somerset and Suffolk. A particularly outstanding porch can be seen at Woolpit, Suffolk.

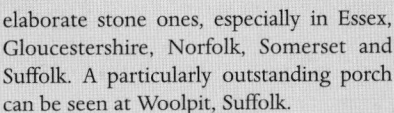

*Shoreham, Kent.*

Although most porches are square or rectangular in shape there are seven hexagonal (six-sided) ones as follows:

1. Bristol (St Mary Redcliffe), Somerset – *c.*1330; on N side.
2. Chipping Norton (St Mary), Oxfordshire – *c.*1450; on S side.
3. Dalton-in-Furness (St Mary), Cumbria – 1882–5; two porches (at SW end of S aisle and NW end of N aisle).
4. Hertford (All Saints), Hertfordshire – 1895; on NW side.
5. Icklesham (All Saints), East Sussex – *c.*1850; at W end.
6. Ludlow (St Laurence), Shropshire – *c.*1330; on S side.

Apart from those at Hertford and Icklesham, the above porches all have two storeys. St Mary Redcliffe's is unquestionably the finest and most richly carved porch in England or Wales.

Another noteworthy porch can be seen at Sunningwell, Oxfordshire. It is unique in being heptagonal (seven-sided) and was given by Bishop Jewel, who used to be rector of Sunningwell in 1550 before fleeing the country to escape Mary Tudor's persecution. He later returned to become Bishop of Salisbury.

## Painswick GLOUCESTERSHIRE

Sᴛ Mᴀʀʏ This charming Cotswold town is situated on the A46, between Cheltenham and Stroud; the tall spire of its church dominates the surrounding area.

 The prominent spire rises to a height of 53 m (174 feet) and has been rebuilt several times, most recently in 1883.

 There are over 100 yew trees in the churchyard, most of which were planted *c*.1779, making these the largest number in any churchyard in Britain.

 The churchyard also contains the most varied collection of eighteenth-century table-tombs in the British Isles. One of the most interesting is on the ɴᴇ side to a Richard Poole (d. 1707). On his tomb are depicted Father Time and a skeleton standing on a globe with a spade beside him.

 The church is unusual in possessing a double chancel, but originally the altar was farther ᴡ with a lady chapel to the ᴇ of it.

 In the ɴ aisle is a fine model of Sir Francis Drake's flagship *Bonaventure* which was made *c*.1885.

 Near the pulpit is the top of the old spire removed in 1950.

 In the sanctuary is a memorial to the Reverend J. Moseley, who is described as 'The Christian! The Scholar!! and The Gentleman!!!'.

 On a nave pillar is carved the inscription 'Be bolde, be bolde, but not too bold'. This may have been carved by a Puritan soldier imprisoned in the church in 1644.

 The superb organ and case date from *c*.1770, made by Snetzler.

 Each year on 19 September or the first Sunday after it, the famous Clipping Ceremony is held. This is nothing to do with the clipping of the yews but is a display of love and affection for each other and the church by encircling the whole building with joined hands and singing a traditional hymn.

 Outside the ꜱᴇ wall of the churchyard are the iron stocks dating from *c*.1840 and known as the 'Squire's Specs' because they resemble spectacles!

## Pamber End HAMPSHIRE

Tʜᴇ Pʀɪᴏʀʏ Cʜᴜʀᴄʜ ᴏꜰ ᴛʜᴇ Hᴏʟʏ Tʀɪɴɪᴛʏ, Oᴜʀ Lᴀᴅʏ ᴀɴᴅ Sᴛ Jᴏʜɴ ᴛʜᴇ Bᴀᴘᴛɪꜱᴛ This priory, founded *c*.1130 during the reign of Henry I, is a very peaceful place in great seclusion with only a farm for company and approached through an avenue of oak trees.

 Although only the former central tower and chancel survive, they are very impressive, with three beautiful lancets at the ᴇ end and four on the ɴ and ꜱ sides, all filled with plain glass.

 In recesses at the ᴡ end of the chancel are three incised coffin lids. There are eight others under the tower, some with beautiful decorations on them.

 On the ꜱᴡ side of the chancel, protected by a modern iron grille, securely padlocked, is a wooden effigy depicting an

unknown knight of *c.*1310. The figure, at 2.13 m (7 feet) long, is shown in chain mail with mail head-covering and coat. His hands are shown in prayer, his right foot is crossed over his left and both feet rest on a lion. There are two cushions under his head, the upper one placed diagonally on the lower. He wears spurs and a sword on his left side. This figure is in an excellent state of preservation. (See Wooden Effigies, page 246.)

◈ On the N side of the chancel are the remains of wall paintings and a well-preserved consecration cross.

◈ Near the gate is the grave of Thomas Chandler (1802–80), woodman, nearly 50 years 'a most faithful and well loved servant of Queen's College, Oxford'.

## Parham       Suffolk

St Mary the Virgin is a light, spacious church with much plain glass.

◈ On a s-facing buttress is a mass dial 13 cm (5 inches) across, complete with numerals. A dial with numerals is a great rarity.

◈ On the s pier of the w tower arch are interesting graffiti of men in ships dating from *c.*1400.

◈ On the N door of the nave is a very unusual feature – a massive padlock dating from *c.*1750 and measuring 17 cm (6¾ inches) across, weighing 2.72 kg (6 lbs). Its key weighs 283.5 g (10 oz).

◈ Behind the Lord's table is a painting of the Last Supper by a Russian artist. (Note that Judas has no halo.)

◈ On the N wall of the chancel is a hat bracket inscribed 'R.H.1716'.

◈ Chained to the communion rail on the s side is a 'poor man's box' dating from *c.*1580.

## Parham       West Sussex

St Peter is situated in the deer park to the s of the superb Elizabethan house and is usually open only when the house's gardens are open. It was rebuilt from 1800 to 1820 when the tower was added.

◈ The lead font standing on its lovely marble plinth dates from *c.*1350 and is unique for three reasons:

† It is the only one dating from the fourteenth century.

† Decorated with the arms of Andrew Peverell it is the only one covered with heraldry.

† With an external depth of 22 cm (8½ inches) and a top diameter of 51 cm (1 foot 8 inches), this is the smallest lead font.

Apart from the shields, the font carries the inscription 'i c h nazar' (Jesus of Nazareth). It has one seam and shows signs of having once been padlocked. (See Lead Fonts, page 74.)

◈ On the pulpit are fixed two plaques of wood which were brought from the Mount of Olives, Jerusalem, in 1917 by a soldier serving in the Sussex Yeomanry and given to the church in 1965.

◈ On the N side of the nave is the private pew for the squire of Parham, complete with its own entrance and fireplace. It is said that if the sermon was too long, the squire would poke the grate vigorously as an obvious hint to the preacher!

◈ In the Elizabethan house near by a wooden font (*c.*1685) is preserved. Adam and Eve stand under an apple tree around which is coiled a serpent. Leaves and grapes adorn the cover. This font used to stand in the now-disappeared chapel and was originally made for the church of St. Peter-in-the-East, Oxford. It was sold to Robert Curzon (1774–1863), who had married Harriet, thirteenth Baroness Zouche of Parham in 1808. (See Wooden Fonts, page 34.)

# Partrishow     POWYS

ST ISSUI or ST ISHOW stands on a s-facing hillside, in remote countryside in the Black Mountains, 8 km (5 miles) N of Abergavenny.

▨ Along the outside s wall of the church is a stone seat facing the churchyard cross. This is a very rare feature.

▨ In the chapel at the w end of the church is a stone altar incised with *six* consecration crosses – a rare survival, as the usual number is five.

▨ The ancient font is one of the oldest in Wales, dating from *c*.1050.

▨ The great treasure of the church, carved from Irish oak, is the magnificent rood screen and loft, dating from *c*.1480. The w front is delicately carved. At some period, perhaps at the Reformation, it appears to have been dismantled as the traceries above and below the gallery have been mixed up and some have been inverted! Unlike most screens, it was never painted.

In front of the screen are two more stone altars but these are incised with five consecration crosses.

▨ On the chancel walls are painted memorial tablets dating back to *c*.1750. The colours remain as bright as when they were first painted, but the secret vegetable dye recipe that was used was lost *c*.1840.

▨ The old building near the path to the lych gate contains a fireplace where the priest could dry out his clothing while he conducted the service! Stabling was also provided for his pony.

# Patrington   EAST RIDING OF YORKSHIRE

ST PATRICK is known as 'the Queen of Holderness' and is claimed to be England's finest village church. Built between 1310 and 1410 it is certainly very impressive both outside and inside and is a superb example of Decorated architecture.

▨ The spire rising from its unusual corona is 57.6 m (189 feet) high.

▨ The capitals of the piers are richly carved with natural foliage.

▨ The s and N transepts are unusual in having aisles on the E and w sides. In the E aisle of the s transept is the lady chapel with an ancient statue of the Virgin Mary in the reredos which was brought indoors in 1985. The lady chapel's position is unique in a parish church.

Notice the beautiful pendent boss above showing the Annunciation.

▨ On the N side of the chancel is the Easter sepulchre showing Christ rising from His tomb while three soldiers sleep below.

▨ Notice how the aisles of the s transept are vaulted but the corresponding aisles in the N transept were never completed. Only the springers were inserted. This was probably the result of the Black Death in 1348 when so many craftsmen died.

▨ In the sw corner of the s transept is a doorway leading to a spiral staircase which goes to the transept roof or into the roof space and out to the unusual stairs, which can be seen over the arch of the transept. This staircase leads to the tower.

▨ The westernmost pier of the nave on the N side rests on the foundations of an earlier pier probably dating from *c*.1250.

# Penn     BUCKINGHAMSHIRE

HOLY TRINITY is set high on the Chilterns and on a clear day there are extensive views from its tower.

▨ The lead font, the only one in Buckinghamshire, is also unique in being quite plain, although graffiti have been made on it since it was cast. Among them is the date 1626, but the font is much older than that. During the Civil War it was

*Peterborough Cathedral, Cambridgeshire, seen from the southeast.*

whitewashed and this undoubtedly preserved it. (See Lead Fonts, page 74.)

⬚ In the S. aisle is a Doom painting on wood dating from c.1450 and only rediscovered in 1938.

⬚ An outstanding brass commemorates someone called Elizabeth Rok of 1540. The remarkable English inscription, set in a Renaissance border, takes the form of an English collect, pre-dating the first *Prayer Book* of 1549.

## Pershore                 WORCESTERSHIRE

THE ABBEY CHURCH OF HOLY CROSS WITH ST EDBURGHA The building that exists today is the former monastic choir of a great Benedictine abbey dissolved by Henry VIII on 20 August 1534. The monastic buildings and nave of the abbey church were destroyed but the townspeople of Pershore paid £400 for the choir, tower and transepts.

⬚ Most of the building dates from c.1220–1290 and is a superb example of Early English architecture, the vaulting being particularly fine. Note the finely carved bosses, of which there are 41 in all.

⬚ Inside the tower is the unique 'cat's cradle' ringing platform designed by Gilbert Scott in the nineteenth century so that the interior of the tower can be seen from the floor.

⬚ In the s transept – a good example of Norman work – is the tomb of Abbot William de Herrington (1304–40). His head rests on a mitre.

⬚ Also in the s transept is a damaged figure of a knight – unique because he holds in his right hand a hunting horn.

⬚ On the w wall of the s transept is a monument to someone called Thomas Hazelwood (d. 1624).

⬚ On the w wall of the shortened N

transept is a monument to Fulke Hazelwood (d. 1595), father of Thomas.

⬚ In the N aisle notice how the decoration on one of the capitals of the piers is incomplete. I wonder why?

⬚ In the triforium at the E end is a beautiful modern figure of Christ with His arms outstretched in blessing.

⬚ The fine tower is similar to the that of Salisbury Cathedral (see page 303), but without its spire, is 35.4 m (116 feet) high to the parapet and 43.9 m (144 feet) high to the top of the pinnacles.

## Peterborough            CAMBRIDGESHIRE

THE CATHEDRAL CHURCH OF ST PETER, ST PAUL AND ST ANDREW This magnificent cathedral was a Benedictine abbey before the Dissolution.

⬚ The w front with its three imposing Early English arches ranks as one of the finest in Europe. Above the three rose windows in the gables are thirteenth-century figures of St Peter, St Paul and St Andrew.

Notice that the sw tower was never built above the s gable to correspond with the NW tower and also the differences between the spires on the extreme NW and sw towers.

⬚ In the w porch is a boss depicting an extremely curious example of the Holy Trinity. The Father is shown with a 'sun face' holding the Son's left hand, raised in blessing. The Son's hands show the nail marks clearly. The Holy Spirit as a Dove appears to be speaking into the right ear of the Father!

⬚ The doorway leading into the cathedral from this porch has a middle post of marble, either Purbeck or local Alwalton, which rests on a carving of an upside-down man reputed to be Simon Magus

(*Acts* 8, vv 9–24) being tormented by demons.

⊠ High on the w wall are two paintings of Robert Scarlett, who was the town sexton and died on 2 July 1594, aged 98. He buried two queens (Katharine of Aragon and Mary Queen of Scots). The wall painting on the N side was uncovered when the oil painting of Scarlett (1747) was taken down for cleaning and subsequently replaced on the s side of the doorway. Underneath the wall painting is this inscription:

'You see old Scarlett's picture stand on high
But at your feet there doth his body lie
His gravestone doth his age and death time show
His office by these tokens you may know
Second to none for strength and sturdy limb
A scarebabe mighty voice with visage grim
He had interred two Queens within this place
And this town's householders in his lives space
Twice over: but at length his own turn came
What he for others did for him the same
Was done: no doubt his soul doth live for aye
In Heaven: though here his body clad in clay.'

(See also, Selby Abbey, North Yorks., page 308.)

⊠ On the E side of the N doorway in the N nave aisle a slab shows Father Time with a scythe resting on a skull and crossbones; it is not inscribed.

⊠ The alternating round and octagonal piers in the N and s transepts are the oldest examples in England, dating from c.1130.

⊠ At the E end of the nave, suspended from the ceiling, is an impressive 4.6 m (15 feet) high crucifix, given in 1975 by the Reverend William Elborne in memory of his wife. The rood figure is by Frank Roper and the cross by George Pace.

⊠ The nave ceiling is the oldest painted wooden ceiling in England and the longest painted ceiling in the world. Painted originally in c.1220 it was repainted c.1745 and again in 1834 to the original design.

As one looks at the complete length it will be seen that it is raised in the middle. If you run your eye down the entire ceiling the diamond shapes gradually create the overall effect of a roof supported on rafters – an ancient optical illusion!

⊠ In the choir is a superb medieval brass eagle lectern. An inscription, now gone, stated that it was given by Abbot William Ramsey (Abbot from 1471 to 1496) and Prior John Malden.

At the base are four lions turning right. The eagle's beak is closed and its eight talons are complete. Also at the base is scratched 'Peter Phelips 1555–1556' but no records exist to say who he was! (See Medieval Brass Lecterns, page 362.)

⊠ In the N choir aisle is the grave of Katharine of Aragon, first queen of Henry VIII and hanging over it the royal standards of sixteenth-century England and Spain. According to tradition, Henry spared the abbey of Peterborough because of Katharine's grave when he dissolved the monastery on 29 November 1539, and Peterborough became a cathedral on 4 September 1541.

The inscription on the tomb of Queen Katharine of Aragon reads:

'+ Here lies the body of Katharine of Arragon [sic] Queen of England first wife of King Henry VIII who died at Kimbolton Castle on the 8th day of January, 1535/6 aged 49 years.'

The black marble slab was placed over the grave in 1895. It was paid for by women all over England whose name was Katharine. The original tomb was destroyed in 1643 but fragments remain near by.

▨ Also in the N choir aisle is the fine effigy of Benedict, Abbot of Peterborough, 1177–93. He added the greater part of the nave to the abbey church. This remarkably well-preserved effigy is the finest tomb of local Alwalton marble in the cathedral. Only the crozier was damaged by Cromwellian soldiers.

▨ In the N choir aisle is a model of the cathedral made by R. F. Rigby, J. R. Simpson and I. G. Tidd in 1955.

▨ At the E end of the cathedral is the retro-choir, still known as the 'New Building'. The magnificent fan vaulting and decorative panelling under the windows was probably the work of John Wastell, who later designed King's College chapel, Cambridge, on a much larger scale. The New Building dates from 1438 to 1518. (See Fan Vaulting, page 152.)

▨ In the retrochoir is the Hedda Stone, carved with figures of Christ and the Apostles. Dating from c.800 it is a fine piece of Anglo-Saxon sculpture.

▨ Where the New Building adjoins the E arches of the apse are flying ribs – a rare feature.

▨ In the s choir aisle is the site of the grave of Mary Queen of Scots, who was executed in 1587 and whose body was later moved to Henry VII's chapel, Westminster Abbey, London (see page 219). The inscription on the pier reads:

'The body of Mary Queen of Scots who was beheaded at Fotheringhay Castle on the 8 February 1586/7, was buried a little to the North of this pillar on the 1 August, 1587 and was

removed to Westminster Abbey on the 11 October, 1612 by order of her son King James 1st.'

This pier and the one on the opposite side of the choir are the only 12-sided Norman piers in existence.

▨ Also in the s choir aisle is the recumbent effigy of an unknown abbot in superb condition. Together with the other five recumbent effigies of abbots in the cathedral, this comprises the finest series of Benedictine memorials in England.

▨ In the Chapel of St Benedict off the s transept is a modern stained-glass window (1958) by W. T. Carter Shapland showing St Dunstan and St Ethelwold on either side of St Benedict.

▨ In the adjoining Chapel of St Kyneburgha and St Kyneswitha is a beautiful Annunciation scene in a glass case carved in 1968 by Alan Durst in memory of his wife Clare.

▨ On the sixth pier from the w in the s nave aisle is a memorial in Irish marble to Edith Cavell which reads:

'Right dear in the sight of the Lord is the death of His saints.

In thankful remembrance of the Christian example of Edith Louisa Cavell who devoted her life to nursing the sick and for helping Belgian French and British soldiers to escape was on October 12th 1915 put to death by the Germans at Brussels where she had nursed their wounded this Tablet was placed here by the Teachers Pupils and Friends of her old School in Laurel Court.'

▨ The third piers from the w on each side of the nave are much larger than the others and the theory is that they were designed to support western towers. In the triforium above on the s side is a newel staircase, which would seem to support this idea.

◈ The following roof bosses inside the main building are of particular interest:

† In the choir is a boss showing the Devil as a very strange figure with a second face on his belly! (The Devil is found on only one other roof boss in a church – Norwich Cathedral.)

† Also in the choir is a boss showing a shield on which is depicted a set square and a pair of compasses.

† In the w bay of the nave is a unique boss. The angle between the ribs is ornamented with trefoil foliage, but the centre of the boss is uncarved and has a small hole in the centre. Was something suspended from this hole?

◈ On the N side of the nave at triforium level is the original wooden windlass or tread-wheel used for raising stone in the construction of the cathedral, c.1200. Only five others exist – at Beverley Minster, Canterbury Cathedral, Durham Cathedral, Louth and Salisbury Cathedral (see pages 26, 61, 110, 226 and 303 respectively).

◈ On the night of Thursday 22 November 2001 a fire started in a stack of 200 plastic chairs behind the organ. The intense heat was funnelled upwards through the organ pipes and caused the lead in a window above to melt, blow the window out and suck out much of the heat also. This, together with the prompt intervention of the fire brigade to the base of the fire, certainly saved the famous roof and much else in the cathedral. A mere ten-minute delay on the part of the fire brigade would have resulted in the heat at the ceiling reaching spontaneous combustion point! However, the resultant chemical soot from the plastic chairs took nearly three and a half years to clear from the cathedral, as *every* nook and canny was covered.

# Petworth        WEST SUSSEX

CHAPEL OF PETWORTH HOUSE This chapel dates essentially from c.1309.

◈ The Early English window arcades incorporate Purbeck marble and Sussex stonework

◈ The medieval *bronze* eagle lectern dates from c.1380 and is the oldest medieval metal lectern in the British Isles. Standing at a total height of 1.73 m (5 feet 8 inches) with a wingspan of 48 cm (1 foot 7 inches) it is almost black in colour and is in superb condition. The eagle's beak is closed, there is a slit in the base of the tail and a hole on the top of its head. Its eight talons are complete and one is slightly polished. At the base of the lectern are three lions with heads turned to the right. A unique feature of this lectern is the fact that the eagle (and the orb on which it rests) can be turned sideways. (See Medieval Brass Lecterns, page 362.)

◈ The other furnishings in the chapel date from 1685 to 1692. At the w end is the huge family pew resting on a screen of Ionic columns.

◈ The heraldic glass in the windows dates from c.1550–1620.

# Piddinghoe
(pronounced 'Pidding Who')    EAST SUSSEX

ST JOHN is situated on a hill quite close to the River Ouse.

◈ The round tower is one of only three in Sussex and dates from c.1130. (The other towers are at St Michael's, Lewes, and nearby Southease.)

◈ On top of the shingled spire is a wind vane in the form of a salmon or sea trout. In his poem 'Sussex', published in 1902, Rudyard Kipling wrote, 'where windy Piddinghoe's begilded dolphin veers'. It was regilded in 1980.

An ancient oak ladder leads to the belfry.

The church is quite dark because of a lack of large windows and too much stained glass in the small windows!

## Playford                              SUFFOLK

ST MARY is situated high above the village. It is approached by several steps.

On the w front of the tower is a fine cross in knapped flints.

On the N wall of the chancel is the famous brass to one Sir George Felbrigg (1400). It is 1.45 m (4 feet 9 inches) long.

On the N wall of the nave is a bust to Sir George Biddell Airy, KCB (27 July 1801–2 January 1892), Astronomer Royal, 1835–81. The bust is by F. J. Williamson of Esher.

On the s side of the chancel is a bust to Thomas Clarkson (28 March 1760–26 September 1846) 'the friend of slaves' who worked with Wilberforce for the abolition of slavery. He is buried near the chancel door and a granite obelisk, erected in 1857 near the s porch, commemorates him.

## Plymouth                              DEVON

ST ANDREW, the parish church of Plymouth, was destroyed by incendiary bombs on 22 March 1941 and only the walls, pillars and tower remained. It was reconsecrated on 30 November 1957, the architect being Frederick Etchells, FRIBA.

The flooring is of Delabole slate slabs – the largest floor ever constructed of this material.

The six impressive stained-glass windows were designed by John Piper and made by Patrick Reyntiens:

† The E window of St Philip's chapel in the N transept is predominantly yellow and is in memory of Dr Harry Moreton, organist from 1888 to 1961.

† The E window of the lady chapel is dedicated to the Virgin Mary and depicts many of her medieval symbols.

† The central E window represents the four elements: air, earth, fire and water, and is predominantly red, blue and green. It is in memory of Lady Astor, MP for Plymouth 1919–45 and the first woman MP.

† The E window of St Catherine's chapel is predominantly red and pink. It shows St Catherine's wheel in the centre superimposed on St Andrew's cross. In the four corners are the symbols of Matthew, Mark, Luke and John.

† The small window in the s transept represents the Creation and the Holy Trinity. In the centre notice the Hand of God over Creation.

† The w window under the tower depicts the Instruments of the Passion. It is in memory of Waldorf, Second Viscount Astor, MP 1910–19.

In St Philip's chapel is a recumbent figure in Purbeck marble dating from c.1200. This is from an earlier building on the site.

On the s wall is a plaque commemorating William Cookworthy – a chemist and potter, the discoverer of English china clay and the first maker in England of true porcelain (b. 12 April 1705, Kingsbridge, Devon, d. 17 October 1780, Plymouth).

Under the tower are three versions of the Royal Arms – an unusual feature. One is of Charles I, another of George III and yet another of George IV which came from St Catherine's Church.

On the ledge of the first window w of the s door is a rough sketch known as the 'Drake Crest', believed to show the arms granted to Sir Francis Drake in 1581 after he became the first Englishman to sail around the world (in the *Golden Hind*).

The marble font dates from 1661 and was once used as a birdbath before it was presented to St Catherine's Church and eventually returned to this church.

## Polstead      SUFFOLK

St Mary In quiet countryside, away from main roads, the church stands at the top of a hill, next to Polstead Hall, with fine views from its churchyard.

This church has the oldest stone spire in Suffolk at 22.3 m (73 feet) high.

The Norman piers in the nave support rounded arches of brick with blocked brick clerestory windows above. The chancel arch is also of brick. These are the oldest English bricks surviving.

On the s side of the chancel arch is a tiny wall tablet showing a father and son kneeling at a desk. The inscription reads, 'Heare lieth the body of Jacob Brand, Gentleilman and his youngest sonne Benjamin Brand which died the 3 day of December, 1630.' He is said to have died having fallen from one of the windows of Polstead Hall.

The Communion rails date from c.1670 and enclose the holy table on three sides.

Among fragments of ancient glass in a s chapel window is the head of a bishop.

Near the s wall of the tower, a little to the w, is the grave of Maria Marten, the victim of the 'Red Barn' murder in 1827. There is no headstone due to its having been plundered by souvenir-hunters.

## Portsmouth      HAMPSHIRE

The Cathedral Church of St Thomas of Canterbury This cathedral, with its newly completed w end, is situated in Old Portsmouth and is clearly visible from the sea.

The tower was completed in 1691 and was originally a naval watch tower. The cupola was added in 1703.

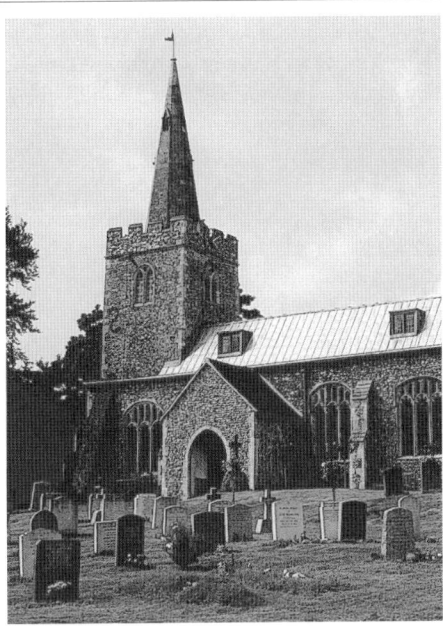

*Polstead, Suffolk.*

On the n side of the nave is the original golden barque wind vane, which stood on the tower from 1710 until it was blown down in gales in December 1954. It was restored in 1958.

In the s presbytery aisle is a large monument to George Villiers, Duke of Buckingham, who was assassinated at 11 High Street, Portsmouth, on 23 August 1628.

In the s aisle a plaque on the floor covers a sailor from the *Mary Rose*, Henry VIII's flagship, which sank off Spithead on 19 July 1545 and was raised on 11 October 1982. His body was interred on 19 July 1984.

In the s transept is a D-Day window in memory of Admiral Sir Bertram Ramsay, who was killed in 1945.

In the n tower transept is a Della Robbia wall plaque of the Virgin and Child dating from c.1500.

At the E end of the N choir transept is a relief effigy in bronze of William Wyllie, who was killed at Montauban, 19 July 1916.

Above this bronze is a wall painting of the Last Judgement dating from c.1250.

The arcades on each side of the choir are unusual in having two smaller arches inside a larger semicircular one. This feature of two pointed arches inside a semicircular one is found in just one other church – Boxgrove Priory, West Sussex (see page 38).

Inside the SW porch is a plaque commemorating the completion of the W end of the cathedral with its twin towers. It reads, 'This stone was set here on the 16 October, 1990 by Her Royal Highness the Princess of Wales to mark the final stage of the building.'

## Poynings      EAST SUSSEX

HOLY TRINITY The present church, nestling under the South Downs, was commenced in 1369.

The N porch, which has elaborately cut and squared flint facing, contains ancient wooden seats on either side, each made from one length of wood. Arthur Mee, who edited 'The King's England' series of county books, describes them in his 'Sussex' volume as 'two of the longest and roughest benches we have come upon in all our journeyings'.

The huge central tower is supported on four massive arches which provide a large open space underneath. An ancient ladder leads to the belfry.

Among the fragments of ancient glass is the Annunciation in the top two lights of the E window of the N transept. It dates from 1421 and is composed of pale yellow and plain glass. On the right are the Virgin Mary, a hovering Dove and a lily in a pot in the shape of a cross with flowers at the top

and at the end of each arm. This is an interesting variation on the lily crucifix (see Lily Crucifix, page 338.)

In the S transept, against the S wall, is an oak tie-beam which once formed part of the roof of this transept. It bears a name and date: 'Francis Killingbecke, 1625'.

The window above this beam came from Chichester Cathedral and dates from c.1640 when it was restored following the damage done by Cromwell's soldiers.

In the chancel are two family pews dating from the seventeenth century.

In front of the communion rails are some tiles dating from c.1290.

At each corner of the communion rails are modern carved angels by William Court given in memory of Anthony Stanislaus, who died in the Second World War.

## Preston      EAST SUSSEX

ST PETER On the E side of Brighton, the church has an unusually slim W tower with red cap and extremely narrow lancets at the top.

Behind the pulpit is a wall painting showing the murder of Thomas Becket in 1170. Dating from c.1260 this is one of the oldest extant representations of this subject.

The carving on the choir stalls is reputed to have been done by Grinling Gibbons, who lived at nearby Rottingdean for a while until his death in 1720.

## Probus      CORNWALL

ST PROBUS & ST GRACE This church, with its imposing tower, lies a little way from the busy A390, between St Austell and Truro.

The magnificent tower, at 38.1 m (125 feet) high, is the finest church tower in

*The superb granite tower at Probus, Cornwall, is reminiscent of the great towers of Somerset.*

# CHURCH MAZES

The word 'maze', for most people, summons up Hampton Court (Greater London) and its famous maze dating from 1690. Visited by over 500,000 people a year, it is probably the most famous maze in the world.

However, it is not generally known that there are many pavement mazes in cathedrals and churches, especially in France and Italy. The characteristic feature of the Christian maze is its symmetry, supposedly representing the mystery of God. Some authorities believe that the maze was introduced to symbolize the perplexities and intricacies of the Christian life. Others have said that it typifies the entangling nature of sin, larger examples being used for the performance of miniature pilgrimages.

It is interesting to note that while many kinds of maze exist in England and Wales, only five churches boast floor mazes. They are as follows:

1. Alkborough (St John Baptist), Lincolnshire
2. Batheaston (St John the Baptist), near Bath, Somerset
3. Bourn (St Mary), Cambridgeshire
4. Ely Cathedral (The Holy and Undivided Trinity), Cambridgeshire
5. Itchen Stoke (St Mary), Hampshire

Alkborough's maze is on the floor of the s porch and it was constructed c.1887. It is a copy of the famous turf maze that can be seen about 183 m (200 yards) from the church in a basin-shaped depression which is known as Julian's Bower on the side of the hilltop overlooking the meeting of the River Trent and of the River Humber. Its origins are obscure, but one theory holds that it was used for a Roman game and cut out by Roman soldiers stationed in the nearby camp of Aquis. But another theory suggests that it was cut by monks c.1190 and used in some form of penance.

The maze is circular and the paths are symmetrical, leading to the centre. It has a circumference of 42.18 m (138 feet 5 inches) and a diameter of 13.41 m (44 feet). The length of the path is 18.66 m (61 feet 3 inches). The copy in the church porch is 1.88 m (6 feet 2 inches) in diameter. Other copies of the maze are in a stained-glass window at the E end of the church and on the gravestone of James Goulton-Constable, who restored the church in 1877 and had the maze design put in the porch. The copy on his gravestone is a bronze replica set in the head of a Celtic cross.

The maze in Bourn Church is on the floor of the church under the tower at the W end of the nave. It is rectangular and made of red and black tiles; the centre is occupied by the font, the path to the centre finishing at the step up to the font. The general plan is similar to that of the Hampton Court maze and it was constructed in 1875 when the church was closed for three years for extensive renovations. It may replace an earlier maze, or have been designed by someone who was conversant with one that was constructed a few years earlier at nearby Ely Cathedral.

Batheaston's maze is a copy of a square pavement that once existed in the Abbey of St Bertin in St Omer, northern France. This was destroyed c.1750 but fortunately a copy had been made of its design.

The maze at Ely Cathedral is under the w tower. It was designed by Sir Gilbert Scott in 1870 as part of his restoration of the cathedral. The maze is enclosed inside a square and composed of black and white tiles. The distance from the entrance to the centre is 65.53 m (215 feet), the same as the height of the w tower.

The maze at Itchen Stoke occupies

the entire floor of the apsidal chancel under the communion table. Made of brown and green glazed tiles it is based on the maze in Chartres Cathedral, France, and was made by Henry Conybeare in 1866. His brother, the Reverend Charles Conybeare, was vicar at the time and paid £7000 for the entire building, which is a miniature replica of La Sainte Chapelle, Paris.

Another churchyard maze is on the gravestone of maze expert Michael Ayrton (d. 1975), at Hadstock, Essex.

At Compton near Guildford, Surrey, is the Watts Memorial chapel, designed by Mary Watts in 1896 as a memorial to her husband, the artist George Frederick Watts (1817–1904), who is buried nearby.

Inside, the decoration dates from 1901 and is a superb example of the Art Nouveau style. Four roof corbels each depict terracotta angels holding  circular mazes based on the design in

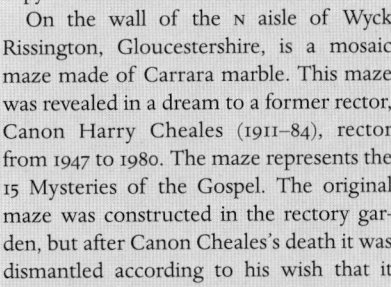 Ravenna Cathedral, Italy, and a further copy of the maze is on the altar itself.

On the wall of the N aisle of Wyck Rissington, Gloucestershire, is a mosaic maze made of Carrara marble. This maze was revealed in a dream to a former rector, Canon Harry Cheales (1911–84), rector from 1947 to 1980. The maze represents the 15 Mysteries of the Gospel. The original maze was constructed in the rectory garden, but after Canon Cheales's death it was dismantled according to his wish that it should never fall into secular hands.

In Lewannick, Cornwall, there is a depiction of a maze on the SW face of the Norman font and, finally, there are two churches in England containing roof bosses that show mazes. One boss is in the N nave aisle of St Mary Redcliffe, Bristol, and the other is in the country church of South Tawton, Devon.

Cornwall. Built of granite, it was constructed c.1523–1610.

 Under the tower is a Tudor wooden screen carved with the letters ABCDE. This would seem to indicate that a school was once here.

 At the E end of the S aisle is a memorial to Thomas Hawkins (d.1 December 1766, aged 42), owner of the nearby eighteenth-century house of Trewithen. An angel above holds the text, 'He is not dead but sleepeth'.

# Puncknowle
(pronounced 'Punnell')     DORSET

ST MARY An interesting church, it stands in a beautiful country village, about 2.4 km (1½ miles) from the sea.

 On the S wall of the nave near the tower is a plaque to Sir Robert Napier (d. 1700). The unusual inscription reads:

> 'Reader when as thou hast done all thou cans't thou art but an unprofitable servant therfore [sic] this marble affords no roome for fulsome flattery or vaine [sic] praise. SR R.N.'

*Queen Camel, Somerset, dominates this beautiful village.*

## Queen Camel    SOMERSET

ST BARNABAS

 Outside the N gate of the churchyard is the following notice:

FLOOD LEVEL

30 MAY, 1979

 On the outside W face of the tower is a fibreglass statue of St Barnabas made by Charles Hopkins in 1971.

 Outside the church on the S side are some grotesque gargoyles, a sundial and unusual eighteenth-century porch.

 The very tall W tower contains the second heaviest ring of six bells in the world. The tenor weighs 1870.2 kg (1 ton 16 cwt 3 qr 7 lb). (See Bells, page 293.)

 The fine entrance screen of plate glass has sand-blasted emblems signifying the province of Canterbury (Y) and the diocese of Bath and Wells (X).

 The unusual church-wardens' staves commemorate the silver jubilee of Queen Elizabeth II (1977). They were designed and made by Charles Hopkins.

 There is evidence on the inside E face of the tower of the earlier steeply pitched roof.

 In the N aisle roof are several interesting bosses, including one depicting the Green Man with a large projecting tongue!

 The chancel arch is richly panelled while above, the roof has beautifully gilded bosses.

 On the S side of the beautiful screen a child's head peeps over the top!

 In the chancel the elaborate piscina and sedilia on the S side have canopied hoods.

 In a glass case at the E end of the N aisle there is some beautiful eighteenth-century embroidery.

## Quorn or Quorndon    LEICESTERSHIRE

ST BARTHOLOMEW This granite-built church (unusual for this part of the country) stands in a large village to the S of Loughborough.

 In the Farnham chapel a monument to Sir John Farnham (d. 1587) shows him standing in front of a battle scene in which tents and guns are visible. This is a very early example of a relief picture enclosed within a rectangular frame. The sculptor may have been Epiphanius Evesham.

 Also in the Farnham chapel are several incised tomb-slabs standing upright against the wall. One of the best depicts Thomas Farnham (d. 1500) and his wife, Margaret. These incised slabs, which resemble brasses, are unique in England but are found in Italy.

## Ranworth NORFOLK

ST HELEN, known as 'the Cathedral of the Broads', is situated near the Broads and has a fine view from its 29.3 m (96 feet) tower.

The magnificent rood screen is unique in that it stretches right across the church and still has the parclose wings enclosing the two side altars. Dating from c.1485 it has its original colouring and paintings. On the back of the screen are original panels showing the white rose of York against rust- and green-coloured backgrounds. For 457 years they were hidden by six miserere stalls attached to the screen and only revealed in 1996. These stalls came from St Benet's Abbey when it was dissolved in 1539.

The cantor's desk dates from c.1500 and was used by singers for their music. It is the only one remaining in England.

The famous *Ranworth Antiphoner* dates from c.1478 and was written by the monks of Langley Abbey near Loddon (Norfolk). Lost c.1620 it was bought back for Ranworth in 1912 for £575. One of the pages for Easter Day is missing.

## Reading BERKSHIRE

GREYFRIARS is not only one of the most complete examples of Franciscan architecture left in England but the *only* one actually still in use as a church. (The only other complete friary church is in Priory Park, Chichester, but this is now used as a museum.)

Completed in 1311 it was suppressed by Henry VIII in 1538 and in 1540 the choir was granted to Robert Stanshawe, a groom of the King's chamber, together with other buildings and land. The choir was probably pulled down then.

On 24 April 1543 the nave became the Guildhall of Reading for a short time, but by 1578 it had become a hospital or workhouse.

In 1613 part of the nave became a House of Correction and cells were erected in the church on the s side and later in the N aisle. This was the Borough Bridewell and prison until 1844 when the county gaol was erected in the Forbury. Some of the pillars in the church have prisoners' initials carved on them. John Howard, the prison reformer, visited the Bridewell and found it in a deplorable state. By 1810 the roof had been removed from the nave to make an open courtyard, allowing fresh air and light in as well as serving as an exercise space for the prisoners. The beautiful w window was bricked up to the tracery to preserve it.

On the site of the s transept was a public house called 'The Pigeons'.

Around 1728 and then again c.1805 houses were built on the site of the choir but when the latter was replaced by the present vicarage in 1963 it was not allowed to encroach on the chancel site.

After many vicissitudes and at the instigation of the Reverend William

*Ranworth, Norfolk. A fine church dominating the Broads.*

Whitmarsh Phelps, the church was restored to something of its former glory and reconsecrated on Wednesday 2 December 1863 by Samuel Wilberforce, Bishop of Oxford. The Reverend Phelps died on 22 June 1867, aged 69.

The w window is a superb example of reticulated (or net-like) tracery, considered by some to be the finest example in existence.

On the w wall of the N aisle are a number of paving tiles dating from c.1350. They are neither religious nor heraldic and show numerous animals and a geometrical design.

At the springing of the arch-mouldings are a number of delightful carved heads. Sixteen of these are Victorian, but six, at the w end, are original and show signs of exposure to the weather when the roof was removed.

## Redenhall NORFOLK

ST MARY In a village just off the A143, SW of Bungay and near the River Waveney, the church, with its superb tower, is a prominent landmark.

The magnificent w tower, built c.1520, is enriched with impressive flush-work. The w door is decorated with a hammer, horseshoe and pincers – possibly given by the Guild of Farriers.

The medieval brass eagle lectern, dating from c.1490, is the only one in the British Isles with two heads! It is 1.91 m (6 feet 3 inches) high with a wingspan of 70 cm (2 feet 4 inches). It has eight brass talons and solid brass eyes. The eagles' beaks are open but only small coins could be inserted into their mouths. This brass lectern is a magnificent piece of work and it is said that it was hidden in the moat of Gawdy

Hall during the Cromwellian upheaval. (See Medieval Brass Lecterns, page 362.)

🔲 In addition to the brass eagle lectern there is a wooden eagle lectern also dating from c.1490.

🔲 At the E end of the N aisle is an ancient wooden chest dating from c.1450 which came from Gawdy Hall before it was demolished. It is reputed to have held vestments in the chapel there. This chest came from Venice and inside the lid are fine paintings of fifteenth-century ships; the lid itself, however, looks as if it might have been adapted from something else.

🔲 The nave is lit by 16 large clerestory windows which also show up the fine hammer-beam roof.

🔲 The beautiful oak screen was restored in 1920 but still has 12 medieval paintings of the Apostles.

## Ringmore                        DEVON

ST NICHOLAS is situated in a quiet valley near Shaldon, overlooking the River Teign.

🔲 On the N side of the churchyard is the grave of William Newcombe Homeyard (d. 6 July 1927) – inventor and manufacturer of Liqufruta cough syrup – and his wife, Maria Laetitia Kempe Homeyard (d. 20 April 1944). When he died, his widow wanted the name inscribed on his tombstone, but this was refused, so she had 'ATURFUQIL' engraved instead ('LIQUFRUTA' backwards)! Maria was a great benefactress in this area and among other things constructed the Homeyard Botanical Gardens above Shaldon.

🔲 On the W wall of the nave is a tablet to the memory of an only child, James Brockinton Hore, who died aged 21 years. He was 'drowned while bathing in the river that flows by these walls, August 13th 1858'.

🔲 Near by is a tablet commemorating Hugh William Francis Cates, who was killed by a fall from the rigging of the *Waitangi* near Dunedin, New Zealand, on 6 November 1898, aged 18 years.

🔲 On the N side of the E wall is an unusual little circular window showing a leper kneeling at a low-side window receiving Holy Communion from a priest.

## Ripon                  NORTH YORKSHIRE

THE MINSTER AND CATHEDRAL CHURCH OF ST PETER & ST WILFRID This beautiful cathedral with its impressive W front stands in an extensive churchyard, surrounded by trees, on a small hill, sloping down to the River Ure.

🔲 The fine Perpendicular nave constructed 1502–25 was one of the last to be built before the Reformation.

🔲 The central tower is unique because it was only partly reconstructed in 1450 after a partial collapse of the original tower. On the S side of the nave the new pier was built to receive the new arch but work then ceased.

🔲 The N transept, an excellent example of Norman transitional architecture, contains a rare Perpendicular stone pulpit. (See Medieval Stone Pulpits, page 348.)

🔲 The stone choir screen, dating from c.1450, contains modern figures with the exception of the representation of God the Father in the apex of the arch.

🔲 In the choir are some fine choir stalls with 34 interesting misericords, including the following :

† Samson carrying off the gates of Gaza – a unique subject.

† An angel holding a shield bearing the date 1489. Dated misericords are very rare.

† A mermaid with a mirror and hairbrush.

† Four misericords featuring a fox.

*Rochester Cathedral, Kent, is overlooked from the west by the magnificent Norman castle.*

✝ On the finial of a stall-end is an excellent carving of an elephant with a castle on its back, complete with soldiers peering over the battlements! This is one of the finest examples of an elephant carved in wood and dates from 1494.

▨ In the choir are a number of interesting roof bosses dating from *c.*1300. The third boss from the E shows Adam and Eve being driven out of the Garden of Eden.

▨ On the E side of the choir screen is a wooden hand which was once used to beat time and which can still be moved – a unique survival.

▨ The great E window is an excellent example of Geometrical tracery and dates from *c.*1280.

▨ On the S side of the nave, behind the choir stalls, is the entrance to the famous Saxon crypt. This was built by St Wilfrid in 672 under the high altar of his church.

▨ In the chapter house are two circular 'splay' windows which throw the light upwards to the roof. They are unique in the British Isles.

# Rochester      KENT

THE CATHEDRAL CHURCH OF CHRIST & THE BLESSED VIRGIN MARY is well seen from the magnificent Norman keep of nearby Rochester Castle.

▨ The great W doorway dates from *c.*1130 and is not only one of the most richly decorated late Norman doorways in England, but also the only surviving example of a column-figure doorway, showing the Queen of Sheba and King Solomon.

▨ Each pair of piers in the Norman nave is different – six different pairs altogether.

▨ In the triforium above, the small arches *inside* the narrow pairs of pillars exhibit pointed arches – among the earliest pointed arches in England, dating from *c.*1130.

▨ On the SE side of the nave is a Norman capital richly decorated with foliage. This carving dates from *c.*1300 when two bays of the Norman nave were demolished and reconstructed in the Early English style, but funds, fortunately, ran out before all the work could be completed.

▨ The N transept dates from *c.*1240–55 and is a superb example of Early English work. The triforium's pointed arches, enriched with dog-tooth mouldings, are particularly noteworthy.

▨ On the N wall of the choir is a thirteenth-century painting of the Wheel of Fortune.

▨ Also on the N wall of the choir is a very beautiful corbel head of a monk. (Among the Early English architecture (*c.*1200–1300) in the cathedral are about 200 corbel-head sculptures of the builder-monks, many of them carved out of Petworth and Purbeck marble.)

▨ Some of the arcaded woodwork in the back row of the front stalls in the choir dates from *c.*1227 and is the oldest stall-work in England.

▨ In the NE transept is the fine tomb of Bishop Walter de Merton (d. 1277), founder of Merton College, Oxford. The alabaster effigy dates from 1598. The glass in the window at the back dates from 1911 and shows Jesus, the Virgin and Child, St William of Perth and John the Baptist.

▨ The presbytery, where the high altar is situated, has only two storeys, which makes it unique in an English cathedral.

▨ On the N side of the presbytery, in the sanctuary, is a piscina now covered with wood. This is a very unusual position since piscinae are usually found on the S side.

▨ In the SE transept is a magnificent doorway leading to the chapter room. Dating from *c.*1340 it is enriched with carvings of saints and angels. (Compare this doorway with the prior's doorway at Norwich Cathedral, see page 257.)

Near this doorway are leaning columns made safe in 1825.

On the E wall of the S transept is a rare marble memorial by Grinling Gibbons commemorating one Sir Richard Head (d. 1689).

Here also is the tomb of Samuel Reynolds Hole, dean from 1888 to 1904 and founder of the National Rose Show.

The extensive crypt is one of only two Early English crypts in an English cathedral (the other being at Hereford, see page 174). This crypt is the earlier (c.1205-1210) and it is also the third largest crypt of an English cathedral; only St Paul's (see page 214) and Canterbury (see page 63) are larger.

On walls facing each other in the centre of the crypt and protected by glass are two similar graffiti showing Jesus holding a chalice in His right hand and a paten in His left. Below are two figures, possibly representing the supper at Emmaus recorded in *Luke* 24, v.30.

On the third pier from the W on the N side of the nave is a graffito showing the Baptism of Jesus with the Holy Spirit as a Dove. Elsewhere throughout the cathedral are numerous graffiti, particularly on the nave piers.

Outside on the S side of the SE transept are the remains of the monastic cloister, which occupies a unique position as the normal siting of cloisters was on the N or S side of the nave.

## Rodborough          GLOUCESTERSHIRE

ST MARY MAGDALENE Apart from the Perpendicular tower, the remainder of this church was rebuilt in 1842.

A unique stained-glass window by Alfred Fisher commemorates the Reverend W. Awdry (1912–97), creator of Thomas the Tank Engine. Awdry, who

lived near by, is shown reading the first stories to his children, while another panel shows him opening an engine shed to reveal the engines Thomas and Gordon.

## Rolvenden          KENT

ST MARY THE VIRGIN On the A28, just S of Tenterden, this large church is set in a picturesque village which also has an attractive windmill.

Outside, the S buttress of the E window serves as a tombstone dated 1770 – a curious use for a buttress!

Outside on the E side of the S porch doorway is a mass dial still carrying the rusty end of the gnomon. This is in an unusually high position.

In the W porch is an alms-box (c.1600) with three locks.

On the S side of the chancel is the Chapel of Saints Katherine and Anne, which contains a gallery reached by a staircase from the chancel. This gallery is occupied by the Hole Park family pew and contains an eighteenth-century table and red-upholstered Chippendale chairs – an almost unique survival.

In the arch of the Scott chapel on the N side of the chancel is a memorial designed by Sir Edwin Lutyens, RA to Lieutenant H. Tennant, Royal Flying Corps, killed in the First World War.

A wall tablet commemorates Frances Hodgson Burnett (1849–1924), who lived at Great Maytham Hall and wrote *Little Lord Fauntleroy*, *The Secret Garden* and many other books.

## Romsey          HAMPSHIRE

THE ABBEY CHURCH OF ST MARY AND ST ETHELFLAEDA This magnificent Norman building is the finest and greatest surviving nuns' church in the British Isles. Its foundation dates from 907 and the present building c.1120–1250. The deed of sale, whereby it was sold to the townsfolk for £100 by King Henry VIII's commissioners in 1544, is still preserved.

On the outside w wall of the s transept is a famous Saxon crucifix dating from c.1040. The figure of Christ with the Hand of God reaching down from above is carved from a single block of stone.

Standing at the w end of the nave notice the difference in shape of the last three arches and the other four further E. The rounded arches at the E end date from c.1150 to 1180 while the pointed ones were constructed c.1230–50.

A beautifully embroidered curtain of 1966 at the E end of the s aisle covers the abbess's doorway.

In the s transept there is a seventeenth-century Cromwellian monument to the St Barbe family, who formerly owned 'Broad-lands', 1.61 km (1 mile) south of Romsey.

Near by is an impressive ogee canopy covering a Purbeck marble effigy of an unknown lady of c.1250.

In the s transept is the grave of Lord Louis Mountbatten of Burma, KG (1900–79), who was buried here on 5 September 1979 following his assassination in Eire on 27 August.

Near the s transept at the w end of the s choir aisle is the Threadgold treasury. Among the items is the original bill of sale of the abbey in 1544, the *Romsey Psalter* c.1450, a clump of Allium bulbs, two hazel nuts, some box leaves and the remains of a bird's nest which included fragments of woollen cloth. These latter items were discovered inside the wall behind the twelfth-century wall painting at the E end of the abbey when the painting was restored in 1976; they are the oldest botanical specimens in Europe, dating from c.1150.

At the E end of the s choir aisle (St Anne's chapel) the Norman capital on the left is richly carved. It shows a crowned figure holding a pyramid, while near by an angel and seated figure hold a scroll inscribed *'Robertus me fecit'* ('Robert made me') – but who was Robert?

Over the altar of St Anne's chapel, inside wooden panelling, is the other famous Romsey crucifix, dating from c.960. On the arms of the cross are angels swinging censors, with the figures of Mary and John on each side.

At the E end of the N choir aisle is St George's chapel. Just in front of the altar, tiles dating from c.1250 depict rosette designs and the Crusades.

Over the high altar there is a fine bas-relief of the Virgin and Child by Martin Travers dating from c.1946. (See page 23 for a similar bas-relief in Beaulieu.)

On the s side of the choir is the Mountbatten family pew with bronze heads in relief of Earl Mountbatten and Edwina, Countess Mountbatten, who died on 21 February 1960 in North Borneo and was buried at sea.

Also in the choir is the organ built in 1858, rebuilt 1888 and one of the finest organs by J. W. Walker.

Over the interior arches of the triforium in the chancel and nave are shafts unique to Romsey, which replace the usual stone tympana.

In the Chapel of St Lawrence in the N transept is a fine painted wooden reredos dating from c.1500 and depicting Christ rising from the tomb while above are saints of the Church. In the bottom left-hand corner is the abbess who donated the reredos.

The NE window of this chapel commemorates the Reverend E. L. Berthon (20 February 1813–28 October 1899), who was a boat-builder, painter, astronomer and inventor. The subject of the window is Jesus reading with Mary and Joseph the

*Rottingdean, East Sussex. A beautiful church with outstanding stained glass.*

Carpenter. Notice the boat, telescope and Joseph's tools!

▨ Behind the choir screen on the N side of the crossing in the N transept are the remains of the foundations of the Anglo-Saxon church which once stood on this site, dating from 999.

▨ The w end of the N aisle was once used as a schoolroom and on the sides of the end windows the initials of boys who were taught here c.1650–1800 can be seen. The dates 1754, 1781 and 1788 are clearly visible and one boy's name, 'R.Watson', is particularly clear.

At the sw corner of the nave is the recumbent figure of Sir William Petty (1623–87) by Westmacott.

▨ Opposite, on the N side of the nave, is the tomb of Alice Taylor, who was born in June or July of 1841 and died of scarlet fever at the age of two years and five months on 10 December 1843 after an illness of four days. Her father was the local doctor, Dr Francis Taylor. Alice holds a rose in her hand which has become broken through being handled.

▨ In the wooden octagon on top of the tower are eight bells, the tenor weighing 1219.3 kg (1 ton 4 cwt).

## Rottingdean      East Sussex

St Margaret Situated on the A259 coast road, between Brighton and Newhaven, the impressive church stands facing the village green.

▨ Inside the tower some of the stonework is reddened from a disastrous fire in 1377 when French pirates set fire to the church, in which several villagers had taken refuge.

The three lancets at the E end are filled with stained glass by Edward Burne-Jones and William Morris. Dating from 1893, this is some of their best work. Some of the other windows were made to their designs after their deaths.

Outside the church near the w wall of the s aisle are the graves of Sir Edward and Lady Burne-Jones who had lived in Rottingdean for many years at North End House. They were the uncle and aunt of Rudyard Kipling (see Wilden, Worcestershire, page 410).

## Rowlestone    HEREFORDSHIRE

ST PETER is situated in the remote countryside off the A465 Hereford to Abergavenny road.

The s doorway is Norman with Christ in Glory in the tympanum above.

The superb Norman chancel arch has many carvings of doves. Notice the two figures on the right which are upside down!

Rare candle brackets can be found in the chancel on the N and s walls. This is simple village blacksmith's work of the fifteenth century. Each bracket holds five candles and is decorated with 12 golden birds, cocks on the left and swans on the right. The left bracket is 1.42 m (4 feet 6 inches) long and the right is 1.23 m (4 feet ½ inch).

On the N side of the nave a fine stained-glass window (1964) depicts St Peter and Rowlestone Church in memory of the Kennedy family, who have been associated with the village since 1864.

## Rudston    EAST RIDING OF YORKSHIRE

ALL SAINTS The church stands above the small village, commanding beautiful views over the Wolds, 8 km (5 miles) w of Bridlington on the B1253.

On the NE side of the church is Britain's tallest standing stone – a prehistoric monolith capped with lead. It is 1.70 m (5 feet 7 inches) wide, 0.88 m (2 feet 11 inches) thick at the base and 7.8 m (25 feet 6 inches) high.

It probably came from near Scarborough (16.1 km/10 miles away) between 1600 and 1000 BC and was set up near a spring that rises to the w.

In the s aisle a wall tablet commemorates Godfrey Wentworth Bayard Bosville, who lived at Thorpe Hall, about 0.8 km (½ mile) E of Rudston and died on 11 October 1866, aged 40. His sorrowing wife holds their baby.

Near the wall tablet is another fine one to a couple, Richard Beaumont (d. 2 November 1877, aged 78) and Susan, his wife (d. 5 November 1879, aged 72). Two plaques show their head and shoulders while on each side sorrowful angels kneel.

Near the finely carved Norman font a plaque reads:

'In this churchyard is the grave of Winifred Holtby (1898–1935).
Born at Rudston House in this village, educated at Queen Margaret's School, Scarborough and at Somerville College, Oxford, she won a high place amongst the writers of her day. Her work was notable for understanding, insight and sincerity. Her charm as a woman came from gentle grace of manner, high courage and purpose, practical sympathy for others and an endearing selflessness. Some of the many who called her friend or who knew her through her writings have set here this tribute to her memory. *Beati Immaculati*'

Winifrid is buried due w of the church. An open book on her grave states:

1

1

1

'In loving memory of Winifrid, daughter of David and Alice Holtby. Died in London 29 Sept., 1935 aged 37 years.

> God give me work
> Till my life shall end.
> And life
> Till my work is done.'

Next to her grave is the burying place of the Macdonalds.

On the N side of the chancel is a window to the memory of Sir Alexander Macdonald of the Isles (26 September 1865–26 March 1933), who played the organ here for 50 years. In 1888 he designed and paid for the organ – the first electric-action organ built in England outside London. The window shows him playing the organ surrounded by men and choir-boys.

In the S aisle is an unusual window showing the Parable of the Sower dating from 1955.

# Rugby WARWICKSHIRE

ST ANDREW is the only church in the world that has two towers, each with a complete ring of bells.

The old fourteenth-century W tower has a ring of five bells made by Joseph Smith of Edgbaston, Birmingham, in 1711 including a tenor of 483.9 kg (9 cwt 2 qr 3 lb). This tower was probably built for defence purposes and is unusual in not possessing corner buttresses. Its lower windows are far from the ground and it also has a fire-place with a chimney going up through the thickness of the W wall to the battle-ments, 21.3 m (70 feet) from the ground.

The Victorian tower and spire (55.5 m/182 feet high) dates from 1895. It stands on the NE side of the church and contains a ring of eight bells, the tenor weighing 1261 kg (1 ton 4 cwt 3 qr 8 lb). They were cast by Mears and Stainbank of White-chapel, London in 1895.

The remainder of the church dates from 1877 to 1885 but contains a fine reredos (1909) by Alec Miller with a copy of Fra Angelico's 'The Transfiguration', which is in St Mark's Church, Florence (Italy).

The uniqueness of two rings of bells in a parish church once caused some con-sternation in Rugby on a busy Saturday afternoon. Visiting members of the Warwickshire Guild of Church Bellringers were so intrigued by this fact that they decided to ring both peals simultaneously, with the result that shoppers below were somewhat astonished and not very pleased!

After the rebuilding and enlarging of the old church, the former nave was named after a previous vicar, the Reverend Moultrie, and became the N aisle or 'Moultrie Aisle'. At the NW corner is a plaque that states:

> 'This aisle
> formerly the nave of
> the parish church was
> rebuilt in loving memory of
> the poet pastor
> the good John Moultrie
> fifty years Rector of Rugby born
> December, 31st 1799
> and died December 26th 1874 of illness
> caught in visiting
> the sick of his flock
> His life for the sheep
> the good shepherd giveth
> his life for the sheep.'

The Reverend Moultrie died having contracted smallpox after it broke out in the town in 1874 – he insisted on minister-ing to those inhabitants who were struck down with it.

## Rushbrooke SUFFOLK

ST NICHOLAS The main structure of this church dates from 1540.

The nave seating is arranged like that in a college chapel with facing pinnacled stalls returned at the w end. Above these stalls is an organ case with pipes but there is no organ, nor is there room for one! The carving and installation were done by Colonel Rushbrooke c.1850.

Above the beam at the entrance to the chancel is the unique and huge Royal Arms of Henry VIII, which is the only large example in the country. Believed to date from 1540 it shows a large portcullis on the left and a Tudor rose on the right with a dragon and a greyhound on either side. There is much doubt as to the authenticity of these Arms as they may in fact be a nineteenth-century copy by Colonel Rushbrooke. (See Royal Arms, page 351.)

Fragments of ancient glass are in the E window and in the nave, much of it surrounded by bright blue glass.

In the s chapel is a charming memorial to 'Mr. Thomas Jermyns. A Hopefull Youth, the only and most dearly beloved Sonne of Thomas Lord Jermyn, and Mary his wife, who most unfortunately lost his life by the accidentall fall of a Mast, on the 27th Day of December 1692: a day never to be forgotten by his unhappy Father and Mother. He was aged 15 Years and 26 Days.' The accident happened on the Thames during a gale.

Near the s door is a rare wooden font dating from c.1850. (See Wooden Fonts, page 34.)

## Rye EAST SUSSEX

ST MARY THE VIRGIN The church, with its low tower surmounted by a short spire, stands at the top of this hilltop town.

The clock is the oldest church turret clock in England still with its original works. It was made by Lewys Billiard of Winchelsea in 1560. The long pendulum swings to and fro under the tower. The clock face and 'quarter-boys' (fat gilded cherubs) on the N face of the tower were added in 1760. They strike the quarters not the hours. The quarter-boys, removed in August 1969 and replaced by fibreglass copies as the originals were badly decayed, stand in the Clere chapel. The clock is now driven electrically.

Also in the Clere chapel is a fine mahogany table, richly carved, dating from c.1735.

In the N aisle is a stained-glass window by Burne-Jones to the memory of Mary Tiltman (d. 30 December 1881). It shows the Magi visiting the Infant Jesus, who leans forward on His mother's lap while five attendant angels look on.

The Royal Arms of Queen Anne, dated 1704, hang above the chancel arch.

Almost every church in England and Wales has at least one bell with which to call people to prayer. Sometimes they have two and many have at least four or more. When the number exceeds two, they are usually hung in a tower, which is stronger than a bellcote and is necessary if the bells are to be rung instead of being merely chimed. Bell-ringing involves the bell being attached to a wheel and turned 360 degrees. This is a British invention and is not found elsewhere except where it has been taken abroad by people anxious to copy the British tradition. Chiming involves swinging the bell from side to side by pulling on a rope until the clapper inside the bell hits the bell itself.

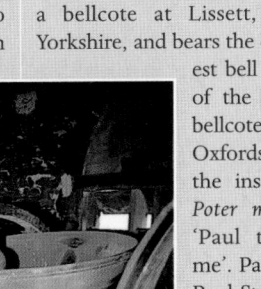

*Eynsham, Oxfordshire.*

On the Continent and elsewhere bell-ringing is effected by means of a hammer striking a hanging bell. Where a number of bells are involved these are called a carillon. In Loughborough, Leicestershire, there is a famous carillon in Queen's Park dating from 1923; it is a memorial to those who died in the First World War.

The lightest bell in a ring is known as the treble, while the heaviest is the tenor. The weights of tenor bells vary considerably from tower to tower. It should be pointed out that a number of bells are called a 'ring'; the word 'peal' refers to the sound made by the bells.

The oldest tower bell in the British Isles hangs in Hardham, West Sussex. Dating from before 1100, it weighs 50 kg (1 cwt). The oldest dated bell hangs in a bellcote at Lissett, East Riding of Yorkshire, and bears the date 1254. The oldest bell bearing the name of the maker hangs in a bellcote at West Challow, Oxfordshire, and carries the inscription, '*Povel le Poter me fist*', meaning 'Paul the Potter made me'. Paul's full name was Paul Stahlschmidt and he was known to have been bell founding in London between 1283 and 1312. The use of the Norman-French form of '*fist*' instead of '*fecit*' suggests that the Challow bell was cast at the beginning of Paul's business career, *c*.1284. (Many years ago I was chiming this bell and its neighbour in the bell-cote prior to an evening service. The acting clergyman, (not the resident one), did not know where the church was, and had begun to make his way down a track leading to a farmyard. On hearing the bells chiming, however, he was able to locate the church exactly, thus proving the point that bells do have a purpose!)

Other old bells can be seen at Caversfield and Goring-on-Thames (both in Oxfordshire). The bell at Caversfield can be dated to *c*.1200-10 and is no longer rung, but claims to be the oldest inscribed bell in the British Isles. The inscription reads, 'In honour of God and St.Lawrence, Hugh Gargatt and Sibilla his wife had these bells erected.' The bell at Goring carries a prayer for Peter Quivil, Bishop of

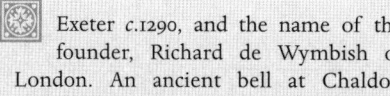

Exeter *c*.1290, and the name of the founder, Richard de Wymbish of London. An ancient bell at Chaldon (Surrey) was stolen many years ago but a plaster replica of it now hangs in the porch.

The vast majority of church towers with rings of bells carry six or eight, but some of the larger churches and cathedrals have ten or 12 bells that can be rung although they may have extra bells that are chimed or used as clock bells. As will be noticed, bells are usually hung in even numbers for ringing but at All Saints in Basingstoke (Hampshire) the only true ring of nine bells in the world can be found.

St Andrew in Rugby, Warwickshire, is the only church in the world with two separate rings of bells – five in the w tower and eight in the NE tower.

Once a bell has been cast in the bell foundry (normally a little thicker than required) it has to be tuned by removing slivers of metal until the required note has been reached. The thickness of the metal determines the note, as does the bell's size – a large bell has a deeper tone than a small one. The six bells at St Veep (Cornwall) are reputed to be the only 'virgin' ring in the world, meaning that the bells were cast perfectly tuned. Bell metal is usually a bronze alloy comprising approximately 70 per cent copper and 30 per cent tin.

It is impossible to establish where the oldest original rings of bells are, as individual bells are frequently recast when they have become cracked or damaged. However, St Bartholomew-the-Great, Smithfield (London), and St Lawrence, Ipswich (Suffolk), both possess rings of five bells dating from *c*.1510, making them the only churches in England and Wales with more than four pre-Reformation bells. St John the Baptist in Cirencester, Gloucestershire, has the distinction of having the first ring of 12 bells in the world. Dating from 1722, they were cast by Rudhall of Gloucester. Unfortunately, some of the bells have had to be recast, most recently in 1952.

Crowland Abbey (Lincolnshire) claims to have had the first ring of bells in England, dating from *c*.1000, but the six bells there now are not the originals. St Peter in North Hayling (Hants.) contains the oldest ring of three bells in England, each one dating from *c*.1350. They are unconventional in that they are fixed to half shafts and only rung once. Horham (Suffolk) is the proud possessor of the oldest ring of eight bells in the world. The oldest bell is dated 1568 (the tenor bell), while the youngest bell is the treble and dates from 1673. They were silent from 1911 until they were rehung in a metal frame and ringing commenced again in 1990.

Harwell (Oxon.) possessed the oldest ring of six bells in England until they were increased to eight in 1932, but the old bells were left untouched. The six ancient bells are dated 1590, 1597, 1611 (two bells), 1612 and 1615. Derby Cathedral has the oldest ring of ten bells in the world.

The following list, to the best of my knowledge, includes the lightest and heaviest rings of bells that can be rung in churches *and* cathedrals of England and Wales, along with the weights of their respective tenor bells. As you will see, they are not only the lightest/heaviest in England and Wales, but also in the world!

*Bells at Eynsham, Oxfordshire.*

12 BELLS
Lightest ring in the world: Grundisburgh, Suffolk – 416.86 kg (8 cwt 0 qr 23 lb)
Heaviest ring in the world: Liverpool Anglican Cathedral, Merseyside – 4171 kg (82 cwt 0 qr 11 lb)

10 BELLS
Lightest ring in the world: Tollesbury, Essex – 363.78 kg (7 cwt 0 qr 18 lb)
Heaviest ring in the world: Wells Cathedral, Somerset – 2864.03 kg (56 cwt 1 qr 14 lb)

8 BELLS
Lightest ring in the world: Highbridge, Somerset – 147.42 kg (2 cwt 3 qr 17 lb)
Heaviest ring in the world: Sherborne Abbey, Dorset – 2339.22 kg (46 cwt 0 qr 5 lb)

6 BELLS
Lightest ring in the world: Warden Hill in Cheltenham, Gloucestershire – 28. 58 kg (0 cwt 2 qr 7 lb)

5 BELLS
Heaviest ring in the world: St Buryan, Cornwall – 1909.20 kg (37 cwt 2 qr 9 lb)

5 BELLS
Lightest ring in England and Wales: Swineshead, Bedfordshire – 130.18 kg (2 cwt 2 qr 7 lb)
(The lightest ring of 5 bells in the world is in Fettes College Chapel, Edinburgh, Scotland; the tenor bell weighs 120.20 kg/2 cwt 1 qr 13 lb.)
Heaviest ring in the world using conventional ropes and wheels: East Pennard, Somerset – 1261.46 kg (24 cwt 3 qr 9 lb)
Heaviest ring in the world (this has no ropes and the bells are rung by force of hand applied directly to the bell): East Bergholt, Suffolk – 1324.51 kg (26 cwt 0 qr 8 lb)

NOTE: visit the Central Council of Church Bell Ringers website on www.cccbr.org.uk for the most up-to-date information.

St Albans Abbey, Hertfordshire, has the oldest cathedral tower in England constructed by the Normans with Roman bricks.

# St Albans     Hertfordshire

THE CATHEDRAL AND ABBEY CHURCH OF
ST ALBAN This massive cathedral and
abbey on its hill dominates the surrounding countryside on its s side and can
be seen from the M25 motorway that
encircles London. It is, in fact, the highest-
situated cathedral in the British Isles, the
floor of the nave being 97.54 m (320 feet)
above sea level. It only became a cathedral
in 1877.

 At the Dissolution of the Monasteries in
1539 the monastic buildings (except the
church and Great Gateway) were demolished. In 1553 the church was bought by
the townspeople for £400 and became
their parish church.

    This cathedral stands on the site of the
execution of St Alban, Britain's first
Christian martyr (d. c.250). Refusing to
worship the pagan gods of Rome, Alban
declared, 'I worship and adore the true
and living God Who created all things.'

 The central tower, at 43.89 m (144 feet)
high, is the oldest cathedral tower in
England and the only ancient one over an
English cathedral to be built of brick. The
Normans built it between 1077 and 1115,
using Roman tile-like bricks from the
ruins of nearby Verulamium. Its walls are
2.13 m (7 feet) thick.

 The w front and the N and s ends of the
transepts were almost entirely rebuilt at
the expense of Lord Grimthorpe from
1880 onwards. The work has been much
criticized, but there is no doubt that had

nothing been done, much of the abbey
would have been reduced to ruins. Some
people positively like the 'Grimthorpe
Pepperpots' at the w end!

 Inside the central w porch on the N wall
a face is carved in the middle of eagle's
wings. This is said to depict Lord
Grimthorpe.

 On the s wall of the N porch at the w
end is a large graffito of an eagle. Many
other graffiti including several dates
remain throughout the cathedral including much defacing of the lower parts of
the nave piers. Some of the graffiti represent masons' marks such as symbols and
geometric patterns.

 The nave is 84 m (275 feet 6 inches) long,
the longest medieval nave in existence.
The total length of the cathedral is
167.64 m (550 feet) – the second longest
church in the British Isles; Winchester
Cathedral (see page 415) is 1.83 m (6 feet)
longer.

 The nave is unusual in possessing three
distinct styles of architecture – six
Norman and four Early English bays on
the N side and five Decorated and five
Early English on the s side.

 On seven Norman piers on the NE side
of the nave are finely preserved wall paint-
ings dating from c.1215 and c.1350. Several
depict the Crucifixion and were done by a
group of painters who made St Albans
famous. In pre-Reformation times an altar
would have existed underneath all of the
paintings since they would have acted as a
reredos.

The rood screen, separating the nave from the chancel (or the monks' church from the people's church) dates from c.1350. It has lost all its statues and is much damaged but its processional doors are a fine feature.

In the triforium of the s transept are interesting Saxon baluster shafts which came from the first abbey church, built by the Saxons c.790. They were re-used by the Normans.

The five lancets on the s side of the s transept are the second tallest in England, the centre one being 18.29 m (60 feet) high. (The tallest are in the central tower of Liverpool's Anglican Cathedral.) The three central lancets are taller outside than inside!

Behind the high altar is the beautiful reredos, one of only two great screens in England that stand so high (the other being at Winchester Cathedral, see page 415). It was built in 1484 by William de Wallingford. At the Dissolution all the statues were destroyed, but from 1884 to 1899 the first Lord Aldenham had new figures made and the tabernacle work, above, restored.

Immediately below the Great Screen is a smaller reredos directly above the altar. This depicts Christ rising from the tomb and was carved by Sir Alfred Gilbert, RA from 1890 to 1899. It is made of marble and shells and is, in fact, unfinished.

On the floor of the choir in front of the high altar is a slab covering 11 abbots and four monks who were buried here when their bones were removed during the building of the new chapter house.

On the n side of the sanctuary is the chantry chapel of Abbot Thomas Ramryge (1492–1521). Built of clunch (tough clay) it completely occupies the bay in which it is built and rises almost to the top of the choir arch. This chantry, of the stone-cage type, has two storeys. In the lower stage is a beautiful fan-vaulted roof.

In the spandrels of the arch over the s doorway are carvings showing St Alban's martyrdom. Look out for the abbot's rebus – a ram wearing a collar on which appear the letters 'RYGE'.

The choir ceiling shows interesting painted panels and has been virtually untouched since it was painted between 1368 and 1377.

Behind the high altar are the remains of St Alban's shrine, which was destroyed in 1539 and re-erected between 1872 and 1875 from over 2000 pieces found in the wall that formerly blocked the lady chapel from the remainder of the cathedral. The missing pieces of the Purbeck marble shrine were originally replaced in wood, but in 1991 these were in turn replaced by Purbeck marble with a new red silk canopy above. The Shrine today looks very much as it did in the Middle Ages.

The ironwork around the shrine was designed by George Pace and dedicated in 1967.

On the n side of the shrine is the oak watching loft dating from c.1400. This is one of only two watching lofts surviving in the British Isles. (The other is near St Frideswide's shrine in Oxford Cathedral, see page 263.) The watching loft was occupied by a monk who kept watch on pilgrims visiting the shrine to ensure that nothing was damaged or stolen.

On the s side of the shrine is the fine tomb of Humphrey, Duke of Gloucester (1391–1447), brother of Henry V and founder of the Bodleian Library, Oxford. It dates from 1446. On the outside of the tomb is a fine grille of Sussex ironwork dating from 1275.

In the n ambulatory, behind the watching loft, is the magnificent brass of Abbot Thomas de la Mare (1349–96). At 3.04 m (10

*St Albans Abbey, Hertfordshire – the longest medieval nave in the world with a Victorian west end.*

feet) long and 1.22 m (4 feet) wide, it is the largest ecclesiastical brass in England and one of the finest in existence.

 Note the fine carvings of rural scenes on the back of the watching loft.

 High on the wall near Ramryge's chantry in the N ambulatory is one of the original painted panels from the tower ceiling dated *c.*1450. It was taken down in 1952 and at the same time a new ceiling was erected beneath the old to a similar design.

 At the E end of the N ambulatory near the lady chapel are the remains of the shrine to Amphibalus (*c.*1350), the Christian priest who, after fleeing Roman persecution, was given shelter by Alban. After Alban became a Christian he gave himself up in place of Amphibalus, refusing to denounce his faith in Jesus, and died a martyr's death.

 At the E end of the cathedral is the lady chapel (*c.*1300–20). The little statues in the jambs and centre mullions of each window are an interesting feature, although many are damaged. Around the edge of each window are fine examples of the ball-flower ornament.

After the Dissolution, the lady chapel was used as a school and a wall built at the w end to separate it from the cathedral. This was finally removed in 1872 when the lady chapel was reunited with the remainder of the cathedral. During the restoration new corbels were added where the roof ribs spring from the wall – superb examples of Victorian carving by John Baker.

 The chapter house to the s of the cathedral was officially opened by HM the Queen on 8 July 1982 on the site of the medieval one. It houses a refectory, shop,

library and numerous other facilities including a crypt and educational centre.

▩ Outside the s door of the s transept in the entrance lobby of the chapter house are the two original w doors of the abbey dating from c.1450. They were removed by Lord Grimthorpe when he rebuilt the w end.

▩ In Sumpter Yard to the SE of the cathedral is a fine cedar tree brought from Lebanon by Countess Spencer and planted on 25 March 1803.

▩ To the w of the abbey church is the original gatehouse to the abbey dating from 1362 and now forming part of St Albans School.

## St Audries                    SOMERSET

See WEST QUANTOXHEAD, page 403.

## St David's                PEMBROKESHIRE

THE CATHEDRAL CHURCH OF ST DAVID
This ancient cathedral stands in a valley in the extreme w of Pembrokeshire, almost hidden from the small town that lies to the SE.

▩ The octagonal tower attached to the gatehouse at the SE corner of the churchyard contains a ring of eight bells.

▩ The unique magnificent nave roof of Irish oak is attributed to the Treasurer, Owen Pole (1472–1509). It consists of pendent bosses running in two rows down the entire length of the nave and connected by a series of arches.

▩ The rood screen, dating from c.1340, occupies half of the easternmost bay of the nave and is one of the finest examples of a medieval stone screen. The s side contains the tomb of Bishop Gower (Bishop from 1328 to 1347), the builder of

the screen. Inside the vault are rare 'flying ribs'; other examples may be seen at Bristol Cathedral, Lincoln Cathedral, Southwell Cathedral and Warwick (see pages 51, 199, 326 and 384 respectively).

▩ The space below the tower is used by the choir and is unique in possessing a second parclose screen, thus totally enclosing it.

The first prebendal stall, marked by the Royal Arms, is always held by the reigning monarch – an honour unique to St David's. It was occupied by Queen Elizabeth II on 7 August 1955.

Many of the fifteenth-century misericords in the choir are worth inspecting. One shows a carpenter building a boat, in another a man is rowing, and in one, a man leans over the side of a boat as if seasick! Yet another shows two men, possibly suffering from sciatica.

On the s side of the sanctuary is a very rare *wooden* sedilia dating from c.1450. It has rich delicate carving.

▩ Behind the high altar are three blocked lancet windows, magnificent examples of Early English work. The mosaics are by Salviati of Venice and were completed in 1871.

▩ On the N side of the sanctuary are the remains of St David's shrine, dating from 1275.

▩ Behind the three blocked lancet windows is the Holy Trinity chapel, which has a beautiful fan vault that was erected c.1510. It carries the arms of Henry VII and of Bishop Vaughan (1509–23), who had constructed it. (See Fan Vaulting, page 152.)

▩ In the w wall of the Holy Trinity chapel, underneath the blocked lancets, is an oak casket containing bones believed to be those of St David.

▩ In the E wall of the s transept is the Abraham stone commemorating Bishop

Abraham's sons Hed and Isaac who were killed by the Norsemen c.1050.

Elsewhere, throughout the cathedral, ancient stones can be seen on which are carved crosses. These make up one of the most important collections anywhere in the British Isles.

▨ At the E end of the cathedral is the lady chapel. This was restored and re-roofed c.1900. At its extreme E end is an unusual fifteenth-century roof boss depicting three hares but with only three ears between them. (See The Three Hares, page 412.)

## St Enodoc     CORNWALL

ST ENODOC This church, which can only be approached over the golf course, was buried in the sands until it was dug out in 1860 and restored from 1863 to 1873.

▨ Near the lych gate, on the s side of the churchyard, the famous poet laureate Sir John Betjeman (28 August 1906–19 May 1984) is buried. Born in Parliament Hill Mansions, in northwest London, he died in his cottage near here.

▨ Near Sir John's grave is that of his mother, Mabel (d. 1952).

▨ Inside the church, which is still lit by paraffin and candles, is a plaque to Sir John's father, Ernest Betjemann (the family later dropped the second 'n'), who died in 1934.

▨ In the churchyard also are the graves of a John Mably and Alice, his daughter (1687), who died within six days of each other. The slate memorial is reputed to be the last incised slab with effigies in England.

## St Just-In-Roseland     CORNWALL

ST JUST & ST MAWES occupies a unique position on the edge of a creek amid a wealth of sub-tropical foliage. Writing in his book *In Search of England*, H. V. Morton says of the churchyard:

'I would like to know if there is in the whole of England a churchyard more beautiful than this. There is hardly a level yard in it. You stand at the lychgate and look down into a green cup filled with flowers and arched by great trees. In the dip is the little church, its tower level with you as you stand above. The white gravestones rise up from ferns and flowers.'

▨ Inside the church are some unique wooden roof bosses on the fine medieval barrel roof over the chancel. They are square and flat and have designs painted on their flat lower faces. Some of the paintings show emblems of the Passion and there is also some good Greek lettering. (The only other example of Greek lettering on bosses is at Spreyton, Devon.)

The late C. J. P. Cave, an authority on medieval roof bosses, said that the bosses here were the only uncarved painted bosses known to him.

## St Mary-in-the-Marsh     KENT

ST MARY The church can be found in a small village in the middle of Romney Marsh, about 3 km (2 miles) from the sea.

▨ Under a simple wooden board in the churchyard, carved by her husband, lies the writer E. Nesbit (1858–1924), author of *The Railway Children*, *Five Children and It*, and other stories. There is a plaque to her memory inside the church, by the door. Her real name was Mrs Hubert Bland.

# WEDGWOOD FONTS

As far as I know there are five baptismal fonts in existence made of black basalt by the founder of the famous pottery firm, Josiah Wedgwood (1730–95). Only two of these still remain in churches – at Cardington, Bedfordshire, and a few miles away at Essendon, Hertfordshire.

The other three fonts are located in the Lady Lever Art Gallery at Port Sunlight, Merseyside, the Wedgwood Museum at Barlaston, Staffordshire, and the Buten Museum of Wedgwood at Merion, Pennsylvania, USA.

Interestingly, three of the five known Wedgwood fonts are connected with Samuel Whitbread I (1720–96), founder of the brewery that still bears his name and a great friend of Josiah Wedgwood. Whitbread's daughter, Harriot, donated the font to Cardington Church in 1783. Samuel Whitbread I was born in Cardington

In 1765 Samuel moved to Bedwell Park in the parish of Essendon, Hertfordshire. In 1777–8 the parish church underwent a complete rebuilding. On completion in 1778 Mary Whitbread, half-sister of Harriot, presented a Wedgwood font to the church, almost identical to that given by Harriot to Cardington. This font nearly left Essendon c.1880 when the present building was being constructed and Richard Green, who had lived at the Mill, Essendon, emigrated to Australia. Anxious to have a tangible reminder of his native village in England he wrote to the vicar requesting the Wedgwood font for his church there. The font had been discarded in the belfry since c.1850 and the vicar agreed to its removal to Australia. Fortunately for Essendon, however, no one was willing to pay the freight charges and, happily, the font remains in Essendon, though not of course in the original church to which it was donated, the present building having been completed in 1883.

When the fonts were used for baptisms, a small silver bowl to hold the water would be placed on a pedestal inside them. On the bottom of the Essendon bowl the inscription reads:

'Mary Whitbread
Born at Bedwell Park gave the font and this vase to the Church of Essendon in the County of Hertfordshire.
MDCCLXXVIII'

The font that is now in the Buten Museum was probably the one made for Emma Whitbread, Lady St John, third daughter of Samuel Whitbread I, and given by her to Melchbourne Church, Bedfordshire, in 1786. It is marked 'Wedgwood and Bentley'. Melchbourne Church was rebuilt by Samuel Whitbread I in 1788. For some reason this font also was removed from the church c.1850 (the same time as the one at Essendon), but instead of being lodged in the tower it was put in Melchbourne House, where it remained until c.1938, when the contents of the house were sold and dispersed. After numerous adventures a font identical to the Melchbourne one was sold in 1959 in Kettering, Northamptonshire, to Mr Harry Buten, founder of the Buten Museum of Wedgwood in Merion, USA. There is little doubt that this is the missing font from Melchbourne Church.

Of the five known Wedgwood fonts, two are in churches and are dated as follows:

1. Essendon (St Mary the Virgin), Hertfordshire – 1778
2. Cardington (St Mary), Bedfordshire – 1783

How many more fonts remain to be discovered, perhaps being used as flower vases or garden ornaments?

# St Mellion or Mellion    CORNWALL

ST MELANIUS stands in a little village just outside Saltash on the A388.

On a wall of the chancel is a brass to Peter Coryton (d. 1551) and his wife, Jane, with their 17 sons and seven daughters! This is the largest number of children by one mother that survives in brass. He wears armour and she is dressed in a long gown with an attractive triangular head-dress.

# Salisbury    WILTSHIRE

THE CATHEDRAL CHURCH OF THE BLESSED VIRGIN MARY Dominating the surrounding countryside, this beautiful cathedral is unique in being the only one to be built entirely in the Early English style of architecture (with the exception of the spire) and in which the plan remains the same today as when it was built, c.1220–84. This cannot be claimed of any other ancient cathedral in England.

The original cathedral, at Old Sarum, was founded by St Osmund, bishop from 1078 to 1099.

The spire is the highest in England at 123.14 m (404 feet) and the third highest in Europe. It was built c.1334–80 and is only 23 cm (9 inches) thick.

The spire leans 74 cm (29 inches) to the SW. A brass plate in the centre of the crossing marks the spot where the centre of the spire should be.

The Purbeck marble piers supporting the central spire on the NW side are markedly bent due to the excessive weight being carried above – about 6,604,416 kg (6500 tons)!

Between the NW and NE piers and the SW and SE piers supporting the central tower and spire are Perpendicular strainer arches built by Bishop Beauchamp c.1450 in order to counteract the great weight above.

In the choir is a pair of inverted arches erected c.1380 to prevent the choir from being pushed outwards, due again to the excessive weight of the spire. They are similar to the arches at Wells Cathedral, Somerset, but earlier.

At the base of the spire, but invisible from the floor, is the original fourteenth-century windlass, which was used for lifting materials during the building of the tower and spire. It is still used today for raising stone and timber for the maintenance of the fabric and is one of only six ancient tread-wheels remaining in our churches. (The others are at Beverley Minster – see page 26; Canterbury Cathedral – see page 61; Louth – see page 226; and Durham and Peterborough cathedrals.)

The original timbering used in the construction of the spire is still retained inside to strengthen it.

On each side of the N door are two beautiful engraved windows by Laurence Whistler depicting the rose of fulfilment, radiant with the light of eternity. They were dedicated on 23 March 1985 in memory of two sisters of Christopher Booker.

In the N aisle is the famous clock – the oldest remaining mechanical clock in working condition in the world. It was made in 1386, probably on the orders of Bishop Ralph Erghum, who later moved to Wells in 1388 where he may have ordered the clock there to be made in c.1390. Both clocks are almost certainly by the same craftsman.

This clock was originally installed in the now-demolished detached bell tower, and is designed to strike every four hours – like all clocks of this period. It has neither face nor quarter-jacks and is now connected to the bishop's bell in the triforium which used to warn the bishop as the times of services approached.

🔲 In the N transept is a cope chest dating from c.1290 that is still in use and a beautiful plaster model of the cathedral, dating from c.1825. This is the work of Sir James Pennethorne, chief assistant of John Nash, the Regency architect.

🔲 On the N wall of the N transept are two of the remaining 19 consecration crosses that survive from the original 24 painted or incised on the walls at the original consecration of the cathedral in 1258. They are painted in their original colours of red, green and gold.

🔲 On the N side of the choir near the gateway is the ancient hand-winch. This was used to raise and lower the Lenten veil. Its preservation is due to its being hidden under panelling.

🔲 Also on the N side of the choir is the chantry chapel of Bishop Edmund Audley (d. 1524). It has a fan-vaulted ceiling and is the only remaining chantry chapel in the cathedral still in its original place.

🔲 Notice the finely carved playful 'dragon' with two young ones at the base of the NW pillars in the E or Trinity chapel.

🔲 The E lancets of the Trinity chapel are filled with glowing blue glass and are known as the Prisoners of Conscience Window. Unveiled on 14 May 1980, they were designed and made by Gabriel and Jacques Loire at Leves near Chartres, France.

🔲 At the E end of the s choir aisle is a large monument to Edward Seymour (1539–1621), Earl of Hertford, son of Protector Somerset and nephew of Jane Seymour, Queen of England and cousin to Edward VI. At his side lies his wife, Lady Catherine Grey, sister to Lady Jane Grey, who was Queen of England for nine days.

The kneeling figures are their sons, Edward and Thomas.

🔲 In the s choir aisle is the former *iron* chantry chapel of Walter, Lord Hungerford (d. 1449). This was restored in 1778 by the Earl of Radnor for use as the Radnor family pew. It has a painted ceiling comprising shields and pendants.

🔲 Near the SE transept is the beautiful tomb of Giles de Bridport (Bishop from 1257 to 1262). He was bishop when the cathedral was consecrated. The tomb is one of the earliest of its kind and is a rare specimen of Geometrical architecture similar to the thirteenth-century triforium in Westminster Abbey (see page 219). The carvings on the sides represent scenes from the bishop's life and his recumbent effigy is of Purbeck marble.

🔲 At the E end of the s nave aisle is the mailed stone effigy of William Longespee (d. 1226) with a superb shield over his left arm. Very unusually it rests on a *wooden* tomb-chest. He was the first person to be buried in the cathedral and his is the oldest effigy of a soldier in England.

🔲 Near Longespee's effigy are the remains of St Osmund's shrine. It has three recesses on the N and s sides to allow crippled pilgrims to insert their afflicted limbs as closely as possible to the bones of the Saint in the hope of being cured.

🔲 The w window of the nave contains early glass dating from c.1270 and French glass from c.1450-1550.

🔲 In the NE transept is a unique brass to Bishop Wyville (Bishop from 1330 to 1375, during which time the spire was built). The brass is 2.29 m (7 feet 6 inches) long and shows the bishop in ecclesiastical vestments looking out of his many-turreted Sherborne Castle (Dorset), while below him stands his champion on guard armed with a shield and something like a coal pick! At the foot of the brass are quaint little figures of rabbits disappearing into their burrows.

*The cloisters on the south side of Salisbury Cathedral, Wiltshire, showing an ancient cedar tree.*

The cloisters on the s side of the cathedral are the largest and earliest of any English cathedral. Dating from 1263 to 1270 the walks are 55.17 m (181 feet) long. One of the cedar trees in the garth was planted in 1837.

The n walk of the cloisters is very unusual in being placed a short distance from the s aisle of the cathedral, the intervening space now being occupied by the cathedral shop, refreshment room and toilets. Originally called the Plumbery, it allowed room for materials and workmen to effect repairs to the cathedral.

Along the w walk are numerous carved stones and four ancient bells, one dated 1585.

Over the e walk is the library, built in 1445 and housing many interesting unique books and manuscripts including an original copy of Magna Carta (1215). This is one of four contemporary copies and only lacks the seal. (The others are in Lincoln Cathedral [one] and two in the British Library, London.)

From the e walk a passage leads into the octagonal chapter house, built in the Geometrical Decorated style, c.1280. A single central pillar supports the vaulted roof. Above the niches around the walls are sculptures depicting Old Testament stories. Some of the glass dates from the sixteenth and seventeenth centuries.

The close around the cathedral was completely walled in c.1333. In 1331 King Edward III gave the bishop and chapter all the stone from the old cathedral at Old Sarum for the building of the wall and many of them still display Norman carving. Salisbury Close is the largest and most beautiful close in the world.

## Sandon          STAFFORDSHIRE

ALL SAINTS is situated in a lovely position with extensive views from its churchyard.

On the NE side of the chancel is an alabaster slab bearing the incised effigies of Hugh and Cecile Erdeswicke (1473) – the finest incised slab in Staffordshire. The Erdeswickes descended from the Normans, and one of the most famous among them was Samson Erdeswicke, an antiquary (d. 1603). Other Erdeswickes are also commemorated.

Next to a monument commemorating Samson Erdeswicke (d. 1603) on the n side of the chancel is an extremely rare *trompe l'oeil* painting showing a Y-traceried window (a window with one central mullion that divides into two at the top to make a Y shape). On each side of this are two family trees carrying shields on their branches which grow out of the family tombs below them.

Under the n side of the Harrowby pew is a carving of Lady Harrowby's Cairn bitch, Tory, and on the s side one of Tory's puppies whose sale helped to pay for this work! It was completed in 1928. Lady Harrowby was the wife of one of the earls of Harrowby who lived at nearby Sandon Park.

Near the main door is a pillar alms-box in memory of Francis Perkin, aged 24, who died 6 June 1848 when a stone fell on him during the fire that destroyed the hall. A piece of this stone forms the base of the alms-box.

## Scarborough          NORTH YORKSHIRE

ST MARTIN'S-ON-THE-HILL, regarded as a shrine of the Pre-Raphaelites, was consecrated on 11 July 1863. The architect was G. F. Bodley and the work was financed by a Miss M. Craven at a cost of £10,000.

At the end of the front pew in the nave is a small brass plaque inscribed, 'Miss Mary Craven's pew'. She died in March 1889.

There are nearly 30 stained-glass windows by such famous artists as Burne-Jones, Ford Maddox Brown, William Morris, D. Rossetti and Philip Webb. Other windows by these artists can be seen at Harris Mansfield College Chapel (Oxford), Middleton Cheney (Northamptonshire), Selsley (Gloucestershire), Speldhurst (Kent) and Wilden (Worcestershire).

## Scopwick     LINCOLNSHIRE

HOLY CROSS The church is found in a pretty village set in quiet countryside; much of it was rebuilt in Victorian times.

On the jambs of the s doorway are some interesting graffiti, including numerous crosses.

About 228.6 m (250 yards) N of the church is the churchyard extension dominated by the Cross of Sacrifice. Here several British and Commonwealth servicemen are buried, as well as Germans. On the left side of the Cross, in the middle of the second row, is buried PO John Gillespie Magee (9 June 1922–11 December 1941). He died while Cloud Flying from RAF Digby when his Spitfire VB AD291 collided with an Oxford aircraft from RAF Cranwell. He bailed out, but his parachute failed to open properly and he was killed instantly on impact.

He is especially remembered for his poem 'High Flight', which was quoted by President R. Reagan on the occasion of the *Challenger* disaster at Cape Canaveral in January 1986. There is a copy of the poem in the church. It runs as follows:

'Oh! I have slipped the surly bonds of Earth
And danced the skies on laughter-silvered wings;
Sunward I've climbed, and joined the tumbling mirth

Of sun-split clouds, – and done a hundred things
You have not dreamed of – wheeled and soared and swung
High in the sunlit silence. Hov'ring there,
I've chased the shouting wind along, and flung
My eager craft through footless halls of air . . .
Up, up the long, delirious burning blue
I've topped the wind-swept heights with easy grace
Where never lark, or even eagle flew –
And, while with silent, lifting mind I've trod
The high untrespassed sanctity of space,
Put out my hand, and touched the face of God.'

PO Magee wrote this beautiful poem on 3 September 1941.

## Seal     KENT

ST PETER & ST PAUL is situated high above this large village. On its N side this church has fine views from its churchyard.

At the E end of the s aisle is a very beautiful unique bronze figure of a child encased in an angel's wings. It is in memory of an Elizabeth Louise Mills (21 March 1902–11 June 1908), only daughter of Geoffrey and Grace Mills.

On the s wall of the s aisle is a tablet to Grace Ellis (1828–1909), 'placed here by the Mills family in remembrance of 54 years' constant love and devotion. "God gives us love: something to love He lends us."'

Grace would have nursed Elizabeth Mills.

In the s aisle is part of a palimpsest brass dated 1577.

A finely preserved brass commemorates

Sir William de Bryene (d.1395). It is 1.37 m (4 feet 6 inches) long and shows a lion at his feet and a bugle at his head.

## Selborne      HAMPSHIRE

ST MARY is in the village of the Reverend Gilbert White (1720–93), the famous naturalist who wrote *The Natural History of Selborne*, published in 1788.

▦ Gilbert White's grave is NE of the church, close to the vestry door. A plain rounded headstone is engraved simply, 'G. W., 26 June, 1793'.

▦ The base of the famous yew tree mentioned by Gilbert White can be seen near the s porch. The tree was blown down on 25 January 1990; it was about 1400 years old!

▦ Inside the porch is a section of the main bough of the tree, the growth rings of which go back to 1549.

▦ On the s door is ironwork dating from *c.*1250.

▦ On the s side of the church a beautiful window depicts St Francis preaching to the birds. Given in 1920 in memory of Gilbert White, it shows 82 birds (all mentioned in his book) as well as his home, the church and former yew tree and the White coat of arms.

▦ The E window near by also commemorates Gilbert White and carries the inscription, 'God be praised. For a faithful priest. A humble student of nature. And writer of genius. *Anno Domini*, 1993.'

Three roundels depict a fox, rabbits, tortoise, hedgehog and stoat with numerous flowers superimposed on a green cross, adorned with lilies.

▦ Below this window is an unusual communion table designed by Philip Hussey and Peter Legg and made from the largest boughs of the old yew tree. It took eight years to complete and was first used on 25 January 1998.

▦ Over the main communion table in the chancel is a triptych attributed to Jan Mostaert, a Flemish painter, *c.*1510. It shows the Adoration of the Magi and was given to the church in 1793 by Gilbert White's brother, Benjamin.

▦ On the N wall of the chancel is a wooden panel from a reredos, also Flemish, *c.*1520.

## Selby      NORTH YORKSHIRE

THE ABBEY CHURCH OF OUR LORD, ST MARY AND ST GERMAIN is the church of a former Benedictine abbey dissolved in 1539 and dominates this Yorkshire town.

▦ The magnificent w doorway is a fine example of Norman work and dates from *c.*1170. The two w towers were raised to their present height in 1935.

▦ The great E window represents the Tree of Jesse and about a quarter is made up of original fourteenth-century glass. It was restored beautifully by William Liversidge in 1891. There are 67 figures in seven lights and the figure of Jesse reclines across the three centre lights.

In one of the clerestory windows, high up on the s side of the choir, is the Washington coat of arms in fourteenth-century glass – the earliest known example of stars and stripes, which formed the design of the American flag. John de Washington was a prior of the abbey and can be traced to the same family as George Washington.

▦ The medieval roof bosses in the nave and chancel are carved from wood and are all gilded. The following are worth noting:

† At the E end of the chancel Christ is represented with His hand raised in blessing.

† Beyond this, farther E, are Joshua's spies carrying grapes.

† At the w end of the chancel is a fine Crucifixion.

*The Gilbert White window at Selborne, Hampshire, installed in 1920.*

†  At the E end of the nave is a depiction of the Holy Trinity three heads with four eyes between them!

†  Near by are three hares with three ears between them and a fourth hare not connected with the other three. (See The Three Hares, page 412.)

†  An elephant with a castle on its back.

These wooden bosses survived the disastrous fire of 19 October 1906 when the nave and chancel roofs were destroyed. They had been fastened with wooden pins which meant that they dropped to the floor as the fire raged and most of them were saved.

▦  The easternmost arches of the fine Norman nave are extremely distorted due to the wet clay on which the abbey is built and the sinking of the foundations of the heavy central tower adjoining it.

▦  The first pillar in the nave on the SE side is called 'Abbot Hugh's Pillar'. Abbot Hugh came from Durham and this pillar is identical to an incised pillar there. Notice that some of the carving on it is incomplete.

▦  As one looks down this Norman nave, notice the differences in the triforium on both the N and S sides above the lower Norman arches.

▦  At the E end of the S nave aisle is a plaque inscribed:

'Near to this Stone lies Archer (John)
Late Saxton (I aver)
Who without Tears thirty four years,
Did Carcases inter,
But Death at last for his works past,
Unto him thus did say,
Leave off thy Trade be not afraid,
But forthwith come away;
Without reply or asking why,
The summons he obey'd,
In seventeen hundred & sixty eight
Resigned his Life and Spade.
Died Sept.15 Aged 74.'

(See also Peterborough Cathedral, Cambs. – page 270 – where another sexton is commemorated.)

# Selworthy       Somerset

All Saints is beautifully situated above the thatched houses of the village and provides a fabulous view of Exmoor from its S door. The outside of the church is periodically coated with a mixture of lime and tallow to protect the stonework – the only church in the district so whitened.

▦  Over the S door is an upper storey, now used as a vestry, which was formerly the Acland pew for the Lord of the Manor and contains its own fireplace. Opening into the church it looks like a private box at the opera. This private pew was installed in 1804.

▦  The W gallery, on which the organ now stands, dates from 1750 and has been described as 'one of the best designed galleries in England'. The workmanship is excellent.

▦  The S aisle is one of the great examples of Perpendicular architecture, with delicate window tracery and a magnificent wagon roof containing many bosses. High up in the W end is the date 1538.

▦  Also at the W end of the S aisle are two sculptured heads by Sir Francis Chantrey to members of the Dyke Acland family. Dating from 1828 and 1837, one is described as 'a good little boy'. His brother died of fever at sea and was buried on Ascension Island.

▦  Behind the altar is a fine reredos depicting angels. It looks like wood carving but is, in fact, exquisite *leather* work, made in 1900 by Philip Burgess, a local tanner.

▦  In the E window of the N aisle are six panes of original medieval glass recovered from a barn at Selworthy Farm.

▦  On the pulpit, which dates from c.1490,

*A Perpendicular window at Selworthy, Somerset.*

is an iron stand with an old hour glass to time the sermons! The pulpit was carved from one tree.

 In the tower are six bells, all of which were cast in 1757 by William Evans of Chepstow. One is inscribed, 'Prosperity to this Parish', and another, 'God preserve our King and kingdom and send us peace'.

## Selsley  GLOUCESTERSHIRE

ALL SAINTS Situated on the side of a hill commanding magnificent views, this church was built 1861–2 by G. F. Bodley and partly financed by Samuel Marling, the wealthy textile manufacturer.

The tower is over 30.5 m (100 feet) high and has a saddleback roof.

The interior is aglow with Pre-Raphaelite stained glass made by William

Morris, Philip Webb, Burne-Jones, D. Rossetti, Ford Maddox Brown and Campfield. This was the first complete scheme of stained glass by William Morris's newly founded firm. The exquisite rose window at the w end depicts the Creation of the World.

## Sheldwich  KENT

ST JAMES The church stands in a small village nestling in beautiful countryside on the A251, s of Faversham.

A brass here, commemorating someone called Joan Mareys (1431) in a shroud and holding an engraved heart, is the earliest shroud brass in England.

## Shelland  SUFFOLK

KING CHARLES THE MARTYR is one of only six churches in England carrying this dedication.

Rebuilt in 1767 by Richard Ray, the box pews and three-decker pulpit date from this time.

On the w wall the Royal Arms commemorate the sovereigns from George III (1760) to Victoria (1837).

The barrel organ was made by H. Bryceson c.1810 and is the only one in regular use. It can play 36 tunes.

## Shenley  HERTFORDSHIRE

ST BOTOLPH was turned into a private chapel in 1978 having been declared redundant in 1972.

In the churchyard under a plain tomb lies Nicholas Hawksmoor (1661–1736), famous architect and pupil of Sir Christopher Wren.

The famous racing driver Graham Hill (15 Feb 1929–29 November 1975) is also buried here.

# STAINED-GLASS SUNDIALS

Following the destruction of much medieval stained glass in churches during the seventeenth century, on the grounds that it was considered idolatrous, stained-glass artists turned their attention to secular subjects. Some chose sundials in stained glass or, more accurately, sundials painted on glass. Because of the difficulty in making them, however, they are not very common.

Sundials were painted on fairly large panes of glass through which a hole had to be drilled to receive the brass gnomon or pin that was used to show the time by its shadow. Inevitably the glass would crack and frequently the gnomon is found to be missing.

Several of the glass sundials still in existence have flies painted on them – a pun on the maxim 'time flies'. In some cases the body of the fly was painted on one side of the glass and the legs on the other, the final result being very realistic. An excellent example of such a fly can be seen at Bucklebury Church, Berkshire. It is dated 1649 and is in a window on the N side of the chancel. Since the sun cannot shine on this side of the church, this sundial is obviously not in its original position. The reason for this is that it came from a neighbouring house!

As far as I know, only eight churches in England and Wales have stained-glass sundials. They are as follows:

*A modern 17th-century-style glass dial, in the Merchant Adventurers' Hall, York*

1. Bucklebury (St Mary), Berkshire – 1649
2. Ledbury (St Michael), Herefordshire – seventeenth century
3. Litchborough (St Martin), Northamptonshire – seventeenth century
4. Lullingstone (St Botolph), Kent – seventeenth century
5. Merton (St Peter), Norfolk – seventeenth century
6. Old Basing (St Mary), Hampshire – 2000 (by John Hayward)
7. Toller Porcorum (St Peter & St Andrew), Dorset – 2000 (by John Hayward)
8. Widdington (St Mary), Essex – 1664

It is interesting to note that two stained-glass sundials from Northill Church, Bedfordshire, are kept in the Church Museum. One is inscribed *'Dum spectas fugio'* ('While you watch I fly'), has a plain glass centre with a painted fly and is complete with its gnomon. It has one crack across the glass. The other, inscribed *'Sic transit gloria mundi'* ('So the glory of this world passes away'), has a decorated centre with two pieces of fruit (possibly apples or plums) and a painted fly. The gnomon is unfortunately missing and the glasswork, although complete, is badly cracked.

*Grimacing gargoyles at Sherborne Abbey, Dorset.*

## Sherborne DORSET

THE ABBEY CHURCH OF ST MARY THE
VIRGIN This beautiful abbey church dominates the lovely Dorset town in which it is
situated. It was dissolved with all the
monasteries in 1539 and sold to the townsfolk for £230 as their parish church in 1540.

On the outside at the s side of the w end
is a smaller blocked arch inserted into a
Norman arch by the monks. This narrow-
ing of the archway in 1437 was one of the
causes of a dispute between the monks
and the townspeople that resulted in a
disastrous fire destroying the nave roof
and tower. The town was compelled to
pay for its reconstruction, which took
about 50 years to complete!

The nave piers are the original Norman
ones encased with Perpendicular
panelling c.1450.

The superb fan vaulting of the nave
dates from c.1490. It is interesting that
there are no pinnacles or flying buttresses
outside to counteract the thrust of the
roof, whereas the choir vault has both.

The fan vaulting of the choir dates from
c.1430 and the base of one of the fans on the
s side has been reddened by the great fire of
1437. Evidence of the fire can also be seen
under the tower arch at the E end of the
nave where the stonework is very reddened
at the bottom, but stops abruptly where a
former stone screen was placed against it.

The fan vaulting of the abbey exhibits
interesting panels between the fans,
similar to lierne vaulting, with numerous
carved bosses where the ribs intersect.
There are 115 bosses in the nave vault and
75 in the choir.

Among the most interesting bosses are
the following:

*Sherborne, Dorset.*

† In the choir: a flaming arrow pointing in the direction in which it was reputed to have been fired by the priest of All Hallows in 1437 when the choir was being fan vaulted. (All Hallows Church was attached to the w end of the abbey but was demolished *c.*1540 when the abbey was dissolved.)

† In the nave: near the tower wall a boss shows a man with a crossbow aiming at the bottom of another man! This may again relate to the quarrel between the monks and townspeople.

† In the e bay a superb boss shows a mermaid holding a comb in one hand and a mirror in the other – the finest example of a mermaid on a roof boss.

† Two bosses have representations of window tracery on them. (Only four other bosses show window tracery and they are all in St Mary Redcliffe, Bristol, see page 52.)

† Another boss has the initials H. E. commemorating the marriage of Henry VII to Elizabeth of York.

† Three bosses show Abbot Ramsam's rebus – the letter 'P' (for Peter), a ram inside the loop and 'SAM' above on a label.

▣ In the s transept is a magnificent marble baroque memorial to John Digby, Third Earl of Bristol, 1698, and his two wives. The sculptor was John Nost. Supporting the roof of this transept are 12 life-size corbel heads dating from *c.*1370.

▣ In the s choir aisle is a Purbeck marble effigy of an abbot, probably Laurence de Bradford (Abbot from 1246 to 1260). The crook of the staff is very unusual and is well preserved.

▣ In the choir are ten misericords dating from *c.*1440. The central one on the n side shows Christ in Majesty, while on the s side there is a depiction of a schoolmaster beating a boy and of a woman beating her husband with a stick!

Some of the elbow rests are also finely carved, especially one depicting a monk reading a book.

▣ At the e end of the abbey are the ambulatory and lady chapel. The latter dates from *c.*1250 and is not quite in line with the Perpendicular choir, which replaced the Norman one. It was difficult for the builders of the fan-vaulted roof to the ambulatory to connect the two and the pendent corbels show their skill in achieving this.

▣ The e end of the lady chapel dates from 1934, when it was returned to the abbey having been the house for the headmaster of Sherborne School from 1560 to 1860. The beautiful engraved glass reredos in the lady chapel was designed and made by Laurence Whistler in 1968. In the centre is

*The nave roof at Sherborne, Dorset.*

the Virgin Mary's crown of lilies and roses and from her initial 'M' spring symbolic vases filled with wheat and grapes.

The candelabra above is inscribed, 'The gift of Mary Whetcombe of Sherborne, 1657'.

⬦ In the N choir aisle is a fragment of the tomb of Abbot Clement (Abbot from 1155 to 1165). This is the earliest English portrait on a tomb.

⬦ The great W window contains modern stained glass by John Hayward and was dedicated on 8 May 1998 in the presence of HM Queen Elizabeth II. It replaced a window by Augustus Pugin which had been badly fired, losing many of the details in the faces of the figures.

⬦ In the tower hangs the heaviest ring of eight bells in the world. The tenor bell weighing 2339.22 kg (2 tons 6 cwt 0qr 5 lb), carries this inscription:

'By Wolsey's gift I measure time for all;
To mirth, to grieffe, to church I serve to call.'

It was presented by Cardinal Wolsey in 1514 (see Bells, page 293.)

## Shipley                    WEST SUSSEX

ST MARY THE VIRGIN is situated in quiet countryside near the little River Adur with a view to the beautiful smock windmill that once belonged to Sussex poet and writer Hilaire Belloc (1870–1953).

⬦ The original lower windows in the central tower and chancel are splayed inside *and* outside – a rare feature.

⬦ On the S side of the chancel is the tomb of one Sir Thomas Caryll (1616) and his wife, Margaret. On the base, their three daughters kneel facing their baby brother in a cradle – another rare feature. (See also Westminster Abbey, London, page 218.)

▩ On the front pew in the nave a brass plate records the visit of the Queen, the Queen Mother and Princess Margaret on 18 October 1952.

▩ A niche in the N wall of the chancel is where Shipley's most treasured possession – the Shipley reliquary – used to be kept. Found in the churchyard and dating from c.1250, it was covered in Limoges enamel. It was stolen during the night of 25 September 1976 and has never been recovered. A cheap replica now stands in the niche.

▩ To the E of the church is the former fourteenth-century porch, moved from the N wall of the church and now used as a tool shed.

▩ Also in the churchyard, s of the s porch, is the grave of the composer John Ireland with the inscription, 'Many waters cannot quench love'.

A plaque fixed to a rough Sarsen stone is inscribed, 'In grateful and loving memory of John Ireland, Hon. D. Mus., Hon. RAM, FRCM, FRCO, Composer, 1879–1962. One of God's noblest works lies here.'

Among other music, John Ireland wrote the famous hymn tune 'Love Unknown' which is usually sung to the hymn 'My song in love unknown'.

## Shobdon                    HEREFORDSHIRE

ST JOHN THE EVANGELIST is approached down a long drive from the main road.

▩ This is the only ecclesiastical example of the Rococo style of architecture in England. It was built by Lord Richard Bateman from 1752 to 1756 when he demolished the Norman church, retaining only its font and thirteenth-century tower.

▩ The interior is very light and all white except for some pale blue decoration.

▩ The N transept was used by the servants at Shobdon Court (now demolished); they sat on benches, while the family from the house occupied the family pew in the s transept, complete with eight chairs and an elegant fireplace in the w wall! The E wall opposite contained the doorway (now closed) leading to the house and approached by steps from the outside.

▩ On the w wall of the s transept is a fine marble bust in memory of Marian, widow of the Third Baron Bateman, who died on 5 July 1970.

▩ Near the s transept is the original Norman font with four curious beasts on the pedestal.

▩ The chancel and transepts are approached through fine hanging triple ogee arches with pendants and all outlined in pale blue.

▩ In the chancel there are two fine eighteenth-century chairs.

▩ Some distance N of the church can be seen the re-erected Norman chancel arch and two doorways from the original church. Exposure to the weather over 200 years has almost completely obliterated the detail. What a tragedy!

## Shoreham                    KENT

ST PETER & ST PAUL is beautifully situated in the village with an avenue of yew trees leading up to the fine fifteenth-century porch.

▩ Across the chancel and s aisle is a fine rood screen dating from c.1490. On the N side are the original doors leading to the loft above.

▩ On the N side of the nave is a wall tablet commemorating the Reverend Vincent Perronet (1694–1785), who was vicar for 57 years and his wife, Charity. Their son,

Edward, wrote the famous hymn 'All Hail the Power of Jesus' Name'. John Wesley was a great friend of Vincent Perronet and Edward's hero. Wesley said of Vincent when he died, 'O that I may follow him in holiness!'

In the s wall is a beautiful Burne-Jones window depicting Joy, Creation and Love in memory of the famous geologist Joseph Prestwick (12 March 1812–23 June 1896).

This was the only window to survive the bombing in the Second World War.

On the w wall is a memorial tablet inscribed thus: 'In remembrance of Harold Copping, born 1864, died 1932 for thirty years resident in this parish. A painter distinguished as an illustrator of Biblical subjects and of the Pilgrim's Progress his pictures inspired the religious imagination of people of many races.'

Many Shoreham residents were among the models used for his biblical pictures and other work.

He is buried in the churchyard directly N of the tower. The inscription on his gravestone reads:

'Here lie Harold Copping, Painter who died 1 July, 1932 and Edith his wife who died 9 December, 1932.

"Nothing is here for tears, nothing to wail

Or knock the breast, no weakness, no contempt,

Dispraise, or blame, nothing but well and fair,

And what may quiet us in a death so noble."

Milton.'

High up at the w end of the church is a painting depicting the return of Lieutenant Verney Cameron, RN from Africa having made the first East–West crossing of that continent in the nineteenth century. He was the son of the vicar. Note the creeper covering the tower and most of the church.

In a window of the N aisle is a roundel of medieval glass depicting a pelican against a red background.

## Shottesbrooke      Berkshire

St John the Baptist This former collegiate church is beautifully situated in parkland near the headquarters of the Landmark Trust and is approached via a road marked 'Private'.

The whole church, with its delicate stone spire (43.3 m / 142 feet high 'to the top of the vane') was built in 1337. Note the fine flint work of the chancel, surpassing that of the nave and transepts. (Designed by Benjamin Ferrey in 1852, Kingswood, St Andrew, near Reigate, Surrey, is a full-size copy of this church.)

The tomb under the window of the N transept commemorates Sir William Trussell, founder of a former college here, and his wife. The effigies have disappeared. Notice that the tomb is wider than the transept!

In the centre of the nave is an excellent brass to a priest and a layman dating from c.1390. Note the swastikas on the priest's robes.

On the N side of the chancel is a unique and curious tomb to William Throckmorton, priest, 1535. He was doctor of laws and was the last warden of the college. He is shown lying in a coffin with a band of stone across his waist to which is fixed a brass inscription. (See Worcester Cathedral, page 430.)

# SEVEN-SACRAMENT FONTS

Seven-sacrament fonts date (with one exception) from *c*.1468 to 1544 and are octagonal in shape. They depict each of the following seven sacraments:

1. Baptism
2. Confirmation
3. Extreme Unction
4. Holy Eucharist or Mass
5. Matrimony
6. Ordination or Holy Orders
7. Penance

The eighth panel is decorated with various subjects, some of which are listed later.

As far as I know, there are 41 seven-sacrament fonts although, sadly, some have been completely defaced or mutilated by the iconoclast. Their exact locations are:

✠ Norfolk

1. Alderford (St John the Baptist)
2. Binham Priory (St Mary) – mutilated
3. Brooke (St Peter)
4. Burgh-next-to-Aylesham (St Mary the Virgin)
5. Cley-next-the-Sea (St Margaret) – mutilated
6. Croxton (All Saints) – completely defaced
7. Earsham (All Saints) – badly disfigured
8. East Dereham (St Nicholas) – dated 1468
9. Gayton Thorpe (St Mary the Virgin)
10. Glandford (St Martin) – Victorian
11. Gorleston (St Andrew) – much mutilated
12. Great Witchingham (St Mary the Virgin)
13. Gresham (All Saints)
14. Little Walsingham (St Mary the Virgin and All Saints)
15. Loddon (Holy Trinity) – some mutilation

16. Marsham (All Saints)
17. Martham (St Mary the Virgin)
18. Norwich (St Peter Mancroft)
19. Norwich Cathedral
20. Salle (St Peter & St Paul)
21. Seething (St Margaret)
22. Sloley (St Bartholomew)
23. South Creake (St Mary the Virgin) – greatly mutilated
24. Wendling (St Peter & St Paul) – some mutilation
25. West Lynn (St Peter)

✠ Suffolk

26. Badingham (St John Baptist)
27. Blythburgh (Holy Trinity) – completely defaced
28. Cratfield (St Mary the Virgin)
29. Denston (St Nicholas)
30. Great Glemham (All Saints)
31. Laxfield (All Saints)
32. Melton (St Andrew)
33. Monk Soham (St Peter)
34. Southwold (St Edmund) – completely defaced
35. Wenhaston (St Peter) – completely defaced
36. Westhall (St Andrew)
37. Weston (St Peter)
38. Woodbridge (St Mary the Virgin)

✠ Cambridgeshire

39. Walsoken (All Saints) – dated 1544

✠ Somerset

40. Nettlecombe (St Mary the Virgin)

✠ Kent

41. Farningham (St Peter & St Paul)

Decoration of the eighth panel

The eighth panel often depicts the Crucifixion or other themes, as follows:

✠ *Last Judgement*
Gorleston (St Andrew), Norfolk
Marsham (All Saints), Norfolk
Martham (St Mary the Virgin),
Norfolk

✠ *Blessed Virgin, crowned, with the Holy
Child*
Gayton Thorpe (St Mary the Virgin),
Norfolk

✠ *Assumption of the Blessed Virgin*
Great Witchingham (St Mary the
Virgin), Norfolk

✠ *Communion of the People*
Farningham (St Peter & St Paul),
Kent

✠ *Holy Trinity*
West Lynn (St Peter), Norfolk

✠ *Martyrdom of St Andrew*
Melton (St Andrew), Suffolk

✠ *Christ in Glory*
Nettlecombe (St Mary the Virgin),
Somerset

PRESERVATION – HOW DID
SOME FONTS ESCAPE THE ICONOCLAST?

It is often asked how some of these beautiful fonts escaped mutilation. One answer is that a few of them were covered in plaster and after all fear of damage had passed, the plaster was removed. The superb font at Sloley, Norfolk, was probably protected in this way.

Another possibility is isolation. A lonely church, a long way from a village, stood a better chance of escaping the destroyer. Yet another means was the complete dismantling and hiding of the font until less troublesome times.

It is a great pity that so many of these fonts did suffer disfigurement, but where only a little damage has occurred, the beauty and detail that can still be seen are exquisite.

WHICH ARE THE FINEST SURVIVING
SEVEN-SACRAMENT FONTS?

Everybody has a view on which church possesses the finest seven-sacrament font. The best thing is to visit the churches in question and then decide for yourself! However, there are exceptionally beautiful fonts in the following churches:

1. Badingham (St John Baptist), Suffolk
2. Brooke (St Peter), Norfolk
3. Cratfield (St Mary the Virgin), Suffolk
4. Little Walsingham (St Mary the Virgin & All Saints), Norfolk – considered by many to be the finest
5. Nettlecombe (St Mary the Virgin), Somerset
6. Seething (St Margaret), Norfolk
7. Sloley (St Bartholomew), Norfolk – Pevsner states that this is the best preserved
8. Walsoken (All Saints), Cambridgeshire

The font at Glandford (St Martin), Norfolk, is a Victorian marble copy of that at Walsoken; the eighth panel shows the Crucifixion. And the fine font at Badingham (St John the Baptist), Suffolk, shows a sick man in bed in the Extreme Unction panel and under the bed can be seen a fifteenth-century chamber pot!

Of all the seven-sacrament fonts in East Anglia, the one at Denston (St Nicholas), Suffolk, is carved from a different-coloured stone; according to H. Munro Cautley (a former diocesan surveyor of Norfolk and Suffolk churches) this was imported from Aubigny in Normandy.

## Sidmouth                    DEVON

ST GILES & ST NICHOLAS The church can
be found in Church Street, quite near the
sea front of this popular seaside resort.

In the tracery of a window in the lady
chapel is a unique piece of glass dating
from *c.* 1450 and showing the five wounds
of Christ in red glass, each surrounded by
a golden crown.

The w window, depicting St Nicholas,
was given by Queen Victoria in memory
of her father, the Duke of Kent, who died
at Woolbrook Cottage, Sidmouth, on 23
January 1820 during a winter holiday with
his wife and baby daughter.

## Singleton                    WEST SUSSEX

THE BLESSED VIRGIN MARY The tower of
this church dominates this beautiful
downland village, which is very close to
the famous Weald and Downland Open-
air Museum.

There are some fine eighteenth-century
headstones in the churchyard.

The porch and n door jambs are full of
graffiti depicting such things as pilgrims'
crosses, Solomon's knot and the ragged
staff.

The rood loft stairway on the n side of
the nave is lit from the outside by an
unusually small window.

Above the chancel arch is a two-light
window filled with fragments of medieval
glass.

In the e window of the n aisle are two
roundels of modern stained glass. The
right-hand panel depicts the Blessed Virgin
Mary and the left-hand one commemorates Miss Pansy Wells (1918–78); she was a
church-warden and also worked as a telephonist at St Richard's Hospital, Chichester.
It depicts church-wardens' staves, an ATS

(Auxiliary Territorial Service) badge and
telephonist's earphones and mouthpiece.
The earphones are unique in stained glass.
Above and below the roundel is a pansy.

## Skenfrith                    MONMOUTHSHIRE

ST BRIDGET This attractive village is dominated by its ruined castle and spacious
church, whose fine w tower is capped with
an unusual dovecote. In times of scarcity
this housed pigeons as well as bells.

In the n aisle is the fine tomb of Sir John
Morgan (d. 1557) and his wife, Ann (d.
1564). Their effigies show excellent details
of the costumes worn at this time. Their
four sons are depicted on the s side and on
the n side are their four daughters. The
Morgans were an influential family who
lived in the village. One, John Morgan,
was the last governor of the castle;
another, Sir Richard Morgan, became
Chief Justice during the reign of Queen
Mary I and pronounced the death sentence on Lady Jane Grey. The family were
members of the Roman Catholic Church.

Close to the Morgan tomb is the Morgan
family pew carved in the Jacobean style.

A treasured possession of the church is
the Skenfrith Cope – a wonderful example
of English embroidery dating from *c.*1450.

## Skirlaugh                    EAST RIDING OF YORKSHIRE

ST AUGUSTINE This small Perpendicular
church dating from *c.*1403 was built by
Bishop Walter of Skirlaw, who was born in
the village. Extremely impressive outside
with many pinnacles and large windows, it
is one of the best specimens of Perpendicular architecture in England. The exterior
has not been altered from its original design.

The ancient glass has been arranged in

strips set in clear glass, giving the church a very bright appearance.

🔲 There is no chancel arch or aisles – a rare occurrence.

## Slindon                    WEST SUSSEX

ST MARY THE VIRGIN With its prominent spire, the church stands in a peaceful village off the A29, between Fontwell and Pulborough.

🔲 On a stone table at the E end of the S aisle is the oak effigy of one Sir Anthony Leger (d. 1539). It is 1.57 m (5 feet 2 inches) long and shows him in plate armour with his head resting on a tilting helmet and his hands at prayer. His armour is a good example of the middle Tudor period. Renaissance scrollwork can be seen on his oddly shaped shoes, elbows and knees. This is the only wooden effigy in Sussex. (See Wooden Effigies, page 246.)

🔲 On the N wall of the nave is a plaque which states that 'Stephen Langton, Archbishop of Canterbury, A.D.1206–1228, Upholder of English Liberties in Magna Carta, June 15 A.D.1215, died in this parish at Slindon Manor, July 9 A.D.1228. This tablet was given in A.D.1939 by Rhoda M. Muriello Langton' – presumably a descendant. Langton is also famous for dividing the Holy Bible into chapters and verses, which, with a few modifications, is what we still follow today.

## Slough                    BERKSHIRE

ST MARY This red-brick church with its soaring spire was built in 1876.

🔲 The W window of four lancets is filled with abstract stained glass in rich colours, designed by a Polish artist, Alfred A. Wolmark (1877–1961). It was made from 1915 to 1917 and is unusual in that it does not conform to the traditional church stained-glass window. (Abstract glass did not appear again until 1962 when Coventry Cathedral, West Midlands, was built). This window was presented by Miss Elliman – a relation of the firm that made Elliman's Embrocation.

🔲 The font was designed by J. Oldrid Scott. The bowl is made of onyx with marble shafts.

## Snarford                    LINCOLNSHIRE

ST LAWRENCE This disused church (now in the care of the Churches Conservation Trust) is situated in a secluded setting down a tiny lane off the busy A46.

🔲 The fifteenth-century octagonal font is one of the finest in Lincolnshire. It displays emblems of the Passion and a superb face of Our Lord.

🔲 On the N wall of the nave is a simple handwritten roll of honour commemorating seven men who died in the First World War. Five of these were from the seven serving sons of a former rector, the Reverend Beechey.

🔲 Behind the communion table is a magnificent 'six-poster' monument to Sir Thomas St Paul (d. 29 August 1582) and his wife. The inscription ends, 'Reader, you see what I am, you know what I have been. Consider what you yourself must be!' The St Pauls (or St Pols) were wealthy and successful lawyers during the reign of Queen Elizabeth I.

The monument is canopied and lavishly coloured. On the canopy, supported by six richly carved pillars, are eight kneeling children at prayer, while a ninth child kneels on a raised canopy in the centre. Sir Thomas wears armour and his wife wears typical Elizabethan dress.

⬛ In the N chapel is another fine monument, strengthened with iron bars, to Sir George St Paul (d. 28 October 1613) and his wife, Frances. They are shown in the reclining position and Frances holds a book. The backdrop is embossed with various emblems of death. Below is their only child, a daughter, Mattathia, who died aged just one year and ten months in 1597. She is shown with beads and lace around her neck. Beneath an alcove in the S chancel wall is her resting place. The brass inscription in Latin was written by the rector, John Chadwick.

⬛ To the w of this monument is a plaque to Robert, Lord Rich (d. 1619) and Frances Wray, whom he married in 1616 three years after she was widowed from Sir George St Paul. She is therefore depicted twice in this church! The second time she had become a countess. She died in 1634. Robert and Frances are buried at his ancestral home, Felstead, Essex.

This wall tablet was probably designed by the famous sculptor Epiphanius Evesham.

## Snettisham                          NORFOLK

ST MARY THE VIRGIN The village is located off the A149, about 6 km (3¼ miles) s of Hunstanton and the tall spire of the church is visible from the sea.

⬛ The spire at 53.34 m (175 feet) high is a rare feature in Norfolk; it was rebuilt in 1895.

⬛ At the w end is a Galilee porch with three arches – another extremely unusual feature.

⬛ Above the porch is a fine w window with elaborate tracery. (A whole chapter is devoted to describing the w front in L. P. Hartley's book *The Shrimp and the Anemone*.)

⬛ The clerestory windows in the nave are round and arched alternately – a very rare feature but similar to those in Cley-next-the-Sea, Norfolk.

⬛ The fine roof has lost its angels at the base of the braces with the exception of one survivor at the w end.

⬛ In the sw corner of the s aisle is a wafer oven, originally used for baking the communion bread.

⬛ The fine medieval brass eagle lectern dates from c.1500. The eagle's claws are missing.

⬛ The E window and windows on the s side are replacements for those destroyed on 19 January 1915 when a German zeppelin dropped a bomb near by. (This was the first church in the British Isles to be damaged by a bomb.)

⬛ The holy table and reredos are fine pieces of modern craftsmanship. Among the rosettes on the reredos are two little faces – can you spot them?

⬛ The original chancel fell into ruins in the sixteenth century and the cruciform church, with crossing tower, now has a tower at the E end.

## Somersby                          LINCOLNSHIRE

ST MARGARET Here was born Alfred Lord Tennyson on 6 August 1809.

⬛ A fine bronze bust of Tennyson stands near the chancel arch. It is by Thomas Woolner, dated 1873. This is a replica of the original and was placed here on 6 August 1911 by the Tennyson Centenary Committee.

Alfred Tennyson was baptized in the plain font.

⬛ On the s wall of the chancel is a brass to a George Littlebury, who died 13 October 1612 'being about the age of 73 yeares'.

⬛ Near the s porch is the original fifteenth-

*Sompting, West Sussex, photographed from the south.*

century churchyard cross in a fine state of preservation.

# Sompting WEST SUSSEX

ST MARY The church is on the side of the Downs and is well seen from the busy A27, which separates it from the village.

 The famous Saxon tower is unique in England although there are Victorian copies. Dating from *c.*1020, the tower is crowned by a helm roof similar to towers found in the Rhineland, Germany. Note the different belfry windows on the s and w faces. (See Rhineland Towers, page 375.)

 The s transept was built by the Knights Templar *c.*1180 as their private chapel and originally had no connection with the parish church, the present open archway being modern. This accounts for the dif-ferent levels between the two buildings. The rectangular vaulted sanctuary where the font now stands is the smallest of its kind.

 Carved stones from the original Saxon church can be seen inside, including eight lengths in various positions in the chancel.

 In the recess of the nave N door is a figure of Our Lord in Glory dating from *c.*1250.

 On the N wall of the chancel is an Easter sepulchre erected in 1527 by Richard Burre. This is one of the last Easter sepulchres to be erected before the Reformation; the last is probably at Tarrant Hinton, Dorset, and was constructed between 1514 and 1536.

 N of the tower is a parish room which occupies the site of a chapel built by the Knights Hospitallers. The inscription on the plaque reads:

*The unique Saxon tower at Sompting, West Sussex, seen from the southeast.*

'The Order of St. John returned to Sompting as Patrons of the Benefice in 1963. This room was built within the ruins of the medieval chapel of the Order of the Hospital of St. John of Jerusalem and was dedicated by the Lord Bishop of Chichester in 1971.'

## Southampton HAMPSHIRE

ST MICHAEL This is the oldest building in Southampton, dating from 1070. It was the only ancient church to escape destruction in the bombing of 1940.

🔲 The spire, a notable landmark for shipping, is 50.3 m (165 feet) high and is crowned by a weathercock 0.99 m (3 feet 3 inches) long, dating from 1733.

🔲 In the sw corner of the church is one of the seven Tournai marble fonts in Britain and one of only four in Hampshire. Its faces are crudely carved with grotesque creatures and an angel on the w face. It dates from c.1170 (see Tournai Fonts, page 439).

🔲 In the nave is the oldest medieval *brass* eagle lectern in the British Isles. (See also Petworth House Chapel, West Sussex, page 273.) Dating from c.1420 it has a triangular base and was rescued from the burning Holy Rood Church at the height of an air raid in 1940 when that church was destroyed. The jewels are now missing from the eyes but the eight silver claws are still intact. An unusual feature is a little demon with a long tail looking up at the eagle from between its claws. There is no blocked hole in the base of the tail. At one time this lectern was painted brown and thought to be made of wood.

Nikolaus Pevsner says of this lectern that it is 'perhaps the most beautiful in England'.

🔲 In the NE chapel is another brass eagle lectern dating from c.1450. The jewelled

eyes and claws are missing and parts of three feathers of the right wing. The hole in the base of the tail has been filled up.

(Note: this is the only church in the British Isles possessing *two* medieval brass eagle lecterns. See Medieval Brass Lecterns, page 362.)

🔲 In the E jamb of the window in the N wall is a merchant's mark; a square sunk panel with a shield bearing a monogram – the sign of the Woolstaplers' Guild.

🔲 By the NE corner of the tower is part of a gravestone (c.1150) with a carving of a bishop in mass vestments, holding a crosier.

🔲 At the E end of the S aisle there is a fine wooden statue of St Michael, carved in yew by Josephine de Vasconcellos. He holds a spear, at the end of which is a cross.

🔲 The nave arcades one composed of cast iron, brick and stucco pillars. Notice the small faces among the leaf decoration at the top.

🔲 In the NW corner of the church is the tomb of Sir Richard Lyster (d. 1553), Chief Baron and later Lord Chief Justice of the Common Pleas. Erected in 1567, it has Perpendicular and Renaissance features.

🔲 The beautiful E window depicts the five medieval churches of Southampton as they were before 1708.

🔲 In the N aisle is the gravestone of Mary Watts, sister of Isaac Watts, the famous hymn writer.

## South Dalton EAST RIDING
or Dalton Holme OF YORKSHIRE

ST MARY The church faces the entrance to Dalton Hall; it stands in beautiful countryside, off the B1248, NW of Beverley.

🔲 The spire of this church rises 63.4 m (208 feet) above the ground and is visible from a long way off.

The building was designed by John Loughborough Pearson and built from 1858 to 1861 for the Third Baron Hotham. Pearson was the architect of Truro Cathedral and there are marked similarities between the two buildings.

The stone used inside is dressed Hildenly stone in the thirteenth-century style with rich carving everywhere, especially just below the roof and in the chancel. Only the tower space and s porch are vaulted in stone. Some of the interior stonework, especially in the chancel, is flaking badly, probably due to damp.

The E window is by Clayton and Bell and depicts the Last Judgement.

In the Hotham chapel on the s side of the choir is a superb monument to Sir John Hotham (d. 1689) attributed to John Bushnell. Sir John, as a knight in armour, reclines on a slab supported by figures representing four of the virtues. Truth holds a mirror, Fortitude carries a broken column, Justice has a sword and Temperance caries two water jars. Underneath is a skeleton resting on a mattress – a reminder of this transient life. Its right foot is broken.

The monument came from the old church. (See John Bushnell, page 212.)

## South Harting     WEST SUSSEX

ST MARY & ST GABRIEL'S green, copper-covered spire is a notable landmark, especially from the nearby South Downs.

Just outside the churchyard are the old stocks.

The churchyard gate and hanging lamp on the NE side of the church feature in a famous painting – 'Christening Sunday' by James Charles (5 January 1851–27 August 1906). Painted in 1887 it portrays typical Victorian villagers leaving church and stopping at the foot of the churchyard steps to look admiringly at the newly baptized child. The model for the baby was the artist's daughter, Marion, and for her mother his wife, Ellen. The painting now hangs in the City Art Gallery, Manchester.

Inside the gate is the superb war memorial designed by Eric Gill.

Anthony Trollope (1815–82), author of many works including the *Barchester Chronicles*, lived in this village towards the end of his life, although he is buried in Kensal Green Cemetery, London. His pen, paperknife and scales are kept in the church.

The magnificent Elizabethan roof dates from 1576 when the church suffered a disastrous fire.

In the N transept is a remarkable Victorian wooden newel staircase.

On the w wall of the s transept is a memorial to James Guthrie, painter, author, poet and printer, who lived in this village from 1902 to 1907.

High up on the left side of the chancel arch is a piscina which indicates a former altar that stood on the rood screen – a rare survival. (See also Lambourn, Berks., page 191.)

Until Victorian times there were no windows in the E wall behind the high altar. This is *very* unusual.

## Southwell     NOTTINGHAMSHIRE

THE CATHEDRAL AND COLLEGIATE CHURCH AND MINSTER OF THE BLESSED VIRGIN MARY This magnificent building dominates the small town in which it is situated. The two Norman towers are crowned with two lead spires, rebuilt in 1880, which makes the w front unique in England.

The N porch is a rare example of a Norman porch with barrel vaulting. The

*Southwell Cathedral, Nottinghamshire. The famous chapter house can be seen on the left.*

room above can only be entered from the nave triforium. Notice the circular chimney on the w side.

🔷 The lintel over the inner doorway in the w wall of the N transept is a fine piece of Saxon carving, depicting St Michael with the Dragon.

🔷 Other superb examples of late Saxon work can be seen in the richly carved figures on the capitals supporting the E arch of the crossing. These may have been re-used from an earlier church on this site.

🔷 The central tower contains a ring of 12 bells. These are rung from a peculiar 'gallery', which is 18.3 m (60 feet) high and is perched on the tower walls. There is a 6.1 m (20 feet) square opening in the centre. (Only one other similar gallery exists in England – at Merton College Chapel, Oxford.)

🔷 The magnificently carved choir screen dates from c.1340 and has 289 small figures on it. On the E side of the screen, at the s end, is the bishop's stall, the back of which is comprised of delicately carved stone panels depicting foliage, no two being exactly alike! Inside the screen are rare 'flying ribs'; other examples of these may be seen at Bristol Cathedral, Lincoln Cathedral, St David's Cathedral and Warwick (see pages 51, 199, 300 and 384 respectively).

🔷 In the choir are three extremely well-carved roof bosses depicting dragons, and several others showing natural foliage.

🔷 The sedilia on the s side of the chancel is rare in having *five* seats. Some of the damaged stone carving was restored with plaster cement in the nineteenth century.

🔷 The stained glass in the four lower

*The east end of Southwell Cathedral, Nottinghamshire.*

lancet windows at the E end of the choir dates from c.1550 and came from the Temple Church in Paris. It was presented by Sir Henry G. Knight in 1818.

▦ The fine medieval brass eagle lectern dates from c.1500 and is inscribed thus: '*Orate pro animabus Radulphi Savage et pro animabus fidelium defunctorum*' ('Pray for the soul of Radulph Savage and for the souls of all the faithful departed'). This, a cross and a pair of candlesticks were found in the lake at Newstead Abbey c.1750, purchased from the Fifth Lord Byron in 1775 by Sir Richard Kaye, prebendary of Southwell and later Dean of Lincoln, and presented to the cathedral in 1805. The cross and candlesticks are the only original ancient set remaining in England. (See Medieval Brass Lecterns, page 362.)

▦ The arcading leading to the chapter house, its magnificent doorway and superb interior are richly decorated with naturalistic carvings of the following trees and plants: buttercup, hawthorn, hop, ivy, maple, oak, potentilla, ranunculus, vine, white bryony, whitehorn, crab apple and wild rose. Among the other carvings is one showing a man playing a horn while his goat nibbles on some trees. (What a pity that some of the leaves on the capitals and on the sides of the chapter house doorway have been broken and removed!)

This is the finest example of thirteenth-century stone carving in Britain.

▦ The octagonal chapter house, which was begun in 1292, is the only one to have a *stone* vault without a central supporting pier. Again, the bosses depict varieties of natural foliage.

*Southwell nave from the west, showing superb Norman arches on three levels.*

# Southwold        SUFFOLK

ST EDMUND, KING AND MARTYR is a large, spacious church, similar to nearby Blythburgh (see page 31).

▨ The fine W tower, at 30.5 m (100 feet) high, displays excellent flushwork. Note the absence of battlements and pinnacles.

▨ Around the outside of the tower's W window is the inscription 'S. A. T. EDMUND ORA P. NOBIS' (St Edmund, pray for us). Each letter is crowned. (See St Edmundsbury Cathedral, Bury St Edmunds, page 58.)

▨ The chancel screen dates from c.1450 and has original colouring and gilding.

▨ In the chancel are some fine choir stalls with interesting arm rests including a jester, a knight and a monkey.

▨ On the N side of the chancel is an engraved window by John Hutton, 1971, representing the martyrdom of St Edmund. It was presented by Sir Charles Tennyson in memory of his wife, Ivy (1880–1958), and his sons, Penrose (1912–41) and Julian (1915–45), from funds provided by his friends for his ninetieth birthday on 8 November 1969.

Underneath, a plaque records Tennyson's own death on 22 June 1977, at the age of 97.

▨ In the lady chapel are two interesting wooden roof bosses. One depicts Henry VIII's sister, Mary, and the other her second husband, Charles Brandon, Duke of Suffolk. Mary wears a 'netted' head-dress and Charles has a beard arranged like four 'corkscrews'.

▨ On the N side of the tower stands 'Southwold Jack'. He holds a battleaxe in his right hand, used to strike the bell at the beginning of services. Dating from *c.*1470 the colouring is original except for the gilding. (See also nearby Blythburgh, page 31 and Minehead, Somerset, page 241.)

On the two pillars of the tower arch are several masons' marks with many more throughout the church.

# Sparsholt                     OXFORDSHIRE

HOLY ROOD This church is situated in a beautiful village at the foot of the Berkshire Downs.

On the w side of the s transept, on a stone table-tomb, lies the wooden effigy of Sir Robert Achard (d. 1353). (Henry I gave the manor of Sparsholt to the Achard family.) His head rests on a tilting helmet with his feet on a lion. His hands and feet are mutilated and he has lost his sword and shield. The length of the effigy is 2.08 m (6 feet 10 inches).

In one recess of the s transept is another wooden effigy depicting Joanna, first wife of Sir Robert (she died in 1336). She wears a wimple with a long, flowing gown. Her hands are in prayer while her head rests on two cushions, the top one of which is supported by two angels. A lion cub lies at her feet. The effigy is 1.85 m (6 feet 1 inch) long.

The third wooden effigy in the other recess represents Agnes, second wife of Sir Robert, and dates from *c.*1360. This is an excellent figure, well preserved, although a forearm is missing. Her head is covered with a veil and she wears a plaited wimple and a long gown. Her head rests on two cushions – the top one supported by two nuns because she entered a nunnery after her husband's death. There are two plump dogs at her feet. The length of the effigy is 1.83 m (6 feet). (See Stories Associated with Wooden Effigies, page 445.)

The wooden screen across the s transept dates from *c.*1250 and is a very rare survival.

In the nave windows are fragments of stained glass dating from *c.*1250 to 1450. Among them is a head of the Virgin Mary on a background of roses, and a picture of Christ in Glory, His right hand raised in blessing.

Also in the nave are several plain glass windows, most of the glass being ancient. In the w window on the N side of the nave in the left light, two and a half quarries up from the bottom, the following words are scratched: 'Joseph Tuff cleaned some of these windows and that's enough.' Underneath these words he added, 'Bright Glazier'! This was probably done in the eighteenth century.

On the N wall of the chancel is the priest's doorway adjoining the Easter sepulchre. On one of the stones that form the jamb, about halfway up on the right-hand side, is a roughly cut design for the game of nine men's morris. If the design here was intended for playing the game, it must have been used in a horizontal position before being placed vertically *c.*1325! (See Nine Men's Morris, page 210.)

Inside the Easter sepulchre is the stone effigy of a thirteenth-century priest, unearthed in 1992–3 when a trench was dug across the site of the now-vanished N transept.

The N transept, opposite the s transept, was demolished *c.*1785. Part of the archway into it is still visible forming the head of the window, and a blocked squint to the chancel also remains.

Three stone arches behind the communion table in the chancel once comprised the top of the E window. When the present window was inserted, these arches were taken down, reversed back to front and cut in half to form a unique reredos. What you see here is the top of the outside of the former window with the original holes for the bars to support the glass.

# Speldhurst                    KENT

ST MARY THE VIRGIN This Victorian church contains one of the finest series of Burne-Jones stained glass in existence.

▨ Two lancets on the s side of the chancel depict the Baptism of Christ and Naaman washing in the River Jordan.

▨ The E window depicts the Crucifixion with the two Marys at the foot of the Cross surrounded by angels.

▨ The w window of the N aisle is one of the best and is called 'the Window of Praise'.

▨ The E window of the N aisle, seen between the N and s parts of the organ, is also very fine and depicts six saints. Dating from 1876, it commemorates a former organist.

Most of these Burne-Jones windows were given by Canon F. H. Hickens, Curate of Speldhurst (1864–79).

▨ The woodcarving is excellent, especially the font cover and the reredos, which portrays the Annunciation.

# Stamford               LINCOLNSHIRE

ST MARTIN is a fine example of a Perpendicular church with a w tower similar to that of Great Ponton in the same county.

▨ The fifteenth-century stained glass in the E window and the s chapel came from Tattershall Church, Lincs., c.1750. This was arranged by Peckitt of York.

▨ To the N of the chancel is the Burghley chapel. It contains the magnificent monument to Sir William Cecil, Lord Burghley (13 September 1520–4 August 1598), High Treasurer of England.

On the E wall a monument depicts his wife, Jane (d. 1587), kneeling at a prayer desk.

▨ In a separate churchyard to the E of the church Daniel Lambert (1770–1809) is buried. He had a waist of 2.84 m (9 feet 4 inches) and weighed 335.21 kg (52 stone 11 lb).

# Stansted House          WEST SUSSEX

The chapel stands in the grounds of Stansted House, which is situated in the extreme w of Sussex in the beautiful countryside, about 4.8 km (3 miles) N of Emsworth.

▨ Apart from the w and s fronts which are of Tudor brick, the remainder of the chapel was built by Lewis Way in 1816 in the Gothick style and restored by H. S. Goodhart-Rendel in 1926.

▨ John Keats, the poet, was present at the reconsecration of the chapel in January, 1819. He was staying at Bedhampton and the arms of the Fitzalan earls of Arundel, 1138–1579, on the N side of the nave were his inspiration for the first two stanzas of 'The Eve of St Agnes'.

▨ The elaborate chancel was inspired by the Sainte Chapelle in Paris. The E window is unique in being the only window in a Christian place of worship with entirely Jewish symbols in it.

▨ Also in the chancel are two unique plaques showing the Ten Commandments in Hebrew! Lewis Way tried, unsuccessfully, to convert all the Jews to Christianity, which explains why there is so much Jewish symbolism here.

▨ Young Samuel Wilberforce, the future bishop, preached his first sermon from this pulpit.

▨ The unusual wooden eagle lectern dates from 1816.

▨ At the w end near the door is a fireplace – an unusual feature outside a manorial pew.

*Staunton Harold, Leicestershire – a beautiful rural scene.*

## Staunton Harold Leicestershire

Holy Trinity Built 1653–65 this is one of the few churches commenced during the Commonwealth. Unlike other contemporary buildings, it is constructed completely in the Perpendicular style. It was presented to the National Trust in 1954 by the Twelfth Earl Ferrers and occupies a beautiful site overlooking a lake.

◈ Over the w door is this famous inscription:

'In the yeare 1653
when all thinges sacred were throughout
   ye nation
Either demolisht or profaned
Sir Robert Shirley, Barronet,
Founded this church;
Whose singular praise it is,
To have done the best things in ye worst
   times,

And
hoped them in the most callamitous.
The righteous shall be had in everlasting
   remembrance.'

◈ Around the *outside* of the chancel the following is inscribed: 'Sir Robert Shirley baronet founder of this church *anno Domini* 1653. On whose soul God hath mercy.'

◈ The organ at the w end is contemporary with the church. Made by Father Schmidt in 1630 it is one of the earliest examples to have survived in its original condition.

◈ The nave ceiling is of wood and the painting dates from 1655, executed by Zachary and Samuel Kyrk. Note the Greek word for 'God' and the Hebrew for 'Jehovah'.

◈ The delicate wrought-iron chancel screen is reputed to be by Robert Bakewell and dates from *c*.1711.

*Steeple Ashton, Wiltshire – a magnificent example of Perpendicular architecture.*

 All the walls inside the church are beautifully panelled and even the nave pillars.

 The contemporary box pews have candle holders on them but electric heating inside!

 On the s side of the chancel is the recumbent effigy of Sir Robert Shirley, who died of smallpox, 5 July 1714, aged 22.

 The altar frontal and pulpit hangings are contemporary with the church.

## Steep                                    HAMPSHIRE

ALL SAINTS As the name implies, this church stands high up on the Downs on the outskirts of Petersfield, commanding extensive views over the beautiful Hampshire and Sussex countryside.

 In the s aisle are two memorial lancet windows by Laurence Whistler to the First World War poet Edward Thomas (pseudonym 'Edward Eastaway', 1878–1917), who was killed at Arras. He lived in Steep from 1906 to 1915, when he enlisted in the Artists' Rifles.

The designs on the windows are engraved on the inside and outside of the glass and depict the countryside, one of Thomas's poems and a Flanders battlefield. The windows were dedicated on 3 March 1978, the centenary of Edward Thomas's birth.

(Another window by Laurence Whistler celebrating the lives of Edward Thomas and his wife, Helen, can be seen in St James's Church, Eastbury, near Lambourn – see page 115.)

 The fine hexagonal font on six pillars dates from *c*.1310. The sculpted cover was made by George Taylor.

# Steeple Ashton     WILTSHIRE

ST MARY THE VIRGIN This is the most richly ornamented church in Wiltshire.

The lofty, elegant tower, at 28.35 m (93 feet) high, dates from *c*.1420.

The s porch has a fine vaulted roof with a central boss depicting the Assumption of Our Lady.

The nave vaulting is of oak and plaster and dates from *c*.1510. It was severely damaged when the spire collapsed on 15 October 1670.

The vaulting of the aisles is of stone. The s aisle was also damaged by the fall of the spire and the repair to the vaulting can be seen near the baptistery. Two of the newest bosses contain the letters I. T. and I. S. – the initials of the church-wardens in 1670.

The s aisle chapel contains fragments of medieval glass including a crowned king and queen.

The N aisle vaulting contains several interesting bosses including one at the E end showing a rebus on Ashton – an ash and a 'tun' or barrel.

Near by, in the N aisle also, a fine boss shows Our Lord holding an orb.

At the E end of the N aisle are more fragments of ancient glass showing a chalice and wafer and the symbols of the Evangelists.

On the wall of the N aisle are the remains of an interesting palimpsest brass showing Queen Anne, Prince George and some bishops with a drawing of a church inscribed, 'The Church of Eng.' What remains of the title reads, '. . . and the Divil overballenced by the Bible'. The missing side probably depicted the Devil and the Pope in the other pan of the scales. This is all shown in reverse.

On the other side of the brass (which is hinged) is the following inscription, 'To the Memory of Deborah Marks who Departed this Life the 8th day of March, 1730. Aged 99.'

The roof vaulting in the N and s aisles terminates in niches that once held statues. The supporters underneath are very fine.

In the baptistery is a fine old chest and an impressive monument in coloured marbles to John Smith (1726–75) and his wife, Ann (1724–65). He was MP for Bath in the reign of George III.

# Steyning

(prounced 'Stenning')     WEST SUSSEX

ST ANDREW St Cuthman, whose feast day is kept on 8 February, is reputed to have pulled his aged mother in a handcart from Cornwall to Steyning! He allegedly built a wooden church here *c*.810. The church we see today is one of the most majestic fragments of Norman architecture in Sussex and dates from *c*.1160.

Each of the s doors possesses its sanctuary ring and the inner one still has its Norman hinges.

In the s porch is a large stone known as the Steyning Stone. It may have been an upright stone, similar to those standing in Cornwall, from which Steyning got its name – Steyning meaning 'dwellers by some prominent stone'.

Also in the porch is an ancient coffin lid bearing two incised crosses to indicate the burial of an important person – probably King Ethelwulf (d. 858), who was buried here but later re-interred at Winchester near his son, King Alfred.

In the nave, the elaborate decoration on each arch and capital is different but three arches are quite plain – two on the N side and one on the s. Note particularly the NW arch on which the mouldings are uncarved in the middle. This would seem to indicate that the carving was done in situ, but why is the work incomplete? Was the mason called away elsewhere and nobody felt able to complete his work when he failed to return?

▨ Between the clerestory windows is a vertical strip of moulding giving the effect of a pair of half-columns. This is a unique feature.

▨ At the E end of the S aisle is an interesting Norman arch, the rich capital on the S side being a good example of Norman work. It shows two lions, back to back, with their tails joined. One head on the angle serves the bodies of both lions!

Towards the top of the pier below this capital is a carved scene of two men grasping tree stems.

▨ At the E end of the S aisle is St Cuthman's chapel. The delightful stained-glass window (dedicated in July 1983) shows St Cuthman pulling his mother.

▨ A fine eighteenth-century seven-branch candelabrum is suspended in the chancel on a rod of Sussex iron.

▨ Against the E wall of the chancel is a reredos of Tudor panelling. Comprising 48 panels of the highest quality workmanship, it bears the date (1522) in words and the following: 'Give glory to God who made all this'.

In the middle panel of the top row are the splendid Royal Arms of Henry VIII with Katharine of Aragon's pomegranate, Tudor rose and portcullis.

▨ The massive W tower, built of stone and flint chequer work, dates from c.1600 and contains much reused material including chevron work, probably from when the W end of the nave was demolished.

▨ The Royal Arms of Queen Anne are on the W wall, dated 1703 – four years before the parliamentary union of England and Scotland. Note the motto 'Semper Eadem' instead of the usual 'Dieu et Mon Droit'.

## Stillingfleet     NORTH YORKSHIRE

ST HELEN This little village with its interesting church stands on the River Ouse, about 13 km (8 miles) S of York on the B1222.

▨ The N and S doorways are superb examples of Norman architecture dating from c.1150, but the S doorway is the more elaborate, comprising five orders of decoration.

▨ The ironwork on the S door is original and comprises elaborate crescent hinges, each of which terminate in a serpent's head. At the top is what may be a Viking ship complete with its great steering paddle.

▨ In the S transept is the fine effigy of Sir Robert de Moreby (c.1286–c.1336). His legs are crossed and he carries a shield on his left arm. The de Morebys were a wealthy family in the Middle Ages, one of whom founded the Moreby chapel in the S transept in 1336 – possibly Sir Robert, just before he died.

▨ On the N side of the church is a stained-glass window by H. Harvey (1956) showing the Resurrection. It is in memory of a Gladys Mary Preston (d. 7 June 1955, aged 71).

▨ An adjoining window depicting the Nativity is in memory of Thomas Preston (d. 2 July 1966, aged 80).

▨ In the churchyard, S of the church, is the grave of nine of the 11 choristers who were drowned on 26 December 1833 when the boat bringing them from singing carols capsized as it struck the tow-rope of a barge. The bodies of Sarah Eccles and Sarah Spencer, two of the victims, were never found.

*The south door and doorway of Stillingfleet, North Yorkshire, dating from c.1150 and showing the original ironwork.*

# Stoke d'Abernon     SURREY

ST MARY is prettily situated near the fast-flowing River Mole.

🔲 In the chancel is what is generally acknowledged to be the oldest remaining figure brass in the British Isles. It is 2 m (6 feet 6 inches) long and commemorates Sir John Daubernoun (d. 1277). Although always claimed to be the oldest brass, some authorities now date it to c.1320 because of the style of armour depicted. It shows the knight in chain mail with a surcoat around his shoulders. His legs are uncrossed (unlike contemporary effigies). On the knight's left arm is a shield bearing a chevron with traces of Limoges enamel.

This is the only brass in existence depicting a knight with a lance and pennon. He holds it in his right arm while a lion at his feet grasps part of it in his teeth!

An inscription in Norman French ran around the edge of the slab on which the brass is fixed. Translated, this said, 'Sir John Daubernoun Knight lies here. May God have mercy on his soul'.

🔲 Near Sir John's brass is that of his son, Sir John Daubernoun the Younger. Dating from 1327 it shows the knight in mail and plate armour. The arms and legs are additionally protected by plate armour and the feet stand on a lion. This brass is 1.65 m (5 feet 5 inches) long.

🔲 Between the chancel and N chapel (or Norbury chapel) at the E end of the arch separating them is the brass of Dame Norbury. She was the wife of Sir John Norbury, who fought at the Battle of Bosworth Field, 1485, and built the Norbury chapel, c.1490. The brass (1464) is 0.46 m (1 foot 6½ inches) long. An unusual feature is that her children are shown engraved in the folds of her dress!

🔲 At the w end of the arch between the N chapel and chancel is a small brass, 30 cm (1 foot) high, to an Elyn Bray (1516). She died within a month of being baptized and is shown in her baptismal chrysom with a cross on her forehead.

A very rare feature of the Norbury chapel (erected c.1490) is a Tudor fireplace; this is usually only found in later manorial pews.

🔲 On the E wall of the chapel is a brass inscription in eight rhyming lines commemorating the Reverend John Pynnoke (d. 1 August 1521). This is a rare example of a brass depicting a chantry priest who was the first to serve here.

🔲 Also in the Norbury chapel are the following interesting monuments:

† On the E wall a monument to Dame Sarah Vincent (d. 1608). (She was married to Sir Francis Vincent, who gave the church its magnificent pulpit.) Dame Sarah wears a Paris hood and ruff and a long, tight-waisted bodice. Below are the kneeling figures of her five sons and two daughters.

† On the N wall is a fine monument to Sir Thomas and Lady Vincent, 1613 and 1619. He is shown on his side in plate armour but his wife is shown in prayer. No children are depicted.

† High up on the E wall is a small kneeling figure of Sir John Norbury, who founded this chantry in 1490 but whose later effigy, replacing an earlier one, shows him dressed in the style of c.1640.

🔲 The vaulted chancel dates from c.1210 and is a beautiful example of Early English architecture.

🔲 The fine Jacobean pulpit dates from c.1620. Near by is the original hour-glass bracket.

Medieval art traditionally showed Mary and Gabriel separated by a lily – the flower that always symbolized purity associated with the Annunciation. In the Middle Ages however, from *c*.1375 to *c*.1540, an addition, unique to England and Wales, was made whereby the tiny figure of the crucified Christ was sometimes superimposed on the lily stem. This is known as a 'lily crucifix'.

According to medieval legend, the Crucifixion of Jesus occurred on the anniversary of the Annunciation to Our Lady (traditionally 25 March or Lady Day, and exactly nine months before Christmas Day), and so the crucified Christ affixed to a lily symbolized the shared suffering of Mother and Son at the Crucifixion. It is interesting that in the *Book of Common Prayer* (1662) the Collect for the Annunciation of the Blessed Virgin Mary includes these words, '. . . as we have known the incarnation of Thy Son Jesus Christ by the message of an angel, so by His cross and passion we may be brought unto the glory of His resurrection . . .' This could be seen as a hidden reference to the symbolism of the lily crucifix.

At the time of the Reformation many lily crucifixes disappeared and those that have survived are often shown without the accompanying figures of the Blessed Virgin Mary and the Angel Gabriel. Today, the lily crucifix is very rare and, as far as I know, occurs only in the following churches (as well as in some libraries and museums):

1. Abergavenny (St Mary's Priory Church), Monmouthshire – glass. Annunciation and Lily Crucifix at the bottom of the chancel's E window and made in 1922 by F. C. Eden (1864–1944). Given by Mrs Randle Barker in memory of her husband, Brigadier Barker, killed in the First World War.

2. Abingdon (St Helen), Oxfordshire – panel on painted ceiling of lady chapel, *c*.1391; unique on a painted ceiling.

3. Ampney (St Mary), Gloucestershire – glass. At the base of the central light of the three-light E window and made by F. C. Eden in 1914.

4. Chantry (Holy Trinity), Somerset – glass. In southern window of W wall and made *c*.1846 by William Wailes (1808–81). Probably copied from the lily crucifix at nearby Westwood, Wiltshire, this single-light window does not show an Annunciation scene but underneath is a panel showing Christ washing the disciples' feet.

5. Crockham Hill (Holy Trinity), Kent – marble. On the W face of the chest supporting the effigy of Octavia Hill (*c*.1912) and delicately carved by Dora Abbott. Octavia was one of the co-founders of the National Trust in 1896 and is buried on the S side of the church.

6. Kenn (St Andrew), Devon. On the S side of the rood screen, *c*.1500. This is not very clear as the paint is quite dark and the image has been defaced.

7. Long Melford (Holy Trinity), Suffolk – glass. Set in the centre of the seven-light E window of the Clopton chantry chapel, *c*.1400. This is probably the most famous surviving lily crucifix.

8. North Cerney (All Saints), Gloucestershire – wood. On a wooden screen at entrance to the lady chapel. Designed by F. C. Eden (1864– 1944) in 1914 carved by Lawrence Turner.

9. Norwich (St Julian), Norfolk – glass. Made c.1950 by Dennis King of George King and Son, Norwich, this window is in Mother Julian's cell and shows Julian kneeling at the feet of the crucified Christ on lily stems. Above her are her famous words, 'All shall be well'.

This church was virtually destroyed in 1942 during air raids on Norwich and was rebuilt after the Second World War. The cell where Mother Julian (1342–c.1416) lived for 40 years of her life and wrote her book *Revelations of Divine Love* was also rebuilt.

10. Nottingham (St Mary the Virgin) – carved in alabaster. On the table-tomb of John de Tannesley (d. 1414 ) in the N transept, it is about 25 cm (10 inches) high and is located on the side of the tomb-chest, about a third of the way along the panel on the left-hand side.

11. Oxford (St Michael at the North Gate) – glass. NE window of the N aisle, set in the tracery of the window, c.1410. The lily plant is shown with five open flowers.

12. Oxford (Queen's College Chapel) – glass. Situated in extreme W window on N side of the chapel. Annunciation with Christ on the lily, probably painted by Joshua Price, c.1710, but incorporating glass from c.1500.

13. Portsmouth (St Agatha), Hampshire (in Market Way, Landport). Free-standing altar crucifix. Made c.1935 by Martin Travers (1886–1948). Wood and gesso, painted a dull gold. It came from St Matthew's Church, New Kent Road, Southwark, London.

14. South Kilworth (St Nicholas), Leicestershire. Tomb side panel of stone, now used as a reredos at the E end of the S aisle. Originally in the N aisle but was out of sight behind the  organ. This may have come from the tomb-chest of Richard Wythnale or Whitenhall (d. 1439) but Nikolaus Pevsner dates it to c.1300. If he is correct, it would make this lily crucifix our earliest depiction. Unfortunately the carving is very worn having been outside in the churchyard for many years. (Under an arch in the N wall of the chancel is a recumbent stone figure which may represent Richard Wythnale, who was rector c.1410–39 and may have rebuilt the church.)

15. Tong (St Mary the Virgin with St Bartholomew), Shropshire – wood. The Annunciation with lily crucifix on a misericord on the S side of the chancel. Dated c.1410 this is now unique as a misericord although one may have existed at All Saints in Gresford, Wrexham, but no clear trace of it now remains.

16. Wellington (St John the Baptist), Somerset. On the centre mullion of the E window in the S aisle is a lily flower with five buds and Christ crucified on it. Underneath is a small corbel depicting a woman's face. Dating from c.1450, this lily crucifix is unique on a window mullion. There may have been figures of the Virgin Mary and Gabriel in ancient glass on either side of it to complete the Annunciation scene. Because this feature is on a window containing clear glass, it is very difficult to get a satisfactory result when photographing it against the light, or even to view it clearly from the floor without binoculars.

17. West Wittering (St Peter & St Paul), West Sussex. On the side of the Caen stone tomb of William Ernley (d. 1545), erected by Bridget Ernley, his second wife and daughter of

Thomas Spring, 'the rich clothier of Lavenham, Suffolk'. Lavenham is quite near Long Melford and Bridget's inspiration for this tomb may well have come from seeing the famous lily crucifix there. This particular tomb is the smaller of the two Ernley tombs on the N side of the chancel and is situated inside the communion rails. This depiction of the lily crucifix is extremely beautiful and is shown in relief near the base of the tomb on the S side. The complete Annunciation scene is portrayed and the crucified Christ is shown on the central lily flower with the backs of His hands against the two side stems of the lily. The legs below His knees are missing.

*Godshill, Isle of Wight.*

18. Westwood (St Mary), Wiltshire – glass. Situated in the central light of the E window, it dates from *c.*1480. In the lights on either side are angels holding instruments of the Passion, but these are placed against bright red backgrounds that are clearly incongruous and indicate from their shape that they have been removed from elsewhere in the church, probably from the tracery of other windows. It is almost certain that these two side lights would have contained depictions of the Virgin Mary and Angel Gabriel, thus forming a complete Annunciation scene. Most of the original canopies still survive at the top of the two side lights, but the original

medieval glass underneath was probably removed in *c.*1840 when other medieval glass from the lady chapel was substituted in its place.

19. York (The Minster Church of St Peter) – glass. Situated in the N choir aisle, the first window from the Q (n 10 or window 8, following the York Minster booklet) was given by Henry Bowet – Archbishop of York, 1407– 23. Underneath the central figure of the Blessed Virgin Mary is an Annunciation scene with Christ shown crucified on a lily stem. Binoculars are needed to see the details of this window containing England's most northerly example of a lily crucifix.

An interesting variation on the lily crucifix can be seen in the tracery of a window on the E side of the N transept of the country church of Poynings, West Sussex. A complete Annunciation scene is shown with the Blessed Virgin Mary on the right and the Angel Gabriel on the left. Although no crucifix is depicted, the lily in the pot is shown with three flowers in the shape of a cross. The glass dates from 1421.

A pot containing a cross-shaped lily is also shown inside the W recess of the seven-sacrament font at St Mary's in Woodbridge, Suffolk, and around the stem of the font at Great Glemham, Suffolk.

At All Saints in Godshill, Isle of Wight, Christ is shown crucified on what appears to be a tree rather than a lily, and neither Mary nor Gabriel is shown. This representation is found on the E wall on the S transept (*c.*1450); while some authorities do not classify this as a lily crucifix, it is announced as such in its home church and is unique as a mural.

Yet another variation on the lily crucifix can be seen in St George's Chapel in Windsor Castle, Berkshire. It is on the desk front of the sovereign's stall on the s side of the choir, the first stall on the right when entering the choir from the w. In the spandrels of the desk front are depicted the Virgin Mary on one side and the Angel Gabriel on the other. Between them is a lily supporting a heart with a spear wound symbolizing the crucified Christ.

In the church of St Giles in Bredon, Worcestershire, on the s wall of the chancel is a beautiful stone coffin lid dating from *c*.1320. This shows the busts of an unknown man and his wife underneath two canopies. Below them is the figure of Christ crucified on a tall cross of thorn branches.

Note: examples of the lily crucifix can also be found in: the National Library of Wales, Aberystwyth (a miniature inside the *Llanbeblig Book of Hours*, *c*.1390); Lambeth Palace library (a miniature Annunciation and lily crucifix inside the *Lewkenor Book of Hours*, *c*.1450); the Victoria and Albert Museum, London (an alabaster panel in wooden housing, *c*.1400, given by W. L Hildburgh in 1946, and a painted wooden panel from a parclose screen, *c*.1480).

## Stoke Lacy HEREFORDSHIRE

ST PETER & ST PAUL The present building was restored in 1863 under a local architect, F. R. Kempson, son of William Brooke Kempson, who was rector from 1839 to 1858. He retained the Norman chancel arch with its scalloped capitals.

 The oak chancel screen, at 2.13 m (7 feet) high, dates from *c*.1550 but is not original to the church, as can be seen from the fact that it does not fit properly into the space provided!

 From 1871 to 1887 the Reverend H. Morgan was rector here, followed by his son, Pebendary Henry Morgan, from 1887 to 1937. His son, Henry F. S. Morgan, founded the Morgan Motor Company of Malvern in 1909. According to tradition, the first prototype three-wheeler Morgan car was assembled in the rectory garage!

 Inside the s porch are two small trefoil windows containing stained glass depicting the Morgan connecion. The one on the E side shows Peter Morgan, the active patron of the church and son of H. F. S. Morgan, above his blue Morgan car and the Morgan factory. It is inscribed, 'In memory of P. H. G. MORGAN 1919–2003'.

The other window depicts two three-wheeler Morgan cars (one red, one blue one) and is inscribed, 'To the memory of

*The Morgan Window at Stoke Lacy, Herefordshire.*

John and Bridget Leavens California USA 1997'. They were benefactors of the church.

## Stoke Poges     BUCKINGHAMSHIRE

ST GILES can be found in a small patch of countryside just N of Slough.

In the churchyard, under the E wall of the church, is the brick table-tomb of Thomas Gray (1716–71), who wrote 'Elegy written in a Country Churchyard'. This is generally acknowledged to be the named churchyard, but the churchyard of St Lawrence, Upton, near Slough, also lays claim to this!

In the E window of the Hastings chapel is the earliest representation of a bicycle that is rather like a hobby-horse. A man sits astride it blowing a long trumpet. The glass dates from 1643.

## Stoke St Gregory     SOMERSET

ST GREGORY The village is in quiet countryside and is dominated by its impressive church.

The central tower is unusual in being octagonal and is crowned with a small recessed spire. Inside are four arches and smaller arches making up the octagon.

The clock in the tower dates from 1898. Its chimes are unusual in being Gregorian (not the normal Westminster).

Over the S door is an original and unrestored fifteenth-century statue of St Gregory. Note the Dove on the book and pen in the right hand.

The excellent and well-preserved Elizabethan bench-ends date from c.1570.

In the S transept are two stone monuments to a Court family dating from 1705. One bears the following quaint inscription:

'O reader now prepared to die,

Thy thread is almost spun
Live like this lady just for why
Her virtues did outshine the sun.
This virgin lady pure and chaste
Beneath doth sleeping lie.
Apace her body now doth waste,
Her soul is in the heavens high.'

Under the ancient yew tree opposite the S porch are some well-preserved stocks, used by the church-wardens to punish offenders at church services!

Note on leaving the churchyard, on the left, beneath the wall, a black headstone inscribed in gold as follows:

'Phyllis Konstam Austin
Actress, wife, adored mother
And friend
1907–1976
She loved Jesus and
The world was her stage.

H.W. Bunny Austin
Tennis Player
Greatly Loved
1906–2000
He served God
The world was his
Court.'

Henry Wilfred 'Bunny' Austin was a tennis finalist from the golden age of British tennis in the 1930s. He was the first male competitor to wear shorts at Wimbledon.

## Stow     LINCOLNSHIRE

ST MARY THE VIRGIN is one of our famous Saxon churches and one of only two where the arches under the crossing tower are all the same height and width. (The other is Norton, Co. Durham.) Each arch is 10.67 m (35 feet) high to the apex and 4.34 m (14 feet 3 inches) wide, making them the tallest Saxon arches in the British Isles. They date from c.1004 to 1016.

*Stow, Lincolnshire – the beautiful Norman chancel of an outstanding church.*

Inside the Saxon arches are four pointed arches inserted *c.*1350 to support the present tower, built inside the Saxon tower.

On the s pier of the outer chancel arch is a graffito depicting a Viking ship dating from *c.*1000 when the arches were built – the oldest drawing of a Viking ship in England.

In the N transept is a wall painting of Thomas à Becket dating from *c.*1210 – one of the earliest representations in England.

The font, dating from *c.*1200, is an excellent example of Early English work.

The vaulting of the chancel was constructed *c.*1850 by J. L. Pearson using about 40 stones from the original Norman vaulting, which had been taken down – much of it embedded in the chancel walls.

On the s side of the chancel is an early floor memorial in English (*c.*1300), part of it in mirror writing. (See also East Budleigh, Devon, page 114, Morwenstow, Cornwall, page 244 and Trent, Dorset, page 368.)

Between the four pinnacles on the tower are four sculpted figures – an unusual feature, probably unique.

## Stow Bardolph          NORFOLK

HOLY TRINITY With its Norman tower, the church is unusual in having a nave without any aisles.

Inside a cupboard, behind a sheet of glass, is the wax effigy of Sarah Hare, who died in 1744 after pricking herself with a needle while sewing on a Sunday. Only the head and shoulders are featured but they are life size and extremely lifelike; the figure is dressed in Sarah's own clothes! When one first opens the cupboard, the sight of it is quite frightening.

On the N side of the chancel is the brick Hare chapel, dating from 1624 and containing several monuments to successive members of the Hare family.

# Stratford -upon-Avon    WARWICKSHIRE

THE COLLEGIATE CHURCH OF THE HOLY TRINITY This beautiful church is situated on the bank of the River Avon, its E end only a few metres from the water's edge.

The elegant spire is 55.78 m (183 feet) high. The circular windows in the tower dating from c.1350 are very unusual.

On the inner door of the N porch is a sanctuary ring dating from c.1250.

The w window of the N aisle has two lights filled with stained glass depicting St Nicholas and St Christopher (given in 1904 and 1907), but the extreme left-hand light is a *mosaic* and *painting* depicting St Faith and given in memory of one Edith Louisa Colbourne James (1871–1910). This left-hand light is covered by a buttress outside – a very unusual feature.

At the E end of the N aisle is the Clopton chapel. Against the N wall is the altar tomb of William Clopton (1592) and Anne, his wife. The Cloptons were originally medieval clothiers who built the Clopton chapel.

Against the E wall is the magnificent tomb of George Carew, Earl of Totnes and Baron Clopton (d. 1629) and his wife, Joyce Clopton, Countess of Totnes (d. 1635). This tomb has been described as 'the finest Renaissance tomb in Europe'. Note the guns, powder barrels and cannon balls at the base of the monument.

Against the NW pier of the central tower is the beautiful silver processional cross, given c.1905 by the Shakespeare Memorial Theatre Company in memory of one of their fellow actors, Frank Rodney, who died in 1902.

Under the crossing is a 20-branch candelabra dated 1720.

On the N side of the spacious chancel is the tomb of William Shakespeare (1564–1616), the famous playwright. The words on the floor read:

'Good frend for Iesvs sake forbeare,
To digg the dvst enclosed heare:
Blese be ye man y spares thes stones
And cvrst be he ye moves my bones.'

On the N wall of the chancel is a bust of William Shakespeare engraved with these words:

' Stay passenger, why goest thou by so fast?
Read, if thou canst, whom envious death has placed
Within this monument: Shakespeare, with whom
Quick nature died; whose name doth deck this tomb,
Far more than cost, sith all that he hath writ
Leaves living art but page to serve his witt.'

In the chancel are 26 very fine misericords dating from c.1450 and depicting numerous unusual and amusing subjects. Affixed to the chancel walls are two more misericord seats.

# Sturminster Newton    DORSET

ST MARY THE VIRGIN stands away from the centre of the town, down a little side street.

The wagon roof of the nave dates from c.1500 and is the only one in Dorset.

The stained-glass windows are outstanding and among the most interesting are the following:

*Sudeley, Gloucestershire. The glorious church nestles close to the castle.*

† The 'Nativity' window in the w tower was the first window ever made by Mary Lowndes (1857–1927), Britain's first woman stained-glass maker. It commemorates her mother.

† The 'Resurrection' window in the s aisle, also by Mary Lowndes, commemorates her father, Canon Richard Lowndes, vicar here for 36 years (d. 3 October 1898).

Both of these windows are in the Arts and Crafts style.

† The se aisle window, brilliantly coloured, is a rare one in the Art Deco style by Harry Clarke of Dublin (1889–1931). It commemorates someone called Roma Spencer-Smith and was very controversial at the time because Clarke was a Roman Catholic!

† In the n aisle is the 'Crucifixion' window by Geoffrey Webb (1879–1954). Notice his signature and date in the bottom left light – a spider in its web and the date, MCMXI (1911). This window commemorates a member of a family called Mansel-Pleydell.

## Sudeley GLOUCESTERSHIRE

ST MARY This church, which adjoins the castle, was built *c*.1460. It is not the private chapel of the castle.

Queen Katharine Parr (1512–1548), last wife of Henry VIII, is buried on the n side of the chancel. Her beautiful effigy and sumptuous tomb by J. B. Philip, 1859, were designed by Sir Gilbert Scott. The inscription around the tomb is copied from the words scratched on the original lead coffin, which was opened in 1768.

## Sulhamstead Abbots    BERKSHIRE

ST MARY This is a small church, keeping company with an ancient yew in the quiet countryside s of the M4.

▨ The altar frontal, reredos and E window were designed by Sir Ninian Comper from 1936 to 1938.

▨ A memorial tablet in the chancel commemorates Robert Fenn (1816–1912), who was awarded the Victorian Medal of Honour for his work in hybridizing and improving the potato.

▨ Another tablet near by dates from 1521. Translated it reads:

> Meditate, O passer-by, on the last end of life
> Seeing that all things so soon shall die,
> Turn thine eyes to heaven,
> Embrace that which shall endure to the end
> And avoid the accursed allurements of Eve.
> Ralph Eyre, Rector of Sullimstead Abbot, erected this monument in his own lifetime in the year of Our Lord 1521.'

▨ At the NW corner of the churchyard is an interesting gravestone inscribed with these words:

> 'All you that do behold this stone, pray think how quickly I was gone,
> Death does not always warning give, therefore be careful how you live.'

## Sunningwell    OXFORDSHIRE

ST LEONARD The small village, just N of Abingdon, has a cruciform church with a tower placed unusually on the N side.

▨ The W porch or Jewel porch is unique in English architecture for being heptagonal (seven-sided). It was built between 1550 and 1552 by John Jewel (1522–71), a former rector who later became Bishop of Salisbury. It has Renaissance columns at the angles with Tudor windows and doorway. There are some fine old hinges on the door.

▨ The beautifully carved Elizabethan communion table was also given by John Jewel.

▨ On the N side of the chancel is buried Samuel Fell, a former dean of Christ Church, Oxford, and rector from 1625 to 1649. He died on 2 February 1649, a few days after hearing the sad news that Charles I had been executed in Whitehall, London (30 January). Fell's wife is buried on the s side of the chancel.

▨ In the nave are 21 large old poppy-heads at the ends of the pews. They are very impressive.

▨ Roger Bacon (c.1214–92), the famous scientist, is said to have carried out experiments in the tower.

## Sutton Courtenay    OXFORDSHIRE

ALL SAINTS is a beautiful church, located in a large and picturesque village, facing the green.

▨ On the E side of the churchyard is the grave of Eric Arthur Blair (25 June 1903–21 January 1950), better known as George Orwell, author of *Animal Farm* (1945), *Nineteen Eighty-Four* (1949) and other novels.

▨ Near by is the grave of Herbert Henry Asquith, Earl of Oxford and Asquith (12 September 1852–15 February 1928). The inscription describes him as 'Prime Minister of England, April 1908 to December 1916' – a curious omission of Scotland, Wales and Northern Ireland!

▨ Inside the church is the pew where Herbert Asquith sat for Sunday services.

# Sutton Valence     KENT

ST MARY THE VIRGIN This church stands high up in the village with beautiful views from its churchyard.

John Willes (1777–1852), the first man to introduce round-arm bowling in cricket, is buried in the churchyard.

# Swimbridge     DEVON

ST JAMES This is a treasure house of carvings in wood and stone with a broach spire, covered in lead shingles and rising to a height of 36 m (118 feet).

The screen (c.1490) is one of the oldest in Devon and was well restored in 1887. It contains delicate carving. On the ancient rood-beam is a trumpeting angel.

The hexagonal stone pulpit also dates from c.1490 and stands on a tall pedestal. Carved with saints and angels, it displays traces of its original colouring. (See Medieval Stone Pulpits, page 348.)

The Reverend Jack Russell (1795–1883), famous for the breeding of the terrier that bears his name, is buried in the churchyard.

# Swinbrook     OXFORDSHIRE

ST MARY This little church stands in a delightful Cotswold village in the valley of the River Windrush, not far from Burford.

The small W tower was built in 1822 in just six weeks!

To the W of the tower are the graves of the writer Nancy Mitford (1904–73) and her sister Unity.

In the window at the E end of the S aisle are fragments of stained glass dating from c.1450. These formerly filled the upper tier of the chancel's E window. The inscription reads:

'A German land-mine, with parachute attached, was dropped in a field between the church and the river at 9.20 in the evening of 26 September, 1940. The explosion shattered the windows, displacing roof tiles, and shook down plaster throughout the church. All adjacent houses suffered in the same way, but no one was hurt. This inscription has been placed here in thankfulness to God for our merciful deliverance and in memory of William Grenville Boyd, Vicar, 1938–1941 who collected and began arranging this old glass.'

In the chancel are five fine misericords dating from c.1450; these probably came from Burford Priory.

On the N side of the chancel are the famous Fettiplace effigies – two fascinating trios of reclining figures. Those on the W were ordered by Sir Edmund Fettiplace I (d. 1613) for his grandfather, father and himself; those inside the sanctuary on the E were ordered by Sir Edmund Fettiplace II (d. 1686) for his uncle, father and himself. It is interesting to compare the two styles of workmanship.

The last baronet in the direct male line of Fettiplaces was Sir George Fettiplace (d. 1743), who is commemorated by a marble bust sculptured by James Annis. (For another link with the famous Fettiplace family, see also Childrey, page 79.)

# MEDIEVAL STONE PULPITS

There are 75 medieval stone pulpits (dating from before 1530) in England. They are found chiefly in the counties of Devon, Gloucestershire and Somerset, but some of the finest are found outside these counties like those at Arundel, Nantwich and Wolverhampton. They nearly all date from c.1450, although a few are older.

In monastic times it was the custom to read from the Holy Bible or some other sacred book during meal times when monks were not allowed to talk. This was usually done from a pulpit that was built against the wall, access being via steps inside the wall. These have survived in some places, but in only one case is the reader's pulpit still used as an ordinary pulpit in a church today. This is at Beaulieu, Hampshire, where the former refectory became the parish church after the Dissolution.

Besides the one at Beaulieu, only four other monastic stone refectory pulpits survive. These are at: Carlisle, Cumbria; Chester, Cheshire; Shrewsbury, Shropshire; and Tupholme, Lincolnshire. Shrewsbury's is the most unusual since it survives in a secluded garden to the south of the abbey church, the remainder of the refectory having disappeared. A road, constructed in 1836, runs between the former refectory and church, so making the pulpit's isolation complete. The pulpit at Tupholme is in the ruins of the refectory.

As mentioned above, some stone pulpits are approached via staircases built inside the wall. These are located as follows:

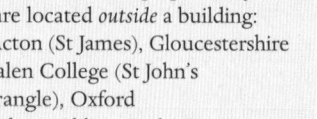
*Arundel, Sussex.*

1. Beaulieu (Blessed Virgin and Child), Hampshire
2. Carlisle Cathedral (Holy and Undivided Trinity), Cumbria – former refectory
3. Chester Cathedral (Christ and the Blessed Virgin Mary), Cheshire – former refectory
4. Chipping Sodbury (St John the Baptist), Gloucestershire
5. Cromhall (St Andrew), Gloucestershire – entered from behind up steps from the vestry
6. Holton (St Nicholas), Somerset
7. Nailsea (Holy Trinity), Somerset – approached via stairs to vanished rood loft
8. Rangeworthy (Holy Trinity), Gloucestershire – approached from behind, from vestry up former rood-loft stairs
9. Staunton (All Saints), Gloucestershire
10. Weston-in-Gordano (St Peter and St Paul), Somerset

Of all the medieval stone pulpits, only the following are located *outside* a building:

1. Iron Acton (St James), Gloucestershire
2. Magdalen College (St John's Quadrangle), Oxford
3. Shrewsbury Abbey (Holy Cross), Shropshire

The pulpits at Banwell and Bleadon, Compton Bishop, Hutton, Locking and Wick St Lawrence (all in Somerset) are almost identical and were probably carved by the same craftsmen. They are beautiful examples of fifteenth-century workmanship.

The pulpit at St Saviour's in Dartmouth, Devon is heptagonal (seven-sided) and has wooden ornaments in the panels depicting a portcullis, harp, fleur-de-lis, lion, rose and thistle, each with a crown over them. They were placed there c.1640.

The pulpit at Okeford Fitzpaine, Dorset, was cut down to make a font c.1790 but reverted to a pulpit again in 1865.

Apart from the unique Early English pulpit in Beaulieu Abbey refectory, the oldest existing stone pulpit is probably at Combe, Oxfordshire, dating from c.1370. Those at Arundel and Clymping, West Sussex, and Cromhall, Gloucestershire, date from c.1390.

As far as I know, the following is a complete list of medieval stone pulpits in churches in England and Wales by county:

✠ CAMBRIDGESHIRE
1. Witcham (St Martin)

✠ CHESHIRE
2. Nantwich (St Mary)

✠ CORNWALL
3. Egloshayle (St Petroc)
4. Truro (St Paul)

✠ DEVON
5. Bovey Tracey (St Peter, St Paul and St Thomas of Canterbury)
6. Chittlehampton (St Hieritha)
7. Dartmouth (St Saviour)
8. Dittisham (St George)
9. Harberton (St Andrew)
10. Paignton (St John)
11. Pilton (St Mary)
12. South Molton (St Mary Magdalene)
13. Swimbridge (St James)
14. Totnes (St Mary)
15. Witheridge (St John the Baptist)

✠ DORSET
16. Frampton (St Mary)
17. Okeford Fitzpaine (St Andrew)

✠ GLOUCESTERSHIRE
18. Ampney Crucis (Holy Rood)
19. Aylburton (St Mary)
20. Chedworth (St Andrew)
21. Chipping Sodbury (St John the Baptist)
22. Cirencester (St John the Baptist)
23. Colesbourne (St James)
24. Coln Rogers (St Andrew)
25. Cowley (St Mary)
26. Cromhall (St Andrew)
27. Hawkesbury (St Mary)
28. Lasborough (St Mary)
29. Naunton (St Andrew)
30. North Cerney (All Saints)
31. Northleach (St Peter & St Paul)
32. Rangeworthy (Holy Trinity)
33. Staunton, near Coleford (All Saints)
34. Thornbury (St Mary)
35. Turkdean (All Saints)
36. Westerleigh (St James)
37. Winson (St Michael)

*Wick St Lawrence, Somerset.*

✠ HAMPSHIRE
38. Beaulieu (Blessed Virgin and Child)

✠ ISLE OF WIGHT
39. Shorwell (St Peter)

✠ OXFORDSHIRE
40. Black Bourton (or Burton Abbots) (St Mary)
41. Combe (or Coombe, Long Combe or Combe-Longa) (St Laurence)
42. Cornwell (St Peter)
43. Shipton-under-Wychwood (St Mary)

✠ SOMERSET
44. Banwell (St Andrew)
45. Bleadon (St Peter & St Paul)
46. Brockley (St Nicholas)
47. Charlcombe (St Mary)
48. Cheddar (St Andrew)
49. Chesterblade (St Mary)
50. Compton Bishop (St Andrew)
51. Glastonbury (St Benedict)
52. Holton (St Nicholas)
53. Hutton (St Mary)
54. Kewstoke (St Paul)
55. Locking (St Augustine)

56. Loxton (St Andrew)
57. Meare (St Mary)
58. Nailsea (Holy Trinity)
59. Shepton Mallet (St Peter & St Paul)
60. Stogumber (St Mary)
61. Stratton-on-the-Fosse (St Vigor)
62. Westbury-sub-Mendip (St Laurence)
63. Weston-in-Gordano (St Peter & St Paul)
64. Wick St Lawrence (St Lawrence)
65. Worle (St Martin)

✠ SUSSEX (West)
66. Arundel (St Nicholas)
67. Clymping (St Mary)

✠ WEST MIDLANDS
68. Coventry (Holy Trinity)
69. Wolverhampton (St Peter)

✠ WILTSHIRE
70. Berwick St James (St James)
71. Bremhill (St Martin)
72. Horningsham (St John the Baptist)
73. Limpley Stoke (St Mary)
74. Nettleton (St Mary)

✠ YORKSHIRE (North)
75. Ripon Cathedral (St Peter & St Wilfrid)

*Chipping Sodbury, Gloucestershire.*

Following the break with the Church of Rome and Henry VIII declaring himself 'Supreme Head on Earth of the Church of England' in 1534, Royal Arms were placed in churches as symbols of loyalty and obedience to the Crown.

Curiously enough there is only one large example of the Arms of Henry VIII still surviving, and this is at Rushbrooke, Suffolk. It is attached to a wooden beam at the entrance to the chancel, but this may be a nineteenth-century copy installed by Colonel Rushbrooke, a former lord of the manor. Smaller examples of Henry VIII's Arms can be seen in the following churches:

1. Cirencester (St John the Baptist), Gloucestershire – carved in stone in the apex of the window over the chancel arch, c.1520.
2. Crudwell (All Saints), Wiltshire – on a bench-end, c.1510.
3. Malmesbury Abbey (Blessed Virgin Mary, St Aldhelm, St Peter & St Paul), Wiltshire – carved in stone on the frieze of the pulpitum (a large stone screen dividing the choir from the nave, usually only found in larger churches and cathedrals) at the E end, c.1530.
4. Milverton (St Michael), Somerset – on a bench-end, c.1540.
5. Steyning (St Andrew), West Sussex – in the middle panel of Tudor panelling against the E wall of the chancel, c.1540.
6. Tawstock (St Peter), Devon – on a bench-end, c.1540.
7. St George's Chapel in Windsor Castle, Berkshire – on a roof boss in the centre of the crossing, c.1528.

Edward VI's Royal Arms are found in just one church, namely Westerham (St Mary the Virgin), Kent. Similarly, Queen Mary I has only one depiction of her Royal Arms and this is at Waltham Abbey (Holy Cross and St Lawrence), Essex. At Burstwick (All Saints), East Riding of Yorkshire, the Royal Arms of Charles II can be seen (and on the back there is a painting of his father's execution on 30 January 1649).

At Furneux Pelham (St Mary), Hertfordshire, are some unusual Stuart Arms carved on both sides, dated 1634 on one side and 1660 on the other. The lion and the unicorn each have two heads! The Arms are on the screen at the w end of the s aisle.

*The sturdy tower of Tamworth contains a double spiral staircase, unique in a church.*

# Tamworth STAFFORDSHIRE

COLLEGIATE CHURCH OF ST EDITHA The large, imposing tower of this church dominates the centre of the busy town, near the border with Warwickshire.

In the sw angle of the tower (built 1380–1420) is a double spiral staircase – unique in a church. The floor of one stairway is the roof of the other and since it has two independent entrances (one from the outside and the other from inside the church) a person can go up one, while another is coming down the other at the same time! There are 106 steps in the outer staircase and 101 in the inner. Over the outside doorway is a statue of St George.

The fine screen separating the nave and chancel is made of wrought iron and dates from c.1750.

In St George's chapel and the chancel are fine stained-glass windows by Burne-Jones, William Morris and Ford Maddox Brown.

A window in the nave commemorates the Reverend Maurice Berkeley Peel, BA, MC, who as Chaplain to the Forces in France was killed while tending the wounded on the 14 May 1917.

The great w window under the tower is filled with modern stained glass, the theme of which is 'the New Jerusalem coming down from God' (*Rev.* 21, v.10). It was unveiled by Princess Margaret on 2 July 1975 and the glass was designed by Alan Younger and G. G. Pace.

Under the s aisle is a fine vaulted crypt dating from c.1250, and now restored as a refectory in 1977.

# Tattershall LINCOLNSHIRE

HOLY TRINITY stands in the shadow of the spectacular red-brick keep of the castle. It was a collegiate church founded on 16 July 1439 and built within 30 years.

Except for the E window, there is an absence of stained glass, which makes the church very light. Much of the glass was removed c. 1750 to St Martin's Church, Stamford, where it can still be seen (see St Martin, Stamford, page 331.)

Among the scenes in the fifteenth-century glass of the E window is a baptism in the right-hand light, a bishop blessing a man, his wife and child in the left-hand light and a king and queen in the centre light.

There are no cusps in the window tracery – a precursor to the forthcoming Tudor style of architecture.

On the N side of the font is the reputed grave of Tom Thumb inscribed, 'T. Thumb. Aged 101. Died 1620'.

In the N transept there are several old brasses. The brass to a warden of the former college has 12 figures of saints on his cope, which is fastened by a clasp showing a figure of Our Lord.

The transept is normally kept locked.

*Tattershell, Lincolnshire. The Perpendicular church is viewed from the nearby castle.*

## Tewkesbury GLOUCESTERSHIRE

THE ABBEY CHURCH OF ST MARY THE VIRGIN This magnificent abbey dominates the town in which it is situated and the surrounding countryside. When it was dissolved by Henry VIII in 1539, the church was bought by the townspeople for £453.

🔲 The central tower is the largest Norman tower in existence. It is 14.02 m (46 feet) square and 45.11 m (148 feet) high to the pinnacles and battlements, which were added in 1600.

🔲 The 14 Norman pillars in the nave are the tallest in England at 9.35 m (30 feet 8 inches) high. Their circumference measures 6.04 m (19 feet 10 inches).

🔲 Directly to the w of the second free-standing pillar from the E is a step which runs across the whole church. This indicates the position of the pulpitum or stone screen that separated the monks' church to the E from the people's parish church to the w.

🔲 Under the centre of the tower is a modern brass marking the burial place of Edward, only son of Henry VI. The inscription (translated) reads, 'Here lies Edward, Prince of Wales, cruelly slain while still a youth, on 4 May, 1471. Alas, the fury of men. You are the sole light of your mother, and the last hope of the flock.'

🔲 High up on the N wall of the choir is an oak pyx canopy. Only four exist in England. The other three are at Dennington, Suffolk, (see page 101), Milton Abbey, Dorset, and Wells Cathedral (see page 388).

🔲 In the choir are three superb stone-cage chantry chapels as follows:

† On the s side is that of Lord Edward Despenser (d. 1375). It has the earliest

*Tewkesbury Abbey, Gloucestershire, seen from the south. Notice where the original nave roof reached on the side of the tower.*

miniature example of fan vaulting in its ceiling. On the roof, under a canopy, is the kneeling figure of Lord Despenser facing the high altar. This particular pose on top of a chantry chapel is unique. The Despensers were one of the noble families associated with the royal family. Hugh le Despenser was hanged in 1326, a year before Edward II was murdered in Berkeley Castle.

† Opposite the Despenser chantry is that of Robert Fitzhamon (d. 1107), who founded the abbey. The chantry was erected *c.*1397 and is similar to the Despenser one, also having a fan-vaulted roof.

† Also on the N side of the choir is the Beauchamp chantry. It commemorates Richard Beauchamp, Earl of Worcester, and was built in 1422. A unique feature is the canopy over the W, with one half supported on two slender shafts. Both roofs

are fan-vaulted. (See Fan Vaulting, page 152.)

▨ The high altar slab is the largest surviving in England. Made of Purbeck marble it is 4.16 m (13 feet 8 inches) long, 1.07 m (3 feet 6 inches) wide and 12.5 cm (5 inches) thick.

▨ The five stained-glass windows above contain excellent medieval glass dating from *c.*1350.

▨ Behind the high altar is a modern stainless steel statue depicting Our Lady, Queen of Peace, by Anthony Robinson.

▨ At the extreme E end, opposite the wall that led to the now-vanished lady chapel, is an iron grating covering the Clarence vault. George, Duke of Clarence, brother of Edward IV and Richard III, whose bones rest here, is reputed to have drowned in a cask of Malmsey wine.

▨ Near the Clarence vault is the chapel of St Dunstan, in front of which is the memorial to John Wakeman, last abbot of

*The tallest Norman arch in England graces the west front of Tewkesbury Abbey, Gloucestershire.*

Tewkesbury. Note the numerous animals on the decaying body, including a frog on the neck and mouse on the stomach! The abbot became the first Bishop of Gloucester and is not buried here.

▦ The roof bosses are noteworthy, those in the nave depicting scenes from the life of Jesus and being the earliest story bosses in England. They date from *c*.1330. The boss showing the Ascension is the finest example in England of this subject; likewise that showing Pentecost, where Mary is shown with the 12 Apostles and the Dove descending from above. There are only three other bosses in England showing Pentecost – two at Norwich Cathedral and one at York Minster (see page 441).

▦ At the w end of the nave is an enormous window inserted in 1686. The recessed Norman arch outside is 18.9 m (62 feet) high, making it the tallest Norman arch in England.

## Theale                    BERKSHIRE

HOLY TRINITY The w front of this impressive nineteenth-century stone-built church is modelled on that of Salisbury Cathedral.

▦ On the N side of the chancel is Bishop Waynflete's chantry (founder of Magdalen College, Oxford), removed from the college chapel in 1830 by Dr Routh, the college President and rector of Theale!

▦ On a tomb inside the chantry, a beautiful monumental brass commemorates Sophie Sheppard (1768–1848), a widow (and sister of Dr Routh), who gave Theale this church (except the chancel). The little dog at her feet is particularly endearing.

## Theberton                  SUFFOLK

ST PETER is a very picturesque church with a round tower located in quiet countryside, near the North Sea, NW of Leiston.

▦ The round tower of this church has an octagonal top richly decorated with flushwork, including alternate belfry openings which look like windows. (See also Round Towers, page 398.)

▦ The nave and chancel are thatched – a rarity.

▦ In the s aisle are memorials to the Doughty family, among them a plaque to Charles Hotham Montagu Doughty-Wylie (23 July 1868–26 April 1915). He was awarded the Victoria Cross for great bravery. His inscription reads:

'To God be the Glory. The Land they loved shall wear the fadeless crown her warriors gave her, when, wrapped in death's dark cloud, they laid them down dying to save her. Yet being dead they die not, in the grave tho' they be lying, these be the souls to whom high valour gave glory undying.'

▦ In the porch, in a glass case, are the aluminium remains of L48, the German zeppelin that crashed near the village on 17 June 1917. Sixteen German airmen died and were buried here, but they were re-interred at Cannock Chase German Military Cemetery, Staffordshire, *c*.1975.

## Thockrington            NORTHUMBERLAND

ST AIDAN is situated in remote countryside on a little hill, commanding magnificent views from its churchyard.

▦ At the w end is a large external buttress supporting a simple stone bellcote.

▦ Near the w end is the grave of William Henry, Lord Beveridge of Tuggal (5 March

*The pseudo-Norman church at Tickencote, Rutland, partly rebuilt in 1792.*

1879–16 March 1963), pioneer of the National Health Service and Social Services.

🔲 Inside is a plain Norman chancel arch and another at the E end surrounding the single lancet window.

## Thornton Curtis    LINCOLNSHIRE

ST LAWRENCE is situated in a beautiful village not far from the River Humber.

🔲 The famous black Tournai marble font dates from c.1150. It is 89 cm (2 feet 11 inches) deep by 93 cm (3 feet) wide and is carved with fabulous animals and birds, four on each face in twos, facing each other. (See Tournai Fonts, page 439.)

🔲 Three of the piers of the S arcade are enriched with dog-tooth ornament of the thirteenth century.

🔲 At the W end of the S aisle are the head and shoulders of a lady (c.1300) sunk into the floor – a very unusual feature.

🔲 The nave and chancel are divided by a fine modern oak screen in the Perpendicular style.

🔲 The communion table dates from c.1610 and has fine bulbous legs.

🔲 On the S side of the chancel is a rare Norman piscina.

## Thurlby    LINCOLNSHIRE

ST FIRMIN stands on the E bank of the Cardyke, a Roman catch-water drain and canal connecting Peterborough and Lincoln.

🔲 The upper parts of the tower and spire date from c.1320 and reach a height of 24.4 m (80 feet). There is a ring of six bells.

🔲 The lower stages of the tower date from c.925. The Saxon tower arch has been infilled with a Norman one dating from c.1100.

🔲 On the S side of the chancel is a rebuilt

Norman arch, which was probably the original Norman chancel arch. It is decorated with chevrons.

🔲 Ancient glass in the S transept depicts Elizabeth greeting Mary.

🔲 The N chantry chapel, dating from 1359, has windows of an unusual double ogee design.

## Thursford    NORFOLK

ST ANDREW Arthur Mee describes this church, situated near Fakenham, as being 'of no great interest'. This is probably because much of it was rebuilt in the nineteenth century. Nikolaus Pevsner, however, says of the glass in the E window (designed by the Reverend Arthur Moore in 1862) that it is 'one of the most beautiful of its time in England, or indeed Europe, as good as the early Morris glass, which is saying much'.

## Tickencote    RUTLAND

ST PETER Situated quite near to the busy A1 road, the magnificent chancel arch of this church is worth coming to see.

🔲 Composed of five orders, it dates from c.1160 to 1170. The decoration includes zigzag, beakhead, billets and other motifs, the outside pattern of foliage being unique. The arch is depressed in the centre.

🔲 In the chancel is a unique example of Norman sexpartite (six-celled) vaulting with a rare roof boss in the centre consisting of a circular plaque inside three heads – two muzzled bears and a monk's head. (This sexpartite vaulting is only found elsewhere in Gothic architecture at Canterbury Cathedral, Kent.) This Norman boss is probably the oldest in England.

🔲 In a recess in the S wall of the chancel is

*The 'Cathedral of the Peak' at Tideswell, Derbyshire.*

a wooden effigy which probably depicts Sir Roland Le Daneys, c.1390. (He was a lord of the manor, an MP and fought in the French wars, probably at Crécy, 1346.) The effigy is 1.9 m (6 feet 3 inches) long and wears a helmet and hauberk. His hands are at prayer, his head rests on a cushion and his uncrossed legs rest on a lion. The effigy is in a mutilated condition. A hole is visible in the side through which charcoal was placed to absorb moisture. (See Wooden Effigies, page 246.)

The fine font dates from c.1250.

Over the outside of the s doorway an inscription records that someone called Eliza Wingfield repaired this church in 1792 in the neo-Norman style.

## Tideswell     DERBYSHIRE

ST JOHN THE BAPTIST Known as 'the Cathedral of the Peak', this is the largest church in the British Isles and stands at an altitude of 304.8 m (1000 feet) or more above sea level.

Built between c.1340 and 1390 the church is a superb example of Decorated and Perpendicular architecture. The tower has eight pinnacles, four of which rise from polygonal turrets on the corners.

The large chancel has square-headed windows and a square-headed sedilia – very unusual features.

In the centre of the chancel is a large tomb-chest to Sir Sampson Meverell (1388–1462). The Purbeck marble slab on top has five incised crosses showing it was once used as an altar before the Refor-mation. It is now set with memorial brasses, the central one depicting the Father, Christ on the Cross and the Holy Spirit.

Underneath the tomb-chest is a cadaver. It carries the date 1462 but was restored in 1875.

Behind the altar is a stone reredos, which encloses a sacristy – a rare feature in a church.

## Tillington     WEST SUSSEX

ALL HALLOWS The church commands beautiful views towards the Downs from its position in the village on the A272, near Petworth Park.

The tower, with its imposing 'Scots crown', dates from 1807 and is situated at the E end of the s aisle. It is featured in a painting by John Constable.

This is Britain's most southerly 'Scots crown', but only nine others survive, as follows:

† Faversham, Kent
† Hillesden, Bucks. (a small separate tower at the NE side)
† London, St Dunstan-in-the-East
† Newcastle upon Tyne Cathedral, Tyne & Wear
† Sutton, Surrey (Trinity Methodist Church, 1907);

and four in Scotland as follows:

† Aberdeen (King's College Chapel)
† East Kilbride (Lanark)
† Edinburgh (St Giles Cathedral)
† Glasgow (Tolbooth Tower).

The circular w window dates from 1906 and is in memory of Arthur Nuttall and Frances, his wife. It is in the Pre-Raphaelite style.

A window at the E end of the s aisle is a good reproduction of Holman Hunt's 'The Light of the World'.

In the NE corner of the N aisle is a brass plate referring to the window above, which was inserted by Cicely and William Kenyon Mitford in thankfulness for the recovery of their son, William Slade Mitford (1898–1966), from a serious accident on 5 August 1909.

# MEDIEVAL BRASS LECTERNS

As far as I know, there are 49 medieval brass or bronze lecterns (before 1530) remaining in the British Isles, 43 of which are in the form of the familiar eagle or falcon. Five are of the double-desk type and one depicts a pelican. A double-desk lectern has a sloping plate on two sides for holding books (e.g. the Holy Bible and a prayer book), whereas a normal lectern has just one plate.

The eagle lecterns were cast in several pieces, usually 13 – head and body in one piece, two wings, two legs and eight talons or claws – and then joined together. In some instances the talons were made of silver and jewels were placed in the eyes, explaining why so many are now missing!

According to C. C. Oman, the great authority on these lecterns, several different moulds were used. In his scholarly work *Medieval Brass Lecterns in England*, Oman identifies the numerous moulds and lists those medieval lecterns that probably came from the same workshop (of which there were possibly no more than four). These may well have been situated in Norwich, King's Lynn, Bury St Edmunds and London. All of these towns are situated on good waterways and within easy reach of the Continent. They were particularly well located for the importation of raw materials and for the exportation of lecterns.

It is perhaps significant that nearly all of the surviving medieval brass lecterns are found in places that are near navigable rivers and seaports.

In Oman's article in the *British Archaeological Association Journal* (1931) he lists various groups of lecterns but the following that I have discovered do not appear to fit into any of these:

1. The pelican lectern in Norwich Cathedral, Norfolk – the only pelican in the British Isles surviving from medieval times.
2. The eagle lectern now in St Michael's in Southampton, Hampshire (where there already was a medieval one!), but which came from the blitzed church of Holy Rood, Southampton. Dated *c*.1420, this is the oldest medieval 'brass' lectern and is considered by Nikolaus Pevsner to be the most beautiful. During the Civil War it was painted brown to resemble wood and thus escaped being melted down. Traces of brown paint still remain.
3. The eagle lectern at Outwell, Norfolk, that rests on a wooden base.
4. The eagle lectern at North Cerney, Gloucestershire, dating from *c*.1480 and a Flemish work.
5. The eagle lectern at Wells-next-the-Sea, Norfolk; this was dug up in a field.
6. The eagle lectern in the chapel of Petworth House, West Sussex – made of 'bronze', not 'brass'. Dating from *c*. 1380, this is the oldest medieval metal lectern.
7. The eagle lectern at Cheddleton, Staffordshire – a Flemish work dating from *c*.1450.
8. The eagle lectern in the chapel of St Mary's Roman Catholic College at New Oscott, Birmingham. This also came from Belgium and dates from *c*.1500.
9. The very unusual lectern at Methley, West Yorkshire, was also made *c*.1500 and is Flemish work with a Victorian eagle added *c*.1850.

## HOW EAGLE LECTERNS WERE MADE

First, a wooden pattern was made by an expert woodcarver and placed upside down in an iron container called a flask. Sand was packed around it to produce an impression of the model. The wooden pattern would then be removed and a slightly smaller duplicate made of hardened sand (probably sand mixed with clay, although in modern sand-casting, resins are usually mixed with sand) was placed inside. This was supported on iron bars at right angles to each other to prevent it from touching the outer casing. Molten metal would then be poured between the two and, after cooling, the sand would be removed using the same holes through which the iron bars had been passed. As with modern castings, provision had to be made for the escape of the gases that built up inside the mould.

Polishing and engraving took place after the various pieces of the eagle had been joined together and attached to the less complicated stem and pedestal. Holes in the eagle were usually blocked up by the insertion of pieces of metal, particularly noticeable in the base of the tail.

Oman dismisses the common theory that brass eagle lecterns were used in the Middle Ages for the collection of alms, Peter's pence and so on (money being inserted into the beak and passing through the tail into an attached collecting bag). As previously explained, the hole in the tail was used to pass an iron bar through at the time of casting. Oman goes as far as to say that any money inserted into the eagle's beak would most probably have become lodged in the body and never have reached the tail! However, I was interested to note when I inspected the lectern at St Mary the Virgin in Wiggenhall, Norfolk, in 1980, that someone had clearly tested the theory of using the eagle as a collecting box and a two-pence coin could still be seen wedged in the tail.

The 'brass' of these eagle lecterns is an early form known as latten, a material that was also used for the many monumental brasses found in our churches. In the case of the latter, these should *not* be cleaned or polished.

Of all the surviving medieval brass lecterns, only the following examples are dated:

1. Chipping Campden, Gloucestershire – 1618 (but this is the date when the lectern was presented to the church by Baptist Hicks). It is inscribed, '*Ex Dono Baptistae Hikes militis anno domini 1618*'. Underneath on the stem is written, 'Restored November 1881 by M. F. H.'
2. Lowestoft (St Margaret), Suffolk – 1504
3. Norwich (St Giles), Norfolk – 1498. This is inscribed, 'Pray for the soul of William Wiltbrok and his wife 1498'
4. Wiggenhall (St Mary the Virgin), Norfolk – 1518
5. Wrexham (St Giles) – 1524

Some of the other examples have inscriptions that allow them to be dated within a few years of their manufacture.

The following is, as far as I know, a complete list of all the surviving medieval 'brass' or bronze lecterns in religious buildings in England and Wales:

1. New Oscott (St Mary's RC College Chapel), Birmingham
2. Bovey Tracey (St Peter, St Paul & St Thomas of Canterbury), Devon
3. Bristol (St Stephen), Gloucestershire
4. Cambridge (Christ's College Chapel)
5. Cambridge (King's College Chapel)*
6. Cavendish (St Mary), Suffolk
7. Cheddleton (St Edward), Staffordshire
8. Chipping Campden (St James), Gloucestershire

9.   Clare (St Peter & St Paul), Suffolk

10.  Coventry (Holy Trinity), West Midlands

11.  Croft (All Saints), Lincolnshire

12.  Cropredy (St Mary), Oxfordshire

13.  Croydon (St John the Baptist), Greater London

14.  East Dereham (St Nicholas), Norfolk

15.  Eton College Chapel, Berkshire*

16.  Exeter Cathedral (St Peter), Devon

17.  Isleham (St Andrew), Cambridgeshire

18.  King's Lynn (St Margaret), Norfolk

19.  King's Lynn (St Nicholas), Norfolk

20.  Little Gidding (St John the Evangelist), Cambridgeshire

21.  Long Sutton (St Mary), Lincolnshire

22.  Lowestoft (St Margaret), Suffolk

23.  Methley (St Oswald), West Yorkshire

24.  Newcastle Cathedral (St Nicholas), Tyne and Wear

25.  North Cerney (All Saints), Gloucestershire

26.  Norwich Cathedral (The Holy and Undivided Trinity), Norfolk – a pelican

27.  Norwich (St Giles-on-the-Hill), Norfolk

28.  Oundle (St Peter), Northamptonshire

29.  Outwell (St Clement), Norfolk

*Woolpit, Suffolk.*

30.  Oxborough or Oxburgh (St John the Evangelist), Norfolk

31.  Oxford (Merton College Chapel)*

32.  Oxford (Corpus Christi College Chapel)

33.  Peterborough Cathedral (St Peter, St Paul & St Andrew), Cambridgeshire

34.  Petworth House Chapel, West Sussex

35.  Redenhall (St Mary), Norfolk

36.  Salisbury (St Martin), Wiltshire

37.  Snettisham (St Mary), Norfolk

38.  Southampton (St Michael), Hampshire

39.  Southampton (St Michael, from Holy Rood Church), Hampshire

40.  Southwell Cathedral (The Blessed Virgin Mary), Nottinghamshire

41.  Upwell (St Peter), Norfolk

42.  Walpole St Peter (St Peter), Norfolk

43.  Wells-next-the-Sea (St Nicholas), Norfolk

44.  Wiggenhall St Mary the Virgin (St Mary), Norfolk

45.  Windsor Castle (St George's Chapel), Berkshire *

46.  Wolborough (St Mary), Devon

47.  Woolpit (St Mary), Suffolk

48.  Wrexham (St Giles), Wrexham

49.  Yeovil (St John the Baptist), Somerset*

*Double-desk lecterns

❧ + ❧

# SINGLE-CELL APSIDAL CHURCHES

*Nately Scures, Hampshire.*

There are only four single-cell apsidal churches in England. They were built by the Normans as single buildings terminating in an apse without any additions such as aisles or transepts.

The four churches are located as follows:

1. Little Tey (St James the Less), Essex
2. Nately Scures (St Swithin), Hampshire
3. North Marden (St Mary), West Sussex
4. Winterborne Tomson (St Andrew), Dorset

(I am indebted for this information to Rodney Hubbuck, who supplied it to Ian Nairn, who, in turn, wrote *West Sussex* for Nikolaus Pevsner in the 'Buildings of England' series.)

It is interesting to note that the church in Winterborne Tomson nearly became ruinous, but was beautifully restored from 1929 to 1931 under the auspices of the Society for the Protection of Ancient Buildings. Most of the cost was covered by the sale of some of Thomas Hardy's manuscripts found in the archives of the society whose secretary, an architect, Albert Reginald Powys, CBE (1881–1936), was responsible for restoring the church in Hardy's memory. Powys is buried in the churchyard in an unmarked grave but a tablet inside the church records his achievements.

*Tollesbury, Essex, which contains the lightest ring of ten bells in the world.*

# Tollesbury    ESSEX

ST MARY THE VIRGIN stands at the highest point of the village on the N bank of the River Blackwater.

▨ A stained-glass window known as 'The Seafarers' Window' depicts various yachts that have contended for the Americas' Cup, and other coastal vessels associated with Essex. The window was designed by Derek Wilson and dedicated on 26 November 1963.

▨ The font dates from 1718 and is unique. It carries this inscription: 'Good people all I pray take care, That in ye Church you doe not sware. As this man did.' John Norman had come into church drunk and cursed and talked aloud during a service. In order to avoid prosecution he agreed to pay a fine of £5, which paid for a new font! Robert Joyce, then church-warden, ordered that the rhyme be put on the font.

▨ In the tower hangs the lightest ring of ten bells in the world. They were augmented to ten in 1990. (See Bells, page 293.)

# Tolleshunt D'Arcy    ESSEX

ST NICHOLAS The church is located in a small village in remote countryside, quite near the estuary of the River Blackwater.

▨ In a window of the N chapel on the N side of the chancel is a piece of stained glass dating from c.1600 and showing a red tulip. This is the earliest representation of a tulip on glass still surviving. (See also Edington, Wiltshire, page 124.)

▨ The attractive painted nave ceiling dates from 1897 when the church was restored.

# Tong    SHROPSHIRE

ST MARY THE VIRGIN WITH ST BARTHOLOMEW This lovely church is known as 'the Village Westminster Abbey' because of its many monuments.

▨ In the s porch are the rules for ringing the Great Bell of Tong. Originally given in 1518 it was last recast in 1892 by John Taylor of Loughborough. It weighs 2540.16 kg (2 tons 10 cwt).

▨ On the N wall of the N aisle are the Royal Arms of 1814, made of Coade stone – an artificial stone made of china clay and various minerals.

▨ In the chancel are 16 misericords, mostly showing leaves and one with a Green Man, dating from c.1410. The first misericord on the right as one enters the chancel shows the Annunciation with a lily crucifix. This is unique because it is the only lily crucifix on a misericord and also because it is the only one carved in wood. (See Lily Crucifix, page 338.)

▨ On the N side of the chancel is an interesting ancient door leading to the vestry. It has three circular holes cut in the top of it, their purpose probably being for the server to see the sanctuary.

▨ On the s side of the s aisle is the 'Golden chapel', founded in 1515 as a chantry chapel by Sir Henry Vernon. It has a fan-vaulted roof with pendants. On the w wall is a monument, the first of its kind in England. It depicts another member of the famous Vernon family, a priest, Arthur Vernon (d. 1517), as a half figure holding an open book in his right hand. The whole is supported on a beautiful bracket and has an elaborate canopy above. (See Fan Vaulting, page 152.)

▨ Also in this chapel is a unique monument to Sir Edward Stanley (1621–32), who was killed by a ball hitting his head. He is shown holding a ball while his other hand presses his head. (See Elford, page 125 – also a Stanley!)

## Tongham                               SURREY

ST PAUL This church was consecrated in 1866.

▣ Cyril Forster Garbett (6 February 1875–31 December 1955), Archbishop of York, was born in the vicarage and baptized here.

▣ To the E of the church are the graves of his parents, the Reverend Charles Garbett (1813–95) and his wife, Mrs Susan Charlotte Garbett (1843–1934). Near by is the grave of Cyril's brother, Basil Maitland Garbett (1876–1900), who was drowned while crossing a river in India.

## Totnes                               DEVON

THE PARISH AND PRIORY CHURCH OF ST MARY This spacious church dominates the town in which it is situated with its typical West-country tower.

The magnificent rood screen dates from c.1459 and is unusual in being constructed of Beer *stone*, unlike the normal wooden Devon screen. Along the bottom are traceried panels, while above are elaborate traceried windows separated by canopied niches that once held statues. This is one of the finest stone screens in a parish church. Access to the top of it was gained from a winding stair on the N side of the chancel.

▣ The medieval pulpit is also of stone.

▣ In the NW corner of the N aisle is a tablet to Walter Venning (1781–1821), who founded the Prison Society of Russia and died at St Petersburg of gaol fever. The inscription is very rare as it is in Russian and reads (translated), 'I was in prison and you visited me'.

▣ A copper plate engraving of Rubens's painting 'Elevation of the Cross' (in Antwerp Cathedral) was done by H. Withoue in 1638 under the direction of Rubens himself. This is the largest copper plate engraving in existence.

## Trent                               DORSET

ST ANDREW This fine church can be found in a little village just outside Yeovil and near the Somerset border.

▣ The medieval stone spire was rebuilt from 1908 to 1909 and is rare in Dorset.

▣ Archbishop Lord Geoffrey Francis Fisher (1887–1972), ninety-ninth Archbishop of Canterbury, who crowned Queen Elizabeth II on 2 June 1953, retired here in 1962 and died on 15 September 1972. He is buried in a Victorian vault in the churchyard beneath the fifteenth-century cross on the S side of the tower.

▣ On the E wall of the S transept is a fine plaque recording the life of Archbishop Fisher, dedicated in 1974.

▣ The fine rood screen dates from c.1450.

▣ The richly decorated pulpit is Dutch and dates from c.1600.

▣ The beautiful stained glass in the E window dates from c.1550 to 1650 and came from Germany and Switzerland. It was brought here by a former rector c.1850.

▣ In the E respond of the N chapel arch is a monument to Anna Coker, wife of Thomas Gerard. Dating from 1633, the monument has a Latin inscription, but on the soffit of the archway runs the text, 'All flesh is grass and the glory of it is as the flovre of the feilde'. This appears as 'mirror writing' except for the letter 's'. Perhaps the person who repainted this in 1792 was illiterate and did not know which way the letters should be painted. (See also East Budleigh, page 114, Morwenstow, page 244 and Stow, page 342.)

▣ In the N chapel, apart from several monuments to the Gerard family, is a life-size effigy of the Reverend W. H. Turner

*The beautiful church at Trent has a rare stone spire for Dorset.*

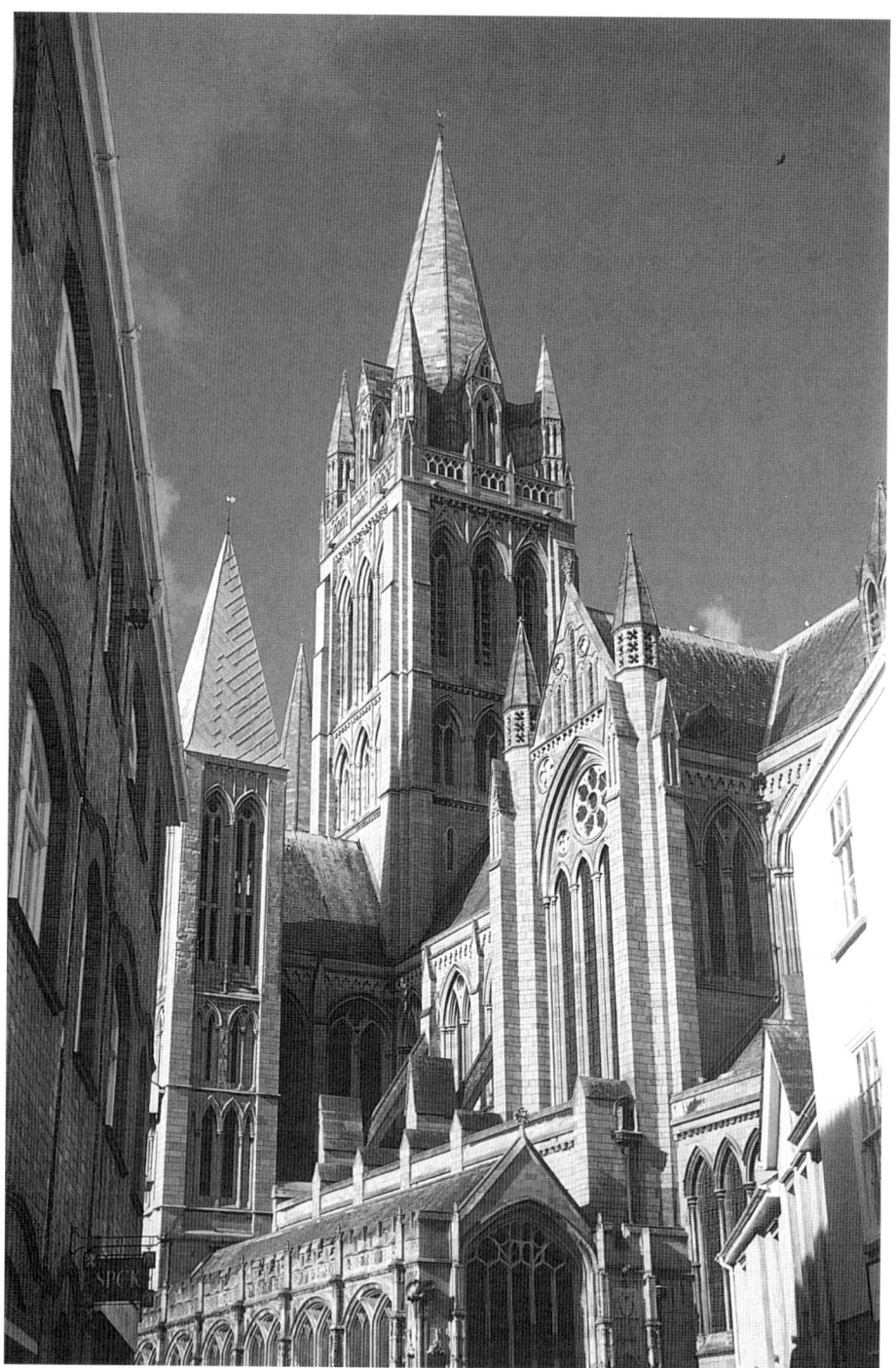

*In spite of being hemmed in by secular buildings, Truro Cathedral rises impressively above the city.*

(d. 1870), who restored the church and lengthened the nave.

Many of the pews in the nave date from *c*.1510 and have carvings depicting emblems of the Passion, a priest holding a chalice and a beautiful carving of the Holy Family. Four of them together form the prayer, *'Ave Maria Gratia Plena Dominus Tecum Amen'*.

## Trottiscliffe (pronounced 'Trosley') KENT

ST PETER & ST PAUL is 2.41 km (1½ miles) from the centre of the village in a remote situation with only a few cottages and Trosley Court near by.

There are interesting box pews and a fantastic pulpit with an elaborate sounding board resting on a palm tree. It was designed by Henry Keene in 1781 and was in use up to 1820 in Westminster Abbey, London. It was not re-erected after the coronation of George IV and came to Trottiscliffe in 1824.

The two wooden plaques on either side of the communion table were given in memory of a Sydney Lee (d. 12 February 1936).

The communion rails date from *c*.1700 and have a unique feature – a small alms-box built between the rails left of the gate and used at churchings.

At the sw end of the nave is a metal plate from the coffin of a lady called Sarah Whittaker (d. 7 September 1782, aged 49 years).

A window on the N side of the chancel by K. and J. Hill, unveiled in 1988, commemorates 1200 years of Christianity on this site.

## Trotton                    WEST SUSSEX

ST GEORGE is situated prettily near the beautiful Trotton Bridge (*c*.1400) spanning the little River Rother.

In the nave floor is the fine brass to Margaret de Camoys (*c*.1310), a member of the famous Camoys family (Lord Camoys – see below – served Richard II and was with Henry V at Agincourt). This is the oldest brass to a woman in the world.

On a table-tomb in the chancel is the magnificent brass of Lord Thomas Camoys (1419) and Elizabeth, his wife. He wears the Garter on his left leg.

High up on the s wall of the chancel a brass plate commemorates Thomas Otway, poet and dramatist, born in Trotton in 1652.

On the w wall of the nave a wall painting (*c*.1380) shows Christ in Judgement and Moses with the Tablets of the Law. On the right is the Good Man surrounded by the Seven Deeds of Mercy and on the left, the Evil Man with the Seven Deadly Sins.

## Truro                    CORNWALL

THE CATHEDRAL AND PARISH CHURCH OF ST MARY The cathedral dominates the city in a style reminiscent of French cathedrals.

The foundation stone was laid on 20 May 1880, the architect being John L. Pearson. It was completed in 1910.

In the N transept hangs a fine painting called 'Cornubia – Land of the Saints', by John Miller. It was unveiled by Prince Charles on 20 May 1980.

Also in the N transept a monument commemorates John Robartes (d. 21 March 1614, 'aged 76 or thereabouts') and Phillippe, his wife.

In the N choir aisle there is a terracotta panel called 'The Way to Calvary'. The work of George Tinworth, it was given by F. Walters Bond as a thank-offering for the safe return of two sons from the Boer War in 1902.

▦ The magnificent organ was built in 1887 by Henry Willis.

▦ On the s side of the choir is St Mary's aisle – all that remains of the original parish church of Truro. Note the many coloured bosses in the barrel roof.

▦ On the s side of the cathedral, almost opposite the N transept, is the baptistery, considered by some to be the most beautiful part of the cathedral. It honours the memory of the missionary Henry Martyn, who was born in Truro in 1781.

▦ In the w window of the s aisle is a picture of John Wesley preaching at Gwennap Pit in Cornwall.

▦ On the N wall of the N aisle a small tablet commemorates Sir Arthur Quiller-Couch (1863–1944), who, it says, as 'author, critic and anthologist kindled in others a lively and discriminating love of English literature'.

▦ The central tower and spire were completed in 1903 as Cornwall's memorial to Queen Victoria. The spire is 76.2 m (250 feet) high – a foot for every mile of the city's distance from London!

## Tudeley                              KENT

ALL SAINTS was rebuilt c.1765 with a plain brick w tower.

▦ Five windows in the N aisle (chiefly of blue glass), two windows on the s side of the nave (predominantly yellow) and nine other windows are filled with abstract glass by Marc Chagall, the Russian-born artist.

▦ Chagall's E window of a beautiful blue was installed in 1967. It was commissioned by Sir Henry and Lady d'Avigdor-Goldsmid, family and friends to commemorate Sarah Venetia d'Avigdor-Goldsmid, who was killed with her friend, David Winn, in a sailing accident off the south coast on 19 September 1963, aged 21. They

had been sailing with Lord and Lady Longford's son, Patrick Pakenham, when their boat capsized some miles from shore. Although Pakenham managed to swim ashore, the other two died from cold and exhaustion.

The window depicts the crucified Christ above sea waves of a brilliant blue with the figure of a girl submerged in the water. At the foot of the cross is a rider on a red horse symbolizing happiness, and other figures can be seen emerging from the water. The window is constructed in 12 major pieces.

This is one of only two churches in the British Isles containing stained glass by Chagall (1887–1985), the other being Chichester Cathedral (see page 72).

▦ In the N wall of the chancel is a monument to George Fane (d. 1572) and his wife, Joan (d. 1545). It is a good example of an Elizabethan tomb with relief inscriptions in Roman capitals and twin shields on the pediment against the wall.

## Twycross                    LEICESTERSHIRE

ST JAMES THE GREAT This church is situated on the busy A444 road.

▦ The piers separating the N aisle from the nave have no capitals – a rare feature.

▦ The main E window is made with superb thirteenth-century glass from St Denis and St Chappelle, Paris. Jumbled fragments are in the tracery. The middle light shows Christ being taken down from the cross while below, Joshua's spies are seen carrying grapes.

▦ The fine brass eagle lectern was presented by Augusta Curzon on 18 November 1901.

▦ Armorial glass in the s nave window shows the Curzon arms in the centre with the motto, 'Let Curzon holde what Curzon helde'.

*The east window of Twycross, Leicestershire, glows with glorious thirteenth-century French glass.*

Roof bosses are an interesting yet often unobserved feature in our churches and cathedrals. They usually take the form of a richly carved block of stone or wood inserted at the point where the ribs of a roof meet, or where wooden beams are joined or meet at an angle. Sometimes they form the keystone but frequently they are merely decorative.

Occasionally a roof boss would be carved in situ, but more frequently the carving was done in a workshop and the completed boss then taken to the church or cathedral for insertion in the roof. Medieval craftsmen often spent hours carving a boss very elaborately and favourite subjects include biblical scenes, heraldry, leaves, flowers, animals and especially scenes from contemporary life. The latter could even include such graphic subjects as a man at stool (as seen in St Mary Redcliffe in Bristol, Gloucestershire, and Wells Cathedral, Somerset)!

Because roof bosses are often high up and can only be viewed clearly with the aid of binoculars, they escaped the iconoclasm that destroyed so much of beauty during the Reformation (which lasted approximately from 1533 to 1558) and the Civil War (1642–51).

The study of bosses is an absorbing one and the acknowledged expert in this field is the late C. J. P. Cave, whose book *Roof Bosses in Medieval Churches* is thoroughly recommended. The beginner who wishes to study the whole range of subjects on medieval bosses would do well to visit either Norwich Cathedral or St Mary Redcliffe in Bristol. Norwich Cathedral has more roof bosses than any other English cathedral (about 900), including five series in the cloisters depicting stories. St Mary Redcliffe has over 1200 bosses, all of which (except those under the tower) have been covered with pure gold.

For those interested in heraldry, Canterbury Cathedral has the greatest collection in stone of medieval heraldry in Europe, with 820 bosses in the cloisters showing coats of arms. Also of interest are bosses that show two or three heads side by side, with eyes common to both or three of them (Canterbury and Chichester cathedrals have examples of these).

Other subjects that may prove interesting are as follows:

## DATED BOSSES

Although there are hundreds of bosses in our churches and cathedrals, it is a curious fact that very few of them carry a date. As far as I know they are found only in the following churches:

1. Beaulieu (Blessed Virgin & Child), Hampshire – 1204; modern boss bearing the abbey arms.
2. Buckden (St Mary), Cambridgeshire – 1665
3. Cirencester (St John the Baptist), Gloucestershire – 1508
4. Crewkerne (St Bartholomew), Somerset – 1784
5. Milford-on-Sea (All Saints), Hampshire – two bosses dated 1639 and 1640.
6. St Neot (St Anietus), Cornwall – 1593
7. South Brent (St Petrock), Devon – 1637
8. Warmington (St Mary), Northamptonshire – 1650
9. Windsor Castle (St George's Chapel), Berkshire – 1528

## St George

In spite of being the patron saint of England, St George is only shown on roof bosses in the following churches:

1. Banwell (St Andrew), Somerset
2. Beverley (St Mary), East Riding of Yorkshire
3. Norwich Cathedral (The Holy and Undivided Trinity), Norfolk
4. Wootton Courtenay (All Saints), Somerset
5. Worcester Cathedral (Christ and the Blessed Virgin Mary), Worcestershire
6. Worcester (St Andrew), Worcestershire

## St Katherine

St Katherine is shown on bosses with the wheel on which she was martyred. Her boss is found only in the following churches:

1. Norwich Cathedral (The Holy and Undivided Trinity), Norfolk
2. Norwich (St Helen in the Great Hospital), Norfolk
3. Patrington (St Patrick), East Riding of Yorkshire
4. Selworthy (All Saints), Somerset

5. Widecombe-in-the-Moor (St Pancras), Devon

## Crucifixion Bosses

Although the Cross is the symbol of Christianity, it is strange that only ten churches contain bosses depicting the Crucifixion. There is one boss in each, except at Exeter Cathedral (where there are five), and they are located as follows:

1. Canterbury Cathedral (Cathedral Church of Christ), Kent
2. Ely Cathedral (The Holy and Undivided Trinity), Cambridgeshire
3. Exeter Cathedral (St Peter), Devon
4. Nantwich (St Mary), Cheshire
5. Norwich Cathedral (The Holy and Undivided Trinity), Norfolk
6. Peterborough Cathedral (St Peter, St Paul and St Andrew), Cambridgeshire
7. Plympton (St Mary), Devon
8. Ripon Cathedral (St Peter and St Wilfrid), North Yorkshire
9. Salle (St Peter & St Paul), Norfolk
10. Tewkesbury Abbey (St Mary the Virgin), Gloucestershire

# RHINELAND TOWERS

On and near the banks of the River Rhine in Germany there are numerous churches whose towers are surmounted by a spire known as a Rhenish helm. In England there is only one ancient Rhenish helm – the famous Saxon one at Sompting, West Sussex.

However, the Victorians admired this tower and spire and copied it when they built or rebuilt the following towers, which still exist:

1. Churcham (St Andrew), Gloucestershire – 1878

2. Flixton (St Mary), Suffolk – 1856
3. Hawkley (St Peter & St Paul), Hampshire – 1865
4. Manchester (St Mary's RC church) – 1848
5. Southampton (St Peter) Hampshire – 1846
6. Wormhill (St Margaret), Derbyshire – 1864

It is said that the roofs in the above cases were constructed like this, with four diamond-shaped sloping faces, to prevent the build-up of snow.

*The beautiful church at Upwell, Norfolk, towers above the River Nene.*

## Uffington OXFORDSHIRE

THE ASSUMPTION OF ST MARY THE VIRGIN Known as 'the Cathedral of the Vale' (the Vale of the White Horse) this church is almost all original Early English (c.1270) – a rarity for a village church.

 To the E of the N and S transepts are projecting chapels – another rare feature for a small church. Notice how the window tracery is missing. (See also Buckland, page 54 and Cheddleton, page 70.)

 Near the S transept is an E-facing porch – a very unusual position for a porch.

 The central tower is octagonal at the top and used to carry a spire; however this was destroyed by lightning on 2 December 1743.

 A wall memorial commemorates Thomas Hughes, QC (1822–96), an MP and county court judge, who lived here and wrote *Tom Brown's Schooldays*.

 Outside the church, around the walls, are 11 out of 12 original consecration crosses set in circular sunken panels. (See also Edington, page 123 and Ottery St Mary, page 260.)

## Ufford SUFFOLK

THE ASSUMPTION OF OUR LADY Just off the busy A12, this church stands a short distance from Woodbridge and quite near the little River Deben.

 The magnificent wooden font cover is the most beautiful in the world. Dating from c.1450 it is 5.5 m (18 feet) tall and contains much original painting. The pinnacles and buttresses are most delicately carved. There is one large statue at the base but the others are missing. Small ones remain inside the pinnacled buttresses.

The cover is telescopic – the lower part slides up over the superstructure. At the top is a pelican pecking its breast.

When the East Anglian iconoclast William Dowsing visited this church in 1643 he was so impressed with this font cover that he only damaged it slightly and removed the statuettes under the canopies.

 Most of the original benches, dating from c.1450, have survived and have lovely carved and traceried ends. Note especially a woman wearing a butterfly headdress.

 On the N wall is a skeleton brass to Richard Ballett (d. 7 June 1598). It shows the arms of the Goldsmiths' Company. The inscription reads,

'Thow mortall mann that wouldest attaine
The happie Havene of hevenly rest
Prepare thy selfe of Graces all
Fayth and Repentance is the best.
Like thee I was somtime
But now am turnd to dust
As thow at length O Earth and slime
Returne to Asshes must
I rest in hope with joye to see
Christ Jesus that redeemed mee.'

 On the floor at the W end of the S aisle is a bell dating from c.1400. The Latin inscription translated reads, 'Make, Margaret, these offices joyful to us'.

The s aisle chapel of St Leonard was designed by Sir Ninian Comper in 1919 in memory of those who died in the First World War. Note in the stained-glass window a modern sailor and soldier assisting Jesus on His way to Calvary.

The vestry is unusually large because it was once used as the village school.

In the churchyard are the stocks and whipping post dating from c.1750.

## Upper Hardres　　　　KENT

ST PETER & ST PAUL is a flint church located in a quiet village just E of the B2068 and s of Canterbury.

The fine brass to John Strete, rector (d. 1405) shows him in academic gown, kneeling in front of a bracket on which stand the figures of St Peter and St Paul. This is a unique arrangement.

The two lancets at the E end contain beautiful glass dating from c.1320 which came from Stelling Church, Kent, in 1795. Red, green and yellow predominate.

In the w window are three roundels of stained glass dating from c.1200; these were damaged by fire in 1972.

## Upwell　　　　NORFOLK

ST PETER This large church, on the border with Cambridgeshire and close to the River Nene, has a square tower with an octagonal top.

The superb angel roofs in the nave and aisles date from c.1450. Some angels hold instruments of the Passion such as a hammer, nails, pincers and a spear.

The N and w galleries dating from c.1810 are a rare survival.

On the N side of the N gallery are two large hooks used for pulling burning thatch off houses.

On the s side of the N gallery is a Stuart Royal Arms, while another superb Victorian wooden Royal Arms is fixed to the w end of the church.

The magnificent brass eagle lectern dating from c.1450 has had a cock's comb added to the head. There is a hole between the feet which have restored talons. The beak is open. The three lions at the base are looking to the right. These three lions were once used as scrapers at the church door until they were replaced and attached to the base by rivets! (See Medieval Brass Lecterns, page 362.)

On the s wall of the chancel is a fine brass of a priest in Eucharistic vestments. It commemorates William Mowbray (d. 1428), presumably a former priest of this church.

A similar brass on the N wall opposite depicts Henry Martin, priest (d. 1435).

On the s wall of the chancel is a memorial to '67 individuals of various age and either sex who in the short period from 21 June to 13 August, 1832 died in this Rectory of Asiatic Cholera, a frightful and previously unknown disease in this country.

Reader! Why hast thou been spared, To what purpose hast thou been left until now?'

## Uxbridge　　　　GREATER LONDON

ST MARGARET is a large flint and stone building with an attractive cupola on the tower; it stands behind the old Market House in the centre of the town.

Leonora Bennet (d. 1638) is shown on an elaborate marble monument in the chancel. (She was the widow of Sir John Bennet, who was Chancellor to Anne of Denmark, James I's wife.) On the side is a grille showing a bony hand grasping the bars from inside! This is unique.

## Wadhurst — EAST SUSSEX

ST PETER & ST PAUL is situated in a beautiful village in the Weald that was, in 1828, the last place to produce Sussex iron.

The spire of this church rises to 33 m (128 feet). The wind vane bears the date 1699 and the church-wardens' initials.

All around the church is an impressive collection of 31 cast-iron tomb slabs or ledgers dating from 1617 to 1799, spanning most of the life of the Wealden iron industry, of which Wadhurst was an important centre.

The slabs are located as follows: 12 in the s aisle; 1 between the s aisle and the nave; 9 in the nave; 7 in the chancel; 1 in the n aisle; 1 in the porch.

There is another on top of a table-tomb in the churchyard, close to the s wall of the church, commemorating an Elizabeth Praysted (d. 16 April 1799). Naturally this slab is not in such good condition as the interior ones, having rusted badly in its exposed position.

This is the largest collection of cast-iron tomb slabs in the British Isles.

Over the altar is suspended a cast-iron cross, which was given in 1967.

On the n side of the chancel is a small alabaster tablet with the kneeling figure of a Mary Dunmoll (d. 1651). Underneath it is the verse:

'Although the earth thy corpse detain,
Yet shall we once more meet again.
For so rejoice and praises sing
To God in Christ our glorious King.'

The E window commemorates the Reverend John Foley, vicar of Wadhurst (d. 1886) and a brass on the s wall of the chancel is in memory of his widow (d. 1898). Six of their children died from diphtheria in the 1850s.

The iron screen between the tower and the nave was designed by Duncan Wilson and erected in 1957.

On the N wall of the N aisle are the Royal Arms of Queen Elizabeth II, designed and executed by R. W. E. Harper in 1977, the year of the Queen's silver jubilee.

## Walpole St Peter — NORFOLK

ST PETER This beautiful church is known as 'Queen of the Marshlands' and 'Cathedral of the Fens'.

The three E bays of the present nave were formerly the chancel and are narrower than the four w bays. Over the third pier from the E end on each side are three sockets; these originally held the rood beam, dividing nave from chancel.

Across the w end is an unusual feature – a wooden screen dating from c.1630.

The font dates from 1532 and has an elaborate cover dating from c.1600.

Also at the w end is a hudd (a shelter resembling a sentry box), which was used by ministers conducting funerals. It dates from c.1750. (See Graveside Shelters or Hudds, page 111.)

The poor box at the w end dates from 1639.

In the nave is a magnificent brass chandelier dating from 1701.

In the chancel are six smaller copies of this chandelier which were given in 1911 in memory of a young woman, Dorothy Hilda Monson, only daughter of Richard and Fanny Monson. She died 1 April 1909, aged 21.

The superb medieval brass eagle lectern dates from c.1475. Its stem is narrower than usual. The eagle has lost its eight talons, its beak is closed but the hole in the tail is open. The three lions at the base are looking slightly to the right. (See Medieval Brass Lecterns, page 362.)

Of the many masons' marks, the best is on the sill of the NW window of the N aisle.

In the chancel, the set of stone canopies over the stalls is very unusual.

Two misericords on the N side of the chancel depict a Pelican in her Piety and an eagle.

Supporting the bookrest on the pulpit are mermaids blowing trumpets!

There are some very fine bosses in the S porch, including the Assumption of Our Lady and the Last Judgement. In the NW corner is a *pietà* – a very rare subject in England.

Outside, at the E end of the nave, is a fine bellcote which still contains the sacring bell, rung during Holy Communion. (When seen in July 1980 the bell was not in use as the bell-clapper had completely rusted away.)

The passage under the high altar is known locally as 'the bolt hole' and contains some good carvings, including a sheep's head. The rings in the walls were used for tethering horses during service time.

# Waltham Abbey      ESSEX

THE ABBEY CHURCH OF WALTHAM HOLY CROSS AND ST LAWRENCE Consecrated on Holy Cross Day, 3 May 1060, this church was founded and endowed by Harold, brother-in-law to King Edward the Confessor. It is the oldest Norman church in the British Isles, having been built by workmen specially brought over from France.

The Norman piers have deeply incised zigzag and spiral patterns on them similar to those in Durham Cathedral, Co. Durham, and elsewhere.

The stained-glass windows at the E end are by Sir Edward Burne-Jones.

In January 2003 much damage was done to the reredos, glass and fittings at the E end by an iconoclast with an axe.

The nave ceiling, reminiscent of Peterborough Cathedral, Cambs., was painted by Sir Edward Poynter in 1860.

Outside the E end of the abbey is the reputed site of King Harold's grave.

The 12 bells in the tower (which was added c.1556–68) are the 'wild bells' that feature in Tennyson's poem 'In Memoriam'.

# Wareham      DORSET

LADY ST MARY This church is attractively situated above the River Frome, near the quay.

The nave dates from 1842 when it replaced a magnificent Saxon nave comparable to Brixworth (Northants.).

At the w end of the nave is the only lead font in Dorset. It is unique in being the only one cast whole and the only one that is *not* circular (it is hexagonal). The bowl dates from c.1100, the base from c.1200. The faces of the Twelve Apostles were

*Warfield Church, Berkshire. The fourteeth-century glass in the tracery complements the Victorian glass below.*

mutilated by Cromwell's soldiers during the Civil War. (See Lead Fonts, page 74.)

 At the E end of the N aisle is a stone coffin that is unique. Traditionally associated with King Edward the Martyr, 978, it is probably much older. Some authorities think it is Roman made in the shape of an Egyptian sarcophagus. Others think it is an early Christian Viking coffin made like a boat that carried dead leaders out to sea after it was set on fire.

 Near this coffin is a stone cresset lamp with two wicks – a rare survival. (See Cresset Stones, page 428.)

 Above the chancel arch is a small window filled with medieval glass.

 On the N side of the chancel is the fine recumbent effigy of Sir William d'Estoke (d. 1294) in chain mail, and on the S side that of Sir Henry d'Estoke (d. 1240) which is not so well preserved.

 On the S side of the sanctuary is the Beckett chapel, built inside a huge buttress and boasting a beautiful stone-vaulted roof.

 At the E end of the S aisle is the crypt chapel of St Edward with another stone-vaulted roof. On the N wall is an icon that came from a Russian church. It was saved in April 1917 by a Wareham man who pulled it from a bonfire where it was about to be burned by the Bolsheviks at the time of the Russian Revolution.

## Wareham                    Dorset

ST MARTIN Dating from c.1030, this is the only Saxon church in Dorset. It was restored and rededicated on 23 November 1936 by the Bishop of Salisbury.

 The central pier of the N arcade dates

from c.1490 and replaced a Purbeck marble one of c.1250.

On the N side of the chancel is a wall painting of St Martin of Tours dividing his cloak and dating from c.1100. Also in the chancel is a Norman consecration cross dating from c.1100 and another at the w end of the nave.

In the N aisle is a fine stone effigy of Lawrence of Arabia (1888–1935) by Eric Kennington. Lawrence lived near by and had a keen interest in the restoration of St Martin's.

# Warfield                    BERKSHIRE

ST MICHAEL THE ARCHANGEL Before the Reformation this church was associated with St Mary's Priory at Hurley, Berks. which accounts for the sumptuous chancel and magnificent E window. The monks came here in the winter when their priory, near the Thames, was flooded. In the chancel is part of the prior's seat.

The N aisle is all that remains of the Early English church, which was rebuilt by the prior from c.1390 to 1410. One original lancet survives.

Across the N aisle and forming the entrance to St Katherine's chapel at the E end is a fine rood screen, which was restored in 1872. The original steps can still be climbed. (This is the only surviving rood screen in Berkshire.)

The beautiful sedilia and piscina in the chancel date from c.1410. Note the carving in one spandrel of a man's head with oak leaves coming from underneath his chin.

The reredos behind the high altar was carved in 1872 from chalk and complements the earlier work.

Behind the altar is a sacrarium or narrow passage, probably used as a vestry or for keeping sacred vessels.

The E window is a superb example of curvilinear or 'flowing' tracery. The glass in the tracery at the top is original and dates from c.1390. Note the flying angels upside down with their censors! The remainder of the glass is Victorian but again, it complements the ancient glass.

In the centre light of the w window of the N aisle is a small figure of St Blaise in a blue cloak. He was the patron saint of wool-combers and this glass dates from c.1500.

On the s wall of the chancel is a mural monument to Thomas Williamson (d. 1611) and his wife. Behind their kneeling figures are shown their eight sons and eight daughters, although the inscription states that they had only seven daughters!

The fine iron-bound chest in the nave dates from c.1690 and is probably German.

On the s wall of the s transept is a memorial plaque to Sir William Herschel which was unveiled on 6 November 1954. He perfected a system of identification by fingerprints. Born at Observatory House, Slough (9 January 1833), he died at Warfield rectory (24 October 1917). Sir William first used fingerprints in 1858 when he was in the Bengal police. Fingerprint classification was invented by Sir Edward Henry and eventually its use spread all over India. When Sir Edward returned to England in 1901 Scotland Yard adopted the same system – that which is now used worldwide.

In the churchyard is a half-timbered building dating from c.1550 which was used as a preparatory school for Eton in c.1870 by the Reverend John Faithful. A bricked-up fireplace has an oven that was used to bake bread for the poor.

# Warlingham     SURREY

ALL SAINTS is located in a village on the North Downs, about 4.82 km (3 miles), NE of Caterham.

A two-light square-headed window on the s side of the church shows Archbishop Cranmer presenting the first *English Prayer Book* to King Edward VI in 1549. Cranmer, who had largely been responsible for its compilation, heard the *Prayer Book* read publicly for the first time in this church on 9 June 1549. He had travelled from his palace at Croydon.

On 30 Nov 2000 the new Church of England *Common Worship Service Book* was used for the first time in this church.

On 24 September 1950 the BBC made history by televising a harvest festival service from this church – the first televised service from a parish church in the British Isles.

On the N wall is a mural of St Christopher dating from *c.*1450.

Near one of the ancient yew trees SE of the church is the table-tomb of Sir Joseph Swan (1828–1914), the great inventor, who lived here at the end of his life. Among his many achievements was the modern electric lamp, the process of making 'half tone' printers' blocks, photographic plates, printing paper and artificial silk.

# Warnford     HAMPSHIRE

OUR LADY OF WARNFORD This church stands isolated in a park near the River Meon. In early spring (February) the snowdrops in the churchyard are a wonderful sight.

Almost opposite the s porch under a holly tree is the grave of George Lewis, who died on Sunday 17 December 1830 when a branch he was cutting fell and killed him. His skeleton, carved on the gravestone, points accusingly at the branch, while his saw leans against the tree on the left.

E of the church, among the nettles, are the ruins of St John House, a fine aisled hall dating from *c.*1210 to 1220 and built by William St John, who succeeded the de Ports as Lord of the Manor of Warnford. Built of flint, the hall originally had four columns 7.6 m (25 feet) high to support the roof. Only two remain.

Aisled halls are very rare. Another, also in ruins, is at Clarendon near Salisbury, Wilts., and a complete example survives at Oakham Castle, Rutland.

Over the s and former N door are inscriptions recording that Adam de Port, Lord of the Manor and patron of Warnford Church from 1171 to 1213, restored and enlarged the building – very unusual inscriptions.

On the s side, inside the s porch, the inscription in Lombardic lettering translated reads: 'Brothers, bless in your prayers the founders young and old of this temple; Wilfrid founded it; good Adam restored it.' (St Wilfrid founded it in 682 and Adam de Port restored it *c.*1190.)

Above the inscription is a Saxon sundial with foliated leaves at each corner. (See also nearby Corhampton, Hants.)

Outside the church, on the N side, a similar contemporary inscription reads, 'May the race signed with the Cross (i.e. Christians) from the rising of the sun bless Adam de Port by whom I have been restored.'

The tower dates from *c.*1130 and is unusual in possessing two circular bell openings on each face.

On the N side of the nave are the Royal Arms of George IV (1821) in very good condition.

On the s side of the altar is a sumptuous

monument to a Sir Thomas Neale (d. 1621) and his two wives, Elizabeth and Mary. The inscription in the back (which is difficult to read) ends:

'. . . What pious mindes should do at such an end.
Then let each one that seeth this with an eye
Quite void of moisture be turned to stone and dry.'

To the N of the altar is the simpler tomb of William Neale and his two wives. William (d. 1601) was the father of Sir Thomas. Both of these monuments boast delicate alabaster carving.

On the N side of the chancel are three choir stalls dating from c.1450; these came from a religious house demolished 1536–9.

# Warwick                    WARWICKSHIRE

THE COLLEGIATE CHURCH OF ST MARY crowns the hill of this county town and is well seen from the magnificent castle.

The impressive tower, built over the street, is 53 m (174 feet) high and was completed c.1706 after a disastrous fire in 1694 had destroyed the original tower and nave along with over 200 houses. The nave was completed in 1704.

The tower was designed by Sir William Wilson and moved a bay westward on Sir Christopher Wren's advice – hence the two large piers at the W end of the nave, originally intended to carry the tower.

The choir dates from c.1390 and has rare 'flying ribs' springing from shafts between the windows and supporting the vaulting; other examples of these may be seen at Bristol Cathedral, Lincoln Cathedral, St David's Cathedral and Southwell Cathedral (see pages 51, 199, 300 and 326 respectively).

In front of the high altar is the tomb of Thomas Beauchamp I, Earl of Warwick and Katherine, his wife. He died of plague at the siege of Calais in 1369.

This alabaster monument was badly damaged in the fire of 1694 so the angels at the head are made of plaster!

About 1.83 m (6 feet) above the sanctuary rail on the N and S walls are two iron rings which formerly carried the Lenten veil.

On the S side of the chancel some steps lead down to three small rooms between the choir and Beauchamp chapel. The one on the E side is known as the 'little chantry' or dean's chapel and is roofed with fan tracery and pendants similar to Henry VII's chapel, Westminster Abbey, London. On the S side is an unusual *wooden* piscina with a leaden drainpipe inside it.

On the N side of the dean's chapel is an oratory restored in 1981 in memory of a lady called Evelyn Mary Rudge (1913–77). Wooden steps lead to a prayer desk with a 'squint' to the high altar at the side.

On the N side of the chancel are the vestries and the chapter house. From the first vestry, steps lead down to the crypt. The three W bays date from c.1123 and the two E bays from c.1367. These later bays were added when Thomas Beauchamp I rebuilt the chancel. He and his wife are buried below their tomb in the chancel above, so their coffins are actually in the roof space over the crypt!

On the N side of the crypt is a chamber that may have been used for depositing relics but since c.1750 has been a private vault for the family of the Earls of Warwick.

At one end of the crypt is the base of a ducking stool. This is one of only two ducking stools surviving in a church. (See also Leominster Priory, page 196.)

In the chapter house, which has stone seats, is the enormous tomb of Fulke

*St Mary's, Warwick, viewed from the castle.*

Grevill (1554–1628), described as 'a friend of Sir Philip Sidney and Servant to Queen Elizabeth'. He was murdered in London and his body brought back here.

⬚ In the s transept, on the e wall, is the fine brass of Thomas Beauchamp II (d. 1401) and his wife, Margaret Ferrers.

⬚ From the s transept on the e side, steps lead down into the magnificent Beauchamp chapel or Chapel of Our Lady. Started in 1443, it was completed in 1464. There are three bays with typical Perpendicular windows, the e one very unusual in having canopied niches and figures which also occur on the central mullions – 30 figures in all. In the e window is some original glass dating from 1447. Coloured jewels have been used in some of the robes. Richard Beauchamp is shown kneeling at the base of the central light, but his head has been lost and the head of one of his daughters inserted in its place!

In the centre of the chapel is the superb tomb of Richard Beauchamp (1381–1439), the Fifth Earl of Warwick. His effigy of bronze gilt rests on a Purbeck marble tomb-chest. His hands are open as if in adoration to the Virgin on the boss above. At his feet are a muzzled bear and griffin and around the tomb are 14 'weepers', between which are 18 angels holding scrolls. The 'weeper' on the s side at the e end is Richard Neville or 'Warwick the Kingmaker'. He married Richard Beauchamp's daughter, Anne, and was buried at Bisham Abbey (Berkshire) after being killed at the second Battle of Barnet (Herts.) in 1471.

Above the effigy is a latten hearse, originally carrying a velvet pall. It consists of six hoops connected by five long bars.

At the ends of the rods are enamel shields inlaid with silver. This is one of three remaining permanent hearses in England. (See also Gloucester Cathedral, page 148 and West Tanfield, page 405.)

Other tombs in the Beauchamp chapel include those of Robert Dudley (1533–88), Earl of Leicester and his wife, Lettice, on the N side of the chapel, Robert, their infant son (d. 1584, aged three) on the s side of the altar and Ambrose Dudley (1528–90), Earl of Warwick, who is shown wearing the Order of the Garter and lies to the w of Richard Beauchamp.

The roof of the Beauchamp chapel has a lierne vault and some of the bosses are coloured.

The tower contains a ring of ten bells, the tenor weighing 1266.45 kg (1 ton 4 cwt 3 qr 20 lb). Five times a day a tune is played on the bells.

# Wasdale Head     CUMBRIA

ST OLAF In the heart of the Lake District among magnificent scenery is this, one of England's smallest churches at 12.2 m (40 feet) long and 5.2 m (17 feet) wide.

One of the windows contains a lozenge of stained glass, 10 cm (4 inches) square, bearing the text from Psalm 121, v.1, 'I will lift up mine eyes unto the hills' – supposedly the smallest inscribed glass window in England.

# Weare     SOMERSET

ST GREGORY stands in a small village near Cheddar; it has a fine pinnacled tower.

The famous comedian Frankie Howerd (1917–92) is buried in the churchyard. He lived near by and was a frequent visitor to this church.

# Welford     BERKSHIRE

ST GREGORY Rebuilt from 1852 to 1855 by Thomas Talbot Bury (1811–77), this church is very unusual in possessing much unfinished carving.

The attractive round tower (and spire) is one of only two round towers in Berkshire. Although rebuilt, it follows closely the pattern of the old one.

Above the s porch is a statue of St Gregory wearing the papal tiara. The porch is stone-vaulted but the bosses and capitals are uncarved, except for one column on the E side.

Inside, the unfinished carving is as follows:

† Ten uncarved roof corbels in the N aisle and ten in the s.

† Eight uncarved roof corbels in the nave. The only two carved ones are those on each side of the chancel arch.

† The corbels at each end of the hood moulds around the nine windows of the N and s aisles are uncarved as are those around the wall recesses in the N aisle, with the exception of the central one.

† The capitals of the tower arch are also uncarved.

Did money run out for the completion of these carvings, or did the sculptor die?

The central recess in the N aisle contains a fine brass depicting William Nicholson seated in his robes, holding a model of Wickham Church in his left hand and Welford in his right. Above it is the inscription:

'In the churchyard at the east end of this church is interred the body of the Rev. William Nicholson M.A. third son of Christopher Armytage Nicholson of Balrath Co. Meath, Esq., and of Catherine his wife, daughter of William Newcome D.D., Primate of All Ireland.

*The round tower of Welford, Berkshire, is one of only two in the county.*

He died December xv AD MDCCCLXXVIII [1878] in the LXXIII [73] year of his age having held the rectory of Welford cum Wickham XLII [42] years. He rebuilt the chapel at Wickham and a great part of the church at Welford.

🔲 Under the tower is a quaint wall monument to an Elizabeth Francisci Mundy (1613–89). She is shown with tight lips and wearing a bonnet.

🔲 At the w end of the s aisle is a wall monument to Anna Fortescue (d. 1585). She was the wife of Queen Elizabeth I's treasurer.

🔲 The fine Norman font has 17 interlacing arches and stands on a Victorian base.

🔲 In the stone-vaulted chancel are four fine sedilia which are original Early English work. Inside them are two brass portraits of a Tudor man and priest.

🔲 In the churchyard is the grave of the Reverend William Nicholson (1 July 1805–15 December 1878).

# Wells                                SOMERSET

THE CATHEDRAL CHURCH OF ST ANDREW
This splendid cathedral looks impressive from any vantage point in the little town in which it is located, especially from the E end.

🔲 The unique w front contains the largest and widest display of medieval sculpture in the world – 286 figures still left in situ, out of an original 461. (During restoration work in the 1980s many of them were brought inside for greater preservation.) The display depicts the Heavenly Jerusalem. The architect of this masterpiece was Thomas Norreys, who began building c.1220. The work was completed by 1242.

🔲 The central tower is supported by inverted strainer arches (similar to great pairs of scissors), which give the interior a unique appearance. When the central tower was raised to its present height in 1315 it started to tilt to the w and large cracks appeared. In 1340 these arches were inserted to strengthen the tower and save it from collapse. They have been severely criticized. What do you think of them?

🔲 The nave, consecrated in 1239, contains the earliest compound Gothic pillars in existence composed of a cluster of massed shafts with delicately carved capitals.

🔲 On the N side the following subjects can be seen on the capitals:
† an animal licking its fur
† birds preening feathers
† a human-headed bird carrying a staff
† a fox stealing a goose
† a merman holding a fish
† a long-billed bird with a frog in its mouth
† a pedlar carrying a pack with a rosary in his hand.

On the s side are similarly carved capitals; one of the finest (facing the s nave aisle) shows several human-headed birds, one of which is wearing a mitre!

These superb capitals are well worth studying in detail – there is so much that one might miss with just a superficial glance.

🔲 On the N side of the nave, in the second bay from the E, is the chantry chapel of Bishop Nicholas Bubwith (Bishop from 1407 to 1424) which he erected c.1420. Now known as the Holy Cross chapel it is hexagonal in plan and has an entrance on the N and s sides. There is only a roof at the E end.

🔲 Opposite the Bubwith chantry is the chantry of Dr Hugh Sugar, erected in 1489. Look for the rebus of Dr Sugar – three sugar loaves underneath a doctor's cap. At the E end is a delicate fan vault.

*The central tower of Wells Cathedral, Somerset, supported underneath on unique strainer arches.*

*Wells Cathedral, Somerset – the magnificent west front with its unique display of medieval sculpture.*

Connected to Dr Sugar's chantry is an early Renaissance stone pulpit dating from c.1540 and given by Bishop Knight.

◈ In the s transept are a number of interesting and amusing capitals depicting a man with toothache (there are several capitals illustrating this theme!), fruit 'stealers' (one of whom is caught) and a cobbler at work.

◈ On the E side of the s transept is St Calixtus's chapel containing the tomb of Thomas Boleyn, Precentor of Wells, 1451–72. Notice the superb delicate carvings of the Holy Trinity and the Annunciation to the Virgin on the side of the tomb and the unique medieval carvings of quire clothing.

◈ The E window of the quire contains glass dating from 1340 and depicts the Tree of Jesse.

◈ In the quire are several finely carved misericords dating from c.1350. Among the subjects depicted are two philosophers talking together, a bat with outstretched wings, a cock, and a cat playing an instrument like a violin.

◈ In the retroquire are carvings of two small animals each of which are biting off three vaulting ribs at the top which do not lead anywhere!

◈ Also in the retroquire is a large cope chest dating from c.1350 and still in use.

◈ The chapter house was completed by 1306. It is octagonal with a central pier supporting the beautiful vaulted roof. Around the arcading are numerous carved heads including six popes and ten bishops.

◈ The worn steps leading into the chapter house continue upwards to the unique chain gate and bridge (built in 1459) and provide a covered way to the vicars' hall and Vicars' Close. The Vicars' Close, built to house the men of the quire, is the oldest continuously inhabited street in Europe.

◈ At the foot of the chapter house stairs notice the corbel of a peasant whose right hand appears to support the vault, while his left holds a staff which he thrusts into a dragon's mouth.

◈ In the entrance to the undercroft (underneath the chapter house) from the N quire aisle, the corbels supporting the roof on the E side are interesting – two have been deliberately inverted!

◈ On the right side of the doorway leading to the undercroft is a finely carved corbel and next to it an old stone lantern in which candles were placed.

◈ The inner door of the undercroft exhibits exquisite medieval ironwork. The doors and barred windows date from when this was the cathedral treasury.

◈ Inside the undercroft, on the right of the entrance, is a stoup, inside which is a delightful carving of a dog gnawing a bone.

◈ On the wall of the N transept is the famous clock with a tournament of horsemen every hour, the same one being struck down in the saddle by his enemy. The clock face (the oldest in the world with its original dials) is divided into 24 hours with noon at the top and midnight at the bottom. A large gilt star represents the sun for the hour hand with a small star for the minute hand on the inner circle showing the minutes.

On the right of the clock is the figure of a man known as 'Jack Blandifer' in early Stuart costume. He sounds the quarter hours with his feet.

The clock dates from c.1390 and is the oldest *complete* mechanical clock in England, although the works were renewed in 1838. (Salisbury Cathedral's clock dates from 1386 but has no face or quarter-jacks.) The old mechanism is now on loan to the Science Museum, South Kensington, London. This clock was probably ordered by Bishop Erghum, who came from Salisbury, Wilts., in 1388. Both clocks were probably made by the same craftsman.

◈ Below the clock is a figure of Christ our Saviour. Carved from yew wood by E. J. Clack, it was erected in 1956 in memory of the Reverend Thomas Henry Sissmore.

◈ On the E side of the N transept is a monument to Bishop Kidder, Bishop of Bath and Wells from 1691 to 1703. The figure of the woman in front, which may represent his daughter, is badly damaged.

◈ In the S quire aisle is a coffin-shaped incised slab commemorating Bishop Bitton II, 1267–74. This is one of the oldest incised slabs in England.

◈ Also in the S quire aisle is the chantry chapel and tomb of Thomas Bekynton, Chancellor of England, Bishop of Bath and Wells, 1443–64. Notice the cadaver underneath. The colouring is original.

◈ The N porch, leading into the N nave aisle, contains unusual interesting arches and chevron mouldings over the door.

◈ Under the NW tower is a pyx canopy, c.1290, which formerly hung over the high altar. This is the earliest example known in England and one of only four surviving. The others are at Dennington, Suffolk, (see page 101), Milton Abbey, Dorset, and Tewkesbury Abbey (see page 354).

◈ The SW tower contains the heaviest ring of ten bells in the world. The tenor weighs 2864 kg (2 tons 16 cwt 1 qr 14 lb) and is called Harewell. It is the fifth heaviest ringing bell in the world. Heavier tenors are at Liverpool, Merseyside, Exeter, Devon, St Paul's, London, and York (see pages 208, 131, 214 and 441 respectively). (See also Bells, page 293.)

◈ The following roof bosses are of interest:

† In the w walk of the cloisters (not far from the cathedral shop) is the rather coarse subject of three men at stool on one roof boss! (This subject is only found on a boss in one other place, namely St Mary Redcliffe, Bristol – see page 53.)

† Also in the w walk of the cloisters, on the w side, is a boss depicting a man playing the bagpipes. This subject is found on only one other roof boss and that is in Winchester Cathedral (see page 420).

† In the lady chapel is a roof boss showing Christ in Glory with the wounds of His crucifixion and wearing the Crown of Thorns. Christ wearing the Crown of Thorns only occurs elsewhere on roof bosses in Ely Cathedral (see page 126) Winchester Cathedral (see page 420) and St Stephen's Cloister, Houses of Parliament, Westminster.)

To the s of the cathedral is the beautiful Bishop's Palace and Gardens surrounded by a moat. To the left of the gatehouse entrance is a small bell with a short rope attached to it. Mute swans on the moat can sometimes be seen ringing the bell for food! Swans were first trained to do this in the nineteenth century and the present swans continue the tradition, passing it on to their young.

## Wells-next-the-Sea      NORFOLK

ST NICHOLAS was struck by lightning on 3 August 1879 and almost totally destroyed by fire (although a fine chest dated 1635 survived). The church was rebuilt very well.

The medieval brass lectern was dug up in a nearby field called Church Marsh. Halfway down the stem is a hole the size of a two-pence piece caused, according to tradition, by the pick of the man who discovered it. Below the hole is a large

dent. At the base are three stylized lions.

The lectern was fortunate to survive the fire of 1879 if indeed it was in the church then. A piece of the tail feathers was cut out in situ and stolen, c.1970. (See Mediaval Brass Lecterns, page 362.)

## Welsh Newton      HEREFORDSHIRE

ST MARY THE VIRGIN This little church comprises a nave, chancel and slim w tower with a short octagonal stone broach spire, all dating from c.1250. The porch dates from c.1350 and has stone seats made out of ancient grave slabs.

The stone rood screen, comprising three arches, dates from c.1320 and is a rare survival. It is decorated with the ballflower ornament.

On the s side is an original dormer window which would have given light to the crucifix on top of the screen.

On the N side of the chancel is a stone seat dating from c.1250 and which may have served as a 'fridstool' or seat of sanctuary.

Immediately w of the churchyard cross is the grave of St John Kemble inscribed, 'J. K. Dyed the 22 of August Anno Do. 1679'. He was hanged for alleged complicity in the Popish Plot of 1678–9.

The last chantry chapel in England was founded here in 1547 during the last year of Henry VIII's reign. No trace now remains of it.

## Westbourne      WEST SUSSEX

THE BEHEADING OF ST JOHN THE BAPTIST is one of only two churches in England with this very rare dedication, observed on 29 August. (The other is Doddington, Kent.)

*One of the bells at West Challow, Oxon, is the oldest in the British Isles bearing the maker's name.*

The yew trees leading to the N door were planted in 1545 and comprise the oldest yew avenue in England.

The fine brass chandeliers in the nave date from 1737.

In the chancel is a memorial to Richard Barwell (d. 1804) by Joseph Nollekens. Barwell was a nabob who made his fortune with the East India Company. To commemorate this he has a carving of an elephant's head at the base of his memorial.

## West Challow        OXFORDSHIRE

ST LAWRENCE This simple little church is situated in a remote village in the Vale of the White Horse.

In an original w bellcote, exposed to the elements, are two bells, one of which is the oldest bell in the British Isles still bearing the maker's name. Inscribed, *'Povel le poter me fist'* (Paul the Potter made me) it was cast *c.*1284. (See Bells, page 293.)

The N porch is a beautiful example of original fifteenth-century woodwork.

In the E window are fragments of stained glass dating from *c.*1450.

## Westdean        EAST SUSSEX

ALL SAINTS is found in a small village, nestling in the Downs, just off the A259 near Seaford; it has an unusual spire on its w tower.

In the churchyard is the grave of Sir John Anderson (8 July 1882–4 January 1958), later Lord Waverley, Home Secretary during the Second World War. He gave his name to an air-raid shelter which was designed by Sir William Paterson in 1938 and which, with some modification, became known as the Anderson shelter.

Lord Waverley lived at Westdean Manor.

Inside the church in the NW corner of the nave is a bronze bust of Lord Waverley by Sir Jacob Epstein which was unveiled by Harold Macmillan on 19 April 1960.

In a niche in the S wall of the nave is a bust of the painter Sir Oswald Birley. Sculpted by Claire Sheridan, it was unveiled by Lady Churchill on 1 June 1958.

Against the N wall are two fine tomb canopies.

## West Dean        WEST SUSSEX

ST ANDREW This church was badly damaged by fire on 26 November 1934 and was rebuilt by the architect Frederick Etchells.

The tower was built in 1726 and the date appears on the sundial on the S side.

On the N side of the nave is a blocked Saxon doorway, the stonework reddened by the fire.

Among the names on the war memorial in the N transept is that of Simon Eden, son of Sir Anthony Eden, a former prime minister.

Under the window in the S transept is the bronze effigy of William Dodge James (1854–1912). He lived in West Dean House and was a great friend of King Edward VII, who he often entertained here. This effigy was sculptured by Sir William Goscombe John.

The triple E window has modern glass by Armitage of Powell's and depicts Jesus with St Andrew on the left and St Richard on the right.

On the N side of the chancel is the Lewknor memorial commemorating the son and grandson of Judge Sir Richard Lewknor. Dating from *c.*1640, the figures were badly damaged in the fire.

# Westerham     KENT

ST MARY THE VIRGIN is positioned overlooking the town green on which stands a statue of Sir Winston Churchill.

The church comprises two aisles and a nave of equal length – an unusual feature.

A rare timber spiral staircase inside the tower dates from c.1390. It shows signs of restoration.

Also under the tower on the N side are the Royal Arms of Edward VI (1547–53) with a Latin inscription, which translated says, 'O Lord, save the King'. These are the only arms of Edward VI in existence.

Opposite, on the S side, are the arms of George III dating from 1804.

In the N aisle is a fine Burne-Jones window made in the William Morris workshops and depicting the Nativity. Underneath a plaque reads:

'This window was erected in 1909, to the memory of Major General James Wolfe, conqueror of Quebec, who was killed in the hour of victory on Sept., 13, 1759. James Wolfe was born in this parish on Jan., 2, 1727, baptized in this church on Jan., 11, 1727, and spent the first twelve years of his life in Westerham.'

In the S or St Katherine's chapel is a sanctuary lamp given by Sir Winston and Lady Churchill in 1950. It is maintained in memory of Sir Winston.

Attached to the wall of the S chapel are three palimpsest brasses. The largest commemorates Richard Potter (d. 4 May 1563). The reverse shows it is part of a larger brass from Broadway, Worcestershire.

Another brass commemorates a priest, Sir William Dye (d. 1567). He is shown wearing a cassock and surplice, while around his neck is a large scarf arranged like a stole. This is the only example of a post-Reformation brass to a parish priest showing him dressed like this. Other brasses to post-Reformation priests show them in civilian dress or in a preaching gown.

Of the six other brasses in this chapel, the brass to a lady called Anne Hayward and her children (1529) was once used as a fender in a shop of the parish clerk, a cobbler!

On the N wall of this chapel is a monument to a John Thorpe (d. 1703) with a curiously arranged inscription.

One of the piers separating this chapel from the chancel is encased in six straps of iron to prevent it from breaking.

# West Hendred     OXFORDSHIRE

HOLY TRINITY is picturesquely situated in a quiet village by a small stream.

In the chancel and nave are several medieval floor tiles dating from c.1500 – a rare feature.

A unique inscription can be seen in the SW window of the S aisle. On the right-hand side, near the top, is a small piece of plain glass scratched roughly, 'C. Parker glazed this Church Mar. 2, 1784 and glad of the job'. He was paid £3.68 (£3 13s. 8½ d) for the work – a sizeable sum in those days.

# Westley Waterless     CAMBRIDGESHIRE

ST MARY THE LESS is situated at the end of a quiet lane near a farm.

In the S aisle are the magnificent brasses of Sir John and Lady Alyne de Creke, c.1325. Each figure is 1.65 m. (5 feet 5 inches) long and the brasses are in excellent condition. Each brass is also in two pieces. Sir John carries a shield and his uncrossed legs rest on a lion, while his wife's rest on a lapdog.

These brasses are:

† the earliest in England representing a man and his wife

† the earliest of six depicting the cyclas (a type of surcoat) period of armour

† among a few bearing the craftsman's mark, as opposed to an actual signature.

The craftsman is believed to have been Walter le Masun.

## West Malling       KENT

ST MARY THE VIRGIN is at one of end of this small town, which lies just s of the M20; the spire of the church dominates the scene.

The nave and aisles were rebuilt in 1901.

The N porch was built in 1903. Inside, on the E wall, is the following notice:

'1903. Thanks be to God. The Porch and Pews of this church were made by the sale of a jug having silver mount- ing with the London hallmark for 1581.'

On the s side of the chancel is a fine marble monument, richly coloured, to one Sir Robert Brett (d. 1620), Lady Brett (d. 1617) and Henry Brett – only son and child (d. 1609). On the left side is a skeleton draped in a shroud while opposite kneels a child.

On the w gallery is a rare and magnifi- cent example of the Royal Arms of King James II (1685–8).

## West Malvern       WORCESTERSHIRE

ST JAMES This church was built by G. E. Street between 1870 and 1871.

On the s side of the churchyard, near the war memorial cross, a large marble slab covers the grave of Peter Mark Roget, MD, FRS who died at West Malvern on 12 September 1869, aged 90, and his daughter, Catherine Mary Roget (d. 20

February 1905, aged 79). Roget was author of the now famous *Thesaurus of English Words and Phrases*.

## West Meon       HAMPSHIRE

ST JOHN THE EVANGELIST Built in 1844, the entire outside of this church has superb knapped flint work.

On the top of the screen at the w end is a fine wooden Royal Arms of 1712. These were removed from the old church when the present one was built and placed in the loft of the builder's house. They remained there until 1951!

In the lower churchyard, near the steps leading to the s door, is the large table- tomb of Thomas Lord (d. 13 January 1832, aged 72.) He was the founder of Lord's Cricket Ground (London) in 1787.

## Westonzoyland       SOMERSET

ST MARY Its huge tower dominates Sedgemoor, where the last battle on English soil was fought on 6 July 1685. About 500 prisoners were locked in the church overnight, many of them wound- ed. Five men died here.

The magnificent tie-beam roof is decorated with 24 angels, pendants and foliage bosses.

A chest near the door is inscribed:

'WD NH
1670'

The 500 prisoners from the battle would have seen this!

The beautiful fan-vaulted screen is modern and dates from 1933 to 1939.

The Victorian brass eagle lectern is inscribed: 'To the Glory of God and in loving memory of the Rev. Edgar Huxtable, M.A., for 15 years Vicar of this Parish. Died 10 July, 1897 aged 87 years.'

*The magnificent tower of Westonzoyland, Somerset, dominates the surrounding countryside.*

# ROUND TOWERS

Churches with round towers always come as a surprise to people who see them for the first time. Most of those in England are located in the counties of Norfolk and Suffolk, but a few can be found elsewhere, in Cambridgeshire, Essex, Sussex, Berkshire and Hertfordshire. There are also three in Wales.

No one knows for certain why round towers were built as opposed to the traditional square or rectangular ones. The theory is, however – based on the fact that they are found in regions where there is usually a shortage of good building stone – that a round tower eliminated the need for squared stones for quoins or corners. A round tower could be built of flints or odd stones that did not need to be shaped. Interestingly, though, the square tower of Beeston Regis, Norfolk, is built of flints without quoins and therefore could have been built circular, thus disproving the theory that a tower without quoins had to be circular. (An explanation often given by country folk many years ago as to why there are so many round towers in East Anglia was that these towers were originally well linings that remained when the waters of Noah's flood subsided!) The only dressed (squared, cut) stone in round towers is used around windows or later doorways and battlements. Although most of them are built of flint, Bessingham and Bexwell (Norfolk) are built of an orange-coloured stone called carstone.

*Herringfleet, Suffolk.*

Originally, the early round towers did not have any doorways at ground level. For people to gain access a ladder had to be let down from an opening high up and then drawn back up again after they had entered. This supports the theory that these towers were originally places of refuge from the attacking Vikings and is, perhaps, another reason why the majority of them are in East Anglia.

### ADDITIONS TO ROUND TOWERS

Most of our round towers are Saxon in origin but succeeding generations have often altered them by adding extra storeys with decorative flint work, blank (or blind) arcading and battlements. Octagonal upper storeys form impressive features, some of the most beautiful being at Acle and Potter Heigham (Norfolk), Mutford and Theberton (Suffolk) and Great Shefford, Berkshire. Mutford's round tower is the only one to which a Galilee porch (usually at the W end and often used as a chapel in the Middle Ages) has been added, while Roydon near Diss, Norfolk, has an octagonal top which houses the bells.

Quidenham, Norfolk, has a round tower surmounted by a spire. It is curious that two of only three round towers in East Sussex have spires! Other spires on round towers are at: Welford, Berkshire; Great Leighs and Broomfield (Essex); Higham near Newmarket, Suffolk; Croxton, Norfolk (which has a short spire of slate); and Stockton, Norfolk (which has a recessed lead spire). Attractive conical roofs can be seen on the towers at Aslacton, Bawburgh, Freethorpe, Howe, Little Snoring, Moulton St Mary and Welborne (all in Norfolk), Southease (East Sussex), Llandysilio and Betws Penpont (Powys). The tower at Hemblington (Norfolk) has an odd little cap.

## OLDEST, LARGEST, SMALLEST AND MORE . . .

The oldest round tower in England is said to be East Lexham, Norfolk, reputedly dating from c.AD900, but some authorities consider that it may have been constructed by Saxon builders influenced by the Norman conquerors after 1066! No one knows for sure which is the oldest round tower.

The largest round tower in England is at Wortham, Suffolk; it has an internal diameter of 8.84 m (29 feet) and is 18.9 m (62 feet) high but it is partially ruined and open to the sky. It has been ruinous since at least 1870. The smallest round tower is at Ashmanaugh, Norfolk, and has an internal diameter of only 1.82 m (6 feet). The tallest and narrowest round tower in East Anglia is at Blundeston, Suffolk, but the tallest in Norfolk is at Rollesby.

All the round towers are truly circular although Ramsholt and Beyton (Suffolk) are often described as being oval. This, however, is because they both possess buttresses giving this illusion. At Ramsholt there are three buttresses on the N, S and W sides and at Beyton, only two (one on the SW, the other at the NW). These two are the only round towers in East Anglia with buttresses built against them although Great Leighs, Essex, has four very typical shallow Norman buttresses and the remains of another over the Norman W doorway.

Of all the round towers, only two exist that are separate from the church. These are at Bramfield, Suffolk, and Little Snoring, Norfolk, although the tower of St Benedict's in Norwich, Norfolk, now exists alone because the remainder of the church was destroyed by German bombs in 1942. St Peter in Ringstead, Norfolk, also had a round tower, which stands alone in a private garden, the church being demolished in 1771.

The most curious tower is at Denton, Norfolk, and is only half round (or semicircular) of stone. The W half collapsed many years ago and was rebuilt square in brick in Victorian times!

The round tower at Sustead, Norfolk, is unique in that it is the only one with no access into the nave of the church. And the most imposing round tower? That's a difficult one, but many authorities would put Haddiscoe, Norfolk high on the list, although other fine towers are at Forncett St Peter, Acle and Bessingham (Norfolk) and Little Saxham, Theberton and Thorington (Suffolk).

Perhaps the most famous round tower is at Letheringsett, Norfolk. It was pictured on a set of British postage stamps featuring village churches issued on 21 June 1972.

## ROUND TOWER RUINS

Over the centuries several round towers have collapsed. The tower of Spexhall, Suffolk, partially collapsed in 1720 and the upper part was rebuilt in 1910. The most recent tower to fall was Cockley Cley, Norfolk, which fell on 29 August 1991 and Morton-on-the-Hill, Norfolk, which collapsed in 1959. Through-out Norfolk and Suffolk other ruined round towers that have never been rebuilt can be seen. Among them are the following:

 NORFOLK
- Appleton – ruins of round tower and church.

– Dilham – base of round tower; remainder fell c.1890.
- Feltwell (St Nicholas) – base of round tower; remainder fell in 1897.
- Fleggburgh St Mary (part of the parish of Burgh St Margaret – the ruins of a round tower and church are in a cultivated field but a right of way runs to them from Tower Road.
- Hardwick – remains of a round tower; remainder fell in 1770.
- Ingworth – base of tower only; remainder fell in 1822.
- Kirby Bedon (St Mary)– ruins of round tower and church.
- Norwich (St Julian) – destroyed by German bombs in 1942; church rebuilt and round tower partially rebuilt.
- Thorpe Parva – ruins of round tower only.
- Wolterton Hall – ruined round tower near house entrance; church demolished by Horatio Walpole c.1740 to improve estate!

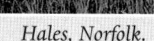

*Hales, Norfolk.*

✠ SUFFOLK
- Ashfield Thorpe (St Peter) – ruins of round tower.
- Buxlow – remains of round tower only.

As far as I know, the following is a complete list of the round towers in England and Wales that are still in good condition (with the exception of Wortham, Suffolk):

*England*
✠ BERKSHIRE (2)
1. Great Shefford or West Shefford (St Mary)
2. Welford (St Gregory)

✠ CAMBRIDGESHIRE (2)
3. Bartlow (St Mary)
4. Snailwell (St Peter)

✠ ESSEX (7)
5. Bardfield Saling or Little Saling (St Peter & St Paul)
6. Barking (St Patrick)
7. Broomfield (St Mary)
8. Great Leighs (St Mary)
9. Lamarsh (Holy Innocents)
10. Pentlow (St Gregory & St George)
11. South Ockendon (St Nicholas)

✠ HERTFORDSHIRE (1)
12. High Wych (St James)

✠ NORFOLK (118)
13. Acle (St Edmund)
14. Ashmanaugh (St Swithin)
15. Aslacton (St Michael)
16. Aylmerton (St John the Baptist)
17. Barmer (All Saints)
18. Bawburgh (St Mary & St Walstan)
19. Bedingham (St Andrew)
20. Beechamwell (St Mary)
21. Beeston St Laurence (St Laurence)
22. Belton (All Saints)
23. Bessingham (St Mary)
24. Bexwell (St Mary)
25. Bradwell (St Nicholas)
26. Brampton (St Peter)
27. Brandiston (St Nicholas)
28. Breccles (St Margaret)

29. Brooke (St Peter)
30. Burgh Castle (St Peter & St Paul)
31. Burnham Deepdale (St Mary)
32. Burnham Norton (St Margaret)
33. Bylaugh (St Mary)
34. Catton (St Margaret)
35. Clippesby (St Peter)
36. Colney (St Andrew)
37. Cranwich (St Mary)
38. Croxton, near Thetford (All Saints)
39. Denton (St Mary)
40. East Lexham (St Andrew)
41. East Walton (St Mary)
42. Eccles, near Attleborough (St Mary)
43. Edingthorpe (All Saints)
44. Fishley (St Mary)
45. Forncett St Peter (St Peter)
46. Framingham Earl (St Andrew)
47. Freethorpe (All Saints)
48. Fritton (St Catherine)
49. Fritton (St Edmund)
50. Gayton Thorpe (St Mary)
51. Geldeston (St Michael)
52. Gissing (St Mary)
53. Great Ryburgh (St Andrew)
54. Gresham (All Saints)
55. Haddiscoe (St Mary)
56. Hales (St Margaret)
57. Hardley (St Margaret)
58. Hassingham (St Mary)
59. Hautbois (Old Church)
60. Haveringland (St Peter)
61. Heckingham (St Gregory)
62. Hellington (St John the Baptist)
63. Hemblington (All Saints)
64. Horsey (All Saints)
65. Howe (St Mary)
66. Intwood (All Saints)

*Sedgeford, Norfolk.*

67. Keswick (All Saints)
68. Kilverstone (St Andrew)
69. Kirby Cane (All Saints)
70. Letheringsett (St Andrew)
71. Little Plumstead (St Protase & St Gervase)
72. Little Snoring (St Andrew)
73. Long Stratton (St Mary)
74. Matlask or Matlaske (St Peter)
75. Mautby (St Peter & St Paul)
76. Merton (St Peter)
77. Morningthorpe (St John the Baptist)
78. Moulton St Mary (St Mary)
79. Needham (St Peter)
80. Norton Subcourse (St Mary)
81. Norwich (St Benedict) – tower only
82. Norwich (St Etheldreda)
83. Norwich (St Mary at Coslany)
84. Poringland (All Saints)
85. Potter Heigham (St Nicholas)
86. Quidenham (St Andrew)
87. Raveningham (St Andrew)
88. Repps (St Peter)
89. Ringstead (St Peter) – tower only
90. Rockland St Peter (St Peter)
91. Rollesby (St George)
92. Roughton (St Mary)
93. Roydon, near Diss (St Remigius)
94. Runhall (All Saints)
95. Rushall (St Mary)
96. Sedgeford (St Mary)
97. Seething (St Margaret & St Remigius)
98. Shereford (St Nicholas)
99. Shimpling (St George)
100. Sidestrand (St Michael)
101. South Pickenham (All Saints)
102. Stanford (All Saints)

103. Stockton (St Michael)
104. Stody (St Mary)
105. Surlingham (St Mary)
106. Sustead (St Peter & St Paul)
107. Swainsthorpe (St Peter)
108. Syderstone (St Mary)
109. Tasburgh (St Mary)
110. Taverham (St Edmund)
111. Thorpe Abbotts (All Saints)
112. Thorpe-next-Haddiscoe (St Matthias)
113. Threxton (All Saints)
114. Thwaite, near Aylsham (All Saints)
115. Titchwell (St Mary)
116. Topcroft (St Margaret)
117. Tuttington (St Peter & St Paul)
118. Wacton (All Saints)
119. Watton (St Mary)
120. Weeting (St Mary)
121. Welborne (All Saints)
122. West Dereham (St Andrew)
123. West Lexham (St Andrew)
124. West Somerton (St Mary)
125. Whitlingham (St Andrew)
126. Wickmere (St Andrew)
127. Witton, near North Walsham (St Margaret)
128. Woodton (All Saints)
129. Worthing (St Margaret)
130. Wramplingham (St Peter & St Paul)
131. Yaxham (St Peter)

✠ SUFFOLK *(38)*
132. Aldham (St Mary)
133. Ashby (St Mary)
134. Barsham (Holy Trinity)
135. Beyton (All Saints)
136. Blundeston (St Mary)
137. Bramfield (St Andrew)
138. Brome (St Mary)
139. Bruisyard (St Peter)
140. Bungay (Holy Trinity)
141. Frostenden (All Saints)
142. Gisleham (Holy Trinity)
143. Gunton (St Peter)
144. Hasketon (St Andrew)
145. Hengrave (St John Lateran)

146. Herringfleet (St Margaret)
147. Higham, near Bury St Edmunds (St Stephen)
148. Holton (St Peter)
149. Ilketshall St Andrew (St Andrew)
150. Ilketshall St Margaret (St Margaret)
151. Little Bradley or Bradley Parva (All Saints)
152. Little Saxham or Saxham Parva (St Nicholas)
153. Lound (St John the Baptist)
154. Mettingham (All Saints)
155. Mutford (St Andrew)
156. Onehouse (St John the Baptist)
157. Ramsholt (All Saints)
158. Rickenhall Inferior (St Mary)
159. Risby (St Giles)
160. Rushmere (St Michael)
161. South Elmham (All Saints)
162. Spexhall (St Peter)
163. Stuston (All Saints)
164. Syleham (St Mary)
165. Theberton (St Peter)
166. Thorington (St Peter)
167. Weybread (St Andrew)
168. Wissett (St Andrew)
169. Wortham (St Mary)

✠ SUSSEX *(East)* *(3)*
170. Lewes (St Michael)
171. Piddinghoe (St John)
172. Southease (dedication unknown)

*Wales*
✠ POWYS *(2)*
173. Betws Penpont (dedication unknown)
174. Llandysilio (St Tysilio)

✠ GWYNEDD *(1)*
175. Llandegwning (St Gwynin)

*Note*: the Round Tower Churches Society, at www.roundtowers.org.uk is an excellent organization devoted to the study of round towers.

*West Tanfield, North Yorkshire – the beautiful church viewed from the bridge over the River Ure.*

# West Quantoxhead
or St Audries             Somerset

St Etheldreda or St Audrey is situated spectacularly against the hillside near St Audries' House in a broad bend of the A39. It was built 1854–6 and designed by John Norton, replacing a much older medieval church.

◈ The nave arcade is supported on cluster columns from single blocks of Babba-combe marble from Devon – a very unusual feature.

◈ At the w end of the nave, on the s internal wall of the tower is a memorial to Henry Acland-Hood inscribed:

'Henry Fuller Acland-Hood
Solicitor
12 Dec., 1863-26 Jan., 1923
Through this toilsome world alas,
Once and only once I pass.

If a kindness I may show
If a good deed I may do
To any suffering fellow man
Let me do it while I can.
Nor delay it, for 'tis plain
I shall not pass this way again.'

◈ The intricate carving of the corbels supporting the roof, especially in the s aisle, is reminiscent of the naturalistic carving in the chapter house at Southwell Cathedral (see page 328). Note also the angels holding musical instruments supporting the nave roof.

◈ Over the priest's reading desk is a brass cross in memory of Prebendary J. R. Vernon, rector 1843–1902. He wrote the book *The Harvest of a Quiet Eye* and the hymn 'There's peace and rest in Paradise' (no.543 in *Hymns Ancient and Modern*, Standard Edition, 1916).

*High above the River Ure, the church at West Tanfield, North Yorks, stands in an attractive village.*

*West Tanfield, North Yorkshire.*

*West Walton, Norfolk.*

# West Tanfield NORTH YORKSHIRE

ST NICHOLAS is situated high above the River Ure, just E of the Marmion Tower with its beautiful oriel window. It presents an attractive picture from the river bridge.

 Outside the vaulted s porch are stone dog-tethers – a rare feature.

 On the N side of the chancel is the Marmion chapel containing several family tombs, the finest being in the centre. This may represent Sir John Marmion (d. 1387) and Elizabeth, his wife. Above the tomb is a wrought-iron hearse with holders for seven candles – one at each corner and three raised ones along the centre. This hearse with candles is unique (but see also Gloucester Cathedral, page 148 and Warwick, St Mary, page 385).

 At the NW corner of the chancel is a unique stone chamber opening into the Marmion chapel. It measures about 1.22 m (4 feet) square and is 1.98 m (6 feet 6 inches) high and may have been used by a chantry priest.

 On the floor of the chancel near the s door is a fine brass to Thomas Sutton (d. 1492), rector of West Tanfield.

# West Walton NORFOLK

ST MARY THE VIRGIN This famous church was built from 1225 to 1240 and is considered to be the finest example of Early English (thirteenth-century) work in the British Isles.

 The magnificent tower stands 18.3 m (60

*West Walton, Norfolk, possesses one of the finest thirteenth-century towers in England.*

feet) away from the church on the SE side and with its four open arches at the base, forms the entrance to the churchyard. The octagonal buttresses at the corners are some of the earliest in England.

This tower is sited on the firmest ground available in the parish, but the nave and chancel are not so fortunate and stand on typical Fenland. There are nine springs under the floor!

🔷 The angel hammer-beam roof dates from c.1450.

🔷 The clear, handmade glass in every window gives the church a very spacious feel.

🔷 The clustered piers of the nave and superb thirteenth-century capitals are particularly fine. The piers are composed of a central column with four shafts attached by annulet rings halfway up.

🔷 The fine brass eagle lectern stands on a shaft leading to a square base. It bears the inscription, 'To the Glory of God and in memory of the donor Henry Houlden. Churchwarden of this parish 1906 to 1908. R.I.P.'

🔷 At the E end of the chancel is a very unusual feature – *eight* sedilias, four on the N wall and four on the S.

🔷 The two-light window at the SE end of the S aisle is a lovely example of early Geometrical work with dog-tooth carving.

🔷 In the S aisle hangs a flood board erected by John Oxburch (rector in 1677), recording three great floods of 1613, 1614 and 1671.

🔷 The S porch has delicate thirteenth-century detail including much dog-tooth ornamentation.

# West Wittering    WEST SUSSEX

ST PETER & ST PAUL The church stands on the S side of the village, about 0.8 km (½ mile) from the beach, where fine views of the Isle of Wight and Portsmouth can be seen.

🔷 The tower occupies an unusual position on the N side of the nave, its base forming the vicar's vestry. The wooden staircase leading to the three bells is in two flights and consists of roughly hewn triangular blocks of elm fastened by wooden pins to sloping bearers. Note: these stairs date from c.1250 and are now unsafe, so visitors should not attempt to climb them.

🔷 Against the N wall of the chancel are two late Gothic tombs having Renaissance details. The larger tomb dates from 1530 to 1535 and the smaller one from 1545 to 1550. The larger commemorates Elizabeth Ernley and the smaller, William Ernley. Below William Ernley's tomb is a beautiful relief of the Annunciation with a pot containing three lily stems and a crucified figure of Christ on the central stem. The legs below the knees are missing. This is a rare example of a lily crucifix. Bridget Ernley, the second wife of William Ernley who erected the smaller tomb, lived at Lavenham near Long Melford (see page 223) where there is a lily crucifix in glass and this may account for its use at West Wittering. (See Lily Crucifix, page 338.)

🔷 In the lady chapel to the S of the chancel is a small marble slab, 1.10 m (3 feet 7½ inches) long with a Greek cross incised on it and a bishop's pastoral staff. It dates from c.1250. During the restoration of 1875 it was found buried in the sanctuary at the foot of the altar, broken in two pieces.

This slab may have covered a shrine containing the relics of a bishop, possibly St Richard of Chichester (d. 1253), who often visited West Wittering and reputedly performed several miracles here. If such a shrine or reliquary existed, it would have been destroyed by Henry VIII in 1538–9 along with all the other shrines in

*A rare snow scene at West Wittering, West Sussex.*

England, including that of St Richard in Chichester Cathedral (see page 78).

On the E pier of the chancel arch in the lady chapel are a number of graffiti including several pilgrims' crosses – about 40 altogether. In addition to the crosses there is a beautiful graffito showing a young woman. Could this be the Blessed Virgin Mary? These graffiti are further evidence that a medieval shrine may have existed here.

On the N wall of the chancel by the door is a memorial to 20 men from the parish who died in the First World War. It is an example of the early work of Eric Gill, the famous sculptor, whose father was vicar of West Wittering from 1914 to 1930.

On the N side of the chancel stands an ancient pair of stalls with original misericords – one carved with a mitred head and two roses (the left one restored) and the other a Tudor rose. They may have been provided for his own use by Bishop Sherburne (Bishop from 1508 to 1536), who frequently resided at Cakeham Manor and built the imposing brick tower there.

Above these stalls is a two-light stained-glass window commemorating people called Charles and Maria Combes, 1899. Superimposed over the base of the left-hand light is a small roundel of Victorian glass depicting the Agnus Dei. This was rescued by the compiler of this book from the now-demolished church of All Saints, Braywood, Berkshire, c.1960 and presented to this church in 1968 in memory of his mother.

## West Wycombe   BUCKINGHAMSHIRE

ST LAURENCE This church occupies a magnificent position on a hill, 195.1 m (640 feet) above sea level and overlooking West Wycombe village.

*Whissendine, Rutland.*

⊠ On top of the tower, built in 1763, is a unique feature for a parish church – a curious ball inside which are nine seats. This was erected by Sir Francis Dashwood *c.*1765 for the use of members of his 'Hell-Fire Club' who occasionally climbed up a precariously placed ladder to reach the inside for meetings. Painted gold, this landmark is known locally as the 'Golden Ball'. Four large chains hang down from the ball, presumably to hold it in place should it move! Above the ball is a wind vane.

⊠ The interior of the church has some interesting eighteenth-century fittings including a most unusual font and lectern.

## Whissendine      RUTLAND

ST ANDREW is a fine church that dominates this little village, deep in the countryside, N of Oakham.

⊠ This church has a fine w tower of the Decorated period.

⊠ Notice how the piers of the N arcade lean dangerously outwards and have been strengthened by three transverse arches, added *c.*1400.

⊠ The fine nave roof dates from *c.*1450 and rests on 12 figures. It was heavily restored in 1728 as stated on a beam at the w end.

⊠ The octagonal font is unusual in being carved on four faces with tracings only on the other four. Why did the carver never complete his work?

⊠ The superb screen in the s aisle came from St John's College, Cambridge, in 1869. It was presented to that college by Lady Margaret Beaufort (1443–1509), mother of Henry VII, our first Tudor king.

## Wickham      BERKSHIRE

ST SWITHUN This church is a good example of mid-Victorian architecture (apart from the tower). Dating from 1845 to 1849 the architect was Benjamin Ferrey. The exterior flint work is very fine, all the flints being squared!

⊠ The SW tower is Saxon with a Victorian top. Two of the windows have typical baluster shafts between the lights. (It is interesting that nearly 1000 years separate the building of this tower from the remainder of the church!)

⊠ In the N aisle are eight papier mâché elephants' heads at the ends of the hammer-beam roof. When the Reverend William Nicholson restored and rebuilt the church in 1845 he had arranged for angels to be fixed to the roof, but when

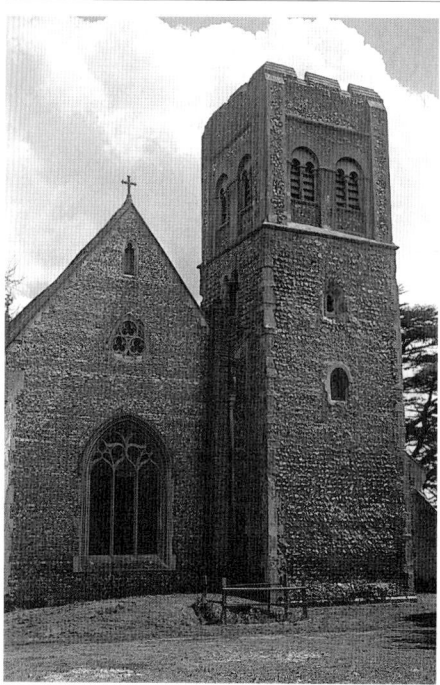

*Wickham, Berkshire.*

## Widecombe-in-the-Moor   Devon

St Pancras Known as 'the Cathedral of the Moor' its tower dominates the countryside. The tower, at 41.15 m (135 feet) high, was built by tin miners.

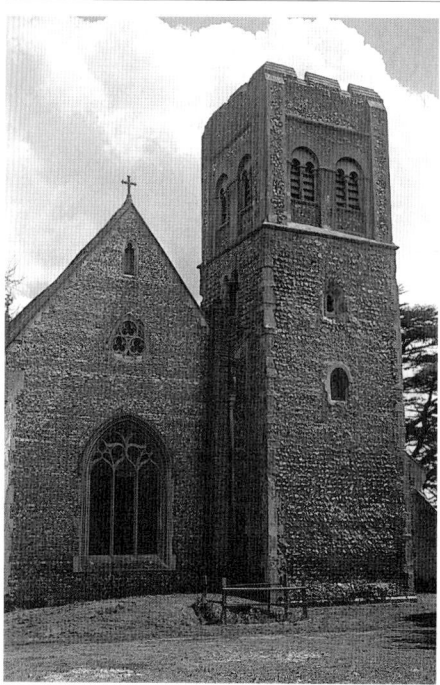 The pillars in the nave are unusual in being monoliths – solid pieces of stone.

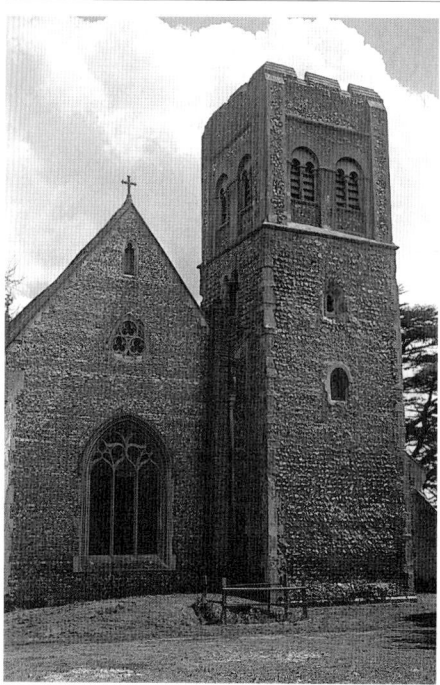 Among many fine roof bosses, two are particularly interesting:

† The third one from the e end shows three hares with only one ear between them (see The Three Hares, page 412).

† Another shows St Katherine – one of only six depictions on a roof boss. (See Roof Bosses, page 374.)

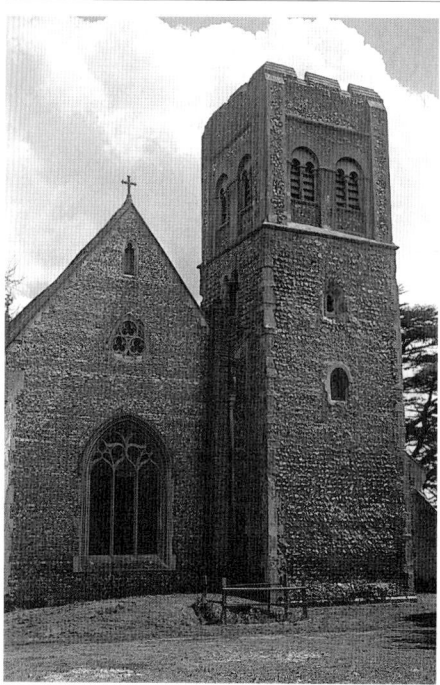 At the w end on the n wall is a wall plaque to a lady called Mary Elford (d. 1642) with an interesting anagram on her name 'Fear My Lord'.

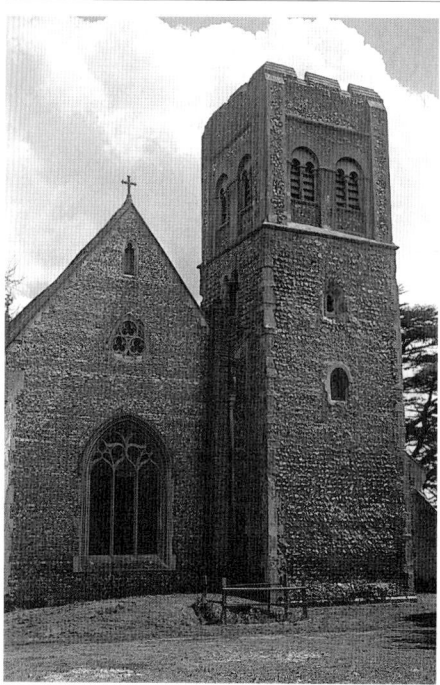 On 21 October 1638 a great thunderstorm occurred which damaged some of the church and killed several people. Boards in the tower record the event.

he saw four papier mâché elephants at the Paris Exhibition of 1862 he ordered a further four and substituted them instead!

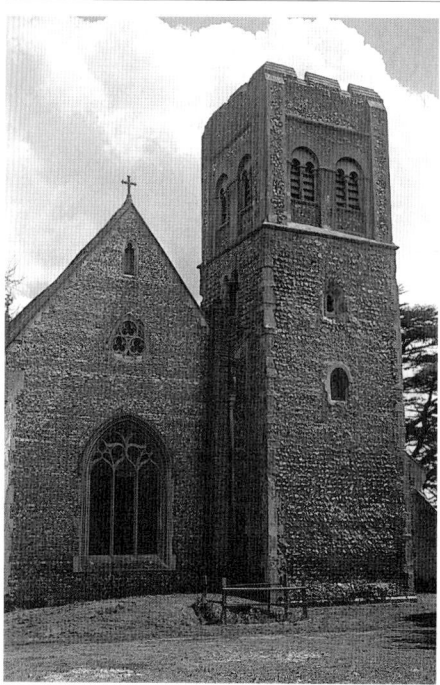 The nave capitals are richly carved. One on the n side has vine leaves with gold-coloured grapes. Other capitals show ivy and different leaves.

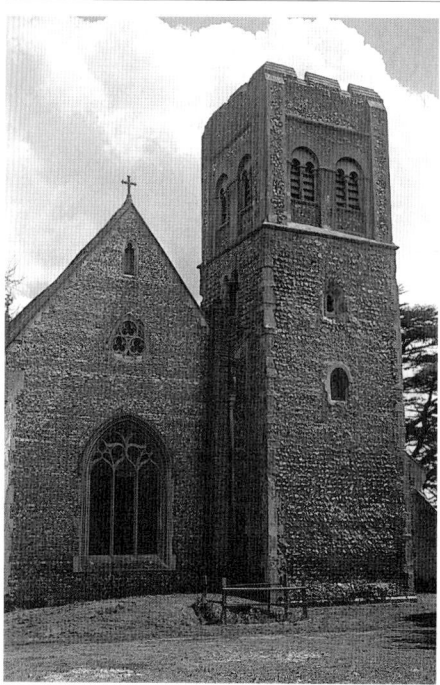 In the nave are eight lime-wood carved angels on the hammer-beams.

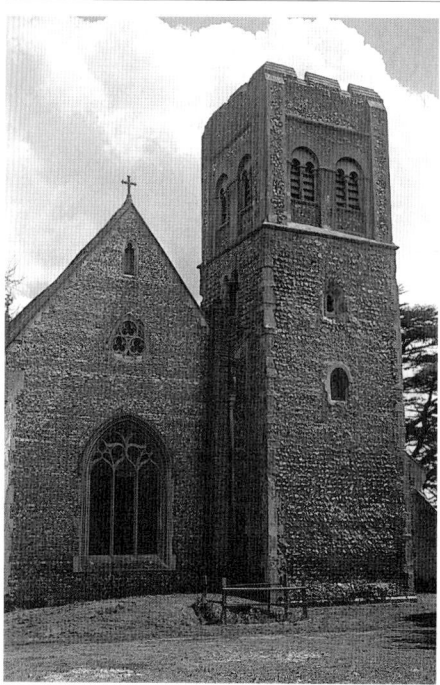 The two carvings on the pew ends at the w end of the church showing an angel and a bishop were personally carved by Sir Giles Gilbert Scott.

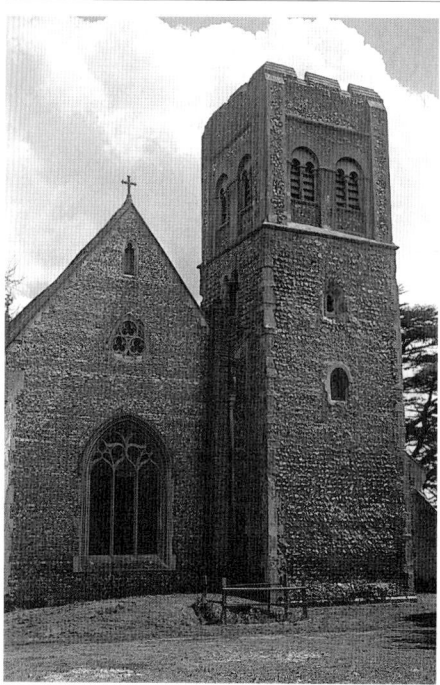 At the w end of the nave is an ancient chasuble dating from *c.*1552 and an embroidered chalice pall from Jerez, Spain, made in 1885.

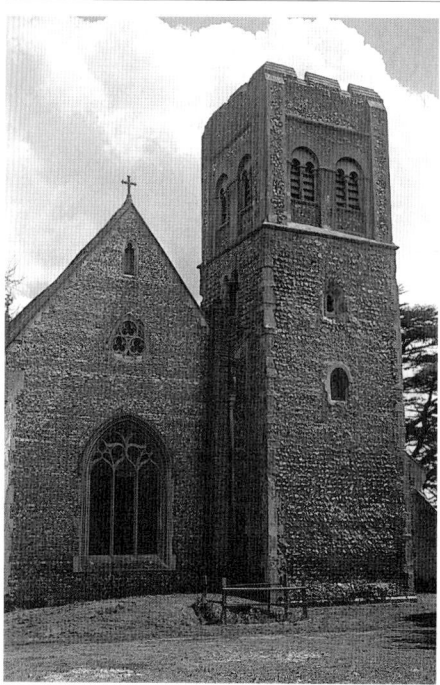 The s door has wyverns, fighting dragons and a Green Man carved in its tracery.

## Wilden   Worcestershire

All Saints The outward appearance of this simple brick church, with a double bellcote at the w end, belies the treasures that await inside! It was built from 1879 to 1880, consecrated on 4 May 1880 and paid for by Alfred Baldwin, who had taken over the Wilden Ironworks in 1879 and who wished to erect a suitable church for his workforce. The architect was W. F. Hopkins.

Alfred Baldwin married Louisa Macdonald, who had six sisters and four brothers. Louisa had one son with Alfred – Stanley (1867–1947), who became Prime Minister in 1923. Of Louisa's six sisters, Mary and Caroline died young and Edith stayed at home to nurse her aged parents.

*Widecombe-in-the-Moor, Devon.*

Her other three sisters married very successfully: in 1865 Alice married John Lockwood Kipling, a sculptor and father to Rudyard; Georgiana married Edward Burne-Jones, the Pre-Raphaelite painter, in 1860; and in 1866 Agnes married Edward Poynter, who later became President of the Royal Academy.

When the church was originally built all the 14 windows were filled with plain glass. Through Georgiana's marriage to Burne-Jones he was persuaded to design stained glass for all the windows to be made in the William Morris workshops. Burne-Jones produced the cartoons but, sadly, both he and Morris died before the windows could be made. However, between 1902 and 1914 the original cartoons were used to make the windows

we see today. Several of them feature acanthus leaves in the background – a typical Morris/Burne-Jones motif.

The E window was given by Alfred Baldwin in 1902 in memory of his happy married life. It shows St Martin, Christ blessing the children and St George. In the bottom centre panel the Wise Men are shown visiting the Infant Jesus, and in the right-hand panel the young Stanley Baldwin is shown beginning his life's journey accompanied by his guardian angel.

Other windows show St Cecilia with her organ, Joshua in red with his trumpeters passing over the River Jordan (given in 1909 in memory of Alfred Baldwin, who died in 1908), the Good Shepherd, Enoch, Samuel, Timothy and St Agnes. The W windows depict Angels of Paradise.

The church is unique in possessing so many (14) Burne-Jones/Morris windows, although Harris/Manchester College Chapel, Oxford, has a set of ten such windows by Burne-Jones including two lights ('Joseph' and 'Mary Magdalene') designed by William Morris and installed 1893–8.

Nikolaus Pevsner says of Wilden Church that 'it is probably the only church provided with Morris glass in all its windows'.

Other treasures include an altar frontal designed by William Morris and worked by Louisa, Georgiana and Edith (the Macdonald sisters); altar hangings from Westminster Abbey used at the Coronation of George VI on 12 May 1937; and the Baldwin silver (chalice, paten and flagon) donated by Louisa Baldwin and containing her jewels and embroidered prayer book of 1893.

The motif of the three hares is an ancient and very interesting one and has been the subject of much study. Examples of these entwined hares show them chasing each other in a circle so that their ears form a triangle in the centre, three ears serving for all of them instead of the usual six.

The three hares can be found across England, Wales and Europe, the Middle East and Far East in Christian, Islamic and Buddhist buildings. Their original meaning is obscure but some scholars have suggested that where they occur in a Christian church they symbolize the Holy Trinity. The noted archaeologist and historian Tom Greaves feels, however, that this is too simplistic an explanation.

Although there is no documentary evidence to support it, in the twentieth century the three hares became associated with the tin miners of Devon and Cornwall. It is said that three hares were imprinted on the special stamp used in such stannary towns as Ashburton, Chagford, Plympton and Tavistock which had ancient rights to test, grade and stamp tin mined in and around Dartmoor. This being the case, it *might* account for the group of 17 churches around Dartmoor containing roof bosses depicting the three hares.

The following is, as far as I know, a complete list of churches containing depictions of the three hares:

On roof bosses in these Devon churches, as follows:

1. Ashreigney (St James)
2. Bridford (St Thomas-a-Becket)
3. Broadclyst (St John)
4. Chagford (St Michael) – two bosses
5. Cheriton Bishop (St Mary)
6. Iddesleigh (St James)
7. Ilsington (St Michael)
8. Kelly (St Mary) – two bosses
9. Newton St Cyres (St Cyriac and St Julitta)
10. North Bovey (St John)
11. Paignton (St John)
12. Sampford Courtenay (St Andrew) – two bosses
13. South Tawton (St Andrew)
14. Spreyton (St Michael) – two bosses
15. Tavistock (St Eustace)
16. Throwleigh (St Mary)
17. Widecombe-in-the-Moor (St Pancras)

On roof bosses in the following churches:
18. Corfe Mullen (St Hubert), Dorset
19. St David's Cathedral (St David), Pembrokeshire – at the E end of the lady chapel, dating from *c*.1450
20. Selby Abbey (Our Lord, St Mary and St Germain), North Yorkshire – although three hares appear on this boss, there is also a fourth hare unconnected with the other three

The three hares can also be seen in other forms besides bosses in the following churches:
21. Chester Cathedral (Christ and the Blessed Virgin Mary), Cheshire – medieval floor tiles
22. Long Crendon (St Mary), Buckinghamshire – on a tile dating from *c*.1235 at the E end of the chancel just below the first step up to the high altar. This tile is unique in that it is the oldest known example of a depiction of the three hares in the United Kingdom.
23. Long Melford (Holy Trinity), Suffolk – medieval stained glass. This church is dedicated to the Holy Trinity, so might this be the reason why the Three Hares are found here?

Owing to their size, there are very few free-standing statues of horses in English and Welsh churches. One of the most famous (c.1860) is in the nave of St Paul's Cathedral, London, on top of the Duke of Wellington's monument, but because it is so high up, few visitors to the cathedral actually see it!

Another famous one is at Gaddesby, Leicestershire, and it occupies quite a large part of the chancel. Carved in marble by Joseph Gott in 1848, it was never intended for a church and came, in fact, from Gaddesby Hall in 1917. Apart from the horse in St Paul's Cathedral this is the only marble equestrian statue inside an English church.

In the N chapel of Mells, Somerset, there is a fine bronze statue of Edward Horner (killed in France, 1917) on his horse. The statue was made c. 1920 by Sir Alfred Munnings, RA and placed on a plinth designed by Sir Edwin Lutyens. There is also a bronze horse statue at Kilkhampton, Cornwall. Dating from c.1900 it depicts Algernon Carteret Thynne on horseback and was executed by Goscombe John, RA.

A unique wooden horse statue in Windermere, Cumbria, shows St Martin on a horse. He is depicted dividing his cloak to give half to a beggar. Two sculptures in Henry V's chantry chapel, Westminster Abbey, London (c.1430), show the king on horseback.

As far as I know, there are only five free-standing statues of horses in England and Wales and two smaller sculptures in Westminster Abbey. They are located as follows:

1. Gaddesby (St Luke), Leicestershire – marble, 1848
2. Kilkhampton (St James), Cornwall – bronze, c.1900
3. St Paul's Cathedral, London – marble horse on top of the Duke of Wellington's monument, c.1860
4. Westminster Abbey, London – two sculptures of Henry V in his chantry chapel, c.1430
5. Mells (St Andrew), Somerset – bronze, c.1920
6. Windermere (St Martin), Cumbria – wood; St Martin on horseback, c.1600

## Wilton WILTSHIRE

ST MARY & ST NICHOLAS Built from 1841 to 1845 this church was one of the first churches in England designed in the Lombardic style of Italy. It is built on a N–S axis (instead of the usual E–W) and has a fine detached bell-tower.

 The four twisted columns in the pulpit date from c.1250 and came from a shrine in Rome.

 Inside the communion rails are the fine tombs of Catherine Woronzow (1783–1856), Countess of Pembroke, and her son Sidney Herbert (1810–61), who built this church.

Other memorials include a monument by Richard Westmacott, RA to George Augustus, erected 1827 and a fine bust by Roubiliac of Henry, Ninth Earl of Pembroke (d. 1750).

There is a large number of interesting

panels of ancient stained glass dating from c.1144 to c.1625, some English and others from France and Germany. The wheel window at the 'w' end contains fifteenth- and sixteenth-century Swiss and Austrian glass brought from Austria to Paris by Napoleon.

# Wimborne      DORSET

THE MINSTER CHURCH OF ST CUTHBURGA This impressive building dominates the town and is well seen from the busy A31 road.

On the inside s wall of the w tower there is an astronomical clock reputed to have been made originally in c.1376. The present mechanism dates from 1743. The earth is shown in the centre with the sun, moon and stars revolving around it! The sun in the outer circle represents the hour 'hand'. A cross at the top indicates midday. Only three other clocks of this type exist – at Exeter Cathedral, Devon, Ottery St Mary, Devon and Wells Cathedral (see pages 134, 261 and 391 respectively).

Outside on the N wall of the w tower is the Grenadier or 'Quarter-Jack', 1.57 m (5 feet 2 inches) high, which dates from c.1815 and strikes the two bells each quarter of an hour.

Under the clock hang two leather water buckets.

In the nave are six pointed Norman arches enriched with chevron decoration – very unusual on *pointed* arches.

The brass eagle lectern was given by an Anthony Wayte in 1623 and carries his initials on a shield. The eagle's eyes are mother-of-pearl.

Near the base of the extreme SE pier of the nave is a small portion of Roman tessellated pavement.

On the Second World War memorial in the s transept are the names of four sons of Canon A. L. Keith, vicar from 1920 to 1946.

Adjoining the s transept is the s choir aisle (or Holy Trinity chapel) and on the sw side is a door through the choir vestry leading to the chained library above, dating from 1686. It contains 240 ancient books and also a collection of early music manuscripts. A piece composed by Thomas Weelkes is not known to exist anywhere else.

Another book on display is Sir Walter Raleigh's *History of the World* (1614). It is particularly interesting because a hole was burned through about 100 pages of the book and yet each one has been very neatly repaired, the repair in many instances being scarcely noticeable.

Walton's *Polyglot Bible* of 1653 is also very interesting. It consists of six volumes and was the first English book whose publication was sponsored. Cromwell allowed the paper on which it is printed to be imported from the Continent free of tax.

The oldest book, and the only manuscript, dates from 1343 and is called *The Direction of Souls*. The oldest printed book in the library dates from 1485. Printed in Germany it is St Anselm's *Annotati*.

Also in the library is a unique thirteenth- or fourteenth-century pewter chrisom which used to hold the consecrated oil. It was discovered in the minster roof in 1856 where it had been hidden from Cromwell's soldiers.

Another item on display is the governor's seal; this depicts the only representation of the minster with its spire, which collapsed suddenly in 1602 and was never rebuilt.

Near the choir vestry under the sw window of the Holy Trinity chapel is the tomb of Anthony Ettrick, 'the Man in the Wall'. As Recorder and Magistrate of

Poole he sent the Duke of Monmouth for trial in 1685. He was convinced that he would die in 1693 and had this date inscribed on his coffin, but in fact he did not die until 1703 and the alteration can still be clearly seen!

▦ Immediately below the chancel is a crypt dating from c.1340 and containing the lady chapel.

▦ On the s side of the chancel above is the alabaster tomb of John Beaufort, Duke of Somerset (1444) and his wife, Margaret. They wear the double 'SS' collar of Lancaster and were the grandparents of Henry VII.

The tomb is covered with graffiti and among the dates inscribed can be seen 1644 and 1647 – the time of the Civil War.

▦ On the n wall of the sanctuary is a brass commemorating St Ethelred or King Ethelred I (866–71), elder brother of King Alfred the Great, who died of wounds fighting the Danes at Martin near Wimborne. The brass was engraved c.1440 but the Latin inscription was added c.1690 citing the king's death as 873 in error. Translated, it reads:

'In this place rests the body of St Ethelred, King of the West Saxons, martyr, who in the year of Our Lord 873 on the 23 day of April, fell by the hand of the pagan Danes.'
The half-figure shows the king wearing a crown and holding a sceptre.

This is the second-oldest memorial brass effigy of an English king. (See Hereford Cathedral, page 175, for the oldest; see also Brasses, page 166.)

▦ The centre light of the e window contains stained glass dating from c.1450 which came from a Belgian convent. It is not easy to identify its theme, the Tree of Jesse.

▦ On the n side of the chancel is the n choir aisle (or St George's chapel). On the n wall is the fine Renaissance monument of Sir Edmund Uvedale (d. 1606). His eyes are open and he is depicted with two left feet!

▦ In this chapel is a Saxon oak chest dating from c.900. It is 1.83 m (6 feet) long and used to contain the church-wardens' accounts. Dating back to 1475, these are the most complete accounts in England.

▦ On the e side of the pillar nearest the main door on the nw side of the church and let into the stonework is a quaint alms-box 1.68m (5 feet 6 inches) above the ground.

## Winchester     HAMPSHIRE

St Swithun-upon-Kingsgate This church has a unique situation above one of the ancient gates into the city.

▦ Fragments of fifteenth-century glass in the e window came from the disused church of St Peter in Chesil Street.

▦ In the last part of his novel *The Warden*, Anthony Trollope makes reference to the church when Warden Harding becomes rector of St Cuthbert's (St Swithun's) after resigning from Hiram's Hospital (St Cross). He describes the church in the 1850s thus: 'The church is a singular little Gothic building, perched over a gateway, through which the Close is entered, and is approached by a flight of stone steps . . .'

## Winchester     HAMPSHIRE

THE CATHEDRAL CHURCH OF THE HOLY TRINITY, ST PETER, ST PAUL AND ST SWITHUN Situated in the centre of the city – the former capital of England – and surrounded by a large open green space, this is the longest Gothic church in the world at 169.5 m (556 feet).

▦ Under the w window of the nave are

*Winchester Cathedral, Hampshire. The trees are now fully grown and obscure this view.*

two fine bronze statues of James I and Charles I by Hubert Le Sueur; these came from a former screen.

 In the N aisle of the nave is the grave of the famous novelist Jane Austen (1776–1817). A brass and window above allude to her literary works.

 On the N side of the nave is the famous Tournai font dating from *c*.1150. The carvings on two faces represent legends in the life of St Nicholas, Bishop of Myra in the fourth century. On the w face the murder of three boys by an innkeeper is shown, as well as their subsequent restoration to life by the Saint. Next to this a nobleman's son, drowned on a sea voyage, is brought back to life.

On the s face St Nicholas gives bags of gold to a nobleman's three daughters and at the end is a Norman church.

 On the E and N faces are round medallions containing carvings of doves, grapes and a salamander. (See Tournai Fonts, page 439.)

 The nave of 12 bays is largely the work of William Wynford, commissioned by William of Wykeham, Bishop of Winchester (1366–1404). Notice the iron hooks on the columns, used for hanging 12 tapestries, each about 9.14 m. (30 feet) long, for the wedding of Mary Tudor to Philip of Spain on 25 July 1554.

In 1979 the Friends of Winchester Cathedral gave a magnificent set of banners to hang on these hooks at a cost of £22,000.

 In the N transept is the back of the organ, dedicated in 1854. Built by Willis for the Great Exhibition of 1851, it was the first cathedral organ to have concave and radiating pedals and the first with pneumatic pistons for governing groups of

*Winchester Cathedral, Hampshire, seen from the southeast.*

stops. Almost 40 of the original stops are in the present organ.

Below the organ is the Holy Sepulchre chapel, famous for its medieval wall paintings.

In the SE corner of the N transept is the entrance to the crypt; this is only open in summer because it floods in winter! It extends from the transepts to the extreme E end of the cathedral and is divided into three sections. There are two wells, one being directly underneath the altar of the Norman church. In a glass case is a piece of beech wood and peat on which the cathedral rested for 700 years!

In the centre of the choir above is the plain stone tomb of either William Rufus (King from 1087 to 1100), who was killed in the New Forest, or Bishop Henry of Blois. The top of the tomb is of Purbeck marble.

The choir stalls are the earliest complete set in England. They, and the canopies above, were carved by Thomas Lyngwood from 1308 to 1310.

Near the choir stalls on the N side of the choir is Prior Silkstede's pulpit. Dating from 1520 it shows skeins of silk in its panels – a rebus on his name.

In the six mortuary chests on top of the screens, each side of the choir, are the bones of some early kings of Wessex and bishops of Winchester. Among them are Ethelwulf (839–58), father of Alfred the Great, and King Canute (1032–5).

During the Civil War the chests were violated and all the bones jumbled up.

The beautiful reredos or Great Screen behind the high altar dates from c.1420, but having been badly damaged c.1540–1600, was restored c.1870. It is very similar to the screen in St Alban's Abbey (see page 298), which also suffered poor treatment. It is 13.34 m (43¾ feet) high.

🔲 In the retrochoir behind the high altar is the largest and oldest area of medieval tiles surviving in this country dating from c.1230.

🔲 A modern shrine to St Swithun was placed on these tiles on 15 July 1962 to replace the one destroyed by order of Henry VIII in 1538. At the E end of the shrine are these words: 'Whatever partakes of God is safe in God. All that could perish of St Swithun being enshrined within this place throughout many ages hallowed by the veneration and honoured by the gifts of faithful pilgrims from many lands was by a later age destroyed. None can destroy his glory.'

🔲 Also in the retrochoir, opposite St Swithun's shrine, are nine separate icons of saints as portrayed by the Orthodox Church. Painted by Sergei Fyodorov they depict local saints such as St Birinus (Bishop of Dorchester, Oxon.) and St Swithun, to whom this cathedral is dedicated. These icons are rarely found in British churches.

🔲 The cathedral contains the largest collection of chantry chapels in England, six of them being of the stone-cage type as follows:

† The most famous is William of Wykeham's chantry, which occupies the whole of the fifth bay from the w on the s side of the nave. It is the tallest chantry in the cathedral and was built in 1403 during his lifetime. In the middle of the chapel is the tomb of the Bishop in episcopal vestments with three seated figures at his feet, their hands together in prayer. They probably represent his secretaries. On the sides of the tomb are heraldic shields and Wykeham's famous motto, 'Manners maykyth man'. At the E end is a restored altar, above which is a reredos with

modern figures in its niches. During the Commonwealth much devastation was done in the cathedral, including the destruction of the statues in this chantry, but the figure of the Bishop was untouched. According to tradition the leader of the Commonwealth soldiers was an old Wykehamite who ordered that the Bishop's effigy should not be damaged. Wykeham died on 27 September 1404 and each year the cathedral observes the day of his death. Apart from his work of largely remodelling the nave of this cathedral, Wykeham is famous as the founder of New College, Oxford, and Winchester College.

† The most splendid chantry in the cathedral and one of the most imposing in the country is that of Bishop Richard Fox (1501–28) on the s side of St Swithun's shrine. In an arched recess on the s side is the cadaver or half-decomposed corpse of the Bishop – a reminder of everyone's mortality. The chantry consists of two stages, the lower composed of solid masonry decorated with canopied niches, many containing figures, and the upper having four Perpendicular windows. There are 55 niches for figures on the entire outside. At the E end of the chantry is a tiny chamber in which the Bishop, when an old man, used to sit listening to the services. Fox founded Corpus Christi College, Oxford, in 1517.

† In the second bay from the E on the s side of the nave is the chantry chapel of Bishop William Edington (d. 1366) containing a superb alabaster effigy of the Bishop. He was the first Bishop of the Order of the Garter.

† On the s side of the retrochoir is the chantry chapel of Cardinal Beaufort (1404–47) with a fan-vaulted roof overlaid with a canopy. Underneath are several niches and buttresses. In the centre of the

roof is an angel holding a shield on which are depicted the fleur-de-lys and cross.

†   On the N side of the retrochoir, directly opposite Beaufort's chantry, is the chantry of Bishop William Waynflete (1446–86) which is very similar in design to Beaufort's chantry. Bishop Waynflete founded Magdalen College, Oxford, in 1448.

†   On the N side of St Swithun's shrine, opposite Fox's chantry, is the chantry of Bishop Stephen Gardiner (1531–55), dating from c.1540. This was the last chantry to be erected in the cathedral and the last in medieval England. It shows the beginning of the Renaissance in its lower walls and inside the E end, which has typical Renaissance recesses. On the N side is a cadaver. There is no altar or effigy inside, but instead the chair in which Mary Tudor sat for her marriage to Philip of Spain is preserved in this cathedral. (See also page 416.)

†   The remaining chantry is unlike all the others in that it is constructed of wood. It is Bishop Thomas Langton's chantry (1493–1501) and lies to the s of the lady chapel. It has been adapted from an original chapel in the cathedral, the roof of the cathedral forming the vault of the chantry. Look for the Bishop's rebus among the bosses – a 'long' (musical note) in a tun (barrel), for Langton and a hen sitting on a tun for the prior, Hunton.

▣   Between the Langton chantry and the lady chapel is a bronze statue to William Robert Walker (1869–1918) – the diver who 'saved this cathedral with his two hands 1906–1912' by underpinning it with tons of concrete and concrete blocks. The total cost of the work was £113,000, a colossal sum in those days. Walker died on 30 October 1918 from influenza and was buried at Elmers End cemetery near Beckenham, Kent, where a plaque commemorates his achievements at Winchester Cathedral.

▣   On the corresponding side of the Lady Chapel to Walker's statue is a statue of Joan of Arc, which was dedicated in 1923, three years after her canonization on 16 May 1920. This statue faces the tomb of Cardinal Beaufort, who was among the men who sentenced her to be burned in Rouen on 30 May 1431!

▣   Near Joan of Arc's statue, on the N side of the lady chapel, is the Guardian Angels' chapel. It contains interesting roof paintings and on the right a superb bronze effigy by Hubert Le Sueur to Richard Weston (Lord Portland, d. 1634), Charles I's Treasurer.

▣   The iron gates at the top of the s aisle steps, dividing the s transept from the retrochoir, consist of the oldest wrought ironwork in England and date from c.1100. They were probably part of the grille protecting St Swithun's shrine.

▣   The E window of Prior Silkestede's chapel in the s transept was given by the fishermen of England in 1914 to commemorate Isaac Walton (9 August 1593–15 December 1683), who is buried in the crypt. He is depicted in the bottom right-hand corner above the words 'Study to be quiet'. A statue of him dating from c.1886 appears in the Great Screen behind the high altar.

▣   In the s transept is the cathedral library and also the triforium gallery, which was opened by the Duchess of York in April 1989.

In the gallery, from which there are superb views of the Norman cathedral, several treasures are exhibited, including: the Shaftesbury Bowl – the only complete late Saxon glass bowl to survive in England; numerous gold and sapphire rings from bishops' tombs; mutilated fragments from the statues that adorned the medieval Great Screen; wooden figures from the organ; the canopy dating from c.1650 which hung over the high altar and hid the defaced Great Screen; and an exquisite model in black basalt of the famous Tournai font, made c.1860.

In the library are the book collection of Bishop George Morley (d. 1684), numerous ancient manuscripts including Bede's *History of the English Church*, written c.1000, and the cathedral's most valuable treasure, the *Winchester Bible*. Dating from c. 1160 it comprises four volumes and 60 of its capital letters are beautifully decorated with miniature pictures. Some of the illuminated capitals have been cut out, but one was recovered from Sledmere House, Yorkshire, c.1950 and has been sewn back in! Apart from two complete pages of illustrations, all the paintings in this Bible are contained inside capital letters.

This library is probably the oldest one in the world that is still in use.

⊠ Among the interesting roof bosses in this cathedral are the following:

† Under the tower are unusual wooden bosses dating from 1635 when the vaulting was constructed. A unique one shows Charles I and his Queen, Henrietta Maria.

† In the choir are 30 bosses depicting Christ's sufferings, including one showing three dice. Others show a portcullis and a Tudor Royal Arms.

† In the N aisle of the nave a boss depicts a man playing bagpipes. This subject is found in only one other place – Wells Cathedral (see page 392).

† In the s aisle of the nave a boss shows Christ's head wearing the crown of thorns. Other bosses depicting this subject occur in Ely Cathedral (see page 126), Wells Cathedral (see page 392) and St Stephen's Cloister, Houses of Parliament, Westminster (London).

† Two fine bosses in the lady chapel date from c.1490. The one at the E end shows Christ in Glory surrounded by angels, while the one at the w end features the Assumption of Our Lady supported by six angels.

⊠ Directly to the w of the cathedral in the churchyard is a solitary gravestone to: 'Thomas Thetcher, a grenadier in the North Regt of Hants militia, who died of a violent Fever contracted by drinking Small Beer when hot on the 12th May 1764, aged 26 years'. Notice the timely warning in verse!

# Windsor                    Berkshire

THE ROYAL CHAPEL OF ST GEORGE, INSIDE WINDSOR CASTLE This magnificent building was started in 1475 during the reign of Edward IV and completed during Henry VIII's reign.

⊠ The fan vaulting of the s and N choir aisles have octagons instead of circles filling the central spandrels. These octagons are unique to Windsor.

⊠ The vaulting of the central part of the chapel is the flattest ever attempted. It was constructed from 1503 to 1511 and several of the bosses carry the arms of Henry VII (r. 1485–1509) and Sir Reginald Bray.

⊠ In the extreme sw corner of the chapel is the polygonal Beaufort chantry, founded in 1506 and contains the tomb of Charles Somerset (d. 1526) and his wife, Elizabeth (d. 1514). Crouching under each of their feet is a tiny figure in a cloak. The unusual grille around the tomb was made c.1517 by Jan van den Einde, a Belgian.

Notice the Spanish Virgin and Child (c.1250), given in 1952.

⊠ Opposite the Beaufort chantry is the recumbent effigy of the Prince Imperial (16 March 1856–1 June 1879), only son of Napoleon III and the Empress Eugenie, who was killed by Zulus. The effigy was

*St George's Chapel, Windsor. Notice the flying buttresses supporting the nave roof.*

carved by Sir Jacob Boehm. On one side of the cenotaph is carved the Prince's prayer in French, written by him in his prayer book. (The Prince's body is buried in the N transept of Farnborough Abbey Church, Hants.).

In the extreme NW corner of the chapel is the polygonal Urswick chantry, which corresponds with the Beaufort chantry. Founded in 1507 it commemorates Dean Urswick (d. 1521), a friend of Henry VII.

The large memorial commemorates Princess Charlotte, only daughter of George IV and heir to the throne, who tragically died in childbirth in 1817. Sculpted by Matthew Cotes Wyatt, the Princess's body is shown covered with a sheet (note the protruding fingers!), while above she is seen ascending to Heaven accompanied by angels. The one on the left holds her stillborn child.

Also in the Urswick chantry is a medieval brass lectern of the double-desk type. One of only five such lecterns, it is unique: instead of a desk of sheet brass (either pierced or engraved) on each side of which a book can be placed, this lectern is composed of two desks of cast brass tracery work. It may date from *c*.1500. An extra book rest on each side and the battlemented grease-pans for the candlesticks were added later. (See Medieval Brass Lecterns, page 362.)

Outside the Urswick chantry is the statue of Princess Charlotte's husband, Prince Leopold of Saxe-Coburg, later first King of the Belgians. Queen Victoria erected this statue in 1879.

Almost opposite the Urswick chantry, between the N nave aisle and the nave, is the tomb of King George V (r. 1910–36) and Queen Mary (r.1910–53). The effigies were carved by Sir William Reid Dick and the base by Sir Edwin Lutyens.

On the N side of the crossing is the polygonal transept containing the Rutland chantry, a feature of which are little carved angels holding scrolls. In the centre of the chantry are the superb alabaster effigies of Sir George Manners (d. 1513) and his wife, Anne (d. 1526). She was the niece of Edward IV. Note the 20 little carved figures or 'weepers' around the base.

On the S side of the chantry are five panels 2.74 m x 1.22 m (9 feet x 4 feet), designed and hand embroidered by Beryl Dean in 1970 and depicting incidents in the early Life of Christ.

🔲 Immediately to the E of the Rutland chantry is the memorial chapel and tomb of King George VI (r. 1936–52). Constructed in 1969, this was the first addition to the chapel since 1528. The stained glass was made by John Piper and Patrick Reyntiens.

🔲 Moving E along the N choir aisle on the S side is the Hastings chantry, which commemorates William, Lord Hastings (executed 1483). This stone-cage chapel contains some fine paintings dating from c.1490 and portraying the life of St Stephen.

🔲 On the N side of the high altar is the tomb of Edward IV (r. 1461–70 and 1471–83), who built this chapel, and his Queen, Elizabeth Woodville (d.1492). He was the first monarch to be buried at Windsor. Protecting the tomb is a grille made by John Tresilian in 1483. This is some of the finest medieval ironwork in England and in places it is only paper-thin!

🔲 Above the tomb of Edward IV is a wooden oriel window built by Henry VIII c.1520 as a gallery for Katharine of Aragon. It shows many Renaissance details.

🔲 On the left of this wooden oriel window is a stone oriel dating from c.1480. Both these oriels form part of the upper chantry of Edward IV.

🔲 The great E window was rebuilt in 1863 in memory of Prince Albert and the reredos added. Around the window are 38 angels holding numerous musical instruments and in the apex is an elaborate boss depicting the Holy Trinity. The Father is shown as an old man while the Son is depicted as a young man. Their hands are placed on a book, above which is the Holy Spirit in the form of a Dove.

The glass was made by Clayton and Bell. Along the base are 15 small panels depicting scenes from the lives of Queen Victoria and Prince Albert.

🔲 The garter stalls were carved from 1478 to 1485 but the two at the extreme E end on the S and N sides were added by Henry Emlyn, c.1780. He also restored the other stalls and canopies. Affixed to the backs of the stalls are 700 copper or brass plates bearing the enamelled or painted coats of arms of knights from c.1390 to the present day. These are the oldest heraldic enamels in the world. The oldest is that of Ralph, Lord Bassett and it is also one of the finest.

Near the sovereign's stall on the S side is the unique diamond-shaped stall plate of Charles the Bold, Duke of Burgundy (1468). On the desk front of the sovereign's stall is a variation on the lily crucifix. (See Lily Crucifix, page 338.)

Above the garter stalls hang the insignia of the Garter Knights – sword, helm and crest with the banner overhead.

🔲 Under the seats of the choir stalls is a wonderful collection of misericords including two men quarrelling over a board game, a demon stealing an old man's food, a mermaid holding a mirror and a comb, and the meeting of Edward IV and Louis XI at Picquigny in 1475. This last misericord is under the sovereign's stall and is one of the finest in England.

In the centre of the choir is the entrance to the royal vault. Several kings and queens are buried here, including Henry VIII and Jane Seymour, Charles I, George III, George IV and William IV.

▣ In the centre of the crossing is a boss showing the Royal Arms of Henry VIII and the date, 1528. Dated roof bosses are rare. (See Roof Bosses, page 374.)

▣ Underneath the crossing is the organ, which stands on top of the beautiful organ screen. The screen blends in well with the architecture of the chapel although it was not constructed until 1790. It was designed by Henry Emlyn and is made of Coade stone – an artificial composition of china clay and different minerals.

▣ From this spot can be seen the great w window, which is 11.6 m (38 feet) high and 8.8 m (29 feet) wide, making it the fourth-largest window in England. It contains 79 lights, 60 of which still contain their original glass dating from 1503 to 1509. Among those depicted are eight archbishops and 24 popes; no other window contains so many popes!

▣ On the s side of the crossing is the polygonal Bray chantry, now the chapel shop. Sir Reginald Bray (d. 1503), principal minister of Henry VII, is buried here. Look for the rebus on his name – the weaver's hemp-bray (a comb-like instrument used in rope making). It is depicted ten times along the top of the screen and 165 times elsewhere in the chapel since Bray bequeathed much money to enable the completion of this building.

▣ On the E side of the Bray chantry is an elaborate bust of Bishop Giles Tomson (d. 14 June 1612), former Dean of Windsor. He holds a copy of the *Authorised Version of the Bible* (1611), which he helped to translate.

▣ On another wall of the Bray chantry is a memorial to Sir Richard Wortley (d. 1603) framed with Della-Robbia pottery.

▣ A large memorial in the Bray chantry depicts Ralph Brideoake (d. 1678), who was Bishop of Chichester and Canon of Windsor. The monument by William Byrd depicts the Bishop lying on his side, his left hand on his breast.

▣ Adjoining the Bray chantry on the E is the Chapel of Oliver King. A former Canon of Windsor, he became Bishop King in 1503 and subsequently rebuilt Bath Abbey.

▣ Opposite the Bray chantry are four paintings of kings. The second from the left depicts Edward V, who was murdered before he was crowned. His crown is suspended over his head like a halo!

▣ Next to the paintings of the four kings hangs the sword of Edward III, the founder of the Order of the Garter. It is 2 m (6 feet 8 inches) long and was made for use in battle.

▣ To the E of Edward III's sword is the stone-cage Oxenbridge chantry (1522) commemorating John Oxenbridge who was appointed canon of St George's chapel in 1509. Look for the rebus on his name over the door – an ox, the letter 'N' and a bridge.

The paintings inside date from 1522 and tell the story of John the Baptist.

▣ Near the Oxenbridge chantry is a painted wooden font dating from c.1650. (See Wooden Fonts, page 34.)

▣ Further E, along the s choir aisle and on the left is the tomb of King Henry VI (1422–71), who was murdered in the Wakefield Tower of the Tower of London, buried at Chertsey Abbey, then reburied here in 1484. He founded Eton College and King's College, Cambridge.

▣ Near by is the pilgrims' wrought-iron offertory box, made in 1484 by John Tresilian. It has 20 slots for coins and four locks.

▣ Adjoining the tomb of Henry VI are the tombs of King Edward VII (1901–10) and

Queen Alexandra. Lying at the King's feet is his faithful terrier dog, Caesar.

◈ At the E end of the S choir aisle is a fine roof boss showing Edward IV and Bishop Richard Beauchamp of Salisbury kneeling on each side of the Cross – a fragment of the True Cross allegedly once owned by St George's.

◈ Nearby in the SE corner is the Lincoln chapel, which contains the tomb of the Earl of Lincoln (1512–85) and his third wife, Lady Elizabeth Fitzgerald. His seven daughters kneeling below were born to his first and second wives.

The earl was Lord High Admiral to Queen Elizabeth I and this accounts for the anchor carved on the side of his knees!

◈ In a niche by the Lincoln chapel is a *Book of Hours* dating from c.1440.

◈ Behind the high altar is the east door (1240), which was originally the W entrance to King Henry III's chapel. The ironwork on the door was made by Gilebertus and is very fine. His name can still be seen!

◈ To the NE of the chapel is the dean's cloister, the windows of which date from c.1354. The grass lawn inside the cloister dates from 1240 – the oldest lawn in England!

◈ On several seats in the dean's cloister nine small holes can be seen; these were used for the playing of nine men's morris. (See Nine Men's Morris, page 210.)

◈ From the dean's cloister one can enter the Albert memorial chapel, which lies outside the E end of St George's chapel and was built by Henry III. It was restored and decorated by Queen Victoria between 1863 and 1873 as a memorial to Prince Albert (d. 1861). Every part of the interior is lavishly decorated – quite a contrast from St George's chapel itself.

◈ In the centre of the chapel is a large, unfinished monument by Sir Alfred Gilbert to the Duke of Clarence (d. 1892), son of Edward VII and brother of George V. To the W of this is the tomb of Queen Victoria's son Prince Leopold (d. 1884), by Sir Jacob Boehm and to the E, near the altar, the monument to Prince Albert by Baron de Triqueti dating from 1872. (Prince Albert is buried in the royal mausoleum at Frogmore.)

◈ On the N side of St George's chapel is a well. It is 24.4 m (80 feet) deep and dates from 1252.

◈ On the exterior walls near by are badges of Edward IV showing a crucifix in the centre of a rose which is inside the sun. This badge is only found at Windsor.

◈ To the NW of St George's chapel is the Curfew Tower; this is the bell-tower for the chapel. Dating from 1227 it contains a ring of eight bells that are rung anti-clockwise. Every three hours the hymn tune 'St David' is played on the bells. The clock dates from 1689 and was electrified in 1985.

# Wing            BUCKINGHAMSHIRE

ALL SAINTS This is one of the famous Saxon churches of England and still retains the early plan of Christian churches – an aisled nave with apse and a crypt under the apse.

◈ At the W end of the nave are two Saxon doorways about 6.1 m (20 feet) above the floor. They probably opened on to a gallery. (See Bosham, page 32.)

◈ The chancel arch is 6.4 m (21 feet) wide and 6.71 m (22 feet) high. It is the widest (though not the highest) Saxon arch in Britain. (The highest is at Stow – see page 342.)

◈ Above the chancel arch is a Saxon window with a mid-wall baluster shaft, discovered in 1893. Apart from this example and three windows in the nave at Worth

*Woodbridge, Suffolk, has a fine flint and stone tower exhibiting good examples of flushwork.*

(see page 434), this is only found in Saxon towers.

🔲 The octagonal Saxon crypt lies about 2.74 m (9 feet) below the level of the chancel floor. It is 3.96 m (13 feet) long, 1.83 m (6 feet) wide and has a 1.22 m (4 feet) walkway around it.

🔲 In the tracery of the E window of the s aisle is original glass of c.1330 showing the Coronation of the Virgin.

🔲 At the E end of the N aisle is the Italianate altar tomb of Sir Richard Dormer (1552). It is not only one of the earliest Renaissance monuments in England, but also the finest of its date.

## Wolborough                    DEVON

ST MARY THE VIRGIN This is the mother church of Newton Abbot and is situated in a beautiful churchyard on the sw side of the town.

🔲 The chief style of architecture is Perpendicular and the windows and nave piers are excellent examples of this. The capitals on the piers are especially interesting and the following should be noted:

† On the s side:
⁙ the third pier from the E shows a pig eating acorns
⁙ on the fourth pier are snails among curly kale
⁙ on the seventh pier against the w wall two dogs are sharing one head!

† On the N side:
⁙ the second pier from the w shows wonderful thistles and leaves
⁙ the fifth pier depicts an owl, pelican and other birds, all superbly carved.

🔲 The beautiful medieval brass lectern (c.1500) has three lions at its feet looking right and is complete with red-jewelled eyes, silver-like talons and an arched bookrest. Apart from the lions, these are Victorian replacements as a small plate

affixed to the lectern states: 'Restored in memory of Elizabeth Anne, widow of James Cornish of Black Hall who died on 22 Dec., 1891. (See Medieval Brass Lecterns, page 362.)

🔲 The beautiful screen across the church dates from c.1520 and originally contained 76 panels showing figures and emblems of saints – the largest number of paintings on any church screen in England. Sixty-six still remain and several of the named saints are unique in England – St Adrian, St Aubert, St Maura, St Paul of Constantinople and St Paul the Hermit.

🔲 Under the pulpit is a large fragment of a German bomb dropped in the churchyard on 4 May 1941.

## Wolferlow                    HEREFORDSHIRE

ST ANDREW stands in remote countryside, on a hillside near the Worcestershire border.

🔲 An effigy to an unknown lady of c.1250 is considered to be the oldest to a lady in England.

## Wolverhampton                    WEST MIDLANDS

THE COLLEGIATE CHURCH OF ST PETER This red sandstone church with its impressive central tower stands on a hill near the town centre and the remains of a famous Saxon cross.

🔲 In the SE corner of the churchyard is a peculiarly shaped stone 1.5 m (5 feet) high with a hole at the top. It is known as the 'Bargain Stone' and tradition states that people used to shake hands through the hole as a sign of having agreed on a bargain!

🔲 On the outside w face of the tower, underneath the pair of windows at the top, is a niche containing a statue of the foundress, Lady Wulfrun.

🔲 The stone pulpit is unique in retaining its original stone staircase. Dating from *c.*1450, its faces are beautifully decorated. It is attached to a pillar in the nave and at the bottom of the steps is a lion. (See Medieval Stone Pulpits, page 348.)

# Wombourne      West Midlands

St Benedict Biscop This is the only church in England dedicated to St Benedict Biscop, who was born in 628. He founded a monastery at Monkwearmouth and, later, one at Jarrow. One of the famous monks at Jarrow was the Venerable Bede, who wrote a life of St Benedict.

St Benedict is said to have introduced glass windows into England and was the first Englishman to patronize the arts in the work of the church.

In the N aisle of the church is a fine sculptured monument to Richard Marsh (d. 1820) by Chantrey. It shows the weeping figure of a woman.

In the s aisle is an alabaster tablet showing the Good Samaritan and the winding road from Jerusalem to Jericho. It was brought to the church from Italy in 1720 by Sir Samuel Hellier.

# Woodbridge      Suffolk

St Mary the Virgin is a very tall, light church.

At the w end of the N aisle is a wall brass inscribed:

> 'Beneath this stone John Sayre the younger sleepes
> Whilst saints on hie, his soule in safety keepes.
> In judgement old, in yeares, in nature's pride
> Thus reader see bothe younge and old he did
> Could wisdome love or learninge purchase breath

> Thou hadst not died nor wee bewaylde thie deathe
> But reader marke the reason thou shalt finde
> Heaven takes the best, still leaves the worste behinde.
> *Obiit Anno Salutis 1622 Aetatis 26'*

The Seven-sacrament font is badly mutilated. The eighth panel depicts the Crucifixion. Note the cross-shaped lily in the w recess.

In the nave is a rare Dutch candelabrum presented to the church by a Robert Elfreth on 15 July 1676.

At the E end of the s aisle is the impressive wall monument to Jeffrey Pitman (d. 21 May 1627), his two wives and two lawyer sons. (Pitman was a tanner in Woodbridge and became Sheriff of Suffolk, *c.*1610.) The monument may have been carved by Gerard Janssen, whose family carved Shakespeare's monument at Stratford-upon-Avon.

On the N side of the high altar is the Renaissance table-tomb of Thomas Seckford (1515–87).

Outside on the tower and the N porch are fine flushwork panels showing the chalice and wafer, various monograms and a Perpendicular window.

At the E end of the churchyard against the Abbey School is an epitaph which reads:

> 'Here lieth the body of
> Benjamin Brinkley
> Who though Lustie and
> Strong was one
> That by misfortune shot
> Himself with's Gun.
> In the 23rd year of his age
> He departed this life
> To the grief of his parents
> Spectators and Wife.
> March the 27, 1723.'

Lighting in medieval churches was usually restricted to candles either on the altar, on each side of a reading desk or even in front of a statue of a saint. Most services took place during daylight hours, however (apart from the monastic offices), so further lighting inside the church was unnecessary.

*Cresset Stone, Collingham, West Yorkshire.*

Occasionally lighting near doorways was provided by means of a cresset stone. This was a flat piece of stone, usually rectangular, containing cup-like depressions filled with some form of oil or tallow in which floated a wick. This could be described as an early 'artificial light' used in addition to the usual candles.

Apart from their use as a primitive form of lighting, cresset stones were also used to burn lights to assist the prayers of the living as well as in memory of the souls of the departed, just as today one can buy special candles in many churches and cathedrals.

Some cresset stones were portable, with only a few cups, but larger ones were heavy and had to be supported by a bracket built into the wall. The largest cresset stone in England and Wales has 30 cups and is found in Brecon Cathedral, Powys.

Variations on the cresset stone can be seen at All Saints in Cawood, North Yorkshire, where an ancient stone can be used for holding candles, and on the SE side of the S transept chapel at St Michael in Buckland Dinham, Somerset, where another stone comprises a shelf with holes for seven candles.

Very few cresset stones remain today as many were discarded by people who were ignorant of their function. To the best of my knowledge, however, the following is a complete list of those cresset stones remaining in churches today:

1. Aldsworth (St Bartholomew), Gloucestershire – enclosed in a niche in the N porch with a flue for the smoke; a unique survival.
2. Alton Pancras (St Pancras), Dorset – has nine cups and is about 30 cm (12 inches) square; found quite by chance *c.* 1970 when a former vicar, the Reverend Derek Parry, saw it leaning upside down against the vestry door where it had probably been used for many years as a door stop, without anyone realizing its true value!
3. Antony (St James), Cornwall
4. Blackmore (St Lawrence), Essex – this had five cups originally but two are damaged. Reputed to date from *c.*1350 this is the only cresset stone in Essex.
5. Bodmin (St Petrock), Cornwall – has eight cups and is octagonal
6. Powys (Brecon Cathedral) – has 30 cups
7. Collingham (St Oswald), West Yorkshire – has eight cups and is circular
8. Dearham (St Mungo), Cumbria – has one cup
9. Gloucester Cathedral – E walk of cloisters
10. Lewannick (St Martin of Tours), Cornwall – has seven cups

11. Lower Gravenhurst (St Mary), Bedfordshire
12. Marhamchurch (St Morwenna), Cornwall – has four cups
13. Monmouth (St Mary), Gwent
14. North Wingfield (St Lawrence), Derbyshire – has five cups
15. Preshute (St George), Wiltshire
16. Romsey Abbey, Hampshire
17. Wareham (Lady St Mary), Dorset – has five cups

18. Westow (St Mary), North Yorkshire – has 12 cups; this cresset stone is unique because it has a twelfth-century carving of the Crucifixion on the reverse.
19. Winterborne Kingston (St Nicholas), Dorset – has two cups
20. Wool (Holy Rood), Dorset – has four cups; this was discovered during rebuilding in 1866

# STONE READING DESKS

Stone bookrests are an unusual feature found in some Derbyshire churches and some outside the county. Usually built into the N wall of the chancel they date from the fourteenth century. They were used at the pre-Reformation Mass for the reading of the gospel. They are found in the following Derbyshire churches:

1. Chaddesden (St Mary)
2. Crich (St Mary)
3. Etwall (St Helen)
4. Mickleover (All Saints)
5. Spondon (St Werburgh)
6. Taddington (St Michael)

Outside Derbyshire they can also be found in these churches:

7. Chipping Warden (St Peter & St Paul), Northamptonshire

8. Crowle (St John the Baptist), Worcestershire
9. Doddington (Beheading of St John the Baptist), Kent
10. Norton (St Egwin), Worcestershire
11. Ottringham (St Wilfrid), East Riding of Yorkshire
12. Paull (St Mary & St Andrew), East Riding of Yorkshire
13. Pitchcott (St Giles), Buckinghamshire
14. Pocklington (All Saints), East Riding of Yorkshire
15. Roos (All Saints), East Riding of Yorkshire
16. Walsoken (All Saints), Cambridgeshire

The reading desk at Norton was dug up in the graveyard at Evesham Abbey in 1813. Similarly the one at Crowle was also buried in a churchyard.

## Woodnewton     NORTHAMPTONSHIRE

St Mary, with its w tower that was rebuilt
c.1570, stands in a little village near
Fotheringhay.

◈ Nicolai Polakovs, OBE (Coco the
Clown, d. 25 September 1974, aged 74) and
his wife, Valentina (d.10 January 1983, aged
82), are buried in the churchyard.

## Woodton     NORFOLK

All Saints is located in quiet countryside,
about 8 km (5 miles) NW of Bungay.

◈ This church has a round tower with an
octagonal top.

◈ The stained glass in the E window came
from Tenterden Church (Kent) in 1934; the
bishop there had refused to dedicate it
because it contained a portrait of the
Devil. At Woodton, however, the window
had to be reduced in size and the Devil
was omitted!

*Woolpit, Suffolk.*

## Woolpit     SUFFOLK

St Mary's stone spire, at 42.7 m (140 feet)
high, and rare in Suffolk, dominates the
lovely countryside. It is supported by
delicate flying buttresses.

◈ Below the parapet of the tower are the
words, 'Glory be to God in the Highest and
on earth Peace, Goodwill to Men'. The
parapet comprises 12 different roundels.

◈ On either side of the clerestory windows outside are excellent examples of
blind windows executed in flushwork.

◈ The superb medieval brass lectern dates
from c.1520. Its wings are 0.51 m (1 foot 8
inches) across and it stands 1.68 m (5 feet 6
inches) high. Three dumpy lions crouch at
the base. The eagle's eyes are incorporated
in the head and never contained jewels.
There is a hole in the base of the tail and
the beak is open. Eight talons are missing;

three are riveted to the globe on which the
eagle stands. (See Medieval Brass Lecterns,
page 362.)

◈ The magnificent double hammer-beam
roof (1439–51) is adorned with angels.

◈ At the ends of all the benches are carved
animals. Notice especially the chained
monkey in the rear row of the nave on the
s side and numerous dogs with appealing
faces!

◈ The s porch dates from 1451 and is a fine
example of the Perpendicular style.

## Worcester     WORCESTERSHIRE

The Cathedral Church of Christ and
the Blessed Virgin Mary This lovely
cathedral occupies a magnificent position
when viewed from across the River Severn.

*The magnificent south porch at Woolpit, Suffolk.*

*Worcester Cathedral, Worcestershire, viewed from across the River Severn.*

◈ The central tower is 62 m (202 feet) high to the tops of the pinnacles and is comparable to Gloucester Cathedral and Great Malvern Priory (see pages 148 and 161 respectively).

◈ Dating from *c.*1130, the chapter house is the earliest of any English cathedral. It has a diameter of 17.1 m (56 feet) and is unique in being circular inside, but a decagon (ten sides) outside!

◈ In the cloisters is a roof boss showing St George killing the Dragon.

◈ In the N cloister is a beautiful boss showing the Virgin and Child.

◈ In the E cloister are five bells from the tower. The old third bell is inscribed, '*In Honore Sci Wolstani Epi*' ('In honour of St Wulstan, Bishop'). This dedication to St Wulstan, Bishop of Worcester 1062–95, is unique. This bell was cast *c.*1374 by William Burford.

◈ On the S side of the choir is the magnificent chantry chapel of Arthur, Prince of Wales (1486–1502), eldest son of Henry VII and Elizabeth of York. He died at Ludlow Castle no fewer than five months after his marriage to Katharine of Aragon. His younger brother, Henry, later married Katharine and became Henry VIII. How different might have been the course of English history had Arthur lived!

In the centre of the chapel is the granite tomb of the Prince without an effigy.

Notice the rich carvings on the S side. Executed by stonemasons from Westminster Abbey, the decoration includes the rose of England, a portcullis, arms and heraldry.

Observe also that the chantry is not symmetrical when viewed from the S side.

◈ In the centre of the choir is the tomb of King John (1167–1216), the oldest surviving

*Worcester Cathedral's magnificent central tower viewed from the west.*

royal effigy in the British Isles. The Purbeck coffin lid is original but the base is later and dates from c.1540.

🔳 In the choir also is a beautiful pulpit carved from a single block of stone in 1642.

🔳 The choir, lady chapel and eastern transepts contain seven figure bosses (c.1220) which are the earliest figure bosses in England. Among the most notable is one depicting the Virgin Mary, crowned, holding her Child and a lily stem with fruit at the end! This boss was featured on the 10p Christmas postage stamp issued on 27 November 1974.

🔳 The crypt, built 1084–9, is approached from the sw transept and is a superb example of Norman architecture. It is the second largest Norman crypt in the British Isles (Canterbury is the largest) and originally occupied a total area of approximately 744 sq m (8000 sq feet) before part of the e section was filled in to support the building above. This crypt is, however, one of the oldest Norman crypts in existence.

🔳 Built into the triforium and clerestory in the easternmost bays on the N and S sides of the nave are large flying buttresses to strengthen the tower – a very unusual feature (but see also Salisbury Cathedral and Wells Cathedral, pages 303 and 388 respectively).

🔳 The two w bays of the nave are Transitional Norman work (c.1185). The chevron ornament in the triforium above is of an unusual design, quite different from the next bays, which are in the Decorated style (c.1370).

🔳 On the NE side of the N nave aisle is an unusual monument to Nicholas Bullingham, Bishop of Worcester from 1571 to 1576. His recumbent effigy is cut in two by a block of stone with an inscription extolling his virtues. (See also Shottesbrooke, page 317.)

🔳 In the N choir aisle is an impressive

model of the cathedral made by Albert T. Harley from 1977 to 1984.

🔳 In the roof space over the s aisle is the cathedral library containing among its treasures some leaves from an old gospel, c.750.

## Worksop                    NOTTINGHAMSHIRE

THE PRIORY CHURCH OF OUR LADY AND ST CUTHBERT This is one of the great Norman churches of England.

🔳 The two w towers are a notable feature. A ring of eight bells is hung in the N tower.

🔳 The ironwork on the yew doors of the s porch dates from c.1250. It incorporates sweeping scrolls and is among the earliest in England.

🔳 In a wall cabinet in the nave lies a skull still penetrated by the tip of an arrow! It was found near the s porch c.1850.

🔳 On 18 May 1974 the new e end of the priory, including a low crossing tower and flèche, was consecrated.

🔳 Towards the s of the building is the ancient gatehouse dating from c.1320 to 1350 with later additions.

## Worth                    WEST SUSSEX

ST NICHOLAS This is one of the great Saxon churches of the British Isles, with the exception of its Victorian tower and spire (1871).

🔳 The nave is lit by three Saxon windows with double round heads divided by plain mid-wall baluster shafts. These three original windows, high up in the walls, are three of only four remaining in a Saxon nave. (The other Saxon window in a nave is over the chancel arch of Wing – see page 424.) The window jambs and shafts have slots in them to hold shutters of wood or horn or possibly glass panels.

🔳 The Saxon chancel arch is 6.71 m (22

feet) high and 4.27 m (14 feet) wide and is the third-largest Saxon arch left in England. (The other two larger arches are at Stow and Wing – see pages 342 and 424 respectively.)

▣ On the s side of the nave is a very tall Saxon doorway that is blocked at the top. This is known as the Knight's Door and was designed to allow the entrance of a man on horseback, who would spend the night in vigil in front of the altar before being knighted.

▣ The fine pulpit (1577) is elaborately carved. It was bought from a London antique dealer in 1841 and probably came from Germany.

▣ The elaborate panelled and carved communion rails of foreign workmanship date from c.1650 and are reputed to have come from an Oxford college.

## Worth Matravers      DORSET

ST NICHOLAS OF MYRA The church is situated in a lonely village, w of Swanage in the Isle of Purbeck and quite near the cliffs overlooking the English Channel.

▣ On the n side of the churchyard, about 13.7 m (15 yards) from the church and slightly w of the buttress dividing the chancel from the nave, are the graves of Benjamin Jesty of Downshay, a farmer, and his wife, Elizabeth. He died on 16 April 1816, aged 79. The inscription on his tombstone reads:

'He was born at Yetminster in this County, and was an upright honest Man: particularly noted for having been the first Person (known) that introduced the Cow Pox by Inoculation, and who from his great strength of mind made the Experiment from the (Cow) on his wife and two Sons in the Year 1774.'

Jesty therefore inoculated before the famous Edward Jenner (1749–1823), who, in 1796, successfully inoculated a boy with matter taken from cowpox bladders. In 1798 Jenner published his discovery that vaccination produced immunity from smallpox.

Elizabeth Jesty died on 8 January 1824, aged 84. On her tombstone these words are inscribed:

'The Time we have allotted here
We highly ought to prize,
And strive to make Salvation sure
Ere Death doth close our eyes.'

## Wouldham      KENT

ALL SAINTS This church is situated quite near the River Medway.

▣ The e window of the s aisle is modern and depicts Jesus the Good Shepherd.

▣ Next to this window is a dainty wall monument to a man called William Bewly (d. 23 December 1611).

▣ A stone bridge with parapets across the n aisle leads to a door that formerly gave access to the rood loft – an unusual feature.

▣ On the n side of the chancel is a brass to Morleius Monox (d. 15 December 1602). He is shown kneeling with his wife and in between them is a Latin inscription.

▣ Near the path leading to the s porch is the grave of Walter Burke (d. 12 September 1815 in his seventieth year). The inscription reads:

'He was purser on His Majesty's Ship Victory in the glorious Battle of Trafalgar and in his arms the immortal Nelson died.'

## Wrexham

ST GILES is situated in a beautiful churchyard and boasts a splendid tower.

▣ The tower, at 41.1 m (135 feet) high, is a superb example of Perpendicular architecture. Its exterior is decorated with life-size sculpted figures of 30 saints, including St Giles. It was built c.1460 and is one of the Seven Wonders of Wales.

Elihu Yale, founder of Yale University, Connecticut, USA, is buried in the churchyard. The university tower is an exact replica of Wrexham's Perpendicular one.

The arch between the nave and polygonal chancel was originally a window at the e end of the nave when the last bay was the old chancel. Fragments of window tracery still remain in the upper part of this chancel arch. Evidence of the removal of the window sill can also be detected. The chancel was added c.1490 which is all the more remarkable.

Over the chancel arch are traces of a wall painting showing the Last Judgement. This was discovered in 1867.

The medieval brass eagle lectern has an inscription around the top stating that in 1524 'John Griffiths gave the Brazen Eagle worth six Pounds to the Altar in Wrexham'. The second feathers of both wings and the tail have been lengthened to support a bookrest. (See Medieval Brass Lecterns, page 362.)

The font dates from c.1450. It was removed during the Commonwealth (1649–60) and used as a garden ornament at Little Acton. It is decorated with Instruments of the Passion and heraldic devices and is in very good condition.

## Wrotham (pronounced 'Root-ham') KENT

St George is located in pleasant countryside just below the Pilgrims' Way and quite close to where the M20 meets the M26.

Under the w tower is the unusual feature of a vaulted passageway; this allowed processions around the church without leaving the churchyard.

The clock dates from c.1620 and is one of the oldest church clocks in the country. It has a carillon and various tunes are played after the hours have been struck.

The s porch has a chamber above it with a chimney on the n side and a stair turret on the w. In a niche over the doorway is a fine bronze figure of St George, made by the sculptor Willi Soukop, RA in April 1973. It replaced the original statue, which dated from 1933 and was stolen in 1971.

On the NE side of the s aisle is the entrance to a staircase that leads to a passage above the chancel arch. Small windows lighting the passage can be seen over the arch. The purpose of the passageway is unknown, but it may well have led to the rood loft.

The fine brass eagle lectern bears the inscription, 'To the glory of God and in loving memory of Ann Webb who died September 12 1879 aged 76 years. This lectern was offered by her son Lieut. Colonel Cecil Webb Cragg.'

The rood screen dates from the fourteenth century and has seven candlesticks on it – a most unusual feature.

In front of the screen at the e end of the nave on the floor are a number of monumental brasses dating from 1498 to 1615.

In the s wall of the chancel is a lovely piscina with a hood mould terminating in ball-flowers – a rare feature in se England.

The e window was brought stone by stone in 1958 from St Alban's Church, Wood Street, London, where it formed the w window before that church was demolished. It was designed by Sir Christopher Wren when St Alban's was rebuilt after the Great Fire in 1666.

The newly installed window was dedicated by the Bishop of Rochester on 18 January 1959, the total cost of re-erection being £2447. It replaced a memorial window of 1856.

*The magnificent tower of Wrexham dates from c.1460.*

## Wyck Rissington    GLOUCESTERSHIRE

ST LAURENCE This church is situated in a quiet village dominating the green.

▣ The thirteenth-century chancel has a rare E end with two two-light windows, each of which is surmounted by a diamond-shaped window and a third larger one above – a forerunner of 'tracery'.

▣ On the floor of the chancel under the Jacobean communion table is the original medieval stone mensa with five consecration crosses. Thrown out at the Reformation it was later used as a memorial stone with an inscription and the date: '27 day of Ianvarei 1580'.

▣ Around the walls of the chancel are 12 dark brown wooden plaques that were found in an attic of Wyck Hill House in 1892. Believed to be sixteenth-century Flemish, they show scenes from the life of Jesus.

▣ On the N wall of the N aisle is a mosaic maze – a copy of one seen in a dream by a former rector, Canon Harry Cheales (6 August 1911–3 September 1984), who is buried outside the E end of the church. This maze is made from Carrara marble from near Florence, Italy. (See Church Mazes, page 278.)

▣ As a pupil at Cheltenham Grammar School, the great composer Gustav Theodore Holst (1874–1934) became organist here in 1891 at the age of seventeen – his first musical post.

## Wymondham

(pronounced 'Windum')      NORFOLK

ABBEY CHURCH OF ST MARY AND ST THOMAS OF CANTERBURY This beautiful Norman building dates from 1130 and with its twin towers dominates the town.

▣ The superb W tower dates from c.1448 when it was built by the townsfolk. They had a dispute over the ringing of the bells in the other octagonal tower that used to be central, but now stands at the E end of the church, the monks' chancel having disappeared. The nave had always belonged to the parish – hence its survival at the Dissolution of the Monasteries by Henry VIII in 1538–9.

▣ The magnificent hammer-beam roof of the nave dates from c.1450. The angels hold shields and texts and down the centre are bosses carved with flowers.

Another hammer-beam roof covers the N aisle.

▣ The arms of George II (c.1750) is one of the largest royal coats of arms in existence.

▣ On the second pier from the W between the N aisle and the nave is a monogram showing the letters 'M' with a crown upon it and 'T', commemorating the church's two patron saints. It has been reset by workmen who have placed it back to front!

▣ The sumptuous reredos at the E end was designed by Sir Ninian Comper (1935) as a war memorial for those who died in the First World War. Beyond this wall would have been the monks' chancel before the monastery was closed.

▣ Among the treasures of the former abbey is a corporas case or burse (c.1290) made of canvas and richly embroidered. It was used to hold the corporal or cloth (which was about 50 cm/1 foot 7½ inches square) on which the bread and wine are placed and consecrated at Holy Communion.

The only other known corporas case is at Hesset, Suffolk, where it is more like a linen bag.

# TOURNAI FONTS

*Tournai font, East Meon, Hampshire.*

Tournai fonts are so called because they were made in Tournai, Belgium, *c.*1150–1200, then shipped down the River Scheldt, across the North Sea and English Channel and unloaded at ports on the south and east coasts. Transportation overland was a laborious business in those days so these fonts are only found in churches near the coast or a river in southern or eastern England.

Each Tournai font was carved from a single block of black marble found in the locality of Tournai. Decorated with symbolic designs, stories from the Bible and legends of the saints, they were probably carved by local artists before being shipped abroad to England. The fonts at Winchester Cathedral and East Meon, Hampshire, are particularly well carved, the former showing scenes from the life of St Nicholas of Myra and the latter the theme of Creation, the Fall and Re-creation.

The seven Tournai fonts are located as follows:

1. East Meon (All Saints), Hampshire
2. Ipswich (St Peter), Suffolk
3. Lincoln Cathedral (Blessed Virgin Mary), Lincolnshire
4. St Mary Bourne (St Peter), Hampshire
5. Southampton (St Michael), Hampshire
6. Thornton Curtis (St Lawrence), Lincolnshire
7. Winchester Cathedral (Holy Trinity, St Peter, St Paul and St Swithun), Hampshire

A mutilated fragment of another Tournai font was found when the town ditch was being filled in at Ipswich. This is now in the Christchurch Mansion Museum, Ipswich.

A completely new base and columns for the font at St Mary Bourne were made in Tournai in 1927 from the marble that is still quarried there. This is the largest of the Tournai fonts.

According to Nikolaus Pevsner there is another Tournai font at Boulge, Suffolk, but the figures have been chipped off. However, H. Munro Cautley, a former diocesan surveyor of Norfolk and Suffolk churches, describes it as a Purbeck marble font dating from *c.*1210

*Yeovil, Somerset, is known as the 'Lantern of the West'.*

## Yarmouth Isle of Wight

St James Much of this church dates from c.1680 with Victorian additions.

 In the Holmes chapel is a standing marble effigy to Sir Robert Holmes (1622–92), Governor of the island from 1667 to 1692. According to tradition, the incomplete statue was intended to depict Louis XIV of France. However, it was captured from the French along with its French sculptor, who was forced to carve Sir Robert's likeness instead!

## Yeovil Somerset

St John The Baptist This grand Perpendicular church is known as 'the Lantern of the West'.

 The tower is 27.4 m (90 feet) high and has an unusual parapet.

 On the n side of the chancel is a beautiful doorway leading to a vaulted crypt once used as a 'bone-hole'.

 The fine medieval brass desk lectern dates from c.1450 and is 1.98 m (6 feet 6 inches) high. The large knob on the top was added c.1750; it probably replaced a statuette of a saint.

Both sides of the desk are engraved with the half-figure of a friar (the head was defaced in 1565) and a scroll which, literally translated states, 'Come, now make your request from this place with humble prayers I pray, and may Brother Martin Forester awake in the Blessed Life'. At the base are four lions looking to the left.

This is the only medieval brass desk lectern in a parish church and in 1930 it was loaned to the Victoria and Albert Museum, London, for an exhibition of English medieval art. (See Medieval Brass Lecterns, page 362.)

 Note the curious pendant-like roof boss with a head on each side showing the Green Man and foliage issuing from his mouth.

 At the e end of the s aisle is the Holy Trinity chapel, dedicated in 1962. It contains four carved mice, the trademark of the famous woodcarver Robert Thompson of Kilburn, North Yorkshire. They are located as follows:

† on the lectern
† on the left communion rail
† on the right corner of the communion table
† underneath the cross that stands on the communion table.

 In the tower hangs the fifth-heaviest ring of ten bells in the British Isles with a tenor weighing 2067.96 kg (2 tons 2 qr 23 lb).

## York

The Minster and Cathedral Church of St Peter This magnificent minster dominates the city and is well seen from the medieval walls. It is the largest Gothic cathedral in England.

 The largest collection of late medieval stained glass in England can be found here in some or all of the 117 windows.

 Some panels of glass in the nave

clerestory date from *c.*1150 and are among the oldest in the minster.

In the N transept is the famous Five Sisters' window dating from *c.*1250. Each lancet is 16.30 m (53 feet) tall and 1.55 m (5 feet) wide and there are over 100,000 pieces of greenish-grey glass in the five lancets. This is the largest expanse of ancient grisaille glass in existence. The five small lancets above contain modern glass.

At the bottom of the central light is a small medallion of Norman glass dating from *c.*1150, showing Daniel in the lions' den. This came from the Norman cathedral. Also in this transept is a modern screen incorporating the names of all the women who died in the conflict of the First World War – the only national memorial.

The second window from the E in the N aisle of the nave is known as the Bellfounders' window and shows the craft of bell-founding. The borders, comprising mostly bells, are unique.

The fifth window from the E in the s aisle of the nave is a Jesse window, dating from *c.*1310, restored in 1789 and again in 1950.

The great w window of the nave dates from 1338 and is a superb example of curvilinear tracery, the central part at the top resembling a heart (often called 'the Heart of Yorkshire'). The glass is contemporary with the stonework.

The great E window in the choir was made 1405–8 by John Thornton of Coventry and is the largest single area of medieval stained glass in the world. At 23.4 m (76 feet 9 inches) high and 9.75 m (32 feet) wide, with the glass covering an area of about 156.1 sq m (1680 sq feet), it is almost the size of a tennis court! It is supported inside by a screen of open stonework.

In the s choir aisle is glass dating from *c.*1380 which came from the w window of New College, Oxford.

At the w end of the N choir aisle is a panel of stained glass dating from *c.*1420. In the middle of the centre light is a depiction of a lily crucifix in an Annunciation scene. Mary and Gabriel in blue and red are surrounded by pale yellow glass. (Binoculars are necessary to see the detail.) (See Lily Crucifix, page 338.)

In the Zouche chapel on the s side of the choir are examples of all periods of stained glass, including superb work by Ervin Bossanyi (1891–1975). Note also the several birds including a delightful wren and spider dating from *c.*1500.

The magnificent stone choir screen was built between 1475 and 1500 and displays kings from William the Conqueror to Henry VI. Apart from the one on the extreme s side (dating from 1810), all the statues are original and escaped destruction at the Reformation because they depict kings and not saints! The figure of Christ over the doorway dates from 1910.

Inside the vaulting over the archway is a fine coloured boss showing the Assumption of the Blessed Virgin Mary.

The chapter house is the largest in England and one of only two that are octagonal. It has a wooden roof and dates from *c.*1280. (Southwell Cathedral's chapter house is also octagonal but has a stone vault, see page 328.) Much of the glass is grisaille, similar to that in the Five Sisters' window.

Near the entrance to the chapter house is a fine astronomical clock dating from 1955. It is a memorial to airmen who died in the Second World War.

In the E aisle of the N transept is the tomb-chest of Archbishop Grenefeld (d. 1315) on which is his brass portrait – the oldest surviving brass of a bishop.

The lierne wooden vault of the choir and remaining woodwork date from 1829 when the originals were destroyed by fire.

*York Minster, viewed from the medieval walls.*

The wooden vault and bosses in the nave were also destroyed by fire in 1840 and replaced by copies of the originals. One of the bosses depicts Pentecost with the Dove and is one of only four in England. (The others are at Norwich Cathedral, where there are two, and Tewkesbury Abbey – see pages 255 and 357.) Another boss showing the Adoration of the Magi was used on the 3½p Christmas postage stamp issued on 27 November 1974.

On the N side of the nave, projecting from the triforium, is a red and gold dragon which may have been used to suspend a font cover.

In the N choir aisle is the only royal monument in the minster. It is the alabaster effigy of Edward III's son, Prince William of Hatfield (d. 1344), younger brother of the Black Prince, who died while still a boy.

At 65.8 m (216 feet) high, the central tower is one of the largest medieval towers in England and was built between 1433 and 1440. Inside, the height of the ceiling is 55 m (180 feet). The central boss depicting St Peter and St Paul is 1.5 m (4 feet 11 inches) across.

In the 1960s the foundations of the central tower were found to be very weak and so from 1967 to 1972 new concrete and stainless steel foundations were laid. An undercroft museum was constructed which is entered from the s transept. This contains many carved stones that were discovered during the work and which date from York's pre-Viking days, through to the arrival of the Normans in c.1080. The superb pre-Conquest sculptures are composed chiefly of interlaced designs.

There is also a beautiful miniature Roman altar, about 14 cm (5½ inches) high.

The entire roof of the s transept was destroyed by fire on 9 July 1984 after people claimed to have seen it struck by lightning. The Tudor Rose s window in the apex, dating from c.1510 and commemorating the marriage of Henry VII and Elizabeth of York after the end of the Wars of the Roses, was badly cracked into thousands of pieces.

The new roof contains several wooden roof bosses, six of which were carved from designs sent in by children who watched 'Blue Peter', the BBC children's programme. Over 32,000 entries were received! The s transept was rededicated in the presence of the Queen on 4 November 1988.

In the E aisle of the s transept is a monument to Archbishop Walter de Gray (d. 1255). Dating from c.1260, it is the finest and oldest mid-thirteenth-century monument in England and is unique in Europe.

Among the treasures in the minster treasury are: the Horn of Ulph made from an elephant tusk dating from c.900, the original coffin lid of Archbishop de Gray and a silver model of Halifax Parish Church made in 1888. In the minster library is the beautiful *York Gospel Book* dating from 1000.

The w front was completed (except for the towers) by 1345. The w doorway is divided into two by a clustered pillar and above it is a circular window of six lights in the space beneath the arch – a very unusual feature in England.

The highest pinnacles on the w towers are 0.46 m (18 inches) *higher* than the parapet of the central tower!

The bells (hung in the sw tower) form the fourth-heaviest ring of 12 bells in the world. The tenor weighs 3020.5 kg (2 tons 19 cwt 1 qr 23 lb). The cathedrals of Liverpool, Exeter and St Paul, London, contain heavier rings (see pages 208, 131 and 214 respectively).

In the NW tower hangs the bell 'Great

# STORIES ASSOCIATED WITH WOODEN EFFIGIES

## BARNBURGH, SOUTH YORKSHIRE

The effigy to Sir Thomas Cresacre, *c.*1345, is one of the finest and best preserved of all wooden effigies. According to tradition Sir Thomas was attacked by a wild cat resulting in his death and that of the animal in the church porch. Some reddened stones are said to mark the spot where they both died!

## BURGHFIELD, BERKSHIRE

The effigy of Sir Roger de Burghfield, dating from between 1330 and 1350, was stolen during the night of 9 January 1978. It was taken to Ghent in Belgium in April of the same year where it was spotted by a London art dealer on sale for £10,000 at an antiques fair! Legal action ensued and continued until 1982 – not over ownership, but over compensation to the man from whom it was seized, since he claimed to have acquired the effigy in good faith. It finally cost the church at Burghfield and a public appeal £10,000 to repurchase the effigy! It is now safely padlocked inside the church.

## DANBURY, ESSEX

In his *Essex* volume of the King's England series Arthur Mee tells a very interesting story about a knight whose wooden effigy can be seen in Danbury Church: on 16 October 1779 a grave was being prepared in the N aisle near a recess containing a wooden effigy. The gravedigger discovered a lead coffin about 0.76 m (2 feet 6 inches) below the pavement. The lid was removed and an elm coffin was discovered inside. On removal of this lid a further shell was revealed about 2 cm (¾ inch) thick and covered with a cement-like substance.

The onlookers who had arrived were amazed to see not a skeleton, but the 1.52 m (5 feet) body of a man, partly floating in a black liquid 'resembling mushroom catchup'. A Mr T. White (possibly the village doctor) who was present actually tasted the liquid, as he had no sense of smell! He sent an account of the discovery to the *Gentleman's Magazine* ten years later in 1789 (volume 59, page 337).

The body was reasonably well preserved but because the coffin had not been quite horizontal, part of the head and neck were not completely submerged in the liquid (which also had feathers and perfectly preserved flowers and herbs floating in it). After several villagers had seen the body, the coffin was again sealed and lowered into the grave.

As for who the embalmed man was? Although Arthur Mee suggests that he was one of the knights depicted as a wooden effigy in the N aisle, this is purely conjecture, as there was no nameplate on the elm coffin when it was first discovered in 1779.

## HILDERSHAM, CAMBRIDGESHIRE

The two effigies of Sir William Busteler and his wife Margaret dating from *c.*1340 were stolen during the night of 14 December 1977 and have never been recovered. The church guide says of this theft: 'If any visitor should ever see the effigies in a museum or private house anywhere, but more probably abroad, the church-wardens would like to be informed.'

## MUCH MARCLE, HEREFORDSHIRE

The effigy of a civilian, Walter de Helyon, *c.*1360, was exhibited in London in 1972 at a special exhibition called 'Chaucer's London'. Until 1970 it had lain on a damp window ledge and when it arrived in London it was found to be in a poor state of repair. Much of it had been restored in plaster and painted during Victorian times to resemble stone.

A reinforcement of fibreglass was made to fit the back of the effigy; nose and fingers were repaired and during this work, traces of colour were discovered. After careful thought and much deliberation it was painted again in these colours, so timely intervention saved a priceless effigy for posterity. I saw it in 1995 and it looked magnificent in its new position in the centre of the nave, *not* on a window sill!

### PAULERSPURY, NORTHAMPTONSHIRE

The two wooden effigies of Sir Laurence de Paveley (*c.*1330) and his wife were exhibited at the Royal Academy, London, in 1987 for an exhibition (entitled 'The Age of Chivalry') on the glories of medieval art.

### SPARSHOLT, OXFORDSHIRE

This church contains three effigies, all in the S transept. These were my first introduction to wooden effigies when, as a small boy, I used to spend holidays with my grandparents in the neighbouring village of Childrey. The effigies commemorate Sir Robert Achard (d. 1353) and his two wives, Joanna and Agnes.

Each year I used to walk to Sparsholt to see the church and effigies until one year, in 1947, I saw that they were missing! I learned later that they had been sent to London, where they were placed in a gas chamber by the London Fumigation Company. They were then treated with a special preservative and finally replaced on their bases, but not before lead studs had been placed between the wood and stone surfaces to ensure a regular passage of air. In 1992–3, during restoration work in the church the effigies were again examined and found to need attention. After cleaning and preservation work was carried out, it was discovered that the stonework of the wall niches underneath the effigies was powdering away. The stone was given special treatment and damp-proofing was inserted under the effigies before the niches were rebuilt.

Peter', weighing 11,008.87 kg (10 tons 16 cwt 2 qr 22 lb) and the third-heaviest church bell in the British Isles; only 'Great Paul' of St Paul's, London (see page 214), and 'Great George' of Liverpool Cathedral (see page 208) are heavier. (See also Bells, page 293.)

According to tradition, York Minster is the only church in the UK that is allowed to use mistletoe in its Christmas decorations!

## York

ALL SAINTS is situated in North Street, a little road on the w side of the River Ouse, sw of the minster; the church has a distinctive tower and spire.

This church contains the finest collection of medieval glass in any of the city churches of York, much of it given by the merchant Nicholas Blackburn, whose letter B appears on the glass.

The most famous glass is in the NE window. It represents the last 15 days of the world and dates from *c.*1450.

Next to this window is another showing

the Acts of Mercy. The detail in the small pictures should be noted.

▦ The E window of the N aisle dates from *c*.1350 and shows the Adoration of the Magi, the Crucifixion and the Resurrection.

## York

ST MARTIN-LE-GRAND is in Coney Street. The church was only partially restored after the Second World War; it stands on the E side of the River Ouse, opposite North Street.

▦ Of the former church of St Martin-with-St Helen only the tower and s aisle remain intact having been restored by George Pace in 1961 following severe war damage on 29 April 1942. The former s aisle is now used as the main part of the church.

▦ In the N wall is the former w window, which was taken out before the war. Dating from *c*.1437 it depicts incidents from the Life of St Martin of Tours. This is the largest and finest stained-glass window of any parish church in York.

## Youlgreave or Youlgrave      DERBYSHIRE

ALL SAINTS The tall w tower with its eight pinnacles dominates the surrounding countryside of the Peak District National Park.

▦ This church has an impressive Perpendicular tower, the finest in Derbyshire after Derby Cathedral.

▦ The Norman font has a stoup attached to it that was used for holding oil at baptism or for holy water. An upside-down salamander grasps it. Originally, in nearby Elton Church, it was placed in the churchyard having been damaged by the fall of the spire. It was brought to Youlgreave in 1838 by the Reverend Pidcock and put in the vicarage garden. The next vicar, the Reverend Wilmot, placed it in the church in 1848, providing it with a new base and shafts. In 1870 the parishioners of Elton claimed it as theirs, so a replica was made for them and now, apart from that one, the Youlgreave font is the only medieval one in England with a stoup.

▦ In the centre of the chancel is the small effigy of Thomas Cockayne (d. 1488). He wears a Yorkist collar around his neck. The effigy is 1.1 m (3 feet 6 inches) long.

▦ The E window (depicting the Four Evangelists) and the s chancel window (showing James, Peter and John) are by Edward Burne-Jones.

▦ On the N side of the chancel is a window depicting St Francis in memory of Isabel, wife of the Reverend Dr Percival Hadfield, vicar of Youlgreave, who died on 10 July 1968.

▦ At the E end of the N aisle is an alabaster reredos showing the Virgin and Child. It is in memory of Robert Gilbert (d. 1492) and his wife, Joan, members of a family who lived in Youlgreave for most of the fifteenth century. She is shown on the right, with ten daughters behind her, and he on the left, with seven sons behind him.

## Zennor CORNWALL

ST SENARA is located in a little village about 6.43 km (4 miles) w of St Ives and 106.7 m (350 feet) above the sea, with magnificent views from Zennor Head.

This church is famous for a bench-end in the chancel. Dating from *c.* 1450, the carving shows a mermaid holding a mirror and a comb. This is a very rare depiction for a bench-end.

# DEDICATIONS OF CHURCHES

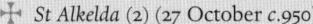

Apart from the churches in Cornwall and Wales that have unusual or unique dedications, there are a number of other unique or rare dedications in the remainder of England. Some of the more unusual, including some double dedications, are listed below. Note: the day and month refer to the date each year on which the patronal festival is celebrated, while the year is usually that in which the saint died.

✝ *St Adeline* (20 October)
Little Sodbury, Gloucestershire – unique dedication

✝ *St Adelwold* or *St Ethelwald* (23 March 699)
Alvingham, Lincolnshire – unique dedication

✝ *St Agatha* (8) (5 February)
1. Brightwell, Oxfordshire
2. Coates, West Sussex
3. Easby, North Yorkshire
4. Llanymynech, Shropshire
5. Portsea, Portsmouth, Hampshire
6. Shoreditch, London
7. Sparkbrook, Birmingham, West Midlands
8. West Gilling, North Yorkshire

✝ *St Aldhelm* (6)
1. Bishopstrow, Wiltshire
2. Broadway, Somerset (St Aldhelm & St Eadburga)
3. Doulting, Somerset
4. Malmesbury Abbey, Wiltshire (The Blessed Virgin Mary, St Aldhelm, StPeter & St Paul)
5. Sandleheath, Hampshire
6. Worth Matravers, Dorset (St Aldhelm's Chapel)

✝ *St Alkelda* (2) (27 October *c*.950)
1. Giggleswick, North Yorkshire
2. Middleham, North Yorkshire (St Mary & St Alkelda)

✝ *St Alkmund* (4)
1. Blyborough, Lincolnshire
2. Duffield, Derbyshire
3. Shrewsbury, Shropshire
4. Whitchurch, Shropshire

✝ *St Alphage* or *StAlphege* or *StAlfege* (6) (19 April 1012)
1. Canterbury, Kent (St Alphege)
2. Greenwich High Road, Greenwich, London (St Alfege)
3. London Wall, City of London (St Alphage)
4. Seasalter, Kent (St Alphege)
5. Solihull, West Midlands (St Alphege)
6. Lancaster Street, Southwark, London (St Alphege)

✝ *St Arild* or *St Arilda* (2) (30 October)
1. Oldbury-on-the-Hill, Gloucestershire (St Arild)
2. Oldbury-upon-Severn, Gloucestershire (St Arilda)

✝ *St Athanasius*
Kirkdale, Liverpool, Merseyside – unique dedication

✝ *St Barbara* (2)
1. Ashton-under-Hill, Worcestershire
2. Earlsdon,Coventry, West Midlands

✝ *St Basil* (2)
1. Deritend, Heath Mill Lane, Birmingham, West Midlands (St John & St Basil
2. Toller Fratrum, Dorset

✠ *St Bede* or *Venerable Bede* (6)
(27 May 735)
1. Carlisle, Cumbria – RC church
2. Clayton-le-Woods, Lancashire
3. Gateshead, Tyne and Wear
4. Toxteth, Liverpool, Merseyside
5. Widnes, Lancashire – RC church
6. Wyther, Stanningley Road, Leeds, West Yorkshire

✠ *St Benedict Biscop* (12 January 703)
Wombourne, West Midlands – unique dedication

✠ *St Bertoline* or *St Bartoline*
Barthomley, Cheshire – unique dedication in England

✠ *St Birinus* (3)
1. Dorchester-on-Thames, Oxfordshire (Abbey Church of St Peter, St Paul &St Birinus)
2. Dorchester-on-Thames – RC church
3. Redlynch – Wiltshire

✠ *St Blaise* (4) (3 February)
1. Boxgrove Priory, West Sussex (St Mary & St Blaise)
2. Haccombe, Devon
3. Milton, near Didcot, Oxfordshire
4. St Blazey, Cornwall

✠ *St Brandon* or *St Brendon* (2) (16 May 577)
1. Brancepeth, County Durham (St Brandon)
2. Brendon, Devon (St Brendon)

✠ *St Brice* or *St Britius*
Brize Norton, Oxfordshire – unique dedication

✠ *St Budock* or *St Budiana* (2)
1. Budock, Cornwall (St Budock)
2. St Budeaux, Plymouth, Devon (St Budiana)

✠ *St Calixtus*
Astley Abbots, Shropshire – unique dedication.

✠ *St Candida* (or *St Wite*) *& Holy Cross*
Whitchurch Canonicorum, Dorset – unique dedication

✠ *St Cassian* (5 August)
Chaddesley Corbett, Worcestershire – unique dedication

✠ *King Charles the Martyr* (6)
(30 January 1649)
1. Falmouth, Cornwall
2. Newtown, Shropshire
3. Peak Forest, Derbyshire
4. Plymouth, Devon
5. Shelland, Suffolk
6. Tunbridge Wells, Kent

✠ *St Clare* (12 August 1253)
Bradfield St Clare, Suffolk – unique dedication

✠ *St Congar* or *St Cyngar* (7 March *c*.550)
Badgworth, Somerset – unique dedication, but nearby Congresbury, about 11.26 km

(7 miles) away, is reputedly the place where St Congar built a church and its name is derived from him.

✠ *St Cosmas & St Damian* (5)
1. Blean, Kent
2. Boyton, Wiltshire – also dedicated to Blessed Mary of Boyton
3. Challock, Kent
4. Keymer, West Sussex
5. Sherrington, Wiltshire

✠ *St Cornelius* (2) (14 September)
1. Cornelly, Cornwall
2. Linwood, Lincolnshire

✠ *St Cuthburga* (31 August *c*.720)
Wimborne Minster, Dorset –
unique dedication

✠ *St Cyr* or *St Cyriac* or *St Cyriacus* or *St*
*Ciricus* or *St Ciricius* or *St Quiricus* (9)
1. Lacock, Wiltshire (St Cyriac)
2. Luxulyan, Cornwall (St Ciricius &
St Julitta)
3. Newton St Cyres, Devon (St Cyriac &
St Julitta)
4. St Veep, Cornwall (St Ciricus &
St Julitta)
5. South Pool, Devon (St Nicholas &
St Cyriacus)
6. Stinchcombe, Gloucestershire
(St Cyr)
7. Stonehouse, Gloucestershire (St Cyr)
8. Swaffham Prior, Cambridgeshire
(St Cyriac)
9. Tickenham, Somerset (St Quiricus &
St Julietta)

✠ *St Decuman* (27 August)
Watchet, Somerset – unique
dedication

✠ *St Deinst* (1)
1. Llangarron, Herefordshire – unique
dedication in England

✠ *St Dinabo*
Llandinabo, Herefordshire – unique
dedication in England

✠ *St Dubricius* (5) (14 November)
1. Ballingham, Herefordshire
2. Hentland, Herefordshire
3. Porlock, Somerset
4. St Devereux, Herefordshire
5. Whitchurch, Herefordshire

✠ *St Eadmor*
Bleasdale, Lancashire – unique
dedication

✠ *St Eata*
Atcham, Shropshire – unique
dedication

✠ *St Eanswith* or *St Eanswythe* (2)
(31 August *c*.650)
1. Brenzett, Kent (St Eanswith)
2. Folkestone, Kent (St Mary &
St Eanswythe)

✠ *St Ebba* or *St Ebbe* (3) (25 August *c*.683)
1. Beadnell, Northumberland (St Ebba)
2. Ebchester, County Durham (St Ebba)
3. Oxford (St Ebbe)

✠ *St Ecgwin* or *St Egwin* (2)
1. Church Honeybourne,
Worcestershire (St Ecgwin)
2. Norton, near Evesham,
Worcestershire (St Egwin)

✠ *St Edward the Martyr* or *St Edward,*
*King and Martyr* (4) (18 March 979)
1. Castle Donington, Leicestershire
2. Chilton Polden, Somerset
3. Corfe, Dorset
4. Shaftesbury, Dorset – RC church
(Holy Name & St Edward)

✠ *St Edwin*
Coniscliffe, County Durham – unique
dedication

✠ *St Edwold* (28 November *c*.870)
Stockwood, Dorset – unique
dedication

*St Egelwine-the-Martyr*
Scalford, Leicestershire – unique
dedication

*St Elgin* or *St Elphin* (2)
1. North Frodingham, East Riding of
Yorkshire (St Elgin)
2. Warrington, Lancashire (St
Elphin)

*St Eloy*
Great Smeaton, North Yorkshire –
unique dedication

*St Esprit*
Marton, Warwickshire – unique
dedication

*St Ethelburga* (11 October *c*.676)
Bishopsgate, London – unique
dedication

*St Eustace* or *St Eustachius* (3)
  1. Hoo, Suffolk (St Andrew &
    St Eustachius)
  2. Ibberton, Dorset (St Eustace)
  3. Tavistock, Devon (St Eustace)

*St Everilda* or *St Emeldis* (2) (9 July *c*.650)
  1. Everingham, East Riding of Yorkshire
  2. Nether Poppleton, North Yorkshire

*St Fabian & St Sebastian*
Woodbastwick, Norfolk – unique
dedication

*St Felix* (4)
  1. Babingley, Norfolk
  2. Felixkirk, North Yorkshire
  3. Kirby Hill, near Ravensworth, North
    Yorkshire (St Peter & St Felix)
  4. Rumburgh, Suffolk (St Michael &
    St Felix)

*St Firmin* (2) (1 September)
  1. North Crawley, Buckinghamshire
  2. Thurlby (near Bourne), Lincolnshire

*St Frideswide* (4, as far as I can ascertain)
    (19 October)
  1. Frilsham, Oxfordshire
  2. Botley Road, Oxford
  3. Iffley Road, Oxford – RC church
    (St Edmund & St Frideswide)
  4.   Water Eaton, Oxfordshire

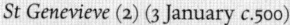
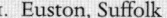
*St Genevieve* (2) (3 January *c*.500)
  1. Euston, Suffolk
  2. Fornham St Genevieve, Suffolk

*St Genewys* or *St Genesius* (seventh-century
    French bishop)
Scotton, Lincolnshire – unique
dedication

*St George & St Lawrence*
Springthorpe, Lincolnshire – the
combined dedication to these two
saints is unique in the British Isles

*St Mary & St Hardulph*
Breedon on the Hill, Leicestershire –
St Hardulph is a unique dedication

*St Hibald* or *St Hybald* (4) (22 September
    *c*.650)
  1. Ashby-de-la-Launde, Lincolnshire
    (St Hibald)
  2. Hibaldstow, Lincolnshire (St Hibald)
  3. Manton, Lincolnshire (St Hybald)
  4. Scawby, Lincolnshire (St Hybald)

*St Hieritha* or *St Urith*
Chittlehampton, Devon – unique
dedication

*St Hubert* (2) (3 November 727)
  1. Corfe Mullen, Dorset
  2. Idsworth, Hampshire

*St Ippolyts* or *St Hyppolyte* or
    *St Hippolytus* (2)
  1. St Ippollitts or Ippollitts,
    Hertfordshire (St Ippolyts)
  2. Ryme Intrinseca, Dorset (St
    Hyppolyte)

*St Kyneburga* (6 March *c*.657)
Castor, Cambridgeshire – unique
dedication

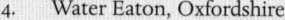

**St Lambert** (2)
1. Burneston, North Yorkshire
2. Stonham Aspal, Suffolk (St Lambert & St Mary)

**St Laud**
Sherington, Buckinghamshire – unique dedication

**St Leodegar** or **St Leodegarius** or **St Leger** (5) (2 October 678)
1. Ashby St Legers, Northamptonshire (Blessed Virgin Mary & St Leodegarius)
2. Basford, Nottingham (St Leodegarius)
3. Hunston, West Sussex (St Leodegar)
4. St Ives, Cambridgeshire – bridge chapel (St Leger)
5. Wyberton, Lincolnshire (St Leodegar)

**St Lucius**
Farnley Tyas, West Yorkshire – unique dedication

**St Lucia** or **St Lucy** (2) (13 December)
1. Dembleby, Lincolnshire (St Lucia)
2. Upton Magna, Shropshire (St Lucy)

**St Magnus-the-Martyr** (2) (16 April 1007)
1. Bessingby, East Riding of Yorkshire
2. Lower Thames Street, London

**St Maxentius** (26 June c.515)
Bradshaw, Greater Manchester – unique dedication

**St Medard**
Little Bytham, Lincolnshire – unique dedication

**St Milburga** or **St Milburgh**
Francis Bond (an eminent ecclesiologist of the early twentieth century) states there are five churches dedicated to this saint, but as far as I know there are only four:

1. Beckbury, Shropshire (St Milburga)
2. Offenham, Worcestershire (St Mary & St Milburga)
3. Stoke St Milborough, Shropshire (St Milburgh)
4. Wixford, Warwickshire (St Milburga)

**St Oswin** (20 August 650)
Wylam, Northumberland – unique dedication

**St Pancras** *(of Rome)* (8) (12 May)
1. Arlington, East Sussex
2. Chichester, West Sussex
3. Coldred, Kent
4. Ipswich, Suffolk
5. Kingston, East Sussex
6. Woburn Place, London
7. Pancras Road, Old Parish Church, London
8. Wroot, Lincolnshire

**St Pancras** *(of Taormina)* (6) (3 April)
1. Alton Pancras, Dorset
2. Exeter, Devon
3. Pancrasweek, Devon
4. Pennycross, Devon
5. West Bagborough, Somerset
6. Widecombe-in-the-Moor, Devon

**St Pandionia** or **St Pandiana** & **St John the Baptist**
Eltisley, Cambridgeshire – unique dedication

**St Pega** (8 January c.720)
Peakirk, Cambridgeshire – unique dedication

**St Petronilla** (31 May)
Whepstead, Suffolk – unique dedication

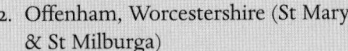

*St Protase & St Gervase* (19 June)
Little Plumstead, Norfolk – unique
dedication

*St Radegund* or *St Radegunda* (5)
1. Grayingham, Lincolnshire
(St Radegunda)
2. Maplebeck, Nottinghamshire
(St Radegund)
3. Postling, Kent (St Mary & St
Radegund)
4. Scruton, North Yorkshire (St
Radegund)
5. Whitwell, Isle of Wight (The Blessed
Virgin & St Radegund)

*St Remigius* (6) (1 October)
1. Dunston, Norfolk
2. Hethersett, Norfolk
3. Long Clawson, Leicestershire
4. Roydon, near Diss, Norfolk
5. Seething, Norfolk (St Margaret &
St Remigius)
6. Water Newton, Cambridgeshire

*St Ricarius* or *St Richard* (26 April *c*.645)
Aberford, West Yorkshire – unique
dedication

*St Robert of Knaresborough* (24 September
1218)
Pannal, North Yorkshire – unique
dedication

*St Rumbald* or *St Rumbold* or *St Rumwold*
(4)
1. Bonnington, Kent (St Rumwold)
2. Cann, Shaftesbury, Dorset (St
Rumbold)
3. Pentridge, Dorset (St Rumbold)
4. Stoke Doyle, Northamptonshire
(St Rumbald)

*St Ruthin*

Longden, Shropshire – unique
dedication

*St Sebastian* (4)
1. Great Gonerby, Lincolnshire
2. Heathland, near Wokingham,
Berkshire
3. Pendleton, Salford, Greater
Manchester
4. Woodbastwick, Norfolk (St Fabian &
St Sebastian)

*St Sidwell* (2) (2 August 740)
1. Exeter, Devon
2. Laneast, Cornwall (St Sidwell &
St Gulval)

*St Sylvester* or *St Silvester* (3) (31 December)
1. Chivelstone, Devon (St Silvester)
2. Inner Liverpool (N), Merseyside – RC
church (St Sylvester)
3. Tetworth, Cambridgeshire (St
Sylvester)

*St Symphorian* or *St Symphonian* or *St
Simphorian* (3) (22 August 180)
1. Durrington, Worthing, West Sussex
(St Simphorian)
2. Forrabury, Cornwall (St Symphorian)
3. Veryan, Cornwall (St Symphonian)

*St Theobald* (30 June 1066)
Although Pevsner states there are
three churches dedicated to this saint,
I have located only two:
1. Caldecote, Warwickshire
(St Theobald & St Chad)
2. Great Musgrave, Cumbria

*St Tysilio* or *St Tesiliog*
Sellack, Herefordshire – unique
dedication in England

*St Vedast* (2) (6 February)
1. Foster Lane, Cheapside, London
2. Tathwell, Lincolnshire

*St Vigor* (2) (1 November 537)
1. Fulbourn, Cambridgeshire

2. Stratton-on-the-Fosse, Somerset

*St Vincent* (5)
1. Ashington, Somerset
2. Burton-by-Lincoln, Lincolnshire
3. Caythorpe, Lincolnshire
4. Littlebourne, Kent
5. Newnham, Hertfordshire

*St Walstan & St Mary* (30 May 1016)
Bawburgh, Norfolk – unique dedication

*St Wandregeselius* (22 July 667)
Bixley, Norfolk – unique dedication

*St Wendreda*
March, Cambridgeshire – unique dedication

*St Weonard*
St Weonards, Herefordshire – unique dedication in England

*St Withburga* (17 March *c.*743)
Holkham, Norfolk – unique dedication

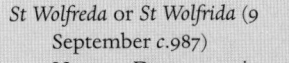

*St Wolfreda* or *St Wolfrida* (9 September *c.*987)
Horton, Dorset – unique dedication

*St Wolstan* or *St Wulstan* (eleventh-century Bishop of Worcester)
Wigston Magna, Leicestershire – unique dedication (but Pevsner gives the dedication as St Wistan)

*St Wystan* or *St Wistan* (3)
1. Bretby, Derbyshire (St Wystan)
2. Repton, Derbyshire (St Wystan)
3. Wistow, Leicestershire (St Wistan)

*St Wulfram* or *St Wulfran* (2)
(20 March *c.*720)
1. Grantham, Lincolnshire – St Wulfram
2. Ovingdean, East Sussex – St Wulfran

And finally, the most bizarre and unusual dedication in England:

*The Beheading of St John the Baptist* (2)
(29 August)
1. Doddington, Kent
2. Westbourne, West Sussex

# Appendix

Transcript of a talk given on 21 September 1967 by Canon William Ernest Purcell (1909–99 – a canon of Worcester Cathedral), on BBC Radio about 'holy places', detailing, in particular, the church at Little Gidding, Cambridgeshire:

'The signpost says Little Gidding; but the road, well off the main route between Huntingdon and Oundle and little more than a thread winding between the wide skies of Eastern England, peters out in a farmyard. Beyond that is a field; nothing more. And if your purpose in going that way has been to search out one of the least known holy places in this island, the spot where Nicholas Ferrar in Charles the First's time, founded a community of men and women the like of which has not been before or since, you may think you've lost your way.

'But no! Look left as you pass from farmyard to field. And there, in the left-hand corner, utterly tucked away, is the church.

'A pond, tree-overhung, wind-wrinkled, lies by the gate. So far, there has been nothing remarkable to be seen. But open the door. You pass into an atmosphere of peace and of what I can only call holiness, breathtaking in its intensity. It's all very simple; a little seventeenth-century altar, a few flowers, and the only sound breaking the quietude, if you happen to be there on a summer day, the little twitterings of birds outside.

'A framed quotation of T. S. Eliot on one of the window ledges announces that, "You are not here to verify, instruct yourself, or inform curiosity or carry report. You are here to kneel where prayer has been valid."

'It all started with a man called Nicholas Ferrar. A brilliant person, fellow of his college, successful in business, at 32 an MP, with a certainty, everyone thought, of worldly success.

'And then, in 1625, in response to an inner urge, he gave up everything, resolved to devote himself to the service of God. "Counting", to use his own words, "the lowliest place in His house better and more honourable than the greatest crown in the world."

'So, ordained deacon, he moved, with his mother, his brother John and wife and children, his sister Susanna with husband and 16 children, into a delightful manor-house at Little Gidding.

'The tiny church they found in use as a hay-loft, the sacristy was actually a pig-sty. Yet within a short while, they had made it a holy place, one which many, including the King, delighted to visit, and there they founded a way of life they never forgot. It was very simple and unpretentious. Nobody ever claimed to see any visions at Little Gidding, no legends of the miraculous grew up there.

'But the heart and centre of their whole community life was worship. Day after day, year after year, whether the rain poured or the sun shone, they all went in procession three times a day, at six, ten, and four in the afternoon, to the church, boys walking with boys, girls with girls, visitors and adults next and Nicholas Ferrar himself, leading his old mother. On Sunday evenings they used to walk over the fields to

Great Gidding church, the steeple of which can still be seen, peeping over distant trees; and after dark, from nine till one, there were always night watches, when the psalms were read from end to end. Nicholas himself had always to be called at one a.m. and a candle left for him, for his own private devotions.

'Such was life at Little Gidding. It soon became famous. But it was healthy and vigorous, and the children grew up sturdy outdoor types, used to fishing, archery and athletics.

'Nicholas died in 1637, after 22 years of utter content. His brother John continued the work for another 20, although many of them were stormy times. The Civil War broke out, you see, and as a punishment for sheltering the fugitive Charles, one night in 1646 a troop of parliamentary cavalry came along and broke the place up. However, he carried on until 1657, and then he died and that was the end.

'But was it? Little Gidding has left a memory. Years later the novelist J. H. Shorthouse wrote a book, *John Inglesant* – quite a bestseller in its time – which is all about Nicholas Ferrar and his community. And here's a passage from it, which seems to sum up much of what such a place has to say to us now:

' "In these sacred places, sacred to the beauty of earth and heaven alike, comes over us a blessed mood, in which all the fair scenes of life, the sunshine and the golden afternoons, come back upon the mind. The loved and lovely appear again. Once again, one roams in that fairy valley that lies behind each of us, into which nothing foul can enter, for the simple reason that only what was pleasant has remained in the memory of that magic time."

'Or, alternatively, you could say the purpose of the whole thing is condensed in the prayer I found in the church: "Lord God, we beseech Thee, make us more worthy of Thy perfect love that, with Thy servant, Nicholas Ferrar, and his household of blessed memory, we may rule ourselves after Thy word, and see Thee with our whole heart." '

❧ + ❧

This is a sentiment that is echoed in a verse I found at Yateley Church, Hampshire:

'Pause ere thou enter, Traveller, and bethink thee
How holy, yet how homelike, is this place.
Time that thou spendest humbly here shall link thee
With men unknown who once were of thy race.
This is thy Father's House, to Him address thee,
Whom here His children worship face to face;
He at they coming in with peace shall bless thee.
Thy going out make joyful with His grace.'

I have chosen the following quotation from the superb guidebook of Long Melford Church in Suffolk, as I feel it sums up what many churches mean to people today.

'Like so many other historic churches, Long Melford is not a place where everything has always been serenity, continuity and peace. But throughout its sometimes turbulent and sometimes depressing history it has always stood witness to the fact that the meaning of life and the meaning of death is to be found in the death and resurrection of Jesus Christ, and that His resurrection is a guarantee that we too can rise from the dead and share in the life of heaven.'

# The Vicar of Bray

1.

In Good King Charles's golden days,
When loyalty no harm meant,
A zealous High Churchman was I
And so I got preferment.
To teach my flock I never missed,
Kings were by God appointed,
And damn'd are those that do resist
Or touch the Lord's anointed.

*And this is law I will maintain*
*Until my dying day, Sir,*
*That whatsoever King shall reign,*
*I'll still be the Vicar of Bray, Sir.*

2.

When Royal James obtained the crown,
And popery came in fashion,
The penal laws I hooted down
And read the Declaration,
The Church of Rome I found would fit
Full well my constitution,
And had become a Jesuit
But for the revolution.

3.

When William was our King declar'd
To ease a nation's grievance,
With this new wind about I steer'd.
And swore to him allegiance.
Old principles I did revoke
Set conscience at a distance,
Passive obedience was a joke,
A jest was non-resistance.

4.

When gracious Anne became our Queen,
The Church of England's glory,
Another face of things was seen,
And I became a Tory.
Occasional Conformists base
I damn'd their moderation,
And thought the Church in danger was
By such prevarication.

5.

When George in Pudding – time came o'er
And moderate men looked big Sir,
I turned a cat-in-pan once more,
And so became a Whig Sir,
And thus preferment, I procured
From our new faith's defender,
And almost every day abjured
The Pope and the Pretender.

6.

The illustrious House of Hanover
And Protestant succession,
To these I do allegiance swear,
While they can keep possession.
For in my faith and loyalty
I never more will falter,
And George my lawful King shall be
Until the times shall alter.

Written *c.* 1720. Author unknown.

# Glossary of Terms

**Aisle** Passage between rows of pews or part of a church parallel to the nave but divided from it by pillars.

**Acrostic** A verse in which the first or first and last letters of each line form a word.

**Ambulatory** A walkway around the semi-circular apsidal end of a church.

**Apse** The semicircular or polygonal E end of the chancel or a chapel.

**Arcade** A series of arches, particularly between the nave and an aisle.

**Aumbry** A small recess in the wall of a church or a small cupboard.

*Baldacchino* A canopy, either suspended or resting on four pillars, over an altar. Usually found in cathedrals or larger churches.

**Baroque** A style of architecture originating from Italy, *c.*1600.

**Barrel roof** A vaulted roof of semicircular design, similar to a barrel cut in half.

**Bellcote** A gabled housing for bells set on the roof.

**Bier** Type of trolley used to convey a coffin into a church or churchyard.

**Boss** A carved block of stone or wood inserted into a roof to hide the joints where the ribs of vaulting meet.

**Box pew** A pew with high sides of an unequal height entered by a door.

**Buttress** A projecting support of stone or brick built against a wall.

**Canopy** A covering over an altar, seat, statue or a niche in a wall.

**Capital** The head of a pillar or column.

**Censer** A special container for holding incense, usually with chains to allow the bearer to swing it in different directions.

**Chancel** The E end of a church containing the communion table or altar; usually the oldest part of a church.

**Chantry chapel** A chapel usually found inside or attached to a church, where a chantry priest was paid to offer prayers for the souls of those who had built it.

**Churching** A special service of thanksgiving for women following childbirth.

**Classical** Any of the styles derived from Greek or Roman architecture.

**Clerestory** The upper storey of the nave walls, above the aisles and containing windows.

**Cloisters** Covered walk usually found to the S of a cathedral or abbey and enclosing a quadrangle with windows on the inside.

**Clunch** A hard type of chalk, sawn into blocks and sometimes used with flint and brick.

**Collegiate** A church associated with a college, usually of priests.

**Consecration crosses** Carved or painted crosses found on the inside and outside of churches. Originally 12 were placed inside and 12 outside and anointed with holy oil by the bishop at the consecration of a church. Few ancient ones still survive.

**Cope Chest** A special chest used for storing robes used by the clergy during Holy Communion services.

**Corbel** A carved block of stone or wood projecting from a wall to support roof trusses or a statue.

**Corinthian** Greek order of architecture.

**Crocket** Carved ornament, usually a bud or curled leaf on the side of a pinnacle, spire, etc.

**Crozier** A special staff carried by a bishop and based on a shepherd's crook.

**Crypt** An underground room or vault usually found beneath the E end of a church and sometimes used for burials.

**Cupola** A small dome forming a roof or ceiling.

**Curvilinear** Flowing tracery found in head of window and based on the ogee arch.

**Cusp** A projecting point between small arcs in Gothic tracery.

**Decorated** Style of architecture from c.1290 to c.1350.

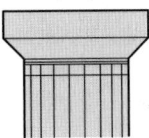

**Doric** Greek order of architecture.

**Early English** English Gothic architecture between 1190 and c.1290.

**Easter sepulchre** A recess, usually found in the N wall of the chancel, where the story of Christ's Resurrection was displayed up to the Reformation.

**Effigy** An image of a person, usually depicted lying down, executed in alabaster, bronze, marble, stone or wood.

**Faldstool** A small, portable stool with folding legs, often used for kneeling.

**Flushwork** Decorative work involving flints and cut dressed stone to form intricate designs and even lettering. Most commonly found in East Anglia.

**Foliated** Decorated or carved leaves.

**Gallery** A balcony or platform projecting from the inner wall of a church and used for musicians or the congregation.

**Gargoyle** An elaborately carved human or animal head through which a pipe is placed to throw water clear of a building. Most frequently found high up on church towers.

**Georgian** Of the period 1714–1830, the reigns of Kings George I–IV.

**Gesso** Plaster of Paris or gypsum, often used as a base for applying paint.

**Gnomon** A metal pin or wedge placed in the centre of a sundial to cast a shadow and allow the time of day to be read.

**Gothic** Style of architecture characterized by pointed arches prevalent in Europe in the twelfth to the sixteenth centuries.

**Graffito** The singular of 'graffiti'.

**Hammer-beam** A wall post supporting a projecting beam or 'hammer-beam' at right angles to the wall which carries vertical posts to support the roof above. Sometimes there are two rows of hammer-beams – hence a double hammer-beam roof.

**Hatchment** A large, diagonal plaque featuring a deceased person's heraldic arms. It was carried at the funeral and then hung in the church.

**Hauberk** Medieval coat of mail with long sleeves.

**Helm Roof** Usually found on towers and comprising four diamond-shaped sloping faces which terminate at each corner of the tower and also form a gable at the top of the four faces of the tower. (Often found on churches in the Rhine Valley, Germany.)

**Iconoclast** A religious fanatic responsible for destroying works of art, monuments, stained glass, etc.

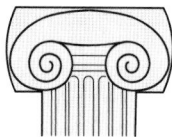

**Ionic** Greek order of architecture.

**Knapped flint** Flint that has been cut carefully and inserted between stonework to give the name 'flushwork'.

**Lady chapel** Usually found at the e end of a church or cathedral, this can be a separate building or enclose part of an aisle or transept. It is dedicated to the Blessed Virgin Mary.

**Lectern** Reading desk, often in the shape of an eagle, and placed near the entrance to the chancel.

**Lenten veil** A piece of cloth that was draped across the chancel in medieval times to hide the altar or crucifix at the beginning of the season of Lent.

**Lierne vaulting** Ribs of wood or stone in a roof that do not radiate from the main springers at the side.

**Lunette** A semicircular opening sometimes containing a window or painting.

**Medieval** The eleventh to the fifteenth centuries.

**Misericord** Carved bracket projecting underneath a hinged choir-stall seat providing a ledge for those who could not stand for long periods during services.

**Morte-safe** Heavy iron grating used to protect a grave against 'body snatchers'.

**Mullion** Vertical bars in a window dividing it into 'lights'.

**Nave** The central part of a church, usually

from the w door to the chancel, excluding any aisles.

**Newel staircase** A spiral staircase curving around a central post or newel, usually constructed of stone but sometimes wood.

**Norman** Style of architecture in the second half of the eleventh century and the twelfth century.

**Ogee** An S-shaped arch with pointed top; popular in the fourteenth century.

**Palimpsest** When referring to a brass, this indicates one which has been engraved on the back of an earlier brass. It can also apply to wall paintings or manuscripts where these have been overpainted or over-written.

**Parclose** A screen separating a chapel from the remainder of the church.

**Parvise** A room over a church porch, sometimes used as a storeroom or vestry.

**Pediment** In classical architecture, a formal style of gable above doors and windows.

**Perpendicular** The third stage of English Gothic architecture from the fifteenth to the sixteenth century.

**Pier** A solid support for arches and another word for 'pillar'.

**Pietà** A picture or sculpture of the Virgin Mary holding the dead body of Christ on her lap or in her arms.

**Piscina** Recess with basin and drain usually found on the s side of a chancel or chapel and used for washing the communion vessels.

**Poppy-head** Carved ornament of leaves and flowers, generally in the form of fleur-de-lys, on the end of pews.

**Presbytery** The part of a church e of the choir where the altar is placed, sometimes called the 'sanctuary'.

**Pulpit** Raised, enclosed platform, approached by steps, in which the preacher stands during a church service.

**Pyx** Special vessel for holding the consecrated bread (host) used at Holy Communion.

**Quire** Another spelling of 'choir' – the E end of a church, normally occupying the chancel.

**Reliquary** Receptacle for holding relics of saints, often richly decorated.

**Reredos** An ornamental screen covering the wall at the back of the altar.

**Retable** A picture or piece of carving fixed behind an altar.

**Retrochoir** The area behind the high altar, only found in larger churches, abbeys and cathedrals.

**Rood** Carved figure of Jesus on the Cross with the Virgin Mary and St John on either side.

**Rood screen** Wooden or stone carved screen usually situated between the E end of the nave and chancel and stretching across the nave and aisles. It may have a loft or gallery, on top of which is placed the rood.

**Sacristy** A room, usually adjoining the chancel or presbytery, in which vestments or church plate are kept.

**Saxon** Style of architecture from 600 to 1066.

**Sedilia** Canopied seats for the clergy (usually three) set in the s wall of the chancel.

**Seven Sacraments** A sacrament is a religious ceremony that enables Christians to draw closer to God and receive His special blessings. According to the Holy Bible, only two were instituted by Jesus – Baptism and Holy Communion. Before the Reformation in England, there were seven sacraments recognized by the Church – Baptism, Confirmation, Extreme Unction, Holy Eucharist or Mass, Matrimony, Ordination or Holy Orders, and Penance. After Henry VIII's break from Rome, the Church of

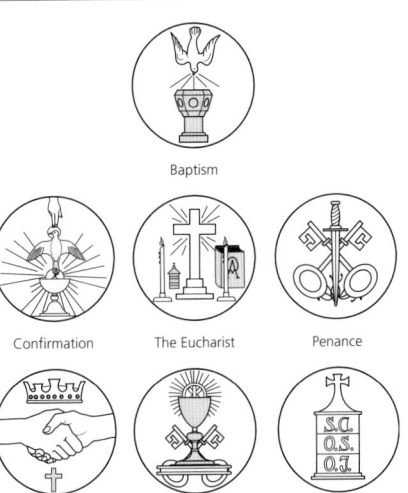

Baptism

Confirmation   The Eucharist   Penance

Holy Matrimony   Holy Orders   Extreme Unction

England retained Baptism, Confirmation, Holy Communion instead of the Mass, Holy Matrimony and Ordination.

**Sexton** Church officer responsible for bell-ringing and other jobs associated with a church.

**Spandrel** Space between the springing of two arches.

**Springers** Carved supports on the side of a wall where ribs of roof vaulting start.

**Squint or hagioscope** An opening cut through a wall, usually on one or both sides of a chancel arch, so that a chantry priest, celebrating mass at the same time as a priest at the high altar, could view the high altar and so synchronize his celebration.

**Stiff-leaf** Carved foliage decoration.

**Stoup** Stone basin, usually set in a recess near the church door, and used for 'holy water'.

**Tester** Also known as a 'sounding board', this is usually a flat, circular board over a pulpit which helps to carry the preacher's voice throughout the church.

**Tierceron vault** A tierceron vault is composed of ribs that spring from the walls to the apex of the vault above, but do not cross any other ribs.

**Tracery** Intersecting bars in the upper part of a window forming patterns, often intricate, in keeping with the period of architecture.

**Transept** Either arm of a church on the N and s sides of the nave.

**Transom** Horizontal bars across a window dividing it in half or more.

**Triforium** A passageway below the clerestory windows and composed of open arches on top of the arches of the nave and chancel. Usually only found in cathedrals and abbeys or large churches.

**Tuscan** Greek order of architecture.

**Tympanum** A triangular or semicircular space over a door between the lintel and an arch which may be carved.

**Vault** An arched stone or wooden roof. Can also describe an underground room where coffins may be placed.

**Victorian** Of the period from 1837 to 1901.

# Select Bibliography

Anderson, M.D., *History and Imagery in British Churches* (John Murray, 1971).

Arnold-Forster, Frances, *Studies in Church Dedications* or *England's Patron Saints*, 3 volumes (Skeffington and Son, 1899).

Betjeman, John. (ed.) *Collins Guide to Parish Churches of England and Wales* (Collins, 1980).

Bond, Francis, *Dedications and Patron Saints of English Churches* (Humphrey Mulford, Oxford University Press, 1914).

Bond, Francis, *Gothic Architecture in England* (Batsford, 1905), Fan Vaulting, pp. 342–9.

Cave, C.J.P., *Roof Bosses in Medieval Churches* (Cambridge University Press, 1948).

Cook, G.H., *Medieval Chantries and Chantry Chapels* (Phoenix House, 1963).

Daniel, Christopher St J.H., *Sundials* (Shire Publications Ltd, 2004).

Delderfield, E.R., *Church Furniture* (David and Charles, 1966).

*Dove's Guide for Church Bell Ringers* (Central Council Publications, 2000).

Duggan, E.J.M., *The Fabulous Icon. A Catalogue and Study of the Lily Crucifixion, 1375–1500* (University of Wales Lampeter, 1990).

Esdaile, Katharine A., *English Church Monuments 1510–1840* (Batsford, 1946).

Fewins, Clive, *The Church Explorer's Handbook* (Canterbury Press, 2005).

Friar, Stephen, *A Companion Guide to the English Parish Church* (Alan Sutton Publishing Limited, 1996).

Fryer, A.C., *Wooden Monumental Effigies in England* (Elliot Stock, 1924).

Fryer, A.C., 'Fonts with Representations of the Seven Sacraments, Part 2.' *British Archaeological Association Journal*, 87 (1931): 24–59.

Greenwood, Douglas, *Who's buried where in England* (Constable, 1991).

Harvey, John, *Cathedrals of England and Wales* (Batsford, 1974).

Howard, F.E., 'Fan Vaults.' *The Archaeological Journal*, 68, Second Series, 18 (1911): 1–43.

Jenkins, Simon, *England's Thousand Best Churches* (Penguin, 1999).

Jones, Lawrence E., *The Observer's Book of Old English Churches* (Warne, 1965).

Jones, Lawrence E., and Tricker, Roy, *County Guide to English Churches* (Countryside Books, 1992).

Leedy, Walter C., Jnr, *Fan Vaulting: A Study of Form, Technology and Meaning* (Scolar Press, 1980; first published in the USA).

Little, B., *English Historic Architecture* (Batsford, 1964).

Mee, Arthur (ed.), *The King's England Series* (published on individual counties, Hodder and Stoughton, 1937); reprinted after 1945, currently out of print, but reprint by the King's England Press, Goldthorpe, Rotherham in progress.

Morris, E., *Towers and Bells of Britain* (Robert Hale, 1955).

Needham, A., *English Weathervanes* (Charles Clarke, 1953).

Oman, C.C., 'Medieval Brass Lecterns in England.' *British Archaeological Association Journal* 87 (1931): 117–49.

Pevsner, Nikolaus and others, *The Buildings of England* (46 volumes, Penguin Books, 1951–74). These are being updated.

Prior, E.S., and Gardner, A., *Medieval Figure-Sculpture in England* (Cambridge University Press, 1912).

Pritchard, V., *English Medieval Graffiti* (Cambridge University Press, 1967).

Randall, Gerald, *Church Furnishing and Decoration in England and Wales* (Batsford, 1980).

Scott, R.A., Sir Gilbert, *Lectures on the Rise and Development of Medieval Architecture* (John Murray, 1879), pp. 217–27.

Williams, E. Carleton, 'Mural Paintings of the Three Living and the Three Dead.' *British Archaeological Association Journal* 7, Third Series (1942): pp. 31 ff.

I highly recommend the Ecclesiological Society, whose website is found at http://www. ecclsoc.org, and the wonderful Churches Conservation Trust, at http://www.visitchurches.org.uk.o

# Index

Page numbers in *italic* refer to the illustrations

# ACKNOWLEDGEMENTS

The compilation of this book could never have been accomplished without the invaluable help of many clergy and friends. It is impossible for me to name them all, but the following deserve special mention:

The BBC – for permission to use the late Canon William Ernest Purcell's broadcast on 'Little Gidding' (21 September 1967), with the agreement of his daughter, Alison Cunningham, and her two brothers.

Lambeth Palace Library, London – for their unstinting help with church dedications, in particular their Assistant Librarian, Gabriel Lineham.

West Lindsey District Council, Lincoln-shire – for permission to use some of the glossary of terms from their Churches Festival guide book.

Ron and Sandy Bannister – who read through the draft of this book and proffered many useful suggestions.

Robert P. M. Bonnington of St Albans – for permission to use his material on the Dunkeld lectern in my feature 'Medieval Brass Lecterns'.

Kenneth Munn, a Fairford parishioner – for valuable information on the construction of the fan-vaulted roof in the south porch at Fairford, Gloucestershire.

Christopher St J.H. Daniel, FSA, Consultant Sundial Designer and a member of the British Sundial Society – for his list of stained-glass sundials inside churches.

Reverend Canon Peter G. Cobb of Bristol – for supplying me with very helpful information on the lily crucifix.

Mr W. J. Goode, President and Founder of the Round Tower Churches Society, for important information on round towers.

Douglas Tyrrell, who gave of his time to transfer this book on to computer disk.

BRIAN L. HARRIS

# PICTURE CREDITS AND PERMISSIONS

The following images are reproduced by kind permission of E&E Picture Library: p.24, p.106, p.157, p.229, p.401, p.398 by D. Burrows; p.44 by J. Turner; p.76 by H. Harrison; p.105 by R. Flowers; p.136, p.139, p.182, p.247, p.249, p.265, p.293, p.340, p.348, p.349, p.350, p.365, p.428, p.439 by I. Sinden; p.137, p.138, p.204, p.205, p.121, p.230, p.364 by P. Mott; p.152 by S. Watersen; p.156 by P. Gatenby; p.159 by L. Jonas, p.293, p.295 by N. Hawkes; p.400 by K. Murrell; p.122 by G. Easby; p.140 (4 photographs) by R. Pilgrim; p.204 by Bill Andrews.

Photograph on p.312 © Christopher St J.H. Daniel. Photograph on p.341 reproduced by kind permission of John Caiger, The Old Rectory, Stoke Lacy. All other photographs © Brian Harris. Illustrations on p.xiv, p.460, p.461–3 by Rodney Paull.

Quotation from H.V. Morton's *In Search of England* on p.301 reproduced by kind permission of Methuen Publishing. Quotation of *High Flight* by P.O. John Magee on p.307 reproduced from the book *John Magee the Pilot Poet* by kind permission of *This England Books*, PO Box 52, Cheltenham, Glos GL50 1YQ. The Publishers would like to thank the Rector and Churchwardens of Long Melford, Suffolk, for permission to quote from their excellent guidebook on p.458.